COLD WAR **ANTHROPOLOGY**

David H. Price

COLD WAR **ANTHROPOLOGY**

THE CIA,
THE PENTAGON,
AND THE GROWTH
OF DUAL USE
ANTHROPOLOGY

Duke University Press | Durham and London | 2016

© 2016 Duke University Press
All rights reserved

Text designed by Mindy Basinger Hill
Typeset in Minion and Futura by Westchester Publishing Services

Library of Congress Cataloging-in-Publication Data
Names: Price, David H., [date] author.
Title: Cold War anthropology : the CIA, the Pentagon, and the growth of dual use anthropology / David H. Price.
Description: Durham : Duke University Press, 2016. | Includes bibliographical references and index.
Identifiers: LCCN 2015037300|
ISBN 9780822361060 (hardcover) |
ISBN 9780822361251 (pbk.) |
ISBN 9780822374381 (e-book)
Subjects: LCSH: Anthropology—Political aspects—United States—History—20th century. | Anthropologists—Political activity—United States—History—20th century. | Military intelligence—United States—History—20th century. | Science and state—United States—History—20th century. | Cold War. | United States. Central Intelligence Agency. | United States—History—1945-
Classification: LCC GN17.3.U5 P75 2016 | DDC 301.097309/04—dc23
LC record available at http://lccn.loc.gov/2015037300

FOR MIDGE WITH LOVE, SQUALOR, AND THANKS FOR HAVING THE STAMINA TO SO OFTEN APPEAR INTERESTED ENOUGH THROUGHOUT THE YEARS OF ONGOING UPDATES ON THIS SEEMINGLY ENDLESS PROJECT.

Anthropology since its inception has contained a dual but contradictory heritage. On the one hand, it derives from a humanistic tradition of concern with people. On the other hand, anthropology is a discipline developed alongside and within the growth of the colonial and imperial powers. By what they have studied (and what they have not studied) anthropologists have assisted in, or at least acquiesced to, the goals of imperialist policy.

RADICAL CAUCUS OF THE AMERICAN ANTHROPOLOGICAL ASSOCIATION | 1969

Anthropologists who study South Pacific cargo cults have come to expect and receive research grants as much as Melanesians expect to receive cargo.

TERRENCE BELL | 1989

CONTENTS

xi Preface
xxv Acknowledgments
xxix Abbreviations

PART I COLD WAR POLITICAL-ECONOMIC DISCIPLINARY FORMATIONS

3 ONE Political Economy and History of American Cold War Intelligence

31 TWO World War II's Long Shadow

54 THREE Rebooting Professional Anthropology in the Postwar World

81 FOUR After the Shooting War: Centers, Committees, Seminars, and Other Cold War Projects

109 FIVE Anthropologists and State: Aid, Debt, and Other Cold War Weapons of the Strong

137 Intermezzo

PART II ANTHROPOLOGISTS' ARTICULATIONS WITH THE NATIONAL SECURITY STATE

143 SIX Cold War Anthropologists at the CIA: Careers Confirmed and Suspected

165 SEVEN How CIA Funding Fronts Shaped Anthropological Research

195 EIGHT Unwitting CIA Anthropologist Collaborators: MK-Ultra, Human Ecology, and Buying a Piece of Anthropology

221 NINE Cold War Fieldwork within the Intelligence Universe

248 TEN Cold War Anthropological Counterinsurgency Dreams

276 ELEVEN The AAA Confronts Military and Intelligence Uses of Disciplinary Knowledge

301 TWELVE Anthropologically Informed Counterinsurgency in Southeast Asia

323 THIRTEEN Anthropologists for Radical Political Action and Revolution within the AAA

349 FOURTEEN Untangling Open Secrets, Hidden Histories, Outrage Denied, and Recurrent Dual Use Themes

371 Notes
397 References
433 Index

The analytic branch of the CIA is given to tweedy, pipe-smoking intellectuals who work much as if they were doing research back in the universities whence many of them came. It probably has more Ph.Ds than any other area of government and more than many colleges. Their expertise ranges from anthropology to zoology. Yet, for all that, they can be wrong.

STANSFIELD TURNER | former director of Central Intelligence, 1985

PREFACE

This book considers some of the ways that military and intelligence agencies quietly shaped the development of anthropology in the United States during the first three decades of the Cold War. Whether hidden or open secrets, these interactions transformed anthropology's development in ways that continue to influence the discipline today. This is an anthropological consideration of anthropology; studying up in ways I hope help the discipline reconsider its inevitable engagements with the world it studies (Nader 1972).

In many of the early Cold War interfaces connecting anthropology and military-intelligence agencies documented here, the anthropologists producing research of interest to governmental agencies pursued questions of genuine interest to themselves and their discipline. Sometimes gentle nudges of available funding opportunities helped anthropologists choose one particular element of a larger topic over another; in other instances anthropologists independently pursued their own intellectual interests, producing work that was only later of interest or of use to military or intelligence agencies. In some instances anthropologists recurrently produced work of no value to, or opposing policies of, these agencies. Anthropological research was sometimes directly commissioned to meet the needs of, or answer specific questions of, military and intelligence agencies, while other times sponsorship occurred without funded anthropologists' knowledge.

Laura Nader argues that one of anthropology's fundamental jobs is to provide context: to enlarge the scope of study beyond particular instances and encompass larger contexts of power, mapping power's influence on the creation and uses of social meanings. Understanding power involves studying the economic and social systems from which power relations arise. Given the military-industrial complex's dominance in postwar America, anthropologists might well expect to find the explanatory systems of our culture to be embedded in and reflecting these larger elements of militarization in ways that do not appear obvious to participants. Cultures frequently integrate, generally without critical reflection, core features of their base economic systems into widely shared ideological features of a society. Most generally these are seen as naturally occurring features of a culture, often ethnocentrically assumed to be views shared by any society. Among pastoral peoples this may mean that religious systems integrate metaphors of gods as shepherds (who shall not want), pristine despotic hydraulic states worshipping their chief bureaucratic administrators as god-kings, or capitalists constructing versions of a Jesus whose Sermon on the Mount somehow supports the cruelties of laissez-faire capitalism. Such ideological integrations of a society's economic foundations are common subjects of anthropological inquiry, though the disciplinary histories of the last half century have seldom consistently focused on political economy as a primary force shaping the theory and practice of anthropology.

Anthropologists, sociologists, and some disciplinary historians study the interplay between political economy and the production and consumption of anthropological knowledge. Since Karl Mannheim's (1936) observations on the sociology of knowledge systems, there has been broad acceptance of such links. Thomas Patterson's *Social History of Anthropology in the United States* (2003) connects political and economic impacts on the development of the discipline. Anthropologists like June Nash, Eric Wolf, Gerald Berreman, Kathleen Gough, or Sidney Mintz direct attention to the political and economic forces shaping field research or the selection of research topics (whether peasants or geopolitical regions) (Berreman 1981; Gough 1968; Mintz 1985; Nash 2007: 3; Jorgensen and Wolf 1970). Eric Ross's *Malthus Factor* (1998b) brilliantly shows how the development of demographic theory from the age of Malthus to the Cold War was inherently linked to the political economy of the age. In different ways, William Roseberry's essay "The Unbearable Lightness of Anthropology" (1996) and Marvin Harris's *Theories of Culture in Postmodern Times* (1998) challenged anthropologists to connect postmodernism's explicit neglect of the importance of political economy with broader disciplinary political disengagements. Critiques of colonialism's impact on anthropology by Asad (1973), Gough (1968), and others dominated discourse in the 1970s and significantly shaped anthropology's understanding of its role in political and economic-colonial formations.

Yet, while the Central Intelligence Agency (CIA), the Pentagon, and facets of American militarism marked political crises from Project Camelot to the Thai Affair, anthropologists' scholarly attempts to put the agency back in the Central Intelligence Agency have been episodic and fleeting. Joseph Jorgensen and Eric Wolf's (1970) essay, "Anthropology on the Warpath in Thailand," provided a framework and sketched enough details to launch the serious academic pursuit of such questions, yet the academic pursuit of documenting such disciplinary interactions remained largely ignored.

I have gone to great lengths to base this narrative and analysis on documents that meet standards of academic research, striving to provide citations for each piece of this puzzle—which both limits and strengthens what can be said of these relationships; in several instances I have excluded discussion of apparent connections with intelligence agencies because of the limited availability of supporting documents. This book is not an exhaustive study of these relationships; it provides a framework for further work and a sample of these pervasive mutually beneficial interactions. I made extensive use of the Freedom of Information Act (FOIA) to file hundreds of requests with the CIA, the Federal Bureau of Investigation (FBI), the Department of Defense, and other agencies, requesting documents on anthropologists and organizations where anthropologists worked during the Cold War. I have also drawn heavily on governmental and private archival sources, as well as previously published materials. While FOIA allowed me to access tens of thousands of remarkable documents from the CIA and other agencies, the CIA continues to guard much of its history and usually complies with FOIA requests in the most limited way, resisting intrusions into its institutional history. Yet even with this resistance, it is possible to document specific incidents and infer general patterns from the sample of available documents.[1]

While portions of my research for this book began during the early post–Cold War years, the emergence of the post-9/11 security state significantly and inevitably shaped my analysis of past and present interactions between anthropologists and military-intelligence organizations, just as my historical analysis of post-9/11 developments was influenced by my historical research on past intelligence agency abuses (see, e.g., Price 2004a). In struggling to add political context to our historical consideration of the development of Cold War anthropology, I hope to have sufficiently complicated the narrative by stressing the dual use nature of this history: showing that anthropologists often pursued questions of their own design, for their own reasons, while operating in specific historical contexts where the overarching military-industrial university complex had its own interest in the knowledge generated from these inquiries. The dual use dynamics of these relationships are of central interest to this book.

For some readers, writing about the CIA raises questions of conspiracies, but I find no hidden forces at work here any larger than those directing capitalism itself. As social forces of significant breadth and power, and playing important roles in supporting America's militarized economy, the Pentagon and the CIA can be difficult to write about in ways that do not make them out to be totalizing forces that explain everything, and thereby nothing, at the same time. While some may misinterpret my focus on the importance of these military and intelligence elements, exaggerating their significance to the exclusion of other social features, my focus on these militarized elements of midcentury American political economy is as central to this work as Richard Lee's (1979) focus on !Kung San hunting and collecting, June Nash's (1979b) focus on Bolivian mining labor relations, or Roy Rappaport's (1984) focus on Tsembaga Maring horticulture and feasting cycles. Anthropological analysis of systems of knowledge production (even its own) needs to contextualize the worlds in which this knowledge exists. As Steve Fuller argues in his intellectual biography of Thomas Kuhn, "Part of the critical mission of the sociology of knowledge . . . is to get people to realize that their thought stands in some systemic relationship to taken-for-granted social conditions" (2000: 232). And while the Cold War's national security state was not the only force acting on anthropology during this period, it is the subject of this book—and a force with significant power in midcentury America—and it thus receives a lot of attention here.

Dual Use Anthropology

The phrase "dual use" appearing in the book's title is borrowed from the physical sciences, which have long worried about the symbiotic relationships between the "pure" and "applied" sciences, relationships in which academic theoretical developments are transformed into commercial products or military applications. Dual use science became a central feature of experimental natural sciences during the twentieth century. This transformation shaped branches of physics, chemistry, biology, and medicine, and scientists from these and other fields increasingly came to surrender concerns about the applied uses of the knowledge they produced as being part of the natural order of things if they were to be able to do their work. As physics moved from answering questions with mathematics, pen and paper, and simple apparatus, to requiring the manufacture of massive, expensive machinery built not by a dozen scientists but by hundreds or thousands of scientists, to plumb secrets of the subatomic realm, it needed sponsors whose uses of such knowledge were fundamentally different from those of pure knowledge and discovery. With the increased weaponization of physics, such funds came to flow from militarized sources with such frequency that the silence surrounding such occurrences became a common feature of the discipline's milieu.

The dynamics of these processes and the outcomes of this dual use nature of scientific advancements are well known, and the general understanding that "pure science" has both "nonpractical" and "applied" uses has widespread acceptance in American society. During the second half of the twentieth century, this dynamic became a thematic element of Americans' shared beliefs in scientific progress. The tragedy of Robert Oppenheimer's slow comprehension that he and his colleagues would be excluded from decision-making processes concerning how their weapons would be used became part of the American dual use narrative. Most scientists understand that the knowledge they produce enters a universe in which they likely have no control over how this knowledge is used; some of this awareness comes from the legal conditions governing the labs where they work, conditions in which employers often own the intellectual rights to the fruits of their labors, but these dynamics go far beyond such legal concerns.

For decades the phrase "dual use research" has described the militarized applications of basic science research, at times describing scientific breakthroughs that have both commercial and military applications, such as developments in global positioning satellites that led to both precision weapons targeting systems and commercial dashboard navigation systems for family cars. Debates over dual use science often focus on biomedical breakthroughs that simultaneously hold the potential both for cures and for the development of devastating weapons. Such potential applications often mix "pure science" research with commercial or military dual uses in ways that confound or mix understandings of "defensive" and "offensive" uses of biomedical knowledge (Miller and Selgelid 2008). Approaches to such biological research are far from uniform. Some groups of scientists, like the Cambridge Working Group, raise public concerns posed by research into viruses and other transmittable diseases; others, like members of Scientists for Science, advocate for the right to continue such research (Greenfieldboyce 2014).[2] But even with these disputes, this awareness of the dual use potential of such work helps focus and clarify the fundamental issues of these debates.

Dual use research programs significantly altered the trajectories of twentieth-century physics, and the payouts for commercial interests and the weapons-industrial complex have been so sizable that the U.S. government supports massive funding programs for supercolliders and other large expenditures that appear to have no direct applications to weapons work. But if past performance is any predictor of future uses, either applications or new frontiers of adaptable useful knowledge will follow. David Kaiser (2002) argues that many of the expensive large physics projects with no apparent military applications, such as supercolliders, functionally create a surplus of physicists who can assist military projects as needed.

The dynamics governing the direction of the knowledge flow of dual use research appear to often favor transfers of knowledge from pure to applied research projects, but a close examination of interplays between theory and application finds any determinative statements far too simplistic to account for the feedback between theory and application. Notions of "applied" and "pure" science are constructions that, although useful, have limitations. In 1976, Stewart Brand asked Gregory Bateson about the roots of his cybernetic research. Bateson explained that his initial interest in developing cybernetic theories of cultural systems came not out of abstract, nonapplied theoretical musings but from applied military research. Bateson's interest in cybernetic feedback in cultural systems was, ironically, itself propagated by an instance of reverse feedback insofar as his abstract theoretical interest came from concrete problems arising from designing self-guiding missile systems. In a move reversing what might appear to be general trends of dual use information flow, Bateson took applied military knowledge and transferred it into the basis of a theoretical abstraction analyzing biological and cultural systems.

Distinctions between "applied" and "pure" research shift over time. Sometimes the abstractions of theoretical or pure research follow from applied problems; other times theoretical developments lead to applied innovations in ways that diminish the utility of these distinctions. The physical sciences long ago acknowledged the dual use nature of their discoveries: assuming that discoveries or inventions made with one intention necessarily were open to other, at times often militarized, uses. Some scientific developments like radar, the Internet, GPS navigation systems, walkie-talkies, jet propulsion engines, night vision, and digital photography were initially introduced as military applications and later took on dual civilian uses; in other cases, what were initially either commercial or "pure research" scientific discoveries took on military applications, such as the discovery that altimeters could become detonation triggers, or the chain of theoretical physics discoveries that led to the design and use of atomic weapons.

Field research projects in other disciplines have also brought dual uses linked to the Cold War's national security state. Michael Lewis's analysis of the Pacific Ocean Biological Survey (POBS), a U.S.-financed ornithological study in India in the 1960s involving ornithologist, Office of Strategic Services (OSS) alumnus, and Smithsonian director S. Dillon Ripley, shows a project that provided scientists and American intelligence agencies with the data they separately sought: the ornithologists gained important data on migratory bird patterns, and the Defense Department gained vital knowledge it sought for a biological weapons program. Lewis found the survey was not simply a "cover" operation but instead "exactly what it was purported to be—an attempt to determine what diseases birds of the central Pacific naturally carried, and to determine bird migration patterns in that region. And it is also clear that POBS was connected to the US biological warfare programme" (Lewis 2002: 2326). The project was directed from the army's Biological Warfare Center at Fort Detrick, with plans (apparently never enacted) to test biological agents to monitor disbursement patterns. As Lewis observed, "Studying the transmission of biological pathogens by birds for defensive purposes is only a hair's-breadth from turning that information to an offensive purpose" (2326).

American anthropology has been slow to acknowledge the extent to which it is embedded in dual use processes, preferring to imagine itself as somehow independent not only from the militarized political economy in which it is embedded but also from the traceable uses to which American academic geographic knowledge has been put. The Second World War and the Cold War years that followed were an unacknowledged watershed for dual use anthropological developments. During the war, cultural anthropologists worked as spies, educators, cultural liaison officers, language and culture instructors, and strategic analysts. Not only did anthropological linguists prove their worth in learning and teaching the languages needed for waging the war, but their research into language training made fundamental breakthroughs in language teaching techniques; one dual use of these developments was that pocket foreign language phrase books, based on model sentences with inserted vocabulary words, became the basis of Berlitz's commercial foreign language pocketbook series (D. H. Price 2008a: 76–77). Physical anthropologists contributed forensic skills to body identifications and were in demand to assist in anthropometric designs of uniforms and new war-fighting machines. Diverse technological innovations (from developments of isotope-based absolute dating techniques to adaptations of radar and new forms of aerial stenographic photography) derived from advancements pushed forward during the Second World War.

While it is seldom acknowledged, many anthropological projects during the Cold War occurred within political contexts in which the American government had counterinsurgent (or, occasionally, insurgent) desires for studied populations. Counterinsurgency encompasses various practices designed to subdue uprisings or other challenges to governments. Some forms of counterinsurgency rely on what political scientist Joseph Nye (2005) termed "hard power"; others draw on soft power. Hard power uses military or paramilitary force and other forms of violence to attack insurgents; soft power uses co-option and corrosion to win favor among insurgents. Whether anthropologists provided cultural information to military or intelligence agencies or assisted in the implementation of international aid programs to stabilize foreign regimes, this book finds that they played many roles linked to counterinsurgency operations—at times undertaking these roles while pursuing their own research projects.

In part, cultural anthropology's self-conception as a discipline generally removed from the processes of dual use science arose from how so many of its practitioners appeared to remain in control of their disciplinary means of production. While grants or other funds that allow anthropologists to spend months or years in the field make life easier, self-financed ethnography or the production of social theory still occurred with relatively meager funds. Most anthropologists do not need to work in expensive teams and do not rely on cyclotrons or particle accelerators; at its most basic, ethnography needs time, people, libraries, theory, reflection, and colleagues.

Although archaeologists routinely work on large, multiyear, coordinated, expensive research projects, relatively few cultural anthropological research projects during the postwar period had high-budget needs similar to those spawning the expansion of dual use trends in chemistry or physics. Few cultural anthropological research designs required significant material support beyond the basic essentials of travel funds, pencils, paper, pith helmet, mosquito nettings, and portable typewriters. Early Cold War anthropology projects rarely required expensive equipment or brought together numerous scholars working on a single project.

Government-financed language programs, like the Army Special Training Language Program or Title VI–funded basic language acquisition, gave scholars the academic skills needed for field research, but these programs lacked mechanisms of coercive focus that could automatically capture funded scholars for some sort of later state purpose. Some postwar projects hired unprecedented large teams of anthropologists to undertake forms of coordinated fieldwork projects. Some of these were governmental programs like the Coordinated Investigation of Micronesian Anthropology (CIMA, funded by the U.S. Navy); others were largely funded by private foundations with ties to U.S. political policy like the Ford Foundation's Modjokuto Project—run out of MIT's CIA-linked Center for International Studies.

Because so much of anthropology's postcolonial history all but ignores interactions between anthropologists and military and intelligence agencies, I worry that my focus on these direct and indirect relationships risks creating its own distortions by creating the impression that an overwhelming majority of anthropological research directly fed military and intelligence apparatus. This was not the case. I assume that the majority of anthropological research had no direct military or intelligence applications, though the indirect ways these programs informed military and civilian agencies about regional knowledge were often significant, and the desires of these agencies routinely shaped the funding of anthropologists' research.

These dual use relationships also nurtured dual personalities among some anthropologists who attempted to balance disciplinary and state interests.[3] The postwar years leave records of anthropologists seeking funding opportunities directly and indirectly linked to Cold War projects through patterns reminiscent of Talal Asad's depiction of Bronislaw Malinowski as a "reluctant imperialist" (1973: 41–69). Although Malinowski at least partially understood the potential negative impacts of such funding relationships, beyond the rare dissent of soon-to-be-disciplinary outsider Jerome Rauch (1955), there was little public consideration of such impacts until the mid-1960s. These silences birthed schisms within anthropologists, like Julian Steward, who developed stripped-down Marxian materialist ecological models while campaigning for Cold War area study funds, even while training a new generation of scholars whose work more directly drew on Marx. There were schisms within archaeologists and cultural anthropologists exploring the rise of pristine state formations using theories of Karl Wittfogel, a Red-baiting anticommunist, whose own dual personality openly quoted and used Marx's writings with impunity while he informed on Marxist colleges and students to the FBI and the tribunals of McCarthyism (D. H. Price 2008c). Other dual personality traits developed as anthropologists like Clyde Kluckhohn and Clifford Geertz worked on projects with direct or indirect connections to the CIA or the Pentagon, even as they omitted such links from the textual descriptions they thinly constructed.

Even during the early days of the Cold War, some anthropologists were critical of encroachments of American Cold War politics into anthropological practice. Elizabeth Bacon, John Embree, and Jerome Rauch voiced insightful critiques of the sort familiar to contemporary anthropologists. Their work and other examples of early critical analysis can inform contemporary anthropologists seeking alternatives to military-linked anthropological prospects in a world increasingly seeking to draw on anthropological analysis for post-9/11 military, intelligence, and security projects.

One lesson I learned by studying the work of Cold War anthropologists is that individual anthropologists' beliefs that they were engaged in apolitical or politically neutral work had little bearing on the political context or nature of their work. Instead, these scientists' claims of neutrality often meant they had unexamined alignments with the predominating political forces, which went unnoted because they occurred without friction. But as Marvin Harris argued in *The Rise of Anthropological Theory* almost half a century ago, "Ethical and political neutrality in the realm of social-science research is a limiting condition which cannot be approached by a posture of indifference. Neither the researcher who preaches the partisanship of science, nor [he or she] who professes complete political apathy, is to be trusted. Naturally, we demand that the scientific ethic—fidelity to data—must be the foundation of all research. But we must also demand that scientific research be oriented by explicit hypotheses, whose political and moral consequences in both an active and passive sense are understood and rendered explicit by the researcher" (1968: 222). Extending this observation to this project, I find that my own political and ethical orientations align with my academic critiques of the CIA and the Pentagon as organizations threatening rather than protecting democratic movements at home and abroad, though during the two decades of this research, my political and ethical views themselves have been transformed by the act of historical research. But, as Harris argues, regardless of declared or undeclared ethical or political positions, it is the fidelity to the data by which research is judged, as should the moral and political consequences (both active and passive) derived from the seeds we sow.

Situating This Book

This is the final book in a trilogy chronicling interactions between American anthropologists and military and intelligence agencies. The first volume (chronologically, though not published in this order), *Anthropological Intelligence* (2008a), detailed how American anthropologists contributed their disciplinary knowledge to meet the military and intelligence needs of the Second World War. The second volume, *Threatening Anthropology* (2004b), explored how loyalty hearings and the FBI's surveillance of American anthropologists during the McCarthy period limited the discipline's theory and practice—deadening what might have been critical theoretical developments and discouraging applied forms of activist anthropology tied to issues of social justice and equality.

This final volume connects elements of these earlier books; whereas *Threatening Anthropology* told the story of victims of the national security state's persecution of anthropologists who questioned the justice or rationality of America's Cold War era political economy, this volume analyzes how Cold War anthropologists' work at times aligned with the interests of rich and powerful agencies, such as the CIA or the Pentagon. This volume connects with the exploration in *Anthropological Intelligence* of how the needs of World War II transformed anthropology in ways that would later take on new meanings during the Cold War. Few Americans who came to see anthropological contributions to military or intelligence agencies while fighting fascism and totalitarianism during the Second World War critically stopped to reconsider the impacts of extending such relationships into the Cold War.

This book traces a historical arc connecting transformations in anthropologists' support for military and intelligence activities during the Second World War to the widespread condemnation of anthropological contributions to American military and intelligence campaigns in the American wars in Southeast Asia. This spans a complex historical period marked by cultural revolutions, startling revelations of FBI and CIA illegal activities, secret wars, cynical neocolonial governmental programs, and increasing awareness of anthropology's historical connections to colonialism. In less than three decades the discipline shifted from a near-total alignment supporting global militarization efforts, to widespread radical or liberal opposition to American foreign policy and resistance to anthropological collaborations with military and intelligence agencies. This was a profound realignment of intellectual orientations to the state.

Cold War Anthropology focuses on how shifts in the Cold War's political economy provided anthropology with rich opportunities to undertake well-funded research of interest to anthropologists, while providing this new national security state with general and specific knowledge. Once-secret documents now show funding programs and strategies that were used to shape the work of scholars conducting international research. Many Americans continued to interpret early Cold War political developments with views linked closely to the world of the previous war. Occupations and other postwar programs found anthropologists continuing to use many of the skills developed during the last war, now in a world pursuing new political goals. The postwar reorganization of the American Anthropological Association (AAA) anticipated new funding opportunities.

Area study centers and other postwar regroupings of social scientists studying questions of interest to the Department of State, the Department of Defense, and intelligence organizations broadly impacted postwar anthropologists.

Anthropologists and military or intelligence agencies interacted through four distinct types of relationships: as witting-direct, witting-indirect, unwitting-direct, and unwitting-indirect participants (D. H. Price 2002: 17). After the war, many anthropologists transformed elements of their wartime service into governmental research, policy, development, or intelligence work. Some developed careers at the Department of State or the CIA. Some of the work involved seamless applications of wartime work, adapted to shifts in the postwar world.

Investigative reporting and congressional hearings identified several CIA-linked social science research projects financed by CIA funding fronts. Press reports from 1967 revealed the Asia Foundation as a CIA funding front, and the Asia Foundation's relationship with the AAA is examined. The Human Ecology Fund is also examined as a CIA front that financed and harvested anthropological research of interest to the CIA.

One way that anthropologists' fieldwork intersected with intelligence agencies was through their writings being accessed without their knowledge; in other instances, cultural anthropologists and archaeologists used fieldwork as a cover for espionage. I examine one instance in which a CIA agent received anthropological funding and was sent to the field under the guise of conducting anthropological research.

In several cases, anthropologists or research groups used military-linked funds for basic research, producing knowledge that had national security uses. During the 1950s and 1960s, the Human Relations Area Files (HRAF) subcontracted army area handbooks and used the funds from this work to finance basic theoretical research of interest to HRAF anthropologists. American University's Special Operations Research Office (SORO) and Counterinsurgency Information and Analysis Center (CINFAC) wrote counterinsurgency reports drawing on anthropological writings. One SORO program, Project Camelot, significantly impacted the AAA, and records from Ralph Beals's post-Camelot inquiries into military and intelligence interactions with anthropologists provide significant new information detailing how the CIA sought assistance and information from anthropologists during the early Cold War.

After leaked documents revealed that American anthropologists were undertaking counterinsurgency work in Thailand, several anthropologists became embroiled in public clashes within the AAA over the political and ethical propriety of such work. Anthropological research for the RAND Corporation on Vietnam and anthropologists' contributions to USAID, ARPA, and AACT counterinsurgency projects in Thailand show increased uses of anthropological knowledge for counterinsurgency. The fallout from the Thai Affair pressed the AAA to adopt its first ethics code, prohibiting secret research, orienting anthropological research toward the interests of research subjects, and requiring new levels of disclosure. The AAA's focus on ethical issues raised by anthropological contributions to military and intelligence projects identified some of the disciplinary problems with military uses of anthropology, yet many of the core questions about the dual use nature of anthropological research remain unanswered within the discipline today.

ACKNOWLEDGMENTS

When I began publishing work on anthropologists and the Cold War and was not sure whether to do a single book spanning the materials covered in this volume, *Threatening Anthropology*, and *Anthropological Intelligence*, three wise women (Nina Glick-Schiller, Janice Harper, and Laura Nader) independently told me to break the stories up into separate volumes and to lead with the McCarthy story. Janice Harper explicitly told me that anthropologists love stories in which we are victims (McCarthyism) but won't like being shown as "collaborators." I had no idea it would take me two decades of largely unfunded, but highly rewarding, research to document this story.

The influences for this project are broad, but the seeds for these volumes were planted three decades ago when I was an undergraduate reading the work of June Nash, Laura Nader, Delmos Jones, Joseph Jorgenson, Gerry Berreman, Eric Wolf, and others on how powerful forces and organizations like the CIA and the Pentagon have directed anthropological inquiries. My graduate work with Marvin Harris strengthened my writing and focused my attention on political-economic forces shaping the worlds in which anthropological knowledge was produced and consumed. My years as a pre-Internet human-Google working as Marvin's research assistant in his largely abandoned campus office found me surrounded by his old 1960s and early 1970s issues of the *American Anthropological Association Fellows Newsletter*, reading accounts of some of the history recorded here. Though Marvin Harris and Marshall Sahlins famously clashed over significant epistemological differences, and even with my clear links to Harris, Sahlins has encouraged me and supported my efforts to document these past connections between anthropologists and military and intelligence agencies.

My friendship and work with Alexander Cockburn and Jeffrey St. Clair and writing for *CounterPunch* strengthened my writing voice, and helped me connect what are often misunderstood as separate academic and political worlds. Nina Glick-Schiller was the first editor to take my political historical work seriously enough to get me into print without dampening my critique; her encouragement and support helped me continue to work on a topic that most editors found intriguing but were hesitant to publish (see Price 1998). I am deeply grateful for the editorial guidance and friendship provided by Gustaaf Houtman, who helped me publish post-9/11 critiques of militarized social science in the Royal Anthropological Institute's *Anthropology Today* during a period when it was difficult to publish such work in the U.S. When I experienced difficulties publishing a report documenting the AAA's 1951 covert relationship with the CIA described in chapter 3 in the *American Anthropologist* (after three split reviews questioning the wisdom of exploring such matters in public), AAA president Louise Lamphere convened a panel at the association's 2000 business meeting (late in the evening, after the infamous Darkness in El Dorado public airing of grievances) to discuss these findings. Without Louise's support and Laura Nader's encouragement, I might have chosen to abandon a topic that was impossible to find research grants to sponsor, and nearly impossible to publish on when I started and returned to working in the Middle East. Roberto González's detailed comments on the manuscript helped me better focus elements of my argument. Karen Jaskar's librarian sensitivities wisely convinced me to not hyphenate "dual use" in the title, or elsewhere, to avert future searching and cataloging catastrophes. I am indebted to Jack Stauder for generously giving me a treasure trove of documents and artifacts from his years in the AAA's Radical Caucus and Anthropologists for Radical Political Action.

This book was not funded by traditional research grants. The failures to secure research grants early on in this project led me, without regrets, to finance this research by other means. Many of the archival trips were added on to invited speaking engagements at universities (American University, Berkeley, Brown, Chicago, Columbia, UC Irvine, George Mason, University of New Mexico, Syracuse, Yale, etc.) or academic conferences, or I used small funds from Saint Martin's University: a teaching excellence award cash prize, two one-semester sabbaticals (in the last twenty years), and some sparse faculty development funds. Funds for some FOIA processing were provided by the Institute for the Advancement of Journalistic Clarity. My dear friends Cathy Wilson and David Patton hosted me at their home during many archival trips to Washington, DC. Ken Wissoker's guidance and support at Duke University Press have been invaluable in helping all three of these volumes come into print. I am deeply grateful to all the scholars who hosted my campus talks or helped publish my work, at times weathering criticisms and setbacks for bringing these critiques directly to the environments where they work.

I have been researching this book for two decades. Earlier versions of some of the historical episodes recounted here have appeared in different forms: *Anthropology Today* published earlier analyses of the Human Ecology Fund (D. H. Price 2007b, 2007c) and the M-VICO System (D. H. Price 2012b). I published a chapter exploring anthropological responses to American military actions in Southeast Asia as part of a School for Advanced Research seminar volume (D. H. Price 2011b). I also published an early analysis of CIA-AAA interactions (D. H. Price 2003a), although documents I discovered later reshaped significant portions of that analysis.

Among the many other colleagues and friends who played important roles in shaping the production and form of this work during the past decades are David Aberle, Philip Agee, John Allison, David Altheide, Thomas Anson, Olivia Archibald, Julian Assange, Alan Bain, Sindre Bangstad, Russ Bernard, Gerry Berreman, Bjørn Enge Bertelsen, Catherine Besteman, Andy Bickford, Jeff Birkenstein, Father Bix, Karen Brodkin, Brenda Chalfin, Noam Chomsky, Harold Conklin, Lorraine Copeland, Dalia Corkrum, Jonathan Dentler, Dale Depweg, Sigmund Diamond, Jim Faris, Greg Feldman, Brian Ferguson, Les Field, Sverker Finnström, Carolyn Fluehr-Lobban, Maximilian Forte, Kerry Fosher, Andre Gunder Frank, Charles Frantz, Irina Gendelman, Deborah Gewertz, McGuire Gibson, Aaron Goings, Jonathan Graubart, Linda Green, Hugh Gusterson, Erik Harms, Chris Hebdon, Alan Howard, Jean Jackson, Bea Jauregui, Barbara Rose Johnston, Adrian Resa Jones, Linda Jones, John Kelly, Chun Kyung-soo, Roger Lancaster, Robert Lawless, Richard Lee, Sara Leone, Robert Leopold, Kanhong Lin, Thomas Love, Catherine Lutz, Andrew Lyons, Harriet Lyons, Jon Marks, Ray McGovern, Brian McKenna, Father Kilian Malvey, Erika Manthey, Stephen X. Mead, David Miller, Sidney Mintz, Bill Mitchell, Sean Mitchell, John Moore, Laura Nader, Steve Niva, Greg Orvis, Mark Papworth, Bill Peace, Glenn Petersen, Jack Price, Milo Price, Nora Price, Steve Reyna, Eric Ross, Mike Salovesh, Schuyler Schild, Robert Scott, Daniel Segal, Michael Seltzer, Gerry Sider, Duane Smith, Molly Smith, Roger Snider, Lawrence Guy Straus, George Stocking, Ida Susser, David Vine, Eric Wakin, Jeremy Walton, and Teresa Winstead.

ABBREVIATIONS

AAA   American Anthropological Association
AACT   Academic Advisory Council for Thailand
ACLS   American Council of Learned Societies
AFME   American Friends of the Middle East
AFOSR   Air Force Office of Scientific Research
AID   Agency for International Development (see also USAID)
AIFLD   American Institute for Free Labor Development
AIR   American Institute for Research
ALS   Army Language School
APRA   Angkatan Perang Ratu Adil
ARD   Accelerated Rural Development (Thai government project)
ARO   Army Research Office
ARPA   Advanced Research Projects Administration
ARVN   Army of the Republic of [South] Vietnam
ASA   Afghan Student Association
CENIS   Center for International Studies, Massachusetts Institute of Technology
CFA   Committee for Free Asia (later became Asia Foundation)
CIA   Central Intelligence Agency
CIMA   Coordinated Investigation of Micronesian Anthropology
CINFAC   Counterinsurgency Information and Analysis Center (part of SORO)
COINTELPRO   Counter Intelligence Program (FBI domestic counterinsurgency program, 1956–1971)
CORDS   Civil Operations and Revolutionary Development Support
CRESS   Center for Research in Social Systems
DCI   Director of Central Intelligence (CIA)
DOD   Department of Defense
DSB   Defense Science Board
ECA   Economic Cooperation Administration (Marshall Plan)
ERP   European Recovery Plan (Marshall Plan)
FARGC   Foreign Area Research Coordinating Group (also called FAR)
FASD   Foreign Area Studies Division (a division of SORO)
FBI   Federal Bureau of Investigation

FISEE Fund for International Social and Economic Education
FMAD Foreign Morale Analysis Division
FOA Foreign Operations Administration
FOIA Freedom of Information Act
FSI Foreign Service Institute
FULRO Front Unifie de Lutte des Races Opprimees
GVN Government of [South] Vietnam
HEF Human Ecology Fund
HRAF Human Relations Area Files
HRIP Harvard Refugee Interview Project
ICA International Cooperation Agency
IDA Institute for Defense Analysis
IIAA Institute of Inter-American Affairs
IFIS Institute for Intercultural Studies
IHR Institute of Human Relations
IPR Institute of Pacific Relations
MSA Mutual Security Agency
MSUG Michigan State University Group
NACA National Advisory Committee for Aeronautics
NAS National Academy of Sciences
NFSS National Foundation on Social Science
NIMH National Institute of Mental Health
NLF National Liberation Front (Vietnam)
NRC National Research Council
NSA National Security Agency
NSC National Security Council
NSF National Science Foundation
ONI Office of Naval Intelligence
ONR Office of Naval Research
OPC Office of Policy Coordination
OPS Office of Public Safety
OSRD Office of Scientific Research and Development
OSS Office of Strategic Services
OWI Office of War Information
POBS Pacific Ocean Biological Survey
PPR Principles of Professional Responsibility
PSB Psychological Strategy Board
RACP Remote Area Conflict Program (an ARPA program)

RAND Research ANd Development (RAND Corporation)
RCC Research in Contemporary Cultures
RRC Russian Research Center (Harvard University)
SEADAG Southeast Asia Development Advisory Group
SI Secret Intelligence Branch, Office of Strategic Services
SIHE Society for the Investigation of Human Ecology
SIL Summer Institute of Linguistics
SMC Student Mobilization Committee to End the War in Vietnam
SORO Special Operations Research Office, American University
SPARE Statement on Problems of Anthropological Research and Ethics
SRI Stanford Research Institute
SSRC Social Science Research Council
SSU Strategic Services Unit
STEM U.S. Special Technical and Economic Mission
TCA Technical Cooperation Administration
UNESCO United Nations Educational, Scientific and Cultural Organization
URPE Union of Radical Political Economy
USAID U.S. Agency for International Development
USIA U.S. Information Agency
USIS U.S. Information Service
USOM U.S. Operation Mission
WAHRAF Washington Area Human Relations Area Files

PART I COLD WAR POLITICAL-ECONOMIC DISCIPLINARY FORMATIONS

> The CIA, after all, is nothing more than the secret police of American capitalism, plugging up leaks in the political dam night and day so that shareholders of US companies operating in poor countries can continue enjoying the rip-off.
>
> PHILIP AGEE | ex-CIA agent, 1975

ONE POLITICAL ECONOMY AND HISTORY OF AMERICAN COLD WAR INTELLIGENCE

The end of the Second World War left the United States in a unique position among the victors. Not only was it the only nation on earth possessing a new weapon capable of instantly leveling entire cities, but the lack of damage to its industrial home front gave America the exclusive economic opportunities befitting a global conqueror.

The United States entered an era of economic prosperity the likes of which the world had never seen. With an expanding global economic system, and much of the world slowly recovering from the war, America found itself with what George Kennan secretly described as a nation holding "about 50% of the world's wealth but only 6.3% of its population.... In this situation, we cannot fail to be the object of envy and resentment. Our real task in the coming period is to devise a pattern of relationships which will permit us to maintain this position of disparity.... To do so, we will have to dispense with all sentimentality and day-dreaming; and our attention will have to be concentrated everywhere on our immediate national objectives.... We should cease to talk about vague and ... unreal objectives such as human rights, the raising of living standards and democratizations" (1948: 121–22). Kennan understood that U.S. foreign policy could not seriously support efforts to improve human rights, raising standards of living and introducing democratic reforms, though he underestimated the importance of the need to "talk about" these vague and unreal objectives as tools of domestic and international propaganda. Kennan's cynicism was matched by the inability of many U.S. social scientists of the era to acknowledge that such self-serving motivations lay at the base of many Cold War American foreign policies and programs linked to American academics.

The war's end brought uncertainty for American intelligence agencies. Under President Truman's Executive Order 9621, the OSS disbanded on October 1, 1945, and the agency's functions were reassigned to the Department of State and the War Department. Had President Roosevelt lived to the postwar period, the OSS may have remained a permanent agency, but OSS director William Donovan lacked Truman's support. Truman's fiscal approach to government envisioned a smaller postwar military and intelligence apparatus, and he initially opposed expanded postwar intelligence functions.[1]

Before the war, the United States had no permanent agency devoted to international intelligence. When Truman disbanded the OSS, 1,362 of its Research and Analysis Branch personnel were reassigned to the Department of State's Interim Research and Intelligence Service, and another 9,028 of OSS Operations personnel (such as covert action) were transferred to the War Department (Troy 1981: 303; 313–14). The OSS's Research and Analysis Branch was renamed the Interim Research and Intelligence Service and placed under the leadership of Alfred McCormack.[2] When OSS's Secret Intelligence (SI) Branch and Counterespionage (X2) Branch were relocated to the War Department, they became the new Strategic Services Unit (SSU). Three months later, in January 1946, President Truman created the Central Intelligence Group which took over the responsibilities, and many of the personnel, of the War Department's SSU. All of this shifting, realigning, and relocating of intelligence personnel was short-lived. The permanent restructuring and relocation of both the analysis and the covert action functions of American international intelligence shifted to a new centralized agency in the summer of 1947, when Truman signed the National Security Act on July 26, establishing the Central Intelligence Agency.

During the 664 days between the dissolution of the OSS and the creation of the CIA, American intelligence personnel continued many of the types of tasks undertaken by OSS during the war, though there was greater institutional disarray, with less intense focus than had existed under a culture of total warfare.[3] Had Truman stuck with his initial decision to divide intelligence analysis and operations into two separate governmental agencies (analysis at State, operations at the War Department), the practices and uses of American intelligence might have developed in profoundly different ways than occurred during the Cold War. Combining analysis with operations structurally fated the CIA to a history of covert action and episodes of cooking analysis to meet the desires of operations and presidents.

When the National Security Act of 1947 established the CIA, the American military and intelligence apparatus was reorganized with the establishment of the National Security Council (NSC), and the June 12, 1948, NSC Directive of Special Projects (NSC 10/2) authorized the CIA to undertake covert action and intelligence operations. The Central Intelligence Agency Act of 1949 later provided budgetary authority to the agency and authorization to undertake domestic and international activities.

During the CIA's early years, its employees' work was divided between the Intelligence Division (Office of Collection and Dissemination; Office of Reports and Estimates) and the Operations Division (Office of Operations; Office of Special Operations). The CIA sought to become the eyes, ears, and mind of America. It envisioned itself as an elite body harnessing the intellectual power of its citizens to gather information. The CIA's charter authorized no domestic or international law enforcement authority; instead, the agency was charged with the collection and analysis of intelligence relating to national security. The CIA was administered by the executive branch, with a bureaucracy providing oversight by a group known as the Forty Committee, which could authorize CIA covert operations in consultation with the executive branch. The looseness of its charge allowed the agency to undertake a wide range of operations with no oversight outside of the executive branch.

From the CIA's earliest days, its analysts monitored postwar, postcolonial shifts in global power. As postwar independence movements reshaped global relations, CIA analysts considered how these shifts would pit American anticolonialist historical values against America's emerging role as a global superpower.

"The Break-Up of the Colonial Empires and Its Implications for US Security"

The CIA's confidential report *The Break-Up of the Colonial Empires and Its Implications for US Security* (1948) described the global setting in which the anthropological field research of the second half of the twentieth century would transpire (CIA 1948). Most anthropologists undertook this fieldwork without reference to the dynamics described in this report, yet these dynamics shaped the funding of particular research questions and geographic areas. The report stated the agency's understanding of the problems facing the postwar world, where shifting power relations presented threats and opportunities to the new American superpower:

> The growth of nationalism in colonial areas, which has already succeeded in breaking up a large part of the European colonial system and in creating a series of new, nationalistic states in the Near and Far East, has major implications for US security, particularly in terms of possible world conflict with the USSR. This shift of the dependent areas from the orbit of the colonial powers not only weakens the probable European allies of the US but deprives the US itself of assured access to vital bases and raw materials in these areas in event of war. Should the recently liberated and current emergent states become oriented toward the USSR, US military and economic security would be seriously threatened. (CIA 1948: 1)

The report identified upcoming dominant Cold War dynamics, as the United States and the Soviet Union would spend trillions of dollars in the next four decades struggling over postcolonial loyalties around the globe. The key elements to future strategies were the collapse of European colonialism, growing native nationalism, the likelihood of Soviet efforts to capture clients in these new states, the presence of (cheap) raw materials needed for U.S. economic growth, and envisioned conflicts with the Soviet Union over control of these nations and resources.

The CIA observed that the postwar collapse of existing European and Japanese colonialism in Asia and Africa fueled "the release of bottled-up nationalist activities," and it conceded the "further disintegration" of global European colonial holdings was "inevitable" (CIA 1948: 1). It stressed the economic impact of anticolonial movements, lamenting that "no longer can the Western Powers rely on large areas of Asia and Africa as assured sources of raw materials, markets, and military bases" (2). Capturing the "good will" of nations achieving their independence was vital, and a failure to do so would result in antagonism toward the United States and a loss of vital clients (3).

At this moment in history, the CIA could have positioned itself to side with the liberation of people of the world who were ruled and taxed without direct representation, but agency analysts instead framed this primarily as a proxy struggle between the United States and the Soviet Union, noting that "the gravest danger to the US is that friction engendered by these issues may drive the so-called colonial bloc into alignment with the USSR" (CIA 1948: 2). The CIA explained native nationalist liberation movements as deriving from a mixture of historical, social, political, and economic forces, and it identified the five primary causes as increased awareness of stratification, colonial powers' discriminatory treatment of subject populations, the "deep-seated racial hostility of native populations," the global spread of Western values favoring independence and nationalism, and "the meteoric rise of Japan, whose defeats of the European powers in the Russo-Japanese War and especially World War II punctured the myth of white superiority" (5).

The CIA noted the neocolonial control of the British in Egypt, the French in Algeria, Morocco, and Tunisia, and the Italians in Libya and mentioned burgeoning independence movements in Indonesia, Madagascar, and Nigeria. It understood that "states like India and Egypt have already brought colonial issues into the UN and may be expected increasingly to take the leadership in attempting to hasten in this and other ways the liberation of remaining colonial areas" (CIA 1948: 7).

Even in 1948, the CIA recognized the role that foreign aid and promises of technical assistance and modernization could play in courting would-be independent nations. As explained in its report, "The economic nationalism of the underdeveloped nations conflicts sharply with US trade objectives and these countries tend to resent US economic dominance. On the other hand, they urgently need external assistance in their economic development, and the US is at present the only nation able to supply it. The desire for US loans and private investment will have some effect in tempering the antagonism of these states toward US policies" (CIA 1948: 8). Under the direction of Cold War economists and strategists like Walt Rostow, Max Millikan, and Allen Dulles, aid later became a powerful soft power component of American international policy.

The CIA viewed coming colonial collapses as "inevitable" and predicted these developments would favor the Soviet Union (CIA 1948: 9). The agency was concerned about the Soviet alignment with international liberation movements. Without addressing Leninist critiques of imperialism, the CIA observed the Soviets were "giving active support through agitators, propaganda, and local Communist parties to the nationalist movements throughout the colonial world" (9). The agency acknowledged the USSR held advantages over the United States because

> as a non-colonial power, the USSR is in the fortunate position of being able to champion the colonial cause unreservedly and thereby bid for the good will of colonial and former colonial areas. Its condemnation of racial discrimination pleases native nationalists and tends to exclude the USSR from the racial animosity of East toward West. The Communists have sought to infiltrate the nationalist parties in the dependent and formerly dependent areas and have been, as in Burma,

Indonesia, and Indochina, among the most vocal agitators for independence. The Soviet Union has found the World Federation of Trade Unions an effective weapon for penetrating the growing labor movements in Asia and Africa and for turning them against the colonial powers. (9)

Nationalism was expected to have increasing importance for poor nations undergoing rapid transformations, and the CIA believed that cultural differences between colonizers and the colonized would increase antagonism in historic colonial regions like Indochina, Indonesia, and North Africa (10).

The CIA identified opportunities for American interests given that newly independent nations would need help from "the great powers for protection and assistance" in the new "power vacuum" (CIA 1948: 11). Establishing the "good will" of the leaders and peoples of these countries would be key, and the report noted that American racial segregationist policies allowed the Soviets to portray the United States as a bigoted nation.

The report identified five impacts that the collapse of the global colonial system would have on U.S. security. First, colonial liberation would economically weaken America's European allies, which would diminish access to cheap minerals and other natural resources and strategic military outposts. Second, political upheaval could leave the United States with reduced access to these same resources. Because of this threat, the CIA insisted that "the growing US list of strategic and critical materials — many of which like tin and rubber are available largely in colonial and former colonial areas — illustrates the dependence of the US upon these areas. The US has heretofore been able to count upon the availability of such bases and materials in the colonial dependencies of friendly powers; but the new nations arising in these areas, jealous of their sovereignty, may well be reluctant to lend such assistance to the US" (CIA 1948: 12). Third, if the Soviet Union established close relationships with new nations in Asia, such relationships would undermine U.S. interests. Fourth, the CIA recognized dangers for American interests if the United States was identified as supporting colonial powers. Finally, the Soviet Union was expected to create unrest in colonial regions and to exploit any resulting upheaval to its political advantage (12–13).

The agency concluded it was vital for the United States to generate goodwill in these new nations. It recommended that the United States temper its support for European allies engaged in colonial control of foreign lands in order to not be identified with colonialism. The CIA predicted colonialism would become a losing venture for Europe and that "attempts at forcible retention of critical colonial areas in the face of growing nationalist pressure may actually weaken rather than strengthen the colonial powers" (CIA 1948: 13).[4]

It is worth speculating on what lost strands of U.S. intelligence analysis favoring postcolonial independence might have developed in an alternate universe where Truman left the OSS's former intelligence and operations branches disarticulated into the State Department and War Department, but in a world where intelligence and operations were conjoined, and Kennan's Cold War game plan aggressively guided American policy, such developments were not to be. As a result, CIA reports questioning the wisdom of aligning American interests with colonial powers were destined to be ignored and overwritten by emerging hegemonic Cold War desires.

Seeing Like a CIA

From its beginnings, the CIA established links with academia. These earliest links exploited connections with academics with wartime OSS service who returned to university positions after the war. An article in the CIA's journal *Studies in Intelligence* noted that "close ties between the Central Intelligence Agency and American colleges and universities have existed since the birth of the Agency in 1947" (Cook 1983: 33). Given the connections of OSS personnel to Harvard, Yale, Columbia, and other elite universities, it was natural that "a disproportionate number of the new recruits came from the same schools. Similarly, professors who had joined the Agency often turned to their former colleagues still on campuses for consultation and assistance. This 'old boy' system was quite productive in providing new employees in the professional ranks. Thus, there was an early linkage between the Agency and the Ivy League, or similar schools" (Cook, 34; Jeffreys-Jones 1985).

In 1951, the CIA launched its University Associates Program, which secretly connected the agency with university professors on fifty U.S. campuses. Select universities became "consultant-contacts who would receive a nominal fee for spotting promising students, steering them into studies and activities of interest to the Agency, and eventually nominating them for recruitment" (Cook 1983: 34). But the CIA's recruitment techniques narrowed rather than expanded its views. In 1954, the Doolittle Commission Report found the CIA's close link to World War II networks hampered its development, and that the heavy use of elite universities for recruitment limited the agency's potential. It recommended that the CIA fire some of its OSS-era employees and expand its campus recruitment efforts to a broader variety of university campuses (Doolittle et al. 1954: 25).[5]

The CIA secretly groomed campus contacts, known within the agency as "P-Sources" (professor sources) (Cook 1983; Price 2011f). P-Sources, who had high value within the agency, sometimes provided debriefings after travel to foreign nations and at other times wrote papers relating to their academic expertise. The number of these P-Sources is unknown, but William Corson, a historian and a Marine Corps lieutenant colonel, estimated that by the mid-1970s as many as five thousand academics were cooperating with the CIA on at least a part-time basis (Corson 1977: 312). During the early 1950s, professional organizations like the American Anthropological Association at times secretly, or unwittingly, worked with the CIA, providing it with membership lists and lists of area specialists (see chapters 3 and 7).

The agency sometimes secretly drew on groups of academics possessing desired knowledge to supplement its understanding of issues. One such group, known as the Princeton Consultants, was established in early 1951 and was tasked with complementing the work of the CIA's newly established Office of National Estimates. The original group consisted of eight scholars who were paid a modest stipend and met in Princeton with CIA personnel four times a year to discuss specific problems of interest to the agency, bringing outside views and broader approaches to problems (Steury 1994: 111; see CIA 1959b: 2). The group, which grew in size, continued to meet in Princeton for decades (CIA 1959a; see table 1.1).

When the existence of the Princeton Consultants became public in the 1970s, members Cyril Black and Klaus Knorr "denied any relationship between the National Intelligence Estimates and the CIA's covert activities" (Cavanagh 1980). Black's and Knorr's denials were in one sense true given that most of their work was aligned with making projections for the Office of National Estimates and the improbability that they had access to details about covert actions. However, as Cavanagh (1980) noted, Calvin Hoover's memoirs suggest some of the work provided by the Princeton Consultants was consistent with the preparatory work undertaken in plotting the CIA's 1953 Iranian coup.

In 1963, the CIA's 100 Universities Program sought to improve the agency's public image and to boost campus recruitments by expanding its presence on American campuses (see CIA 1963c). Former CIA case officer John Stockwell described the agency's Foreign Resources Division as its "*domestic* covert operations division," linking CIA case officers with professors and students at "every major campus in the nation. They work with professors, using aliases on

TABLE 1.1. Listing of the CIA's Princeton Consultants

NAME	INSTITUTIONAL AFFILIATION	CITATION
Norman Armour	Former ambassador	(Steury 1994: 110)
Hamilton Fish Armstrong	*Foreign Affairs*	(Montague 1992: 135; CIA 1959b)
Samuel Bemis	Yale University	(Steury 1994: 110)
James Billington	Princeton University, History	(Cavanagh 1980)
Richard Bissell	CIA, Deputy Director of Plans	(Steury 1994: 110)
Cyril Black	Princeton University, Soviet Studies	(Cavanagh 1980; CIA 1959b)
Robert Bowie	Harvard, International Studies	(Cavanagh 1980)
Vannevar Bush	OSRD, NACA	(Montague 1992: 135)
Burton Fahs	Director of Humanities, Rockefeller Foundation	(Steury 1994: 110; Montague 1992: 136)
Gordon Gray	Secretary of the Army/ national security adviser	(Steury 1994: 110)
Joseph Grew	Former ambassador	(Steury 1994: 110)
Caryl P. Haskins	Carnegie Inst., director	(Cavanagh 1980)
Barklie Henry	New York businessman	(Montague 1992: 136; Steury 1994: 110)
Calvin Hoover	Duke, Soviet Economics	(Cavanagh 1980; CIA 1959b)
William H. Jackson	CIA, Deputy Director	(Steury 1994: 110)
George Kennan	Career, Foreign Service etc.	(Montague 1992: 135)
Klaus Knorr	Princeton University, Strategic Studies	(Cavanagh 1980; CIA 1959b)
William Langer	Harvard, History	(Steury 1994: 110)
George A. Lincoln		(CIA 1959b)
Harold F. Linder	Chair, Export-Import Bank, Asst. Sec of State	(Cavanagh 1980)
Max Millikan	MIT, International Studies, Econ	(Steury 1994: 110)
Philip Mosely	Columbia University	(Steury 1994: 110; CIA 1959b)
Lucian Pye	MIT, Political Science	(Cavanagh 1980)
Raymond Sontag	UC Berkeley, European History	(Steury 1994: 110)
Alexander Standing		(Montague 1992: 136)
Joseph Strayer	Princeton, Medieval history	(Steury 1994: 110; CIA 1959b)
T. Cuyler Young Sr.	Princeton, Near East studies	(Steury 1994: 110)

various programs. Their activities include building files on students whom the professors help them target" (Stockwell 1991: 102–3).

Curating Knowledge and Intelligence at the CIA

As part of its effort to monitor and control international developments, the early CIA collected and curated global knowledge. The agency envisioned that even the almost random collection of knowledge could eventually, if organized and retrievable, later be used in intelligence capacities. The scope of its approach to collecting disarticulated bits of knowledge is shown in Jane Schnell's classified article "Snapshots at Random" (1961), which described a CIA collection known as the "Graphic Register." This was the agency archive of photographs collected from all over the world showing routine features and elements of physical culture. These photographs were cataloged and analyzed for use at some unknown date in CIA operations.

Schnell encouraged CIA employees planning future trips to "some less well frequented place" to contact agency personnel maintaining the Register to see if it was interested in providing them with film and a camera (Schnell 1961: 17). The CIA wanted almost any image from abroad. Schnell wrote, "The fact that an object may have been photographed previously by no means disqualifies it: changes, or the absence of changes, in it over a period of years or of weeks may be important. And changes aside, it is amazing how many pictures of the same object can be taken without telling the whole story" (18).

The scale of Schnell's project revealed core CIA conceits from this period, as if the unguided particularist collection of at-the-time meaningless information could inevitably lead to useful breakthroughs later. The CIA believed that if enough information was collected from enough angles, American intelligence could develop a comprehensive view of the world it sought to control. No mundane event or artifact was too insignificant for collection. According to Schnell:

> If a new gas storage tank is being built in the city where you are stationed and you drive past it going to work every day, why not photograph it once a week or once a month? The photos will tell how long it takes to build it, what types of materials and methods of construction are used, and how much gas storage capacity is being added. Maybe you don't know what a gas storage tank looks like, and all you see is a big tank being built. Take a picture of it anyway; obviously it is built to store something. What you don't know about it the analyst will. That is what he is an analyst for, but he can't analyze it if you don't get him the pictures. (1961: 18–19)

This project was an emblematic representation of the CIA's midcentury project: it was well funded, global, brash, panoptical, without borders or limits. It was funded despite the unlikelihood that it would ever produce much useful intelligence, and working under conditions of secrecy removed normal general expectations of outcomes or accountability.

Other Cold War intelligence agencies also established massive collections they imagined could be of use at some hypothetical future date. While enrolled in a spycraft lock-picking class, former British MI5 counterintelligence agent Peter Wright encountered a massive cellar room with thousands of keys, meticulously cataloged and arranged on walls. His instructor told the class that MI5 made it a practice to secretly collect key imprints "of offices, hotels, or private houses ... all over Britain." The instructor's explanation for the collection was simply that "you never know when you might need a key again" (Wright 1988: 51). In *The File* (1998), Timothy Garton Ash described the East German intelligence agency, Stassi's, massive collection of personal items (including underwear and other articles of clothing) that might be of use at some unknown future date if Stassi needed to use tracking dogs to locate the owner of the stolen item. These items were processed and placed in plastic bags, then sorted and stored in Stassi's immense, efficient archival filing system for unknown future uses. Edward Snowden's more recent disclosures of rampant National Security Agency (NSA) electronic monitoring establish that the agency collected previously unfathomable amounts of data on billions of people on the assumption the information might be of use at some future date (Greenwald 2014; Price 2013c).

Intelligence agencies' vast collections of (immediately) useless objects illustrate institutional commitments to establishing stores of intangibly useful resources that *might* have intelligence uses at unforeseen future times. A powerful national security state collecting unlimited numbers of obscure, useless snapshots with no conceivable direct applications thought nothing of supporting area study centers (teaching a spectrum of languages, which ranged from having obvious to nonexistent security applications), and a broad range of nonapplied anthropological research grants without direct applications to intelligence work. Academics might well collect needed bits of unconnected knowledge that CIA analysts could later use for tasks yet to be determined.

But this rapid growth in intelligence activities also brought unease as President Eisenhower (1961) raised awareness of the "danger that public policy could itself become the captive of a scientific-technological elite." The secret report, titled "Conclusions and Recommendations of the President's Committee on

Information Activities Abroad" (CIAA 1960), more commonly known as "The Sprague Report," captured the unease, philosophical position, and growing reliance on academics as the CIA embarked on a new phase of the Cold War. The report described the agency's use of U.S. labor unions to establish relationships with labor union movements in communist countries and noted political gains from open academic exchange programs funded by public or private means (CIAA 1960: 53–54, 65). Academic exchanges were acknowledged as important Cold War weapons that needed funding because "in our exchange programs we must outdo the Sino-Soviet Bloc in selection of leaders and students with leadership potential, quality of programs offered, and treatment accorded visitors" (78).

George Ecklund's secret article "Guns or Butter Problems of the Cold War" unapologetically noted that "the world now spends about $135 billion annually on the war industry, roughly as much as the entire income of the poorer half of mankind. The United States spends a little more than a third of the total, the USSR about a third, and the rest of the world a little less than a third" (1965: 1–2). Ecklund described the negative impacts of such high levels of military spending on the Soviet economy and the problems this presented for the Soviets' ability to spend funds on human needs at home and on those they hoped to influence in international technical assistance programs. He projected that such continued levels of military spending would be devastating to economic growth for the Soviet Union.

Ecklund did not consider whether American runaway military spending would establish *domestic* crippling economic deficits or direct federal spending priorities away from national health care, mass transit infrastructure, education, and other programs. Instead, Ecklund asked and answered questions in ways that ignored what these developments meant for the homeland while stressing the anticipated devastating impact on the Soviet system.

The Fourth Estate Reveals Ongoing Patterns of CIA Lawlessness

The decade between 1966 and 1976 brought numerous journalistic exposés that revealed CIA involvement in widespread covert and illegal activities. White House and congressional investigations followed, as did startling revelations by disillusioned former CIA agents. Both mainstream and alternative newspapers and magazines played crucial roles in uncovering these activities. Many Americans viewed these secret programs as undermining the possibility of American democracy. These revelations shocked the public and pushed Congress to pass legislation limiting specific practices and establishing increased congressional oversight of the CIA through the Hughes-Ryan Act of 1974.

The CIA used dummy foundations known as funding fronts to provide the appearance of neutral funds for scholars conducting research of interest to the agency. Early public revelations about these fronts financing academic research and travel were made by Sol Stern in *Ramparts* magazine in 1967. Stern discovered this CIA connection as a result of Representative Wright Patman's 1964 congressional hearings investigating the impacts of nonprofits on American political processes (U.S. Congress 1964). Patman's subcommittee investigated Internal Revenue Service (IRS) documents of various groups and uncovered anomalies in the records of several foundations. When Patman inquired about irregularities in the Kaplan Fund's records, Mitchell Rogovin, assistant to the IRS commissioner, privately told him that the fund was a CIA front, used to finance programs of interest to the agency, an arrangement that was confirmed by the CIA representative Patman contacted. Patman identified eight nonprofits that had financially supported the Kaplan Fund while it was operating as a CIA conduit: the Gotham Foundation, the Michigan Fund, the Andrew Hamilton Fund, the Borden Trust, the Price Fund, the Edsel Fund, the Beacon Fund, and the Kentfield Fund (U.S. Congress 1964: 191; Hailey 1964). Patman publicly revealed these CIA-Kaplan connections after the CIA refused to comply with his requests for information about these relationships (U.S. Congress 1964: 191).

After Patman's revelations, several newspapers condemned these practices. The *New York Times* called for the end of CIA funding fronts, arguing that they allowed "the Communists and the cynical everywhere to charge that American scholars, scientists, and writers going abroad on grants from foundations are cover agents or spies for C.I.A. All scholars — especially those involved in East-West exchanges — will suffer if the integrity of their research is thus made suspect" (NYT 1964: 28). On September 7, 1964, the *Pittsburgh Post Gazette & Sun* wrote that "the CIA's intrusion into policy-making, its reported defiance of higher executive authority on occasion and its secret operations in the domestic field are enough to make citizens wary of its role in a democracy" (reproduced in U.S. Congress 1964: Exhibit 48). Because Patman did not further pursue CIA wrongdoing (Pearson 1967), even with such concerns over unlawful interference in domestic activities, there were no further investigations into the agency's use of these fronts until three years later, when Sol Stern published his exposé in *Ramparts*. Stern's article established that the CIA secretly had provided the National Student Association with $1.6 million since 1959, during a period in which the association was experiencing funding difficulties.

Starting with information from 1964 news reports on Wright Patman's hearings, Stern used Patman's discoveries and identified more CIA funding fronts, conduits, and recipients. Stern determined that the CIA had used fronts identified by Patman to fund the National Student Association and to manipulate policies within the association. He learned that, in 1965, the CIA had approached the president of a "prominent New England foundation" requesting access to the foundation's list of funded organizations. After viewing the list, CIA agents explained that they would like to use the foundation to support some already funded and new organizations of interest to the CIA, so that they could "channel CIA money into the foundation without it ever being traced back to the CIA. They said they were very skilled at these manipulations" (Stern 1967: 31). This foundation's board rejected the CIA's proposal, but other foundations accepted CIA funds and passed them along to unwitting individuals and programs.

One *Ramparts* reporter found that when he tracked down CIA front foundation addresses, he "usually found himself in a law office where no one was willing to talk about the Funds" (Stern 1967: 31). Stern traced CIA funds passing through several intermediary foundations (e.g., the J. Frederick Brown Foundation and the Independence Foundation) that were themselves funded by CIA fronts (31), with other money coming from the CIA-linked Rabb, Kaplan, Farfield, San Jacinto Foundation, Independence, Tower, and Price Funds and eventually reaching the National Student Association with no visible links to the CIA (32).

Stern's report had a significant impact on the public. *Ramparts* purchased large ads in the *New York Times* announcing the piece, and there were widespread reactions to the story. Art Buchwald (1967) wrote a humorous piece, spinning ridiculous CIA cover stories, including one in which the CIA had accidentally funded the National Student Association, thinking it was giving money to the National Security Agency. While numerous editorials on these fronts criticized the CIA, Thomas Braden published "I'm Glad the CIA Is 'Immoral'" (1967) in the *Saturday Evening Post*, describing his role in passing CIA funds to the American Federation of Labor to bolster anticommunist unions in Europe. Braden disclosed that CIA funding had helped the Boston Symphony Orchestra, the International Committee of Women, and the Congress for Cultural Freedom advance against the forces of international communism. He bragged about the CIA secretly using Jay Lovestone, the former leader of the Communist Party USA and an anticommunist, to subvert communist advances in French labor struggles. Carl Rowan, former director of the U.S. Information Service (USIS), claimed in his syndicated column that the National Student Association exposé in *Ramparts* was part of a communist plot (Richardson 2009: 78). Stern's investigation did not need communist agents passing on CIA front identities: his information was in the congressional record, and Rowan's USIS background suggests his attack was nothing more than "disinformation from the CIA propaganda machine" (Richardson 2009: 78).[6]

Stern's revelations led mainstream media outlets to investigate the CIA's use of funding fronts to infiltrate domestic organizations (see *Newsweek* 1967). Public concerns led President Johnson to appoint Under Secretary of State Nicholas Katzenbach to lead a commission investigating CIA programs that stood to "endanger the integrity and independence of the educational community." But with Director of Central Intelligence (DCI) Richard Helms on the committee, there was little chance of uncovering anything that the agency did not want made public, and even less chance that the committee would recommend criminal trials for CIA employees violating the agency's charter limiting its domestic activities. President Johnson later received political payback for appointing a committee supporting the status quo; "having 'saved' the Agency, he demanded its loyalty on the Vietnam issue. His demand produced further cosmetic exercises, including an attempt to discredit political protest against the war and the suppression of dissent within the CIA" (Jeffreys-Jones 1989: 156). But even as the Katzenbach Commission downplayed CIA criminal wrongdoing, it confirmed widespread CIA infiltration of domestic political organizations and revealed that the agency covertly funded the publication of more than a thousand books for academic and general audiences, as well as magazines like *Encounter* and *Partisan Review* (Wilford 2008; U.S. Senate 1976: 189).

Movements to keep the CIA off American campuses began in 1966; with time this campaign spread and focused on keeping both CIA recruiters and sponsored research off campus (Mills 1991; Price 2011e). A confidential 1968 CIA report titled "Student Reaction to CIA Recruitment Activities on Campus" summarized the stages of the movement's growth and credited *Ramparts* with spawning antirecruitment campaigns at Grinnell College, the City College of New York, San Jose State, and Harvard in 1966 (CIA 1968b: 1). The CIA found that while these protests brought unfavorable publicity to the agency, a "*New York Times* series of articles on the Agency's world-wide activities did much good and no perceptible harm. On the whole, the publicity and free advertising did more good than harm for the recruitment effort—inspiring a great many write-in candidates of whom we might never have heard otherwise—and emphasized the fact that the press and the reading public will take a special interest in what the Agency does" (1).[7] The following year brought more anti-CIA campus campaigns, with an increase from four campus incidents in 1966 to twenty-seven in 1967, including "a physical incarceration of two recruiters at Columbia University" (2). By 1968, there were seventy-seven anti-CIA campus protests, with the agency identifying the [Students for a Democratic Society] as the "primary instigators" (2).

In 1968, Julius Mader published *Who's Who in the CIA*, claiming to identify hundreds of individuals with CIA connections. Mader's methodology was crude, drawing mostly on published biographical details of Americans working in diplomatic and other capacities, focusing particularly on individuals with wartime intelligence links, but also on those in roles traditionally fulfilled by CIA agents at foreign embassies. Mader's scattershot approach led to several errors, and his work was rumored to have been produced with KGB and Stassi assistance.[8] This book and a growing number of nonscholarly works making untrue claims about the CIA fed growing public concerns about the agency's unchecked powers.

President Johnson's efforts at damage control and at managing public opinions about the CIA had limited results. The period from 1967 until the mid-1970s brought ongoing revelations about CIA, the FBI, and military intelligence engaging in widespread illegal activities, including unlawful use of these agencies to monitor and manipulate domestic political developments. These activities affected American college campuses, with the FBI not only monitoring anthropologists and other students on campus but at times also using young future anthropologist agent provocateurs to infiltrate, disrupt, and spy on campus political movements (see Divale 1970). In 1970, Christopher Pyle, a former army employee, revealed that the army had a secret intelligence network devoted to spying on U.S. citizens protesting the Vietnam War. Pyle disclosed that "The Army employed more than 1,500 plainclothes agents, coast to coast, to watch every demonstration of 20 people or more" (2002). Investigations led by Senator Sam Ervin and the Judiciary Subcommittee on Constitutional Rights substantiated Pyle's revelations.

On March 8, 1971, a small group of activists broke in to the FBI Field Station in Media, Pennsylvania, and stole records documenting the FBI's illegal Counter Intelligence Program (COINTELPRO), which harassed and spied on leftist political groups (see Medsger 2014). These records established how groups ranging from the American Indian Movement to the Black Panthers were infiltrated, harassed, and at times encouraged to engage in illegal activities by the FBI. With each revelation, the American public came to understand that open democratic processes had been covertly subverted by a hidden network of intelligence agencies; with further leaks documenting CIA and FBI lawlessness, pressures built for congressional investigations.

The CIA's Family Jewels

Richard Helms resigned as the director of the CIA in February 1973 and was replaced by James R. Schlesinger.[9] In May 1973, Schlesinger directed the agency to conduct a classified secret in-house study identifying all past and present CIA operations that were likely outside of its operational charter. By the time the report was completed, William Colby had replaced Schlesinger as DCI. The report, known as "The Family Jewels," was a 693-page compilation of portions of memos and files that provided a detailed account of the CIA's illegal activities. "The Family Jewels" described the agency's involvement in extensive illegal domestic intelligence operations including broad surveillance of U.S. news reporters and American political dissidents (including compiling almost 10,000 pages of files on anti–Vietnam War protesters); break-ins at homes of defectors, former CIA employees, and CIA critics; forging of ID documents; and kidnappings and assassination plots against state leaders (Fidel Castro, Patrice Lumumba, and Rafael Trujillo). News reporting on this document caused a political eruption that the executive and legislative branches could not ignore.

On December 22, 1974, Seymour Hersh published a *New York Times* story, titled "Huge CIA Operation Reported in US against Anti-war Forces, Other Dissidents in Nixon Years," that drew on leaked portions of "The Family Jewels" (Hersh 1974b); President Ford and members of Congress first learned of this program from Hersh's article. After Hersh revealed Operation CHAOS' illegal monitoring of more than one hundred thousand U.S. citizens, Ford asked DCI Colby for a background report on CHAOS. Colby briefed the president on a range of illegal activities revealed in the report, including the Inspector General's 1967 report on the CIA's program for assassinating foreign leaders. A few weeks later, in an "off-the-record" meeting with the *New York Times* editorial board, President Ford raised concerns that congressional investigations could unearth the existence of CIA's assassination programs.

The *Times* did not report on the CIA's assassination program. But when CBS newsman Daniel Schorr, who had no ties to the *Times*, learned that Ford had acknowledged CIA involvement in assassinations, Schorr (incorrectly) assumed these were domestic assassinations, and when Colby responded to Schorr's efforts to get more information on the program, Colby inadvertently redirected Schorr's focus to international assassinations. With this information Schorr broadcast the news of an international CIA assassination program on CBS television on February 28, 1975 (see Schorr 1977: 144–49). The Church Committee hearings later examined CIA efforts to assassinate a number of foreign leaders, including Fidel Castro of Cuba, Ngao Dinh Diem of Vietnam, Patrice Lumumba of the Congo, General René Schneider of Chile, and Rafael Trujillo of the Dominican Republic.

Wishing to preempt a disruptive congressional investigation, President Ford appointed Vice President Nelson Rockefeller to chair the eight-member fact-finding commission.[10] The Rockefeller Commission report (*Report to the President by the Commission on CIA Activities within the United States*, June 1975) identified several illegal CIA activities and issued recommendations for CIA reform, including that a CIA database on hundreds of thousands of Americans be destroyed (N. Rockefeller 1975). The commission provided descriptive summaries rather than specific accounts of a range of illegal activities, and its weak recommendations reduced its impact and indicated Ford's desire to limit Americans' knowledge of CIA activities.

The Rockefeller Commission established that the CIA had read more than 2.3 million pieces of American mail in its Soviet mail monitoring program; indexed 7 million individual names (under Operation CHAOS) (Rockefeller 1975: 24–34, 41); and used the Agency for International Development and an unnamed American university to run a CIA counterinsurgency "training school for foreign police and security officers" in the United States, which also "sold small amounts of licensed firearms and police equipment to the foreign officers and their departments" (39). Despite the report's admonitions that the CIA should not repeat these illegal and inadvisable acts, no one at the agency was arrested, and no concrete forms of oversight were forthcoming as a result of the Rockefeller report.

In 1975, former CIA agent Philip Agee published *Inside the Company: CIA Diary*, providing detailed accounts of his activities as a CIA operative in Ecuador, Uruguay, and Mexico. Agee identified 250 CIA agents or officers, as well as Latin American presidents who collaborated with the CIA, and he recounted bugging operations and CIA torture and described how he had recruited and managed CIA spy networks abroad. *Inside the Company* publicized how the agency undermined foreign democratic movements aligned with socialism, depicting it as a cynical organization supporting authoritarian governments aligned with U.S. business interests.[11] Agee's later work with Louis Wolf on the book *Dirty Work* and in the magazines *CounterSpy* and *Covert Action Information Bulletin* led to the publication of hundreds of other CIA employee names.

The Church Committee

In response to the revelations of ongoing press reports on "The Family Jewels," Watergate, and COINTELPRO and growing suspicions of illegal activities undertaken by the FBI and the CIA, in 1975 the U.S. Senate Select Committee to Study Governmental Operations with Respect to Intelligence Activities held hearings investigating the CIA's illegal activities. The committee, which came to be known simply as the Church Committee (after its chair, Senator Frank Church, D-ID), produced fourteen volumes of reports documenting hundreds of illegal activities ranging from kidnapping, murder, and drugging of unsuspecting civilians to the widespread infiltration and subversion of domestic academic institutions.

Book 1, section 10, of the Church Committee's report summarized the committee's findings on the CIA's ability to covertly influence the production of academic knowledge. The committee found that the CIA's Domestic Collection Division routinely contacted American academics traveling abroad, and that the Foreign Resources Division was "the purely operational arm of the CIA in dealing with American academics." Between these two divisions, the CIA had contacts "with many thousands of United States academics at hundreds of U.S. academic institutions" (U.S. Senate 1976: 189).

The CIA's Office of Personnel secretly worked with university administrators to facilitate the recruitment of students. The CIA's operational use of academics raised "troubling questions as to preservation of the integrity of American academic institutions" (U.S. Senate 1976: 189). The report described extensive covert contacts with American academics, yet the committee chose not to identify specific individuals or institutions compromised by the CIA.

The Church Committee's investigations into the use of funding fronts for international research projects had significance for anthropology, as the committee determined the following:

> The CIA's intrusion into the foundation field in the 1960s can only be described as massive. Excluding grants from the "Big Three"—Ford, Rockefeller, and Carnegie—of the 700 grants over $10,000 given by 164 other foundations during the period 1963–1966, at least 108 involved partial or complete CIA funding. More importantly, *CIA funding was involved in nearly half the grants the non-"Big Three" foundations made during this period in the field of international activities.*[12] *In the same period more than one-third of the grants awarded by non-"Big Three" in the physical, life and social sciences also involved CIA funds.* . . . A 1966 CIA study

explained the use of legitimate foundations was the most effective way of concealing the CIA's hand as well as reassuring members of funding organizations that the organization was in fact supported by private funds. The Agency study contended that this technique was "particularly effective for democratically-run membership organizations, which need to assure their own unwitting members and collaborators, as well as their hostile critics, that they have genuine, respectable, private sources of income. (U.S. Senate 1976: 182–83, emphasis added)

In most instances the academics receiving these funds were unaware that the CIA funded their work. The committee identified "several hundred" instances in which the CIA had established covert relationships with academics at more than a hundred university campuses performing CIA-backed jobs, including "making introductions for intelligence purposes" and writing books or "material to be used for propaganda purposes abroad" (U.S. Senate 1976: 190). At most universities no one outside of the CIA contact knew of these relationships, and all such contacts were guarded by the agency, which considered "these operational relationships with the United States academic community as perhaps its most sensitive domestic area and [imposed] strict controls governing these operations" (190).

One of the ways that the CIA shaped the funding of international research was by planting agency employees in key positions on foundations. In 1955, DCI Dulles responded to a request by Don K. Price, acting president of the Ford Foundation, to loan a CIA employee to serve on the Ford Foundation staff, writing that he would make a CIA employee (female, identity redacted) available to the foundation for two years, adding that "we consider her competency such that, with a period of service with you, she and this Agency will gain significantly" (FOIA CIA-RDP80B01676R004000140015–9, AD to DKP, 8/13/55). The strategic placement of one such CIA employee within Ford or other Foundations could influence untold numbers of funding decisions; though the record is incomplete (due to the CIA's refusal to publicly release its own records), we can assume that this relationship at Ford was replicated at other key foundations.[13]

Recently declassified CIA reports have shed light on some of the ways that the CIA, the Pentagon, and other governmental agencies working on counterinsurgency projects or other intelligence matters influenced and benefited from government-funded social science research during the Cold War. Henry Loomis (of the Psychological Strategy Board [PSB]) produced "Report on Social Science Research in Cold War Operations" (1952), a CIA report outlining strategies for using American social science research to further the agency's knowledge and goals (FOIA CIA-CIA-RDP80R01731R001700230005-8, 4/11/52). Loomis worked with Max Millikan (FOIA CIA-RDP80R01731R003300090002-9, 5/5/52) where he advocated letting the PSB oversee this CIA-linked research within and outside the agency (FOIA CIA-RDP80R01731R003300090003-8, 5/19/52). The articulations of such relationships were described in some detail in a 1962 CIA report:

> The External Research Division maintains an index of government sponsored contractual research on foreign areas, obtaining the pertinent data from the sponsoring agencies. Each calendar quarter it publishes an inventory of contracts. (The publication is classified "Secret.") A tabulation of some 400 contracts reported in the publication over a period of several quarters reveals that the Agency for International Development reported roughly 155 contracts, Air Force reported 125 and CIA reported 56. Other agencies varied from a low of one (NSA and Arms Control, one each) to a high of 22 for Army. The information on these contracts is usually gathered and published after the research contracts have been let. Advance coordination through the External Research Division is not required and, therefore, there is not a uniform method of coordination. Some offices (OSI for example) conduct a search of the quarterly published inventory prior to entering into new contracts. ORR, in addition to searching the published inventory, coordinates its external research requirements through the Economic Intelligence Committee (USIB) and the EIC, in turn, requests the External Research Division to conduct a search of its records. The offices do, however, make consistent use of the inventory. The value of a central record such as that maintained by the External Research Division was demonstrated recently when the Division, in response to a request from Senator Fulbright, was able to supply the Senator with a consolidated report of government sponsored external research on the USSR and Communist China.
>
> ... In addition to the records maintained and published on government sponsored research, the Division maintains a private research catalogue of social science research conducted in the United States on foreign areas and international affairs. Information for the catalogue is obtained through annual surveys of universities, foundations, research centers, etc. The catalogue is unclassified and is open to the public. External Research lists of current private research on foreign areas and international affairs are published and distributed throughout the government and to university libraries, department heads, individual scholars, and foreign academic institutions. (FOIA CIA-RDP80B01676R002400030004-1, 7/26/62)

During 1962 discussions on how the CIA, the U.S. Agency for International Development (USAID), Air Force Intelligence, and other governmental agencies might best coordinate the use of the social and behavioral science research being produced, the CIA suggested the formation of a "working group" with "a number of coordinating specialists thoroughly familiar with the literature in the relevant fields whose duty it would be to maintain liaisons with all government agencies and research scholars" (FOIA CIA-RDP80B01676R002400030004–1, 7/26/62).

Between 1952 and 1967, the CIA covertly funded U.S. scholars to write more than a thousand books representing views the agency wished to propagate. Of these books, the Church Committee determined that "approximately 25 percent of them were written in English. Many of them were published by cultural organizations which the CIA backed, and more often than not the author was unaware of CIA subsidization. Some books, however, involved direct collaboration between the CIA and the writer" (U.S. Senate 1976: 193). Former CIA agent E. Howard Hunt's testimony confirmed CIA books were distributed in the U.S., and the Church Committee concluded "that such fallout may not have been unintentional," adding that U.S. citizens were "a likely audience" when this propaganda was published in English (U.S. Senate 1976: 198–99). When asked by the committee (which was concerned that the CIA had illegally engaged in domestic propaganda) if the agency took steps to limit domestic exposure to the CIA books published by Praeger or others, Hunt replied:

> It was impossible because Praeger was a commercial U.S. publisher. His books had to be seen, had to be reviewed, had to be bought here, had to be read.... If your targets are foreign, then where are they? They don't all necessarily read English, and we had a bilateral agreement with the British that we wouldn't propagandize their people. So unless the book goes into a lot of languages or it is published in India, for example, where English is a *lingua franca*, then you have some basic problems. And I think the way this was rationalized by the project review board ... was that the ultimate target was foreign, which was true, but how much of the Praeger output actually got abroad for any impact I think is highly arguable. (U.S. Senate 1976: 198–99)

In response to Hunt's revelations that Praeger had published CIA propaganda in the United States, the committee concluded that, "given the paucity of information and the inaccessibility of China in the 1960s, the CIA may have helped shape American attitudes toward the emerging China. The CIA considers such 'fallout' inevitable" (U.S. Senate 1976: 199).

Pike Commission

The House investigations of the CIA were more aggressive than the Senate's, and unlike the Senate's Church Committee, the House proceeded largely without the CIA's cooperation. The House Select Committee on Intelligence began its investigation in February 1975 under the leadership of Congressman Lucien N. Nedzi. The initial selection of Nedzi as chair raised concerns that his previous role as chair of the House Armed Services Subcommittee on Intelligence had compromised his ability to conduct an independent investigation. When a *New York Times* story revealed that DCI Colby had privately briefed Nedzi about the CIA's "Family Jewels" in 1973, Nedzi was replaced as chair by Congressman Otis Pike.

Conflicts between Pike and DCI Colby began before the hearings were convened. Pike interpreted congressional oversight of CIA to include the right to declassify documents and information as Congress saw fit. The CIA maintained it had control of what information would be given to Congress (see Haines 1989: 84). Colby was contemptuous of the Pike Committee and refused to disclose the CIA's budget in public session, while within the agency, Colby was despised by many CIA loyalists who resented him allowing any critical public scrutiny of the agency.

In an effort to understand the range of CIA actions and the oversight that the Forty Committee had exercised over CIA activities, the committee reviewed all CIA covert actions between 1965 and 1975 (Pike Report 1977: 187). The committee devised six historical tests to measure the effectiveness of the CIA's analytical abilities to correctly foresee significant political events: the 1968 Tet Offensive in Vietnam, the August 1968 Soviet action in Czechoslovakia, the 1973 war between Israel and Syria and Egypt, the April 1974 coup in Portugal, the CIA's monitoring of India's nuclear arms program, and the 1974 Cyprus crisis. The committee found that the CIA failed to meaningfully anticipate any of these developments, and that these failures left America in a weakened position.

The Pike Committee found that even after President Johnson wrote directives prohibiting the CIA from covertly funding U.S. educational institutions (after the 1967 National Student Association revelations in *Ramparts*), the CIA "unilaterally reserved the right to, and does, depart from the Presidential order when it has the need to do so" (Pike Report 1977: 117). The committee determined that between 1965 and 1975 about one-third of the covert actions approved by the Forty Committee involved CIA efforts to influence the outcomes of foreign elections (190). Another third (29 percent) of the CIA's Forty

Committee-approved covert activities during this period involved "media and propaganda projects" (190). These projects included covert CIA control of the publication of books and magazines within the U.S. and abroad, though "by far the largest single recipient has been a European publishing house funded since 1951," with a "number of similar operations in the region" (190). About a quarter of the funds (23 percent) for the CIA's operations during this period went to the procurement and distribution of arms and covert paramilitary training, and "at times, CIA has been used as a conduit for arms transfers in order to bypass Congressional scrutiny" (191).

The report evaluated three types of CIA covert operations: "election support" (e.g., subverting democratic movements abroad), arms support, and the backing of independence movements of the National Front for the Independence of Angola (FNLA) and the National Union for the Total Independence of Angola (UNITA) in Angola. Investigation into the CIA's use of USAID "foreign police training" programs on American university campuses found these programs were also used by the CIA to monitor campus activities (Pike Report 1977: 228–29).

Whereas the Church Committee found the CIA to at times be a "rogue" agency engaging in unauthorized illegal activities, the Pike Committee found that the CIA bypassed congressional oversight and operated under executive branch control. This finding of consistent executive branch CIA oversight was *the* crucial finding of the Pike Report. It showed how presidents, through the NSC, the Forty Committee, and at times directly through DCIs, used the CIA as a covert tool of executive branch policy. As former career CIA agent Ralph McGehee later wrote, "My view backed by 25 years of experience is, quite simply, that the CIA is the covert action arm of the Presidency" (1983: xi). The Pike Report concluded that "all evidence in hand suggests that the CIA, far from being out of control, has been utterly responsive to the instructions of the President and the Assistant to the President for National Security Affairs. It must be remembered, however that the CIA director determines which CIA-initiated covert action projects are sufficiently 'politically sensitive' to require Presidential attention" (Pike Report 1977: 189). While the executive branch exercised control of the CIA's covert actions, proposed CIA covert actions also came from others, including "a foreign head of state, the Department of Defense, the Department of State, an Ambassador, CIA, the Assistant to the President for National Security Affairs, a cabinet member or the President himself" (Pike Report 1977: 187).[14] As Pike put it, "The CIA never did anything the White House didn't want. Sometimes they didn't want to do what they did" (Pike qtd. in Haines 1998: 88). House Republicans blocked publication of the final report, but Daniel Schorr leaked an early draft to the *Village Voice*, which published it in its entirety (Schorr 1976; Pike Report 1977; Benson 1976).

One short-term outcome of press revelations and of the findings of the Rockefeller, Pike, and Church committees was the establishment of new congressional oversight of CIA activities. President Ford signed Executive Order 11905, banning political assassinations, creating the new National Security Committee on Foreign Intelligence, replacing the Forty Committee with the Operations Advisory Group, and clarifying the necessity of reporting illegal activities to the executive branch. In 1978, President Carter signed Executive Order 12036, restructuring oversight groups, a change that was widely interpreted as providing more CIA oversight, yet the executive branch retained oversight control over the agency. The Foreign Intelligence Surveillance Act (1978) established new congressional and judicial oversight of the CIA's domestic surveillance abilities.

Although the CIA appeared publicly complacent with presidential and congressional reform efforts, it resisted efforts to curtail its covert relationships with universities. When pressed by Senator Edward Kennedy to contact individuals and universities that had unwittingly received CIA funding through MK-Ultra projects (discussed in chapter 8), the CIA refused to undertake these most basic of reparations (U.S. Senate 1977: 36, 45).

Writing the CIA into Disciplinary Histories

The United States' postwar global political stance shifted American orientations toward the peoples anthropologists studied. As the United States and the Soviet Union competed for the hearts, minds, debts, and arms contracts of the world's nonaligned nations, there were tangible uses for the forms of intangible knowledge that anthropologists brought home from the remote areas where they worked; whether their work involved esoteric symbolic studies or radical Marxist analysis, the CIA saw prospects of useful knowledge.

Anthropology departments grew with the postwar wealth that flowed from GI Bill tuition, and this growth was nurtured by the dual use dynamics of Cold War research needs. Anthropologists sought training funds, opportunities for field research, linguistic training, and travel funds so that they could pursue research questions of interest to them and their discipline. Postwar governmental agencies needed knowledge about the peoples of the world where the new American superpower developed relationships favoring American dominance. These were often symbiotic relationships allowing academics to research topics of their choosing or to pursue theoretical questions of interest; in other instances, the questions or geographic regions of inquiry were more closely shaped by the availability of funds. Either way, fields of knowledge were funded that benefited individual anthropologists and generated knowledge for a brain trust.

Rarely was this brain trust a concrete conglomeration of scholars, of the type exemplified by the Princeton Consultants; generally the knowledge was far more diffuse and participants pursued knowledge in what appeared to be a mostly free-range manner. Yet the revelations, first from a wave of journalistic investigations, then from a wave of presidential and congressional committees disclosing the CIA's influence on international scholarship during the early Cold War, were "massive."

What is easily lost on readers in later years marked by increased surveillance is the level of shock and outrage that these initial revelations of CIA lawlessness unleashed in America in the 1960s and 1970s. The CIA's reliance on assassinations, lying, cheating, death squads, destabilizing foreign democratic movements, torture, bribery, kidnapping, or cooking intelligence reports to fit the needs of the executive branch directly undermined American ideals of democracy and openness. The American public's lessening ability to be shocked by revelations of CIA lawlessness and domestic programs is remarkable, but anthropologists recognize how the numbing tendencies of enculturation can normalize atrocities. Sustaining shock is always difficult, outrage's half-life is short, and the toll of cognitive dissonance weighs heavy. With time the outrageous and offensive can be seen as the "unfortunately necessary," and the currency of shock is short-lived as once current events become historicized.

Revelations of the CIA's lawlessness, its role in covert actions, its use of funding fronts, and its self-serving use of unwitting citizens have now become staples of the American imagination. In the milieu of these press and congressional revelations were films like Sydney Pollack's *Three Days of the Condor* (1975), Costa-Gavras's *State of Siege* (1972), Francis Ford Coppola's *The Conversation* (1974), and Alan Pakula's *Parallax View* (1974), or even Pakula's Watergate journalistic detective story based on Bob Woodward and Carl Bernstein's book *All the President's Men* (1976). America's popular imagination comfortably incorporated *Condor*'s CIA funding fronts, *The Parallax View*'s assassinations, *The Conversation*'s borderless surveillance panopticon, and *All the President's Men*'s all-encompassing lawless cancer on the presidency.

There remained lasting visible and invisible fallout from the Church and Pike investigations throughout American culture. Initially, a general distrust of the CIA and FBI spread, but the cultural incorporation of this new knowledge of

CIA practices took many forms, some based on fact, others on fantasies or delusions. Revelations of CIA practices spawned a range of paranoid conspiracy theories that often began with facts or partial facts about actual CIA programs unearthed by the press or congressional hearings, but these facts were mixed with a range of delusional fantasies involving supposed successful mind control programs with imagined "monarch slaves" and a host of international conspiracies involving bankers and agents of the Illuminati. While the CIA's MK-Ultra program funded a bizarre range of scientific research exploring the possibility of "mind control," other than some new techniques for "enhanced interrogations," the CIA did not develop any effective "mind control" program (beyond its covert use of newspapers and academic presses to influence public discourse). With time, the mixing of fact and fiction in popular accounts of CIA activities contributed to the American public's confusion about the agency's history, as documented CIA atrocities became indistinguishable in the public memory from absurd claims. This haziness of Americans' shared CIA memory mixed with the popularized paranoid fantasies about this history, along with post-9/11 Hollywood fantasies of CIA saviors operating beyond the law, diminished the likelihood of the American public demanding new levels of CIA accountability.

While the leaked Pike Report and released Church Committee Report expanded public knowledge about CIA wrongdoing and ongoing lawlessness, the findings of these committees brought little long-term change in the way the agency did business, or how Congress exercised due oversight of the agency. Congressional and journalistic revelations increased the American public's distrust of the CIA and the FBI. These disclosures weakened the confidence of many educated Americans in the CIA and strengthened growing movements to keep the CIA off of American university campuses.

Several years after the fact, in the pages of the CIA's in-house classified journal, *Studies in Intelligence*, Timothy S. Hardy gloated that, while Seymour Hersh and other journalists had successfully spawned White House and congressional investigations of CIA activities, "yet Hersh may not even merit a historical footnote, perhaps, because the ball he started rolling never really knocked down all, or even any of the pins.... The CIA is thriving in Langley, its constituent parts all strung together, its basic mission unchanged. The Defense Department still spends more than 80 percent of the billions of national intelligence dollars in ways only vaguely known to the American public" (1976: 1). Given the depth of anti-CIA feelings at the time Hardy wrote this, his remarks may seem like a form of dismissive denial, but if one takes the long view, Hardy's focus on the speed at which Americans came to adjust to and accept news of the CIA's lawlessness proved to be profoundly accurate. Americans were enculturated to learn to accept CIA death squads, wiretaps, kidnappings, covert arms dealing, support for foreign dictators, and even massive NSA metadata surveillance as necessary details of the modern world. In post-9/11 America, the acceptance of CIA torture, invasions of domestic privacy, assassinations, and attacks on international democratic movements updated this enculturation process to a point where increasing numbers of Americans accept these practices as necessary and just, while the agency's history and the public's outrage over past revelations disappear from public memory.

While this overview of Cold War strategies, revelations of CIA lawlessness, and interactions with academics during the Cold War is crucial for our consideration of how American anthropology interacted with military and intelligence agencies during the period, it is important to keep in mind that most anthropologists were then unaware of the secret shifts in American policy and practices during the earliest days of the Cold War, as fighting of the Second World War subsided and the postwar era began. Although this lack of awareness shaped anthropologists' motivations, innocence did not mitigate harm; as Thomas Fowler argued in *The Quiet American*, "Innocence is like a dumb leper who has lost his bell, wandering the world, meaning no harm" (Greene 1955: 36).

> The end of the war brought the anthropologists back to the campuses but with empty notebooks, and the *American Anthropologist* reflected this lack of a research backlog for the first few years of our period.
>
> ROBERT MURPHY | 1976

TWO WORLD WAR II'S LONG SHADOW

Due to wartime publishing interruptions, Cora Du Bois's prewar ethnography of eastern Indonesian culture, *The People of the Alor*, was not published until 1944. A decade and a half after the war's end, she wrote an appendix to the original preface that briefly broke disciplinary standards muting discussions of ways that anthropology had intersected with the war. The years between writing *People of Alor* and its 1960 republication had been active ones for Du Bois. She began the war in Washington at OSS headquarters, using her 1930s ethnographic fieldwork experiences to inform her war knowledge of Indonesia; she later relocated to Ceylon, at an OSS base where she directed operations in Malaysia, southern China, Siam, and Burma (Seymour 2015).

Du Bois's updated appendix acknowledged that the people of Alor described in her book were forever changed by the war and by their prewar contact with her. She wrote that after the war's end she received a "jovial, almost flippant letter" from "a young controleur who was sent to Alor during the Dutch interregnum before Indonesia achieved independence." This young man asked for a copy of her ethnography and passed along news of the island, with some details of the Japanese occupation during the war (Du Bois 1960: xiv). He described how the Japanese had established a station and run patrols near the village, Atimelang, where Du Bois had lived and conducted her fieldwork in 1937–39. He wrote to Du Bois that one day, the Japanese command learned that the leaders of Atimelang "were claiming that Hamerika would win the war"— Hamerika being how they pronounced the name of the strange, distant land from which Du Bois had traveled to live among them. Du Bois added that the notion that the great house of Hamerika would win the war could have been nothing but the most innocent fantasy to my friends in Atimelang since they had never even heard of the United States prior to my arrival. But to the Japanese, suffering from all the nervous apprehensions of any occupying power in a strange and therefore threatening environment, such talk could mean only rebellion.... so the Japanese sent troops to arrest five of my friends in Atimelang. I am not sure who all of them were from the young controleur's letter, but apparently Thomas Malelaka, and the Chief of Dikimpe were among them. In Kalabahi they were publicly decapitated as a warning to the populace.

There is no end to the intricate chain of responsibility and guilt that the pursuit of even the most arcane social research involves. (1960: iv–v)

The personal responsibility Du Bois assumed for her indirect involvement in the execution of these five people was remarkable and arguably beyond a reasonable interpretation of individual guilt; but in acknowledging the rampant killing unleashed in the Second World War, Du Bois broke a fourth wall of postwar ethnographic writing in ways that were unusual for her time. This wall supported the standard narrative contrivance in which not only the ethnographer as a person but also the geopolitical events impacting fieldwork were removed from the focus of the text. Ethnographies adopted tones presenting objective accounts of a natural world where the scientist-ethnographers were neutral observers. Du Bois's blunt acknowledgment that anthropology was part of "the intricate chain of responsibility and guilt" linked to even the "most arcane social research," with generally unacknowledged atrocities and lesser consequences, was reminiscent of Kipling's lama warning Kim that he had "loosed an act upon the world, and as a stone thrown into a pool so spread the consequences thou canst not tell how far" (1922: 334). Many postwar ethnographic works all but erased the war and its wake of slaughter from their narratives. The consistency of the ways that post–World War II ethnographers glossed over the war's transformative impacts informs us about the world in which they wrote.

The Postwar Ethnographic World

Postwar anthropological works recorded and ignored the war's impacts in varying ways. Some efforts, like Joseph Tenenbaum's interviews with survivors and others linked to Nazi concentration camps, appearing in the book *In Search of a Lost People* (1946), were works of tragic salvage ethnography, while other works moved the war's impacts beyond the horizon of the ethnographic present. Some ethnographers studied impacts of the war in New Guinea and elsewhere. Ian

Hogbin's *Transformation Scene: The Changing Culture of a New Guinea Village* (1951) described how the war and the postwar period shaped the villages of New Guinea. Cyril Belshaw's book *The Great Village* (1957) chronicled New Guinea villagers' efforts to rebuild and reestablish their village after it was destroyed during the war. Anthropological studies of cargo cults connected these millennial movements with villagers' experiences with GI culture during the war.

Kenneth Read described how the Japanese, British, and Australian wartime occupations impacted the peoples of New Guinea's Markham Valley, noting that the Japanese, who also "possessed the white man's weapons," were initially viewed much as the European occupiers had been (Read 1947: 98). Read was reproached for the Europeans' hypocrisy that forbade locals to fight, yet "Europeans were engaged in a war with another people" (Read 1947: 99). Anthropologists studied how the war disrupted traditional New Guinea subsistence and altered local foodways (Read 1947; Hogbin 1951).

The Australian government had worried that native loyalties could easily shift during the war. One government report on Japanese interactions with Aborigines noted that aboriginals "openly stated that the Japs told them that the country belonged to the blacks, had been stolen from them by the whites and that 'bye bye' they (the Japs) would give it back to them (the blacks). In fact, the writer suggested that whoever supplied 'food and tobacco' would have the support of the Aborigines" (Gray 2005: 19).

Micronesians first endured Japanese occupations, then an American liberation that became an occupation. In regions where indigenous populations prior to the war had been pacified under the forces of colonialism, the war sometimes found old and new colonial managers rolling back otherwise strictly enforced prohibitions against traditional forms of warfare and other forms of violence (D. H. Price 2008a: 71–72). For those living in the war's path, the end of the war did not bring peace or freedom as much as it brought new relationships of control and domination.

The war transformed the settings of postwar ethnographies around the world. Cultures of Melanesia, Indonesia, and the Philippines experienced combat and occupations, while North African cultures from Morocco to Egypt were caught in the middle of American and European battles. Cornelius Osgood's book *The Koreans and Their Culture* mixed war zone ethnography with lengthy discussions of the Japanese, Russian, and American occupations of the twentieth century, along with sympathetic narratives explaining why villagers would be drawn to align with communism. With acknowledgments thanking Dean Acheson and Edgar Furniss, Osgood noted that attempts "to undertake independent research under the aegis of a military occupation should be avoided if possible for, though cooperation is generous and sincere, it can be even more confusing than the complications of operating as an alien in a country at war" (1951: 9).

Bringing the War Back Home

After the armistice, American soldiers returned home and resumed civilian life. Most anthropologists who had served the war in an alphabet soup of military and intelligence agencies returned to universities, museums, and other civilian workplaces. Classrooms were soon packed with students entering college under the GI Bill. Many anthropologists returned to teaching, and large universities and small colleges expanded curriculum to meet the demands for the growing postwar interest in anthropology courses. A 1947 article in the *News Bulletin of the American Anthropological Association* described how even small colleges expanded their anthropology course offerings and required anthropological faculty to meet the growing demand for courses (NBAAA 1947 1[3]: 45).[1]

Not all anthropologists returned to the classrooms they had left for the war. After the war's end, some continued working in military or civilian positions like those they held during the war. Others applied anthropology to the managerial problems the American victors faced in managing lands they now occupied. Some anthropologists worked on postwar projects in Europe, Asia, or the Pacific. Some continued the work they had done for military intelligence agencies, at times extending questionable methodologies forged in the heat of wartime.

Some scholars repurposed wartime data for peacetime academic research. At Harvard, E. A. Hooton and (future CIA anthropologist) J. M. Andrews analyzed fifty thousand somatotype photographs of military inductees, hopelessly searching for correlations between body type and "education, occupation, military service and achievement" (NBAAA 1947, 1[4]: 49). In 1948, Weston La Barre received a Guggenheim Fellowship to write a book "on oriental character structure based on materials gathered during the war as an officer in [the Office of Naval Intelligence; ONI] and OSS (CBI and SEAC), in China, India and Ceylon" (NBAAA 1948 2[3]: 43).[2] La Barre published two papers from this OSS and ONI work in *Psychiatry*, on Japanese and Chinese personality types (La Barre 1945, 1946a, 1946b).

La Barre's study of Chinese personality reduced the complexity of Chinese culture to brief caricatures. Such overly simplified cultural representations circulated widely as classified memos during the war and helped inform or reinforce the views of military and intelligence personnel, but the publication of such an amateurish work in the peer-reviewed pages of *Psychiatry* after the war indicates the militarist milieu that remained in postwar academia. La Barre's later work studying culture and personality among the Aymara showed levels of nuance and moderation of analysis distinct from the sort of army surplus analysis that he published after the war in *Psychiatry*.

The National Research Council (NRC) and the Social Science Research Council (SSRC) funded the Library of Congress's Document Expediting Project, which salvaged and declassified two thousand army, navy, and OSS civil affairs reports, which were distributed to American universities interested in using these materials for research (NBAAA 1947 1[3]: 34). In 1949, the army's Historical Division sought anthropologists interested in analyzing a cache of military documents collected from overseas military outposts during the war (NBAAA 1949 3[1]: 13).

Alexander Leighton's work bridged the Second World War and the Cold War in ways that illustrate how American social science remained connected to wartime themes. During the war, Leighton managed interned Japanese Americans at Poston, Arizona, and his published writings on his work at the Poston Detention Camp conveyed a detached, observational narrative tone. As described in his book *The Governing of Men*, Leighton strove to study human interactions as a neutral scientific observer measuring the variables of human culture, an effect designed to present this political act with a façade of scientific neutrality as if he were but a passive observer, not an inflictor, of "natural" processes (Leighton 1945; D. H. Price 2008a: 149–51).

Leighton's *Human Relations in a Changing World: Observations on the Use of the Social Sciences* (1949) opened with an account of his December 1945 visit to Hiroshima, four months after its bombing. He described the remarks of the people he encountered, but his narrative was far from the sort of thick description that later anthropological writing would strive to achieve; instead, Leighton's postwar Hiroshima was a world where tragic stories mixed with collections of information on human data points. Leighton approached the Japanese people as variables to be understood so that they could be altered to suit the needs of American interests, in the name of peace in a "changing world." His ethnographic frame was carefully chosen, opening with a skeptical GI Jeep driver assuring him that Hiroshima was no different from any other bombed Japanese city, followed by descriptions of a nuclear bomb–decimated landscape, children playing among ruins, the ways and means of his local Japanese hosts, and his own insistence that the bombing was no more of a crime against humanity than any other wartime bombardment.

Leighton visited Hiroshima while on assignment for the U.S. Strategic Bombing Survey, which continued collecting information on local populations after the war. Leighton's encounters with survivors provided a composite ethnographic narrative of the experiences of the people of Hiroshima. He compiled shared memories of the calm morning before the attack, followed by the flash, the burning air, vaporized people, the shock, dying children, dying parents, and dead bodies everywhere. The vice mayor of a neighboring town told him how, after the bombing, "everybody looked alike. The eyes appeared to be a mass of melted flesh. The lips were split up and also looked like a mass of molten flesh. Only the nose appeared the same as before. The death scene was awful. The color of the patient would turn to blue and when we touched the body the skin would stick to our hands" (Leighton 1949: 29). The Strategic Bombing Survey's sponsorship and anticipated consumption of Leighton's report altered it from a neutral collection of stories into a sociocultural ballistics report detailing the outcomes of a calculated, intentional use of a new weapon. This transformation occurred not because Leighton's narrative lacked human compassion (it had no such deficit) but because the context in which this agency consumed his narrative repurposed it as a part of dual use processes regardless of his compassion, sympathies, or intentions.

Leighton described the routinized processes for using data collected from Japanese prisoners of war: "Interrogation reports were coded and data dealing with morale factors and background information were reduced to punch cards which could be sorted and tabulated by machines. In addition to this, however, extracts were made from the reports and filed in two systems, one dealing with the morale of the *fighting forces* and the other with the *home front*" (1949: 83). Postarmistice Foreign Morale Analysis Division (FMAD) reports included attitudinal data measuring Japanese dissatisfaction as FMAD switched from attempting to spawn wartime insurgent movements to fearing postwar counterinsurgencies (e.g., Leighton 1949: 68).

Human Relations in a Changing World argued that a fundamental lesson learned at FMAD was that science could measure, explain, and control human behavior. Leighton took for granted that such social science control over society would be used for "the prevention of war and the promotion of workable relationships between nations" instead of for one nation or class to exploit the weaknesses of others, or for leaders to manipulate their own populations to support wars serving the interests of elites but not the populous manipulated into supporting and fighting them (Leighton 1949: 101). He advocated that the same sort of analytical techniques developed by FMAD be used by the U.S. government to solve domestic and international social problems.[3] This work betrayed little awareness of the political dimensions of scientific research. Leighton did not acknowledge that individuals and groups used knowledge both for the greater good of all and for themselves; in the book's conclusion, he conceded the existence of a "fear that social scientists will sell their skills to 'conscienceless manipulators,'" and while not dismissing this as a possibility, he diluted such concerns, arguing that these dangers face all branches of science (207).

The Marshall Plan and Postwar Occupations

The Soviet's Molotov Plan of 1947 brought postwar aid to Eastern Europe's Soviet bloc, extending Soviet influence in ways similar to the relationships secured for the United States the following year under the Marshall Plan. The Marshall Plan launched the United States on a new soft power international interventionist trajectory linked to the Truman Doctrine. Named after Secretary of State George Marshall, a retired army general, and designed primarily by William Clayton and George Kennan at the State Department, the Marshall Plan's European Recovery Program (ERP) funneled $13 billion to programs for rebuilding Western European economies and infrastructure. From 1947 to 1951, the ERP spent 3 percent of the U.S. GDP on Cold War European recovery projects (contrast this with the 0.19 percent of GDP the United States spends on all foreign aid; Keating 2014).[4]

The Marshall Plan had general domestic bipartisan support, but on the political right, Senator Robert A. Taft, a Republican, opposed all forms of international aid; on the left, Henry Wallace criticized the plan as a Cold War tactic weakening labor movements, propping up private business interests, and increasing schisms between the United States and the Soviet Union. Michael Hogan, historian of the Marshall Plan wrote that Wallace viewed "the ERP as the work of American monopolists and imperialists who were seeking to promote their interests at home and overseas at the expense of social justice and world peace. Wallace denounced what he saw as the invasion of government by private business and financial leaders who had turned the State Department and other public agencies into servants of monopoly capital" (Hogan 1987: 94).

Wallace found cynical motives behind American plans to rebuild Europe, arguing that "Western European countries can no longer count on colonial loot to sustain their customary standards of living. They must now earn their own way through reconstruction and expansion of their economies" (1948: 6). Wallace believed the Marshall Plan would "underwrite the military budgets of reactionary governments which will do the bidding of American private capital" (18). He criticized the ways the plan undermined European efforts to nationalize industries while empowering private trusts benefiting from the particulars of reconstruction and economic reforms as the plan pressed European nations toward adopting regionally integrated economic relations. Foreseeing critiques of Reaganomics, he argued, "We can draw a just parallel between the [European Recovery Plan] and the [Herbert] Hoover plans for combating depression here at home in the early 30's. Both plans were based on the thoroughly discredited notion that you bolster the wealthy and entrenched interests, and benefits will automatically trickle down to the people" (17). Combined with coming NATO formations, the Marshall Plan entwined American global power and European economic reorganization in ways that sharply divided the world into the Cold War's dichotomous camps of East and West.

The Marshall Plan brought stability to Western Europe, but it also re-formed Europe in a Cold War context adopting specific anticommunist, antisocialist political economic positions. The vision of the Marshall Plan would remain an attractive nuisance for various Cold War development schemes claiming to liberate the underdeveloped world from poverty.[5]

Some European anthropologists, like Pierre Bessaignet of France, worked for the Marshall Plan in their home countries, but anthropologists' involvement with European reconstruction was not as widespread or centrally coordinated as were their involvements in the postwar Japanese occupation, or the Micronesian ethnographic explorations of the Coordinated Investigation of Micronesian Anthropology group (CIMA) (Gaillard 2004: 188). These regional differences in anthropological contributions likely occurred for a combination of reasons, including larger numbers of available State Department personnel who were already familiar with the languages and cultures of Europe.

Occupations starkly demonstrate power relations, and anthropologists' contributions to occupations reveal disciplinary alignments to power. Occupations during and after the war betrayed structural imbalances whose internal logics often suggested retribution could settle scores as wartime collaborators faced their countrymen and countrywomen, and postwar occupiers had to resist temptations to make losers pay for the personal losses the occupiers experienced.[6]

The American military leadership realized that the successful postwar occupation of Japan required significant knowledge about Japanese culture. With the passing of decades, many Americans came to view the occupation as a peaceful, smooth transition. As American strategists contemplated occupations in Iraq and Afghanistan in the early twenty-first century, public discourse often nostalgically referred to the ease and success of the GHQ's postwar occupation of Japan. Japan has been presented as a model occupation that brought peace to a war-torn nation by installing American-style democracy. Notions of a peaceful Japanese occupation were regularly contrasted with the clashing factions using improvised explosive devices to kill and maim American occupiers in Afghanistan and Iraq. Typical of these claims about the Japanese occupation is this passage from a *New York Times* essay from 2003, lamenting the absence of anthropologists to help guide the American occupation of Iraq: "As the occupation of Iraq appears more complex by the day, where are the new Ruth Benedicts, authoritative voices who will carry weight with both Iraqis and Americans?" (Stille 2003).[7] While the occupation of postwar Japan brought relatively low levels of interpersonal or organizational violence directed against occupiers, there were other difficulties and forms of structural violence that such ebullient narratives conveniently neglect.

Many anthropologists have come to believe that Ruth Benedict and other anthropologists influenced decisions to allow the Japanese emperor to retain ceremonial power at the war's end, and that *The Chrysanthemum and the Sword*, Benedict's study of Japan, guided General Douglas MacArthur's postwar occupation. While Benedict's book has been read by millions of Japanese in the postwar period, there is no evidence that Benedict's recommendations to spare the mikado had any direct impact on his fate — MacArthur and others already understood that the emperor should remain (D. H. Price 2008a: 171–99). Likewise, *The Chrysanthemum and the Sword* was not a central text influencing the Japanese occupation in the ways characterized by Stille and others. Like other anthropological counterinsurgency-linked texts, *Chrysanthemum*'s greatest impact was on the home front, as it helped frame American understandings of the conquered Japanese.

As John W. Dower's *Embracing Defeat: Japan in the Wake of World War II* shows, the postwar occupation of Japan was far more complicated than as depicted in popular American retcon narratives. Dower documents a remarkably compliant occupied Japanese population that aligns with popular renderings, but he also reveals the incredible hardships and severe cultural annihilation that lay behind this layer of "nonviolent" compliance, a compliance enforced by GHQ's totalitarian control of traditional Japanese cultural and political processes.

Dower contrasted the sort of nuanced American academic approach to Japanese culture that emerged during the war as a new generation of "American and British anthropologists, sociologists, psychologists, and psychiatrists [entered] into the general areas of intelligence analysis and psychological warfare" (1999: 219) with that of the war's elder generation of Asia experts, who concluded that the Japanese would be incapable of adopting democracy after the war. A cohort of American social scientists who recognized the malleability of enculturation processes and the innate forces of cultural relativism advocated for an occupation based on aggressive social engineering.[8] An older generation of Asia experts with ties to the United Kingdom's Royal Institute of International Affairs judged the Japanese as not being able to adopt democracy because they were an "obedient herd." According to Dower, if this generation of "Asia experts had their way, the very notion of inducing a democratic revolution would have died of ridicule at an early stage. As happened instead, the ridicule was deflected by the views of experts of a different ilk — behavioral scientists who chose to emphasize the 'malleability' of the Japanese 'national character,' along with planners and policy makers of liberal and left-wing persuasions who sincerely believed that democratic values were universal in their nature and appeal" (1999: 218). Dower speculated that had the emperor followed his advisers' counsel and surrendered at the beginning of 1945, Japan not only would have avoided conventional, jellied gasoline, and atomic bombing campaigns but also might have avoided "the occupation's revolution from above. As of early 1945, there was no plan to induce a democratic revolution in the defeated nation. The old Japan hands [e.g., British analysts] who still controlled post surrender planning anticipated a mild reform agenda at best" (220).

Dower reveals an American occupation full of brutalities and degradations, as the Japanese public were denigrated through programs like a government-organized prostitution operation supervised by the local police (1999: 124–26) and a collapse of the production and distribution of basic foodstuffs that was still so severe in October 1947 that a young, honest municipal judge died of starvation after refusing to purchase food on the black market (99). The United States' refusal to shoulder the costs of occupation exacerbated Japanese hardships. In contrast to those living under the Marshall Plan in Europe, many Japanese starved as they were required to pay the costs of the American occupation, a burden that "amounted to a staggering one-third of the regular budget at the beginning of the occupation" (115).

In 1950, anthropologist George Foster was appointed to be the American Anthropological Association (AAA) delegate to the Commission on the Occupied Areas' Second National Conference on the Occupied Countries (AA 1951 53[3]:456). Foster reported on conference presentations describing the state of American occupations of Austria, Germany, Japan, and the Ryukyus, in which he criticized American military officials' grasp of the realities and problems of an occupation, and broad beliefs in faulty cultural engineering assumptions. Foster described a series of upbeat military-linked occupation reports making unrealistic claims of transformed occupied populations that fit Americans' expectations. According to Foster:

> The report of Col. Nugent on Japan was very discouraging because of the attitude and point of view. He painted a glowing picture in which everything is going beautifully in Japan and there are no problems. As a result of the U.S. program, Japanese character, personality and culture have been entirely changed during the past five years and they are well on the road to American democracy. The ethnocentric approach on the part of most delegates and officials toward all of the occupied countries was almost unbelievable. Nearly every discussion and comment was predicated on the assumption that American institutions are perfect and that success in the occupied countries consists only in recasting them more nearly in our own image. It was implied that what is wrong with Japanese culture is that it is so unlike American culture. . . . Japanese universities were thoroughly excoriated because they were copied after the European pattern and not the American pattern. Unquestionably, foreign nationals representing the occupied areas must have felt that most of the discussion was an unvarnished insult to their national cultures. (AA 1951 53[3]: 456–57)

Foster's bitter assessment was ignored not only by American policy makers but also by some in the generation of coming applied anthropologists who avoided such assessments that directly countered American policy positions, instead adopting managerial views that better aligned with American policy.

Several American anthropologists conducted fieldwork in occupied Japan. Douglas Haring took a leave of absence from Syracuse University during 1951 and 1952 to serve on the NRC's Pacific Science Board in the Ryukyus, where he worked on an army program documenting local culture. The Wenner-Gren Foundation later funded Haring's research evaluating U.S.-backed reforms after the American occupation of Japan ended (J. W. Hall 1952: 293–94). Some Americans conducted community studies: Arthur Raper surveyed rural fishing communities, gathering information on the impacts of postoccupation land reform programs (see Raper et. al. 1950); John Bennett modeled his research on Walter Goldschmidt's ethnographic field research on California agricultural communities, as he studied neighborhood associations, the "labor boss" system, and "problems of 'freedom and control'" in a rural forestry community in the Tochigi Prefecture (Bennett 1951: 1–2).[9] These community studies gathered data used for planning and to integrate translated background material gathered by research staff. Japanese staff helped design effective surveys, questionnaires, and other data-gathering methods and collected attitudinal surveys, interviews, and local archival materials (Bennett 1951: 2).

Bennett's analysis adopted a "Weber-Parsons scheme of analysis for institutional economics" to account for studying variations in social integration (1951: 3), while other research was more descriptive and less theory oriented. Bennett's study analyzed how market conditions determined wages and prices, while cultural traditions and intricate systems of obligations, rituals, and values shaped Japanese business relationships. Bennett found that Japanese cultural traditions cultivated "a strong local democratic respect for individual and family rights, [which also led to the] exploitation of workers by 'bosses,' who manipulate the traditionalistic structure and demand loyalty in return for protection" (4).

Occasionally, data and analysis from these community studies impacted occupation policy decisions. In one instance, data from Bennett's fishery rights study were integrated by the Natural Resources Section when it wrote new fisheries laws (Bennett 1951: 4). While some research impacted policy decisions, it is unclear to what extent the social science programs of occupied Japan described by Bennett and others influenced shifts in Japanese cultural policy. Such questions are highlighted by the work of Iwao Ishino, an anthropologist formerly employed by the Japan Occupation's Public Opinion and Sociological Research Division working alongside Bennett, who published an analysis of the shifts in the traditional Matsui labor supply system in which "labor bosses" controlled hiring in certain Japanese job sectors (dockworkers, carpenters, cooks, etc.). Ishino (1956) argued that traditional economic forces, rather than nuanced understanding of cultural meanings, likely accounted for the collapse of the labor boss system.

Many of these occupation studies sought to understand how traditional Japanese cultural systems of obligation interfered with claimed efficiencies of capitalism-unfettered markets. One of Bennett's occupation studies, titled "Economic Aspects of a Boss-Henchman System in the Japanese Forestry Industry" (1958), described his attempts to understand how traditional systems using local networks of employment obligations led to inefficiencies and incurred unnecessary costs.

Bennett detailed the importance of customary loyalties and showed how expectations were embedded in traditional logging and wood-processing occupations. Bennett described this "informal social system, with its web-like fabric, extending *via* kinship, ritual or simulated kinship, and chains of obligations through the whole nation, [which] can be efficiently mobilized for national purposes," while conceding that to American outsiders this traditional system would appear "incompatible" and irrational (1958: 28). He observed that plans to modernize underdeveloped nations generally sought to discard traditional obligation-bound systems, and he conceded that in many instances, such as those involving heavy industry, such changes were appropriate; but Bennett advocated that small Japanese industries, with unskilled, migrant labor, be allowed to continue using these cumbersome (to outsiders and occupiers) systems of obligation. He argued that "in these contexts, the Japanese economy continues to display familistic and traditionalistic social patterns and is able to blend them with standard commercial and business methods" (28–29). He found that the forest industry's boss-henchman system met these criteria and that Western models of development needed to be more flexible and to integrate local cultural practices before assuming that conforming to external top-down managerial changes would increase productivity, profits, or efficiency.

The Japanese Village in Transition

In November 1950, GHQ published *The Japanese Village in Transition*, a monograph based on the research of Arthur F. Raper, Tami Tsuchiyama, Herbert Passin, and David Sills.[10] Raper was a consultant for GHQ's Natural Resources Section, and the other contributors were staff at GHQ's Public Opinion and Sociological Research Division (Raper et al. 1950). *Transition* showcased a level of interdisciplinary collaborative research that was rare in the prewar period. This interdisciplinary team approach grew from the experiences of social scientists who worked on similar interdisciplinary projects at OSS, Office of War Information (OWI), ONI, and other agencies. *Transition* drew on ethnographic research and survey data gathered in thirteen Japanese villages between 1947 and 1948; Raper evaluated agricultural developments, Tsuchiyama summarized social and cultural issues, and a rich collection of photographs and brief descriptions illustrated the layout of villages and farmland, and daily life in postwar rural Japan.

Transition analyzed political participation by women, changes in the form and function of the extended family, marriage, inheritance practices, kinship solidarity, retirement, child rearing, the financial collapse of shrines, schools, youth associations, the black market, land reclamation programs, and the impact of agricultural cooperatives installed by American occupation forces to undermine the power of the traditional agricultural associations. It evaluated impacts of new democratic institutions and land reformation programs mandated by GHQ to undermine the traditional grip of powerful Japanese families and royalty (Lu 1996: 491).

The monograph's ethnographic descriptions of land reform and imposed democracy in Yokogoshi illustrated larger trends in occupied Japan, and its narrative highlighted the counterinsurgency goals at the heart of these policies. An account of a village meeting reported the following:

> A meeting was held in the village hall assembly room. Looking up at the large portraits of six of the former headmen, the present officials stated that not one of the officers in the village hall at that time could have held office under conditions prevailing when these earlier mayors were in authority.... The present mayor owns no land. He had been a clerk in the village office for more than 30 years until he became deputy mayor; in 1947, he was elected mayor. He has long been identified with the farmers' union. His background is generally similar to that of the majority of the present assemblymen, nearly all of whom are new owner-operators who were tenants a couple of years ago. Under the previous seven mayors, practically all of the assemblymen had been landowners despite the fact that just before the land reform program was launched, 46 percent of all farmers rented 90 percent or more of the land they cultivated, and 72 percent rented half or more of their land. (Raper et al. 1950: 166)

Replacing leaders with new individuals from outside traditional circles of power was a counterinsurgency technique to establish new power relations that broke with the past. Raper and colleagues stressed themes of increased representation and equality, while seldom examining how the democratic installation of occupation-ready local leaders undermined the old cultural order.

American social scientists studied farmers' complaints, learning about their worries over increased taxes, inflation, a decline in the black market, increased agricultural production quotas, shortages of consumable goods, limited available farmlands, and a lack of adequate technical assistance (Raper et al. 1950: 182–91). *Transition* contrasted the new democratically controlled agricultural cooperatives with the traditional "feudal" system.

This new imposed counterinsurgent democratic system eroded traditional relationships and obligations in ways that incentivized allegiances to occupiers.

For many farmers, this shift brought opportunities, as Raper and colleagues reported: "The new agricultural cooperatives are generally reported by farmers to be a real improvement over the earlier agricultural associations. Various concrete improvements are mentioned, particularly the fact that the delivery quotas need not be turned in at the new agricultural cooperatives unless the farmer elected to do so. Under the present system, any dealer who has been designated as an official handler can receive quota deliveries, and almost any dealer can be designated as such if enough farmers certify their desire to deliver to him" (1950: 180).

Perhaps the anthropologically riskiest engineered changes in the cultural practices of postwar rural Japan were the postsurrender Civil Code's revisions of traditional inheritance laws. Article 900 of the Civil Code nullified the traditional system of primogeniture and replaced it with rules stating that a surviving spouse would inherit one-third of the property, and surviving children would inherit two-thirds of the property, to be divided equally among them (see Raper et al. 1950: 211). When Raper's team asked locals about the impact of these inheritance changes, they found that "the consensus of most of the farmers interviewed was that if the inheritance provision of the revised Civil Code were carried out, the family as an economic unit would encounter great difficulty" (211). The American occupiers who were designing these changes seemed unconcerned about accelerating the forces of devolution of landholdings, focusing instead on how these laws provided greater equity. Young people uniformly favored the traditional inheritance system, arguing that the responsibilities of care for elderly parents required a greater level of inheritance (212).

The occupation's enforcement of Articles 14 and 24 of the new constitution undermined the traditional "house" system and democratized family arrangements in ways that transformed property relations and intergenerational obligations. Article 24, section II stated, "With regard to choice of spouse, property rights, inheritance, choice of domicile, divorce and other matters pertaining to marriage and the family, laws shall be enacted from the standpoint of individual dignity and the essential equality of the sexes" (Schmidt 2005: 323n165). After 1952, conservative Japanese politicians tried to restore the traditional "house" system, citing the rapid fragmentation of landholdings in rural communities, but these efforts failed "because of the determined opposition mainly from youth and women's organizations, but also due to the fact that the conservatives were losing their rural strongholds in the wake of the effects of industrialization and urbanization" (Schmidt 2005: 328). Petra Schmidt noted that from the postwar occupation until the 1960s, several failed attempts were made to allow a single child to inherit agricultural holdings, with compensation to siblings, and while these efforts failed, other agricultural legislation accomplished these goals (2005: 328–29).

Drawing on fieldwork in the village of Futomi funded by the Rockefeller Foundation and the Office of Naval Research (ONR), John Bennett later expanded some of the work that had appeared in *Transition* (Bennett and Ishino 1955: 41n1). Bennett and Ishino's later publications drew on unpublished data collected by occupation forces, later integrating this research into an anthropological narrative examining how Japanese culture coped with the extreme environmental and economic limitations of this "land-hungry village" (42–43).

Bennett and Ishino examined the impact of ecological limitations on the development of specific cultural formations. Describing Futomi as a village limited by "land scarcity," where economic limitations shaped postwar developments, theirs was an ecological argument in which farmers maximized good soils with high-yield crops, and poor soils were planted with low-yield crops. The local carrying capacities limited population growth (Bennett and Ishino 1955: 43).

Their account of villagers' cultural adaptation to living in such circumscribed environments relied on mechanical structural functionalist metaphors, presenting the village as having "devised elaborate and sensitive machinery to fight the problems brought about by land scarcity and poverty of natural resources" (Bennett and Ishino 1955: 43). This was an innovative ecological analysis, yet the lack of analysis of the political economy of the occupation stunted their explanations of a world occupied and partially restructured by American force, which was acknowledged but not an active force worthy of analysis itself.

The Coordinated Investigation of Micronesian Anthropology

Former theaters of war soon became training grounds for a new generation of anthropologists. Postwar occupations provided funding opportunities for graduate students looking for fieldwork research possibilities, increasingly moving American anthropologists to dissertation fieldwork outside of the United States. William Lessa, Thomas Gladwin, and Ward Goodenough were part of a new generation of American anthropologists whose Micronesian fieldwork was sponsored by postwar funding sources like the ONR (through the NRC Council's Pacific Science Board's) and CIMA (see table 2.1) (Falgout 1995; Fischer 1979).

TABLE 2.1. Postwar CIMA Anthropologists (Source: Spoehr 1957)

PROJECT	INVESTIGATOR	AREA	INSTITUTION
CIMA	Homer G. Barnett	Carolines	University of Oregon
CIMA	C. Bentzen	Carolines	University of Southern California
CIMA	N. M. Bowers	Marianas	University of Michigan
CIMA	Mrs. N. M. Bowers	Marianas	University of Michigan
CIMA	P. H. Buck	Carolines	Bishop Museum
CIMA	E. G. Burrows	Carolines	University of Connecticut
CIMA	A. Capell	Carolines	University of Sydney
CIMA	M. Chave	Marshalls	University of Hawaii
CIMA	I. Dyen	Carolines	Yale
CIMA	S. H. Elbert	Carolines	Bishop Museum
CIMA	K. Emory	Carolines	Bishop Museum
CIMA	P. L. Garvin	Carolines	University of Indiana
CIMA	T. Gladwin	Carolines	Yale
CIMA	Ward Goodenough	Carolines	Yale
CIMA	E. E. Hunt	Carolines	Harvard
CIMA	A. Joseph	Marianas	Institute of Ethnic Affairs
CIMA	N. R. Kidder	Carolines	Harvard
CIMA	C. Lathrop	Carolines	Bishop Museum
CIMA	F. M. LeBar	Carolines	Yale
CIMA	W. A. Lessa	Carolines	University of Chicago
CIMA	J. L. Lewis	Carolines	University of Pennsylvania
CIMA	F. Mahoney	Carolines	University of Wisconsin
CIMA	George P. Murdock	Carolines	Yale
CIMA	A. Murphy	Carolines	University of Oregon
CIMA	R. E. Murphy	Carolines	Clark University
CIMA	V. Murray	Marianas	Inst. of Ethnic Affairs
CIMA	R. I. Murrill	Carolines	AMNH
CIMA	J. Rauch	Carolines	Columbia University
CIMA	S. H. Riesenberg	Carolines	University of California
CIMA	R. S. Rizenthaler	Carolines	Milwaukee Public Museum
CIMA	David M. Schneider	Carolines	Harvard
CIMA	M. Spiro	Carolines	Northwestern University
CIMA	Alexander Spoehr	Marshalls	Chicago, Natural History Museum
CIMA	W. D. Stevens	Carolines	Harvard

(continued)

TABLE 2.1 (*continued*)

PROJECT	INVESTIGATOR	AREA	INSTITUTION
CIMA	B. Tolerton	Carolines	Columbia University
CIMA	J. Useem	Carolines	University of Wisconsin
CIMA	H. Uyehara	Carolines	University of Wisconsin
CIMA	A. Vidich	Carolines	University of Wisconsin
CIMA	J. E. Weckleter	Carolines	University of Southern California
CIMA	C. Wong	Carolines	Yale, Harvard
SIM Project	Isidor Dyen	Yap, Ponape, Truk	Yale
SIM Project	A. M. Fischer	Truk	Radcliffe College
SIM Project	Ward Goodenough	Gilberts	University of Pennsylvania
SIM Project	Leonard E. Mason	Marshalls	University of Hawaii
SIM Project	Alexander Spoehr	Marianas	Chicago Natural History Museum
SIM Project	John E. Tobin	Marshalls	University of Hawaii
SIM Project	H. Uyehara	Marshalls	University of Hawaii
USCC Survey	William R. Bascom	Ponape	Northwestern University
USCC Survey	Edwin H. Bryan		Bishop Museum
USCC Survey	E. E. Gallahue	Marianas	U.S. Department of Agriculture
USCC Survey	E. T. Hall	Truk	University of Denver
USCC Survey	Leonard E. Mason	Marshalls	U.S. Department of State
USCC Survey	Douglas L. Oliver		Director of USCC Survey
USCC Survey	Karl J. Pelzer	Truk	U.S. Department of Agriculture
USCC Survey	John Useem	Palau	University of Wisconsin

In 1946, CIMA directed a project sponsored by the U.S. Commercial Company Economic Survey, sending twenty-two social scientists to field settings throughout Micronesia to gather economic, political, and social data on postwar conditions (see Oliver 1951). Between 1947 and 1948, CIMA hired forty-two field researchers, twenty-five of whom were cultural anthropologists, to gather primary data on the state of Micronesian society. The approach used by CIMA was modeled after previous projects for the U.S. Bureau of American Ethnology and the Philippines Ethnology Survey—an early episode of applied anthropology described by Roberto González as one in which "colonial administration was reduced to a problem of rational scientific management" (2010: 141;

Kiste and Marshall 2000: 267). The CIMA ethnographic research was primarily funded by the ONR, with supplemental funding from the Wenner-Gren Foundation (Spoehr 1951: 2). In 1949 the NRC's Pacific Science Board began sponsoring the Scientific Investigations in Micronesia's ecological studies of island environments and cultural research, including traditional diets and archaeological inventories (Mason 1953). Felix Keesing developed a training program for Micronesian administrators from 1946 to 1949 (Keesing 1947; Mason 1953: 1; NBAAA 1947 1[2]: 15).

Ward Goodenough did fieldwork in the Gilberts on the Onotoa Atoll in 1951 and Bengt Danielsson worked on the Raroia Atoll in 1952 (Mason 1953: 2). As a graduate student at Harvard, David Schneider originally planned on conducting fieldwork in Africa, but after learning of CIMA-funded fieldwork opportunities on Yap, he later wrote, "The jingle of coins attracted my attention" (Schneider and Handler 1995: 85).

The Handbook on the Trust Territory of the Pacific Islands drew on the work of CIMA anthropologists, focusing on managerial outcomes that mirrored wartime Pacific handbooks that Murdock and others had produced a few years earlier (OCNO 1948). The Handbook was a neocolonial administrative guide describing local property relations, work habits, land tenure systems, exchange systems, land disputes, settlement patterns, the primacy of kinship, and so on.

The Handbook described managerial strategies of direct and indirect rule, arguing that adopting an indirect approach "clears the way for normal evolution of the familial local system toward political forms more in keeping with modern world conditions." Notions of "normal evolution" reinforced neocolonial policies within cultural evolutionary frameworks that helped justify changes in local governmental structures that would help local cultures progress, rather than explanations focusing on American geopolitical interests (OCNO 1948: 124). The Handbook identified problems for indirect rule, including local corruption, nepotistic tendencies, and the abuse of authority, at times referring to local leaders as "kings" and using other terms that drew on historical European notions of social structure. The Handbook advocated for a special "double type of leadership," such as was installed in the Marshall Islands, or Ponape, where "the paramount chiefs of the districts hold the top official positions, but district secretaries are held mainly responsible for carrying the load of practical affairs. In the Marshalls, too, the kings are given fullest ceremonial honors, but local administrative responsibilities are in the hands of magistrates" (125). It suggested capturing the loyalties of local youth and recommended creating ceremonial roles for traditional chiefs, with an understanding that, with time, these traditional leaders "will be called upon less for practical leadership" (125). The Handbook supported CIMA anthropologist Saul Riesenberg's suggestion that potential heirs to traditional leadership titles be shipped out for Western schooling in Hawaii and the U.S. mainland (125).

The Handbook warned that external management of native populations could lead to a "growth of political consciousness" and advised administrators to not stir up nativist or nationalist feelings, which can "arise primarily out of the social unrest which comes from disintegration of the old cultures, and from the pressures of alien domination and discrimination" (OCNO 1948: 126). Administrators were cautioned that past uprisings caused foreign administrators to react in ways that strengthened local support, and they were advised to maintain local input on some administrative decisions in order to reduce the possibility of revolts. The Handbook theorized that coming independence efforts would likely be island group–specific, and given the existing linguistic and geographic separation, it was unlikely that separate island groups would develop a sense of "common identity," so threats to American rule would be localized, not pan-Micronesian (126).

Anthropologists at CIMA frequently acknowledged the recent war in their narratives, and in some instances vestiges of the war may have been represented as core cultural features of these societies. As Lin Poyer shows, Thomas Gladwin and Seymour Sarason's work in postwar Truk used psychological inventory tests indicating "food anxiety," a cultural trait they connected to the near starvation faced by islanders during the war (Poyer 2004: 161–62). Some anthropologists characterized the impacts of the war on Micronesian cultures as devastating. Douglas Oliver concluded that the "conquest of the islands by combat and the defeat of Japan destroyed completely the prewar economic structure," and that the war destroyed the islanders' income sources (1951: 32). Oliver described "the presence of [U.S.] armed forces is unduly blocking the economic development of Micronesians" (1951: 11). He recommended that the United States support the restoration of native economies, and that the U.S. military restore some lands taken from natives for U.S. military installations. Oliver advocated developing support programs to supply pigs and chickens for every family.

Alexander Spoehr's 1951 report for the Naval Civil Administration Unit in the Marianas described the ongoing transfer of administration from the U.S. Navy to the U.S. Department of the Interior. Spoehr argued that anthropological insights into Micronesian customs were needed if Americans were to undertake an "enlightened administration" of the islands (Spoehr 1951: 1). Anthropologists provided instructional materials to the School of Naval Administration, anthropologist Lieutenant Commander Phillip Drucker oversaw applied programs in Micronesia, and Homer Barnett took up these duties when the administration was transferred from the navy to the Department of the Interior (Spoehr 1951: 2–3).

Research projects at CIMA provided a broad range of fieldwork opportunities for fledgling and midcareer American anthropologists, fieldwork that was a gateway for the careers of a new generation and led to the production of classic anthropological texts and important theoretical works on kinship and other topics, while simultaneously generating knowledge that was at least conceived of as having managerial uses. With a confluence of naval intelligence needs and anthropological theoretical desires, George Murdock's work for both CIMA and the Institute of Human Relations (IHR) made IHR's project "the largest research effort in the history of American anthropology and a major program in applied anthropology" (Kiste and Marshall 2000: 265). Many CIMA ethnographic reports read as fractured, hurried works, in part because Murdock provided financial bonuses that encouraged this sort of work, but also because the fractured theoretical approach and functional uses of the work reinforced such approaches. David Schneider recalled Murdock offering "a $500 bonus if you wrote up your report real quickly" (Schneider and Handler 1995: 21).

From Fighting Fascism to Supporting Occupations

Many who took part in transforming the postwar world did so while continuing to use the previous war as an ideological reference point. Most anthropologists working on occupations or aid programs conceived of their role as that of a stabilizer or liberator, not an active agent of a new American empire.[11] The Second World War brought a unity of purpose for many Americans, most of whom were impacted by notions of fighting totalitarianism and making the world safe for democracy. The threats of Nazi ideologies championing racial superiority, postwar news of the extent of the horrors of the Holocaust, and Japanese atrocities during Japan's occupation of the Philippines, China, Burma, and elsewhere in Asia helped some justify American war losses and attacks on civilian populations abroad. These postwar residues helped nurture ideological justifications for a new era's conceptions of American exceptionalism.

Anthropology has long been ambivalent about how to cope with the political processes in which it is enveloped. This ambivalence is found in the discipline's contradictory early articulation of the innate equality of all cultures, while simultaneously assisting in the colonial subjugation of those recognized as theoretically equal. Some contradictions can be reduced to differences in individual anthropologists' political perspectives, but the collective positions of disciplinary professional associations have been as inconsistent as these individual positions. Anthropologists, like others of their time and place, internalize the political views of their times in ways that generally coalesce the political processes of their society.

The milieu of the Second World War and shadows of anthropologists' wartime contributions lay draped over the discipline after the war in ways that were not always obvious at the time. American anthropologists' responses to World War II helped them misinterpret and support their nation's Cold War international policies in the late 1940s and throughout the 1950s. This interpretive lag is a crucial element for understanding how American anthropology came to so easily align its orientation with policy agendas supporting American expansion. The normalcy of anthropology's military links is seen in the pages of postwar issues of the *News Bulletin of the AAA*. The front page of the April 1950 issue included two job announcements marking this milieu: one for naval operations field consultants on Yap and Ponape, the second seeking anthropologists for a classified research project at Air University's Arctic, Desert, and Tropic Information Center (*NBAAA* 1950 4[2]: 1).[12]

As Bruce Cumings observed, during the early postwar period, "scholars caught up in one historical system and one discourse that defined discipline, department, area, and subject suddenly found themselves in another emerging field of inquiry, well in advance of imagining or discovering the subject themselves. To put a subtle relationship all too crudely, power and money had found their subject first, and shaped fields of inquiry accordingly" (Cumings 1999: 179). This historical shift can be easily discerned with hindsight, but for those living through these transformations, the preexisting lens of interpretation anchored in past practices was most often used to explain political developments. The range of critiques of American policies developing at the time is impressive. It is not that *some* anthropologists or political writers did not understand the political transformations of the Cold War as they were occurring. Some clearly did, but these were minority views, outside the mainstream consciousness of the time. Most notable among those Americans who understood the transformations of the Cold War to be fundamentally different than America's political purpose during the Second World War were those of the radical left. Publications like the *Nation*, the *Progressive*, and *I. F. Stone's Weekly* provided timely analysis that interpreted American postwar foreign policy as serving fundamentally different ends than those advanced in the war years and before.

Henry Wallace's reasons for rejecting the Marshall Plan highlight the limitations presented by strictly historicist analysis. The presence of Wallace's sophisticated, marginalized critique of 1947 (or the analysis of Jerome Rauch, discussed in chapter 4) demonstrates how strictly "historicist" positions necessarily champion and hegemonically elevate past voices from a dominant majority, most frequently aligned with power, over those from a marginalized minority. It is difficult to imagine who might have funded such marginal critiques during this period so marked by the rise of McCarthyism.

A range of forces align to support the rise of one research project or interpretive school over another. The coming availability of government and private foundation funds to finance postwar academic research helped transform universities and professional associations, like the American Anthropological Association and the Society for Applied Anthropology, as these and other organizations sought to best align themselves with new funding opportunities — alignments that mutually served the funders and recipients of these funds.

> The mighty edifice of government science dominated the scene in the middle of the twentieth-century as a Gothic cathedral dominated a thirteenth-century landscape.
>
> A. HUNTER DUPREE | 1957

THREE REBOOTING PROFESSIONAL ANTHROPOLOGY IN THE POSTWAR WORLD

During the last months of the Second World War, the American Anthropological Association formed the Temporary Organizing Committee to prepare the association for anticipated academic and financial opportunities that appeared to be coming to the postwar world (Frantz 1974: 9).[1] Two weeks after VE Day, future AAA executive secretary Frederick Johnson wrote Julian Steward a letter recapping their recent discussions concerning the desirability of establishing a large, centralized organization of American anthropologists positioned to take advantage of emerging opportunities. With clear enthusiasm, and joking about a drinking session with a colonel described as an "erstwhile 'Wall Street Merchant,'" Johnson wrote:

> As the alcoholic mists cleared during the ride north on the train I had a dream. I pass it on to you for what it is worth. As I thought about your suggestion that there be organized a society of professional anthropologists I had much difficulty in finding a common denominator for the whole field. There is one, of course, but it may be so broad that it is useless. I wondered if it might not be possible to recognize the division of the field into several professional bodies, such as archaeology, ethnography, and social anthropology. This could be done for the purpose of developing criteria for professional status and would have no reference to scientific problems or ambitions. Professionals chosen in this way would be anthropologists and thus be eligible for a general professional body. At the outset this appears

as a complicated thing fraught with all kinds of difficulties. However it might be shaken down to become something of use.

The need for such a body, no matter how it originates, is great and it is urgent. My past experience is sufficient reason to convince me. Sudden developments in the Committee make it even more imperative. Confidentially I can say that even now the status of the Committee is being questioned. I do not know whether this is a real difficulty or a desire to develop the most complicated arrangement possible. I doubt if this is serious because I have just fired off a big gun, if this does not work we might as well quit. I have a couple of more shots but these must be saved to further the work of the Committee rather than simply to form it. (ISA 7, FJ to JS 5/22/45)

Steward replied that Ruth Benedict, Margaret Mead, John Cooper, and Clyde Kluckhohn supported this plan, adding that "if this fine collection of prima donnas is so unanimously for it, I am positive the thing is sure fire" (ISA 7, JS to FJ 5/29/45).

In the month following Japan's surrender, Steward wrote Johnson about "the battle of Washington" over a coming struggle either within the AAA or with the formation of a new central anthropological association "scrambling for status and permanency comparable to the days of the depression and again of the first part of the war." A tentative constitution was drafted, and Steward described the status of generational factions among anthropologists in which "the venerable generation is not interested but won't oppose it. Those of a slightly younger generation who have achieved fame are suspicious of it as a means either of trapping them or of building up their rivals. The younger generation is 100% for it" (ISA 7, JS to FJ 9/20/45). Steward anticipated that new governmental sources of social science funding were coming, and a well-organized professional association could position itself to take advantage of these opportunities. He saw a "great furor about getting social science into some sort of a national research foundation to implement the [Vannevar] Bush plan for the physical sciences. Several bills of the Bush plan are now before Congress and there is a mad scramble to get the social science plan ready before the hearings start in a few weeks" (ISA 7, JS to FJ 9/20/45). Steward initially considered creating a new anthropological association, a "proposed Society for Professional Anthropologists" (RB, JS to RB 10/25/45), but by early 1946, he realized that a reorganization of the AAA would be preferable to splintering off a new organization.

In the fall of 1945, Steward urged the AAA to publish a monograph detailing American anthropologists' contributions to the war. The National Research Council had sponsored a monograph chronicling psychology's contributions to the war, and Steward envisioned producing a larger work detailing anthropology's war years (RB, JS to RB 10/25/45), but this history was never published.[2] In late 1945 Steward drafted a statement titled "Anthropology's Justification of Federal Support for Social Science Research" for congressional hearings considering postwar national science policies. He argued that anthropological knowledge could help explain the root causes of human violence, and that in a nation devoting federal funding to the physical sciences at unprecedented levels, "knowledge of human forces must parallel knowledge of physical forces if World Organization is to discharge its trust" (AAAP 37, Sec. Memos, 9/29/45; see also AA 1946 48[2]: 309). Steward pitched anthropology almost as a form of Comtian social physics, claiming that "as an analyst and source of information, the social scientist has a function comparable to that of the research physicist or biologist" (AAAP 37, Sec. Memos, 9/29/45). He argued that like other scientists, anthropologists produced neutral data that would be used by policy makers because "a scientist as such has no political objectives" (AAAP 37, Sec. Memos, 9/29/45). Steward cited anthropologists' valuable contributions to the war, stressed anthropologists' roles facilitating "Indian Administration," and saluted anthropologists' roles supporting "colonial affairs of Great Britain, Holland, and France" (AAAP 37, Sec. Memos, 9/29/45).

Steward envisioned anthropological knowledge supporting the implementation of American foreign policy on projects ranging from the economic development of China to problems of postwar occupations and the "reeducation" of "backward peoples." He argued:

> In our efforts to aid Japan, Germany, or any other nation to achieve a government acceptable to the family of nations we must understand the native institutions we are dealing with lest our efforts have unexpected results or, at best, amount to nothing more than political imperialism. Reeducation of masses of people to alter their basic values and habits of thinking will succeed only as the values and habits are properly comprehended. Again, if we are to participate in or sanction trusteeship for backward peoples, we are morally obligated to make every effort to ascertain the probable consequences of the policies we underwrite. (AAAP 37, Sec. Memos, 9/29/45)

As other disciplines organized themselves in anticipation of coming funding opportunities, anthropologists settled subfield differences within the AAA and worked to reorganize the association's members to more effectively compete for funding. In December 1945, at the first postwar annual meeting of the AAA, a committee was appointed to collect information from the membership and from "allied societies, and other local groups" concerning their views on reorganizing the structure of the AAA, establishing a permanent secretary, "and other means of furthering professional interests." The committee was in part selected to represent anthropology's four field divisions, with a membership of Julian Steward (chair), Elliot D. Chapple, A. I. Hallowell, Frederick Johnson, George Peter Murdock, William Duncan Strong, C. F. Voegelin, S. Washburn, and Leslie White (ST 177, 3).

At a 1946 meeting of the AAA Reorganization Committee, Steward extolled the benefits of a more centralized association lobbying for new federal funds. When Hallowell and others argued that the NRC and other existing bodies could best achieve these ends, Steward countered that "it will be better in the final pay-off when the money is allotted if anthropology has made a case for itself" (AAAP 131, AAA Reorganization Materials, 3). This small group of men negotiated the basic features of the coming reorganization, determining qualifications for membership; proposing the structure and election of the association's board, president, and liaisons; and arguing for a new structure that could meet more than once or twice a year and best represent members in the anticipated new age of funding opportunities.

New Postwar Funding Horizons

During the 1950s and 1960s, several governmental bodies considered establishing a federally funded social science research agency. Some efforts sought connections with national security–related agencies; others tried creating more independent funding bodies. In 1950, after three years of legislative struggles, the National Science Foundation (NSF) was founded as the primary federal institution responsible for funding scientific research aligned with national science policies, but at its founding the NSF did not fund social science research.

The struggle to establish permanent federal funding of social science had been ongoing since the war's end. On May 20, 1947, Senator William Fulbright failed in his attempts to amend the provisional National Science Foundation Act to include NSF social scientific research funding. Fulbright negotiated Public Law 53A, in the Seventy-Ninth Congress, allowing surplus overseas funds to be used for the training of citizens from these countries for academic study and other related activities in the United States. Later revisions of the Fulbright Act expanded academic opportunities for Americans to travel abroad as scholars. In 1947, the *News Bulletin of the AAA* announced that Fulbright funds were available in countries such as Indonesia, the Philippines, and French Indochina, and that anthropological fieldwork projects could be funded under the Fulbright Act's guidelines (NBAAA 1947 1[2]: 1). Within a few years' time, other countries became available for research: Burma, Jamaica, Gold Coast, Nigeria, the Netherlands, Norway, Greece, Italy, Australia, Iran, Egypt, Malta, Hong Kong, and the Federation of Malaya.

Many in Congress rejected the prospect of large-scale federal funding of academics. American anti-intellectualism in the late 1940s and 1950s fueled skepticism over the contributions that academics could make to relevant Cold War issues. Typical of these views were the remarks of Senator John McClellan (Arkansas) at a 1953 hearing on academics (like Walt Rostow and Max Millikan) receiving funds to "determine how to carry on psychological warfare against the Soviet [Union] and satellites," in which Senator McClellan complained that such research was "simply throwing money away" and that all the taxpayers received from such projects was "just a lot of professor theories and all that stuff" (U.S. House 1952: 345). Such anti-intellectual grandstanding played well with segments of the American public, but it failed to feed the incipient national security state's growing hunger for social science informed intelligence.

Cold War concerns so deeply influenced the establishment of the NSF that the House version of the bill establishing the NSF required all grant recipients to undergo FBI background investigations—though this requirement was cut from the final reconciliation bill (H.R. 4846, March 1950; NBAAA 1950 4[2]: 3).

Anthropology received little federal science funding during the early 1950s (Solovey 2013: 167), and in 1954 the NSF began funding a limited number of anthropological projects under its Biological and Medical Sciences Division (Solovey 2013: 157). In 1958, the NSF recognized anthropology (along with economics, sociology, history, and philosophy of science) as a discipline with its own NSF funding status, under its new Social Science Programs (Larsen 1992: 40–52). Anthropology initially received "more than half (52.9 percent) of the resources allocated to social science" at the NSF (Larsen 1992: 64).

Two months after the launch of *Sputnik*, Julian Steward sent a telegram to AAA president E. Adamson Hoebel expressing concerns that America's new space race would undermine AAA struggles for federal funds to study anthropology. Steward wrote that the government's "increased support for education in the physical and hard sciences while ignoring social science implies a race for the ultimate weapon is the only deterrent to war[;] I hope that anthropologists and our fellow social scientists see behavioral understandings as better solutions to international tensions than threats of total destruction" (AAAP 48, JS to EAH 12/28/57).

While federal funding sources for anthropological research during the 1950s did not emerge at rates anticipated by Steward and others, the rapid growth of area study centers and private foundations funded significant growth in anthropological research. But military and intelligence agencies would eventually identify gaps in the sort of social science research for which they had uses.

In 1963, the Office of Naval Research funded a study, overseen by Ithiel de Sola Pool of the Center for International Studies (CENIS) at MIT, that resulted in a 270-page report titled *Social Science Research and National Security* (Pool 1963).[3] The study sought to answer the question "How can a branch of social science be produced which takes upon itself a responsible concern for national security matters, and how can talented individuals from within social science be drawn into this area?" (Pool 1963: 10). The report discussed a broad range of social science applications: USIS polls of foreign populations, military applications of game theory, assisting counterinsurgency operations, theories of strategy and alliance, nuclear strategy, psychological warfare, "problems of international tensions related to military postures" (56), the production of intelligence information, efforts to anticipate the behaviors of other nations, military developments in new nations, and demographic impacts on national military policies. Pool argued that "social science needs a kind of engineering to go with it" (17). The report identified a need for standardized forms of accessing or organizing cultural data. Human Relations Area Files (HRAF) research was cited as having "contributed substantially" to the strategic collection of global attitudinal information that could be of strategic use to national security sectors (Wilbur Schramm in Pool 1963: 52).

Pool's report informed a congressional revival attempting to establish a federal social science funding agency. In 1966, Senator Fred Harris (Oklahoma) proposed a bill to establish a National Foundation on Social Science (NFSS) to address gaps in federal social science funding at NSF, but it also linked Pentagon and intelligence needs with the production of social science research while maintaining some independence (Larsen 1992). The *New York Times* reported that the proposed NFSS would "be independent of all other Federal agencies, and it would be forbidden to allow interference with its personnel or policies from any other Federal official or department" (Eder 1966a:5).

In response to the academic freedom problems raised by Project Camelot and other military-linked programs (see chapter 10), Harris wanted a federal agency that would steer clear of military, intelligence, or secret research (Solovey 2012: 64). Harris proposed creating a twenty-five-person oversight board to review research proposals. Harris would have allowed CIA- or Pentagon-related research, but "all research would be made available to the public" (Eder 1966a). Harris's proposed NFSS died in 1969 (*AAAFN* 1970 11[1]: 7), but a House amendment proposed by Congressman Emilio Daddario and adopted in 1968 amended the NSF's charter, expanding the funding of social science research (Solovey 2012).

Private Interests Linked to State: Ford, Rockefeller, Carnegie

As the Pike and Church congressional committees would later discover, even without directive Camelot-like federal funding programs for social science research, the CIA had secretly developed ways of directing private foundation funding. But more openly, the leadership of America's most influential private foundations consisted of individuals rotating in and out of federal agencies with national security interests.

Public foundations worked with governmental agencies to prioritize research agendas. In 1949, John Gillin, Sol Tax, and Charles Wagley produced an NRC list titled "Research Needs in the Field of Modern Latin American Culture" (CLAANRC 1949). This was a broad list, including studies on enculturation, culture and personality, urbanization, gender roles, and the impact of culture on notions of "race." That same year, the AAA appointed the NRC Committee on Asian Anthropology, which generated a list of recommended projects that included a mixture of field-based and library research on topics such as community studies, colonialism, national structure, population shifts, land use, and cultural values (CLAANRC 1949). The NRC's Committee on Asian Anthropology at this time recommended that anthropologists could use classified documents to produce a "series of volumes on China, Japan, Indonesia and India would be feasible at the present time and should be encouraged by boards of competent scholars in these fields. Obviously such studies should be undertaken only after a thorough exploration of classified and unclassified materials of a comparable nature have been examined both in the U.S. and abroad" (*AA* 51[3]:540).

Rockefeller, Ford, Carnegie, and other private foundations bearing the names of Rooseveltian malefactors of great wealth shaped the funding of anthropological research during the Cold War. Functioning as intergenerational trusts, these foundations protected against the dissolution of the massive conglomeration of wealth upon the death of the funds' creators. With the establishment of family members controlling boards (sometimes with significant compensation or with family use of trust properties) and following established policies aligned with the desires of the funds' patrons, the interests of wealthy magnates could stretch beyond their corporal existence while estate taxes were evaded in ways that created intergenerational tax shelters. Joan Roelofs described these foundations as "examples of mortmain, the dead hand of past wealth controlling the future" (2003: 20).[4] These foundations funded not only research projects aligned with their intellectual, political, or class interests but also less-aligned projects (with some limitations), though they favored the coverage of specific geographic regions or specific social problems during given periods.

These private foundations funded social science in ways that nurtured the establishment of an academic elite that, as David Nugent observed,

> was to be trained in the virtues of empirically grounded, practically oriented research within one of the philanthropies' remade institutions of higher learning. In order to make it possible to train a new elite along these lines, the philanthropies provided their remade institutions of higher learning with large sums of money specifically for the training of students. The philanthropies made it possible for these institutions to offer scholarships to fund the entire graduate training of "promising" students. The philanthropies thus helped influence entire cohorts of graduate students, who were schooled in the scientific, empirically grounded, practically oriented concepts, methods, and techniques that the philanthropies believed would make a contribution to the pressing social problems of the day. (2002: 11)

Carnegie, Ford, and Rockefeller were selectively predisposed to nurture ideas aligned with their founders' political-economic interests, and funds were disbursed that supported causes ranging from spreading specific forms of American democracy, to advancing the Green Revolution, to studies of foreign labor systems favoring management. These wealthy private foundations were often directed by elite men who moved between these positions and Cold War governmental roles. John Foster Dulles and Dean Rusk moved from Rockefeller Foundation presidencies to becoming secretary of state. When McGeorge Bundy left his White House national security post, where he liaisoned with the CIA, he replaced John McCloy as chair of the Ford Foundation. The Ford Foundation's director of international affairs during the 1950s and 1960s, Shepard Stone, had served in army intelligence and the State Department. With such ties, it seemed natural for the Ford Foundation to provide replacement funds after the CIA's secret funding of the Congress for Cultural Freedom was exposed, providing needed financial support in the CIA's embarrassed absence (Epstein 1967: 16–17n1).

Bruce Cumings's examination of how Philip Mosely linked the CIA, the Ford Foundation, and area study centers at various universities clarifies how the CIA used private foundations, such as Ford, to shape academic research during the 1950s and 1960s. Cumings cited 1953 correspondence between Mosley and Paul Langer discussing how the Ford Foundation would consult with CIA director Allen Dulles to establish how Ford-funded research projects could be selected in ways that coalesced with the CIA's needs (Cumings 1999: 184). Cumings showed how "Mosley provided a working linkage among Ford, the CIA, and the ACLS/SSRC well into the 1960s," with back-channel correspondence between Mosley and the CIA working out who the CIA should use as regional consultants (185). Cumings concluded that this

> suggests that the Ford Foundation, in close consultation with the CIA, helped to shape postwar area studies and important collaborative research in modernization studies and comparative politics that were later mediated through well-known Ford-funded SSRC projects (ones that were required reading when I was a graduate student in the late 1960s). According to Christopher Simpson's study of declassified materials, however, this interweaving of foundations, universities, and state agencies (mainly the intelligence and military agencies) extended to the social sciences as a whole: "For years, government money . . . not always publicly acknowledged as such — made up more than 75 percent of the annual budgets of institutions such as Paul Lazarsfeld's Bureau of Applied Research at Columbia University, Hadley Cantril's Institute for International Social Programs at Princeton, Ithiel de Sola Pool's CENIS program at MIT and others" . . . My own work in postwar American archives over the past two decades has taught me how many books central to the political science profession in the 1950s and 1960s emerged first as internal, classified government studies. (Cumings 1999: 186)

The spread of these funds in postwar area study centers provided opportunities for anthropologists seeking fieldwork, while also shaping the questions they pursued.

The AAA's First Postwar Decade and Select Political Advocacy

The AAA membership grew rapidly during the postwar years, rising from 1,271 in 1946 to 3,000 in 1949 (NBAAA 1949 3[4]: 5). Increased membership funded a full-time professional staff, and in 1949 anthropologist Frederick Johnson was hired as the association's executive secretary. Johnson helped advance the association's standing with New York's and Washington's newly emerging networks of public and private funding sources; as foundations were established, a new generation of funds emerged for overseas fieldwork with programs like the SSRC's Training and Travel Fellowships (NBAAA 1949 3[1]: 7) and fellowships dedicated to studying problems of foreign nations (NBAAA 1948 2[1]: 5–6). The Department of State offered new programs like the Government Fellowship in American Republics for graduate students, which funded six months of study and travel in Central and South America (NBAAA 1949 3[1]: 9). In 1952, the Ford Foundation had opportunities for one hundred Foreign Study and Research Fellowships (NBAAA 1952 6[2]: 8). There were also programs with more obvious governmental applications, with the AAA publishing requests for information from the State Department's Office of Intelligence Research seeking anthropologists' dissertation abstracts for circulation within governmental agencies (NBAAA 1951 5[2]: 5).

During the decade following the war, the AAA struggled with how to address several political issues. At the first AAA meeting after the American bombing of Nagasaki and Hiroshima, the membership adopted a resolution proclaiming the association's dedication to studying atomic energy and to working to guard against the dangers of these new weapons (AA 1946 48[2]: 319). In 1946, the AAA Executive Board appointed Carleton Coon (Chair), Gregory Bateson, Earl Count, Melville Herskovits, and Alfred Métraux to the Committee to Investigate the Possibility of Strengthening Non-Nazi Anthropologists in Enemy Countries (AA 1946 48[2]: 319). The wartime service of these five anthropologists represented the range of activities undertaken by many AAA fellows: Coon and Bateson had both served in Office of Strategic Services (OSS) field operations, Count taught human anatomy to military surgeons in training, Herskovits worked at the Smithsonian's Ethnogeographic Board, and Métraux worked for the U.S. Strategic Bombing Survey (D. H. Price 2008a; Sade 1997).

The committee was charged with determining which specific anthropologists in "enemy or enemy-occupied countries had been on our side and which opposed us," but it soon abandoned this task, arguing that it was unqualified to delineate which anthropologists had been Nazi collaborators. The committee had difficulty evaluating conflicting reports about individual anthropologists and was concerned that some scholars might be settling personal vendettas against colleagues. It reported that the French were "having great sport accusing each other of being collaborators" (AA 1947: 353).

In abandoning its charge, chair Carleton Coon explained that the committee "considered that if a German served in the armed forces of his country he was no more guilty from our point of view than those of us who had done the same thing. At first glance, we considered blackballing those who had used their positions for propaganda, but we soon realized that a great number of our own anthropologists had done the same thing and if we had supported that course of action we would have had to condemn some of our own colleagues" (AA 1947: 353). This argument revealed an understanding of the complexities of duties of service during wartime, as well as lingering misgivings some anthropologists had about their war work, but it also revealed an unexamined argument of assumed political, ethical, and moral equivalence between Axis and Allied applications of anthropology.

This decision by the AAA to ignore political differences between using anthropology for campaigns of genocidal fascist tyranny and, arguably, for liberation from such forms of oppression had later consequences for American anthropology. These would include the association's proclivity to sidestep political concerns in favor of *ethical* considerations in ways that focused on professional "best practices" for fieldwork yet ignored political outcomes of projects using anthropology and anthropologists. Differentiating between ethical and political critiques is not without epistemological and practical difficulties. Yet meaningful distinctions can be made by recognizing that ethical critiques focus on best practices followed by professionals — often in a context of providing disclosure, gaining consent, minimizing harm, maintaining informed autonomy, and so forth — whereas political critiques focus on power relations, including macro questions of empire, neocolonialism, and imperialism. This practice of focusing primarily on ethics while avoiding confronting political issues would become a significant feature of later anthropological critiques of disciplinary militarization (D. H. Price 2014b).

Perhaps the wartime experiences of these committee members influenced this decision. Gregory Bateson's OSS propaganda work in Burma included overseeing black propaganda broadcasts (in which his OSS team pretended to be Japanese radio broadcasters while supplying disinformation) made from a clandestine radio station, work that Bateson later regretted for having been deceitful (Mandler 2013; D. H. Price 1998). While some committee members may have undertaken war work that paralleled some of the war work of German anthropologists, this did not mean their work was morally or politically equivalent, given the differences in the larger Allied and Axis political projects.

The committee stipulated that if "special cases" of Nazi anthropologist collaborators came to its attention, it would investigate and determine the facts of specific alleged instances, but it did not look for any such "special cases." Had the committee investigated, it would have easily found disturbing examples of anthropologists' Nazi collaborations. As Gretchen Schafft's research shows, the contributions of German anthropologists to the Nazi cause were widespread and apparent. Had these scholars investigated, they would have found records of anthropological collaborations ranging from research supporting the Nuremberg Race Laws of 1935 to the cooking of fake scientific racial reports (Schafft 2004: 73, 17–27). The atrocities of professionally trained anthropologist Josef Mengele would have been easily identified examples had the committee chosen to undertaken even the most cursory of investigations (Schafft 2004: 183).

But the AAA found it easier to weigh in on other political issues. Anthropologists' concerns about American racism led to policy changes within the association. In 1947, the Executive Board canceled plans to hold the association's annual meeting in St. Louis because "all large hotels in St. Louis maintain discriminatory practices against some of our members" (NBAAA 1[3]: 1). The meeting was relocated to Albuquerque, where the University of New Mexico graciously provided free accommodations in campus dormitories that were empty for the Christmas break. These progressive moves by the association were the sort of activities devoted to racial equality that would eventually garner the FBI's attention and harassment for activist anthropologists in the 1950s (D. H. Price 2004b).

The AAA joined the efforts of other professional organizations collecting academic books to be sent to devastated academies around the world (AA 1946 48[3]: 490). The association adopted a political statement declaring that native peoples should not suffer under the impacts of increased Western militarization. At the 1946 AAA annual meeting the membership passed a resolution deploring "the proposed action of the British Military Mission in Australia to fire destructive projectiles into an area of Western Australia occupied by many living aborigines, and calls upon the Mission to cancel all such action" (AA 1947 19[2]: 365).

In 1947, Melville Herskovits drafted a "Declaration of Human Rights" that was presented to the Department of State and the United Nations (NBAAA 1947 1[3]: 41). The declaration, which acknowledged the difficulties of identifying fundamental human rights in a context completely independent of cultural processes, stated three fundamental positions:

> 1. The individual realizes his personality through his culture, hence respect for individual differences entails a respect for cultural differences.

2. Respect for differences between cultures is validated by the scientific fact that no technique of qualitatively evaluating cultures has been discovered.

3. Standards and values are relative to the culture from which they derive so that any attempt to formulate postulates that grow out of the beliefs or moral codes of one culture must to that extent detract from the applicability of any Declaration of Human Rights to mankind as a whole. (AA 1947: 541–42)

Julian Steward criticized the statement, voicing doubts that

> in urging that values be respected because "man is free only when he lives as his society defines freedom," we really mean to approve the social caste system of India, the racial caste system of the United States, or many of the other varieties of social discrimination in the world. I should question that we intend to condone the exploitation of primitive peoples through the Euro-American system of economic imperialism, while merely asking for more understanding treatment of them: or, on the other hand, that we are prepared to take a stand against the values in our own culture which [underlie] such imperialism. (1948: 351)

Steward identified problems that arise when anthropological associations use their scientific positions to advocate on political issues. He concluded:

> We have gotten out of our scientific role and are struggling with contradictions. During the war, we gladly used our professional techniques and knowledge to advance a cause, but I hope that no one believes that he had a scientific justification for doing so. As individual citizens, members of the Association have every right to pass value judgments, and there are some pretty obvious things that we would all agree on. As a scientific organization, the Association has no business dealing with the rights of man. I am sure that we shall serve science better, and I daresay we shall eventually serve humanity better, if we stick to our purpose. Even now, a declaration about human rights can come perilously close to advocacy of American ideological imperialism. (1948: 352)

Steward brought questions of scientific neutrality and advocacy, as well as issues of applying anthropological understandings of culture, power, and equality, to the foreground, but most of the discipline remained silently disengaged from weighing in on these issues (see D. H. Price 2014b).[5]

In July 1950, Ashley Montagu (with the assistance of Claude Lévi-Strauss, Ernest Beaglehole, and others) drafted UNESCO's progressive statement rejecting biological essentialist notions of race, known as "The Race Question" (A. Métraux 1951; UNESCO 1969: 30–35). Asserting that "scientists have reached general agreement in recognizing that mankind is one: that all men belong to the same species, Homo sapiens," this UNESCO statement advanced Boasian notions of the social construction of race in an international sphere.

The statement declared that scientists had determined that all of humanity was a single species, and that while genetic differences between groups were evident, using the concept of "race" to describe different populations was scientifically arbitrary. Métraux deconstructed notions that nations or religious groups constituted "races." He described a number of acquired characteristics, such as "personality and character," "temperament," and cultural differences, and rejected the possibility that biological processes were responsible for these differences, declaring that "'race' is not so much a biological phenomenon as a social myth. The myth of 'race' has created an enormous amount of human and social damage" (Métraux 1951: 144). The statement argued for human equality, pointing out that "the characteristics in which human groups differ from one another are often exaggerated and used as a basis for questioning the validity of equality in the ethical sense" (144).

As the AAA membership and the association's focus expanded after the war, some governmental agencies found opportunities to capitalize on this convergence of research opportunities, money, and anthropologists' desires to contribute to building a better world.

A Secret Sharer and the AAA's Membership Roster

During the Second World War, the AAA had helped the OSS's institutional predecessor, the Office of the Coordinator of Information, compile rosters identifying anthropologists' geographic and linguistic expertise; later the Ethnogeographic Board compiled similar lists for military and intelligence agencies (D. H. Price 2008a: 97–101). These rosters were vital tools during the war, and as the Cold War progressed, the American government had renewed needs for such lists.

The CIA's interest in compiling rosters listing biographical information on specialists with skill sets of interest stretched back to the agency's earliest days. A May 12, 1948, CIA memo to the future director of the CIA-funded Asia Foundation, Robert Blum (then working in the office of the secretary of defense), records the CIA already prioritizing the creation of databases containing such records (FOIA CIA-RDP80R01731R003400050047-3, 5/12/48).[6] In 1974, former AAA executive secretary Charles Frantz reported that in the 1950s the NRC, the NSF, and the CIA had been the main agencies pushing the AAA to compile a membership roster (Frantz 1974: 7).[7] Frantz observed that facilitating projects that connected members with federal agencies and funding opportunities was a natural extension of the reorganized AAA's goals. The new association bylaws "further specified that the officers were obligated to maintain records of professional anthropologists, to serve as a clearinghouse for professional and scientific anthropological matters, to publish a bulletin for Fellows on activities of professional interest, to hold referenda on urgent matters, and to establish liaisons with other scientific organizations and institutions" (Frantz 1974: 12).

In February 1951, the AAA's executive secretary, Frederick Johnson, wrote President Howells and the Executive Board (John O. Brew, John Gillin, E. Adamson Hoebel, Morris Opler, Froelich G. Rainey, and Edward H. Spicer) that governmental agencies had contacted the association to request a cross-indexed roster of the AAA membership, noting that the "people who desire the roster are, somewhat justifiably impatient" (AAAP 6, FJ memo 4, 2/21/51). As the only nonrevolving member of the Executive Board, Johnson exerted significant influence on the board's transient members. After exploring several options for agencies to oversee and support the compiling of the roster, Johnson determined that the CIA would do a superior job, though the agency insisted on secrecy. Johnson wrote, "In searching for the ways and means of setting up a roster of Anthropologists I have a general proposal from Central Intelligence Agency. This agency is reluctant to have its name connected with the proposal. It will do the work as generally and tentatively outlined below provided the Association will sponsor the project" (AAAP 6, FJ memo 4, 2/21/51, 2).[8]

Johnson asked board members to signify whether or not they wanted to pursue this offer from the CIA; a second ballot item asked approval for Johnson to investigate how the association might maintain future versions of the roster. The ballot stated:

> The Executive Secretary is empowered to continue negotiations with Central Intelligence Agency for the purpose of compiling a roster of Anthropological Personnel. The final agreement will be based on the idea that the Anthropological Association will sponsor the roster and the Agency will do the technical work connected with it. The [Central Intelligence] Agency will be allowed to keep one copy of the roster for its own use and it will deliver to the Association a duplicate copy the use of which will not be restricted. The final agreement between the Association and the agency shall be such that the Association shall be liable only for mailing charges and such incidental expenses as it may be able to afford. The final agreement shall be approved by the Executive Board. (AAAP 6, memo 4, 2/21/51)

The board approved these arrangements, with five members voting yes, one voting no, and two not voting; the board also authorized Johnson to investigate options for making the roster updatable.

President Howells wrote Johnson:

> The CIA proposal is ideal. We should go along with it, with the understanding that they give us duplicate IBM cards *and* duplicates of the questionnaires, which they can easily do; they are great at reproducing things. If a reasonable questionnaire, suitable to both parties, can be worked out, we will both get what we want, and except for the mailing they will put the whole thing through from beginning to end, and the chances are we will get something that we want; if we don't, then the questionnaire method is no good anyhow, and we don't stand to lose. (AAAP 6, WH to FJ, 3/2/51)

Howells proposed to Johnson that the AAA establish an anthropologist liaison committee that could link the association with government agencies. Responding to a suggestion apparently already made by Johnson, Howells advocated designating an individual to act as a liaison between the CIA and the AAA, writing:

> I think that we should appoint a committee along the lines you suggest, and it can work, and no fooling. We have anthropologists in the CIA, of course and I should think we could get one appointed liaison member for the CIA, and go to work. I suggest: Newman, Fenton, Collins (bad health?), Foster, Flannery, Roberts, Stirling, all obvious as candidates for committee. What have we for a linguist? And yourself, ex-officio. For your information, we shall be in Washington April 6 and 7, and we can make time for some work, e.g. seeing Jim Andrews or somebody about it, if necessary. (AAAP 6, WH to FJ 3/2/51)[9]

The AAA's surviving correspondence provides no further information on what became of Howells's suggestion that the AAA appoint a "liaison member for the CIA."[10]

Johnson, who had his own ideas about which anthropologists should liaison with the CIA, responded, "Of the group you suggested I am only enthusiastic about Foster and with some reservations Bud Newman" (AAAP 6, FJ to WH 3/6/51). Johnson eliminated most of Howells's nominees, complaining that "Stirling does not know what it is all about and usually does not care. Collins' ideas concerning Anthropology are rather narrow. Fenton, on the basis of the record is greatly over-rated. Flannery is almost as restricted as Collins.

Roberts on the other hand might be of use especially since he has had some experience with similar things. However, I happen to know a lot about his situation and what he has to do and I am fairly certain that if he took on the job he would not be able to do as much as he should" (AAAP 6, FJ to WH 3/7/51:2). Johnson wanted liaison members to be based in Washington, but he rejected several suggested Washington-based individuals. He wanted a *certain type* of DC-based anthropologist; as he explained to Howells, they should

> select a group of Anthropologists representing all fields who in-so-far as possible are heads of departments. Ask these men to select from their advanced students people who will do the work under supervision. This accomplishes two things. It gets the work done without overloading the experienced man. It "trains" the younger men in committee work. The later is getting to be important. Now that our, at least my hair is getting gray we are losing touch with the new generation. If we can get some of these men started up the line in the Association it will be that much easier to get more representatives and active committees in the future. The gray-beards are nice and we know what they can do, but there comes a time when they cannot or will not. (AAAP 6, FJ to WH 3/7/51, 2)

Johnson favored creating a closed structure of power, drawing on a young generation of anthropologists, which would establish ongoing bonds between the association and the bureaucratic power structures of Washington.

Howells did not press the issue. He relinquished his authority to Johnson, writing that he could

> keep after this as you like, as far as I am concerned. My suggestions of the Washington people were only the names that occurred to me, and I will not stick to them. On the other hand I do not care much for the idea of advanced students taking the job at hand; they are apt to be too enthusiastic and overdo things, according to my experience. Actually, you on the one hand and the CIA on the other are the key people, and could probably agree on the data wanted in a very short time. Certainly a committee which is representative should help, but too many cooks might spoil the broth. Why don't you and Mr. Kelley draft something up? This might save a lot of time. What I am saying is rather random. I am inclined to suggest that Duncan Strong might come in on it, because of his past experience. (AAAP 6: WH to FJ 3/16/51)

Strong's "past experience" was likely a reference to his war work on the Ethnogeographic Board's roster (D. H. Price 2008a: 97–100). Howells and Johnson recognized that with AAA members' information entered into the CIA's computers, these data could be adapted and rearranged later, and future editions and updates to the roster could be easily adapted. Howells wrote the board a few days later to provide an update on Johnson's progress with the CIA and suggestions for how CIA anthropologists could assist this project, explaining that Johnson "would like to see a working committee set up to collaborate with the CIA; I have suggested that this should be made up of Washington people, especially since there are already anthropologists in the CIA, and the questionnaire could be set up more quickly, always of course under Fred's eye; this is his baby" (AAAP 6: WH to Board 3/6/51). Howells wanted the CIA to produce duplicate computer punch cards so that the CIA and the AAA could both have copies of the data, and he wrote Johnson, saying he wished to meet with anthropologist and CIA employee James Madison Andrews IV to discuss details of the roster. Johnson responded that this sounded like a good idea:

> By all means go and see Jim Andrews and others in the CIA when you are in Washington. If the members of the Board would only return their "ballots" to me I could go ahead with this business. Mr. Francis Kelley who worked out the proposal with me is very anxious to get this started. I had hoped that the Association would act efficiently in this matter simply because we should do our job. In any case, I suspect that the ballots will be in before you get to Washington and that I will have taken the next step. I hope so for then there will be something for you and others to put your teeth into. (AAAP 6, FJ to WH 3/7/51)[11]

As AAA executive secretary, a nonelected position, Johnson exerted extraordinary control over policy decisions. He drafted resolutions and later forwarded these to Howells, who sent them to the board for ratification as if he had written them. Howells facilitated this and even took steps to hide this practice, prohibited by the bylaws, of a non–board member introducing a motion by developing their own "protocol." Howells asked Johnson, "May I make a suggestion about protocol? That is, that if you send out proposals to the Board accompanied by 'ballots,' so marked, it looks like a motion being made and seconded by the Executive Secretary instead of from within the Board, which is unconstitutional, and we might get our lines tangled. E.g., it sometimes might embarrass me in trying to act on your behalf, as in the previous paragraph, when I think you ought to be put on the committee" (AAAP 6, WH to FJ 3/2/51). Johnson replied that this was "certainly food for thought," admitting that he had in the past introduced several motions adopted by the board, a violation of association bylaws, and that on some issues he had skirted procedures, but he assured Howells this was in the interest of streamlining the process: "This was perhaps a little legalistic but I found myself on the verge of tacitly committing the Association to an activity. Theoretically I should have submitted the proposal to you. Members of the Board should move and second it and then vote on it. In my brash way I have short-circuited this and submitted the 'motion' for a vote. I have done this in the interest of saving time and correspondence" (AAAP 6, FJ to WH 3/7/51).[12] Johnson proposed that he and Howells set up an arrangement where Johnson could present proposals that Howells could then restate as a motion coming from him so that the board could vote (AAAP 6, FJ to WH 3/7/51).

Johnson negotiated with the CIA, and by mid-April 1951 an agreement for collaboration was reached. Johnson informed the board that under this agreement, "the C.I.A. will compile a preliminary questionnaire. The people who will do this have had experience with the rosters being made by the NSRB and they will be advised by anthropologists on the C.I.A. staff" (AAAP 6, FJ to EB 4/17/51).

The identities of the CIA anthropologists who assisted in this work were not disclosed in archived AAA correspondence. Johnson collaborated with CIA personnel to produce the questionnaire sent to AAA members. The only appreciable cost for the association coming from this arrangements was the approximately two hundred dollars in postage for mailing questionnaires to members.

In September 1951, Johnson sent a "Memorandum to Committee on Roster" providing a "checklist" of information to be collected for the roster. Johnson supplied a page from the American Council of Learned Societies (ACLS) questionnaire for its political science roster and suggested that the AAA separate out the subfields of social anthropology, applied anthropology, physical anthropology, linguistics, archaeology, and ethnography. Johnson recommended that the AAA collect information on the following "functions": "research, development or field exploration," "management or administration, teaching," "technical writing and editing or library work," "consulting, clinical practice or evaluation," and "student" (AAAP 36, FJ memo, 9/13/51). He wrote the board that "a voluntary registration of specialized personnel is frequently viewed as closely related to recruitment and placement activities. While it is possible that the projected registration will be used in connection with recruitment and placement programs, no definite plans for such use have yet been developed by the ACLS or the Office of Naval Research" (AAAP 6, Johnson memo, 10/15/51).

Though I searched numerous archives and libraries and filed several Freedom of Information Act (FOIA) requests with the CIA and other governmental agencies, I have not located a surviving copy of the AAA roster. In response to a FOIA request, the FBI mailed me a 129-page file relating to the AAA's activities with the ACLS, which included a copy of the final survey instrument that was mailed to AAA members in 1952. The FBI stumbled across this roster questionnaire while undertaking a mail intercept operation involving an (unidentified) anthropologist who received the roster survey.

The FBI recognized the usefulness of this instrument for itself and other intelligence agencies. The FBI reported that "such a repository appears to be [of] great value to the Bureau from an investigative standpoint, and it is suggested that consideration be given to developing reliable sources in the organization and utilizing this material to the fullest advantage. The thought occurs that the questionnaires may have been initiated by some Governmental agency, such as CIA, for the express purpose of obtaining intelligence data" (FBI 100-387756-8).[13] While American anthropologists passed along a wealth of personal information with little apparent concern of how it might be used, the FBI understood how such information would be invaluable to the CIA as it set up covert operations and contacts all over the underdeveloped world.

The FBI reproduced the AAA's original six-page questionnaire, along with a sheet requesting "additional names" that might be included in the roster, and cover letters from AAA executive secretary Johnson, and Bernard V. Bothmer, general secretary of the Archaeological Institute of America. Figure 3.1 reproduces the second page of the roster questionnaire, showing the detailed level of information that was gathered. The questionnaire asked AAA members to provide information on educational background, languages studied, countries visited, academic specialties, citizenship status, professional honors, professional membership, past military service and current military status, employment history, and income levels. The questionnaire did not divulge the CIA's role in the project, only telling members that "the data compiled from this Roster will be used in the analysis of manpower problems and for possible placement and allocation purposes" (FBI 100-387756-2). The roster questionnaire was announced in the January 1952 issue of the *News Bulletin of the AAA* and in *American Anthropologist* (see NBAAA 1952 6[1]: 1; AA 1952 54[2]: 288–89). Association members were told that the roster was being compiled because "the present lack of information concerning specialists in the humanities and social sciences is a serious stumbling block to a kind of planning which is urgently needed. Mobilization activities which will continue over a long period of time have strongly emphasized the basic need for apprising our defense program as related to the concept of national security. Analysis of the data from this registration will throw considerable light on the potentialities of the various fields,

Developed by
AMERICAN
ANTHROPOLOGICAL ASSOCIATION
and
ARCHAEOLOGICAL INSTITUTE
OF AMERICA

NATIONAL REGISTRATION 100-387756-2
THE HUMANITIES AND THE SOCIAL SCIENCES
Checklist of Fields of Speciali[illegible]ion
ANTHROPOLOGY and ARCHAEOLOGY

Budget Bureau No. 45-5104
Approval expires 6-30-52

This checklist as well as the list of functions below, is to be used as a work sheet for the completion of portions of the questionnaire sheets, especially Question 16 on the four-page questionnaire. NOTE: *Any entries written in under one of the "Other, specify" headings should be transferred to the appropriate blanks on the questionnaires.*

Indicate specialized rather than general fields of specialization as far as possible.

Specialty	Code
ETHNOLOGY AND SOCIAL ANTHROPOLOGY (general)	9500
Human ecology, environment and culture	9501
Technology and invention	9502
Folklore	9503
Art, music, recreation	9504
Cultural and social change, acculturation	9505
Reproductive practices and sexual life	9506
Medicine	9507
Ethnobotany	9508
Ethnozoology	9511
Ethnolinguistics	9512
Theory	9513
Other (specify)________	9519
SOCIAL ORGANIZATION (general)	9520
Family and kinship systems	9521
Political systems	9522
Law and social sanctions	9523
Economic systems	9524
Religious systems, ritual, belief, magic, witchcraft	9525
Social stratification and prestige systems	9526
City, town, village organization (including contemporary communities)	9527
Warfare	9528
Associations (Sodalities)	9531
Demography (population, fertility, morbidity, mortality, etc.)	9532
Theory	9533
Other (specify)________	9539
CULTURE AND PERSONALITY (general)	9540
Socialization and education	9541
Life-cycle	9542
Group character, modal personality structure, national character, etc.	9543
Deviant behavior	9544
Personality testing, cross-cultural use	9545
Intelligence testing, cross-cultural use	9546
Life-histories	9547
Theory	9548
Other (specify)________	9549
APPLIED ANTHROPOLOGY (general)	9550
Business administration	9551
Industrial relations	9552
Public administration	9553
Educational institutions	9554
Medical and psychiatric facilities	9555
Personnel selection	9556
Administration of non-Western peoples	9557
Intercultural problems	9558
Minority, ethnic and racial problems	9561
Relocation problems	9562
Technological change problems	9563
Administrative and social change problems	9564
Industrial projects in non-industrialized areas	9565
Propaganda	9566

Specialty	Code
Group morale	9567
Nationalism and nativism	9568
Food habits and diet	9571
Survey techniques	9572
Theory	9573
Other (specify)________	9579
ARCHAEOLOGY (general)	9580
Old World	9581
Palaeolithic and mesolithic	9582
Neolithic	9583
Advanced civilizations	9584
Classical	9585
Greek	9586
Roman	9587
Anatolian	9588
Mesopotamian	9591
Iranian	9592
Egyptian	9593
Palestine-Syrian	9594
Indian	9595
New World	9596
Early Man	9597
Archaic and formative	9598
Advanced civilizations	9601
Other (specify)________	9609
PHYSICAL ANTHROPOLOGY (general)	9610
Human evolution	9611
Fossil	9612
Living	9613
Comparative anatomy	9614
Comparative psychology	9615
Ecology	9616
Human variation	9617
Race	9618
Morphology	9621
Genetics	9622
Blood-grouping	9623
Pathology	9624
Population biology	9625
Human growth	9626
Fetal	9627
Cranio-facial	9628
Post-cranial	9631
Skeletal	9632
Tissue relations	9633
Constitution	9634
Applied physical anthropology	9635
Other (specify)________	9639
Areas of Specialization	
NEW WORLD (general)	9640
Arctic	9641
Eastern North America and the Plains	9642
Western North America (general)	9643
Western North America (Southwest)	9644
Middle America	9645
Andean South America	9646
Tropical Lowland South America and Circum-Caribbean	9647

Specialty	Code
Southern South America	9648
Other (specify)________	9649
OLD WORLD (general)	9650
Northern Europe	9651
Western Europe	9652
Central Europe	9653
Southern Europe	9654
Eastern Europe and Balkans	9655
Egypt	9656
Near East	9657
North Africa	9658
Equatorial Africa	9661
Southern Africa	9662
Madagascar	9663
India and Pakistan	9664
Southeast Asia	9665
Australia	9666
Far East	9668
Central Asia	9671
Soviet Northern Asia	9672
Pacific Islands	9673
Other (specify)________	9679
Other Competences	
Aerial photo interpretation	8512
Biometrics	1803
Botany	1310
Field mapping and surveying	8480
Dendrochronology	9681
Genetics	1400
Geology	3100
Human anatomy	9682
Human physiology	9683
Medicine and public health	2000
Climatology	8412
Nutrition	1170
Palaeobotany	3177
Field photography	8521
Vertebrate Palaeontology	3175
Zoology	1230
RELATED SPECIALIZATIONS (Indicate specialty within a field. Code numbers not required.)	
AESTHETICS (specify)________	
ARCHITECTURE (specify)________	
ECONOMICS (specify)________	
FINE ARTS (specify)________	
GEOGRAPHY (specify)________	
HISTORY (specify)________	
LAW (specify)________	
LINGUISTICS AND LITERATURE (specify)________	
MUSICOLOGY (specify)________	
PHILOSOPHY (specify)________	
POLITICAL SCIENCE (specify)________	
PSYCHIATRY (specify)________	
PSYCHOLOGY (specify)________	
SOCIOLOGY (specify)________	
STATISTICS (specify)________	
OTHER (specify)________	

List of Functions

Function	Code
RESEARCH, FIELD EXPLORATION Analysis of published materials, documents, reports; collection and analysis of new facts, data, materials; testing and evaluation of hypotheses; experimentation; operational research.	0.
PROFESSIONAL CONSULTATION Professional advisory service to private clients, or to governmental agencies; membership on advisory boards, commissions, committees on other than full-time salary basis.	1.
ADMINISTRATION, MANAGEMENT Direction of operating activity; direction and supervision of the work of others; planning and policy determination; administration of research. Includes elective and appointive offices.	2.
OPERATIONAL ACTIVITY Performance of professional or technical activities not classified as research, consultation or administration, in connection with the operation of a government agency or business enterprise.	3.
TEACHING	4.
PROFESSIONAL WRITING AND EDITING Editing technical and professional manuscripts for publication; preparation of text books and manuals, popular articles.	5.
PROFESSIONAL LIBRARY OR MUSEUM ACTIVITY Archival, bibliographical, library or museum activity not classified as subject matter research or administration.	6.
CREATIVE WRITING, CRITICISM Literary composition other than presentation of the results of research, or popularized technical materials.	7.
STUDENT To be checked only in cases where competence in a given occupational specialty has been acquired entirely through study and course work rather than experience.	8.
OTHER, Specify________	9.

FIGURE 3.1. Page 2 of the AAA's 1952 roster questionnaire as reproduced in FBI file 100-387756-2. The FBI collected this questionnaire while conducting surveillance on AAA members, and FBI analysis of the document led them to correctly assume the CIA was likely involved in the collection of this information.

including Anthropology" (*NBAAA* 1952 6[1]:1). A 1952 report of AAA committees listed members of the Committee on the Roster of Anthropologists as W. W. Howells, Frederick Johnson, D. B. Stout (ex officio), David Aberle, Wendell C. Bennett, Marshall Newman, Alexander Spoehr, and Carl F. Voegelin. The CIA drafted components of the questionnaire, and it is unknown what activities this committee undertook, or whether committee members not on the board knew of the agency's links to the roster (*AA* 1952 54[2]: 289).

Other organizations with later-identified CIA links collected information on anthropologists and other scholars for their own roster projects (see Colby and Dennett 1995: 339). In 1955, the *Bulletin of the AAA* carried a small advertisement announcing the National Conference on Exchange of Persons, sponsored and organized by Kenneth Holland, president of the Institute of International Education, which was held in New York in February 1955 (*BAAA* 1955 3[1]: 13). The advertisement reported the roster had records on "210,000 persons who have studied, trained or taught in countries other than their own" and was financed by the Ford Foundation (*BAAA* 1956 4[2]: 4–5).[14]

The AAA produced other membership and departmental rosters in later years, but these did not contain the level of profiling detail of this first CIA-assisted roster and were produced by AAA personnel without assistance from the CIA.

Postwar Applied Anthropology

The Society for Applied Anthropology (SFAA) was founded months before the United States entered the Second World War. With so many anthropologists engaged in war work, the organization's membership grew rapidly, and the postwar years brought opportunities for anthropologists working in the emerging public service sector and on new international aid programs connected with America's Cold War development strategies. The Cold War provided opportunities for applied anthropologists, with some military and intelligence agencies using them for jobs similar to those performed by anthropologists during the war.

Louis Dupree organized the session "Anthropology in the Armed Services" at the 1958 annual meeting of the SFAA. The impetus for this session occurred two years earlier, when, after presenting a paper at a conference on using anthropology to study air force survival techniques, anthropologists C. W. M. Hart and H. T. E. Hertzberg asked Dupree to organize a session for applied anthropologists working for the military. Hart and John Bennett later helped add this armed services session to the 1958 program (Dupree 1958: 2; see NBAAA 1952 6[2]: 16).

For a discipline that had been so thoroughly engrossed in warfare only a decade and a half earlier, this 1958 session found anthropology significantly distanced from the military and now more commonly working in industry, on community-based projects, or on governmental projects financed through the Departments of the Interior or the Department of State. Most of the session topics had anthropological corollaries during the Second World War, yet the papers did not connect with this now-silent past.

Paul Nesbitt's overview of air force projects identified anthropological studies of "social stratification of U.S. Air Force Bases," "combat behavior," "psychological and sociological vulnerability of peoples in satellite tension areas," and studies administering "national intelligence surveys of Africa, Asia and Europe" (Nesbitt 1958: 4–5). Nesbitt argued that anthropology could effectively study and improve people's abilities to use new weapons systems (5). He examined oral histories and other records, finding themes in descriptions of more than a thousand bail-out incidents. Nesbitt artificially created the conditions encountered by a downed crew of a B-52 and then used ethnographers to conduct participant observations with the crew as they enacted what they would do in an actual survival situation (8). Nesbitt described air force uses of HRAF data and other ethnographic sources to produce five-by-eight-inch "ethnic information" cards containing ethnographic data that crew members carried in their flight suit pockets. He found that "each ethnic group is described in terms of populations, range, environment, physical appearance, language, religion, social organization, economy, diet, transportation, and reputation for being friendly or hostile. In addition, each card bears a photograph of a typical male and female and a map which pinpoints the location and range of the particular ethnic group.... To date more than 150 of these studies have been published" (11). These cards, which were produced by civilian and air force anthropologists, supplied ethnographic profiles of seventy ethnic groups within the USSR, twenty in the Middle East, and another twenty in the Far East (11).

Joan Chriswell (1958) summarized some of the World War II navy research by the Institute of Human Relations and connected this work with anthropologists' postwar roles at CIMA and the Scientific Investigation of Micronesia. He highlighted Ruth Benedict and Margaret Mead's ONR-sponsored work at the Research on Contemporary Cultures project, and John Bennett's ONR-sponsored research in Japan. Paul T. Baker, a physical anthropologist who had spent five years working for the army, identified two dozen reports and publications by army physical anthropologists (Baker 1958: 23–25). He described military medical anthropological efforts stretching from the Civil War era to World War II, including projects contributing to survival and area culture guides, forensic methods of identifying war dead, and physical anthropologists' designs for gas masks (23–25). Baker envisioned a bright future for military anthropologists, emphasizing that "the anthropologist employed by the Army will find himself armed with considerably greater funds and resources than in almost any other research position" (26). The paper "The Future of Anthropology in the Department of Defense," by Colonel Philip H. Mitchell of the U.S. Air Force, examined the bureaucratic context in which anthropological research would be used (P. H. Mitchell 1958: 47–50).

Dupree concluded the volume by reporting that despite the optimism of assembled scholars, their enthusiasm for harnessing anthropology for Pentagon uses was not shared by their anthropological audience. He wrote: "What was conceived in optimism died in pessimism. The discussion following the presentation of papers seemed to indicate a current lack of interest in anthropology and social science research in the Armed Services" (L. Dupree 1958: 52). The audience response was tepid, and Dupree concluded that "except to dig up and record the fate of cities at the conclusion of a nuclear war, archaeologists per se have little place in the scheme of modern warfare planning" (52).

Pentagon Careers

While Dupree despaired over the military anthropology session's lackluster reception by mainstream applied anthropologists, he underestimated the variety of work being undertaken by anthropologists at the Department of Defense. A growing cadre of military anthropologists — at times rotating in and out of universities and applied military employment settings — developed in the postwar years. A brief survey of some of these anthropologists' work provides perspective on the range of developments that were occurring beyond the academy.

Donald Stanley Marshall's career combined years of Polynesian fieldwork with national security strategic planning and ethnographic explorations of human sexuality. Educated at Harvard and at the Army Command and General Staff College and the Army War College, Marshall was awarded Fulbright, McConnaughy, Guggenheim, and Peabody fellowships for his fieldwork in New Zealand (1951–52). He conducted extensive fieldwork at various other locations in Polynesia and Southeast Asia during the 1950s, 1960s, and 1970s, widely publishing books and articles based on this anthropological work (e.g., Marshall

1957, 1961). Marshall joined the army in 1942. According to his September 7, 2005, obituary in the *Washington Post,* an encounter with San Blas Cuna Indians while he was stationed in Panama during the war sparked his interest in anthropology. He played multiple military roles, including chief of the army's Long Range Planning Task Force, and deputy director of the SALT Task Force from 1973 to 1974, and wrote counterinsurgency works on Southeast Asia, including the two-volume *Program for the Pacification and Long Term Development of South Vietnam* (1966) and several multivolume reports on Thailand and Vietnam.

At least one anthropologist worked for the National Security Agency. Richard Wesley Howell was an NSA intelligence analyst, working in Washington, DC, and Japan from 1953 to 1958; later sent to Japan as a cryptolinguist with the Army Security Agency and became a professor of anthropology at the University of Hawaii, Hilo (BIC 2014b). Theodore Allen Wertime was an OSS operative in China during World War II. His April 16, 1982, obituary in the *Washington Post* indicated that he then "did further intelligence work with the State Department from 1945 until 1955," later establishing a career as an anthropology research associate at the Smithsonian Institution.

During the 1950s, Thomas Sebeok oversaw the production of sixteen Uralic monographs for the army's chief of psychological warfare and wrote training materials for teaching Hungarian for the War Department (BIC 2014f). Robert Brainerd Ekvall graduated from the Missionary Training Institute in 1922; a decade later he began graduate work in anthropology at the University of Chicago (1937–38), work that informed his U.S. Army intelligence work focusing on Burma and China (1944–51). Ekvall held appointments as a research associate in the University of Chicago's anthropology department (1951–53) and as a research fellow on the University of Washington's Inner Asia Research Project (1958–60) (BIC 2014e).

Sometimes anthropologists working for military organizations came under FBI scrutiny for holding progressive political beliefs. Bela Maday earned his doctorate in 1937 at Pazmany University in Hungary. After the war, Maday worked for the Hungarian Red Cross. The CIA's release of documents under FOIA and the Nazi War Crimes Disclosure Act included reports indicating that Maday came to the attention of intelligence agents working on Project Symphony (an OSS-SSU project designed to identify communist and Soviet agents among Jewish refugees emigrating to Palestine). According to one declassified secret CIA document, Project Symphony identified Maday as directing the Vienna office of the Hungarian Red Cross, where intelligence reports indicated that staff "have been variously suspected of intelligence activities and the smuggling of Nazis into the Allied Zones" (CIA 4/18/46; 1705143 File HQ File LVX 219).[15]

Maday immigrated to the United States on a postdoctoral fellowship in 1947 and in the early 1950s became chair of the Army Language School's (ALS) department of Hungarian language. After an employee at the ALS reported to the FBI that Maday supposedly said "he was happy the Communists came to power in Hungary," the FBI began an investigation of him in October 1955 (FBI 140–10547-8). The FBI interviewed several professors and staff members at the ALS (FBI 140-10547-4) but found no evidence of communist ties or tendencies (FBI 140-10547-5); nor did checks with the Immigration and Naturalization Service and the CIA find anything that suggested communist ties (FBI 140-10547-9). Maday's efforts to become an American citizen were later complicated by this report, although he did become a citizen in 1956 (FBI 140-10547-NR, 12/29/67). Maday began teaching at George Washington University and American University in 1956. His FBI file includes a sixty-page report from 1959 evaluating his "suitability for access to classified information" related to his employment at American University's Special Operations Research Office (SORO) (FBI 140-10547-NR, 12/29/67). At SORO Maday wrote a series of military and State Department manuals: he coauthored *Area Handbook for Brazil* and *Area Handbook for Malaysia and Singapore* and wrote *Magyar Grammar* (1950) for the ALS.

"Just a Lot of Professor Theories and All That Stuff"

In the years following the Second World War, the AAA's Executive Board saw nothing wrong with governmental agencies compiling information on anthropologists for rosters. But two decades later, with increased knowledge of the uses to which military and intelligence agencies put such lists, anthropologists' attitudes were significantly changed as the AAA Executive Board would take steps to limit the U.S. government's access to its members. When the AAA leadership learned in 1971 that the National Science Foundation had been compiling the National Register of Scientific and Technical Personnel, the AAA joined other professional associations in objecting to "its locator function which enabled any government agency to request and receive lists of scientists, with their specialties, in the participating fields" (AAAFN 1971 12[4]: 1). In severing its ties to this project, the AAA announced, "The AAA Board in February unanimously voted to condemn the locator use of the roster, recognizing its potential for misuse. Data for the National Register, a requirement of the National Science Foundation Act of 1950, has been collected since 1954 in biennial surveys of scientists chosen by their professional associations" (NAAA 1971 12[4]: 1).

Given congressional claims of the 1950s that social science research was too biased or too liberal to receive federal funding, it is ironic that an increased flow of militarized funds for directed social science research would, as we will see in later chapters, invert this feared dynamic. These funds fed increasing liberal notions of militarizing the social sciences, with a new generation of counterinsurgency projects that showed the Pentagon and intelligence agencies how easily they could buy a piece of anthropology.

During the decade following the end of the Second World War, American universities were packed with eager students funded by the GI Bill, and a new wave of first-generation college students brought to anthropology mid-twentieth-century hopes of internationalism, theory building, and cross-cultural understanding. Both students and professors remained transformed by the Second World War and Cold War impacts on higher learning in ways that were seldom considered at the time.

Most of the professors who had contributed their anthropological skills to the war effort had worked on large projects, with dozens of other scholars and with goals and outcomes determined by others. This type of workplace environment encouraged working on research questions that had been determined by external forces, and as the Cold War brought new sources of funds for scholars working on certain research topics, these wartime experiences helped inform the approaches to this work.

Anthropologists at times joined interdisciplinary teams. Some of these were new interdisciplinary arrangements of academic departments, such as Harvard's Department of Social Relations; other anthropologists joined new types of ethnographic research teams, such as Columbia University's Puerto Rico Project (funded by the Rockefeller Foundation; see Patterson and Lauria-Perricelli 1999) or Harvard's Modjokuto project in Indonesia (funded by the Ford Foundation), Norman McQuown's Chiapas Project (funded by the National Institutes of Health and the NSF), or George Foster's research at the Institute of Social Anthropology. The postwar availability of substantial support for fieldwork dramatically increased the number of anthropologists working in foreign countries as funds from Fulbright, SSRC, Ford, Rockefeller, NSA, NIH, the Viking Fund, and the Wenner-Gren Foundation provided the ways and means for anthropologists to conduct fieldwork all over the world.

> In very large measure the area study programs developed
> in American universities in the years after the war were manned,
> directed, or stimulated by graduates of the OSS — a remarkable institution,
> half cops-and-robbers and half faculty meeting.
>
> McGEORGE BUNDY | 1964

FOUR AFTER THE SHOOTING WAR

Centers, Committees, Seminars, and Other Cold War Projects

Before the Second World War, there were few centrally important sources of American anthropological funding. Funding was provided predominantly by museums and universities and occasionally by rich patrons sponsoring salvage anthropology or archaeology projects to collect what they envisioned as the dying embers of a once-thriving Native American culture.[1] Outside of a few philanthropically funded, museum-financed, or Department of the Interior projects, most prewar fieldwork developed as modest self- or university-funded self-directed projects.

The most significant difference between pre- and postwar funding was not a transformation in scale of funding (which did occur), but a shift from anthropologists working mainly on projects following their own interests to anthropologists, if not following the questions of others, then following geographic or topical funding streams.[2] It was not that anthropologists abandoned pursuing theoretical questions of their own choosing; the early Cold War brought a renaissance of anthropological theory. But like colleagues in the physical sciences, postwar anthropologists increasingly engaged in dual use research projects, pursuing questions of interest to themselves on topics of interest to sponsors (see D. H. Price 2003b, 2011e, 2012c).

Hopes of increased postwar funding led anthropologists William Fenton, Charles Wagley, and Julian Steward to advocate for area study programs. Fenton's *Area Studies in American Universities* (1947) envisioned centers fostering the type of interdisciplinary environment he experienced during the war at the Smithsonian's Ethnogeographic Board. Fenton conceived of such centers as serving the national strategic needs of the postwar world, and training new generations in the languages and cultures needed to support America's rising global dominance (see Mead 1979: 151).

At the 1947 SSRC National Conference on the Study of World Areas, anthropologists were represented in larger numbers than any other discipline (Wagley 1948: iv) (see table 4.1).[3] Area panels were held for Latin America, Europe, the Soviet Union, Southeast Asia and India, the Near East, and the Far East (Wagley 1948: 28) — with no panels on the Pacific Islands or Africa. Most of those in attendance represented universities, but there were also representatives of private foundations, Congress, and military, policy, and intelligence agencies — including Sherman Kent, historian and future director of the CIA Office of National Estimates (Wagley 1948: 53–57).[4]

Charles Wagley described how, at the war's end, university campuses that had housed wartime Army Specialized Training Programs and the Civil Affairs Training Program shifted their emphasis to area studies graduate programs (Wagley 1948: 1–2). Wagley pitched anthropology as the discipline for area studies to emulate, envisioning centers coordinating interdisciplinary research projects such as Ralph Beals, George Foster, and Robert West's Tarascan research and Gordon Willey's Viru Valley projects (Wagley 1948: 11).

Julian Steward combined academic and national security arguments for conducting community studies research, writing that the value of such projects could be seen in the gap in contemporary studies of China (Steward 1950: xii, 52), observing that "few community studies have been made in China: none have been made of communist towns" (53). Steward stressed the importance of anthropologists' national character studies, noting the work of Linton, Kardiner, Du Bois, Mead, Hallowell, Benedict, Haring, Kluckhohn, Bateson, and Gorer (80). While most anthropologists self-conceived their work outside of Steward's Cold War political framing, these issues elicited interest from the governmental and private bodies funding this research. These differences were seldom addressed; whereas wartime anthropologists had clearly understood the potential uses of their work, postwar anthropologists worked in environments that more easily ignored these issues.

Anthropology students' first encounters with area study centers were frequently as language students. Universities received military funds for language programs, and area study centers benefited from these funds. Funding programs like: Fulbright, Foreign Language and Area Studies, Title VI, and International Research and Exchanges Board became significant means for anthropology students to fund their education. Most programs had no requirements that recipi-

TABLE 4.1. Anthropologists Attending the 1947 National Conference on the Study of World Areas (Sources: Wagley 1948: 53–58; Price 2008a)

ANTHROPOLOGISTS	1947 INSTITUTIONAL AFFILIATION	WORLD WAR II AFFILIATION
Ralph Beals	UCLA	National Research Council
Ruth Benedict	Columbia	Office of War Information
Wendell C. Bennett	Columbia	Ethnogeographic Board
Carleton Coon	Harvard	Office of Strategic Services
Cora Du Bois	Office of Intelligence Research, State Department	Office of Strategic Services
Fred Eggan	Chicago	Civil Affairs Training Program
John P. Gillin	University of North Carolina	U.S. Board of Economic Warfare, Peru
A. Irving Hallowell	National Research Council	None (was chair, University of Pennsylvania)
Douglas G. Haring	Syracuse University	Civil Affairs Training School
Melville J. Herskovits	Northwestern University	Ethnogeographic Board
Felix Keesing	Hoover Institute, Stanford University	Office of Strategic Services
Raymond Kennedy	Yale	Office of Strategic Services
Clyde Kluckhohn	Harvard	Office of War Information
Li An-Che	Yale	(unknown)
Ralph Linton	Yale	Office of Strategic Services
David Mandelbaum	University of California	Office of Strategic Services
George P. Murdock	Yale	Office of Naval Intelligence
R. Lauriston Sharp	Cornell	Department of State
Marian W. Smith	Columbia	None (fieldwork in India)
Julian Steward	Columbia	Institute of Social Anthropology
W. Duncan Strong	Columbia	Ethnogeographic Board
Mischa Titiev	Michigan	Office of Strategic Services
Charles Wagley	Columbia	Department of State
T. Cuyler Young	Princeton	Office of Strategic Services

ents later work for the government or pay back the money they had received. Other than assuring that some segment of the population was familiar with a variety of languages and cultures, there was little connection between the funding sources and those funded. Some area studies centers advanced specific theoretical approaches; in others, specific funding lines helped channel questions and answers. But even without such dynamics, notions of regional culture areas focused inquiries in ways unlike anthropology departments. As area study centers became increasingly important dispensers of funds, they helped shape the questions anthropologists asked and the answers they found.

Harvard's Russian Research Center and Clyde Kluckhohn, Anthropologist Cold Warrior

During the earliest days of the Cold War, Harvard University and Columbia University established area study centers focusing scholarship on the Soviet Union, combining public, openly stated research projects with classified research projects. These early Cold War programs mixed private initiatives with governmental desires, and at times, groups like the Joint Committee on Slavic Studies met privately with CIA personnel to discuss the needs of the agency and academic programs (see FOIA CIA-RDP80B01676R003800020121-7, 1/10/58). Harvard's Russian Research Center (RRC) exemplified some of the ways that area study centers fulfilled politically circumscribed dual use Cold War roles.

Anthropologist Clyde Kluckhohn was the first director of the Harvard RRC. During the Second World War, Kluckhohn worked for George Taylor and Alexander Leighton at the Office of War Information, and many of the intelligence analyst skills he developed there had later applications at the RRC. Kluckhohn had a top secret security clearance (O'Connell 1990: 139), and along with monies from the Departments of State and Defense, "'baseline funding' for the Harvard Russian Research Center came from the CIA" (O'Connell 1990: 186).

Kluckhohn secretly shared students' and staff's research reports with CIA, air force intelligence, and Department of State personnel (O'Connell 1990; Diamond 1992). One declassified CIA document shows Kluckhohn in July 1948 sending the agency's R. H. Hillenkoetter a report titled "The Automobile Industry That's behind the Iron Curtain" (FOIA CIA-RDP80R01731R003100040052-1, 7/6/48).[5] Harvard knew of Kluckhohn's relationships with the CIA, the State Department, and the FBI, and Kluckhohn reported to Provost Paul Buck his success in establishing connections with State Department and Pentagon personnel through Harrison Reynolds, who directed CIA activities in the region (Diamond 1992: 109–10). Military and intelligence personnel at times recommended RRC academic projects to Kluckhohn and later accessed results from RRC scholarship. In 1951, the Boston FBI special agent in charge reported:

> One of the jobs of Kluckhohn is to obtain pertinent information requested by government departments and within limits shape the research program of the center to the needs of the United States. He cited as an instance of the application [sic] the State Department would communicate with him to suggest they were short of a certain aspect of Soviet activity. Kluckhohn would then suggest to a graduate student at the School that he might do a thesis on this particular problem, making no mention to him of the fact that the State Department was also interested. Subsequently the results of the individual research could be brought to the attention of the State Department. (Diamond 1992: 59)

Alfred Meyer, Kluckhohn's assistant director, described how the U.S. government secretly used the RRC to fulfill its research needs using a process whereby "once in a while Kluckhohn would suggest to the entire academic staff of the Center some topic for discussion in a seminar, or a topic on which we all might want to write papers" (qtd. in O'Connell 1990: 145). Meyer reported that in 1952, when he was the assistant director of the RRC, Kluckhohn

> called me into his office for a confidential chat. "Once in a while," he said, "I send a memo around to all the members of the Center in which I suggest that we discuss a specific problem." Of course, I had seen such memos and responded to them. "Well," he continued, "such suggestions of mine usually come from the local field office of the CIA, who phone me, saying, "Our uncle in Washington would like to know what you people think about such a problem." Kluckhohn told me that during the next semester he was going to be on leave, and the CIA agents wanted someone appointed to be their contact person. (Meyer 2000: 21–22)

Kluckhohn's study of the "overseas interrogation of current refugees" was described in a secret 1950 CIA report "Psychological Warfare Research Studies within the Air Force," as "a project primarily designed to obtain sociological, psychological, and political data on defectors from behind the Iron Curtain. This is part of a larger project listed under B-13. The project is under the direction of Dr. Kluckhohn, Harvard University and is now underway in Germany" (FOIA CIA-RDP80R01731R003500150016-5). This CIA report also referenced sociologist Kingsley Davis's study on "methods of interrogation" using "interviews of defectors from the Soviet zone, to arrive at [the] most effective method of interrogation for Soviet defectors" (FOIA CIA-RDP80R01731R003500150016-5).[6]

In the early 1950s, Kluckhohn directed the Harvard Refugee Interview Project (HRIP). This project, sponsored by the Human Resources Research Institute of the U.S. Air Force, interviewed more than three thousand Russian refugees (NBAAA 1951 5[4]: 4). In 1949, future anthropologist Paul Friedrich helped Merle Fainsod with "interrogating non-returnees and recent escapees" in Germany as part of an air force–funded project (Engerman 2009: 53; Diamond 1992).[7] Under Harvard RRC's contract with the Human Resources Research Institute at Maxwell Field Air Force Base's Air University, in 1950–51 Fainsod and Friedrich interviewed over one hundred Soviet refugees for the HRIP. Using standardized interview questionnaires, they collected refugees' biographies, eliciting information on their political background (see HPSSS).

Sociologist Sigmund Diamond documented that the University of Michigan's Survey Research Center interviewed individuals coming to the United States from the USSR in the 1940s without informing them that their survey data would be "turned over to Clyde Kluckhohn, director of the Harvard Russian Research Center, which had its own connections with the FBI and CIA" (Diamond 1993: 409; see Diamond 1988). Despite such secret machinations, Harvard social scientists made audacious public claims about their intellectual independence. Harvard sociologist Talcott Parsons claimed that he and Kluckhohn successfully sidestepped the damages of McCarthyism by handling "with great delicacy the politically sensitive problems of a university organization engaged in the study of Communist society," yet this statement ignored the extent to which his and Kluckhohn's work secretly aligned with government policies and needs (Parsons 1973: 36). Parsons did not make these remarks while unaware of Kluckhohn's entanglements with government security and intelligence agencies.

Even as Harvard professors secretly worked with the CIA and the Pentagon on projects large and small, "Parsons denied the existence of a political directorate composed of corporate, military, and governmental elites as claimed by [C. Wright] Mills" (O'Connell 1990: 484). Given the extent of elite influence on the work of Parsons and his colleagues, O'Connell concluded that "Parsons' criticism of Mills was in bad faith. Parsons knew better than to argue that Mills was wrong because he himself had witnessed Policy Planning Staff covert operations. He himself had seen a Morgan Guaranty Trust director successfully demand the dismissal of Stuart Hughes and threaten to withhold funding of the Russian Research Center if the demand was not met. And he himself knew that Harvard scholars as advisors and consultants were indeed part of an informal political directorate"

(484). As C. Wright Mills complained (following sociologist David Lockwood), Parsons's work "delivers the sociologist from any concern with 'power,' with economic and political institutions," yet Parsons posed as if he were "removed" from politics because his work supported the politics of the status quo (1959: 35).

The University of Michigan's Near East Study Center

The University of Michigan's Near East Study Center emerged after the war, creating an academic environment that brought together historians, language specialists, literary scholars, and anthropologists. In this era in which area study centers comfortably engaged with governmental agencies, summer sessions brought prominent scholars from other universities and State Department personnel (*Daily Michigan*, 3/28/52, 2).

In 1951, Assistant Secretary of State Edward W. Barrett wrote the study center's first director, George G. Cameron, after reading Cameron's remark in a newspaper story that "the Russians still had the edge on us in the propaganda battle in parts of the Middle East." Barrett conceded that the United States faced difficulties, and that American operations would benefit from Cameron's "observations and constructive suggestions." Barrett asked Cameron to share his remarks or meet with him and Shepard Jones ("who is concerned primarily with information operations in that area") the next time he was in Washington (GWU-NSA, EB to GC 10/4/51).[8]

Cameron responded at length, evaluating U.S. propaganda efforts in Iraq and suggesting improvements. Much of his analysis drew on his recent fieldwork in the region. He wrote:

> For about six months we lived among Iraqi and Iranian Kurds, returning periodically to our base in Baghdad or to a secondary base in Iran. We were busy at our own tasks involving teamwork examination of the area from many points of view — history, language, geography, anthropology, archaeology and government. We had little opportunity and inclination to observe the operation of the Department of State in the propaganda battle. Inevitably, however, we saw some of the results, as well as the reaction of the people, especially in the Kurdistan to them. They were not particularly wholesome.
>
> For example, we spent several days in the area of a Baradost chieftain. In his tent we found a little tract with pictures representing a pig with hammer and sickle tail, the pig intent upon gobbling up various quarters of the world. The language of the tract was Kurdish. This chieftain, who presides over some 5,000 Kurds, was highly

indignant. His people, he said, knew of communism, but they knew better their own ill [health] and poverty. "I know," he said, "the Baghdad man who is producing this sheet for your Government. I know how much he is being paid yearly to produce it. If one fourth of that amount was to be made available in medicines or in some other more tangible product of your country which could be used to lessen the poverty or to better the health of my people, would it not be a far more successful propaganda approach?"

According to information which came to me, this area is in truth honeycombed with propagandists for the other side. It was, of course, not wise for us to inquire concerning the techniques of infiltration and we made no effort to do so. I fear, however, that we have taken inadequate accounting of the tremendous power of the radio. In Iran, every teahouse possesses one, and the anti-British and sometimes anti-American propaganda has seriously damaged our position. The Iranians feel that the British tail is all too successfully wagging the American dog. They have not been touched by the animosity of the more western Moslems or Arabs toward America as a result of our backing of the Government of Israel. The Iraqis, on the other hand, are not only vocal — their antipathy to us stems directly from the Palestine war. For them, there is only one side of the matter and they combat any attempt to present the other side. One does become very tired of trying to explain America's position, trying to make them see that American streets are not paved with gold to be had for the asking, or to make them see that there are other countries also which badly need some assistance. It seemed to me constantly that America desperately needs to pass on a little of the information about widespread commitments in all parts of the world which have been made, to explain in terms of the local monetary units just how much in time as in money has been poured into each particular area. (GWU-NSA, GGC to EWB 10/24/51)

Barrett thanked Cameron for his letter. He expressed hopes that upcoming Point IV programs (one of the Cold War's first international aid programs) would provide "the technical know-how" to improve health conditions, and he inquired about whether Cameron had seen "any of the excellent USIE Disney health films — simple, direct explanations in an attractive form on a number of local diseases and how to avoid them," adding that these were "often shown with a Kurdish language sound track" (GWU-NSA, EWB to GGC 11/19/51).

At Michigan, Cameron developed problem-oriented seminars that shared some characteristics with Kluckhohn's RRC seminars. These seminars drew heavily on faculty, as an "interdisciplinary seminar devoted to the analysis of major problems in the Near East, both professors and students present papers"

(Liss 1953). One of these interdisciplinary seminars received Ford Foundation funding to send anthropology professor William Schorger and five graduate students to Syria for fieldwork at the Aleppo Field Session (Liss 1953; University of Michigan 2000: 189; Shiloh 1959: 99). Louise Sweet, an anthropologist on this Syrian team, reportedly later learned the CIA had sent its own people as members of the field research project. This information upset Sweet, who over the years told several colleagues about the distress these discoveries caused her. When she ran for a position on the AAA's newly created Committee on Ethics, her campaign statement directly addressed these issues, indicating that she "would not knowingly, much less willingly, accept support of any kind from or give information to any agency, public or private, of the United States or any other country, which engages in or promotes in any way espionage, manipulation of individuals or groups, interventionism, counterinsurgency, or technological, economic, social, political or ideological domination and coercion over any internal part of its own system or over any other country in whole or in part" (NAAA 1971 12[6]: 10–11). Years later she told archaeologist McGuire Gibson how her unwitting involvement in this CIA-linked project had damaged her career.[9] Gibson recalled:

> She was then teaching in the University of Kuwait or AUB, one of the several places she worked because she couldn't get a permanent job at the time because she was tainted by the CIA involvement in the project that she had taken part in. . . . The gist of the story was that in the early 1950s, the CIA infiltrated a large research project conducted by the University of Michigan in Syria. It was multi-disciplinary (soils, agriculture, botany, public health I think too), with anthropology as a part. Just as it did in Iraq, about the same time, the CIA had its own "scholars" in the program who were supposed to be working on specific projects (in Iraq, one or two actually published short articles of no merit). (MG to DHP, 12/30/13)

In later writings, Sweet cited this interdisciplinary fieldwork project (Sweet 1960: iii–iv), but like other scholars who discovered unwanted interactions with the CIA, she refrained from exposing or critiquing these connections in print. Independent substantiation and details of Sweet's claim that the CIA infiltrated Michigan's Aleppo Field Session are lacking, though colleagues recall the impact of these events on her career.

CENIS as Dual Use Model

In 1952, MIT established the Center for International Studies (CENIS) as a new type of program linking the dual use needs of scholars conducting international research and of American military and intelligence seeking informed input for their own projects. At CENIS, Project Troy brought together diverse scholars who studied intercultural communications to investigate means of countering Soviet jamming of American broadcasts into the Soviet Union and explored the possibility of engineering a collapse of the Soviet Union through remote propaganda broadcasts. James Killian, president of MIT, and Harvard provost Paul Buck recruited faculty for Project Troy, pitching the venture as an interdisciplinary opportunity to "bring together a group of first-rate minds to let them attack the problem in a free-wheeling, uninhibited manner" (Blackmer 2002: 7).

Troy collected interdisciplinary teams of social scientists, physicists, chemists, engineers, economists, and political scientists. Clyde Kluckhohn was among the first four Harvard professors to join the project. Max Millikan came to Troy from his position as assistant director of the CIA, envisioning a program that would "exploit MIT's facilities and connections in science and engineering" and "pioneer . . . inter-disciplinary treatment of the social studies questions" by developing and testing social science theory (Blackmer 2002: 10).

Troy proposed devoting technological research to problems of overcoming Soviet radio jamming technologies that were dominating Eastern Europe and also sought new forms of psychological or political warfare. It envisioned university centers hosting "government research programs in the field of political warfare utilizing university personnel either on a part-time basis or by the use of a rotation plan which would permit university specialists to remain in their 'home atmospheres' during leaves of absence from university duties" (Blackmer 2002: 14). The MIT program aspired to become a prestigious center with the appearance of academic independence, hosting scholars under "a rotation plan" in which they spent time in residence at the center contributing to CENIS Cold War projects such as Troy.

Kluckhohn told MIT's President Killian that Troy was "one of the most fruitful experiences of his professional career and that the world of scholarship would lose something important if MIT did not turn the classified program into a continuing, interdisciplinary, unclassified research center" (Blackmer 2002: 18). But Kluckhohn's hopes for a declassified center were ignored as CENIS's funding source shifted from the State Department to secret CIA funds (2002: 20).

The Center for International Studies collected great minds, but rather than setting them to work on questions of their own choosing, it directed projects that pursued a narrow range of questions linked to American Cold War ideologies. Walt Rostow studied vulnerabilities of the Soviet Union (resulting in his book *Dynamics of Soviet Society*), Clyde Kluckhohn oversaw a study in which researchers interviewed Soviet defectors, and psychologist Alex Bavelas worked on a project apparently designed to subject the Soviets to disinformation (Blackmer 2002: 21). Using Ford Foundation funds, several CENIS social scientists advanced economic development theories, with expectations that western development could divert underdeveloped countries from the attractions of socialism.

The Ford Foundation liked CENIS's hybrid approach to the classified and declassified harnessing of scholarship for the needs of state (see Ross 1998a: 492–95). With Millikan's return to the academy from the CIA, Ford provided CENIS with a million dollars of initial funds to plan and develop research projects on political and economic security and on international communication. Over the next nine years, Ford provided another million dollars for research on political and economic development issues (Blackmer 2002: 35, 67). Psychological warfare experts Jerome Brunder, Harold Lasswell, Paul Lazarsfeld, and Edward Shils sat on the CENIS International Communication Planning Committee, administering Ford's international communication grant (51).

Ithiel de Sola Pool and the CENIS planning committee established four research criteria for CENIS-funded projects. These were (1) research designs exploring how elite leaders of various cultures "learn about and respond to information from abroad that leads them to try and influence foreign policy"; (2) research contrasting how individuals from rural and urban settings reacted to news of international developments; (3) research studying how "reference groups" influence decision-making processes; and (4) projects examining how communication "lead[s] to political action" (Blackmer 2002: 61).

In 1954, the CIA relied on CENIS social scientists to supply academic cover supporting justifications for the CIA's military coup in Guatemala. One declassified CIA report describes how the CIA's Operational Intelligence Support unit (OIS)

> worked intensively on the preparation of support materials for the American Delegation at the Xth Inter-American Conference, Caracas, 1 March 1954. As the Conference became largely concerned with the question of communism in Guatemala, the task was considered as a phase of PBSUCCESS [the CIA's code name for its 1953–54 Guatemala coup] support. OIS staff members produced a considerable volume of research and presentation, including text and charts, and carried out the coordination of State ARA and OIR contributions with CIA production, as well as most of the editing, typing and all of the work of reproduction and assembling

of the main American documentary exhibit and reference paper, under the title of "Communism in Guatemala (150 pages). Contributions to this study were obtained from CENIS (external research), OCI, ORR, Staff C, and WH Division." (CIA 1954: 8–9)

Through such arrangements, CENIS offered first-rate copying and clerical services as scholars produced intellectual propaganda supporting the CIA's Guatemalan coup, turning academics into outsourced operational support personnel. Yet the first public criticism of CENIS's linkage of academics and the CIA would not come from American progressives; it came from the reactionary right.

William F. Buckley Exposes CENIS's CIA Connection

In February 1957, a column published in *National Review* criticized CENIS's violations of the CIA's charter by advocating a foreign policy approach based on what it called "a permanent foreign aid program to give underdeveloped nations a 'sense of progress'—without regard of course, to U.S. political or strategic interests." The article questioned why the U.S. Senate had provided CENIS $200,000 for producing *A Proposal: Key to an Effective Foreign Policy* (Millikan and Rostow 1957):

> The Center for International Studies, according to persistent rumor, was set up and financed for the most part by the Central Intelligence Agency (through what is called a "cut-out"). Unless this rumor is false, we have the following circle on our hands:
>
> 1) The Senate votes fund to CIA. 2) CIA defying a law (that prohibits CIA's operating within the United States), uses some of the funds to create a domestic research institution, the MIT Center, and the Center regularly publishes slanted books and articles, advocating partisan policies for the US Market. 3) The Center, putting itself forward as a bona fide scientific outfit, asks a Senate committee to give it further funds with which to conduct a study of foreign aid problems. 4) The Center obliges with a propaganda brochure.
>
> Gentlemen of the Foreign Relations Committee, it looks to us as if you have been conned. Why not a few pertinent questions to Professors Max Millikan and W. W. Rostow, who authored the brochure, and to their backers? (National Review 1957)

William F. Buckley's magazine's attack on CIA collusion highlights conservatives' distrust of the agency during the early Cold War. Yet such distrust was far from universal, and five years earlier Buckley himself had worked as a CIA operative in Mexico, under E. Howard Hunt (Buckley 2007). Buckley's indignation sharply contrasts with how comfortable Americans would later become with what he identified as the polluting effects of secrecy and CIA influence on the production of academic knowledge. Yet Buckley misunderstood that Rostow and Millikan's formulation of international development policies based on U.S. aid expressed not some sort of generous gift of American charity, but a calculated arm of American anticommunist foreign policy and a key element of U.S. counterinsurgency campaigns. The *National Review*'s concerns were generally ignored, and this critique did not gain traction for another decade, though the next attack on CIA infiltration of academia would come from the left, not the right.

In 1962, CENIS's oversight Visiting Committee raised concerns that receipt of CIA funds jeopardized perceptions of the center's legitimacy. Three years later, CENIS was publicly accused of interfering in India's domestic policy, and the center agreed that "over the next several years either a policy of full disclosure should be worked out or the Center should move in the direction of further reducing its contractual commitments with the Agency" (Blackmer 2002: 194). The center's public relationships with the CIA ended in June 1966, but in what would be a well-established pattern, the shortfalls in CIA funding were conveniently made up by a "multiyear Ford grant" that came "just in time to replace CIA funding of work on international communism" and other ongoing projects (203). The Ford Foundation continued supporting what had been CIA-funded projects.

Most critiques of CENIS's receipt of CIA funds failed to understand that this money was but a small part of the military-intelligence complex's funding of CENIS. As Blackmer observed, "In the six years before 1963, the Center had received an average of $69,000 per year from government agencies other than the CIA. In six years from 1963 to 1968, the average rose to over $600,000 per year, primarily from agencies of the Department of Defense" (2002: 203). Further, the seamless substitution of Ford Foundation funds to continue the CIA-initiated project received no critical public scrutiny concerning what this revealed about the ways that Ford's political orientation overlapped with the CIA's.

Public awareness of CENIS's military and intelligence connections increased with time. In October 1969, 150 student demonstrators amassed outside of CENIS, protesting its military research; Millikan, Pool, Pye, and others "were tried by a mock revolutionary tribunal and found guilty of 'crimes against humanity'" (Nelkin 1972: 110–11). While indignation over academic's complicity with the CIA at CENIS raged in the late 1960s, there was only minor concern with the political implications of the social science that CENIS-linked projects like Modjokuto produced. The Modjokuto Project's affiliation with CENIS exemplifies how mainstream anthropology at times operated around the edges of CIA-funded projects and how Cold War agendas that were often beyond the focus of particular anthropologists' interests.

Geertz, Modjokuto, and CENIS

The Modjokuto Project (1952–59) became known as the classic postwar multisite ethnography project, sending teams of bright young fieldworkers to Indonesian villages to study traditional cultures coping with modernization, postcolonial independence, and emerging topics that captured the fancy of these ethnographers. The idea for the Modjokuto Project originated with Douglas Oliver, with later input coming from Clyde Kluckhohn and Max Millikan.[10] But Oliver's contacts with governmental officials during Modjokuto's planning stage remain unclear, and his 1948–49 service as a State Department special assistant for Far Eastern affairs provided him with significant governmental contacts (Browman and Williams 2013: 453). When Clifford Geertz and other Modjokuto participants went to the field in 1952, the project was funded by the Ford Foundation and administered through Harvard.[11] By the time the fieldwork was completed, its administration had been relocated to CENIS, where the agency's former assistant director of the Office of Research and Reports, Max Millikan, directed the center, and a host of Pentagon- and CIA-linked scholars worked.

In 1995, Douglas Oliver explained to me that Modjokuto had been his idea and that Max Millikan had been involved in the project's planning and funding from its earliest stages. Indonesia had been selected for this cooperative interdisciplinary research project in order to "fill a gap in the ethnographic record" (Oliver interview 7/10/95). In 1995, Clifford Geertz told me that he understood Kluckhohn had played an important part in designing Modjokuto and that Talcott Parsons may also have had a role. Geertz did not know why Indonesia had been selected, given that none of the principals involved in the project were Indonesian specialists (Geertz phone interview 7/19/95). Geertz's "theory of what went on was that" Kluckhohn and Millikan

> were thinking of establishing something like the Russian Research Center except . . . the Center for International Studies at MIT and [Kluckhohn] suggested that when the actual Modjokuto Project was going — and this part is actual fact — it became

the first sort of enterprise of CIS [CENIS] really before CIS existed. Now whether Millikan was already on board as head of CIS, or whether CIS was still on the drawing board I'm not sure when we left, but I do think the Ford money and all that — which is what supported us — was got[ten] by Clyde or maybe by Millikan that's conceivable. . . . But I'd never met Millikan [before going to Indonesia], and I'm almost certain . . . nor did any of the other members of the group — in fact I'm probably the only member of the group who knew him very well [later]. But we were sent out, and CIS existed as a kind of "paper thing," but when we came back it existed as a reality. By then the economists were there . . . so it was formed in our absence. (Geertz phone interview 7/19/95)

After returning from Indonesia, Geertz wrote his dissertation and worked on his book *Agricultural Involution* at CENIS. He developed a friendship with Millikan (Hander 1991: 604, 605), describing him as "very supportive, but again, he had no intellectual input into it. His interests were elsewhere, and of course he was involved in various kinds of CIA research. The places were divided by people [who] could go in certain doors and people who couldn't. Whether they were clear or not" (Geertz phone interview 7/19/95; cf. Gilman 2002: 5). Geertz told me he did not recall who could and who could not go through these doors, describing CENIS as having "this sort of split personality of being just a bunch of economists mainly, and the odd anthropologists, myself, working on research on the three I's, Indonesia, Italy, and India. And then there was this other dimension of it, which was murky. I think that some of my colleagues were — reasonably enough — and so was I, a little bit dubious about that" (Geertz phone interview 7/19/95).[12]

Geertz had no knowledge of any work that Millikan might have done with Oliver before leaving for Indonesia, but when I told him that Oliver said Millikan helped secure Modjokuto funds even before CENIS existed (CENIS began in 1952), he said: "That sounds right to me. That's what I'd really assumed. I didn't really know this, but there was a certain mild paranoia among us — not so much me, but some of the people on the project — about CIS, and Millikan and so on, especially after we got back." According to Geertz, some people "worried about its involvement in the CIA and so on. I mean, they weren't really deeply worried about it. Most of them stayed away from [CENIS], in fact, once they got back they didn't want to be deeply involved" (Geertz phone interview 7/19/95). Geertz explained that he did not feel the same need to stay away from CENIS as his cohorts:

> It's just that they wanted to do their thesis and didn't want to become involved with CIS as an institution. I didn't mind. I didn't have a thing to do with the secret

part—as I said—but I worked for them. I had a project for a year, I worked for them—and it was Max who decided. I remember I went to see him and he said, "Yeah, OK." It wasn't my idea that I should do this, it must have been [Benjamin] Higgens or somebody that they should hire me and then they said yes, and then I worked there for a year. All that I did was write *Agricultural Involution*, I didn't do anything else at all. (Geertz phone interview 7/19/95)

Although Geertz's anthropological analysis generally downplayed political forces, he understood how such forces framed his first Indonesian fieldwork opportunity. Geertz said that Indonesia in the early 1950s "was an important part of the world, and it was one of the earliest states to get independence, and there was a big communist movement and so on. [If Modjokuto had links to intelligence agencies,] it would have been totally unwitting, because nobody ever said anything to us about gathering . . . any kind of information that would have been of any use to the government" (Geertz phone interview 7/19/95). Geertz liked the economists at CENIS and would talk with them, but he did not have an office at CENIS and mostly wrote at his home. When Geertz said that he did not know what Millikan had done before coming to CENIS, I told him that Millikan had been an MIT economist after the war, then assistant director at the CIA. Geertz said he had not known this, but that CENIS "had a split personality," with people like Norman Weiner mixing with Rostow and Millikan types. He thought that probably "half of the people . . . had nothing to do with the secret part of [CENIS], and what the secret parts was, I have no idea, but it had a CIA dimension all right" (Geertz phone interview 7/19/95).

The Ford Foundation's Interest in Indonesia

The Modjokuto Project was only a small part of the Ford Foundation's sponsorship of research efforts to understand and control the economic fate of Indonesia. As David Ransom wrote, in 1954 "Ford launched its efforts to make Indonesia a 'modernizing country' with field projects from MIT and Cornell. . . . Working through [CENIS] . . . Ford sent out a team from MIT to discover 'the economic causes of stagnation in Indonesia.' Part of this effort was Guy Pauker's CENIS study of Indonesian 'political obstacles' to economic development, obstacles such as armed insurgency" (1975: 96). Ford also guided the production, interpretation, and consumption of knowledge about Indonesia by funding Cornell's Academic Center for Indonesian Studies and establishing Cornell's Modern Indonesia Project in 1954.

Though Geertz insisted that CENIS's economists did not impact his work, his analysis aligned neatly with theirs. Geertz explained away the systemic poverty and political brutality of Indonesia with models of "involution" steeped in cultural traditions. He found colonialism's Pax Nederlandica a stabilizing influence, and he downplayed the devastating effects of colonialism and Cold War relations of dependency (Geertz 1963a: 80). He found the Javanese solution to the conditions of diminishing returns for agricultural intensification under conditions of population growth was a strategy of what he called "shared poverty," a concept that was an application of the sort of Parsonian political doctrines he had learned in Harvard's Department of Social Relations (Gilman 2002: 7). Geertz blamed Javanese poverty on ideology, not on the material forces of colonialism: for Geertz, the values and social constructs of poverty were independent of poverty itself. Javanese poverty was caused by cultural values that gave primacy to sharing and communalism, values that inhibited external efforts to modernize. Java was caught in a homeostatic feedback loop in which increases in production designed to modernize led to increased population and entrenched systems of shared poverty. Gilman later argued that Geertz's analysis of peasant behavior paralleled American military policy in Vietnam; insofar as the United States "could be seen as justifying wars against insurgent peasantries on the grounds that their radicalism had to come from without, Geertz's narrative of recent Indonesian economic and cultural history fit the ideological needs of those justifying the Vietnam War" (13).[13] Geertz's later involvement with University of Chicago's Committee for the Comparative Study of New Nations extended his early theoretical contributions to development-linked programs.[14]

Anthropologists' critiques of the political orientation of Geertz's work first appeared in the early 1970s, when some, such as John Moore, attacked the political message of *Agricultural Involution* as "an economic plan for the capital penetration of every region in Indonesia" (1971: 40). Geertz's *Involution* followed Rostowian modernization logic, calling for Western administrators to interrupt the Javanese involuted economic stagnation. Despite Geertz's insistence that he was not impacted by CENIS's economic theoreticians, his model of traditional society and the solutions he endorsed aligned with the economic policies developed by Edward Shils, Guy Pauker, Millikan, Rostow, and others at CENIS. Geertz's economic history of Java featured resilient traditional social structures that coexisted with external economic change. Because he argued that national identity could be impervious to economic penetration and captivation, his work rebutted indigenous critics of global development strategies (see Knight 1982). The developing markets and entrepreneurs in Geertz's *Peddlers and Princes* (1963b) awaited one of Rostow's or Millikan's capital infusion development projects.

Geertz's involvement with the Modjokuto Project, the Ford Foundation, and CENIS fits a dual use model of the half-unwitting scholar who was not directly concerned with the forces and politics of the Cold War, even while contributing to the intellectual discourse in ways that supported American hegemony. Geertz was not privy to CENIS's classified projects, but his lack of access to classified materials did not diminish the fact that Millikan, Rostow, and the others at CENIS had access to *his* research. Geertz's work was shaped by the milieu of CENIS. As Gideon Sjoberg observed, irrespective of an individual's ties to classified work, the presence of CIA funding for even some CENIS projects "may well leave a subtle impact upon the research process itself, especially where researchers are interested in attracting continued support from this agency. For example some projects may have been selected over others because they are congruent with the goals of the funding agency" (1967: 156).

Geertz's memoir *After the Fact* (1995) revealed too little too late about the Cold War struggles he removed from the foreground or background of his classic thick descriptions of Bali. As Nancy Scheper-Hughes observed, "Geertz's celebrated Balinese 'cockfight' scenario was developed within the larger context of a national political emergency that resulted in the massacre of almost three-quarters of a million Indonesians, though it took Geertz three decades to mention the killing that had engulfed his Javanese field site, now forever associated in our minds with those semiotic fighting roosters" (1995: 437; see also Reyna 1998). Geertz's silence over Modjokuto's links to CENIS and his involvement in politicized social science projects had links to Parsons's notion of power, particularly the denials of any universal commonality to the political economy of the human condition. Instead, for Geertz, "All politics is quarrel, and power is the ordering such quarrel sorts out: that much is general. What is not general is the nature of the quarrel or the shape of the ordering" (1995: 39).

Cold War RAND*thropology*

Anthropologists served as consultants at the RAND Corporation throughout the Cold War, producing work that included village studies in Thailand or Vietnam, analysis of cultures of the Himalayas, research on Laotian traditions and innovations, studies of Japanese social organizations, analysis of authority structures in Soviet society, or linguistic simulation studies (see Phillips and

Wilson 1964; Pearce 1965; Hickey 1967b; Hays 1962; Halpern 1960; Kay 1969; Mead 1951).

Ruth Benedict was the only anthropologist, and the only woman, who attended RAND's First Conference of Social Scientists. This New York conference, held in 1947, was conceived by John Williams, a RAND game theoretician, and Warren Weaver, social science chairman of the Rockefeller Foundation, "to get RAND started on a social science program that would be useful to national security" (RAND 1948: viii). A classified restricted transcript of the conference recorded candid conversations focusing on the range of Cold War–related research projects that RAND might fund. Benedict discussed methods for studying Communist Party members in the United States, differences in cultural perceptions of atomic weapons, the extent of pro-Russian feelings in the United States, and other Cold War research topics. She sought to use anthropology for peace, but the resulting discussions show a general lack of participants' interest in pursuing these goals (RAND 1948: 16). Instead, the projects under consideration had titles like "Psychology of Attack Behavior," "Public Apprehension of Threats to Physical Security," "Morale Policy in Wartime," "Emotional Impact of Atomic Bombing," and "Psychological Effects of Reconnaissance Satellite" (19–23). There were proposals outlining the construction of a "Belligerency Index," numerous counterintelligence programs, and new methods of tracking Russians, and while there was much talk of peace, most proposals explored new ways to wage war.

Conference participants considered research ideas in free-flowing discussions of how social scientists could reshape the postwar world with methods developed during the recent war. The ethnocentric insouciance of the discussions is striking. Harold Lasswell discussed the cultural mitigation of aggression and prospects of a social science for the "management of peoples' responses" (RAND 1948: 110). Benedict stressed the necessity of understanding cultural subtleties before attempting such changes, though she appeared to accept as a given that such work should be undertaken (111).

A project called "Pro-Russian Feeling in U.S." proposed using public opinion surveys to track Americans' pro-Russian sentiments. This proposed study would be secretly "carried out in cooperation with the FBI; public opinion surveys at regular intervals [would] study variations in the magnitude of the group in relation to current events" (RAND 1948: 26). Some participants found potential methodological problems with this research, but no concerns were raised about the ethical propriety of assisting the FBI in spying on Americans. Ernst Kris commented, "I find here cooperation with the FBI, which is fine, but then also, public opinion surveys, which I can't by any stretch of the imagination combine with information coming from the FBI" (123). While Kris was confused about the FBI's involvement, Herbert Goldhamer understood the FBI would not passively digest survey data collected by others; it would use the pretext of a legitimate survey to spy on citizens. Goldhamer observed that "the FBI, or whatever agency keeps track of these things, might specify individuals who fall in the group we are discussing. It might then be feasible to send out public opinion interviewers with an arranged list of questions who would interview these people, supposedly at random" (123). The fate of this proposal is unknown, but Clyde Kluckhohn's involvement in the University of Michigan's Survey Research Center project interviewing Russian émigrés demonstrates that similar projects were undertaken (see Diamond 1988; 1993: 412).

Research on Contemporary and Distant Cultures

In 1946, Ruth Benedict launched a cross-cultural anthropological seminar at Columbia University to teach the wartime techniques developed by the Office of War Information to study enemy cultures (R. Métraux 1980: 367). Benedict's students were enthralled with this approach, and Benedict's $100,000 Office of Naval Research (ONR) grant empowered Columbia University's Research in Contemporary Cultures (RCC) project to fund a large group of students and senior scholars (R. Métraux 1980: 367). The RCC piggybacked on the institutional successes of the Institute for Intercultural Studies (IFIS).[15] The RCC research was unclassified and used interviews with foreign-born individuals living in the United States, combined with published resources (Caffrey 1989: 329–30).

Among the anthropologists employed by RCC were Conrad Arensberg, Gregory Bateson, Jane Belo, Ruth Bunzel, William Chen, Francis L. K. Hsu, Rosemary Spiro, and Eric Wolf (Peterson 2005: 47). At Cornell Medical School, neurologist Harold Wolff directed the RCC project "Studies in Human Ecology-China" (R. Métraux 1980: 362). Other projects studied the cultures of France, Czechoslovakia, Poland, shtetls of Eastern Europe, Syria, pre-Soviet Russia, and prewar China. Margaret Mead and Geoffrey Gorer directed the RCC Russian group (Mead 1959: 435; Mandler 2013: 223–53).

Mead later admitted there were initial concerns about academic freedom when Benedict first gathered anthropologists for this project, writing that everyone knew "that a study of Russia was vitally important. We knew, equally, that it could be done — if at all — only under government auspices because of the hazards, if not to the senior people, at least to any beginners who ventured to show any interest in Soviet materials" (1959: 432). McCarthyism's academic orthodoxy made it difficult to interpret RCC findings without considering the climate of doublethink permeating academic research during this period.

There was a flurry of activity after Benedict announced the receipt of the ONR grant, as Mead and Benedict recruited junior and senior scholars to build a prototype interdisciplinary project to expand techniques pioneered at OWI, OSS, and other intelligence agencies. Mead wrote that they recruited "the gifted people who had somehow managed in wartime but who did not fit into the peacetime mold — the aberrant, the unsystematic, the people with work habits too irregular ever to hold regular jobs" (1959: 434).[16]

The RCC struggled to establish work space at Columbia. Once the ambitious project was under way, its sizable funds began to look inadequate, and in 1948 Benedict applied for, and received, supplemental funds from RAND (Mead 1959: 434, 438). Mead worked to overcome the sort of hierarchical culture of rank that had predominated in war work. The large seminars had their own dynamics. As many as seventy-five people participating, and "every individual — including the secretaries and the youngest graduate student — was regarded as a full member of the group" (435). Mead thought of this project as the spiritual descendent of a Boasian seminar (436); yet, unlike in Boas's seminars, participants focused not on esoteric features of language, culture, or mythos as a tool for understanding the psychic unity of humankind but on cultural features for ends linked to Cold War contexts. This shift enticed some anthropologists to refocus their intellectual depth of field from one of theoretical abstractions to a plane of interest aligned with the growing militarized state.

After Ruth Benedict died in 1948, Mead took on most of Benedict's RCC duties. Much of this work was later run through the Council for Intercultural Relations and the Institute for Intercultural Studies, organizations that over the years employed more than one hundred people conducting cultural research (Peterson 2005: 47; R. Métraux 1980: 371). Rhoda Métraux wrote that after Benedict's death, Mead recruited anthropologists, many of whom after the war had "left government agencies, vowing never again to work within restrictions on open discussion and publication or to become involved in activities that might affect the lives of others, for good or ill, without their knowledge or consent. I was one of those who had to be convinced that there would be no undisclosed uses of our research. Margaret did convince me" (1980: 368). Métraux's initial concerns were not without some basis. As described in chapter 8, her naive trust in those she met though Mead led to her work on Harold Wolff's research on Chinese personality types — a project that linked RCC to CIA espionage efforts.

Margaret Mead's *Soviet Attitudes toward Authority* (1951), published by RAND, simplistically characterized Soviet national character with references to authoritarianism and political police, ironically writing during a period in which the forces of American McCarthyism were already undertaking Red-baiting attacks on academic freedom.[17] Other RCC projects had Cold War applications. Among the proposals Mead pitched to the National Institute of Health were Mark Zborowski's pain research project and Martha Wolfenstein's examination of "children's expectations and fears which are developing in response to the civilian defense programs, the war news, the draft, etc." (MM, M17, MM to JE 1/31/51).

In late 1956, while overseeing CIA-funded MK-Ultra research (see chapter 8), Harold G. Wolff wrote Margaret Mead, asking her for the IFIS mailing list so that he could alert IFIS-affiliated scholars to "the possibility for future research funding" (MM C37, HW to MM 12/3/56). Wolff did not disclose that his Society for the Investigation of Human Ecology was a CIA front, and Mead provided access to the mailing list (MM C37, MM to HW 1/4/57). Mead and Wolff had been friends since at least the 1940s, and over the years she had offered constructive comments on Wolff's research papers (e.g., MM C19, MM to HW 1/2/48) and shared papers that she thought would be of interest to him, such as Daniel Gajdusek's 1958 work on the "'laughing death' of New Guinea'" (MM C41, MM to HW 7/21/58).[18]

At IFIS, Mead worked with Brookings Institution pollster and social psychologist Donald N. Michael on the Man in Space project. Man in Space research tracked the spread of knowledge about satellites following the launch of *Sputnik*, tracking measurable shifts in the American public's consciousness on topics ranging from popular understandings of satellites to how surprised Americans were that the Soviets had launched the first satellite (55 percent were surprised, 44 percent were not) (Michael 1960: 576). For this project, in the days after the satellite's launch, Mead asked Melville Jacobs to poll Seattleites for their reactions to *Sputnik*, instructing Jacobs to not disclose to research subjects any information about this project (see Michael 1960: 573; MJ 5, 20, MM to MJ 10/6/57). Adopting techniques similar to those used in British anthropologist Tom Harrisson's mass research project, Mead and Rhoda Métraux helped Michael gather and analyze these data (Michael 1960: 575).

The Salzburg Seminars

Another way that American Cold War political forces drafted anthropologists to spread particular forms of Americanized democracy after the war was as participants in programs exposing foreign scholars to American intellectuals. The 1947 Salzburg Seminar in American Civilization symposium collected promising European student scholars at Salzburg's Leopoldskron Castle to foster postwar intellectual growth and the spirit of a specific form of American internationalism. The seminar was conceived of by Harvard graduate students Clemens Heller and Richard Campbell and one of their professors, Scott Elledge. After being refused funding by Harvard's President James B. Conant, Heller and Campbell received a few thousand dollars from the university's student government to finance the basic needs of the seminar; later, after the Seminar was established, in the early 1950s, the Rockefeller Foundation provided $30,000 a year (Rockefeller Foundation 1952: 417).

Margaret Mead was one of eleven American scholars who attended the first Salzburg Seminar. The first seminars were low-budget operations. The first year, the organizers traveled throughout Europe interviewing "about 150 students" and with 92 students attending the conference (Mead 1947: 2). Attendees read classics of American literature and political history in an informal setting that allowed select Americans to cultivate contacts with future leaders of postwar Europe. Conceived as an internationalist project fostering intellectual growth and humanitarianism in a land still decimated by the war, the seminar was controlled by the war's victors.

The American presence at the seminar was significant. Not only was "American civilization" the central topic, but the seminar's unsubtle political message was that it was time for Europe to learn intellectual lessons from the American victors (Mead 1947: 4). Representations of domestic American oppression were generally absent from Salzburg; academic press reports emphasized European student participants' surprise at the levels of academic freedom and dissent. An account of the screening of the film *Grapes of Wrath* stressed a student's amazement at Americans' willingness to show such a depiction of abject poverty (H. N. Smith 1949: 35–36).[19]

The U.S. Army Intelligence Service "dispatched agents to infiltrate [a Salzburg Seminar] session and report on the activities." One army intelligence report, which summarized a spirited debate contrasting U.S. and Soviet economic and political systems, led to Clemens Heller being labeled as a "dangerous Red." The State Department began proceedings to ban Heller from future entry to Austria and canceling future seminars, but calmer heads at State prevailed, and these plans were canceled (Ryback 2009).

Talcott Parsons participated in the second Salzburg Seminar, and the most notable political outcome of his attendance was that this trip marked the beginning of his efforts to bring accused Nazi collaborator Nicholas Poppe to the United States (Gerhardt 1996).[20] Given Kluckhohn's documented reporting to the FBI and CIA during this period, his selection as the seminar's anthropologist during its third year (Gleason 1949) raises the possibility of intelligence agencies gathering dossiers on seminar participants. By the end of the 1950s, rumors were circulating that the seminars had secret connections with the American intelligence community, though these accusations are unsubstantiated (see Wachman 2005: 44). But we do have documentation of the CIA funding other international seminars at this point in time following similar patterns of organization.

During this period, the CIA began providing funds that would total $135,000 for similar international summer sessions at Harvard organized by Henry Kissinger (NYT 1967b). In 1950, Henry Kissinger, then a Harvard graduate student, began planning a ten-week seminar that would bring fifty young European professionals to the university. This International Summer School program was run through Harvard's Summer School, which a decade and a half later was discovered to have secretly operated with funding supplied by Frank Wisner's Office of Policy Coordination (OPC) at the CIA. As Heller, Campbell, and Elledge had traveled throughout Europe collecting top participants for the Salzburg Seminars, Kissinger traveled in Europe, interviewing prospective students to attend the International Summer School, in some instances making political contacts that would have future uses. After CIA funding for the program was exposed, Kissinger insisted he had no knowledge of such support from the agency, but correspondence between Kissinger and William Elliott establishes his knowledge of CIA links (Wilford 2008: 126).

Although the CIA did not release any records in response to my FOIA requests relating to the Salzburg Seminars, it remains an open question whether the CIA or other governmental agencies had nondisclosed contacts or influence with the students or others who attended. Given the CIA's interest in, and covert financial support of, Harvard's International Summer School during this period, this remains a possibility, and we know that military intelligence and State Department intelligence were monitoring seminar participants. Whatever the CIA's involvement or noninvolvement in the Salzburg Seminars, the seminar's propaganda value was clear, and anthropologists' contributions to these efforts became a natural Cold War addition. A March 29, 1962, memo from the under secretary of state for political affairs advising DCI John McCone on various ways to infiltrate and influence international organizations mentioned the Salzburg Seminars as a model that the CIA could use for such efforts (CIA 1959c: Annex B, 2).

The Rise of Centers and Seminars

The rise of area study centers, international seminars, and research centers focusing on research problems framed by U.S. international concerns was shaped by Cold War political developments, and these centers and seminars were birthed with an infusion of governmental and private foundation funds. As David Nugent's work shows, the value of social science to military and corporate foundations interested in maintaining power over, and controlling markets in, foreign countries "resulted in an unusual willingness on their part to subsidize the production of that knowledge" (2010: 2). At the time, the ways these funds supported American hegemony were not always apparent to those receiving the funds. It would not be until press revelations of CIA involvements became public in the 1960s that anthropologists began to consider the larger political context in which these systems of knowledge production were embedded.

This increasing availability of foundation funding was welcomed by anthropologists, who seldom considered what obligations might accompany such gifts or how the gifts might shape avenues of inquiry or analysis. But whether or not such issues were considered, these funds brought their own transformations. To receive this financial support, anthropologists "had only to learn to formulate research problems in categories established by the foundations and government agencies in the bureaucratic mold of rational procedure. The research proposal, and the thought process required to successfully fulfill it, therefore superseded the older, more individual approaches to the pursuit of knowledge. The changes in anthropology constituted just one small part of a wider process leading to the present situation in which government funding, tax-exempt foundations, and grant applications permeate all levels of American society, with their abstract formulas to which applications must either conform or die" (Denich 1980: 173). The conflux of the rise of tax-exempt foundations named after dead millionaires and anthropologists seeking research funds provided new life to Marx's observation that "the more a dominant class is able to absorb the best people from the dominated class, the more solid and dangerous is its rule" (Marx 1894: 736).

In part, the area study centers rapidly appearing on American campuses during the early Cold War were intellectual extensions of wartime innovations made at the OSS and other intelligence agencies (Winks 1987: 115). Bruce Cumings observed how personal connections, skills, and mind-sets developed during the war influenced the interdisciplinary structural formation of area study centers; in addition, the centers frequently employed academics who maintained contacts with members of intelligence agencies in ways that mixed their academic pursuits with those of the CIA and other intelligence agencies (Cumings 1999: 173). Drawing on correspondence between Philip Mosely and Paul Langer from 1953, Cumings described how the Ford Foundation consulted with CIA director Allen Dulles to establish how Ford-funded research projects could be selected in ways that coalesced with the CIA's needs (184). Cumings showed that Mosely was a "working linkage among Ford, the CIA and the ACLS/SSRC" extending from the early 1950s into the early 1960s to help "shape postwar area studies" (185).

Saunders (1999), Wilford (2008), Diamond (1992), Ransom (1975), and others document some of the ways that the CIA influenced intellectuals during the Cold War, at times using agencies like the Ford Foundation, as well as CIA front foundations, to steer intellectual movements (see chapters 7 and 8). The Ford Foundation played a vital support role, invigorating flaccid CIA-linked social science projects that were in need of support and legitimization. The pattern shown in the Ford Foundation volunteering to make up for the shortfall of funds at CENIS left by the CIA's 1966 withdrawal was repeated in other CIA-exposed programs discussed in later chapters.

As one of the Cold War's classic large, multisite ethnographic research projects, the Modjokuto Project demonstrated how large-scale projects required large, centralized funding sources. Such projects suggest similarities with how physics was transformed during the twentieth century, as it became tied both directly and peripherally to weapons lab research in classic dual use ways that nurtured the curiosity of those engaging in theoretical research and also produced findings that had implications for developing weapons systems.

Anthropologists and other scholars working at area study centers sometimes supported and sometimes scrutinized Cold War assertions of American hegemony, but even with occasional strong academic critiques, these centers produced the levels of technical cultural and linguistic knowledge needed to train those who supported American policy—and even the work of critics or politically neutral scholars was cannibalized for military or intelligence ends (Condominas 1973; D. H. Price 2003b, 2012a). These critiques of area study centers' political alignments are almost as old as the programs themselves, with remarkably sophisticated critiques being made by anthropologist Jerome Rauch in his article "Area Institute Programs and African Studies" (1955). As an anthropology graduate student at Columbia University, Rauch traced the roots of the Cold War's area study centers to the Second World War, writing that "the war-emergency agencies placed great emphasis on area organization," producing information needed by agencies like the Office of Strategic Services, the Foreign

Economic Administration, and the Office of War Information (Rauch 1955: 409). Rauch described the Ethnogeographic Board's coordination of the collection and distribution of ethnographic data to various military and intelligence agencies during the Second World War. He stressed how the board's confidential reports and rosters "formed the backbone" of postwar area study center rosters (410). Rauch connected the 1950s area studies approach directly to U.S. cold war military and intelligence needs.

Rauch understood "the mantle of world hegemony" as providing "the propelling force behind foreign area research" (1955: 413). Rauch quoted George Peter Murdock's realpolitik observation that "we shall have reason to believe that area research is prompted by pure science objectives when, for example, there suddenly appear in our universities ten times as many area programs concerned with Madagascar or the Fan Chaco as with Russia or China" (413).

Rauch understood the government outsourced needed analysis and training functions to area studies centers, a process in which "the subordination of area research to government and business policy has at times assumed war-time 'crash project' undertones" (1955: 415). While Rauch critiqued this approach, he recognized that others, like Karl Wittfogel, argued that just as the United States should dispense economic aid to underdeveloped nations only in ways that furthered the national interest, social science programs that were aligned with furthering the national interest should also be funded as a priority (415; Wittfogel 1950).

Rauch critiqued the Wenner-Gren Foundation's role in funding anthropology and area studies, in what must be the first published academic criticism that alleged Axel Wenner-Gren's connection with Nazis.[21] The directness of his critique of the largest funder of anthropological research was unusual for the 1950s.

Rauch argued that "the themes underlying current African research" were aligned with America's quest for "raw materials and investment opportunities, strategic and military import, the status quo and/or colonialism" (1955: 422). He rejected prevailing views that colonialism in Africa had brought positive impacts to those living under colonial rule, and he derisively quoted comments by Bryce Wood at a Princeton conference on Africa that called for American scholars to rethink their anticolonialist attitudes (423).

It is not surprising that Rauch's critique of the dual use Cold War functions of area study centers did not garner praise: such interpretations were decidedly unwelcome in 1955. In 2001, Rauch wrote me that the publication of his paper produced unexpected results: "I had no great expectation that this analysis would be received as front page news, but I was taken aback by the way it was totally rejected and assigned to oblivion. Over the years and to no avail I have submitted it to several bibliographic surveys hoping only that it would be listed" (JR to DHP 2/22/01). After Rauch published his analysis of area study centers, his adviser, Julian Steward, told him such forthright critiques were a form of academic suicide and suggested that he leave the field, which he did (D. H. Price 2011c: 350).

Critiques of Cold War agendas during this period brought career setbacks, and alignments with these agendas brought rewards. While anthropologists like Jack Harris, Bernhard Stern, Gene Weltfish, and Richard Morgan struggled to keep jobs or, after suffering the attacks of McCarthyism, left academia entirely to work as an insurance salesman or a chicken farmer, Clyde Kluckhohn's career rose as a consequence of his alignment with nontransparent Cold War projects. Anthropologists who aligned their work with Cold War topics or regions of concern found broad career opportunities.

These campus-linked area study centers, seminars, and other research centers were not the only means of linking anthropologists to Cold War research projects. A wealth of governmental development projects focusing on global economic inequality and military-linked projects brought anthropologists into the orbits of the State Department, the CIA, and other governmental agencies.

In this context, anthropology's neglect of the critique by sociology, its intellectual cousin, of the military-industrial complex through the writings of C. Wright Mills coalesced with the needs of state. The attacks on Mills at Harvard by Parsons and his followers produced dual use outcomes, as anthropology's disciplinary elites drew attention away from power relations embedded in political-economic relations, even as anthropologists increasingly undertook fieldwork in societies of the "Third World," where America fought for the hearts, minds, and bodies of those living on the Cold War's proxy battlefield.

> USAID is the CIA's little sister.
> FATHER GEORGE COTTER | 1981

FIVE ANTHROPOLOGISTS AND STATE

Aid, Debt, and Other Cold War Weapons of the Strong

Assuming the role of a powerful victor in the postwar world, the U.S. State Department asserted new global powers that brought opportunities for anthropologists interested in working for State or other civilian governmental agencies or as civilians working for military branches. One mid-1950s anthropologist working for the U.S. government described the activities of Mutual Security Agency anthropologists as ranging from helping "explain to American businessmen the differences in cultures to be taken into consideration in planning aid and reorganization of foreign industries" to acting as advisers to R. L. McNamara on developments in Southeast Asia (MacGregor 1955: 423).

Anthropologists found a broad range of civilian governmental employment opportunities at home and abroad. In 1950, Edward Jandy left his anthropology professorship at Wayne State University to become cultural officer at the U.S. embassy in Tel Aviv (*NBAAA* 1950 4[3]: 3). In 1948, Philleo Nash, Harry S. Truman's presidential specialist on minority matters, helped draft Executive Order 9981, which racially integrated the armed forces (MacGregor 1985: 309–14). T. Dale Stewart helped identify the remains of dead U.S. soldiers for the army during the Korean War; Edward T. Hall and Glen Fisher taught cultural sensitivity training courses at the State Department's Foreign Service Institute (FSI) (424). Civilian archaeologists worked on many military cultural resource management projects that were at times linked to development or acquisition of American military bases.[1]

Responding to a request from John Bennett and Clyde Kluckhohn, in late 1950, Harvard anthropologist John Pelzel produced a report on two Korean villages occupied by North Korean forces (Oppenheim 2008: 228). The American embassy in Lebanon developed a "special branch of the Foreign Service Institute" that employed anthropologist Kepler Lewis and linguist Charles Ferguson to provide "intensive training for younger foreign service officers preparing for a career in the Near East" (MacGregor 1955: 426). Secretary of State John Foster Dulles appointed David Mandelbaum to the U.S. National Commission to UNESCO (BAAA 1957 5[3–4]: 1). During the late 1940s, several anthropologists took positions at the FSI, where they continued in roles that had become familiar for the discipline during the war. At FSI, Edward Kennard became a professor of anthropology, Henry L. Smith directed the FSI's School of Language Training, and George Trager took on a professorship of linguistics (NBAAA 1949 3[1]: 5). And while these and other anthropological contributions to civilian governmental tasks at the State Department and elsewhere were considerable and widespread, many anthropologists considered this work as peripheral to the discipline's core.

After the war, Cora Du Bois moved from OSS to the Department of State, where she was the chief of the department's Intelligence Research Southeast Asia Branch from 1945 to 1949. The FBI investigated Du Bois as a possible communist because of her anticolonialist views, her participation in progressive political movements, and her past employment by Owen Lattimore, American scholar of China accused by Senator Joseph McCarthy of being a Communist spy (see D. H. Price 2004b: 293–97). Du Bois's exit from governmental employment illustrates the narrowness of political thought that was tolerated in governmental service during the postwar years.

During the late 1940s and throughout the 1950s and into the early 1960s, advertisements for military, intelligence, or State Department positions routinely appeared in the *News Bulletin of the AAA* (e.g., NBAAA 1952 6[6]: 4). One advertisement from 1952 described positions in the State Department's Office of Intelligence Research, which was seeking anthropologists to conduct "interpretive studies of areas, ethnic and linguistic groups"; the advertisement requested that applicants provide their dissertation abstracts for governmental distribution (NBAAA 1961 5[2]: 5). Among those anthropologists who answered the State Department's call was John Embree, one of America's most knowledgeable scholars of East Asia.

John Embree's Vision for Anthropologists of State

Because of his prewar fieldwork in Japan and his travels in Asia, John Embree's ethnographic knowledge was in high demand by military and intelligence agencies during and after the war (D. H. Price 2008a: 152–53, 173–76). In 1947,

Embree became the first cultural relations adviser at the U.S. embassy in Bangkok; a year later he took a USIS position at the American embassy in Saigon, then soon left to assume a position in Yale's Southeast Asia Area Studies Program (*NBAAA* 1947 1[1]: 8; *NBAAA* 1948 2[1]: 12).

Embree's governmental work led to a significant critique of governmental applied anthropology. He questioned the likelihood that anthropologists' efforts could remain unentangled from the corrupting influences of governmental sponsors (*NBAAA* 1948 2[4]: 61). In recounting the problems facing anthropologists working as cultural officers abroad, Embree described the double binds anthropologists faced as they tried to spread "knowledge among nations for the ultimate good of all," while their governmental sponsors expected them to spread knowledge in ways favoring U.S. geopolitical interests as defined "by the current government in Washington." Embree warned his colleagues that "an anthropologist who serves as cultural officer is thus soon faced with a problem in professional ethics" (1949: 156).

Embree broadly critiqued the philosophical basis and implementation of postwar applied anthropology. He attacked the commonplace rankings of cultures as either simple or complex, noting that before World War II Japan was widely described as a "progressive" nation, yet when the war broke out, many anthropologists described Japanese culture as "evil," "pathological," or "adolescent" (Embree 1950: 430). He ridiculed wartime anthropologists who had tried "to show that Japanese society was not only different from western European — an acceptable anthropological proposition — but also tried to demonstrate that their peculiar culture made the Japanese warlike and aggressive as individuals and expansionist as a nation. This was done by resort to ingenious theories concerning toilet training, Emperor worship and food habits" (430).

Embree described U.S. anthropologists' work in Micronesia as demonstrating a paternalistic "white man's burden" (1950: 430) attitude toward Micronesians that was reminiscent "of French and British colonialists who have devoted their lives unselfishly to administration of the affairs of their little brown brothers" (431). He critiqued George Murdock's ethnocentrism, writing that Murdock had brought the discipline "full circle," back to the "views and sentiment of the nineteenth century foreign investors, convert-seeking missionaries, and writers such as Kipling singing the praises of the docile brown man — when ruled by western man" (431).

Embree was outraged that anthropologists managed people in ways that served administrators, instead of giving voice to the desires of studied peoples. He denounced the "recent trend" of applied anthropology, declaring that international projects managed local populations in ways that met the needs of government administrators abroad, while industrial applied anthropologists sold out workers to their managers at home. Embree argued that America needed to "learn some self restraint if she is not to ruin the people and cultures of the world." He hoped American anthropologists would play a role in offering "intellectual leadership" while remaining aware of the dangers of "falling in love with their own culture and their own professional folkways to such an extent as to lose sight of their primary object: to study the nature of man and his culture, of the relations between men and their cultures" (Embree 1950: 431–32).

Embree's critique brought several responses that were published in *American Anthropologist*. John Fischer, an anthropologist working for the Civil Administration Unit of the Ponape Trust Territory of the Pacific Islands, admitted that Embree's piece "struck a very sympathetic note," acknowledging that governmental anthropologists must support the rule of administrators and reduce "trouble" with the locals, and that most administrators essentially want to Americanize those they administer. Fischer conceded that "an applied anthropologist who devoted his major effort to opposing this general goal would, I believe, accomplish very little except the eventual termination of his employment" (1951: 133). Yet Fischer defended these practices, arguing that these applied anthropologists were not "simply a tool of the administration" (133).[2] He stressed that an applied anthropologist working between the cultures of administrators and the culture he was hired to study must "be careful of passing judgment on the ways of the inferior group (inferior in the social sense), he must also be careful about passing judgment on the ways and values of the superior group which employs him" (133). With such derogatory language, Fischer only dug deeper the hole begun by Embree; he appeared only a few quatrains away from channeling Kipling.

Fischer argued that "when a politically and economically powerful society takes over a weaker society we may expect the weaker society to change more in conformity with the more powerful than the reverse." Fischer claimed the directionality of these changes existed not because of differences between military might, but "partly because the weaker society *seeks* to imitate the more powerful in order to become more powerful itself" (1951: 133). Fischer claimed this situation would be made worse if the "superior culture" inhibited the "inferior culture's" emulation, but he acknowledged things would be different if the "inferior group" hired its own applied anthropologists (134). Fischer compared the role of applied anthropology to that of past waves of American missionaries sent to proselytize in the undeveloped world, writing that he hoped "perhaps in the present age there would be some public support for anthropological 'missionaries,' who would however try to help dependent peoples hold, develop, and realize their own systems of values in the face of alien domination instead of imposing on them a foreign system" (134).

Douglas Haring rejected Embree's critiques, declaring that he upheld "the right of native tribes to adopt civilized ways, and the right of any ethical human being to encourage such adoption, especially if by education and experience he is fitted to foresee the probable extinction of natives who fail to make the change. This does not for a moment grant the right of superior military or political power to enforce such acculturation merely in the interest of power politics. If this be ethnocentrism, I accept the onus" (1951: 137).

But Jules Henry embraced Embree's critique, adding his own attack on the dominance of personality and culture studies that focused on "studies of the enemy" and pointing out how frequently these studies found enemy cultures to be "rigid," "hypochondriacal," "paranoid," "neurotic," or suffering from "mass megalomania" (1951: 134). Henry declared that "a study of 'enemy' personality that finds the enemy [to have a] diseased mentality is hardly worthy of scientific consideration" (135).

In December 1950, Embree was killed by a drunk driver, and thus he was unable to respond to these comments; his death left American anthropology without a clear voice that could critically straddle the gap between Ivy League academia and governmental anthropology. Embree's critique of the political realities of Cold War applied anthropology remained largely dormant for the next decade and a half, and the rising political chill of McCarthyism provided incentives for anthropologists to develop other arguments (D. H. Price 2013b).[3] Within this silence, the ubiquity of the dysfunctions identified by Embree came to be seen as normal features of these interactions. Increasing numbers of anthropologists and bureaucrats working on these projects internalized these contradictions in ways that helped camouflage ethical and political shortcomings as inevitable parts of the workplace environment.

As Cold War global patron-client relations developed, the Pentagon and State Department supported new economic assistance programs. Some of these provided agricultural or technological assistance, others provided military aid, and some supplied both. During the first sixteen years after World War II, several agencies (under both State and Defense, with names like the Technical Cooperation Administration (TCA), the Mutual Security Agency (MSA), and Point IV) distributed this aid, and anthropologists provided a steady supply of labor for these programs. The birth, life, and death of these short-lived postwar assistance programs can best be understood in the context of a larger administrative evolutionary framework stretching from the creation of the Institute of Inter-American Affairs (IIAA) in 1942 to the establishment of the United States Agency for International Development (USAID) in 1961.

USAID's Prehistory: Alphabet Soup, TCA, MSA, and Others

In 1942, the Institute of Inter-American Affairs (1942–55) began as a wartime agency collecting regional intelligence and providing economic and technical assistance to poorer nations of North and South America.[4] In Europe, the Marshall Plan was overseen by the Economic Cooperation Administration (ECA), an agency directed by both the Department of Commerce and the State Department, though the ECA's charge and operations were temporally limited to the years 1948–52, as specified war restorations ended and new agencies took up variations on these initial postwar projects. Many of these economic assistance programs were elements of American counterinsurgency operations, broadly defined as practices designed to prevent uprising and to support the legitimacy or powerbase of existing regimes (see Price 2010a: 162).

As the Cold War developed, two new agencies emerged. The Technical Cooperation Administration (1950–53) delivered humanitarian technical assistance programs (Point IV) without direct military aid, while the Mutual Security Agency (1951–53) mixed technical assistance with military aid. Both programs developed independently until political forces favored the creation of a single agency (into which the remains of IIAA, MSA, and TCA were merged): the Foreign Operations Administration (FOA, 1953–55). The FOA provided technical assistance and "mutual security activities" to politically aligned nations—a shift that explicitly transformed the supposedly neutral aid of Point IV into a soft power Cold War weapon. The FOA needed people with anthropological skill sets to help implement these assistance programs, and anthropologists contributed to FOA projects in India and the Philippines (MacGregor 1955: 424).

In 1955, the International Cooperation Administration (ICA, 1955–61) was formed as an agency administering nonmilitary assistance projects. Finally, the creation of USAID in 1961 established an agency that merged humanitarian assistance and development assistance with what would develop as a broad range of counterinsurgency programs (figure 5.1).

The institutional evolution of agencies housing these Cold War aid programs reveals congressional and executive ambivalence over which types and programs to fund, as well as connections between aid and raw Cold War politics.

FIGURE 5.1. The evolution of United States' Cold War aid organizations: Agency for International Development (USAID, 1961–present), Economic Cooperation Administration (ECA, 1952), Foreign Operations Administration (FOA, 1953–1955), Institute of Inter-American Affairs (IIAA, 1942–1955), International Cooperation Administration (ICA, 1955–1961), Mutual Security Agency (MSA, 1951–1953), Technical Cooperation Administration (TCA, 1950–1953) (Illustration, Nora Jean Price).

Establishing the IIAA during the war presented few political problems, especially because it was overseen by Nelson Rockefeller, one of the world's richest men, who at times mixed his own long-term financial interests with the interests of the institute. Creating the MSA and TCA, as two separate agencies, enabled the United States to spread military power and the appearance of humanitarian goodwill. The lack of political backing for Point IV as a relatively more neutral political tool demonstrated America's low commitment to soft power projects and nonmilitary aid during the period. With time, this evolution through transitional forms (FOA and ICA) led to the establishment of USAID as an agency supporting passive military- and diplomatically linked counterinsurgency operations that were extensions of U.S. international political agendas.

Point IV

In his 1949 inaugural speech, President Harry S. Truman announced a four-point plan for his administration. First, there would be continuing support for the United Nations; second, the United States would support the postwar global economic recovery; third, the United States would exhibit solidarity with the North Atlantic alliance; and fourth, the United States would "embark on a bold new program for making the benefits of our scientific advances and industrial progress available for the improvement and growth of underdeveloped areas" (Truman 1949). The last item in this four-point plan, the commitment to global development aid, came to be known as "Point IV," and anthropologists were soon identified as important agents in its development. As historian Peter Mandler noted, Point IV "portended both opportunity and danger. On the surface the tremendous opportunities opened up by Point IV gave at last a point of direct entry into postwar international politics for anthropologists interested and expert in the less-developed world. However, by blurring the boundaries between multilateral UN programmes and bilateral US programmes, Point IV also had the potential to draw anthropologists who were either uninterested in or overtly hostile to America's interests overseas into compromising situations" (Mandler 2013: 262).

In 1949, the AAA established the Committee on Anthropology and Point IV, chaired by Gordon Willey and composed of Gordon Bowles, Wendell Bennett, John Embree, George Foster, and Frederick Johnson (AA 1951 [3]: 447, 449). Willey wanted to position the discipline so that once Congress funded Point IV, "an anthropologist [would] be appointed to the staff of the General Manager of Point IV, and others be attached to Technical Cooperation Missions in those countries where there will be sizable Point IV operations, and that still others be attached to action field projects dealing with fundamental education, public health, maternal and child welfare, nutrition, irrigation and reclamation, housing and general industrialization" (AA 1950 52[1]: 155). The Smithsonian's Institute of Social Anthropology, with its wartime roots and governmental connections, was seen as the logical point to coordinate anthropological contributions to Point IV, and George Foster was to facilitate these links (ISA Series 1, Box 1 "Resolution").

Willey worked as a liaison with the State Department, and in May 1950 he began writing "a general anthropological indoctrination manual" to be used by Foreign Service personnel (AA 1951 [3]: 448). The manual used anthropological perspectives to ease difficulties in culture contact. A month before his death, John Embree was appointed to work with the NRC and Point IV to oversee the production of a Point IV training manual, a task that was later taken on by Conrad Arensberg (AA 1951 [3]: 449; AA 1952 [2]: 285).[5]

Gordon Willey's report, titled "Anthropology and the Point IV Program," described the value of anthropology's relativistic outlook for Point IV and outlined how anthropologists working as members of academic teams with economists, agricultural technicians, and other experts could implement development programs abroad. Willey envisioned anthropologists working as intermediaries, helping translate "native" viewpoints to Western developers; he provided hypothetical examples of ways that "native beliefs in the supernatural nature of disease and its treatment by . . . medicine" or traditional beliefs about agriculture could be mitigated by anthropologists taking active roles in the development process (ISA 1, 1, 9/22/49). He acknowledged that some anthropologists would be critical of linking research with such an overtly political project, conceding that "scientific research which is administratively united to the applications of the results of the research stands always in [a] very real danger of having its objective investigative function warped by the administrative outlook and desires" (ISA 1, 1, 9/22/49). Willey argued against dismantling the ISA or transforming it into an agency that was primarily devoted to Point IV. Instead, he recommended that a board of anthropologists (and the AAA's executive secretary) with diverse geographic areas of expertise consult with a chief Point IV anthropologist (ISA 1, 1, 9/22/49).[6]

The State Department's TCA, established in 1950, oversaw Point IV's development. The TCA did not sponsor military aid, instead focusing on programs to transfer technology or agricultural techniques to underdeveloped nations. Separate from the TCA, but with some overlapping functions, was the MSA, established in the following year), which provided both military and technical assistance to underdeveloped nations that were of strategic interest to the United States.

A 1952 Point IV job advertisement in the *News Bulletin of the* AAA described Point IV assistant program officer position openings in South Asia, the Near East, and Africa. The ad, which sought applicants trained in cultural anthropology, linked Point IV to past governmental projects drawing on anthropological expertise; it stated that "qualification for these positions requires previous field experience with people of two or more cultures, experience in the applied social science field, for example community analysts with War Relocation Authority, or teaching at the assistant or associate professor level" (NBAAA 1952 6[3]: 4). In general, anthropologists who supported Point IV publicly characterized it as a politically neutral program. Elliot Chapple claimed that it "asked nothing in return" from the countries it would aid, unlike other programs such as the MSA, which "operated on the simple principle that in return for its cooperation it expected military assistance and political allegiance in the struggle against communism" (Chapple 1953: 2).

Point IV was terminated in 1953, after having enacted only pilot projects in Iran, Israel, and Pakistan. Anthropologists held key positions, with H. Naulor, R. Minges, and R. C. Albers working on TCA Point IV projects in Iran and K. Orr working on the early stages of a planned project assisting Bedu in Jordan (MacGregor 1955: 424).

Walt Rostow and Cold War Theories of Global Development

Point IV's political difficulties with Congress arose in part because its supporters lacked a clearly articulated ideological justification for these projects. Walt Rostow's modernization theory later became a prominent persuasive ideological tool used by Cold War academics and policy makers to rationalize these kinds of Third World economic interventions. It mattered little how flawed Rostow's theory was; it provided a useful rationalization for establishing valuable patron-client relationships of dependence, but such arguments were not well developed in the early 1950s.

The Center for International Studies supported Rostow as he wrote numerous articles and contributed to nine books that endorsed the strategic philosophy behind these economic aid programs. A mixture of CIA, Ford Foundation, and Rockefeller Foundation funds financed the development of arguments for using foreign aid as an arm of U.S. policy. Rostow's *Stages of Economic Growth: A Non-Communist Manifesto* (1960) provided rationalizations for development policies linked to American counterinsurgency strategies. Rostow argued that the United States could counter the spread of international communism by identifying and replicating the same historical stages that had occurred within American capitalism. In Rostow's world, nations' successful economic development progressed through four universal stages of capitalism: a traditional stage, a take-off stage, the drive to technological maturity, and high mass consumption. Modernization theory's unilinear evolutionary schema maintained that if underdeveloped countries could progress through the same historical stages of economic development as had occurred in the West—with foreign aid accelerating their technological development—then prosperity would follow. Rostow envisioned an evolutionary progression for underdeveloped nations, culminating in their achievement of a lifestyle of high mass consumption; or, as Marshall Sahlins put it, Rostow was "among the first to perceive that the culmination of human social evolution was shopping" (2000c: 504).

Modernization theory provided the intellectual veneer needed by policy makers seeking to rationalize neocolonial ventures, and the accompanying international economic programs became key components of U.S. Cold War counterinsurgency strategy. Rostow was but one of many postwar American social theorists who focused on "modernization"; others who did so included Edward Shils, David Apter, Lucian Pye, Cyril Black, and Daniel Lerner, and even Talcott Parsons's adaptations of Weberian notions of traditional and legal rational authority were rooted in analyses of societies mired in traditions that inhibited modernity. Nils Gilman observed that efforts by Parsons, Millikan, and Rostow to reinvent Weber as an optimistic supporter of development capitalism required some academic sleight of hand. Gilman noted, "Just as Marx used the Hegelian dialectic to read the economic history of mid-nineteenth-century Britain, so the modernization theorists used Parsonian theory to understand the postwar changes in impoverished parts of the regions" (2003: 94). Rostow argued that the economic prosperity or poverty of nations could not be reduced to economics, and that prosperity could be engineered by rich nations providing technological infusions along with accompanying ideological overhauls. Rostow's materialist infusions of hardware provided the poor with new technologies—often sold under interest-bearing loans—while calling for ideological shifts channeling Norman Vincent Peale, as cultures needed to *think* themselves into modernity and prosperity.

As former colonial states in Africa and Asia gained independence, the attractions of socialism and communism for people ravaged by northern imperialism were obvious, and Rostow recognized the threat that decolonialization represented to American hegemony. Rostow argued that in the 1950s, global decolonialization and the rapid expansion of Chinese and the Soviet economic aid programs in Asia and Africa undermined American authority in would-be client states, developments that could lead to the spread of communism. Because of the necessary parallels to Leninist theories of imperialism Rostow was reluctant to directly critique the historically crippling effects of colonial imperialism. However, he advocated large-scale U.S. economic assistance in the form of technological infusion programs to modernize agricultural or industrial processes, or to bring improved roads or sanitization facilities. Cold War anthropologists and other social scientists often worked as foot soldiers, interacting with local populations, solving logistical problems, or getting "local buy-in" for development projects. Yet many of these programs were of the type later excoriated by John Perkins in *Confessions of an Economic Hitman* (2004) as undertakings that delivered minimal goods or services and established debts that were used to manipulate domestic policies in client states.

In May 1952, Millikan and Rostow sent DCI Dulles a memorandum titled "Notes on Foreign Economic Policy," which argued that developed nations should invest in development projects in order to create a "higher real income [to] every free world citizen" (FOIA CIA MORI ID 30405, 5/21/54, 1).[7] They advocated capturing underdeveloped economies as dependent allies in the struggle between capitalists and socialists. They believed underdeveloped nations could be converted into consumers or producers of goods in ways benefiting developed nations. They identified two fundamental "weaknesses" in the current system of economic relationships. First, underdeveloped nations cannot sustain growth. Second, industrial nations lack a source for inexpensively produced goods, which "in the free world economy, properly handled, could be converted into assets: the underdeveloped areas need the products and markets the industrialized areas can supply; the industrialized areas need the markets and products of the underdeveloped countries" (FOIA CIA MORI ID 30405, 5/21/54, 6–7). Millikan and Rostow believed that "in the short run communism must be contained militarily. In the long run we must rely on the development . . . of an environment in which societies which directly or indirectly menace ours will not evolve. We believe the achievement of a degree of steady economic growth is an essential part of such an environment" (FOIA CIA MORI ID 30405, 5/21/54, 3). They argued that the United States had "a particular responsibility in this regard in view of its twofold position as the largest creditor country and as leader of the free world partnership" (FOIA CIA MORI ID 30405, 5/21/54, 17).

Rostow's work informed CIA approaches to counterinsurgency. On March 15, 1960, he wrote DCI Dulles a memo predicting that at the Paris Summit that was to take place that May, Soviet Premier Nikita Khrushchev would make grand gestures of offering international aid. Rostow advised Dulles that the United States needed to be prepared with contingency plans and listed advantages to the United States producing its own aid initiatives (FOIA WWR to AD, CIA-RDP80B01676R003700040046-0).

There was nothing hidden about the political role Rostow envisioned modernization theory playing in America's Cold War struggle against communism. While Rostow subtitled his magnum opus *A Non-Communist Manifesto*, the governmental agencies initiating programs based on modernization theory's propositions (such as USAID) were seldom viewed as implementing *counterinsurgency* programs. Many development anthropologists have been uncomfortable acknowledging Rostow's ideological end goal for world development, instead preferring visions of Third World self-sufficiency that ignore development programs' legacies of debt and their failures to live up to envisioned outcomes.

The United States was not the only superpower funding Cold War economic development and educational and cultural exchanges; the Soviet Union and the People's Republic of China launched their own programs. The CIA worried that communist-financed aid programs presented serious soft power threats to American international dominance (see discussion of Edward S. Hunter in chapter 7). In its secret working paper titled "Soviet Policy toward the Underdeveloped Countries" (1961), the CIA analyzed Soviet efforts to win the hearts and minds of the underdeveloped world and voiced fears of an impending aid race. Summarizing the Soviet Union's efforts to expand its global influence through economic development projects, the CIA noted a 1954 Soviet Institute of Ethnography symposium that focused on African "cultural achievements and political and economic developments." The Soviet Africanists at the symposium argued that Western policy for Africa was mired in racist assumptions and sought economic exploitation, whereas these Soviet scholars "advanced an interpretation of African developments based on a 'long and original path of historical development,' of a past golden age which was destroyed by Western political and economic intrusion, and in general attributing to Western influence all negative features of African life" (CIA 1961: 24).

A CIA secret intelligence report titled "Communist Cultural and Propaganda Activities in the Less Developed Countries" (1966a) described two Nepalese cultural agreements with the Soviet Union. One program called "for the exchange of delegations, publications, exhibits, films, and radio programs" on an annual basis; under this program, Nepal received a Soviet performance ensemble, an exhibit of Soviet stamps, one lecturer, an exhibit of photography, and the services of radio experts and "the USSR would receive an 18-member cultural delegation, 25 Nepalese students, three literacy experts, and an exhibit of photography," as well as exchanges of books and musical recordings, with most of the incurred costs being funded by the host nation (CIA 1966a: 8). The CIA report detailed a similar exchange program between Nepal and China and noted that many of these programs created financial difficulties for poorer nations as they struggled to reciprocate (CIA 1966a: 8); in these struggles, the CIA found opportunities for the United States to capitalize on these hardships. American programs such as Fulbright Scholar Program (which had no CIA links), as well as programs with CIA links, established relationships similar to those with the Soviets, but without requiring these poorer nations to provide funds.

Dual Use Aid: USAID as Assistance and Counterinsurgency

After the relatively rapid succession of short-lived international aid organizations (e.g., ECA, MSA, TCA, FOA, ICA), at times clumsily mixing technical assistance and military aid, the establishment of the United States Agency for International Development (USAID) in 1961 marked a new era in international assistance. The range of Cold War USAID projects spanned agricultural improvement, technology infusion, postharvest production transportation plans, irrigation improvement, rural education, rural electrification, and road improvements to democracy reform operations or police training programs. The diversity of projects, themes, motivations, and outcomes of thousands of USAID projects negates the possibility of isolating simple themes that connect all the Cold War USAID projects to which anthropologists contributed.

Many of USAID's Cold War era projects supported the general tenets of counterinsurgency in its broadest definition. These projects used soft power to support political regimes aligned with U.S. geopolitical interests, effectively using aid to pacify potential challenges to U.S. clients' political legitimacy. Economic assistance programs became important parts of these schemes. From the perspective of dual use science, the individual motivations or ideologies of the participating anthropologists mattered little (there were free-market capitalists, Marxists, and theorists who were little interested in particular projects but wanted access to the field): these projects served larger counterinsurgency goals. Many of these dynamics shifted with time; as Steve Weissman observed, as the Cold War developed, there were shifts in the ways that funds for foreign aid as "a tool for instant counterinsurgency" moved from coming directly from USAID and other branches of the U.S. government to coming from multilateral agencies like the World Bank and the Asian Development Bank (1974: 15). From USAID's earliest days, anthropologists contributed to projects that expressed humanitarian motivations and altruistic desires to improve the lives of others, yet many anthropologists working on these projects ignored the political contexts in which the projects were embedded, which included leveraging the clients' significant debt resulting from these projects.

A now declassified CIA executive memorandum from 1962 described a six-week training program in which the CIA added a USAID counterinsurgency training course consisting of two weeks focusing on area studies and a special two-day course titled "Communist Theory, Communist Threat in Developing Countries, Soviet Economic Potential, Communist Global Propaganda, Unconventional Warfare, and Communism and Free Labor." The CIA reported that approximately seven hundred USAID personnel received this counterinsurgency training each year and that "USAID intends to coordinate with FBI to determine where the program can be drawn in more direct counterinsurgency terms." Middle-grade USAID personnel attended a twenty-one-week course at Johns Hopkins University's Institute for International Development or a similar program at Boston University's African Area Studies Program. Stressing the central importance of counterinsurgency for USAID, the memo continued: "Nearly all of the major USAID training programs are in a terminal stage and set to be replaced or reviewed. In whatever substantive continued form, counterinsurgency training will be appropriately emphasized." The memorandum mentioned USAID's counterinsurgency operations training of foreign nationals through the Inter-American Police Academy and other U.S. training programs (FOIA CIA-RDP80B01676R000100100032-7, 6/21/62).[8]

The CIA and USAID combined forces to run the Office of Public Safety (OPS), training political figures and paramilitary units around the world (see Blum 1995: 200–206); in Vietnam, these police training sessions taught aggressive paramilitary techniques. During the 1960s and 70s, USAID's oversight of the OPS police training programs linked USAID with CIA personnel. During the Vietnam War, soldier, strategist, and Kennedy Administration advisor Roger Hilsman and British counterinsurgency expert Robert Thompson trained special branch police units to establish counterinsurgency operations designed to monitor and control communist activities in the Vietnamese countryside (Valentine 1990: 73–75). Specially trained "policing" units were the key components of this program, acting as counterinsurgency operations' eyes and ears; USAID was the administrative body publicly responsible for the program, and the policing program was run as a CIA operation.

Anthropologists were an enticing prospect for USAID functionaries looking for someone to interface between USAID and rural communities. They were hired by USAID to work on projects such as Latin American science exchanges and as staff advisers for programs like the newly established Community Development Division (*AAAFN* 1962 3(2): 1). Many anthropologists viewed these programs as altruistic means of assisting poorer nations, yet views within the CIA recognized other uses. The humanitarian face of USAID was an effective public distraction from the other roles USAID played in supporting CIA efforts to disrupt certain political developments. Eva Golinger described the impact of these USAID efforts to subvert foreign elections:

> One of the first documented misuses of USAID funds was during the early 1960s in Brazil. The CIA was heavily involved in attempts to thwart João Goulart from succeeding in the Brazilian presidency because he was viewed as a leftist who supported "social and economic reforms" that in the eyes of the CIA had "communism" written all over them. The CIA and USAID spent approximately $20 million to support hundreds of anti-Goulart candidates for gubernatorial elections in 1962. USAID was used as a cover to invest heavily in the Brazilian labor movement. The funds were filtered through the international branch of the AFLCIO, then American Institute for Free Labor Development (AIFLD), now known as the American Center for International Labor Solidarity (ACILS), and were controlled on the ground by the CIA. In 1964, President Goulart was overthrown by a CIA-backed coup that resulted in a brutal US-sponsored dictatorship that lasted nearly twenty years.
>
> In the 1980s, as part of the move toward "democratic intervention" models, the State Department established the USAID Office of Democratic Initiatives, with the goal of supporting and "strengthening democratic institutions." From 1984 to 1987, USAID utilized that office to filter more than $25 million into electoral processes in Latin America. Although NED later assumed similar operations, USAID has continued to use the office, now known as the Office of Transition Initiatives (OTI), to intervene in nations involved in crises that "threaten democracy." USAID and the NED also overlap in funding initiatives for the IRI and the NDI both core NED grantees. A large portion of USAID and NED funds are channeled into electoral intervention efforts and civil society penetration. In the case of Venezuela, more than $20 million has been invested by USAID and NED since 2001 to foment conflict and instability in the name of "promoting democracy." (2006: 21–22)

In Chile in 1963, the CIA and USAID cofunded anti-communist social programs organized by Jesuit priest Roger Vekeman, shifting political forces in an effort to undermine Chilean democracy in favor of American hegemony (Blum 1995: 207–8).

In Southeast Asia, USAID's counterinsurgency projects included agricultural development programs promoting economic stability or rewarding groups that were working with the Americans and South Vietnamese authorities. The "Land to the Tiller" (LTTT) law supported counterinsurgency goals by providing free land to farmers who were willing to live on and farm lands in military zones, with differing amounts of land available in different regions (Newberry 1971: 1), and more land available for those who actively cultivated rice (see Newberry 1971; Russell 1971). As a counterinsurgency operation, LTTT offered tangible rewards to soldiers and families of soldiers aligned with the Americans, though it inverted the forms of "land reform" advocated by their communist opponents.

Control Data Corporation surveys measured whether or not the LTTT program was taking lands away from the families of soldiers who were serving in the Army of the Republic of Vietnam (ARVN), who were fighting alongside the Americans. Most ARVN soldiers supported the program, and other data showed that few of these soldiers came from landowning families. These reports contained statistical breakdowns of comments by ARVN soldiers and also included profiles of sample statements of those interviewed. Many respondents complained that even with family serving in the army, they still did not qualify for land (Newberry 1971: 18). But the law was popular among ARVN soldiers, as Newberry concluded, because "the consensus seems to be that LTTT is the type of law no poor man could oppose" (26).

In a 1969 briefing on USAID activities and programs in Vietnam, Joseph Mendenhall, the USAID assistant administrator for Vietnam, summarized USAID's mission in the region by highlighting the crucial counterinsurgency support role for the Civil Operations and Revolutionary Development Support (CORDS) paramilitary program. Mendenhall described USAID's objectives not in the humanitarian language generally used in public discussions but in strategic military terms. Mendenhall stated that USAID continued

> to support prosecution of the war and to mitigate the effects of the war on the people and the economy of Vietnam. In this field which is primarily the field of the military of course — ours is not the primary role; ours is the supporting role, but it is nevertheless an important one. About twenty percent of the funds that we're seeking in the Fiscal Year 1970 are for programs that are directly connected with

the war effort, with the military conflict — that is refugees, medical care, pacification and police. In addition, more than fifty percent of the funding that we're seeking in Fiscal Year '70 will be spent on combating the inflationary pressure which is brought about as a result of the military conflict and the very heavy military expenditures in the Vietnamese budget.

The second objective is that we seek through economic and social development assistance to strengthen the non-communist political forces in South Vietnam. (1969: 1–2)

Mendenhall emphasized the importance of USAID's mission as an element of counterinsurgency strategy that was "necessary to improve living conditions in the poorer quarters in the urban areas to help prevent the communists from gaining a toehold there" (3). He said that USAID's goal was to essentially work itself out of a job as South Vietnam reached economic stability in independence, but he assured his internal audience that significant levels of foreign aid would be needed to maintain stability for a decade after an armistice (4). He summarized USAID's work to resettle the four million Vietnamese who became homeless during the war, especially after the 1968 military offensive, spending more than $60 million on various refugee projects (4, 6).

The involvement of CORDS in village relocation programs linked with the Strategic Hamlet Program and other counterinsurgency operations was extensive, with USAID providing $25 million a year for Vietnam in the late 1960s; the military provided about six thousand individuals working on CORDS, with USAID supplying one thousand CORDS advisers (Mendenhall 1969: 10). Along with a national ID card program, the police's role included "the campaign for eliminating the Viet-Cong political infra-structure at the village and hamlet level," a polite phrase that allowed Mendenhall to gloss over the bloody tactics used by Vietnamese CIA operatives to "eliminate" such Vietcong operations, as well as efforts to block the flow of arms from the Vietcong (10).

Mendenhall described the discomfort of some USAID workers in rural provinces as they came to understand the contradictions of having "two bosses," one being the humanitarian calling of working on issues like public health, the other being CORDS's military links, with CORDS necessarily trumping such conflicting dual use needs (1969: 27). Mendenhall optimistically reported on the successes and popularity of new high-yield rice varieties, arguing that agricultural development in Vietnam was a measure of stability and offered the promise of peace in the war-torn land (16–18). With the help of anthropologists and other aid workers, development, economic assistance, agrochemistry, debt, and dependency became tools of waging war by other means, as wars in Asia and Africa became opportunities to expand development's patronage of hope, with little accounting for USAID's serial failures. When it came to international development schemes, failure was a marketable commodity that sold itself with built-in financing.

SEADAG: USAID's Soft Power War Brain

In 1966, USAID established the Southeast Asia Development Advisory Group (SEADAG), which funded conferences, publications, and research opportunities that helped scholars of Asia from a variety of disciplines to address Asian development issues. This group's parent organizations were USAID and the Rockefeller Foundation–funded Asia Society (SEADAG 1969: vii). To stimulate research that would be of use to U.S. governmental development agencies, SEADAG fostered communication between scholars and government officials. Its network of scholars and officials freely exchanged information relating to Southeast Asian development. The group avoided using the word "counterinsurgency" in its documents, though with the central importance of the period's Southeast Asian wars, counterinsurgency was the reason for undertaking many of the development-related research projects funded by SEADAG.[9]

Each year, SEADAG organized three topical seminars and reimbursed participants for related expenses (SEADAG 1969: ix). With funds from Rockefeller and USAID, SEADAG seminars were held in enticing locations (such as Hawaii) where academics could relax and USAID personnel could benefit from their expertise (see SEADAG 1969: ix).[10] The United States Agency for International Development played a central role in setting the agenda for these seminars and also directed "ad hoc meetings" when problems arose that needed specific consultation.

The relationships between SEADAG, the Asia Society, and USAID blurred institutional boundaries in ways that bypassed normal peer review processes and connected university scholars with the needs of state. An overview of SEADAG activities in the late 1960s reported that "the Asia Society initiated an AID-funded program of research grants through SEADAG, and recommended to AID, after a large number of proposals from various sources had been screened by appropriate seminars and then by a Screening Committee of eminent scholars from outside the SEADAG organizations structure — according to criteria of evaluation established by the Executive Committee. A final approval by AID of these grants will be made directly to researchers and will be administered by the Asia Society" (SEADAG 1969: x). On the surface, this appeared like a normal academic conglomeration bringing together groups of scholars through a generous funding source, but the flow of funds, proposals, and screening occurred within a small circle of actors with shared political concerns.

Through these procedures, SEADAG facilitated the distribution of peer-reviewed proposals, and while the three separate administrative bodies (USAID, Asia Society, and SEADAG) each technically played a separate role, they functioned as one, and the conflicts of interests between them narrowed SEADAG's range of vision and short-circuited an impartial peer review process. This community of scholars linked public (USAID) and private (Rockefeller's Asia Society) groups interested in Southeast Asian research that could inform American policies in Asia. Some scholars applying for these funds met at meetings sponsored by USAID or the Asia Society, where participants learned which research topics were being funded. Although almost everyone involved scrupulously avoided stating it as such, counterinsurgency was a thread connecting many of these projects.

With the rise of Rostow's modernization theory, the measurable outcomes for development often had little to do with improving the lot of underdeveloped nations per se; development aid was a weapon against communism, a tool to be used against insurgents. In the context of the wars of Southeast Asia, aid became a tool of the powerful against the weapons of the weak (Scott 1985). In the mid-1960s, anthropological research became increasingly connected to counterinsurgency theory. In his SEADAG paper titled "Political Consequences of Rural Development Programs in Indonesia" (1967), Guy Pauker described the Indonesian massacres of 1965–66 as arising from "overcrowded rural areas" due to recent rapid population growth, while "the peasant-cultivated area was enlarged by only 11 percent," resulting in high population densities of about two thousand people per square kilometer (1967: 1–2). Pauker conceded that earlier work on agricultural involution by his protégé Clifford Geertz described a process that "had probably already gone as far it could" (2). Pauker analyzed the successes of the PKI (Indonesian Communist Party) in terms of taking advantage of these economic and demographic crises by "inciting the poor and landless peasants" (2), and he used Geertzian and Parsonian theory to analyze the background of the PKI's insurgent tactics:

> If the Javanese village—as Clifford Geertz describes it—lacked structural solidity and traditional resiliency and was therefore open to penetration by ideologically based structure originating in supra-village political life, the unilateral action of the PKI and BTI must have introduced or in any case sharpened social conflicts in

the village. A population which was delicately matching agricultural output with population growth by a complex pattern of land ownership rotation systems, communal work requirements, elaborate reciprocal labor lending customs, sharply defined rights to work on one's relatives' land . . . [etc.] — in short, the pattern of response to a worsening economic situation through a division of the economic pie into smaller and smaller pieces — which Clifford Geertz has so aptly called "shared poverty" — was bound to experience greatly enhanced tensions as the result of "unilateral action" and the ensuing violent clashes. (2–3)

Pauker theorized that the killing of several hundred thousand individuals in the uprisings of 1965–66 was caused by a "disruption of village solidarity" brought about by the PKI and BTI's "unilateral action" (3). Geertz's images of the social forces guiding village life were used to explain the massacre, hypothesizing that these individuals were identified by villagers as "trouble-makers" and labeled as "Communists." When it was time to deal with them, the other villagers did so in what Pauker described as "the Javanese way," which was, "as Geertz graphically puts it — is to 'do all things quietly, subtly, politely, and communally — even starve,' these individuals acted in stark contrast with local custom. [The PKI- and BTI-linked local insurgents] had therefore made themselves not just enemies of the more prosperous elements in the village, in a class-conflict sense, but enemies of the community as a whole, whose ancient ways they were disrupting. I suspect that these considerations, more than genuinely ideological controversies, may have been the decisive factor behind the killings" (3). Embracing modernization's central talisman, namely, bioengineered rice varieties, Pauker advocated for further reliance on high-yield rice to bring peace through increased food production and theorized coming reductions in population levels.

Anthropologist Terry Rambo's doctoral research in Ca-Mau on Vietnamese peasant social systems was funded by SEADAG (see Rambo 1973). On the surface, the published version of Rambo's dissertation reads like a typical early-1970s ecological anthropology dissertation. The literature he addressed cited Leslie White, Julian Steward, Morton Fried, Marvin Harris, Andrew Vayda, Roy Rappaport, Eric Wolf, Elman Service, and other leading ecological anthropologists of the period, yet his analysis also had clear political applications to the Vietnam War. Rambo analyzed the evolution of social organization in the northern Red River region and the lower Mekong Delta, "with the Northerners constituting a closed corporate peasantry and the Southerners being an open peasantry" (1973: 362). Rambo argued these variations in social structure followed adaptations to different ecological niches: in the North, the fundamental unit of social structure was the "corporate village," while in the South, it was the "nuclear family." Differences in population density (lower in the South, higher in the North) followed different subsistence strategies (cash crop rice in the South, a more mixed economy in the North), and differences in exchange types (vertical in the South, horizontal in the North) led to different levels of specialization (high in the South, lower in the North) and fundamentally different forms of social organization (Rambo 1973: 362).

Rambo speculated on whether Edmund Leach's pendulum model of *gumsa* and *gumlao* shifts explained these different structures, or whether some other form of cyclical evolution or linear evolutionary model was at work (1973: 363–69), with more applied reports to USAID and SEADAG exploring how these shifts might relate to exposures to the Vietcong. Rambo and Neil Jamieson (1973: 35–46) used Florence Kluckhohn's value orientation scale to measure communist-linked shifts in social structure. Rambo's theoretical analysis engaged with the ecological cultural evolutionary anthropology of his day, but he avoided addressing the political realities of war impacting the people he studied, as well as the reasons that SEADAG and USAID funded his, and others', fieldwork. The ethnographic present created by Rambo was an ecological laboratory without politically active sponsors or Vietnamese deaths complicating his efforts to measure, model, and explain Vietnamese social structure.

While much of the social science research funded by SEADAG was linked to development projects designed to bring stabilizing counterinsurgency ends (for example, anthropologist Jasper Ingersoll's work on the Nam Pong Project in northeast Thailand), SEADAG also funded more critical progressive or radical work, including that of antiwar critics (e.g., Ingersoll 1968; Scott 1975). By funding a range of political work, SEADAG exemplified the broad Cold War funding strategy successfully used by public and private organizations to generate knowledge, even extremely critical knowledge. In financing scholarship that could at least in part inform military and civilian policy in Southeast Asia, SEADAG got what it paid for, but it also sponsored critiques and radical analysis not to the liking of many policy makers.

USAID and "The Family Jewels"

When news of the CIA's "Family Jewels" report was released in 1974 (see chapter 1), the public first learned of the CIA using USAID for a range of clandestine operations. The report included a folder (on pages 594–609) relating to the CIA's Counter Intelligence Staff, Police Group (CI/PG). The CI/PG maintained a "liaison with the Office of Public Safety, Agency for International Development (OPS/AID) and its training facility, the International Police Academy (IPA)" (CIA 1973: 597). The CIA coordinated daily information exchanges with USAID, including information on training programs and "arranging for IPA/OPS AID briefings and tours for foreign police/security representative sponsored by CIA Area Divisions" (597).

"The Family Jewels" included a memo by CIA counterintelligence specialist James Angleton explaining how USAID supported foreign CIA operations. As Angleton wrote:

> ▬ [redacted, but likely "The CIA"] does not maintain direct contact or liaison with any law enforcement organization, local or federal at home or abroad. When the need arises, such contact is sometimes made on our behalf by ▬▬▬▬ [likely "USAID"] has such contacts at home and abroad because of the nature of its activities (training of foreign police/security personnel at home and abroad), and its Public Safety programs around the world.
>
> ▬ has such contacts at home—local and federal level—because its personnel are personally acquainted with law enforcement officers throughout the United States. Members of the ▬▬▬▬ have appeared as guest lecturers at such federal institutions as the U.S. Park Police, IPA, the U.S. Secret Service, and the U.S. Treasury Enforcement Division. (CIA 1973: 599)

Angleton described Dan Mitrione as "a bona fide OPS/AID officer assigned to the AID mission in Uruguay, and was never a CIA employee or agent" (599). Mitrione was a USAID "policing" specialist who worked with the CIA to teach South American anticommunists the arts of interrogation and torture, until he was kidnapped and murdered by the Tupamaros while working on a USAID assignment in Uruguay, advising Uruguayan police on the use of torture techniques when conducting interrogations. Mitrione was the shadowy archetypal American torturer, providing the basis for the Philip Michael Santore character in Costa-Gavras's film *State of Siege* (1973) (Norman 2005).

Angleton also described a joint CIA-USAID training program for foreign law enforcement personnel in which CIA personnel taught counterterrorism tactics, techniques for making booby traps, methods for neutralizing explosives, and so forth. Angleton indicated that the course had "26 participants from ten (10) foreign countries. Nine (9) are financed by AID, eight (8) by CIA and nine (9) by their own governments" (CIA 1973: 601). The CIA estimated that about seven hundred foreign police officers received training each year in this CIA/USAID program (602). "The Family Jewels" included portions of a chapter by

James R. Schlesinger ("Strategic Leverage from Aid and Trade") in which he argued that foreign aid could be used for policy leverage (J. R. Schlesinger 1963, reproduced in CIA 1973: 608).

Other CIA sources detail how USAID worked with the CIA during the Cold War. William R. Johnson, a CIA veteran, described USAID missions as a "major source of information" providing intelligence directly from in-country sources (1976: 50; see also 63–64, 66). Victor Marchetti and John Marks described how during the 1960s and 1970s in Laos and Vietnam, the CIA's "Clandestine Services had a fairly clear idea of how many local tribesmen were in its pay, but the operators were never quite certain of the total number of mercenaries they were financing through the agency's numerous support programs, some of which were fronted for by the Department of Defense, the Agency for International Development, and, of course, the CIA proprietary, Air America" (1974: 87).

Several former CIA employees later described the agency's close relationship with USAID in the 1960s and 1970s, with DCI Helms testifying before the Senate Foreign Relations Committee in 1970 that the CIA had used USAID as cover for operations in Laos (Marchetti and Marks 1974: 90; Prados 1986: 292). Former CIA agent Philip Agee (1975: 264) detailed how USAID functioned as a front for CIA work in Ecuador in the 1960s. Marchetti and Marks described a CIA employee who sometimes "posed as an official of the Agency for International Development to entrap unsuspecting [National Student Association] officers, revealing his 'cover' only after extracting pledges of secrecy and even [National Student Association] commitments to cooperate with specific CIA programs" (1974: 77).[11] Ted Shackley, a CIA operative, described how in the 1960s, the CIA in Southeast Asia worked with the USAID on counterinsurgency operations, at times transferring CIA funds to USAID for needed projects (Shackley and Finney 2005: 108–9). In other instances, Shackley took locals who had been hired by USAID to work on agricultural development projects and used them to gather intelligence for the CIA; in one instance he relocated them from working on vegetable gardens to working as "trail watchers" gathering CIA intelligence (Corn 1994: 144–45). Sometimes, CIA pilots operating illegally in Laos were paid through USAID contracts; by the early 1970s, USAID had provided Air America with more than $83 million for chartered flights (Blum 1995: 142; Marchetti and Marks 1974: 168).

At times USAID was a channel used to secretly fund CIA-supported programs. The CIA used USAID as cover when funding their agent Tony Poe in Laos, and CIA operations in Laos depended on networks maintained by USAID (Branfman 1975: 57–58, 64). During the 1960s, Sam Wilson, chief of USAID's Pacification Program in Vietnam, used his USAID position to coordinate elements of the Intelligence Coordination and Exploitation Program (also known as ICEX) assassination program linked to CORDS and the Phoenix Program (Trento 2001: 339). In 1963, USAID began oversight of the CIA's Vietnamese defector program (named Chieu Hoi, "open arms"), which combined field recruitment techniques with political indoctrination (Valentine 1990: 51). While employed by USAID in the late 1960s, John Paul Vann, a retired U.S. Army lieutenant colonel, helped oversee the U.S. military's CORDS counterinsurgency program designed to pacify resistance in South Vietnam (Milne 2008: 2004). A 1967 address by CIA officer Richard Bissell to the Council on Foreign Relations described the CIA's reliance on public and private institutions to provide "deep cover" for agency operations. Bissell described the use of nonsecret "exchange-of-persons programs" through which foreigners are exposed to American ideas. Among the organizations involved in these open exchanges was USAID, and at times the CIA was also secretly involved in these exchanges. In a passage originally redacted by CIA censors but restored in their published book, Marchetti and Marks explained, "On occasion, the agency [i.e., CIA] will sponsor the training of foreign officials at the facilities of another government agency. A favorite site is AID's International Police Academy in Washington. The academy is operated by AID's Public Safety (police) Division, which regularly supplies cover to CIA operators all over the world. And the CIA takes advantage of exchange programs to recruit agents" (1974: 81).

Frank Wisner, chief of the CIA's Office of Policy Coordination (the CIA's covert action division), at times used USAID to direct funds to foreign students attending universities in the United States, under an operation through which the CIA would later establish contacts with students the agency hoped would return home and assume positions of power. William Corson, a retired marine lieutenant colonel and a onetime deputy director of the Southeast Asia Intelligence Force, later claimed that many of these students were "'recruited' by blackmail and coercive techniques"—though further evidence of this claimed practice is lacking (1977: 310–11).

The Agency for International Development functioned in tandem with the CIA so well that after the CIA was caught in 1967 secretly passing funds to the AFL-CIO in order to "create counter-revolutionary labor movements in under-developed countries," USAID publicly carried on what had previously been the CIA's covert role in this operation (Greider 1969, A1). The CIA had formerly used the Andrew Hamilton Fund (a CIA front) to finance the Granary Fund, which acted as a conduit to pass money to Retail Clerks International to finance CIA-backed international labor programs, and USAID took up this CIA work without difficulty. According to William Greider, writing for the *Washington Post*, "This 'union to union' diplomacy, 'uninhibited by formal Governmental relations,' as one AID official explained, is just the sort of thing which the Central Intelligence Agency used to pay for secretly — before the CIA's cover was blown [in 1967] and it had to abandon its network of dummy foundations" (1969, A1). The CIA, and later USAID, backed labor unions not because the capitalists it protected wanted labor unions but because they were a useful tool to agitate its communist enemies.

Gifts of Coercion

A half decade after the Church and Pike congressional investigations documented multiple connections between USAID and intelligence agencies, Father George Cotter, a Maryknoll Catholic priest who had worked for years on humanitarian projects in Latin America and East Africa, described the interactions between humanitarian development projects, USAID, and the CIA that he had witnessed during the Cold War. Cotter observed that CIA agents rarely visited missionaries in the field, instead establishing contact through the nongovernmental organizations with which missionaries worked. He described the connections between humanitarian-based missionaries, nongovernmental organizations, and intelligence agencies as "silken threads which grow into strings. With such strings, spies can fish out sensitive information about leaders" in regions that were of special interest to the CIA and others (Cotter 1981: 324). Cotter wrote that his curiosity led him

> to learn about sources of funds for mission work, I spent two years visiting private voluntary organizations (PVOS) in Europe, Canada and the United States. Many directors of American organizations told me they had received government grants. These grants enabled the PVOS to fund certain types of church work. During these years I also attended a course given by USAID on how to write project proposals, and I studied USAID's practices. Around this time I learned that its administrator, John Gilligan, had said that the agency had served as a sort of graduate school for CIA agents. "At one time, many AID field offices were infiltrated from top to bottom with CIA people," he said. "It was pretty well known in the agency who they were and what they were up to.... The idea was to plant operatives in every kind of activity we had overseas, government, volunteer, religious, every kind." His statements startled me. (321)

Father Cotter understood that because some American humanitarian groups received funds from USAID, their reports made the groups they assisted legible to USAID, and through USAID, this information was passed along to the CIA (321–22). He described USAID as "the CIA's little sister" (323), and he worried that those working on humanitarian and assistance projects were being "plugged into an information network that starts with the U.S. government and to which the CIA is connected" (322).

Cotter also understood that the CIA valued missionaries because, like anthropologists, they tended to "spend years working with grass-roots people and helping the unfortunates among them, they win trust and confidence. People will tell them about their hopes and fears, about village happenings, and about whatever there is of interest. They learn who are the most promising leaders, what are the region's problems, and they are often given access to people and areas closed to most outsiders. This is the information wanted by the CIA, and wanted in steadily flowing streams" (Cotter 1981: 323–24). While groups such as Anthropologists for Radical Political Action (see chapter 13) developed critiques of military-linked anthropological projects, at times singling out USAID projects directly linked to war zone counterinsurgency operations, during the Cold War, American anthropologists were slow to develop such broad critiques of the ways that modernization theory, USAID, and other development projects directly and indirectly connected with the CIA and Cold War politics.

Modernization theory provided a philosophical justification for hundreds of development projects in which anthropologists played supportive roles on the ground. This work seldom required anthropologists to critically evaluate the successes or failures of their projects: they simply needed to complete assigned work in a well-funded bureaucratic process of institutional self-replicating reification. Some applied anthropologists found themselves serving as cheerleaders of progress, or working as apologists for the failures of the Green Revolution, facilitating evacuations of indigenous peoples in the way of hydraulic projects, acting as brokers for overpriced irrigation or technology transfer projects, or advising the World Bank, International Monetary Fund, or major corporations interested in "developing" new markets and sources of (or dumping ground for) goods in the Third World. Perhaps the most measurable outcome of modernization theory's development projects was underdeveloped nations' posture of alignment — through debt and policy control, not Rostow's claimed goals of economic development (see Frank 1997; Ross 1998a; D. H. Price 2007a).

The national debts created by many of modernization theory's development projects had a greater societal impact than the intended demographic, social, health, economic, or agricultural benefits. Development strategies built on debt damaged the autonomy and health of underdeveloped nations as the creditors set and manipulated national policies, ranging from setting food prices to determining debtor nations' military policies. As Eric Ross states in his analysis of Cold War applied anthropology's Vicos project in Peru, that project was "far more productive for the discipline (and its need for professional status) than it has been — and should have been — for those it studied" (2011: 149).

While development, modernization, and USAID brought anthropologists working on international projects into the CIA's orbit of influence, the Cold War also brought other, more direct, connections between anthropologists and the CIA, as some anthropologists made careers working within the CIA.

INTERMEZZO

On Christmas Day, 1966, anthropologist Elizabeth Bacon wrote Ralph Beals a letter containing the following short historical overview:

> Before World II, the U.S. had little in the way of intelligence for limited activities of the Army and Navy. Even the State Department had no resident representatives in some areas, relying on British or other consular and diplomatic officers to care for the occasional American traveler. With U.S. entry into World War II, U.S. interest became global. The State Department opened legations where it had had none before, and raided the universities for area specialists to staff the Washington office. The first attempt at organizing an information agency, COI (Coordinator of Information), proved too cumbersome, and was divided to form OWI (Office of War Information), a propaganda agency, and OSS (Office of Strategic Services).
>
> OSS had five branches: R&A (Research and Analysis); SI (Secret Intelligence); and three cloak and dagger branches whose exploits have been widely publicized, most recently by Allen Dulles' new book. SI, the fact-gathering branch, and R&A, the analysis branch, worked together quite closely; they had no contacts with the cloak and dagger branches. At the end of the war, R&A was taken over by State, where it became OIR (Office of Intelligence Research). SI and the cloak and dagger branches formed the basis of CIA (Central Intelligence Agency).
>
> The dangers of subordinating fact-gathering to planners conditioned by experience and temperament to daredevil exploits are obvious. The imbalance was accentuated by the fact that most of the R&A people did not remain with OIR. A majority returned to academia; others transferred to other governmental departments where research was less subject to the vagaries of political crises. Not surprisingly, CIA flowed in OIR to fill the vacuum.
>
> For example, it had been discovered during the war, in areas not involved in fighting, that much useful intelligence could be obtained openly more readily than secretly. After the war, a new type of post was established in the State

Department, that of research attaché. This, as far as I know, worked well enough. No government would object to a research attaché any more than it would object to a military attaché. But when the Eisenhower administration came into office, with John Foster Dulles [as] Secretary of State, and adventure-minded brother Allen head of CIA, this position was abolished "for economy reasons." This, of course, meant turning over to CIA the open fact-gathering activities which State was trying to develop. The present resident CIA agent in Afghanistan is presumably doing the work of research attaché. If he had that title, there would be no problem. Instead, he operates under three academic covers (one a front organization, the other two bona fide academic institutions), and proclaims himself an anthropologist at the top of his voice.

... With the vast expansion of intelligence activities during World War II, there was an urgent need for personnel with real experience. The people who had this background and were able to use it effectively were to a considerable extent academics and other professionals. At the end of the war one might have expected a program to train professional operatives who, with varied covers, could settle in a country and blend into the landscape. Instead, the emphasis seems to be on "quickie" operations, to get information on areas where the need is immediate, using the easiest cover that comes to mind.

There have, of course, been training programs usually with the emphasis on language. You will perhaps remember the number of special language training programs for "businessmen and government officials" that burgeoned among the universities after World War II. There are still plenty of intensive programs for "exotic" languages (vide the last ACLS Newsletter for next summer's programs). It would be interesting to discover what proportions of the students enrolled in such programs are casuals — that is, not graduate students planning to specialize in an area or teach languages.

Before World War II, there were very few area programs in the U.S. The Army ASTP during the war gave great impetus to area studies, and after the war a number of area programs were established in universities around the country. Also the Ford Foundation set up its program for Foreign Area Training. In some universities the area programs were presumably set up on the initiative of university personnel. In others, it seems likely that CIA provided the *initiative. I suspect this of one university, and consider it possible that the UCLA Middle East Center may have this background.*

... To sum up, CIA is conducting its intelligence operations as if it were a cloak and dagger organization in wartime and seems never to have adjusted to the normal peacetime pattern of other countries, of trained professional agents located permanently at strategic locations. Instead, it seems to be going in for "saturation coverage," sending everyone it can find into strategic areas. For years, the proliferation of CIA and psychological warfare people in Bangkok has been notorious. In Saigon there are bars patronized only by CIA operatives. And these operatives are so obvious that everyone knows who they are. I have heard the same stories of obviousness from parts of Africa....

Anthropological research is certainly being endangered by the activities of CIA. (RB 75, EB to RB 12/25/66)

PART II ANTHROPOLOGISTS' ARTICULATIONS WITH THE NATIONAL SECURITY STATE

Most of the knowledge of the outside world that the CIA collects it collects by social-science research methods, that is, through reading newspapers, listening to radio broadcasts, and asking people questions. Social research including area studies, history, anthropology, sociology, political science, and statistics provides both important inputs and important knowledge of methods of analysis to the intelligence community. The CIA, as its name implies, should be the central social research organization to enable the federal government to understand the societies and cultures of the world.

ITHIEL DE SOLA POOL | 1967

SIX COLD WAR ANTHROPOLOGISTS AT THE CIA

Careers Confirmed and Suspected

To understand how some American anthropologists came to work for the CIA during the early Cold War, it is necessary to consider anthropologists' wartime experience and to disentangle what the Cold War became from what it appeared to be to those living through its earliest days. From the present we can see distinct differences between America's World War II fight against totalitarianism and Cold War America's increasing support for neocolonialism, but for many who had served in military or intelligence capacities during the war, the nation's shifts in postwar international political orientation was invisible.

For anthropologists who served in the Office of Strategic Services, Office of War Information, G2, or other wartime intelligence agencies, later being approached by the CIA for debriefings upon returning from fieldwork in foreign lands, or joining the agency, often seemed like a natural extension of wartime work. While anthropologists' interactions with the CIA raise significant ethical questions today, the steps that led postwar anthropologists to these engagements raised few concerns at the time. During the earliest transitions from hot to cold war, news of these decisions by anthropologists and others to join the CIA often remained public.

One *New York Times* article from 1950 announcing recipients of grant awards from the Guggenheim Fund listed "Dr. Edward Wyllys Andrews 4th, division chief, Central Intelligence Agency, Washington. Early Maya archaeology in northern Yucatan" as the recipient of one of three anthropological/archaeological awards that year (NYT 1950: 15). In 1948, a "News of the Members" column in the *News Bulletin of the* AAA carried the following entry: "James Andrews left Cambridge late in December, 1947 to join the Central Intelligence Agency, Washington. For more than a year prior to that time he had been in charge of the Anthropometric Laboratory, Department of Anthropology, Harvard University, in which 50,000 separatees are being somatotyped for the Quartermaster Corps under direction of E. A. Hooton" (NBAAA 1948 2[2]: 27).[1] This same issue of the *News Bulletin* announced that Eugene Worman was leaving the University of Chicago for the CIA (NBAAA 1948 2[2]: 30). In later years, anthropologists who moved in and out of the CIA did so quietly, without public announcements or fanfare. Some anthropologists moved between the agency and the academy; others moved between the agency and private consulting or research positions.

Several archaeologists and cultural anthropologists established careers within the CIA, offering valuable skill sets ranging from aptitudes for envisioning complex systems from sample data sets to analytical linguistic skills that were needed for translation or cryptographic work. Richard Hallock, an archaeologist trained at the University of Chicago, used skills he had developed in translating dead languages in his work on deciphering Soviet encrypted VENONA intercepts. During the 1950s, Waldo Dubberstein left a career in archaeology to work as a CIA intelligence analyst, though he later became embroiled in scandal for his associations with former CIA agent turned arms dealer Edwin P. Wilson, who was convicted in 1983 of arms smuggling, specifically, shipping twenty tons of plastic explosives to Libya (Ayres 1983).[2]

Archaeologist Richard Francis Strong Starr served in the Office of Naval Intelligence during the war; after the war, he became a research specialist on the Middle East at the State Department and the CIA (Saxon 1994). The CIA offered anthropologist Charlotte Gower job opportunities that were rare for women in the postwar years (Lepowsky 2000).[3] William Sidney Stallings Jr. worked for years as a dendrochrologist at the Laboratory of Anthropology in Santa Fe, later joining the CIA's Photographic Intelligence Division, where his group identified the Russian missiles at the heart of the Cuban missile crisis (Browman and Williams 2013: 425).

Sometimes, spousal CIA connections brought travel or research opportunities. Marjory Cline, a longtime research editor at the National Geographic Society, was married to CIA employee Ray S. Cline and accompanied him on numerous assignments, including moves to England (1958) and Taipei, where he became the new CIA station chief. When Ray Cline took on the responsibility of running Chiang Ching-kuo as a major CIA asset, Marjorie Cline became Ching-kuo's English tutor (Taylor 2000: 239). Ray Cline later became the deputy director of intelligence at the CIA (Quirk et al. 1986: i). During the Second World War, Derwood Lockard did intelligence work for ONI and OSS, and after the war he extended this work at the CIA. In 1954, he returned to the academy, working on Middle Eastern ethnography and archaeology (D. H. Price 2008a: 221; Browman and Williams 2013: 429). He worked on archaeological projects in Iran and Turkey and accompanied his wife, Barbara Lockard, on several Middle Eastern archaeological projects; in 1967, he became associate director of Harvard's Center of Middle East Studies, where he worked until his retirement in the early 1970s (Browman and Williams 2013: 429).

Anthropological research was sometimes used in CIA training programs. In response to my FOIA request, the CIA released a declassified program from a 1963 midcareer training course that included sessions on current political and economic developments. One daylong presentation was made by an anthropologist (identity redacted) in a session titled "American Problems in Understanding Foreign Cultures," described in the program bulletin as "an anthropological view of the newly developing countries with emphasis on their deep-seated cultural characteristics." This anthropologist's presentation lasted from 9:00 AM until 3:30 PM, followed by discussion and a reception. The supplemental readings accompanying this presentation consisted of Ruth Benedict's essay "The Growth of Culture" (1956), Margaret Mead's article "The Underdeveloped and the Overdeveloped" (1962), and George Murdock's "How Culture Changes," (1956) as well as Brookings Institution publications on development (Brookings Institution 1962), Dan Kurzman's *Subversion of the Innocents* (1963), Max Millikan and Donald Blackmer's book *The Emerging Nations* (1961), and Eugene Staley's book *The Future of Undeveloped Countries* (1961) (CIA 1963c).

Staley, Millikan, Blackmer, and the Brookings Institution provided a baseline for Rostow-derived, CIA-backed modernization schemes. Murdock's sunny cultural evolutionary model provided a simplistic "great man" view of culture change for CIA trainees who would soon be looking for interlocutors in the underdeveloped world. Mead's article "The Underdeveloped and the Overdeveloped," which had been published in *Foreign Affairs*, situated global inequality by downplaying determinants of global stratification, arguing that economic development could bring wealth to all, not simply exacerbate and continue internal and global stratification. Mead's article also argued that "riches are no longer somebody's disproportionate, though legitimate, share of a scarce supply; poverty is no longer the consequence of someone else having a large proportion of the existing supply" (1962: 81; CIA 1963c).

Anthropologists at CIA Desks

Several anthropologists established careers at CIA desk jobs, working as analysts, or in other capacities within the agency's bureaucracy. Most of these careers developed as extensions of wartime work.

The child of American missionaries, Eugene Clark Worman Jr. was born in and lived the first dozen years of his life in India. He studied anthropology as an undergraduate at Harvard, then did graduate research in Central Europe, India, and New Mexico. When the war interrupted his studies, he served at the U.S. Navy Division of Naval Intelligence tracking Japanese naval and merchant marine positions. At the war's end he completed his dissertation, "The Problem of a Neolithic Culture in India" (1946), and undertook NRC-funded research connecting Indian prehistory with the prehistory of other areas in the Near East and Far East (NBAAA 1947 1[3]: 5).

Worman took a visiting professorship at Chicago, filling in for Robert Braidwood while he conducted an excavation in Iraq, and in the summer of 1948, Worman joined the CIA (NBAAA 1948 2[1]: 30). The CIA drew upon Worman's academic and anthropological skills. Beyond his analyst duties, Eugene Worman also became the official historian of the CIA's Office of Current Intelligence, writing the agency's internal, five-volume unpublished, but completed in 1971, "History of the Office of Current Intelligence" (see Westerfield 200: 126–27n18).[4] Worman remained active in the AAA while working at the CIA; in 1950–53, he served as the AAA's representative to the American Association for the Advancement of Science and was appointed as the AAA's delegate to the National Conference on Citizenship (NBAAA 1950 4[4]: 6; BAAA 1952 2[3]: 2; AA 1951 53[4]: 454; AA 1952 54[2]: 289; AA 1952 54[3]: 307).

Worman's dual position, working within the CIA while acting as an official representing the AAA on national committees, did not raise concerns within the association. His CIA connections were known within the AAA (see Worman to Stout 11/7/51; NBAAA 1952 6[4]: 12–13).[5] The 1951 report of the Anthropological Society of Washington noted that Eugene Worman (then a full-time CIA employee) organized a speaker series held at the U.S. National Museum (Gilbert 1951: 309). Worman hosted George Murdock, who described his fieldwork in Truk; Ralph Soleki, speaking on "ancient man in Northern Alaska"; Duncan Emrich on folklore; Frank Setzer on aboriginal Australia; Cornelius Osgood presented a paper titled "Koreans and Their Culture"; Schuyler Cammann, who spoke on "Tiber, the Land and Its People"; and George Foster, who gave his "Ethnographic Impressions of Spain" (Gilbert 1951: 309).

James Madison Andrews IV worked as a Peabody Museum archaeologist before joining the ONI during the war. After a brief return to archaeology at the war's end, he joined the CIA in 1948 and worked at the agency until retiring in 1957.[6] At the CIA, Andrews directed the Office of Collection and Dissemination (OCD); as discussed in chapter 3, he was mentioned as one of the CIA's anthropologists who could help facilitate communications between the agency and the AAA during the association's membership roster project in 1951 (AAAP 6. WH to FJ 3/2/51; Darling 1990: 328; Montague 1992: 183). Andrews rose to the position of assistant director of the CIA, where he "was in charge of development of programs for automated information retrieval. He received the Intelligence Medal of Merit for his service" (AN Oct. 1988, 4; see also Browman and Williams 2013: 435).

As director at OCD, Andrews transformed the structural organization and functioning of the CIA. While directing OCD, he was at the forefront of recognizing the vital role that computers could play in organizing all variety of databases and records, serving as "an enthusiastic advocate of the use of business machines for the indexing, retrieval, and analysis of information" (Montague 1992: 182). Agency historian Ludwell Montague credited Andrews with fundamentally reshaping how the CIA undertook the collection and distribution of intelligence data, ending institutional practices wherein holders of intelligence had certain control of its uses. According to Montague, "Andrews sought to instill in OCD personnel the idea that OCD existed only to serve the other components of the CIA, and the departmental agencies as well, insofar as practicable. They must forget about pretensions to superior coordinating authority and do their utmost to service every demand or request that came to them, no matter what the source" (1992: 182). Andrews argued for building an independent OCD that would collect, catalog, and distribute intelligence data and academic sources from within the collection of documents he helped the agency amass. He convinced DCI Walter Bedell Smith to ignore a recommendation made by NSC 50 (a 1949 document also known as The McNarney Report, recommending significant restructuring of the CIA) and the Dulles Report to disband OCD and localize the collection and organization of intelligence data (Montague 1992: 181).

Anthropologists did not always garner respect from others within the CIA. In his memoir recalling his years at the agency, Dino Brugioni described DCI Smith's distaste for Andrews. According to Brugioni, Smith mistakenly thought Andrews was an ornithologist and considered him too much of an academic, who wrote "with a flowery flourish." Brugioni continued: "Smith sent back one of Andrews' papers with an attached note: 'This is the biggest pile of unadulterated crap I've ever read.' He once remarked that he had hoped for an energetic go-getter in collection, but they had hired a 'fucking birdwatcher'" (Brugioni 2010: 38).

Harvard-trained archaeologist E. Wyllys Andrews IV, who had served the OSS in Africa and Europe, joined the CIA when it was first formed (Stirling 1973: 295). Andrews later claimed he stayed with the CIA for only a few years and returned to archaeology for the remainder of his career. One report of his CIA years described him as working for the "CIA for several years after the war, working in Africa and the Middle East, finally leaving the CIA in 1955 to accept a position at [the Middle American Research Institute] at Tulane" (Browman and Williams 2013: 410). Claims by scholars that they left CIA careers and returned to life outside the agency are often met with skepticism and are difficult to evaluate conclusively. There is a well-documented history of the CIA using former employees, especially those who travel to exotic locations or have contacts with persons of interest to the agency, for agency business (see Winks 1987; A. C. Mills 1991; Lawrence 1979). While the extent of Andrews's connections with the CIA after he left the agency is unknown, one set of CIA records (released by FOIA researchers investigating the assassination of President John F. Kennedy) indicate that Professor Andrews was in contact with a CIA employee in Mexico City in 1962, years after he stated he ceased working for the agency (FOIA CIA 104–10419–10321). This released CIA record does not state the nature of this contact beyond describing Andrews as a "reputable American businessman in Mexico" who had been in contact with Richard C. Cain (the subject of the CIA's inquiry).[7] While the nature of this contact remains unclear, it demonstrates the agency's practice of recontacting individuals with past CIA connections when agency needs arise at later dates, a practice that raises questions about the possibility of such contacts with anthropologists who were former CIA employees.

CIA Anthropologists in the World at Large

Frank Bessac served in the OSS in China during the Second World War. When the OSS was disbanded at the war's end, Bessac moved to the War Department's

Strategic Services Unit, later joining the Secret Intelligence Branch, where he was assigned duties as an intelligence officer in Shanghai (NARA FBI 9/11/46). Bessac maintained that he first joined the CIA in July 1947 after he was recruited by his old OSS handler, Marge Kennedy.[8] As part of Bessac's spycraft training, Kennedy provided him with a protocol phrase and reply to identify fellow CIA agents in the field. Kennedy and Bessac "agreed that in the fall of 1947 Frank would be a student in Peking's Fujen University, and that would also be his cover. The Outfit [CIA] would pay his return to China and keep him on the payroll" (Laird 2002: 42).

Bessac later claimed he had misgivings about using his status as a student in China as his CIA cover, telling his superiors that "he simply did not enjoy looking at China through the lens of government employment" (Laird 2002: 52). He later claimed he resigned from the CIA in October 1947, but this assertion seems contradicted by many of his later actions in China.

In 1948, Bessac traveled in Inner Mongolia and worked for the United Nations Relief and Rehabilitation Administration, and he continued to study in China with his Fulbright scholarship in the fall. Bessac's travels to Inner Mongolia have obvious political interpretations given his admission of having already agreed to work as a paid CIA contractor and the American intelligence community's interest in gathering up-to-date intelligence on Chinese Communists' rapid advances. While Bessac later insisted that his travels and UN work in Inner Mongolia had nothing to do with the CIA, Sechin Jagchid, a Mongol with direct knowledge of U.S. intelligence activities in Inner Mongolia supporting Prince De during the late 1940s, dismissed Bessac's claims, arguing that Bessac worked for a CIA agent named Raymond Meitz in Inner Mongolia in 1948–49 (see Jagchid 1999: 410).[9]

In the fall of 1949, waves of Americans were evacuated from China as Mao's soldiers seized control of rural and urban areas. Yet instead of joining his fellow expatriates' exodus to ships leaving China's eastern coastal cities, in September 1949, Bessac headed west to the interior. Bessac flew to Tihwa, where he was met by Vice Consul Douglas Mackiernan. Bessac claimed this meeting with Mackiernan was pure chance. Mackiernan brought Bessac to the Tihwa American consul compound, where over the course of a few days they hurriedly burned consul documents and destroyed vehicles, radios, and other U.S. equipment before the impending arrival of Chinese Communist troops.

Using State Department cover, the CIA sent agent Douglas Mackiernan to the outer reaches of western China with top secret equipment designed to monitor the Soviet Union's eastern Kazakh region, searching for indications of the

Soviets' anticipated first nuclear bomb test. With this equipment, on August 29, 1949, Mackiernan detected the Soviet Union's first successful detonation of a nuclear weapon in Semipalatinsk, Kazakhstan.

Using the CIA's secret identification pass-phrase protocol that Bessac had learned in his 1947 CIA training, Mackiernan identified himself to Bessac as a CIA operative. Bessac's response confirmed his CIA identity to Mackiernan, an act that complicated Bessac's later claims that he was not then a CIA agent (Laird 2002: 109).[10] Bessac's 2006 account of how he joined the CIA, resigned from the CIA, traveled in China on a Fulbright scholarship, and then rejoined the agency only after meeting up with Mackiernan strains credulity and raises questions about whether this story was later concocted to smooth over the ethical and legal problems of a Fulbright scholar spying for the CIA abroad.[11] As Bessac later argued, when Mackiernan approached him with his secret CIA code phrase, if he "was recruiting me again as an agent for the CIA, asking me to take on a mission, he should have outlined the task, the conditions of employment, government employment, with payroll taxes and a pension, the whole bit" (Bessac and Bessac 2006: 51). Bessac claimed that upon his reply, "Doug just asked, 'Do you want to join Osman Bator (the great Kazakh leader of Chinese Turkestan) with me? Maybe we can be of assistance to him.' That was all, but enough for me" (51).

Because the CIA operated on a strict "need to know basis," Bessac's knowledge of the mission he undertook was limited, but he joined Mackiernan and Osman Bator and a group of White Russians and Mongols, packing gold, machine guns and an assortment of other light arms, ammunition, hand grenades, a shortwave radio, and Geiger counters on an overland trip to Tibet. Bessac loosely understood the group's mission to be supportive of Tibetan nationalism in the face of what appeared to be an impending Chinese occupation. Mackiernan sewed a small fortune in gold wafers into his clothing and other hiding places, to be used to finance their mission as they traveled.

In January 1950, the Chinese press denounced Mackiernan as an American spy. The group avoided capture by Chinese forces during their eleven-month, fifteen-hundred-mile trek across the Kara Desert toward Shegarkhung Lung, and then to Lhasa, Tibet. They entered Tibet in April 1950, and during an encounter with Tibetan border scouts Mackiernan was shot and killed, and another member of their party, Vasili Zvansov, was seriously wounded. This left Bessac cut off from the outside world, with limited mission knowledge and no understanding of the CIA's encoded radio contact protocols. These Tibetan forces captured Bessac and took him prisoner, but he was treated as an honored guest after the Department of State contacted the Tibetan government.

Bessac, who remained in Tibet from April to July 1950, was one of only a few Westerners to visit Tibet before the Chinese occupation. He had an audience with the Dalai Lama and held closed-door discussions with Tibetan officials. The Tibetans were desperate for U.S. military support in the face of an impending Chinese invasion. Bessac stressed that he was not an American governmental representative, but he also told his hosts that he would convey their concerns to U.S. officials after returning home (Laird 2002: 224).

Bessac's account of his trek in *Life* magazine stressed the high adventure of the journey, with no mention of the political dimensions of the mission or of Mackiernan being a CIA agent. Bessac wrote that he was in western Asia "to study Mongolian anthropology," claiming that he headed to Inner Mongolia from Chengtu after recovering from eye surgery because this was the region he considered "least likely to be bothered by the Communists" (Bessac 1950: 131). His account provided scintillating details of going days without water, the ravages of an all-meat diet, ongoing sickness, monotonously trudging onward in the freezing cold, Mackiernan's killing, and Bessac's audience with the Dalai Lama.

In 2006, the CIA publicly recognized Douglas Mackiernan as the first CIA agent killed in the line of duty. The agency revealed Mackiernan's name in its "Book of Honor," which listed, usually without publicly providing names, CIA agents killed while serving the agency (Dujmovic 2008: 7).

After returning to the United States, Bessac studied anthropology at the University of California, Berkeley, later earning his doctorate at the University of Wisconsin, briefly teaching in Texas and Kansas before becoming a professor of anthropology at the University of Montana, where he remained from 1970 to 1989. Throughout his life, Bessac insisted he had not traveled to China using a Fulbright scholarship as cover for CIA activities.

There are credibility problems with Bessac's claim that he resigned from the CIA in October 1947, so soon after he joined. For instance, Bessac's insistence that he had not traveled to China using a Fulbright scholarship as cover for CIA activities contradicts the fact that the CIA later paid him for his entire service in China and Tibet, and, more significantly, that he responded to his CIA recognition code and agreed to undertake a risky CIA mission.[12]

Former CIA agent Frank Latrash rejected Bessac's claim that he had not been a CIA agent while studying under a Fulbright fellowship. As described by

Thomas Laird, the CIA told Latrash in 1950 "that Frank Bessac was a contract CIA agent using Fulbright cover. He claims that this is the very reason why Bessac is so insistent that he was not a CIA agent — it was, and is illegal for the CIA to use a Fulbright scholarship as cover for any agent" (2002: 103).

Louis Dupree

Louis Dupree began World War II in the Merchant Marine, later joining the army's Eleventh Airborne Division fighting in the Philippines. During the decade following the war, he studied archaeology at Harvard, earning his bachelor's, master's, and doctoral degrees. He first traveled to Afghanistan with an archaeological expedition in 1949, and over the next decades he traveled and at times lived in Afghanistan, conducting cultural and archaeological research. Dupree conducted archaeological excavations in Afghanistan throughout the 1950s, and his years of excavations and publications earned him the reputation of a central figure in Afghanistan anthropology.

Dupree maintained military ties after the war, teaching at Air University and writing numerous publications for Air University's Force's Arctic, Desert, Tropic Information Center, and organized the Society for Applied Anthropology's 1958 session on "Anthropology in the Armed Services" (see chapter 3). During the decades after the war, he became the American anthropologist who spent the greatest amount of time in Afghanistan. His luxurious home in Kabul was a regular stop for Western visitors, and his daily regime of five o'clock cocktails for all comers made him a central collector of expatriate gossip and political rumors. Dupree's report "Anthropology in Afghanistan" (1976) for the American Universities Field Staff (AUFS) described the previous decades of anthropological work in Afghanistan, and his ethnographic map served as the source for numerous reprinted governmental and military maps for years to come (L. Dupree 1976: 5).

Dupree published numerous scholarly reports and skillfully cultivated media coverage of his archaeological discoveries. His primary research affiliation was with the AUFS, a research consortium that combined the resources of scholars from eleven universities, established with funds from the Crane Foundation,[13] with headquarters in Hanover, New Hampshire, and a field office in Kabul.[14] CIA documents establish that one of the ways AUFS interfaced with the CIA was to hold "private round table meetings[s] on political developments," with select invitations issued to CIA personnel (FOIA CIA-RDP80B01676R004000060031-0, 9/15/58). With the support of the AUFS, Dupree maintained a home in Kabul from the 1950s until 1978. Dupree also maintained affiliations with the Archaeological Mission of the American Museum of Natural History in Afghanistan project (JLA, Box 10).

Anthropologist M. Jamil Hanifi has described his first meeting with Dupree, after Hanifi left his native Afghanistan and arrived at Michigan State University to begin graduate work in political science in 1961. Dupree was a guest speaker in a class taught by Wesley Fischel in which Hanifi was enrolled (MJH to DHP 11/5/05).[15] Hanifi found it strange that when they first met, Dupree grilled him for information on Afghanistan's intelligence services, pointedly asking whether Hanifi planned to later work for the intelligence service. Hanifi's studies were sponsored by the Afghan Ministry of Finance, and he told Dupree that he had no intention of working for the intelligence service. Dupree then asked Hanifi to recommend a translator for him to use in Kabul, which he did. According to Hanifi, he "has vivid memories of Dupree going around the country photographing Afghan defense installations and facilities" (MJH to DHP 11/4/050).

Anthropologist John Allison (2012) later described how Dupree, while a visiting professor of anthropology at Indiana University, recruited Allison, with promises of well-funded fieldwork opportunities, to begin fieldwork in Afghanistan. As an anthropology graduate student, Allison traveled with Dupree in 1969 through Kandahar and Herat to Maimana, where they conducted archaeological excavations of a cave site. Allison and his wife traveled by Land Rover into remote regions of Afghanistan with Louis and Nancy Dupree, members of the Kabul Museum and American archaeologists, and others claiming archaeological expertise. According to Allison, "One had an interest in ceramics, another seemed not especially interested in talking about his work; I don't recall their names. They didn't seem to participate in the excavation much, and were often gone off in their Land Rovers" (2012).

A man claiming to be the team's ceramics expert — who "liked to show off his martial arts skills"— got drunk one night and admitted "he was actually there to do ground-proofing and local village investigations around the area to see if it was a possible emergency landing place for a U-2, if necessary" (JA to DHP 11/12/07). Allison combined archaeological excavations with small ethnographic surveys and photographic inventories under the direction of Dupree. He later conducted ethnographic linguistic field research among the Ashkun in the Hindu Kush, all with advice, introductions, and a field assistant (Mohammad Alam Nuristani, a Kabul University anthropology graduate student) provided by Dupree (Allison 2012).

Nuristani provided invaluable assistance, helping Allison gain access to people in this remote area; his solid knowledge of English, Dari, Pashto, and dialects of Kalasha gave Allison the sort of access that would have otherwise been impossible for an American outsider. Allison found that

> as a native speaker of the closely related Waigul people, Mohammad Alam gave us trusted access to the family homes, to the different special places, to work and to participate in gatherings and feasts.... Alam gave me sensitive and patient guidance in some of my understandings of the meanings of Ashkun concepts. He grasped the nature of ethnography and the cognitive nature of culture. He was from a leading family in Waigul, but his acceptance in the urban society of Kabul depended upon his intelligence and upon this charm that led those with power and influence to support his ambitions. His family had little power in Kabul. (2012)

With Nuristani's assistance, Allison collected a significant body of ethnographic data. In June 1970, Dupree convinced Allison that he and his wife needed to leave Afghanistan because of growing threats to Americans. Allison wanted to stay and complete the last six months of his planned eighteen-month study. He recalls that when he was finally persuaded to leave, he

> left a full box of 7 inch reels of tapes with Dupree, who assured me he would get them to me safely. They included a lot of info on the demography of the Alingar River basin area of Nuristan, the eastern edge of the Hindu Kush, where no one had ever done research before, and only one other had passed through that area of the Titin Valley, Schyler Jones, in 1964, simply hiked through and over the top to Waigal Valley. The tapes were never seen again. Dupree claimed he had them sent by diplomatic pouch. He might have done that, but [he] did not send them to me at Indiana University. Since, I have often wondered if that diplomatic pouch went to the CIA in DC. (JA to DHP 11/12/07)

Without his field notes and tapes, Allison was unable to complete his dissertation research.[16] Because international shipping from Afghanistan in the early 1970s was a precarious method for sending materials, Dupree told Allison he would ship his field notes using the secure U.S. embassy pouch. Dupree claimed he had no knowledge of why Allison never received these invaluable field notes (Allison 2012).

Allison later recalled that Dupree amassed a large collection of documents that would have great value to American military and intelligence agencies:

> Dupree and his co-operative colleagues used their access to Kabul government documents and files for US advantage; even when it was explicit that they were

not to make use of such sensitive data as air photos and maps developed from them, they stole copies of the entire set of air photos and topographic maps for all of Afghanistan.... He was part of the US Mission in Afghanistan long before the US was aware of Afghanistan. Charlie Wilson's War came and went late during Dupree's watch; and I think not without his participation. His ethics and morals were related to that foundation in the military Mission. Among his friends, he was always ethical and a Good Man, within that cultural world view and its priorities.... He was not an evil man if judged by his own value system, or a bad anthropologist in the sense of producing valuable works. His *Afghanistan* is still the standing authority in US/NATO on the history, archaeology and cultures of the Afghanistan that existed until 1978. (Allison 2012)

Allison did not learn of Dupree's reported CIA connections until reading Dupree's obituary some years after his death. This revelation helped Allison connect the dots between Dupree's life as an adventurer establishing connections throughout Afghanistan's backcountry, and the expatriates' and Afghan establishment's salons and parties.[17]

Dupree's years in Afghanistan suddenly ended on November 25, 1978, when he was apprehended and interrogated for five days by Afghan security under general accusations that his work with the AUFS was linked to American intelligence agencies. Dupree was questioned about his relationship to Nuristani, and the information he provided appears to have led to Nuristani's death (see Allison 2012; L. Dupree 1980a: 12). His interrogators asked a series of questions about Nuristani's time studying in the United States and about other Afghans Dupree had encountered at Indiana University over the years. Dupree provided many names to his interrogators — names of past students, landlords, and others he had known over the years. Dupree later recounted:

A new interrogator put a sheet of questions in front of me. I was about to write "I don't remember," but reading the questions stopped me cold. "Suppose someone accused you of being a CIA agent, what would you say?" Answer: "Bullshit!?" Question: "How would you justify your answer?" "Quite simple. I don't work for the CIA." The interrogator said, "Come now, you've got to give more reasons than that." I said: "Why? Look, if you're going to accuse me of being a CIA agent, don't go through the routine. Just go ahead and accuse me, and go out into the streets and pick up three witnesses. Pay them 50 afghanis apiece and have them swear I hired them to work for the CIA. They can say, yes, we gave them secret information. I mean, why bother with all this crap? I mean, if you're really going to accuse me of being CIA, why waste your time and mine. Let's both get some sleep.

Instead, he came back with: "Suppose you were confronted with someone who said you worked for the CIA? What would you say?" "Bullshit!" I wrote again, this time adding a short essay on the foreign community "covered wagon" in Kabul. (1980a: 12–13)

Dupree claimed that his activities naturally led many to suspect he had CIA connections, but he dismissed these suspicions as "folklore" among the expatriate community. He wrote that the "collective wisdom" was that he and his wife, Nancy, were with the CIA, and that this "folklore is passed on from one generation to the next. Nancy and I can't defend ourselves. We simply have to live with the folklore" (L. Dupree 1980a: 13). Dupree acknowledged that in light of the forms of research he undertook in Afghanistan, "at times the whole program sounds suspicious even to me" (12).

After a few days of Dupree's detention and interrogation, Muhammad Alam Nuristani was brought before him. Nuristani had obviously been tortured. Dupree wrote that it looked "as though his hair had been burned. His face was totally misshapen, and his upper lip almost reached his chin" (1980a: 13). He had identified Dupree as a CIA agent. Dupree wrote that Nuristani must have had no other choice given the torture to which he had been subjected. When interrogated before Dupree, he screamed, "Everybody knows Dupree is CIA. Everybody knows!" Yet, according to Dupree, Nuristani admitted that Dupree had never tried to recruit him for the CIA, and that he never undertook any clandestine work for Dupree or the CIA (13). Obviously, people will admit to anything when they are tortured, so Nuristani's identification of Dupree as a CIA agent is meaningless.

Dupree was released after six days and expelled from Afghanistan on November 30, 1978. Although he was unable to return to Afghanistan, he continued to work for the AUFS (which he had worked with since 1959) until 1983. Dupree maintained a presence in Pakistan, establishing contacts and networks with members of the Mujahideen, the Islamic fundamentalist group armed, trained, and financed by the CIA, in their war against Soviet forces occupying Afghanistan. He remained interested in Afghanistan politics and sat on the Heritage Foundation–funded Committee for a Free Afghanistan. After his 1978 expulsion from Afghanistan under accusations of being a CIA agent, his alignment with Department of State and CIA political positions became increasingly apparent. His obituary in the *New York Times* listed his consultant work for Austria, Denmark, England, France, Germany, Norway, Sweden, and the United States, including work with the State Department, the NSC, the CIA, USAID, and the UN (Narvaez 1989).

Dupree denied being a CIA operative in Afghanistan. Yet the accounts of John Allison and M. Jamil Hanifi, Dupree's connections with the Afghan Student Association, his role in leading an archaeological expedition with individuals claiming to be intelligence personnel using the expedition as a pretext for intelligence gathering, and public claims (in his obituary and by a member of Congress) that he was a consultant for the CIA lend credence to claims he was a CIA asset, though the extent of his CIA activities remains unclear.

After the coming to power of the Democratic Republic of Afghanistan in the spring of 1978, the CIA increased its presence in Afghanistan. In *Afghanistan — Washington's Secret War*, Phillip Bonosky described Louis Dupree as "the CIA man in Kabul whose activities there among the counterrevolutionaries made him *persona non grata* to the Afghan government, and he was forced to leave in 1978, but only as far as Peshawar where he resumed his work directing counterrevolutionary forces in an attempt to bring a happy ending to his book, *Afghanistan*, otherwise so woefully unended" (2001: 184). Bonosky identified Dupree as one of the U.S. governmental sources who was planting false stories claiming that the Soviets were using nerve gas in rural Afghanistan (217). In eulogizing Dupree after his death in 1989, Senator Gordon J. Humphrey (R-NH) noted Dupree's service as a CIA consultant (U.S. Senate 1989: S4649).[18]

Donald Wilber, Our Man in Iran

In 1930, while an undergraduate at Princeton, Donald Wilber was hired as an artist to draw archaeological architectural features as part of a University of Chicago expedition to Egypt. After working on these Egyptian excavations for three seasons, in 1934 he drove from Egypt to Iran, where he did further architectural surveys and archaeological excavations. Wilber's archaeological travels provided him with the skills, experience, and linguistic training that later served him well as a CIA operative. When he first traveled to Egypt, he was so fearful of locals that he wanted the protection of a pistol, but by the time he left, he "had learned not to feel uneasy or out of place in a foreign land, not to feel superior to others, however humble, because of chances of birth and background" (Wilber 1986: 23).

Wilber's graduate study in Princeton focused on historic and prehistoric architecture. After the United States entered the Second World War, Wilber was assigned by the Office of Coordinator of Information (OCI) to undertake intelligence work, first at OCI and later at the OSS. Wilber observed in his memoir that "there were very few Americans who knew [the Middle East] at all well:

missionaries, archaeologists, research scholars, oil men, and a scattering of businessmen, such as tobacco buyers in Turkey. So, the net gathered many of us, including missionaries whose possible scruples about serving other than the Lord gave way before patriotism" (1986: 101).

Wilber ran OSS operations in Iran, using cover provided by the Iran-American Relations Society and his position as the assistant to the director of the Asia Institute (Wilber 1986: 102). His chief wartime activities involved monitoring the German and Soviet presence in the region. Mixing archaeological discovery and espionage, during one of his OSS missions monitoring Soviet troop movements in Azerbaijan, he surveyed Mongol tombs, where in one village "his excitement at the discovery was tinged by fears that the village was also home to a nest of German agents" (Wilford 2013: 38). At the OSS's request he remained in Iran at the war's end to track Soviet activities in the region.

After the war, some of his OSS contacts talked Wilber into joining the Central Intelligence Group, and he joined the CIA at its inception, spending the next twenty-two years in the agency until his mandatory retirement in 1969 (Wilber 1986: 148–71, 151). Wilber's academic specialty was the early Islamic architecture of Iran. During his years with the CIA, he authored academic publications on Iranian political developments, archaeology, and architecture for academic and popular consumption, while producing an impressive number of internal CIA reports and working on covert operations in Iran. Wilber's *Iran: Past and Present* was a popular text that underwent nine revisions and has remained in print for decades (Wilber 2014). Though Donald Wilber at times made dubious boastful claims about his importance and adventures, substantial documentation exists to establish his role in a number of important CIA operations.[19]

Wilber described how, while he was working covertly for the CIA, he made "thirteen trips to Iran, one trip around the world, and others that took me to Afghanistan, Greece, Cyprus, Lebanon, Egypt, England, Pakistan, India, Ceylon, Turkey, France, Italy and Ghana" (1986: 149–50).[20] As a CIA operative, his specialties were "political action and psychological warfare," and while in the CIA he served as an active member of the board of directors of the Iran Foundation of New York City (150, 186). Wilber had various job titles, including "Consultant and Expert, Intermittent; Consultant, Intermittent; Consultant, Covert; Consultant, Semi-Covert; and again Consultant Intermittent" and Area Operations Officer (149). He worked closely with CIA operatives Kermit Roosevelt and Miles Copeland in the early 1950s (Copeland 1989; Wilford 2013: 160–74, 228).

The CIA sent Wilber to Afghanistan in 1951 using a cover story that he was a "writer on the Middle East." Details of Wilber's mission remain an agency secret, but his assignment appears to have involved monitoring or countering Soviet activities in Afghanistan (see Wilber 1986: 172). Wilber traveled throughout Afghanistan, filling a notebook with reports on the conditions of roads and other infrastructure, noting the presence of military and police, and recording general political attitudes, attitudes toward Soviet philosophy, economic activities, and the presence and activities of expatriates (172–86). Wilber's methods were at least partly opaque, his dual use cover giving his movements a plausible explanation as he spent his days making "the rounds of various offices picking up books, notes on subjects I had requested, and information from just talking and talking" (177).

Back home, Wilber split his time between Princeton and Washington, DC, where he spent three days a week working with Miles Copeland in Kermit Roosevelt's CIA group (Wilber 1986: 192). Wilber wrote that in 1957 he "became the founder and director of the Middle East Research Associations, having persuaded some five of the most highly regarded scholars of the Middle East to join. Of course I obtained prior [CIA] approval. We got a few small jobs but were too far ahead of the times, ahead of the demand for consultants that climaxed in the 1970s" (193; Wilford 2013: 228).

In the late 1950s, Wilber was one of the CIA's leading experts on the Islamic world, writing the CIA reports "Islam in Iran," "Islam in Pakistan," and "Islam in Afghanistan"; he later described these reports as "more exhaustive than any published material" and said "they were to serve as guidelines for working with Muslim groups" (Wilber 1986: 195). Wilber was the architect of Operation Ajax, a CIA coup that Kermit Roosevelt implemented in 1953 against Iranian president Mossadegh; the operation installed Mohammad Reza Shah Pahlavi, who reprivatized petroleum resources and represented American interests in the region. In 1954, Donald Wilber filed an internal CIA report that was a first-person account of the CIA's overthrow of Mossadegh. Almost half a century later, the *New York Times* declassified the report under FOIA and published it (NYT 2000). Wilber later described his role "preparing propaganda material in Persian, directed against Mossadegh.[21] It included cartoons, small wall posters, short articles. Given high priority, it poured off the Agency's press and was rushed by air to Tehran" (Wilber 1986: 188–89).[22]

Wilber was extremely productive, writing, as he recalled, "at least 90,000 words a year for the CIA and about as many for my own purposes" (1986: 195). In the early 1960s, Wilber had CIA assignments in India and Ceylon (196). In 1963, he began working on Africa and wrote a CIA draft titled "Guide to Subversion in Africa," which he described as "breaking the types of subversion into separate categories." Although this guide was never finished, it was used within the CIA as a resource for planning the agency's African psychological warfare campaigns (202).

Careers Traversing Academy and Agency

Many questions remain unanswered about anthropologists and other academics leaving positions at the CIA to establish careers on university campuses. Most academics who leave positions at the CIA and establish university careers maintain they have severed all ties with the agency (see, e.g., Siskiyou 2011), though the secrecy surrounding intelligence work inevitably raises doubts or suspicions about such claims. Declassified reports published in the CIA's journal, *Studies in Intelligence*, clarify that the long history of CIA reliance on university professors for recruiting, contract work, and ongoing reports makes such contacts with former employees an ongoing design feature of university-agency symbiosis (Cook 1983).

Archaeologist Michael D. Coe's memoir, *Final Report: An Archaeologist Excavates His Past* (2006), describes his transitions from the academy to years at the CIA and his later return to academia. Coe became interested in archaeology as a Harvard undergraduate visiting Mayan ruins in Yucatán on a family vacation (Coe 2006: 54). At Harvard, Alfred Kidder, Douglas Oliver, and Alfred Tozzer introduced Coe to anthropology, and in 1949 he began excavating in British Honduras with British Mayanist Eric Thompson (54–57). In 1950, as Coe was preparing for his first year of graduate study in anthropology at Harvard, America entered the Korean War. After Coe was rejected by the navy for medical reasons, Clyde Kluckhohn approached him and recruited him into the CIA, where he became a case officer (64).

At CIA training school he learned spycraft and intelligence skills. Despite the strict use of pseudonyms for all agent-students, Coe recognized a fellow CIA operative as a former classmate from Fay School, the elite boarding school he had attended in his youth (Coe 2006: 73). The CIA trained Coe in its practices and culture. In seclusion he learned how to "recruit agents, how to test them for reliability, how to elicit information without the subject knowing, and how to detect lying. There was amazingly good instruction in modern history, and particularly the history of Marxism-Leninism, and its philosophical roots in the French Revolution and in the philosophy of Hegel. We were never told the names of our teachers, but I'm positive they came to us from the best campuses in the land (much later, when I had just joined the Yale faculty, I would recognize one or two of these instructors in the Sterling Library elevator!)" (74). Coe and his fellow students were taught the skills of tailing people, casing locations, passing messages, clandestine communications, and using dead drops and learned the details of security systems.

Coe was assigned to the CIA's Far Eastern Section, initially undertaking research assignments, by way of training, at the Library of Congress. He was a case officer in a CIA operations group working with General Claire Chennault and Madame Chiang Kai-shek, covertly offering support to guerrillas fighting Mao's Communist forces in China. The CIA used an import-export business with offices in Taipei and Pittsburgh, known as Western Enterprises, Inc., as a front for these operations. Coe was assigned to intelligence analysis, rather than operations, though he ran a series of covert agents on the Chinese mainland.

In January 1952, the CIA sent Coe to Taipei, where he helped train Chinese nationalists; he was soon sent to Kinmen, then Paich'üan, strategic islands off the coast of the Chinese mainland (Coe 2006: 75). On Paich'üan he used an interpreter and CIA networks to establish links with the local nationalist intelligence organization. His primary contact was a lieutenant who, according to Coe, passed along "reports gathered by the mainland agent network of the Ministry of Defense, and I would analyze these and transmit anything new nightly to Taipei. On one wall of our quarters I had stapled up all of the 1:250,000 sheets of the northern Fuchien coast made in the U.S. Army Map Service, with grease pencil notations on the Chicom order of battle, continuously updated" (84).

Coe's most reliable spy was a woman in her thirties who lived near an airfield where Soviet MIGs landed. Pretending to fish at night, she secretly traveled out to Paich'üan to report to Coe (Coe 2006: 85). In 1953, the CIA reassigned Coe to Taipei, where he studied Mandarin, carried out CIA intelligence duties, and was put in charge of running the agency's training camp at the "T-Area" along the T'an-shui River (90).

Coe had a negative assessment of the impact of the CIA's anticommunist operations in China; he found "the infrequent raids against the Chinese mainland had been little more than minor annoyances to Mao, but they did bring one plus to the United States: they tied down along the southern Chinese coast several hundred thousand Communist troops that otherwise would have gone to Korea to fight the United Nations Forces. The true line that was drawn at the 38th parallel might then have been far to the south; perhaps *all* of the peninsula would have ended up in the hands of 'Great Leader' Kim Il-sung" (Coe 2006: 92).

Coe left the CIA in early 1954, returning to the United States to pursue his doctorate at Harvard (Coe 2006: 92). His memoir's discussion of his CIA years ends with his reflection that this time in China "made me"; he notes that if one mentions "'CIA' to the average academic, ... he or she would recoil in horror, yet the three years I spent with the Agency were wonderful ones, and I have no regrets whatsoever" (93). The remainder of his memoir barely mentions the CIA, and Coe's compartmentalization and silence leave readers to assume he had no further contact with the agency after he returned to Harvard to study archaeology. During the next half century, while based at Harvard and Yale, Coe regularly conducted archaeological research in Mesoamerica (192–97).

CIA Connections Primary, Secondary, Hypothetical

During the years I spent researching this book, I collected far more reports of claimed links between anthropologists and the CIA than I have been able to verify, and a wealth of speculative information on such links has not been included here. In some instances I reasonably ruled out claimed anthropological links with the CIA; in other instances such claimed links remain open possibilities. Significant questions remain concerning possible links between specific anthropologists and the CIA that I have not included in this chapter because the information I gathered did not conclusively establish such connections. Yet even without a larger collection, we have enough documented examples of various types of CIA articulations with anthropology to consider how these interactions worked during the Cold War.

Questions about anthropologists' direct and indirect involvements with the CIA have persisted in the discipline for decades. In an essay examining the political and familial background of Richard Critchfield, Timothy Mitchell raised questions about an ethnographer's (in this case a self-trained pseudoethnographer) family links to the CIA. Mitchell identified Critchfield's older brother James Critchfield as "the first director of CIA clandestine operation in the Near East in 1959" (2002: 148). Mitchell acknowledged that it cannot be assumed that both Critchfield brothers were directly involved with the CIA, but Mitchell established social connections, including links to Robert McNamara and others who were prominent in military intelligence circles, indicating some overlap between the brothers' worlds (149). Mitchell showed how Richard Critchfield's writing mirrored the CIA's Cold War narrative lens; for example, Critchfield's

> choice of villages, always portrayed as out-of-the-way places, followed the changing focus of U.S. imperial concerns, some of them at the time quite secretive. He

was in India and Nepal in 1959-62, the years coinciding with probably the largest CIA operation of the time: a secret program based in Nepal to train and arm Tibetan refugees to fight the Chinese occupation in Tibet. Critchfield's visits to Nepal were spaced between spells teaching journalism at the university in Nagpur, the birthplace and headquarters of the rising Hindu fascist movement. By the mid-1960s, an account of the CIA program in Nepal reports, "CIA officer James Critchfield described the guerrillas' achievements inside Tibet as 'minimal.'" (149)

Mitchell conceded the difficulties in determining whether or not Richard Critchfield was a CIA operative, but he noted that "the importance of Critchfield's connections with America's 'national security' regime, whether direct or indirect, lies elsewhere, in unraveling the political genealogy of such expertise on the Middle East, and on the question of 'the peasant' in particular" (151). Mitchell described the CIA's infiltration of academic enterprises during the 1960s and theorized that such clandestine efforts to redirect scholarship may have influenced writings on Middle Eastern culture such as those of Critchfield or Henry Habib Ayrout, whose U.S. publication of *The Egyptian Peasant* (1963), Mitchell notes, coincided "with a renewed American interest in Egyptian affairs," and shaped elements of Critchfield's narrative (151; see 47–52).

While Critchfield's familial links to CIA operations in the Middle East present unusual connections, much of the Cold War's anthropological fieldwork occurred in regions of interest to the American national security apparatus, with ethnographers independently collecting information from local peoples whose views were underreported yet often the core of national movements. Most of our documented knowledge linking academics with the CIA appears as outlines rather than comprehensive, detailed portraits. The secrecy shrouding most of these relationships is intentional, and while it is important that scholars do not go beyond what can be documented, it is equally important to not ignore what can be known about them. Some sources establish ongoing interactions between academics with agency ties, with scholars with onetime agency ties being recurrently contacted for information or facilitating the recruitment of students; yet such activities cannot be automatically assumed (see A. C. Mills 1991; D. H. Price 2011e; Cook 1983). These documented interactions raise questions about how common or widespread such ongoing contacts with the CIA have been.

We are often left only with questions, shadows and other residuals of these relationships; yet anthropology, perhaps more than other disciplines, is used to dealing with such traces of the phenomena we study, with archaeologists grasping spent residues of cultures lost in time and ethnographers straining to understand the ephemeral features of culture. Still, many questions remain, some of them as fundamental as what it means that the AAA representative (Worman) to the National Conference on Citizenship was known to be a full-time CIA employee. Other questions pertaining to these relationships hinge on grappling with the disciplinary meanings to be made from what can be established about ongoing efforts by the CIA and military agencies to secretly finance specific forms of anthropological research.

The [African Studies] Association, which represented the combined strength of those concerned with Africa in this country, would be happy to aid you in any way it can.

MELVILLE HERSKOVITS | first president of the African Studies Association, to the Honorable Allen Dulles, Central Intelligence Agency, February 20, 1958 (qtd. in Martin and West 1999: 91–92)

SEVEN HOW CIA FUNDING FRONTS SHAPED ANTHROPOLOGICAL RESEARCH

A series of investigative press reports in 1967 revealed that beginning in the 1950s the CIA used funding fronts and "conduit" foundations to secretly finance academic research of interest to the agency. The CIA avoided outside scrutiny of the research it funded by working with organizations, projects, or individuals that fulfilled one of three roles: as a front, a conduit, or a recipient.

The front, sometimes also called a "dummy foundation," was frequently a CIA-held "paper foundation" consisting of little more than an address or post office box and a bank account holding CIA funds. Sometimes these fronts were nonprofit foundations — even while failing to provide the IRS with the documentation needed to support this claimed pretense (see table 7.1). The CIA used fronts to pass funds to conduits.

The conduit, sometimes referred to as a "pass-through," was usually a legitimate preexisting foundation receiving funds from a CIA front (see table 7.2). Usually, someone from the CIA contacted a senior-level individual at the foundation and discussed how the agency wished its funds to be used. The CIA representative discussed the funding of specific individuals or programs with designated individuals at the conduit and assured the delivery of CIA funds to the desired project under the pretext of funding from the conduit.

The recipient was the individual or project that received CIA funds from either a front or a conduit (see table 7.3). In many instances recipients did not know they were receiving CIA funds.

Elite social networks played important roles in establishing fronts and conduits. As a Princeton graduate who for years had practiced law at the New York firm of Sullivan and Cromwell, DCI Allen Dulles had contacts he used to quietly approach board members of nonprofits, and others at the CIA used similar elite networks to establish foundation contacts. With CIA links to Ivy League universities, there was no shortage of informal agency connections to nonprofit boards. In a 1967 *Washington Post* exposé, Richard Harwood described how "Samuel Hadley of the prestigious New York law firm of Milbank, Tweed, Hadley, and McCloy allowed his family's Rubicon Foundation to be used as a conduit for CIA funds" (1967d: E1); firm partner John J. McCloy was a former chair of the Carnegie Corporation. Harwood traced connections between Wall Street firms and prominent law offices, where the CIA quietly contacted individual board members and passed along CIA funds or requests for specific funding directives. Harwood identified Eli Whitney Debevoise and Francis T. P. Plimpton of the law firm Debevoise, Plimpton, Lyons and Gates as linking the (CIA-funded) American Council for the International Commission of Jurists, the (CIA-funded) Foundation for Youth and Student Affairs, the United Nations, and the Rockefeller Foundation. The CIA also used the foundations of a Texas oil tycoon (William P. Hobby Jr.) to secretly fund projects. Connections between moneyed families, private foundations, and the CIA ran deep. According to Harwood, "The list of establishmentarians involved with the CIA in its penetration of private institutions is lengthy and includes such other figures as Robert Manning, editor of the *Atlantic Monthly,* and McGeorge Bundy, who has had experience both inside and outside the Government. As a foreign policy adviser to Presidents Kennedy and Johnson, Bundy in effect supervised the CIA operation. Today he is president of the Ford Foundation" (1967d: E1).

The *New York Times* revealed that Richard M. Hunt, assistant dean of Harvard University's Graduate School of Arts, was the director of the Fund for International Social and Economic Education (FISEE), which received CIA funds through the Brown and Pappas Foundations. Howard C. Thomas Jr., FISEE's executive director, had been the Saigon representative of the Asia Foundation, which at the time was a CIA front (Sheehan 1967c). Hunt claimed he did not know FISEE received $50,000 a year in CIA money, saying that "money from the Brown organization was used to support work by his group in Latin America, but 'I'm not at liberty to disclose the nature of that specific project'" (1).

The funding of particular projects shaped disciplinary research agendas. Often research projects' designs were established prior to the receipt of laundered CIA funds, yet the completion of these projects was made possible through CIA assistance, while other projects withered without such support. Foundations exposed in the press as CIA conduits received surprisingly little scrutiny; usually foundation spokespersons refused to answer press questions concerning CIA contacts, and they refused to identify which projects received CIA funding. When the Hobby Foundation was identified as a CIA conduit, William Hobby refused to respond to questions relating to CIA contacts or which projects received laundered CIA funds (Kenworthy 1967a). But Hobby's IRS 990-A filings informed news reports that in 1964 Hobby funded American Friends of the Middle East ($75,000), the Fund for International and Social Education ($50,000), Radio Free Europe ($40,000), the Committee of Correspondence ($5,000), the Institute of International Education ($500), and Berliner Verein ($100,000) (Kenworthy 1967a; see Wilford 2013: 113–32).

Vice President Hubert Humphrey was outraged to learn of the CIA's abuse of foundations to gain access to unwitting Americans, but many politicians defended these programs. Liberals like Robert Kennedy supported the CIA's use of fronts to influence groups like the National Student Association. Kennedy ignored the threats these programs presented to academic freedom and argued that these decisions were "not made unilaterally by the CIA but by the Executive Branch in the Eisenhower, Kennedy and Johnson Administrations" (Harwood 1967d: E1).

At the African-American Institute, in 1953 Waldemar A. Nielsen began accepting CIA funds — funds that continued for eight years, even while Nielsen knew "the inherent imprudence and impropriety" of these actions (Harwood 1967d). In spite of these misgivings, once the funding began, the institute became "like a drunk taking the first drink.... It is easy to overindulge." This indulgence continued until, at the point when this secret relationship was revealed, half of the institute's funding came from the CIA (Harwood 1967d).

Soon after the *Ramparts* story on the National Student Association broke in 1967, other journalists revealed other CIA-linked foundations. Tables 7.1, 7.2, and 7.3 list identified CIA fronts, conduits, and recipients identified by the press after, and including, the publication of Sol Stern's 1967 *Ramparts* article.

Even after press revelations of CIA fronts, and despite the Church Committee's findings that the CIA's influence on the funding of international research had been "massive," the specific details of how this funding influenced American anthropologists' research remain largely unexamined. But the passage of time increases archival resources and the availability of FOIA documents, allowing consideration of how these covert relationships worked.

TABLE 7.1 Thirty-Two Documented CIA Fronts

FOUNDATION	CITATION
Appalachian Fund	(Sheehan 1967c; *Newsweek* 1967)
Asia Foundation (until 1967)	(Turner 1967)
Beacon Fund	(Stern 1967; CQ 1967)
Borden Trust	(Stern 1967; CQ 1967)
Broad High Fund	(CQ 1967*)
James Carlisle Trust	(CQ 1967*; *Newsweek* 1967)
Chesapeake Fund	(CQ 1967*)
Edsel Fund	(Stern 1967; CQ 1967)
Foundation for Youth and Social Affairs	(Farnsworth 1967; CQ 1967*)
Gotham Foundation	(Irwin and Burke 1967; Saunders 2000: 354)
Andrew Hamilton Fund	(CQ 1967; *Newsweek* 1967; Saunders 1999: 354)
Heights Fund	(CQ 1967; *Newsweek* 1967)
Human Ecology Fund (aka SIHE)	(Marks 1979; 147-92)
Independence Foundation Inc.	(Harwood 1967e; CQ 1967*)
International Development Foundation	(Sheehan 1967b)
International Marketing Inst.	(Sheehan 1967b)
Jones O'Donnell Foundation	(Glass 1967)
Kentfield Fund	(Stern 1967; Kenworthy 1967b; CQ 1967)
Knickerbocker Foundation	(CQ 1967*)
Michigan Fund	(see Saunders 1999: 354)
Monroe Fund	(CQ 1967; *Newsweek* 1967)
Munich Institute	(O'Connell 1990: 307)
Northcraft Educational Fund	(CQ 1967*)
Price Fund	(Stern 1967; CQ 1967)
San Jacinto Fund (Houston)	(CQ 1967)
San Miguel Fund	(CQ 1967; *Newsweek* 1967)
Tower Fund	(Sheehan 1967c; CQ 1967; *Newsweek* 1967)
Vernon Fund	(CQ 1967*; Irwin and Burke 1967)
Charles Price Whitten Trust	(CQ 1967*; *Newsweek* 1967)
Warden Trust	(CQ 1967*)
Williford-Telford Fund	(CQ 1967*; *Newsweek* 1967)
Wynnewood Fund	(CQ 1967*; *Newsweek* 1967)

CQ 1967* = *Congressional Quarterly* listed this as "Suspected CIA 'Dummies.'"

TABLE 7.2 Twenty-Six Documented CIA Conduits (aka Pass-Throughs)

FOUNDATION	CITATION
M. D. Anderson Foundation	(CQ 1967; *Newsweek* 1967; Saunders 1999: 354)
Baird Foundation	(CQ 1967; Saunders 2000: 354; *Newsweek* 1967)
J. Frederick Brown Foundation	(Sheehan 1967b; *Newsweek* 1967)
Catherwood Foundation	(CQ 1967)
Dation (Miami)	(Irwin and Burke 1967)
Cleveland H. Dodge Foundation Inc.	(CQ 1967)
Farfield Foundation Inc.	(CQ 1967; Harwood 1967e)
Florence Foundation	(Irwin and Burke 1967)
Geschickter Fund for Medical Research	(Marks 1979: 59)
Granary Fund (Boston)	(Kenworthy 1967b; CQ 1967; cf. Glass 1967)
Hobby Foundation	(Kenworthy 1967a; CQ 1967)
Hoblitzelle Foundation	(CQ 1967)
Kaplan Fund	(Saunders 2000: 354; *Newsweek* 1967)
J. M. Kaplan Fund	(Stern 1967; CQ 1967)
Lucius N. Littouer Foundation	(Irwin and Burke 1967; CQ 1967)
McGregor Fund	(CQ 1967)
Josiah Macy, Jr. Foundation	(Marks 1979: 59)
Marshall Foundation	(CQ 1967; *Newsweek* 1967)
Mount Pleasant Fund	(Kenworthy 1967b)
Aaron E. Norman Fund, Inc.	(Irwin and Burke 1967; CQ 1967)
Jones-O'Donnell Foundation	(CQ 1967)
Pappas Charitable Trust	(CQ 1967)
Rabb (Sidney & Ester) Charitable Foundation	(CQ 1967; *Newsweek* 1967)
Benjamin Rosenthal Foundation	(CQ 1967)
Rubicon Foundation	(CQ 1967; Ross 1976: 104)
Victoria Strauss Fund	(Kenworthy 1967b; Sheehan 1967c)

What CIA Fronts Funded

The CIA used fronts to secretly finance the publication of books and articles propagating CIA-supported views. One CIA front, the Gotham Foundation, financed projects related to political developments in postwar Japan. Gotham published Lawrence Battistini's book *The Postwar Student Struggle in Japan* (1956), and an early 1960s Gotham Foundation project run by former Asia Foundation employee Dr. Gaston Sigur translated Japanese labor publications into

TABLE 7.3 Seventy-One Documented Recipients Funded by CIA Fronts

FOUNDATION	CITATION
African American Institute	(CQ 1967; *Newsweek* 1967; Irwin and Burke 1967)
African Research Foundation	(Irwin and Burke 1967)
American Anthropological Association	(NAAA records)
American Committee for Émigrés in the Professions	(Irwin and Burke 1967)
American Council for the International Commission of Jurists	(CQ 1967; *Newsweek* 1967)
American Federation of State, County and Municipal Employees	(Harwood 1967b; W. A. Price 1967)
American Friends of the Middle East	(Sheehan 1967b; CQ 1967; Irwin and Burke 1967)
American Fund for Free Jurists	(Sheehan 1967a; Irwin and Burke 1967)
American Newspaper Guild	(Sheehan 1967a; CQ 1967)
American Federation of Labor	(de Vries 2012: 1075)
American Society of African Culture	(Sheehan 1967b, 1967c; CQ 1967; *Newsweek* 1967)
Association of Hungarian Students in North America	(Harwood 1967e; Irwin and Burke 1967)
Atwater Research Program in North Africa	(*Newsweek* 1967)
Berliner Verein	(Kenworthy 1967a)
Canadian Union of Students	(CQ 1967)
Center for Christian Democratic Action	(Irwin and Burke 1967)
Committee for Self-Determination	(Kenworthy 1967b; Irwin and Burke 1967)
Committee of Correspondence, Inc.	(Kenworthy 1967a)
Commentary Magazine	(Harwood 1967e)
Congress for Cultural Freedom	(*Newsweek* 1967; Harwood 1967e)
Congre pou la Liberte de la Culture, Paris	(Irwin and Burke 1967)
Dialogue Magazine	(NYT 1967b, 1967c)
M. J. Desai	(Kenworthy 1967b)
Escuela Interamerican de Education Democratica	(Irwin and Burke 1967)
Foreign Policy Research Institute	(Sheehan 1967a; Kenworthy 1967a)
Frente Departmental de Camposinos de Puno	(Irwin and Burke 1967)
Friends of India Committee	(Kenworthy 1967b; *Time* 1967b)
Fund for International Social and Economic Education	(Sheehan 1967c; Kenworthy 1967a)

TABLE 7.3 (*continued*)

FOUNDATION	CITATION
Thomas J. Gilligan Jr.	(Kenworthy 1967b)
Billy Graham Spanish-American Crusade	(*Time* 1967b)
Harvard Law School Fund	(*Time* 1967b)
Independent Research Service	(CQ 1967)
Institute of International Education	(Kenworthy 1967a; *Newsweek* 1967)
Institute of International Labor Research	(CQ 1967; *Newsweek* 1967)
Institut d'Historie Sociale	(Kenworthy 1967b)
Institute of Public Administration	(Sheehan 1967a; *Newsweek* 1967)
International Center for Social Research	(Irwin and Burke 1967)
International Commission of Jurists	(Tolley 1994: xiii)
International Confederation of Free Trade Unions	(CQ 1967)
International Cooperative Development Fund	(CQ 1967)
International Development Foundation, Inc.	(Sheehan 1967c; CQ 1967)
International Federation of Petroleum and Chemical Workers	(CQ 1967)
International Food and Drink Workers Federation	(*Time* 1967a)
International Marketing Institute	(CQ 1967)
International Student Conference	(Shehan 1967a; Farnsworth 1967; CQ 1967)
International Union of Socialist Youth	(Irwin and Burke 1967)
Kenya Federation of Labor	(Sheehan 1967c)
Kossuth Foundation	(Irwin and Burke 1967)
National Council of Churches	(*Time* 1967a)
National Education Assn.	(CQ 1967)
National Student Association	(Ramparts 1967; Sheehan 1967d; CQ 1967)
Oficina Relacionadara Movimientos Estudiantiles Universitarias	(Irwin and Burke 1967)
Operations and Policy Research, Inc.	(Kenworthy 1967b; *Newsweek* 1967)
Pan-American Foundation	(Sheehan 1967c; CQ 1967)
Pax Romana, North American Secretariat	(*Time* 1967b; Irwin & Burke 1967)
P.E.N.	(Harwood 1967e)
Praeger Press	(*NYT* 1967c; Hersh 1974a)
Public Services International	(CQ 1967)
Radio Free Europe	(Kenworthy 1967a; CQ 1967)
Retail Clerks International Association	(CQ 1967)
Service Educational Foundation	(Irwin and Burke 1967)

(*continued*)

TABLE 7.3 (*continued*)

FOUNDATION	CITATION
Stanford Research Institute	(Irwin and Burke 1967)
Synod of Bishops of the Russian Church Outside Russia	(*Newsweek* 1967)
University of Southern California	(Sheehan 1967c)
United Auto Workers	(Flint 1967)
United States Youth Council	(*CQ* 1967)
John Hay Whitney Trust	(Kenworthy 1967b; *Time* 1967b)
Robert E. Witherspoon	(Kenworthy 1967b)
World Assembly of Youth	(Irwin and Burke 1967)
World Confederation of Organizations of the Teaching Profession	(*CQ* 1967)

English (Burks 2011: 53n25). Princeton psychologists Hadley Cantril and Lloyd Free used CIA funds to establish the Princeton Research Council, where they developed public opinion survey methods and administered surveys in the Eastern bloc during the 1960s (Crewdson and Treaster 1977: 37).

In his 2009 memoir, South African Special Branch career intelligence veteran P. C. Swanepoel described his discovery in the early 1960s that the London-based "Transcription Center" (advertised in then CIA-financed *New Africa* magazine) was a CIA-backed operation providing news stories of interest to those studying Africa. The Transcription Center, which published news stories and maintained contact with scholars and journalists working in Africa, was financed by a grant from the Farfield Foundation (Swanepoel 2007 226, 246). Among those identified as having been interviewed (on African oral traditions) by the Transcription Center was anthropologist Godfrey Lienhardt (Swanepoel 2007: 227; see Lienhardt et al. 1966).

The CIA secretly funded the Congress for Cultural Freedom, including the financing of the British journal *Encounter* (see Saunders 1999; D. H. Price 2005; Fox, 1967; Warner 1995) and the Japanese journal *Jiru*, which the CIA used to legitimize desired political reforms in Japan (Takeyama and Minear 2007: 19–21). *Japan Cultural Forum* received CIA funds channeled through the Hoblitzelle Foundation (Takeyama and Minear 2007: 20). The African-American Institute's *Africa Special Report* was financed by another CIA front, the Andrew Hamilton Fund, which used CIA funds to support conferences and other events (African-American Institute 1956–1959). Some CIA fronts, such as the Andrew

Hamilton Fund, paid for scholars' research expenses when they traveled to the underdeveloped world, such as Michigan State University historian James R. Hooker's travels to London, Rhodesia, Zambia, and Malawi in 1959 (Henderson 1989: vii; Lawrence 1979: 83–84).

Several presses published books financed entirely or in part with CIA funds; there was little academic market for many of these books, which would have faced difficulties being published without such underwriting. The Asia Foundation funneled CIA monies as grants to subsidize the publication of books at Franklin Press; the agency also "made editorial contributions" to books published by major publishing houses such as Scribner's Sons (including *The Yenan's Way* [1951] by Eudocio Ravines "from a translation supplied by William F. Buckley, Jr. who was a CIA agent for several years in the early 1950s"), Ballantine Books, and G. P. Putnam's Sons. Several well-known writers, including Peter Matthiessen and George Plimpton, received CIA funds during this period (Crewdson and Treaster 1977: 37).

In February 1967, the *New York Times* disclosed that Praeger Press had published books "at the CIA's suggestion" (NYT 1967c). Praeger's first CIA-backed publication was Milovan Djilas's book critiquing Yugoslavian communism, *The New Class* (Djilas 1957; see Crewdson and Treaster 1977: 37). Frederick Praeger claimed to have published only "15 or 16" books that "dealt fundamentally with facts, history and analysis of event of Communist-bloc countries or of nations susceptible of a fall to Communism," telling the *Times* these books were vetted by specialists before publication, but he refused to answer questions about Praeger's CIA relationship (NYT 1967c).[1]

E. Howard Hunt Jr. later contradicted Frederick Praeger's claims of limited CIA involvement. Testifying in Senate hearings investigating Watergate cover-ups, Hunt described his years at the CIA's Domestic Operations Division, which operated out of CIA covert field stations in Boston, Chicago, San Francisco, Washington, DC, and elsewhere. Hunt had worked out of the National Press Building, using credentials of Continental Press, a CIA front. Hunt told Seymour Hersh, "We funded much of the activities of the Frederick D. Praeger Publishing Corporation in New York City. We funded, to a large extent, the activities of Fodor's Travel Guide, distributed by the David McKay Corporation" (Hersh 1974a: 4).[2]

The CIA did not act alone in negotiating these propaganda publishing ventures at Praeger and other presses. At the U.S. Information Agency (USIA), Louis Fanget, Donald McNeill, and William W. Warner developed a process in which first they "would think of a book that could explain what the Soviets had done to hurt the freedom of its people; then they would offer Frederick Praeger or other publishers an advance to commission an author and publish his work for foreign markets, even if the topic would not normally sell abroad" (Green 1988: 69). Through such hidden moves the CIA did more than fund preexisting academic views looking for support: it created propaganda that was passed off as scholarship and, in the process, warped academic freedom and damaged the credibility of academic projects financed by these funds.

The CIA's secret interference with academic publishing was not limited to the dozen or so books first claimed by Frederick Praeger in the *Times*. Instead, "thousands of books from Praeger and Franklin Press and other publishers flowed into dozens of countries. They were either donated by the USIA posts abroad, or in some cases, sold through local retailers. Field officers liked these results and admired the fact that a government agency could stimulate the appearance of so many good books. Frederick Praeger's enterprise and energy contributed to the program's success as did the willingness of Fanget, McNeill, and Warner to slash red tape" (Green 1988: 69). After reading news reports of Frederick Praeger's CIA links, Marvin Harris speculated that this explained "why Praeger started then stopped publication of my friend Antonio Figueiredo's book on Portuguese Africa for which I had already written a preface. Praeger claimed that he couldn't publish it after he found out that Antonio worked for Narodny, the Russian bank in London. He said no one would believe Antonio because of this connection" (MH to DHP 11/9/94).

The *New York Times* identified several international academic journals as being secretly financed with CIA funds: *Africa Forum* and *Africa Report* (both organs of the American Society of African Culture and the African-American Institute), *Argumenten* (Sweden), *Combate* (Latin America), the *East African Legal Digest* (Kenya), *Preuves* (France), *Forum* (Austria), *Der Monat* (West Germany), *El Mundo Nuevo* (Latin America), *Thought and Quest* (India), and the Asia Foundation's *Asian Student* (Crewdson and Treaster 1977: 37). In 1967, Jason Epstein observed in an essay in the *New York Review of Books* that the CIA's covert support of specific forms of academic inquiry "was not a matter of buying off and subverting individual writers and scholars, but of setting up an arbitrary and factitious system of values by which academic personnel were advanced, magazine editors appointed, and scholars subsidized and published, not necessarily on their merits, though these were sometimes considerable, but because of their allegiances. The fault of the CIA was not that it corrupted the innocent but that it tried, in collusion with a group of insiders, to corner a free market" (16).

The *New York Times* later identified American writer Edward S. Hunter as a "CIA operative who employed the cover of a freelance author in search of a book ... who roamed Central Asia for years collecting material for a work on Afghanistan that eventually was published by the prestigious house of Hodder and Stroughton of London" (Crewdson and Treaster 1977: 37).[3] Hunter wrote articles and books, testified before Congress on communist brainwashing techniques, and was an anticommunist "expert witness" for the House Un-American Activities Committee. His book *The Past Present: A Year in Afghanistan* adopted an orientalist stance to provide an account of mid-1950s Afghanistan for the general public. He traveled to Afghanistan during Nikita Khrushchev's tour of southern Asia in 1955, when the USSR announced it would give Afghanistan $100 million in economic development aid. Hunter viewed Khrushchev's aid as a Soviet strategy to turn Afghanistan into the "keystone of a new psychological offensive in the cold-hot war. If it could not be dislodged, even its loosening might topple the already wobbly Free World arch that extended downwards to the sea, through Iran on the one side and Pakistan on the other" (Hunter 1959: 15; cf. CIA 1961: 30).

Hunter described waves of Soviet technicians working on various technological infusion programs spread throughout the countryside. His accounts of the inferiority of Soviet machinery and aid projects carried dual messages as he questioned the intentions and workable outcomes of the Soviet projects, while bluntly stressing how America's enemies were gaining ground in a struggle for the hearts, minds, and loyalties of Afghans (Hunter 1959: 242–43). Hunter described Americans working on small technical assistance programs, and he included details of an ICA irrigation pump program. Personnel from ICA were skeptical about the long-term impacts of their pump project, and Hunter wished the pumps had clear labels indicating this was a U.S.-sponsored project (147).

The CIA's underwriting of Hunter's book makes his focus on the presence of Soviet advisers throughout Afghanistan seem comical. In one passage Hunter complained about how upset he was when he "saw Soviet Russians mysteriously moving about; nobody could tell me what they were doing. They were 'advisors' and 'technicians' on strange visits from elsewhere. What were they doing in that region was unstated. Indeed, their presence was denied. I watched a small party of them embarking on the King's plane at Kandahar after one of their periodical trips. The Afghan authorities who came to the airport airily denied that the group entering the royal plane were Communist Russians. Other Afghans took me aside later and told me not to be fooled; they were Red agents"

(1959: 236). Hunter did not depict American ICA operations as having similar double motives. As he presented the situation, the Soviets were "mysteriously moving about," while American aid was a generous expression of American compassion, and was simply a neutral observer.

The Asia Foundation, the AAA, and CIA: 1956–1967

The Committee for Free Asia (CFA) was established in 1951 and three years later changed its name to the Asia Foundation (Morehouse 1957: 52). Under the leadership of Brayton Wilbur, the CFA operated the anticommunist Radio Free Asia, produced pamphlets, and "mobilized church groups and garden clubs behind a 'Seeds for Democracy' campaign in the Philippines" (Weissman and Shoch 1972: 3). The committee's staff and board had significant military and intelligence connections (Weissman and Shoch 1972: 3–4).[4] The committee also had links to the CIA's Radio Free Europe program, and it undertook propaganda radio broadcasts (beginning in Manila in 1951). It backed candidates in Philippine elections, funded scholarships and travel grants for Asian students, and ran a bookstore in Hong Kong where it "provided a front for US support for the Asian operations of a host of international organizations such as the World Assembly of Youth and the International Confederation of Free Trade Unions" (Defty 2004: 207), both of which were later revealed to have CIA ties (Saunders 1999: 142; Kelber 2004; Blum 1995: 109).

The CFA published the anticommunist monograph *Land Reform: Communist China, Nationalist China, Taiwan, India, Pakistan* (1953), which was mailed to libraries and journalists with a letter explaining that the volume "is not designed to serve as a detailed analysis of land reform, but as a ready daily reference for use by editors, news commentators and educators."[5] Supplying journalists with such predigested CIA-sponsored analysis was designed to shape American views on Asian land reform.

The CIA trained Tibetan fighters (see McGranahan 2010), and the CFA funded anthropologist and missionary Robert Ekvall to act as a translator and culture broker for the Dalai Lama's eldest brother, Thubten Jigme Norbus, during his visit to the United States (Jackson 2004: 613).[6] In 1953, the CFA became the Asia Foundation, with Robert Blum as its president. Blum had extensive intelligence experience; during World War II, Blum oversaw OSS operations in France, Germany, the Netherlands, and Switzerland, later becoming deputy director of the OSS's European Counterintelligence Clearinghouse (RBP, NARA,

6/25/45). After the war Blum took a position at the CIA, which he left to direct the Asia Foundation.

Blum was a "protégé of CIA Director Allen Dulles," whose CIA work in Asia involved leading the U.S. Special Technical and Economic Mission (STEM) in Vietnam in 1950–54, for which he was dubbed by General Jean De Latire, commander of the French expeditionary forces, "the most dangerous man in Indochina" (Corson 1968: 36). Blum's papers at Yale document his busy Asian travel schedule in his official capacity of Asia Foundation president. His travels allowed him to establish connections with academic and political figures, and he wrote detailed reports on the people and organizations he encountered. Many of these meetings produced memos fit for intelligence dossiers; he wrote monthly and quarterly internal Asia Foundation reports and memos recounting detailed embassy meetings and summaries of political, economic, and academic developments.

These reports contained profiles of individuals in Afghanistan, Burma, Cambodia, Hong Kong, India, Indochina, Indonesia, Laos, Nepal, the Philippines, South Korea, Thailand, and other political hot spots of the 1950s and 1960s. They include accounts of Blum's 1960 visit with Asian leaders (including Prince Norodom Sihanouk of Cambodia and President Suharto of Indonesia) and hundreds of scholars and local functionaries. Blum's Asia Foundation records include receipts for a range of interactions with important intelligence and political functionaries such as lunches with then Harvard Professor Henry Kissinger or dinner with CIA counterintelligence chief, James Angleton (RBP AF Receipts Folder, 4/21/58 and 9/24/54).

Blum compiled dossiers on individuals he met in Asia and collected photographs (meticulously labeled) of individuals attending parties at embassies or Western hotels. For example, the dossiers on individuals encountered during Blum's November 1954 visit to Indonesia included a summary of his encounter with Cornell political scientist George McT. Kahin with the following paragraph:

> Kahin said that the situation in Indonesia was not good and that the government was spending a lot of time talking about the international position of Indonesia as a member of the Colombo group in order to distract attention from domestic failure. He said that [Sukarno] was a revolutionary by training and experience and could not adapt well to the requirements of stable political life. There was no evidence that [Sukarno] was a doctrinaire communist, but [Sukarno] had told Kahin that he admired greatly what the communists had done, for example, in

bringing about unity and political stability in China and their ability to organize their youth. Kahin does not think that there is an early danger of a communist take-over but is worried that political disintegration is gradually setting in. (RBP AF 11/10–13/54 Monthly Report, 6)

Blum's voluminous reports contained evaluations of political developments, and although they were designated for circulation only within the Asia Foundation's board, because Blum was a CIA asset, they would have circulated within the agency, where segments could be incorporated in classified intelligence reports (RBP).

The foundation provided funds, opportunities, and contacts for foreign scholars; these contacts, in turn, provided Blum and staff with links to their homelands. Anthropologist Swami Agehananda Bharati's memoir *The Ochre Robe* (1970) described his impressions of the Asia Foundation. To the young Bharati it appeared as "one of those rich American bodies which the Hindu sages might have likened to the wish-granting tree or the wish-fulfilling cow of mythological fame. It sponsors studies in Asian humanities, and it has its offices all over free Asia, its headquarters in San Francisco. It gave much aid to the Mahāmukuta Buddhist Academy, and it was through the Academy that I became known to the Foundation. It was suggested that I should go on a lecture tour to Japan and I was very pleased with the suggestion" (Bharati 1970: 263). The Asia Foundation was Bharati's gateway to America, where he established his anthropological career with foundation funds.

President Blum used his position to shape academic work. One example of how he accomplished this is seen in a March 20, 1957 letter to the organizer of the upcoming conference seeking funds from the Foundation.[7] Blum mailed the organizer an unsolicited detailed "list of suggestions for participants," and he disparaged some of the scholars previously suggested by the organizer (RB 1, 6, 3/20/57). Because the Asia Foundation helped fund such conferences, these "suggestions" carried significant weight and allowed CIA-linked personnel to alter academic discourse. Blum's correspondence has examples of similar interactions in which he used his influence to shape represented views (RB 1, 6). When these interactions and their secondary aftereffects are multiplied out across all of the CIA funding fronts, and the informal conversations between CIA-linked personnel and non-CIA linked foundation personnel, we can understand some of the returns the Agency received from its investments in funding fronts. By 1957, the Asia Foundation had seventy employees at its San Francisco and New York offices, and another thirty-five in the field (Morehouse 1957: 52–53).[8] During this period the foundation funded diverse projects, including bringing Burmese, Japanese, and other Asian scholars to American universities; translating Boy Scout literature into Burmese and Korean; funding the East Asia Teacher Training Program at the University of California; helping the Camp Fire Girls mail plant seeds to people in Asia; book-buying programs; spreading American business curriculum; producing Asian radio commentaries; and providing economic analysis of Asian developments. The foundation funded various programs at organizations, including the Carnegie Endowment for International Peace, the Association of Asian Studies, the Institute of East Asiatic Studies, the Nieman Foundation for Journalism, the Japan Society, the University of Michigan, the National Association of Foreign Student Advisors, and the Stanford Research Institute.[9]

The AAA: The CIA's Asia Foundation Subsidiary

In 1956, the Asia Foundation, in a program initiated by Robert Blum, began awarding the AAA an annual $2,500 grant to make "it easier for Asians to subscribe to the *American Anthropologist*" and to "provide small sums to enable [Asian anthropologists] to come to scientific meetings if they are already in the USA" (AAAP 13, 14, Sol Tax 7/29/59). As with the CIA's involvement in the AAA's membership roster in 1951–52, the agency's interest in this program appears to have been its desire to identify and contact individual anthropologists. With these funds, supplemented by their own payment of one dollar, Asian anthropologists received a three-year AAA membership, including receipt of *American Anthropologist* (AAAP 49, Mandelbaum memo 1/8/58).[10]

The AAA established a committee to review Asian anthropologists' applications, and AAA publications advertised these subsidized memberships.[11] A letter from Blum to George Foster from December 1956 explained that grant recipients must be from an Asian country of origin located between Afghanistan and Japan, must be involved in teaching or studying anthropology at the graduate level, and must return to their homeland within two years of receiving these funds; the foundation reserved the right to nominate grant recipients (AAAP 48, RB to GF 12/26/56). The AAA's records are incomplete, but they include ledgers listing more than 413 identifiable individual recipients, and a few institutional recipients, between 1956 and 1967 (AAAP 73).[12]

In April 1959, foundation president Blum sent AAA president Sol Tax a $2,500 grant check, stressing that "the Foundation will appreciate continuing receipt of brief reports describing the utilization of funds transmitted to the Association under this grant"; with time, this reporting agreement came to mean the AAA sent lists identifying recipients, including contact information (AAAP 13, 14; RB to ST 4/22/59).

By 1959, Japan and India dominated the program's recipient lists; in 1961, Japan had 101 and India had 38 of the total 168 recipients of the foundation's funds. There were also single-digit numbers of recipients from Pakistan, Indonesia, Thailand, Korea, Formosa, the Philippines, Ceylon, the Andaman Islands, and "other" (AAAP 73, Boggs to Blum 1/27/61; Meggers to Mandelbaum 10/30/59). The foundation gathered detailed information about these recipients (AAAP 73, Blum to Willey 2/20/61). While citing a need to complete accounting of the previous year's grant, in November 1962, Louis Connick, Program Service Division, Asia Foundation (and longtime CIA operative; see later discussion), wrote AAA executive secretary Stephen T. Boggs asking "for as much detail as possible about the awardees themselves" (AAAP 73, LC to SB 11/2/62). When Boggs replied without sending a list of recipients, Connick promptly responded that the foundation still expected "to receive the list of names and addresses of those now receiving subscriptions paid for by The Asia Foundation" (AAAP 73, LC to SB 12/10/62). No explanation was provided concerning why the foundation needed the *addresses* of grant recipients. Connick wrote that he did "appreciate the difficulty involved in providing biographical details on each of the awardees beyond those that will be supplied in the new international directory mentioned in your letter. The data included therein will, I'm sure, be sufficient for our needs" (AAAP 73, LC to SB 12/10/62).

In 1963, Connick and Robert Schwantes asked to meet with Secretary Boggs to discuss a new program of travel grants to "assist Asian anthropologists attending scholarly meetings in the United States." The foundation required the AAA to provide it with the names and addresses of recipients (AAAP 73, LC to SB 5/7/63). Foundation funds were used by AAA Asian scholars to attend academic conferences and other anthropological events within the United States.[13] At times, foundation representatives recommended specific individuals to participate in its sponsored AAA membership program (AAAP 73, Porterfield to Boggs 11/12/65).

In 1966, a year prior to the *New York Times* disclosure that the Asia Foundation was a CIA front, an article in the *Washington Post* with the headline "CIA Front" reported, "Prince Norodom Sihanouk, Cambodia's chief of state, believes the Central Intelligence Agency is using the Asia Foundation, the only US organization remaining in Cambodia. A monitored New China News Agency report quoted Sihanouk as saying his suspicions about the Asia Foundation, a private aid group, were substantiated by its 'persistence' in remaining in Cambodia despite growing hostility from the government and people" (*Washington Post* 1966). The foundation's unusual aggressiveness in contacting scholars and its large amounts of research funds, with little accountability, raised suspicions of CIA ties. Others speculated about possible CIA links. In 1966, UCLA anthropologist Tom Kiefer wrote Ralph Beals with suspicions that the Asia Foundation was a CIA front. Kiefer described how in early 1965 he repeatedly saw the foundation listed as a funding source in articles, and after sending an "exploratory letter" to the foundation, he received an encouraging letter and an application form. Kiefer wrote that he "became suspicious because of the format of the application. No references were required, no testimonials as to scholarly competence. Etc. Rather, the form reminded me of a request for a security clearance (all past addresses, political organizations one belongs to, etc.). I declined to send this in, but received a follow-up request from them two weeks later asking that I complete the form and send it. I rather foolishly did so, before doing any additional checking up on the organization" (RB 75, TK to RB 2/12/66). Kiefer discovered the Asia Foundation was not listed in directories disclosing the sources of foundation funds. He became alarmed when a friend learned from North Borneo contacts that a known CIA operative had made inquiries about Kiefer. This upset Kiefer, who withdrew his grant application. He wrote Beals that other researchers reported "similar experiences of a suspicious nature" (RB 75, TK to RB 2/12/66; a discussion of Elizabeth Bacon's suspicions appears in chapter eleven). During the years before CIA funding was exposed, several anthropologists received Asia Foundation funding, including Robert F. Spencer (BIC 2014c), Agehananda Bharati (Bharati 1970: 263), and Wilton S. Dillon (*AAAFN* 1966 7[7]: 8).[14]

Ramparts *Revelations of* CIA *Funding Fronts*

A March 22, 1967, *New York Times* story disclosed that the Asia Foundation was a CIA cover organization (Turner 1967). The story cited a recently published *Ramparts* article on CIA infiltration of the National Student Association as the impetus for this report. The narrative in the *Times* closely followed the Asia Foundation's press release that acknowledged, but downplayed the extent of, its CIA ties. The foundation announced:

> The Trustees wish to state that in the past they have also knowingly received contributions from private foundations and trusts which have been recently named as

having transmitted Central Intelligence Agency funds to private American organizations. The Trustees' independent decision to accept funds from these foundations and trusts in no way affected the Foundation's policies and programs. All contributions to the Foundation, from whatever source, were accepted on the condition that the expenditure of such funds was to be left to the discretion of the Trustees without any interference and that the funds be used solely for the Foundation's declared purposes. (AAAP 73, Asia Foundation, Trustees Statement 3/21/67)

Foundation spokesman John Bannigan refused to disclose the extent of CIA funds received, nor would he confirm whether the board was aware of these funds. Although a number of prominent Americans (e.g., Paul Hoffman, Grayson Kirk, Adlai Stevenson) were identified by the *New York Times* as sitting on the foundation's board, after the initial flurry of news interest in the story, there was no real follow up by investigative journalists with these individuals concerning the CIA role at the foundation.[15]

The Asia Foundation claimed that employees had "not been used or influenced in any way, directly or indirectly, by any contributor to the foundation" (Turner 1967), but now-declassified documents establish this was not true. One 1966 top secret memo between the CIA and the 303 Committee bluntly described the Asia Foundation as "a Central Intelligence Agency propriety" and expressed concerns about *Ramparts* reporters inquiring into foundation funding sources in case the press discovered the CIA was the Asia Foundation's main funding source.[16] Although the foundation lied to the public about the extent of its CIA ties, the CIA disclosed the truth to its oversight body, the 303 Committee:

> The Asia Foundation (TAF), a Central Intelligence Agency proprietary, was established in 1954 to undertake cultural and educational activities on behalf of the United States Government in ways not open to official U.S. agencies. Over the past twelve years TAF has accomplished its assigned mission with increasing effectiveness and has, in the process, become a widely-known institution, in Asia and the United States.
>
> ... In the long run, we feel [The Asia Foundation's] vulnerability to press attack can be reduced and its viability as an instrument of U.S. foreign policy in Asia can be assured by relieving it *of its total dependence upon covert funding support from this Agency*. In the belief that TAF contributes substantially to U.S. national interests in Asia, and can continue to contribute if its viability is sustained, CIA requests the Committee's study and attention to possible alternative means of supporting it. (CIA 1966b, emphasis added)

This 1966 memo clarified the CIA's awareness of the vulnerabilities of the Asia Foundation and that the foundation had a "total dependence upon covert" CIA funds.

Other declassified documents establish that the CIA used the Asia Foundation to fund projects of interest to the CIA and other agencies. In the 303 Committee minutes of August 5, 1966, reference was made to comments by Walt Rostow "that the CIA had many times taken up the slack [at the Asia Foundation] when other agencies were unable to come up with funds."[17] The Asia Foundation also ran a Books for Asian Students Program that shipped educational books to Asian students, listing 12,040 books and 5,859 journals sent to Afghanistan, 69,464 books and 21,229 journals to the People's Republic of China, and thousands of books sent to other Asian nations. The Books for Asian Students Program appears to have been part of the CIA-operated Asian propaganda program outlined in the CIA's top secret 1953 Draft Psychological Strategy for Southeast Asia (FOIA CIA-RDP80R01731R000700450031-6, pp. 17–18) later described by Victor Marchetti and John Marks (1974: 200–201; AAAP 73, Carlton Lowenberg to S. Boggs 9/23/66).

On April 12, 1967, DCI Richard Helms ordered the CIA to terminate covert funding of the Asia Foundation. The CIA noted that the foundation's recent acknowledgment of CIA funds "produced no serious threat to [Asia Foundation] operations in Asia, and the Trustees are now prepared to attempt to acquire the necessary support for [the Asia Foundation] to go on as a private institution, partially supported by overt U.S. Government grants" (http://www.state.gov/r/pa/ho/frus/johnsonlb/x/9098.htm 4/12/67). The CIA worried that without the steady flow of covert CIA funds, the Asia Foundation could close. The memo expressed the following concerns:

> TAF's present resources are sufficient to sustain operations through July 31, 1967, the end of the Foundation's fiscal year. ▮▮▮▮▮▮▮▮▮▮▮▮▮▮▮▮▮▮▮▮▮▮ [4-1/2 lines of text redacted] To meet these obligations, and to allow TAF management to plan rationally for FY 1968, immediate firm commitments must be acquired on future levels and sources of support. This Agency is prepared to provide whatever assistance remains within its authority and competence to offer. To undertake further necessary action, however, the Agency requests that the Committee now designate the Agency or official to whom TAF management should look for future guidance and direction with respect to United States Government interests. (http://www.state.gov/r/pa/ho/frus/johnsonlb/x/9098.htm 4/12/67 [accessed 3/9/12])

This memo raises questions of what roles the CIA played in helping the Asia Foundation establish non-CIA funds after these disclosures.

On June 26, 1967, the CIA's director of planning, programming, and budgeting terminated CIA funding of the Asia Foundation (FOIA 0001088615, 6/26/67). Victor Marchetti, former special assistant to the CIA's deputy director, later questioned the immediacy of the CIA's break, arguing that the foundation "clearly was one of the organizations which the CIA was banned from financing and, under the recommendations of the Katzenbach committee, the decision was made to end CIA funding. A complete cut-off after 1967, however, would have forced the foundation to shut down, so the agency made it the beneficiary of a large 'severance payment' in order to give it a couple of years to develop alternative sources of funding" (Marchetti and Marks 1974: 200–201). Marchetti and Marks wrote that when the CIA founded the foundation, with its

> carefully chosen board of directors, the foundation was designed to promote academic and public interest in the East. Its sponsored scholarly research, supported conferences and symposia, and ran academic exchange programs, with the CIA subsidy that reached $8 million dollars a year. While most of the foundation's activities were legitimate, the CIA also used it, through penetrations among the officers and members, to fund anti-communist academicians in various Asian countries, to disseminate throughout Asia a negative vision of mainland China, North Vietnam, and North Korea, and to *recruit foreign agents and new case officers*. Although *the foundation often served as a cover for clandestine operations*, its main purpose was to promote the spread of ideas which were anti-communist and pro-America — sometimes subtly and sometimes stridently. (Marchetti and Marks 1974: 200, emphasis added)

This acknowledgment from former CIA personnel raised questions of whether the lists of Asian anthropologists provided by the AAA to the foundation were used by the CIA in attempts to recruit analysts or agents or to assist in the "clandestine operations."

A decade later, the *New York Times* described the Asia Foundation's links to the CIA in more direct terms than those used in the initial disclosure, writing that "the foundation provided cover for at least one CIA operative and carried out a variety of media-related ventures, including a program, begun in 1955, of selecting and paying the expenses of Asian journalists for a year of study in Harvard's prestigious Nieman Fellowship program" (Crewdson and Treaster 1977:37).

Blum was not the Asia Foundation's only career CIA employee. Louis Connick, who collected the AAA's lists of Asian anthropologists receiving memberships subsidized by the foundation, had a long CIA career. In 2008, Connick's nephew Oakley Brooks published an article in the *Christian Science Monitor* that examined Connick's CIA links and described some of the ways he used his position as an apparently "charming humanitarian who ran aid programs in Indochina" during the 1970s, as a front while he "moonlighted for the CIA" (Brooks 2008). According to Brooks:

> While Lou led humanitarian efforts on almost every continent, he ran aid and development programs for the Asia Foundation and the US Agency for International Development (USAID) in Laos at the height of the American military presence in Indochina. As part of those postings, he worked for another organization there — the Central Intelligence Agency.
>
> His involvement with the CIA seemed low-level, passing on information here and there about people. He didn't talk about it much. Like a lot of lives lived on cold-war fronts, his remains shrouded in some mystery. That only fueled my desire to know more about Lou in Laos. As it happens, Lou's past opened up an unexpected portal into my family history as well as life in Laos, then and now.

It is unknown how many other Asia Foundation employees had CIA careers or connections. But even with these gaps, there is a lot we do know. Revelations from the Church and Pike Committee hearings, the disclosure of the CIA's "Family Jewels," and the declassification of CIA documents from this period identify the following elements of the Asia Foundation's relationship with the CIA and the AAA:

> 1. The Asia Foundation was a CIA front throughout the first decade that it subsidized AAA memberships for Asian anthropologists.
> 2. The Asia Foundation during this period had a "total dependence upon covert funding support from" the CIA (303 Committee memo, June 1966).
> 3. Contrary to the intentionally misleading claims in the foundation's 1967 press release, several Asia Foundation employees had CIA ties (Brooks 2008; Turner 1967).
> 4. The CIA used the foundation to "recruit foreign agents," and the foundation "served as a cover for clandestine operations" (Marchetti and Marks 1974: 200).

The Asia Foundation's interest in the AAA was similar to the CIA's 1951 interest in the AAA's comprehensive cross-indexed roster of its members (see chapter 3):

both projects collected information on specific anthropologists that could help identify individuals working in areas of interest to the CIA and that facilitated the CIA's ability to contact anthropologists for interviews, debriefings, or recruitment — practices that we know from Ralph Beals's 1966 AAA inquiries occurred regularly during this period (see chapter 11).

The AAA Reacts to New York Times *Revelations*

After the *Times* story disclosed ties between the Asia Foundation and the CIA, the AAA leadership privately questioned the connections between the CIA, the Asia Foundation, and the association (Turner 1967). On April 29, 1967, Charles Frantz, the AAA's executive secretary, wrote Turner McBaine, secretary of the Asia Foundation, that press coverage of the CIA's covert funding of the Asia Foundation necessitated inquiries into past contacts between the foundation and the AAA. Frantz wrote, "Since you granted this Association funds in the past to subsidize subscriptions for Asian anthropologists to our journal, the *American Anthropologist*, we would like to ask if C.I.A. have been involved in this program or subsidy. We would also appreciate a statement of the full activities the Foundation has carried on during the past with the use of CIA or other intelligence or defense branches of the US government. Finally, may we be honored with copies of your annual and presumably complete financial statements during the past five years?" (AAAP 73, CF to TM 4/29/67). In response, McBaine sent Frantz the foundation's director of program services' statement claiming that CIA funds had been "deposited in the general fund of the Foundation and there intermixed with contributions from a number of other sources" (AAAP 73, TM to CF 6/1/67).

McBaine wrote that "under these circumstances, it would be impossible to determine the source of funds for any particular grant made by the Foundation, including that to the American Anthropological Association" (AAAP 73, TM to CF 6/1/67). This statement tried to normalize the foundation's receipt of CIA funds by listing the names of prominent Americans who had served on its board, a list that included Paul Hoffman, Adlai Stevenson, Robert Blum, and Roger Lapham. The foundation's statement declared:

> The Trustees wish to state that in the past they have also knowingly received contributions from private foundations and trusts which have been recently named as having transmitted Central Intelligence Agency funds to private American organizations. The Trustees' independent decision to accept funds from these founda-

tions and trusts in no way affected the Foundation's policies and programs. All contributions to the Foundation, from whatever source, were accepted on the condition that the expenditure of such funds was to be left to the discretion of the Trustees without any interference and that the funds be used solely for the Foundation's declared purposes. (AAAP 73, Asia Foundation, Trustees Statement, 3/21/67)

The Asia Foundation wanted to have it both ways: claiming that the board was in control, while also maintaining some distance for the board so it could avoid the fallout from the revelation. The foundation claimed its operations had not been corrupted by its reliance on CIA funds even though its operation had been under the supervision of board members with CIA ties.

As the AAA board privately debated its response to these revelations, Boggs was informed by the Asia Foundation that the AAA had fallen behind in submitting reports identifying foundation fund recipients. It had been more than four years since the AAA had submitted the names, addresses, and other materials relating to funded recipients (AAAP 73, LF to SB 12/4/67). Rather than being relieved that the AAA's sloppy bookkeeping protected the identities of several years of Asia Foundation–funded anthropologists from CIA scrutiny, AAA staff worried whether the association could recoup uncollected subsidy funds if it broke from the foundation before receiving the more than $1,500 it was owed for four years of unreimbursed funds.

Frantz, the AAA executive secretary, replied to Lawrence T. Forman, Program Services Division, Asia Foundation, writing that the timing of the AAA annual meeting made it difficult to respond at that time, but he would file a report as soon as he could; he added, however, "We will not be able to give you all [grant recipients'] addresses and nationalities, since a number of the people formerly receiving support through the Asia Foundation are now paying on their own, and it would not be possible to pick them out of our membership files" (AAAP 73, CF to LTF 12/15/67).

Three months later, Frantz wrote Forman, complying with the foundation's request for identifying information on subsidized members (AAAP 73, CF to LTF 3/14/68). Far from appearing ready to sever all ties with the CIA-funded agency, Frantz laid on compliments about how he was "confident that the Asia Foundation program has been most helpful" to various Asian scholars. The AAA had overspent its budgeted Asia Foundation funds by $1,626, and Frantz requested that the foundation cover this debt. Frantz provided a glowing summary of all developments in Asian anthropological scholarship, ranging from the establishment of new journals to the upcoming Eighth International

Congress of Anthropological and Ethnological Sciences to be held in Japan, and he expressed his conviction that the Asia Foundation had "been most helpful in all these matters" (AAAP 73, CF to LTF 3/14/68).

Two weeks later, anthropologist David Mandelbaum who was conducting research in India, wrote Frantz with news that the Indian government was closing down its Asia Foundation offices. Mandelbaum shared "the concern of the Executive Committee about accepting funds from any foundation which may possibly be associated with the CIA" (AAAP 73, DM to CF 3/28/68). On April 26, 1968, Forman wrote Frantz that he was "frankly, somewhat dismayed" to receive his letter of March 14, asking for more funds. Given that the foundation was already in its eighth month of the budgetary year, the request for new funds and for funds to cover losses from the preceding year created some difficulties, but Forman was willing to work with the association by providing $2,000 to cover the AAA's deficit ($1,626) and to provide a small supplement to pay for subscriptions to *American Anthropologist* for Asian scholars (AAAP 73, LTF to CF 4/26/68). Though the loss of CIA funds placed the foundation at risk of collapse, it needed to retain whatever legitimacy it could, and a payment to the AAA during this transition was no doubt calculated as an investment in creating the public appearance that there was nothing unusual about the foundation.[18]

Frantz appeared relieved when he thanked Forman for his offer to send a payment, yet he did not commit the association to accepting the promised $2,000, instead writing that he would bring this to the board's attention at the upcoming meeting on May 17 and 18. Frantz wrote that the AAA had received numerous

> inquiries about the degree to which your activities and that of our members has been supported by Central Intelligence Agency and other intelligence branches of the US Government. One of the most serious questions likely to arise from members of our Executive Board is with respect to the sources of funds to the Asia Foundation for supporting this program of providing Asian anthropologists with subscriptions to our Journal. Since the Board meeting is very soon, I would appreciate your telling me as full as possible 1) the source of funds for the grants we have received heretofore and, 2) the present source of funds that would help carry this program into the future. (AAAP 73, CF to LTF 5/3/68)

Patricia Flanagan, director of the institutional relations for the Asia Foundation, claimed it was impossible to determine which funds were used for particular programs. She assured Frantz that the foundation "does not accept funds from sources alleged to have any connection with the Central Intelligence Agency, nor has it ever been supported by other intelligence branches of the United States Government" (AAAP 73, PF to CF 5/21/68).

The AAA Executive Committee decided at its spring 1968 meeting that President Irving Rouse and Frantz should determine whether the association should accept Asia Foundation payments (AAAP 73, 59th meeting of the E.B. AAA, NYC, May 17–18, 1968).[19] Frantz wrote to President Rouse, summarizing news reports of the CIA's funding of the Asia Foundation and adding that "nothing in our correspondence suggests that since the initial arrangement was made, some ten years ago, any officer of the American Anthropological Association was aware of these sources of funds for The Asia Foundation. It appears clear therefore, that the AAA has unwittingly been receiving money from intelligence agencies to help distribute our Journal to Asian anthropologists at a cost of $1.00 per year" (AAAP 73, CF to IR 6/6/68).

Frantz did not mention the foundation's funding of travel grants for AAA Asian scholars in the United States or its desire to fund students who would be returning home to Asia soon, features that would be ideal for CIA operative/informant recruitment. But Frantz recommended to President Rouse "that this arrangement be terminated immediately, even though Asia Foundation is no longer receiving funds from such sources. You will note in the letter of May 21, 1968, from Patricia Flanagan that (third paragraph) it has not been the policy to publish the names of donors or amounts contributed to The Asia Foundation. The final sentence in that paragraph is deceptive, for while the Foundation may not have ever been supported directly by intelligence branches of the United States Government, all the evidence suggests that it was indirectly so supported" (AAAP 73, CF to IR 6/6/68). Frantz added that if Rouse concurred that the AAA should terminate its relationship with the Asia Foundation, this could be done to coincide with the end of the fiscal year. Frantz noted that the association could still draw upon the $1,626 offered from the foundation to cover its debt, though the foundation might withdraw its offer. Frantz clarified that "in financial terms, as you know, we are in no need of that $1,626.00" (AAAP 73, CF to IR 6/6/68).

President Rouse replied (and sent a carbon copy to Du Bois) that he was inclined to accept Frantz's recommendation, but that he would also like to hear from Cora Du Bois, who had been a member of the AAA committee that had "supervised" the applications for these funds (AAAP 73, IR to CF 6/10/68). Rouse recommended against accepting the offered funds, arguing that the AAA could "afford to pass up this money from an apparently tainted source" (AAAP 73, IR to CF 6/10/68).

Du Bois wrote Rouse that she was not very concerned about the association's receipt of CIA funds. She did not appear to consider that the Asia Foundation had been trying to identify scholars who could be used to provide intelligence or work with the CIA in other capacities. Du Bois wrote that she had

> long been aware of allegations concerning the sources of at least some of the Asia Foundation fund. And I may add that the original committee on which my name appears to the best of my memory really never functioned. I was not aware that the Asia Foundation was covering most of the cost of subscriptions to Asian scholars for the *American Anthropologist*. I consider this a useful and innocent service. It was with some reluctance that I would penalize our Asian colleagues for our moral sensitivities. I am therefore not at all sure that I would go along with the suggestion for discontinuing that service. (AAAP 73, CDB to CF and IR 6/12/68)

In closing, she wrote that she would accept whatever decision Rouse made. President Rouse wanted more input from the board and delayed his final decision until its fall meeting (AAAP 73, IR to CF and CDB 6/18/68, 6/21/68). No doubt Du Bois's years at OSS and the State Department mitigated her negative reactions to the CIA as an agency "supporting" academic endeavors; these years also should have suggested the possibility that a CIA front could use this information for its own ends, but these records show no such concerns.

In November, the Asia Foundation approached the AAA asking for the names, affiliations, and addresses of sponsored Asian anthropologists—even before the AAA had decided whether it would seek reimbursement for the outstanding $1,626. While awaiting the final decision of the AAA's Executive Board, Evelyn Wares of the Asia Foundation's Programs Department wrote Frantz that "whether or not you decide to renew our grant relationship, [the foundation] would like to receive from you for forwarding to our representatives in Asia a listing of the nationalities and Asian institutional affiliations or addresses of the nineteen individuals whose names were circled on the copy of your report enclosed with our letter last April" (AAAP 73, EW to CF 11/6/68).

While Rouse and Frantz had appeared ready to terminate the AAA's connections with the Asia Foundation (even assuming the outstanding debt), at its fall meeting the board rejected Rouse and Frantz's proposal to refuse Asia Foundation funds. Finally, Edward Lehman, AAA director of administration, wrote Evelyn Wares that the board "approved the renewal of our current cooperative grant program to supply the *American Anthropologist* to scholars in Asia." Lehman expressed regrets that the AAA's system did not store addresses of former subscribers, so the association could not send the nineteen missing addresses. Lehman requested, and later accepted, the full $2,000 payment from the foundation (AAAP 73, EJL to EW 11/13/68).

As the AAA leadership privately considered its public response to news of the Asia Foundation's CIA links, the Indian government officially expelled the foundation and forbade it from funding projects within India's borders. The AAA board did not report to its membership on internal debates concerning its response to the decade-long receipt of funds from a CIA front (Lelyveld 1968). Instead, the AAA continued to announce Asia Foundation projects in the AAA Fellow Newsletter (e.g., AAAFN 1968 9[3]: 11). The Fellow Newsletter of May 1968 announced State Department funds were filling the gap left when the CIA ceased funding the Asia Foundation (AAAFN 1968 9[5]: 15). While this announcement acknowledged the Asia Foundation's program for funding Asian anthropologists, no mention was made of the foundation's requests for contact information on program participants, nor did AAA publications discuss the Ramparts findings of how CIA relationships with the NSA allowed the agency to influence that association's business. Rather than fostering public discussions of this CIA front's AAA interface, the association's leadership provided such limited information that it misled its membership about interactions with a CIA-linked organization.

The AAA leadership began curtailing the association's contact with the Asia Foundation. On June 27, 1969, Edward Lehman advised the foundation that the AAA was considering lowering subscription charges for foreign subscribers, and that until the association had decided on this policy change, it would return the $291.60 remaining from the $2,000 Asia Foundation grant (and subtracted $82.40 for copies and shipping of issues of American Anthropologist to the foundation as requested, leaving $209.20) (AAAP 73, EL to Asia Foundation 6/27/69). With the return of this $209.20, the AAA hoped to conclude its relationship with this CIA-tainted organization. But The Asia Foundation, however, did not easily accept rejection; it continued requesting that the AAA renew this relationship until August 1972. But the AAA did not restore this program even after the foundation publicly declared it had severed its CIA ties.

Known Knowns and Rumsfeldian "Known Unknowns" and "Unknown Unknowns"

There are obvious difficulties in analyzing past interactions between unwitting anthropologists and CIA funding fronts. Some of these difficulties are designed; others are of the usual sort encountered in any historical research: purged records, incomplete document collections, loss of knowledgeable informants, the inherent challenges of studying secret classified activities, and a general reticence by many to delve into such troublesome events. This limits contemporary understanding of how these identifiable pieces of intelligence apparatus articulated with CIA analysts, bureaucrats, and spies. Still, we *do* know elements of how these processes functioned. Declassified documents, published reports, congressional testimony, participant accounts, and raw ratiocination help us reconstruct some of these incompletely understood instances of anthropology unwittingly in harness with the needs of the state.

Surviving AAA archival records and information from other archival collections and FOIA requests help us answer some key questions, while other questions remain a mixture of Rumsfeldian "known unknowns" and "unknown unknowns" about two of the CIA's relationships with the AAA. But we actually do know a lot. We know that the CIA approached the AAA in 1951 and established a covert relationship with the board through which the AAA secretly gave the CIA the raw information it had collected for its detailed roster, with the understanding that the CIA would keep the information for its own uses. We know the CIA wanted to identify anthropologists who were working in regions of the underdeveloped world, and it was interested in establishing an agency liaison within the AAA.

We know that the Asia Foundation was established as a CIA asset to help the agency interface with academics working in Asia. We know that the president of this CIA asset (himself a CIA careerist) approached the AAA in 1956, offering to subsidize membership fees of Asian anthropologists; and we know that this CIA asset doggedly sought the names and addresses of those receiving these services. We also know that during this period, the CIA sought contacts with academics, contacts that were used for relationships ranging from onetime debriefings concerning activities in foreign nations to ongoing recruitment of CIA operatives (see Corson 1977: 301–3; D. H. Price 2011e; Cook 1983).

The CIA's use of funding fronts at times damaged the credibility of scholars who received these funds and undermined the academic freedom of all scholars on American campuses. As Jason Epstein wrote in 1967, the CIA's secret use of foundations undermined free academic inquiry, as "the CIA and the Ford Foundation, among other agencies, had set up and were financing an apparatus of intellectuals selected for their correct cold-war positions, as an alternative to what one might call a free intellectual market where ideology was presumed to count for less than individual talent and achievement, and where doubts about established orthodoxies were taken to be the beginning of all inquiry" (16).

Some significant unknowns remain. It is not known which, if any, AAA members may have secretly acted as CIA liaisons during the early 1950s. We do not yet understand exactly what the Asia Foundation did with the information on specific Asian anthropologists it received from the AAA. We do not yet know which, if any, individual Asian anthropologists were contacted by the CIA. Most of these unknowns remain intentionally unknown. One of the reasons we do not know more about the specifics of the CIA's covert funding of American scholars, journalists, and others is because the Church and Pike Committees intentionally chose not to release their identities in the Senate and House reports, as if knowing their identities would be bad for democracy and the free pursuit of knowledge.

The Asia Foundation's interface between the AAA and the CIA compromised the discipline's independence. Yet, this interface only made the discipline as legible and available to the CIA as a twenty-eight-second Internet search today would make any Asian anthropologist. But this episode's key significance is found in what it reveals about larger patterns demonstrating social science's articulation with Cold War America's militarized political economy.

In isolation, this could seem an almost coincidental interface between American anthropology and the CIA, but when viewed in a larger context, it is seen as part of a widespread pattern linking hundreds of anthropologists and other regional specialists with Cold War intelligence agencies. When considered in light of the Church Committee's findings that CIA intrusions into international studies were endemic during this period, perhaps the most unusual thing about this episode is that the AAA ever became aware of the CIA's connection to the Asia Foundation.

Charles Frantz's spring 1968 correspondence with Lawrence T. Forman clarified the fundamental role that financial dependence played in linking the CIA to professional associations and social scientists in general. The AAA wanted to remove the taint that followed from the CIA's funds through the Asia Foundation to its membership. Even though, in 1968, the AAA was flush with money, it did not feel it had the freedom to break free until accounts were settled. Even with President Rouse's position that the AAA could "afford to pass up this money from an apparently tainted source," the association still gave in to pressures to accept these funds, there is little hope of organizations resisting such pressures during more pressing financial times (AAAP 73, IR to CF 6/10/68; cf. D. H. Price 2011f).

While the impacts on those who unwittingly received CIA funds were not always obvious or dramatic, they were nonetheless real. These impacts "nothing so simple as coercion, though coercion at some levels may have been involved, but something more like the inevitable relations between employer and employee in which the wishes of the former become implicit in the acts of the latter" (Epstein 1967: 20). Yet, knowledge and culpability, ignorance and innocence are not always directly linked. Novelist Don DeLillo explores these questions in *The Names*, whose central character realizes that the multinational insurance company where he works as a risk analyst is in fact a front producing classified reports for the CIA. With this realization of his own unwitting CIA work, he wonders if "those who engaged knowingly were less guilty than the people who carried out their designs. The unwitting would be left to ponder their consequences, to work out the precise distinctions involved, the edges of culpability and regret" (DeLillo 1982: 317). As the next chapter shows, sometimes anthropologists' research unwittingly contributed to CIA projects that most would not have chosen to support, leaving the discipline to ponder where the borders of culpability, responsibility, and regret lie.

> Our science is useable, and is often used, in the service
> of imperialism, in the interest of domination and exploitation.
>
> JACK STAUDER | 1972

EIGHT UNWITTING CIA ANTHROPOLOGIST COLLABORATORS

MK-Ultra, Human Ecology, and Buying

a Piece of Anthropology

In the mid-1970s, John Marks, a former State Department Foreign Service employee, used FOIA to release thousands of pages of governmental documents describing covert CIA programs known as MK-Delta and MK-Ultra (Marks 1979; U.S. Senate 1977). Marks's book *The Search for the "Manchurian Candidate"* (1979) summarized sixteen thousand pages of CIA documents, many of which described secret MK-Ultra and MK-Delta projects searching for effective interrogation methods. Some of these CIA programs used fronts to sponsor witting and unwitting scientists to conduct research that would help the CIA understand whether effective forms of "mind control" or "brainwashing" could be developed for interrogation and interrogation-resistance programs. Some studies investigated whether drugs, stress, or specific environmental conditions could be used to "break" prisoners or induce confessions (Marks 1979; SIHE 1960). Some of this research on coercion and interrogation informed the production of the CIA's *Kubark Counterintelligence Interrogation* manual (1963), a foundational document for the agency's interrogation and interrogation-resistance procedures (CIA 1963b, 1983; McCoy 2006: 50–54).

A 1963 CIA report describing MK-Ultra projects stressed the interdisciplinary development of the program, as the CIA's Technical Service Division explored use of "radiation, electro-shock, various fields of psychology, psychiatry, sociology, and anthropology, graphology, harassment substances, and paramilitary devices and materials" to control human behavior (CIA 1963d: 4). In a few cases, the academics working on these projects knew they were funded by laundered CIA funds, but in most instances they were unaware of these connections. The CIA provided the following description of how the MK-Ultra program worked:

> Annual grants of funds are made under ostensible research foundation auspices to the specialists located in the public or quasi-public institutions. This approach conceals from the institution the interest of CIA and permits the recipient to proceed with his investigation, publish his findings (excluding military implications), and account for his expenditures in a manner normal to his institution. A number of the grants have included funds for the construction and equipping of research facilities and for the employment of research assistants. Key individuals must qualify for top secret clearance and are made witting of Agency sponsorship. As a rule each specialist is managed unilaterally and is not witting of Agency support of parallel MKULTRA research in his field. The system in effect *"buys a piece" of the specialist* in order to enlist his aid in pursuing the intelligence implications of his research. His services typically include systematic search of the scientific literature, procurement of materials, their propagation, and the application of test doses [of drugs] to animals and under some circumstances to volunteer human subjects.
>
> The funding of sensitive MKULTRA projects by sterile grants in aid as noted in the preceding paragraph disclosed one of the principal controversial aspects of this program. (CIA 1963d: 7–8, emphasis added)

In his book *A Question of Torture*, Alfred McCoy discussed several CIA-funded MK-Ultra social science research projects producing knowledge to be quietly harvested by CIA personnel who were designing scientific means of conducting interrogation and torture (McCoy 2006: 43–46; cf. Prince 1995). According to McCoy, by using results from MK-Ultra's research programs, "the CIA distilled its findings in its seminal *Kubark Counterintelligence Interrogation* handbook. For the next forty years, the *Kubark* manual would define the agency's interrogation methods and training program throughout the Third World. Synthesizing the behavioral research done by contract academics, the manual spelled out a revolutionary two-phase form of torture that relied on sensory deprivation and self-inflicted pain for an effect that, for the first time in the two millennia of their cruel science, was more psychological than physical" (McCoy 2006: 50).[1] Stress research was a vital area of MK-Ultra's search for effective means of coercive interrogation (40, 45–47, 50).

At the CIA, Richard Helms authorized $25 million in funds for Dr. Sidney Gottlieb and the CIA's Technical Services Division for MK-Ultra projects studying human responses to drugs and environmental conditions that could manipulate individuals to perform behaviors against their will (McCoy 2006: 28–29). Bluebird and Artichoke, two agency operations, studied the possible uses of psychotropic drugs in interrogation. These operations' research methods included dosing unsuspecting people with strong chemical agents like LSD, DMT, liquid concentrates of THC, or opiates (26–28; Marks 1979: 53–121).

Some research placed unwitting prisoner, civilian, or military research subjects at risk, at times leaving individuals with permanent damage (see Weinstein 1990). McCoy observed that the CIA's "alliance with behavioral science seems marvelously synergistic, placing mind-control research at the apex of the academic agenda and providing patronage that elevated cooperative scientists, particularly psychologists, to the first rank of their profession" (2006: 31). The full range of the CIA's MK-Ultra projects is unknown, but a list of projects cobbled together from released FOIA documents indicates a collection of projects studying pleasure, pain, hypnosis, drugs, sex, stage magic, refugees, and other elements of culture and nature seen as useful to the CIA's efforts to interrogate or control the Other.

Human Ecology

Between 1955 and 1965, the CIA relied on a funding front, operating under the names the Society for the Investigation of Human Ecology (SIHE; 1955–61) and the Human Ecology Fund (HEF; 1961–65), to pass on CIA MK-Ultra funds to unwitting social science and medical researchers doing work that had applications for CIA projects, including the agency's *Kubark Counterintelligence Interrogation* manual (CIA 1963b; D. H. Price 2007b, 2007c; Marks 1979; HEF 1963; SIHE 1957, n.d.). The first of these organizations, SIHE, was established in New York City in 1955 by neurologist Harold Wolff, MD. When SIHE was reorganized as HEF in 1961, operations shifted to Cornell University Medical School, with most SIHE personnel remaining with the organization (HEF 1963: 9).[2] While noting this organizational shift from SIHE to HEF, for the remainder of this chapter I refer to both SIHE and HEF simply as "Human Ecology."

Harold Wolff was a highly respected neurologist whose research focused on migraines and other forms of headache pain (Blau 2004).[3] Wolff met Allen Dulles while he was treating Dulles's son for a brain injury, and Dulles later recruited Wolff to direct CIA-funded research on persuasion and interrogation (Marks 1979: 148; D. H. Price 1998: 398–401). Using Human Ecology as a front, the CIA wanted Wolff "to devise ways to use the broadest cultural and social processes in human ecology for covert operations. He understood that every country had unique customs for child rearing, military training and nearly every other form of human intercourse. From the CIA's point of view, he noted, this kind of sociological information could be applied mainly to indoctrinating and motivating people" (Marks 1979: 148–49).

Wolff participated in early LSD research and coauthored an article with Louis Berlin, Thomas Guthrie, Arthur Weider, and Helen Goodell examining the effects of mescaline and LSD on creativity (Berlin et al. 1955). Wolff was joined at Human Ecology by Lawrence Hinkle, MD, whose early career focused on environmental impacts on cardiovascular health (AMWS 2005: 3:753). In 1965, Hinkle described his work with Wolff at Human Ecology as studying "the mechanisms by which the individual man adapts to his particular environment, and the effect of these adaptations upon his disease" (1965: 532). Hinkle and Wolff (1957) pioneered studies of workplace stress and the effects of stress on cardiovascular health and migraines, studies that brought fame and legitimacy of a sort that enticed Human Ecology grant applicants. In the mid-1950s, Hinkle and Wolff began studying the role of controlled stress in "breaking" and "brainwashing" prisoners of war and communist enemies of state (see Hinkle and Wolff 1956). They studied coercive interrogation methods and published their findings in the article "Communist Interrogation and Indoctrination of 'Enemies of the State'" (Hinkle and Wolff 1956). They also produced a classified secret version of this paper for Allen Dulles at the CIA (Rév 2002: 86). As secret reports were passed along to the CIA, Wolff continued to produce Human Ecology–funded research publications on interrogation (Wolff 1960; HEF 1963: 53).[4] Wolff and Hinkle's studies linking stress and disease produced dual use outcomes, with some reports adding to the medical literature and others contributing to CIA interrogation research.

John Marks described Human Ecology as a CIA mechanism for putting "money into projects whose covert application was so unlikely that only an expert could see the possibilities" (1979: 159).[5] Marks illustrated this point by describing a 1958 Human Ecology grant that funded sociologist Muzafer Sherif's study of American inner-city youth gang members. Unbeknownst to Sherif, his data were later used by the CIA to model the management of KGB defectors. Marks discovered that the CIA learned from Sherif's work that "getting a juvenile delinquent [gang] defector was motivationally not all that much different from getting a Soviet one" (see Marks 1979: 159, cf. HEF 1963: 29).

There is no known paper trail establishing how Wolff or others at Human Ecology reported scholars' findings to CIA sponsors, and one declassified internal CIA memo from 1963 indicates the possibility that the reporting of such findings was slipshod. This memo stated that "a substantial portion of the

MKULTRA record appears to rest in the memories of the principal officers," indicating the possibility that Human Ecology findings were usually informally incorporated into the work of individuals working on *Kubark*-related projects (CIA 1963d: 23). Because the CIA destroyed most MK-Ultra records in 1973 (Marks 1979: vii), fundamental questions remain concerning how Human Ecology research made its way into *Kubark*, but *Kubark*'s reliance on citations of Human Ecology–funded scholars, as well as information from declassified CIA documents establishing MK-Ultra's goals and methods, indicate this research was incorporated in *Kubark*.

The *1961–1963 Report of the Human Ecology Fund* (HEF 1963) listed Barnaby C. Keeney (president, Brown University) as the director of the fund's board.[6] James L. Monroe, who had overseen the U.S. Air Force's comprehensive study of Korean War prisoners, was executive director from 1961 to 1963, followed by psychologist David Rhodes (Marks 1979: 156–57).[7] With these established leadership figures, the public face of Human Ecology was a paragon of respectable research; the 1961 directory of the *Encyclopedia of Associations* described the foundation as one that "stimulates and supports studies of man's adaptation to the complex aspects of his environment. Conducts investigations at universities and research centers in such subjects as psychic and physical brain function impairments, sudden environmental change on the health and attitudes of a large immigrant population (conducted among Hungarian refugees), undergraduate adjustments, *ethnopsychiatry*, heteropsychic driving, psycho-social determinants of drug reaction, hypnosis, psychological and physiological variations in personality and personality change, the scientist in the Soviet Union" (EOA 1961: 291). Human Ecology funded anthropological and sociological projects studying Cold War enemies, such as China or Russia, as well as research projects on pain, pleasure, sexuality, stress, and refugees (see D. H. Price 1998: 398–402). Human Ecology lied to some anthropologists concerning the potential uses of their research. In one instance, Cornell University "hired an anthropologist before learning that the CIA security office would not give her clearance, [Harold] Wolff simply lied to her about where the money came from" (Marks 1979: 150–51). Sidney Gottlieb envisioned Human Ecology enabling the CIA to "keep in touch with that part of the scientific research community which were in areas that we were interested in and try to — usually its mode was to find somebody that was working in an area in which we were interested and encourage him to continue in that area with some funding from us" (Weinstein 1990: 139).

Table 8.1 shows reported Human Ecology–funded projects arranged in ascending order of funding level. In 1962, the *AAA Fellow Newsletter* and the

TABLE 8.1 Known Grants Funded by the CIA Research Front Known as the Human Ecology Fund, 1960–1963 (Source: HEF 1963: 13–42)

GRANT	RESEARCHER	FIELD	GRANT AMOUNT
Academy of Science for East Africa			$500
Psychological Effects of Circumcision	Cansever, Gökçe	Medicine	$500
Aspects of Marquesan Behavior	Suggs, Robert C.	Anthropology	$700
Craniological Racial Analysis	Hartle, Janet A.	Anthropology	$948.75
Conceptual Development in Children & Young Adults	Watt, Norman F.	Psychology	$2,250
African Research Foundation			$1,000
Instrumentation in Psychophysiology			$1,000
Internal Migration in Puerto Rico	Macisco, John J.	Medicine	$1,000
Self-Image and Reaction to Isolation	Warbasse, Anne	Psychology	$1,058
Role Conflict in Burma	Guyot, James F.		$1,190
Journal: *Graphologische Schriftenreihe*	Cossel, Beatrice V.	Graphology	$1,470
Three Workshops			$1,500
Antecedents of Revolution	Casuso, Gabriel	Psychology	$1,500
Hungarian Refugees in the Netherlands	Kuyer, H. J. M.		$1,611
Book: *The Psychology of Writing*	Roman, Klara G.	Psychology	$2,000
Self-Instruction Language Program	Carroll, John B.	Education	$2,456
Fallout Shelters and Attitudes Toward Nuclear War	Berrien, Kenneth F.	Psychology	$2,500
Creation and publication of: Bioelectrics Directory	Seels, Saul & Helen F.	Biology	$2,500
Review of Research on Sleep	Webb, Wilse B.	Psychology	$2,500
Psychophysiological Analog Information by Digital Computer	Zimmer, Herbert	Psychology	$2,505

TABLE 8.1 (*continued*)

GRANT	RESEARCHER	FIELD	GRANT AMOUNT
Child-Rearing Antecedents of Dependency and Affiliation	Wardwell, Elinor S.	Psychology	$2,525
Comparative Study of Chinese Personality	Rodd, William G.		$3,000
Aspects of Upper Class Culture among the Internationalized Elite of Japan	Stover, Leon	Anthropology	$3,000
Review and Newsletter: Transcultural Research in Mental Health Problems	McGill University	Psychology	$3,000
Treatment of Psychiatric Disturbances by Yoruba Native Practitioners	Prince, Raymond H.	Psychiatry	$4,060
Factors that Cause individuals to Seek Medical Aid	Groen, J. J.	Medicine	$4,500
A Restudy of Levittown, New York	Liell, John T.	Sociology	$4,525
Publications of *International Resources in Clinical Psychology*	Priester, H. & H. David	Psychology	$5,000
Attitudes of Sierra Leone Students	Bureau of Social Science Research		$5,000
Behavior within the Sociocultural Context	Scott, R., A. Howard	Anthropology	$5,000
Emerging Socio-Political Roles of Scientists & Managers in the USSR	Parry, Albert	Russian studies	$5,000
Volume on Soviet Psychology	Bauer, Raymond/ APA	Psychology	$5,000
Changing Patterns in the Chinese Family	Huang, Lucy Jen	Sociology	$5,775
Child Rearing in Three Cultures	Bronfenbrenner, Urie	Psychology	$6,020
Studies in the Psychology of Aging	Krugman, Arnold D.	Psychology	$6,700

(*continued*)

TABLE 8.1 (*continued*)

GRANT	RESEARCHER	FIELD	GRANT AMOUNT
Computer Simulation of a Simple Society	Browning, Iben	Computer science	$7,500
Studies of Small Group Behavior	Sherif, Muzafer	Psychology	$8,500
Experiments in Extrasensory Perception	Abrams, Stephen I.	Psychology	$8,579
Identification of Individuals Prone to Schizophrenia	Mednick, Sarnoff A.	Psychology	$10,046
Effects of Personality on Drug Reactions	Aaronson, Bernard S.	Psychology	$12,900
Mental Illness and Identity	Hirvas, Juhani Allardt, Erik	Sociology Sociology	$16,479
Psychiatric Rating Scales	Samuel B. Lyerly Preston S. Abbott	Psychology Psychology	$22,551
Measurement of Motivation	Eysenck, H. J.	Psychology	$26,030
Institute for Experimental Psychiatry	Orne, Martin T.	Psychology	$30,000
Neighborhood Family Clinics (Harlem)	Berle, Beatrice	Medicine	$32,817
Study of the Genetic Code	Bledsoe, W. W.	Mathematics	$35,000
Physique and Psychological Functioning	Haronian, Frank	Psychology	$39,000
Artificial Intelligence	Browning, Iben	Computer science	$40,000
Pattern Recognition	Bledsoe, W. W.	Psychology	$45,000
Comparative Learning Behavior of Different Personality Types	Schucman, Helen Thetford, William N.	Psychology	$47,832
Anthropological Identification of the Determinants of Chinese Behavior	Carr, William K.	Anthropology	$48,480
Implications of a Hypothesized Congruence between Personality Systems	Gittinger, David R.	Psychology	$50,000
Panoramic Research, Inc.			$80,000
Cross-Cultural Generality of Meaning Systems	Osgood, Charles E.	Communications	$83,406
Interdisciplinary Conference Program			$116,116

African Studies Review carried Human Ecology funding announcements, soliciting grant applications on a "diversity of research problems and methodology within the behavioral sciences" (AAAFN 1962 3[5]: 4–5; *African Studies Review* 1962, vol. 5: 42). Wolff used his professional relationship with Margaret Mead to recruit anthropologists, gaining an IFIS mailing list from her in 1956, writing that he wanted "to bring to the attention of the members the interests of the Society for the Investigation of Human Ecology and the possibility for future research funding" (MM C37, HW to MM 12/3/56; MM 37, MM to HW 1/4/57).[8] In 1964, the *Fellow Newsletter* announced that anthropologist William Carr had "joined the staff of the Human Ecology Fund" and that the fund contributed to the financing of Raymond Prince and Francis Speed's film *Were Ni! He is a madman*, on Yoruba treatments of mental disorders (AAAFN 1964 5[5]: 6).[9]

Human Ecology financed a wide range of projects, including Frank Westie's (1965) efforts to empirically test American variations in valuations and beliefs; Melvin DeFleur's (1964) study of occupational roles as portrayed on television; scientific studies of the shifts and variations in individuals' attitudes over time (DeFleur and Westie 1963: 17; cf. Glander 2000: 164–65); Raymond Augustine Bauer's trips to gather information for his book *Some Views on Soviet Psychology* (1962); Ronald Taft's (1966) study of immigrant assimilation in Australia; psychologist Dr. Joseph C. Kennedy's research into the educational needs of Ghana, Liberia, and Nigeria;[10] sociologist Richard Stephenson's work on deviant behavior;[11] and a 1960 conference in Cambridge, Massachusetts that led to the publication of the book *International Behavior: A Social-Psychological Analysis* (Kelman 1965). Sociologists Robert Ellis and Clayton Lane used Human Ecology funds to study the effects of social isolation, social strain, and deprivation on low-income students entering high-status universities (Ellis and Lane 1967: 237). Human Ecology funded American psychologists Harold Schlosberg, Neal E. Miller, and Carl Pfaffman's trip to tour psychological laboratories in the Soviet Union and Poland (Kimble 1979: 704). It also funded the travel of anthropologist Marvin Opler and an American delegation attending the First International Congress of Social Psychiatry in London in 1964 (Opler 1965).

At the Human Ecology–sponsored conference "Information and Control Processes in Living Systems," held in 1965, participants covered topics without direct connections to interrogation, yet the CIA's interrogation studies focused on controlling processes in very direct ways, and the agency's theoretical approach was informed by such parallel, but not directly linked, thematic work (see Ramsey 1965). Other projects were smaller in scale, with apparently intangible outcomes.

Human Ecology provided funding for anthropologist Leon Stover's project titled "Aspects of Upper Class Culture among the Internationalized Elite of Japan." Stover later wrote me that his Human Ecology "research report was written up as a science fiction story published in Damon Knight, ed., *Orbit 9*." Stover told me his grant had come "as an act of charity by a close friend who worked for the fund. It supplemented another small grant from the National Institute of Mental Health" on a research project that "was peripheral to my job as a visiting professor in the Department of Cultural Anthropology at Tokyo University (1963–1965)" (LS to DHP 11/28/94). Stover set his story in a futuristic Japan, where movies are not filmed using traditional cameras and actors but instead are the recorded visions of "a young catatonic" who is cajoled into envisioning scenes desired by film producers.[12] The story uses this process of "bionic moviemaking" to analyze postwar Japanese attitudes toward Japanese citizens who have spent time abroad.

In his story, Stover scripted the remarks of a fictional anthropologist, Professor Iwahashi, as commentary on differences between Japanese and American social structure revealed in American mental hospitals' segregation of patients into "violent wards, general wards, or open wards." In Japan, in contrast, as Professor Iwahashi describes it, "mental patients enjoy unmitigated commonality. This equality under one class of confinement is enabled by the fact that we Japanese are so disciplined a race that even when we go mad, we go mad politely, with no disobedience to authority, no unguarded lapse of consideration for others, no unexpected breach of decorum, and no interruption of politesse" (Stover 1972: 197). Focusing on the high-context nature of Japanese society, Stover argued that "it is in the social conduct of your human relations that you are Japanese, if in nothing else" (200).

Stover viewed the secret to being truly Japanese as found in the principle of *ki ga tsuku*, the practice of finding "out what the other person intends to do. It is a game of perception. But it is different from the one played by Westerners. Foreigners want always to know *why* people do things. Foreigners want always to understand each other. Just as they come to Japan and try to understand the Japanese people" (1972: 201–2). Stover's Japanese narrator viewed his society as static, as a world where everyone's role "is fixed and identified like a piece on a chessboard. When we encounter another Japanese we have only to guess what his next move will be" (202).

Stover's fictional narrative contained the theoretical strands of the era's standard intercultural communications research.[13] With MK-Ultra's interest in psychotropic drug research, some might speculate about these images of catatonic hallucinations or the social differences in mental hospitals, but there is no evidence of any such connection here. Stover's research instead best fits within the continuum of Human Ecology–funded cross-cultural communications studies and the fund's interest in "breakdowns." Human Ecology funded many projects with no detectable connection to MK-Ultra projects, those projects appear to have only provided Human Ecology with the necessary appearance of legitimacy within the academic community. It is possible that Stover's work, along with several other projects, including cranial analysis studies, studies of Puerto Rican migration and child rearing, and a study of Levittown, New York, were funded to increase Human Ecology's visibility and to gain access to scholars who might later be approached as consultants.[14]

A Technical Services staff member indicated that grants provided to scholars like Charles Osgood, B. F. Skinner,[15] and Karl Rogers "'bought legitimacy' for the Society and made the recipients 'grateful'. . . . the money gave Agency employees at Human Ecology a reason to phone Skinner — or any other recipient — to pick his brain about a particular problem" (Marks 1979: 160).[16] Human Ecology sponsored Raymond Prince's Nigerian transcultural psychological studies during the late 1950s (see HEF 1963: 50–51; Prince 1962a, 1962b). Prince's *Ifa: Yoruba Divination and Sacrifice* (1964) provides an ethnographic account of Nigerian traditional rituals of sacrifice and divination. The January 1961 issue of the *AAA Fellow Newsletter* announced the three-month research project by Prince and his coworkers, including Dorothea C. Leighton, Charles Savage, and anthropologists Charles and Jane Hughes, as one "identifying and rating sociocultural factors that may be of significance to prevalence of symptoms, problems of identifying and evaluating types of psychiatric disorder in the Nigerian setting" (*AAAFN* 1961 2[1]: 11). Prince later speculated that this research was funded to establish connections in the field that would later be used by the CIA for the recruitment of foreign nationals and "to collect psychocultural data on cultures and countries of interest to the CIA for psychological warfare purposes" (1995: 407). His research contributed to MK-Ultra's data on isolating cultural manifestations of mental illness. A CIA document declassified and accessed by Prince in 1977 clarified that, unbeknownst to him, the CIA believed his research would "add somewhat to our understanding of native *Yoruba* psychiatry including the use of drugs, many of which are unknown or not much used by Western practitioners. It will also assist in the identification of promising young [deleted by CIA censors] who may be of direct interest to the Agency. *Prince* will be located in *Nigeria* thus carrying out the plan of developing the Human Ecology Fund as a world-wide organization. Since *Prince* will learn the *Yoruba* language this project offers a potential facility for [deleted by CIA censors] project 95" (Prince 1995: 412).[17] In Prince's case, the CIA was interested in ethnographic fieldwork not only to access a distant cultural world but as a recruitment tool and to collect new pharmacological samples.

Human Ecology funded projects to develop standardized psychological instruments whose dual uses potentially included gauging variations in individuals' responses to interrogation. In the 1950s, Human Ecology funded an Educational Testing Service (ETS) project examining the Wechsler Adult Intelligence Scales (ETS 1955: 90, 92), and it later funded Eugene Gendlin and Jerome Berlin's study of subjects monitored by a polygraph (1961: 73n1).

Several studies examining childhood conceptual developments supplied information that appears to have informed *Kubark*'s conception of the childlike regressive state induced by "coercive interrogation" (CIA 1963b). Research examining isolation and sleep deprivation, stress, handwriting, and links between personality types and drug interactions addressed topics central to the *Kubark* interrogation manual. Human Ecology received grants from the U.S. Public Health Service (MYP-5699 and MH-08807) to produce the *Handbook of Psychiatric Rating Scale* (Lyerly and Abbott 1966),[18] which compiled nineteen psychiatric scales. The resulting product appeared to serve dual uses: producing knowledge that could be used by mental health practitioners, while simultaneously producing a tool that would be of use to interrogation specialists gauging the impacts of interrogations.

But Human Ecology also funded studies on revolutions, refugees, Chinese personality types, Chinese family structure, Soviet psychology, and cross-cultural communication, as well as various studies that examined elements of psychological profiling.

Human Ecology, China, Hungary, and Elsewhere

The CIA used Harold Wolff's presence at Cornell to investigate ways to take Chinese citizens living in the United States and, as Lawrence Hinkle put it, "steer them to [the CIA], and make them into agents" (qtd. in Marks 1979: 149). Human Ecology sponsored Cornell projects investigating ways to train recruited Chinese agents to resist Chinese brainwashing (150).

Rhoda Métraux assisted Wolff and Hinkle's research on the manifestations of stress on Chinese individuals who were unable to return to China (see Hinkle et al. 1957). After Wolff learned that Métraux would not be granted CIA research clearance, he lied to her about the nature of the project (Marks 1979: 150–51).

Raymond Prince speculated that Human Ecology sought to "use their Chinese sample as a means to identify disgruntled refugees with suitable personality profiles who had fled the Communist regime 10 years earlier and might be persuaded to act as CIA agents back in China" (1995: 411). Hinkle later admitted that this project's secret purpose was to recruit skilled CIA intelligence operatives who could return to China as spies. As an unwitting participant, Métraux collected information on Chinese subjects' performance under stress, which contributed to the CIA's efforts to train agents to resist Chinese forms of interrogation (Marks 1979: 149–50). Human Ecology funded William Rodd's research into Chinese cultural systems of problem solving, values, and logic (HEF 1963: 17), and William K. Carr was awarded $48,480 to work on a project, "Anthropological Identification of the Determinants of Chinese Behavior" (*AAAFN* 1964 5 [5]: 6; Carr and Tullock 1965).[19]

One project used unwitting social scientists to interview Hungarian refugees to gather intelligence for the CIA (see Marks 1979: 153–54; Stephenson 1978; HEF 1963: 30). In the mid-1950s, Human Ecology sponsored two conferences at which scholars examined the political, psychological, and cultural means through which Hungarian refugees retained their identities under Soviet occupation (see SIHE 1958). Stephenson described his discovery in 1977 that the Hungarian refugee research project he had been involved with since the 1950s had been secretly funded by the CIA's MK-Ultra program. He had mixed reactions upon learning of this CIA sponsorship, later writing that he was both "offended and resentful, if not actually angry," that he had "been had"; he also noted, "In view of the nature of the sociological data and its undirected and unclassified status, the idea that the CIA was involved and the Society was its 'cover' assumed a cloak and dagger staging closer to comic opera than serious drama" (Stephenson 1978: 130).

HUMAN ECOLOGY AND A RANGE OF *KUBARK*-LINKED RESEARCH

The CIA's *Kubark Counterintelligence Interrogation* (1963) was an instruction manual, not an academic treatise, and as with other manuals, it cites only a few academic sources. Though most sources remain unacknowledged, the work of some Human Ecology–sponsored scholars appears in its pages, including Martin Orne's research on hypnosis, work that provided the basis of *Kubark*'s discussion of the uses and limits of hypnosis in interrogation (CIA 1963b: 78, 95–98). Biderman and Zimmer's research and published volume on nonvoluntary behavior funded by Human Ecology (Biderman and Zimmer 1961: ix) is quoted and cited extensively in *Kubark* (see CIA 1963b: 77–80, 83, 86–87, 89–91, 99), as is Hinkle's work on pain and the physiological state of interrogation subjects (CIA 1963b: 83, 93). *Kubark*'s discussion of the uses of graphology in analyzing interrogation subjects drew on Karla G. Roman's Human Ecology–sponsored research (CIA 1963b: 81; HEF 1963: 38). Martin Orne and sociologist Albert D. Biderman's Human Ecology–sponsored research is cited in *Kubark*'s scant reference section. *Kubark* incorporated (without attribution) the essentials of anthropologist Mark Zborowski's model of pain, explaining that "the sensation of pain seems to be roughly equal in all men, that is to say, all people have approximately the same threshold at which they begin to feel pain, and when carefully graded stimuli are applied to them, their estimates of severity are approximately the same. . . . Yet . . . when men are very highly motivated . . . they have been known to carry out rather complex tasks while enduring the most intense pain" (CIA 1963b: 93; see Zborowski 1952, 1969; Zipperstein 2010; D. H. Price 2011d).

Kubark discussed the importance of interrogators' learning to read the body language of interrogation subjects. Human Ecology funded early research on body language by anthropologist Edward Hall, whose studies aligned with CIA research needs.[20] Several pages of *Kubark* instructed interrogators how to read a subject's body language with tips such as the following: "It is also helpful to watch the subject's mouth, which is as a rule much more revealing than his eyes. Gestures and postures also tell a story. If a subject normally gesticulates broadly at times and is at other times physically relaxed but at some point sits stiffly motionless, his posture is likely to be the physical image of his mental tension. The interrogator should make a mental note of the topic that caused such a reaction" (CIA 1963b: 55).

In 1977, after public revelations of the agency's role in directing Human Ecology research projects, Edward Hall discussed his unwitting receipt of CIA funds that supported his writing of *The Hidden Dimension* (E. T. Hall 1966). Hall acknowledged that his studies of body language would have been useful for the CIA's goals "because the whole thing is designed to begin to teach people to understand, to read other people's behavior. What little I know about the [CIA], I wouldn't want to have much to do with it. . . . I don't mind training people for the State Department, the United States Information Agency, the Agency for International Development—even the Army . . . within that overall context, here's a group of people out there doing dirty tricks. I don't know what you do about that" (qtd. in Greenfield 1977: 11).[21] Greenfield added, "Hall doubts he would have taken the money, had he known it was coming from the CIA: 'I would want to know why were they backing me? What were they getting out of this? I still don't know'" (11). Despite his later personal objections, Hall's work informed Human Ecology's knowledge base.[22]

Albert Biderman received grants from Human Ecology and the air force to study former U.S. soldiers who had been prisoners of war in North Korea and "Communist China" to test factors leading prisoners to confess (Biderman 1960: 120n1).[23] He found that "prisoners rarely conform to the injunction of silence in interrogation because to do so is inconsistent with more compelling requirements they experience in the actual situation; namely, the maintenance of a viable social role and an esteemed self-image" (121). Biderman studied the difficulties prisoners had in simply remaining silent while facing interrogation and found that silence often became a form of interaction with interrogators, especially interrogators who used a "silent confirmation" trick where they repeatedly asked and answered questions whose answers were already known as a way of tricking prisoners into mentally engaging with them. He found that stress mounted with each question prisoners refused to answer, and that stress was relieved by answering questions.

Biderman interviewed soldiers and amassed reports of torture, coercive interrogation, and "brainwashing," presenting these in an air force report titled *Communist Techniques of Coercive Interrogation* and academic articles on interrogation and forced indoctrination (Biderman 1956, 1960). Human Ecology funded Biderman's book *March to Calumny: The Story of American POWs in the Korean War* (1963). *March to Calumny* critiqued claims that American soldiers in the Korean War who broke under Korean interrogation were weak and also demonstrated that Korean War POWs did not behave significantly differently from soldiers in other recent wars.

Human Ecology funded a variety of so-called mind control studies, including Edgar Schein's (1961) study of Chinese efforts to brainwash American prisoners. Eysenck and colleagues conducted research on the hypnotic potential of the spinning hypno-disk (as seen in dozens of cheesy 1950s science fiction movies) (Eysenck, Willett, and Slater 1962). The 1977 Senate hearings on MK-Ultra programs detailed the CIA's failures in the 1950s and early 1960s to find esoteric means like hypnosis, psychedelics, "truth serums," sensory deprivation tanks, or electroshock to break uncooperative interrogation subjects. John Gittinger testified that by 1963, after years of experimentation, the CIA realized that "brainwashing was largely a process of isolating a human being, keeping him out of contact, putting him under long stress in relationship to interviewing and interrogation, and that they could produce any change that way without having to resort to any kind of esoteric means" (U.S. Senate 1977: 62). The CIA understood that *isolation* and *stress* were the keys to effective coercive interrogation, and it was during this shift away from exotic drugs and equipment that Human Ecology sponsored the stress research discussed below.

In 1964, A. Arthur Sugerman and Frank Haronian published their article "Body Type and Sophistication of Body Concept," which reviewed various efforts to correlate indexes of "body type" to psychological profiling features. The authors, whose study had been funded by Human Ecology, conceded that there were significant reliability problems with Sheldon's somatotype research (other researchers had difficulty replicating his findings), yet they were enamored with the prospect that some means of correlating body type with psychological profiling was possible. Sugerman and Haronian discussed the possibility that there may have been errors in the specific psychological and physical variables measured, and their study combined Sheldon somatotype measurements with Parnell phenotype measurements, concluding that both systems produced comparable results.

Haronian and Sugerman's Human Ecology–funded work from 1965 sought to test the validity of Sheldon's work. Psychologist William Herbert Sheldon had developed his somatotype model as an attempt to correlate human body types with psychological outlooks, believing that physical appearance held decipherable indications of inner psychic worlds or individual potentials. Though his somatological work produced explanatory models that were no more accurate than the phrenology of a century earlier, Sheldon had a following during the 1940s and 1950s (see Rosenbaum 1995). Haronian and Sugerman (1965) contrasted Sheldon's somatotype approach to classifying and interpreting human body forms with Parnell's phenotype scoring methodology.

Haronian and Sugerman conceded that Parnell's methodology was less rigorous and was susceptible to reliability errors, but they liked its advantage of not requiring subjects to disrobe and be photographed in the nude (1965: 135). Their evaluation of these two systems of classifying body type found that they produced varied results. The authors did not attempt to correlate the systems' body type classifications with psychometric data, leaving that for future research.

Haronian and Sugerman's efforts to read bodies fit with Human Ecology's efforts to establish baseline standardized metrics that could also be used to understand interrogation subjects. With deep misunderstandings of the impacts of biology and culture on human behavior, Human Ecology did not realize that the best outcome that Haronian and Sugerman's model could hope to produce was an efficient way of consistently labeling and measuring stereotypes, but their model did not achieve even this misguided end.

Human Ecology's Anthropological Research on Bereavement and Stress

It is unclear why Human Ecology sponsored several anthropological research projects investigating cultural impacts on grieving; it is possible that Wolff or others recognized that bereavement was a universal experience of intense stress *and* isolation mitigated by culture. Human Ecology funded medical anthropologist Barbara Gallatin Anderson's study using American bereavement data to develop a cross-cultural framework for studying bereavement (Anderson 1965: 181n1).[24] Anderson interviewed mental patients and determined that the death of someone close to them had been the single most stressful event of their lives (184). Several MK-Ultra projects investigated the effects of isolation on interrogation subjects as part of efforts to understand states of regression and psychic collapse of the sort "whose covert application was so unlikely that only an expert could see the possibilities" (Marks 1979: 159; cf. CIA 1963b: 83).

Human Ecology funded anthropologists Alan Howard and Robert Scott's (1965–66) investigation of enculturation's impacts on grieving processes. Their work studied how cultural norms and behavioral practices caused isolation, which created different conditions of stress for grieving individuals. Scott drew on sociological literature to examine American ways of death, grieving, and alienation, while Howard applied his ethnographic knowledge to examine how Polynesian Rotuman Islanders were socialized to experience isolation differently and how these differences translated to different cultural reactions to death. In 1994, Robert Scott wrote me, describing in some detail his and Alan Howard's interactions with Harold Wolff and Human Ecology. Scott explained that he and Howard

> had absolutely no idea that the Human Ecology Fund was a front for anything, least of all the CIA. As far as I knew it was a small fund that was controlled by Harold Wolff and used to support projects of various types concerning the study of stress and illness in humans. Its connection with the CIA only came to my attention some years later when Jay Schulman . . . of Columbia wrote an article exposing the connection.[25] Obviously if I had known of such a connection at the time I would never have accepted money from them. I should also explain that the money we got from them was used to support library research I was doing at the Cornell Medical School on studies of stress and that the final product was a theoretical model for the study of stress in humans. . . .

I was interested in studying stress and illness and the work of Harold Wolff, his colleague Larry Hinkle and others was far closer to the mark. I therefore arranged to transfer my postdoc to a unit headed by Hinkle and with which Harold Wolff had an affiliation. The name of that unit was the Human Ecology Studies Program. At the time I was there, Larry Hinkle was completing a study of stress among telephone operators working for New Jersey (or was it New York) Bell Telephone company and he was also beginning a study of stress and heart disease among a group of executives for the New Jersey Bell Company. He invited me to participate in the analysis for the first study and to advise him about the design of several of the instruments used in connection with that project. At the same time, I was also working with Alan [Howard] on an article about stress and it was in connection with this work that I received support from the Fund. Or at least I think that is the reason why I acknowledged the Fund in our paper. I no longer have financial records from that date and therefore do not have a file indicating the amount of support I got or for what period of time I received it. I do remember that either Hinkle or Wolff or both suggested that I write a letter to the Fund requesting a modest level of support for our work (I can't remember the amount, but I am reasonably certain it came to no more than a few thousand dollars). As I recall, I used it to supplement my Russell Sage Foundation stipend, probably for summer income in order to finish the paper.

It will be obvious to you from reading this that I knew Harold Wolff for a brief period of time during this period. As I recall, Wolff [died] either in 1962 or 1963. From the manner in which the matter was handled I gained the impression that he had available to him a small fund of money that could be used to support research and writing of the sort I was doing and he gave me some for my work. At that time there were lots of small pots of money sitting around the medical school and there was no reason to be suspicious about this one. Moreover, Wolff was a figure of great distinction in Neurology and was well known outside of his field as well. For all of these reasons I simply assumed that everything was completely legitimate and was astounded when the connection between the Fund and the CIA was disclosed.

... As I recall the only application I made was in the form of a letter. I should also mention that during the course of our collaboration Alan [Howard] and I co-authored a second paper on cultural variations in conceptions of death and dying which was also published and in which there is an acknowledgment to the Fund. . . . [26] My association with the Human Ecology Studies Program came to an end early in 1964. (RAS to DHP 11/2/94)

Scott confirmed that Wolff and Hinkle shielded participants from knowledge of CIA funding and interests.

Howard and Scott's article "Cultural Values and Attitudes toward Death" (1965–66) reads like a typical synthetic literature review of the period, though the literature cited shows the influence of Wolff, Hinkle, and Human Ecology; references drew on Philip E. Kubzansky's chapter in Biderman and Zimmer's Human Ecology volume, *The Manipulation of Human Behavior*—the volume most heavily cited in *Kubark* (Howard and Scott 1965–66: 163n11).[27] Out of the universe of writings on death and bereavement, Howard and Scott's selection of Kubzansky's prison research illustrates how Human Ecology's environment shaped sponsored studies. Howard and Scott's views of isolation reflected Human Ecology's focus on the isolation and vulnerability of prisoners. As they wrote in their article:

> While a fear of death may stem from anxieties about social isolation, it seems equally true that the process of becoming socially isolated stimulates a concern about death.... When social isolation is involuntary... the individual experiencing separation from others may become obsessed with the idea of death. Ordinary values, those previously associated with primary groups or with society in general, may pale into insignificance when they are no longer shared with significant others.... the fear of death may come to outweigh the fear of dying, and the person may be motivated toward ego-destructive behavior. (164)

For hidden CIA sponsors, the focus on isolation and vulnerability transcended the circumstances of death and bereavement. This work had uses for Human Ecology's secret sharers considering captive individuals facing other forms of total social isolation, who shared characteristics with those experiencing the social isolation of mourning.

Howard and Scott's Stress Model and Kubark's *Approach to Stress Mastery*

Human Ecology's grant supported Howard and Scott's library research and the later write-up of their findings. Scott was based at Cornell, where he had some contact with Hinkle, Wolff, and other Human Ecology personnel, while Howard wrote in California and never visited Cornell. Prior to 1961, they submitted a copy of their Human Ecology–sponsored paper developing a "proposed framework for the analysis of stress in the human organism" to *Behavioral Science*, and a copy of the paper was submitted to their sponsor (RS to DHP 6/11/07; Howard and Scott 1965). Although the paper was submitted in 1961, it was not published in *Behavioral Science* until 1965 (AH to DHP 6/5/07).

In 1977, John Gittinger testified to the Senate Select Committee on Intelligence and the Subcommittee on Health and Scientific Research of the Committee on Human Resources that the CIA's funding of Human Ecology allowed it to be "run exactly like any other foundation," which meant the CIA had "access to any of the reports that they had put out, but there were no strings attached to anybody. There wasn't any reason they couldn't publish anything that they put out" (U.S. Senate 1977: 59). This was the principal way that the findings of Human Ecology research were channeled to those at the CIA who selectively harvested elements of this work for their own uses.

The scope of Scott and Howard's work aligned with Wolff's ongoing research on stress and health, as well as Wolff's secret search for successful "coercive interrogation" methods. Both Scott and Howard had worked together on their cross-cultural stress model before they knew of Human Ecology, and Scott argued they would have undertaken this work even without this funding (RS to DHP 6/11/07). Human Ecology's semiannual report described their research as developing an "equilibrium model . . . based upon a view of man as a 'problem solving' organism continually confronted with situations requiring resolution to avoid stress and to preserve well-being" (HEF 1963: 24). Understanding individuals' efforts to "avoid stress" through cooperative "problem solving" was just one abstraction away from transforming an informative general model on stress into a useful interrogation tool for the CIA.

Howard and Scott's 1965 article on stress could be "reverse engineered" for information on how to weaken a person's ability to adapt to stressful environments, such as those present during an interrogation. Thus, when Howard and Scott wrote that "stress occurs if the individual does not have available to him the tools and knowledge to either successfully deal with or avert challenges which arise in particular situations," they were simultaneously scientifically describing factors mitigating the experience of stress (*their* purpose), while also unwittingly outlining what environmental factors should be manipulated if one wanted to keep an individual under stressful conditions (*their hidden CIA patron's* purpose) (Howard and Scott 1965: 143).

Howard and Scott reviewed literature that established how stress alters regular gastric functions and can cause or increase the severity of diseases. They described how individuals cope with stressful situations through efforts to "maintain equilibrium in the face of difficult, and in some cases almost intolerable circumstances" (1965: 142). Howard and Scott's "problem-solving" model for conceptualizing stress began with the recognition that individuals under stress try to reduce their stress and return to a state of equilibrium. It posited that "disequilibrium motivates the organism to attempt to solve the problems which produce the imbalance, and hence to engage in problem-solving activity" (145).

To apply Howard and Scott's model to situations involving coercive interrogation, interrogation subjects would be seen as trying to reduce the "imbalance" of discomfort or pain and returning to a state of equilibrium by providing the interrogator with the requested information. Their model could be adopted to view cooperation as the solution to the stressful problems faced by interrogation subjects, and rational subjects would cooperate in order to return to noncoercive states of equilibrium. This philosophy aligned with a basic *Kubark* paradigm, which maintained the following:

> The effectiveness of most of the non-coercive techniques depends upon their unsettling effect. The interrogation situation is in itself disturbing to most people encountering it for the first time. The aim is to enhance this effect, to disrupt radically the familiar emotional and psychological associations of the subject. When this aim is achieved, resistance is seriously impaired. There is an interval—which may be extremely brief—of suspended animation, a kind of psychological shock or paralysis. It is caused by a traumatic or sub-traumatic experience which explodes, as it were, the world that is familiar to the subject as well as his image of himself within that world. Experienced interrogators recognize this effect when it appears and know that at this moment the source is far more open to suggestion, far likelier to comply, than he was just before he experienced the shock. (CIA 1963b: 65–66)

Thus a skilled interrogator "helps" subjects move toward "compliance," after which subjects may return to a desired state of equilibrium.

Howard and Scott found that individuals under stress had only three response options. They could mount an "assertive response," in which they confronted the problem directly and enacted a solution by mobilizing whatever resources were available; they could have a "divergent response," in which they diverted "energies and resources away from the confronting problem," often in the form of a withdrawal; or they could have an "inert response," in which they reacted with paralysis and refused to respond (Howard and Scott 1965: 147). They concluded that the "assertive response" was the only viable option for an organism responding to externally induced stress: if these findings are transposed onto an environment of coercive interrogation, this would mean that cooperation was the only viable option for interrogation subjects.

In the context of MK-Ultra's interest in developing successful interrogation methods, these three responses took on other meanings. Interrogation subjects producing an "assertive response" would cooperate with interrogators and provide them with the desired information; subjects producing a "divergent response" might react to interrogation by mentally drifting away from the present dilemma (like Sam Lowry, at the end of Terry Gilliam's film *Brazil*), or by fruitless efforts to redirect inquiries; and subjects producing an "inert response" with frozen states without external response — like that of the torture machine's victims in Kafka's *Penal Colony* (see D. H. Price 2010b).

Kubark described how interrogators use "manipulated techniques" that are "still keyed to the individual but brought to bear on himself" that create stresses for the individual and push him toward a state of "regression of the personality to whatever earlier and weaker level is required for the dissolution of resistance and the inculcation of dependence" (CIA 1963b: 41). As presented in *Kubark*, successful interrogators get their subjects to view them as liberators helping them find a way to return to the desired state of release: "As regression proceeds, almost all resisters feel the growing internal stress that results from wanting simultaneously to conceal and to divulge. . . . It is the business of the interrogator to provide the right rationalization at the right time. Here too the importance of understanding the interrogatee is evident; the right rationalization must be an excuse or reason that is tailored to the source's personality" (40–41). *Kubark* conceptualized the stress created in an interrogation environment as a useful tool to be manipulated by interrogators who understood their role of helping subjects find release from this stress: "The interrogator can benefit from the subject's anxiety. As the interrogator becomes linked in the subject's mind with the reward of lessened anxiety, human contact, and meaningful activity, and thus with providing relief for growing discomfort, the questioner assumes a benevolent role" (90). Under Howard and Scott's learning theory model, the interrogator role becomes not that of the person delivering discomfort but of the individual acting as the gateway to obtaining mastery of a problem.

Howard and Scott found that once an individual under stress conquers this stress through an assertive response, then "the state of the organism will be superior to its state prior to the time it was confronted with the problem, and that should the same problem arise again (after the organism has had an opportunity to replenish its resources) it will be dealt with more efficiently than before" (1965: 149). These findings suggest that interrogation subjects will learn to produce the desired information "more efficiently than before." But as *Kubark* warned, this could also mean that an individual who endured coercive interrogation but did not produce information on the first try may well learn that he can survive without giving information (see CIA 1963b: 42; 1983: H-5).

Kubark "suggests that the specific coercive techniques employed should be chosen based on the personality of the subject. The 'usual effect of coercion is regression.' The subject will become more 'childlike as his/her adult defenses breakdown. While this is happening, the subject will feel guiltier and the interrogators should exploit this" (Gordon and Fleisher 2006: 187). *Kubark*'s philosophy of choosing "specific coercive techniques" "based on the personality of the subject" explains why the Human Ecology Fund sponsored so many different efforts to develop standardized profiling tools that could be used to identify and exploit individual variations in personality.

Most of the noncoercive interrogation techniques described in *Kubark* focus on the specific tactics that interrogators can employ (e.g., using joint interrogators — one the "good cop," the other the "bad cop"; rapidly switching the language of interrogation; using "news from home" to the interrogator's advantage), with little direct information presented on the level of analysis presented in Howard and Scott's 1965 paper. Howard and Scott found that "if an organism is ultimately to attain mastery over a problem, the problem must be solvable" (1965: 146); in the world of *Kubark* interrogations, one corollary of this finding would be that if coercive interrogation subjects have no useful information, they are in a world of hurt, without any options available to gain relief.

Howard and Scott's problem-solving model aligns with *Kubark*'s rationalization of effective uses of coercive interrogation. *Kubark* explained:

> The confusion technique is designed not only to obliterate the familiar but to replace it with the weird. Although this method can be employed by a single interrogator, it is better adapted to use by two or three. When the subject enters the room, the first interrogator asks a doubletalk question — one which seems straightforward but is essentially nonsensical. Whether the interrogatee tries to answer or not, the second interrogator follows up (interrupting any attempted response) with a wholly unrelated and equally illogical query. Sometimes two or more questions are asked simultaneously. Pitch, tone, and volume of the interrogators' voices are unrelated to the import of the questions. No pattern of questions and answers is permitted to develop, nor do the questions themselves relate logically to each other. In this strange atmosphere the subject finds that the pattern of speech and thought which he has learned to consider normal have been replaced by an eerie meaninglessness. The interrogatee may start laughing or refuse to take the situation seriously. But as the process continues, day after day if necessary, the subject begins to try to make sense of the situation, which becomes mentally intolerable.

Now he is likely to make significant admissions, or even to pour out his story, just to stop the flow of babble which assails him. This technique may be especially effective with the orderly, obstinate type. (CIA 1963b: 76)

One of *Kubark*'s techniques, called "Spinoza and Mortimer Snerd," described how interrogators could gain cooperation by interrogating subjects for prolonged periods "about lofty topics that the source knows nothing about" (CIA 1963b: 75). The subject is forced to honestly say he or she does not know the answers to these questions, and some measure of stress is generated and maintained. When the interrogator switches to known topics, the subject is given small rewards, and feelings of relief emerge when these conditions are changed. Howard and Scott's model was well suited to be adapted to such interrogation methods, as release from stress was *Kubark*'s hallmark of effective interrogation techniques.

Kubark described how prisoners come to be "helplessly dependent on their captors for the satisfaction of their many basic needs" and release of stress. *Kubark* taught that, "once a true confession is obtained, the classic cautions apply. The pressures are lifted, at least enough so that the subject can provide counterintelligence information as accurately as possible. In fact, the relief granted the subject at this time fits neatly into the interrogation plan. He is told that the changed treatment is a reward for truthfulness and as evidence that friendly handling will continue as long as he cooperates" (CIA 1963b: 84). Translated into Howard and Scott's stress model, this subject mastered the environment by using an "assertive response" that allowed him or her to return to the desired state of equilibrium. There remain basic problems of knowing when a "true confession" is actually a false confession — elicited simply to return to the desired state of equilibrium.

When comparing the theoretical explanations in Howard and Scott's 1965 stress article with *Kubark*'s underlying guiding paradigms, there are clear overlapping models. But when reading both texts with hindsight, it remains unclear where an academic model of stress independently developing similar explanations (from those in *Kubark*) for stress release begins, and where MK-Ultra's focused interest in these questions ends. Given the destruction of documents and the nature of secret agencies, some specific elements of these questions remain unanswerable, but we do know that MK-Ultra funded stress research and other projects at Human Ecology to gather data that could be used to refine interrogation methods. Steven Kleinman (2006) summarized *Kubark*'s paradigms as relying on psychological assessment, screening, the creation and release of controlled stress, isolation, and regression, all of which are used by interrogators to "help" the interrogation subject "concede."

The Impacts of Funding Fronts

Harold Wolff died in 1962, a year before the CIA finished the *Kubark* manual; Hinkle remained at Cornell for decades. Without fanfare, the Human Ecology Fund closed its doors on June 30, 1965 (AAAFN 1967 7[4]: 8). A decade later, its CIA ties were exposed. In the end, psychology was the discipline that provided the most useful MK-Ultra-funded interrogation research, but anthropology also unwittingly contributed to these programs.

It was no accident that the Senate's 1977 hearings investigating MK-Ultra's co-option of academic research did not probe into the details of Human Ecology's few witting academicians who sought and coordinated academic research that aligned with the covert interests of the CIA. When CIA psychologist John Gittinger's testimony drifted into discussions of the individuals working within Human Ecology who knew of the CIA's secret sponsorship of unwitting researchers, Senator Edward Kennedy stopped Gittinger and told him that the committee was "not interested in names or institutions, so we prefer that you do not [identify them]. That has to be worked out in arrangements between [DCI] Admiral Turner and the individuals and the institutions. But we're interested in what the Foundation really was and how it functioned and what its purpose was" (U.S. Senate 1977: 59).[28] The Senate's decision to not delve further into the campus-CIA articulations leaves us with only outlines of how these interactions worked.[29] Though the Senate did not investigate the specific individuals involved in MK-Ultra's academic links, John Marks documented how cardiologist Lawrence E. Hinkle Jr. and neurologist Harold G. Wolff became the heart and mind of Human Ecology's CIA inquiries.

In one sense, the details of Human Ecology's use of CIA funds to commission specific research are extraordinary; in another sense, they are not. Given congressional and media revelations of the extent of covert CIA funding of unwitting academics during this period, perhaps the most remarkable feature of this Human Ecology research is that we can trace the CIA funds and what CIA project it was used for — *not* that it was financed by CIA funds (U.S. Senate 1976: 182).

MK-Ultra's covert use of Human Ecology to fund this stress research gave the CIA what it wanted: access to selective pieces from an elegant analytical cross-cultural model explaining human responses to stress. It did not matter that the model was produced in public by scholars with different intentions; the CIA had its own private uses for the work it funded. As Alan Howard clarified, the abuse of his and Scott's work was facilitated by the CIA's secrecy and the unknown dual use dimensions of the project:

> I could liken our situation to the discovery of the potential of splitting atoms for the release of massive amounts of energy. That knowledge can be used to create energy sources to support the finest human endeavors or to make atomic bombs. Unfortunately, such is the potential of most forms of human knowledge; it can be used for good or evil. While there is no simple solution to this dilemma, it is imperative that scientists of every ilk demand transparency in the funding of research and open access to information. The bad guys will, of course, opt for deception whenever it suits their purposes, and we cannot control that, but exposing such deceptions, as you have so ably done, is vitally important. (AH to DHP 6/7/07)

Howard, Scott, and most other scholars who received Human Ecology funds did nothing wrong. They undertook research designed to understand stress in an environment they had every reason to believe was striving to improve health and the understanding of stress's role in disease; that hidden sponsors had other uses for this work was not their fault.

But the same cannot be said of the CIA. The agency's ethical misconduct in using the Human Ecology Fund to conduct research hinged on lying to the scholars the CIA funded about where grant money came from; lying about what their results would be used for; and, more fundamentally, designing and implementing inhumane interrogation methods. But despite the ethical depravity of using unwitting outsourced scholars to gather data to be used for degenerate ends, the CIA understood that open academic research conducted by scholars operating "freely" outside of the constraints of an agency like the CIA produced high-quality work.

Military and intelligence agencies' misappropriation of anthropological research for their own ends creates serious problems for unwitting academic servants. Howard and Scott intended for their stress research to add to a literature concerned with *improving health*, yet their research was selectively funded and reviewed by those who would use it for *harm*, not healing.

> In the 1950s ... fledgling anthropologists went into field situations innocent of counterinsurgency plots spawned in the emergent globalization system, and of the role that we might unconsciously play. Now too much is known about undercover plots to ignore or deny U.S. intervention in the field sites we choose.
>
> JUNE NASH | 2007

NINE COLD WAR FIELDWORK WITHIN THE INTELLIGENCE UNIVERSE

Over the decades, numerous anthropologists in the field have falsely come under suspicion of being spies. Such accusations are thematically linked to why intelligence agencies *have* occasionally sought to use anthropologists to collect intelligence. These reasons include expertise in foreign cultures, familiarity with local languages, ease of traveling in remote areas, reliance on participant observational methods, and working in regions with colonialist histories that remain of interest to military and intelligence agencies of the global north.

False accusations of spying were among the dangers facing anthropologists conducting fieldwork identified by Nancy Howell in *Surviving Fieldwork*, her monograph on dangers facing anthropologists in the field. Howell recounted archaeologist Bruce Schroeder's arrest by the Syrian Border Patrol while he was surveying sites in Lebanon as an example of dangerous outcomes of these widespread suspicions (1990: 97). Fifteen percent of anthropologists surveyed by Howell reported accusations or suspicions that they were spies; her research identified these accusations by geographic regions — with the Pacific Islands and Asia being associated with the most accusations, though we may assume geopolitical developments can quickly alter such trends.[1] While false accusations of spying have been an ongoing threat to anthropologists in the field, Howell acknowledged that "sometimes the suspicion is correct," pointing out that Louis Leakey used his fieldwork to broadcast anti-insurrection propaganda during Mau Mau uprisings in Kenya (98).

False accusations of spying can have devastating impacts. Former CIA agent John Stockwell once recounted how after a lecture on a university campus, one of the organizers of the event described how, when she began studying in Zambia, she had been warned that an American scholar there was known to be CIA. Stockwell later wrote, "Her story made me want to cry. As supervisor of CIA activities in Zambia during the time she was there, I was intimately familiar with every 'asset' the CIA had in the country and the person she named was *not* one of them. Americans in Zambia mistrusted and avoided one another because the CIA had poisoned the environment. Frankly, my guess is that if Congress were investigating this aspect of CIA operations, they would find that most CIA managers actually *preferred* that other Americans in the country not trust one another" (1991: 104).

Anthropologists occasionally benefited from mistaken beliefs that they are CIA operatives. While conducting Malayan fieldwork in 1968, anthropologist Douglas Raybeck spent days in a rural police station collecting historical demographic data from birth and death records. After several days of this work, one of the police officers asked Raybeck how long he had worked with the CIA. Raybeck protested vigorously against this suggestion, and he produced his passport and letters of introduction from his dean at Cornell to demonstrate his academic legitimacy. The police officer looked at the documents but remained unconvinced, assuming that any CIA plant would also be able to produce such papers. Raybeck later learned that most of the Malayan governmental officials he had contact with assumed he was a CIA operative collecting information on Chinese Communists because, "after all, there I was staying in a small village only fifteen miles from the Thai border.... This whole misperception could have greatly altered my relationship to the villagers, made my work difficult or impossible, and possibly even endangered Karen and me. Fortunately the governments of Malaysi and Klantan, as well as the villagers, thought the CIA was a wonderful organization because it was opposed to Communism" (Raybeck 1996: 87–88). While Raybeck may have benefited from the misconception that he had CIA ties, most anthropologists suffer when such misconceptions occur.

In 1982, Jon Kalb, an American geologist, was expelled from Ethiopia after false rumors circulated that he was a CIA agent. Ethiopia soon banned all foreign scientists, and fears that similar rumors could lead to research bans in other countries spread through the paleoarchaeological community (*New Scientist* 1982: 552). Kalb argued that these false claims grew from his past disputes with a colleague (*New Scientist* 1982: 552). Kalb believed these claims first appeared during the peer review process for his 1977 NSF grant application, and he filed more than a hundred FOIA requests seeking NSF records. After Kalb showed the NSF had been party to discussions in which Kalb's colleagues and funding competitors raised rumors that he was secretly a CIA operative, he won an out-of-court settlement from the NSF for damages (see Kalb 2001).

At times, CIA operations intruded into fieldwork settings, spreading suspicions of anthropologists in ways that impacted their interactions with locals. June Nash has written that when she began fieldwork in Bolivia in 1967, "Che Guevara was still fighting in the tropics of Santa Cruz," and political tensions were high (1979b: 4). Nash's and anthropologist Doris Widerkehr's interests in mining and labor organizations led to accusations of their being CIA agents of "*Yanqui* imperialism" (Nash, 1979a: 359–60). Nash published articles in local outlets demonstrating her allegiances with the miners' struggles, but the political upheaval cast suspicion on her. She responded to accusations with a letter and a meeting with union officials to explain her methodology and her analytical approach to Bolivian mining. These incidents intensified during the political upheaval of October 1970, and Nash took precautions to protect her field notes and family during this time, while student protesters blew up the doors of the USIS building and burned its books. Crowds of protesters were fired upon, and some protesters were killed; Nash's home was targeted by sniper fire (362). Later, when one of her research audiotapes accidentally came to be played for others (after she had loaned out her tape recorder with a tape accidentally still in it), suspicions were again raised. After Nash explained what had happened, though, the union believed her because, "despite their hatred of the CIA, they had a very high regard for the agency's performance, and this blunder did not fit the image" (363).

It was common for American anthropologists during the Cold War to be falsely suspected of spying (e.g., Mars 2003; Verdery 1996: 7). Stuart Kirsch recounted how when he was doing fieldwork in New Guinea in the mid-1980s, he encountered a university scientist trying to determine if rabies had entered the country with dogs accompanying refugees. The scientist wanted Kirsch to ask refugees about their dogs, but other work kept him from making inquiries. Years later, a refugee told Kirsch that when he first arrived he was suspected of being a spy. Kirsch wrote, "Curious about this claim, I asked him whether they had ever seen a spy. He said that an Australian spy visited the camp the year before I arrived. I asked him how they knew that the Australian visitor was a spy. He explained that it was obvious, because the Australian man claimed to be a doctor, but spent all of his time talking to people about their dogs" (2006: 239n15).

In Nicaragua in the 1980s, Roger Lancaster found himself accused of being a CIA operative one day while shopping for a chicken. A drunk man started raving that Lancaster was a CIA agent, come to spy on Nicaragua. This man's "proof" was that when he spoke to Lancaster in English, he "pretended" to not understand, arguing, "Now why else would he do that unless he was trying to conceal his nationality? And why would he conceal his nationality unless he were trying to hide something? He must be CIA. Arrest him!" But Lancaster was defended by the shopkeeper's wife — whom he had never met, but who surprised him by listing his credentials as a UC Berkeley anthropologist and even the specific topic of his dissertation, noting, "When he goes back [to the United States] he's going to tell the truth about Nicaragua, and our revolution, and it will be good for us" (Lancaster 1992: 75–76).

While accusations of spying from locals are common motifs in ethnographic writings, anthropologists have rarely discussed being investigated by the FBI or the CIA, although such investigations occasionally intersected with fieldwork during the Cold War. In 1958, a CIA field agent stationed in East Africa became suspicious of anthropologist Leo Silberman, who claimed to have a grant from the Carnegie Endowment for International Peace to study the "Somaliland-Ethiopia border disputes." The FBI made inquiries at the University of Chicago's anthropology department. Entries in a compilation of CIA reports claimed, "L.S. has reputation for being glib, slick, quick-tongued, fast-talker, creates impressions which are not true" and indicated that Silberman "[has] a marvelous gift of gab, writes exceedingly well, and has considerable experience in Africa" (FOIA CIA DOC_0001152250, 4/3/58). In 1959, the FBI monitored Oscar Lewis's research in Mexico and Cuba, while some people in Mexico falsely accused him of being an FBI agent; the FBI also suspected that Lewis might be a communist because they misread his work on poverty as having Marxist undertones (D. H. Price 2004b: 237–54).[2] In 1957, Marvin Harris was expelled from Mozambique for researching practices of racial segregation. On the advice of a Ford Foundation representative, he shipped his field notes home to New York using the U.S. embassy pouch, only to later discover that once his notes and data finally arrived, they had been repackaged and obviously combed through (D. H. Price 2002: 16). Stanley Diamond's FBI file indicates that he contacted the FBI in October 1960 to report that his car had been broken into on the streets of New York, and his field notes documenting his recent political and economic research in Central Africa were taken (FBI 105–131338–4. 10/12/60). June Nash wrote that she learned years later that in 1970 the "Dirección de Investigaciones Criminales, the Bolivian equivalent of the U.S. FBI, had, under orders from the CIA, investigated me" (Nash 2007: 165).

But it was Stanley Diamond who most succinctly explored the circumstances of anthropologists being suspected of spying, writing that, "Logically enough, anthropologists are frequently taken as spies because of the inquisitive nature of their work; their concern with local affairs in the remote places to which they go, their tendency to fade into the background of local custom in living up to the canons of participant observation. They have, also, a certain limited academic immunity; they travel freely, and what better cover could a secret agent desire." But Diamond did not stop there, drawing attention to the dual use dynamics supporting such fieldwork, noting that, "Of course anthropologists are spiritual double agents. That is, they are marginal to the commercial-industrial society that created them, but they eagerly explore the areas opened up to them by colonialism" (1974:89; see D.H. Price 1998: 419n1).

Actual spies have at times posed as anthropologists conducting fieldwork, a practice that creates problems for real anthropologists. During the Second World War, Special Intelligence Service (a now defunct US intelligence division) agent William Clothier (who later worked for the CIA from 1952 to 1979) used archaeology as a cover, while working on a Harvard expedition, to spy in Peru (see D. H. Price 2008a: 210–11). Archaeologist Payson Sheets described how once, when traveling in El Salvador, he took a side trip to visit Ixtepeque, a Salvadoran obsidian source site. When he asked for directions in a small town along the way, the mayor told him that "two CIA agents, masquerading as archaeologists, had been discovered and killed by guerillas the year before. One body had been fished out of the Motagua River and the other had not been found. Local people were ready to kill any other self-declared archaeologist who wandered into the area" (Sheets 2001: 3). In 1967, Ralph Beals described the killing of an archaeologist in Guatemala: "The murder was believed to have been committed by guerrillas who thought the victim was an agent of the Central Intelligence Agency" (1967: 18). Beals later noted that the same issue of the *New York Times* that reported news of this murder published a front-page story in which he had been quoted as saying "there was good reason to believe that the CIA had used anthropologists as agents abroad or that CIA agents had passed themselves off as anthropologists" (18; see Raymont 1966). Michael Lewis writes of Smithsonian administrator and conservationist David Challinor's account of an unidentified "young man who the Smithsonian helped fly to India, supposedly to do anthropological research, who unknown to them was also using a grant from the department of defense to interview refugees from Communist China-controlled Tibet" (M. Lewis 2002: 2325).

During the 1950s and 1960s, the CIA focused concerted efforts on recruiting sociologists, anthropologists, historians, political scientists, and others working in Africa. In 1965, Rene Lemarchand was approached by Miami's CIA station chief while on the campus of the University of Florida and asked to provide information on developments in Burundi politics: Lemarchand rejected these advances in no uncertain terms (Blanchard and Scheinbaum 1977b). Sociologist Jay Mullen spied for the CIA while living in Uganda, where he used his position as an instructor at Makerere University to gather intelligence about Idi Amin. Mullen later bragged that his operatives planted bugs and wiretaps in Amin's headquarters and in the homes of various Russian and Chinese individuals living in Uganda (Lawrence 1979: 86; see also Mullen 1979; Siskiyou 2011). Historian James R. Hooker was recruited by the CIA in the 1950s, and during his years living in Africa he kept files on individuals he met in the Federation of Rhodesia and Nyasaland during the 1950s and 1960s (Lawrence 1979: 84–85). When Hooker famously and disparagingly claimed that "anthropology could not escape its European origins; it remained a discipline peopled by whites who looked at darker, dependent persons," he did not similarly reflect on the impact of his own position within the CIA on his professional writings (see Hooker 1963: 458).

Many interactions between the CIA and anthropologists and other academics occurred on university campuses. Theodore Graves described CIA efforts to recruit anthropologists at the University of Colorado and UCLA, where CIA representatives roamed the campuses with promises of laundered "research" funds for anthropologists who would align their work with agency interests. Once Graves began teaching at the University of Colorado, he had annual visits from a CIA employee offering funding for graduate students willing to do fieldwork in "sensitive parts of the world." Graves refused to cooperate, yet the CIA representative returned each year. Graves was told these funds would be "channeled through 'respectable' agencies" to hide any CIA connection." He encountered scholars funded by these CIA grant programs while he was conducting fieldwork in East Africa in 1967–68, and he learned that "one of the tenured faculty at UCLA apparently recruited students for research in politically sensitive areas of the world for many years, with secret financial support from our government" (Graves 2004: 315).

In the wake of the Church Committee hearings' revelations of CIA activities on campus, Paul Doughty, chair of the University of Florida's Department of Anthropology, reported that it had become routine for him and other anthropologists, upon returning from fieldwork abroad, to "receive debriefing and personal information forms from the CIA" asking for "personal information about persons whom Doughty said he has been closely involved for many years." Doughty ignored these queries, and the CIA eventually stopped contacting him (Blanchard and Scheinbaum 1977a: 14–15). Other anthropologists presumably briefed the CIA; the extent of such briefings remains unknown, but ongoing reports of such requests by those who refused to cooperate suggest the likelihood that others did comply with these requests (Blanchard and Scheinbaum 1977b).

Anthropological field research sometimes facilitated intelligence operations by nonanthropologists. For example, in 1952, F. Trubee Davison, assistant director of the CIA, planned to use his connections to the American Museum of Natural History to join a trip to Sarawak to collect artifacts and make an ethnographic film. But Davison's CIA links brought additional political attention to the trip. Declassified CIA memos show agency interest in Davison gathering firsthand information on "what appears to have been Communist terrorist activity [that has] taken place in recent months in the southwestern part of Sarawak in and around Kuching" (FOIA CIA-RDP80R01731R000500020001–8, 9/24/52).[3] Davison, who had only recently stepped down from two decades serving as museum president, wrote Allen Dulles, describing his plans to travel with his wife

> under the auspices of the American Museum of Natural History. In broad terms, the purpose is to obtain documentary motion pictures of the tribal life and collect artifacts used by the various tribes. I am naturally concerned to know whether or not the political conditions are suitable and safe.
>
> Our contact in Sarawak is one Tom Harrisson, Government Ethnologist and Curator of the Sarawak Museum. I am enclosing a copy of a letter which has just been received by the head of the Department of Anthropology at the American Museum who is organizing our end of the trip. I thought you might be interested in seeing Mr. Harrisson's letter. (FOIA CIA-RDP80R01731R000500020005–4, 9/11/52)[4]

In June 1952, Harrisson reported delays in securing a houseboat because of political troubles, explaining that "there is now a state of emergency declared." He noted that it was "not practical to plan very much for the moment" and that movements were currently restricted. He wrote that the current situation was "not unpleasantly serious," but he advised the museum to postpone its plans for the present (TH to Shapiro, FOIA CIA-RDP80R01731R000500020005–4, 8/23/52).

Field Agents

During the Cold War, the CIA occasionally used archaeological projects as cover for collecting foreign intelligence. A onetime CIA chief of station, Baghdad, Wilbur Eveland later described the agency using archaeology covers in Iraq during the 1950s, when "part of the CIA station in Iraq operating under diplomatic cover was so understaffed that even its two secretaries arranged communications drops and safe-house meetings with agents. Wives of the few CIA officers under 'deep cover' (education and archaeological) typed their reports and sequestered their children while their husbands met with informants at home" (1980: 46).

Engineer, philanthropist, and archaeological enthusiast John M. Dimick had no formal training in archaeology, but he was an active presence in major archaeological excavations in Guatemala, Egypt, Turkey, Italy, Greece, and elsewhere from 1946 into the late 1960s. His memoir, *Episodes in Archaeology*, described how observing excavations at the Herculaneum in 1939 kindled his passion for archaeology. This interest led to fund-raising and managerial roles in archaeological excavations on three continents (Dimick 1968). But there was more going on than Dimick described in his memoir; as his November 29, 1983, *Washington Post* obituary disclosed, "Following service in Spain during World War II, Dimick combined government assignments with archaeological interest while working in Latin America for the U.S. Central Intelligence Agency."

In 1946, Dimick contacted United Fruit Company founder Sam Zemurray and persuaded him to provide $430,000 for three years of work on Mayan monumental archaeological remains in Guatemala (1968: 26). From 1946 to 1960, Dimick directed the project, hiring Alfred Kidder to undertake the initial surveys. Dimick selected Zaculeu for major restoration efforts, and the crew cleared and excavated the massive temple complex (NBAAA1949 3[3]: 4).

Missing from Dimick's account of Zemurray's Guatemala is any depiction of a Yankee banana republic; instead, we have a description of Zemurray as a kind benefactor looking out for Guatemalans' interests. Dimick praised his patron, writing that during his "own years in Guatemala the usual derogatory comment on the Fruit Company was invariably sweetened with stories of how it had conquered the Latin Americas by force. That is not only unjustified, but untrue. The conquistador was Zemurray. He with his wisdom, his love for the country as well as for self-benefit, was the power who employed the force of arms" (1968: 20).

In 1954, two years after Nasser's Officers Revolution in Egypt, Dimick directed University of Pennsylvania excavations of the Apis embalming house at Mit Rahineh (Dimick 1968: 66). Dimick and his wife, Teena, took an apartment on the top floor of the Semiramis Hotel in Cairo, where they were near "the living quarters for King Saud of Saudi Arabia" (67). Dimick claimed his work with Arab colleagues in Egypt generated mutual aid and assistance, with "no subterfuge, no double talk" (81). Documents from the Eisenhower administration's negotiations with the Nasser administration during Dimick's time in Egypt include notes from diplomatic meetings of American envoy Robert Anderson (who traveled with several CIA personnel in his party) and establish that Dimick provided briefings on the political climate of Egypt, including his own evaluations of Nasser and his administration. Records from a U.S. Egypt Evaluation Team meeting of May 19–20, 1955, report "an Egyptologist," identified in Alterman's endnotes as "Dimick," "with experience in the CIA and OSS [who] opined that Abdel Nasser was 'well intentioned and reasonably capable, within his limits. He does not know how to run a government. His advisers are totally incapable'" (Alterman 2002: 130, 163n130). Alterman wrote that, "although the precise details of the CIA's involvement with the Anderson mission remain classified, many years later CIA regional chief Kermit Roosevelt admitted to playing a leading role as an intermediary between Anderson and the Egyptians" (118). These records confirm Dimick's later claims of being a CIA operative, yet the specific details of how his CIA position articulated with his years of archaeological adventuring remain unclear. At a minimum, his presence in developing nations undergoing revolutions and counterrevolutions provided the CIA with background reports on what he saw while working on archaeological projects; but he may also have played less passive roles, either running CIA operatives, working as a CIA currier, or performing other tasks for the agency.

Archaeologist Frank Hibben told *New Yorker* writer Douglas Preston that while he was on an expedition in the 1950s retracing the route of Roy Chapman Andrews's Mongolian travels, he smuggled a device into Outer Mongolia that was capable of remotely monitoring Chinese atomic bomb tests at Lop Nor (Preston 1995: 80–81). Hibben claimed Chinese troops chased and shot at him. While Hibben's central role in the Sandia Cave scandal (in which Hibben claimed to have excavated undisturbed 25,000 year old human remains — a claim rejected by many other archaeologists), diminishes his general credibility, some evidence supports his claims. In response to my FOIA requests, the FBI released portions of Hibben's FBI file, including a report indicating that the FBI conducted a background investigation on him for an unspecified sensitive project administered through the Department of Energy, raising the possibility that this was the governmental agency that possibly hired him for this claimed operation in western China.

Fieldwork in a Time of Crisis

June Nash has written about her lack of political awareness during her initial Guatemalan fieldwork in 1953, referring to herself as naive. Her later reflections capture the political orientation of the era, when she and her husband, Manning Nash, "were not concerned with paramilitary or guerrilla operations, nor did we feel that we had to justify our presence. America had just won a war against Fascism, and had not yet embarked on our own imperial campaigns. The ethnographic frame was on the functioning of traditional societies and the structures that maintained coherence in the face of modernizing changes" (Nash 2007: 105–6).

For her dissertation fieldwork, Nash planned to study a community of textile factory workers and the contexts of modernization, ethnicity, village governance, class, and education. But the political backdrop for this research came to dominate her experience. The Guatemalan election of 1950 brought Jacobo Árbenz to the presidency, and his land reform policies alarmed the U.S. State Department and the CIA because they threatened American corporate interests in Guatemala, especially large landowners like United Fruit.

Tensions mounted in May 1954 as a Czechoslovakian shipment of Soviet-manufactured arms arrived in Guatemala, and the U.S. government denounced the spread of Soviet influence in the Western Hemisphere. As June and Manning Nash completed a year of fieldwork that summer, they heard rumors that Colonel Carolos Castillo Armas was planning a revolt with five hundred soldiers to seize lands taken by Germans during the Second World War. Government security agents arrived in the town where the Nashes lived, asking questions about the U.S. researchers staying there, but the locals lied and told the officials they had no such foreign researchers (Nash 2007: 108). On June 25, 1954, the CIA toppled President Árbenz's government, and after a series of presidential successions, Armas was installed as the American-backed president, rolling back Árbenz's nationalization project. Nash later wrote that, after the coup,

> rumors circulated about who was being jailed and who had fled. The jails were filled with five thousand suspects when Richard Adams received a grant to study the penetration of Communist ideology in the countryside. He asked us to assist him, assigning Manning [Nash] and a number of Guatemalan students to the jail interviews and me to compile the results. Among the prisoners was a student who advised the team about the prisoners' interpretation of the questionnaire. Convinced that the interviews were part of a scheme to distinguish militant Com-

munists from those who were apolitical, the prisoners had worked out responses that minimized their involvement in the revolutionary government, and indeed, our summation of the interviews confirmed this. But the moderate views they expressed reflected a well-grounded support for the Arévalo-Árbenz government that was not based on fomenting a violent revolution. This was the allegation of the U.S. National Security Council when they approved plans for a coup against a government that had for the first time in Guatemalan history made strides in advancing rural education and health, and that had permitted democratic participation in unions and cooperatives. (110)

The Nashes were later denounced as "communists" to the U.S. embassy by the factory weaving master, but an intervention by friends halted efforts to force their return to the United States (110).

In July 1954, June and Manning Nash were unexpectedly visited at their Chicago apartment by a CIA agent. Without forethought on how to respond to such intrusive pressures, their answers to the agent's request for specific information they had learned from the fieldwork were a model for anthropologists concerned with protecting those they study. June Nash later recalled that this CIA agent "waited in the stifling heat of our basement apartment for Manning to rouse himself, only to be told that he could read whatever Manning might publish, but that he (Manning) had nothing to say. Although the agent had not tried to debrief me, it was then that I began to realize our research might fit into a larger domain of state intrigue that may even have influenced the funding of our research. The book, *Machine Age Maya*, probably had little that would have interested the CIA, then or even later" (2007: 110–11). This awareness that research areas influenced funding came late, yet for many anthropologists such awareness was never voiced. And the interest or usefulness to the CIA was not always apparent. As Asia Foundation president Russell Smith later observed, often research projects that appeared to have little importance or to be "frivolous" to CIA interests turned out to be valuable, especially given the usefulness of firsthand information from regions of interest (FOIA CIA 1/28/63, DTPILLAR VOL. 3_0024, 2).

Using the pseudonym Stokes Newbold, Richard N. Adams published a report on his interviews with Guatemalan prisoners in the journal *Economic Development and Cultural Change* (ISA 4, GF to RNA 5/10/51). Adams interviewed a sample of the fifteen hundred to two thousand pro-Árbenz Guatemalans who had been arrested and imprisoned in the Guatemala City Jail soon after the coup. Manning and June Nash assisted with these interviews (Newbold 1957: 338n1). Adams observed that, "while interviewing jailed persons immediately after a highly emotional revolution is obviously a most unsatisfactory method of obtaining data, it was considered more realistic to attempt the study in this way than after the jailed population had been released and dispersed once more through the countryside" (342). These interviews collected socioeconomic and demographic data on the prisoners. Adams found that Árbenz's supporters had "more contact with outsiders and would as a result tend to be more literate than non-members" and would be more likely to come from municipal capitals (348); he also found higher-than-average literacy rates and that the population was largely rural, religiously active, and relatively economically well off (349, 360; cf. S. C. Schlesinger and Kinzer 1983: 220).

Because Adams's report found that few of those arrested appeared to be communists or to know much about communism, it supposedly irritated many at the CIA and the State Department (see S. C. Schlesinger and Kinzer 1983: 22), and any uses to which governmental agencies might have put it are unknown. This report significantly impacted Adams's later life and career, as news of this collaboration with a State Department intelligence venture limited his access to work and travel in Central America (RNA to DHP 10/1/96). But, as Marc Edelman observed, "During the rest of his long career, Adams developed a pronounced concern about research ethics and a strongly critical stance regarding US policy in Guatemala and the Guatemalan military's abysmal human rights record, as did June Nash, who also participated in the survey" (2009: 252n23).

Indonesian Fieldwork on the Front Lines of the Cold War

During the Second World War, Raymond Kennedy worked at the OSS Morale Operations Branch, helping design anti-Japanese propaganda operations in Indonesia; he also worked with the OSS's secret Marigold Unit (Soley 1989: 161). As the war's end approached, Kennedy expressed strong opposition to America aligning its national interests with the colonial and neocolonial policies of European nations hoping to return to dominance in Asia. Kennedy's anticolonial views were not well received in the State Department. In his reports he bluntly expressed concerns. In one 1945 State Department memo discussing U.S. postwar policy options, he argued that "American military operations in Southeast Asia involve potential danger to American prestige among the peoples of the area, because the latter are bound, regardless of our protestations to the contrary, to link American military forces with the reentering Anglo-Dutch-French military and civil administrations" (Kennedy in G. Smith 1999: 2). He cautioned that "America should take care to pursue a policy which will ensure that the 'emerging nations' of Southeast Asia will be ideologically sympathetic to the United States" (RK 1, 2/22/45). The Atlantic Charter of 1941 was signed as a war statement designed to destabilize Axis occupations, but at the war's end its declaration of self-determination for people under occupations undermined colonial and neocolonial claims of legitimacy. While many in the United States ignored these contradictions at the war's end, Kennedy argued for American policies that remained consistent with principles of liberation, anticolonialism, and self-determination (see Kennedy 1944, 1945a, 1945b; Kennedy and Kattenburg 1948; D. H. Price 2013b).

Kennedy returned to Yale after the war, but he continued working as an intelligence consultant at the Propaganda Intelligence Section of the Secret Intelligence Branch,[5] commuting to Washington, DC, on a regular basis.[6] He read intelligence reports and made "suggestions concerning the form and content of reports, and [suggested] Intelligence guidance for field operations in Southeast Asia" (FOIA CIA MORI Doc ID: 242537, RD to RCR 1/9/46). Given his contributions to postwar intelligence, it is likely that Kennedy continued consulting at the newly formed CIA. No records confirming such a relationship were released in response to my FOIA requests, though this may reflect CIA unwillingness to supply documents in response to FOIA requests more than it reveals whether or not Kennedy had an ongoing relationship with the agency.

Kennedy took a sabbatical from Yale in 1949, using a $3,000 Viking Fund grant for fieldwork studying "acculturation in selected sections of Indonesia" (Viking Fund 1951: 39, 132). In Indonesia, Kennedy visited new villages every few days, studying acculturation and focusing on topics ranging from folk knowledge to political divisions and orientations.

On April 27, 1950, Raymond Kennedy and Robert Doyle, a *Time-Life* correspondent traveling with him, were murdered in rural Indonesia (Gardner 1997: 68). Kennedy had been en route to meet Paul M. Kattenburg, a State Department employee who was a fellow OSS alumnus, and Southeast Asian scholar (OSS *Society Newsletter*, Fall 2004: 10–11).[7] Kennedy had mentored Kattenburg in government and academic settings (Gardner 1997: 68), and they coauthored several scholarly works on Indonesian political developments. The Australian press reported that Kennedy and Doyle were "shot by a gang of four or five Indonesians dressed in military uniform, according to stories told by villagers who were forced by the murderers to bury the bodies" (*West Australian*, April 29, 1950, 1).

Four decades later, Kattenburg remained unsure who murdered Kennedy and Doyle, writing that "we thought then that the Darul Islam, an early extremist

Islamic movement, was responsible for the assassinations. It is also possible that Kennedy and Doyle were set up by criminals in Jakarta or simply victims of local thugs intent on capturing the several thousand U.S. dollars that many in West Java knew Kennedy had with him" (qtd. in Gardner 1997: 68). George Kahin and Clifford Geertz later assumed Kennedy was killed either by men working for Turk Westerling (Raymond Pierre Paul Westerling) or by Darul Islam (Kahin 1997: 39n3; cf. Geertz 2010: 213).[8]

Former OSS analyst and State Department officer John F. Cady later described Kennedy's Indonesian trip not as ethnographic fieldwork but as Kennedy being "sent to Indonesia" to "keep abreast of developments there" as part of a larger effort by the U.S. government sending American experts "out to the field to examine the potentialities of particular situations and to explain what could happen" (qtd. in McKinzie 1974: 23–24).[9] Robin Winks wrote that Kennedy continued his intelligence work "after the war [when] the intelligence community called on Kennedy again, for his field notes, his photographs, and his political point of view, which had so cogently put the anticolonial position, were valued as they had not been during the war" (1987: 50).

After a four-month investigation in Indonesia, Alexander Marshack published an exposé titled "The Unreported War in Indonesia" in *American Mercury*. Marshack wrote that Kennedy had angered Dutch loyalists in Indonesia by publishing an article "condemning the activities of the Netherlands official" (1952: 39). Marshack determined that days before their deaths, "Doyle and Kennedy registered in Bandung at the beautiful ultramodern Dutch-owned Savoy Homann Hotel, which was at this time (though they did not know) the center of the NEFIS-IVG and Dutch intelligence organization for West Java. And having registered they began circulating through the city asking questions" (1952: 39). Kennedy's questions were not drawn from the 267 questions listed in his detailed ethnographic research questionnaire; these were more immediate political questions that "concerned the roots of the Westerling-NEFIS affair. Immediately two Indonesians riding a blue sedan began tailing Doyle and Kennedy in their movements" (39). Marshack concluded:

> The motive evidently was not robbery. It was political assassination of two Americans. Significantly, villagers near the killing were brusquely ordered by the Dutch troops to bury Kennedy and Doyle, forget them, and keep quiet. One woman, hesitantly, talked, and Indonesian military police went in and dug Doyle and Kennedy up. The identification papers, passport, and notes of Professor Kennedy had been taken. For he was the already well-known hated member of the twosome. Doyle

of *Time-Life* was newly arrived, had not yet filed his story, and was therefore unknown to those interested in Kennedy. And so Doyle's notes were found, complete, on his person. It was Kennedy they were after. (40)

Doyle's notes showed that he had made inquiries in Bandung about Angkatan Perang Ratu Adil (APRA). This paramilitary unit, which Westerling formed with sympathetic Dutch expatriates after resigning from the Dutch armed forces, hoped to seize power from the coming Indonesian government and to restore Dutch rule. After Westerling's botched coup attempt, APRA launched small-scale rural paramilitary operations against the new Indonesian state.

Most of the reporting on Doyle's and Kennedy's deaths ignored the political context of Americans collecting information on the "culture change" of a nation rapidly heading toward what appeared to be widespread rural commitment to communism in the wake of its postcolonial freedom (e.g., *Life* 1950: 42).

Unresolved Questions about Kennedy's Fieldwork

Three years after Raymond Kennedy's death, HRAF published the first of three volumes of his *Field Notes on Indonesia: South Celebes, 1949–1950* (1953b). These volumes were transcribed and edited by Harold Conklin, whose knowledge of Dutch and Indonesian was vital for the publication of the notebooks (Kennedy 1953b: xiv; see also Kennedy 1953a, 1953c), which were published by HRAF as HRAF coded texts — indexing Kennedy's notebooks using HRAF's cross cultural index system.[10] In the introduction to *Field Notes*, Ruby Kennedy described how she and Raymond sailed to Indonesia from Norfolk, Virginia, bringing a jeep, books, and other supplies (Kennedy 1953b: vii). Raymond Kennedy was a frenetic fieldworker, often working more than twelve hours a day and typing a dozen pages of field notes in a single evening. During eight months of fieldwork, he produced more than nine hundred pages of single-spaced typed notes, as well as detailed letters home that supplemented these observations and analysis (viii).

Kennedy planned to investigate at least three villages in six Indonesian culture areas, focusing on the impact of Islamic, Christian, and local religious traditions. He spent the last months of his life in eastern Indonesia and completed surveys in South Celebes, Flores, Ambon, Ceram, and Borneo. The South Celebes field notebook was published by HRAF in 1953, with limited microfiche editions of the notebooks from his work in Flores, Ambon, Ceram, and Borneo released next.

Field Notes described changing Indonesian social relations, with notes on Kennedy's random encounters. Kennedy hired local research assistants to administer a standardized questionnaire of 267 items, many of which focused on agricultural practices and were adapted from a turn-of-the-century British survey. He intended to contrast contemporary responses with existing data for a longitudinal understanding of culture change.

The questionnaire's sections on economy and political life included questions on technological changes, ownership and distribution of automobiles, landownership, debt, wage labor systems, shifts in political organization, the role of family, and class relations in everyday life. The section on political dimensions included the following questions: "Are there parties in the village, for instance, conservative, radical, etc.?"; "Have there been changes in the horizons of political thought?"; and "To what extent is there knowledge of world politics? How have the people obtained this?" Other questions explored the role of religion in politics, and still others inquired about political parties' organization and function (Kennedy 1953b: 235–37).

Field Notes contained information on social structure, sexual mores, rituals of life and death, and agricultural production, and it recounted local political observations. Kennedy evaluated the extent of socialist or communist thought in the new Indonesian state. He interviewed locals about political "radicals" and views of anticolonialism, and he gathered information on the relative strength of various military factions (1953b: 216–17).[11] Kennedy recounted discussions with Riekerk, a civil servant, who believed that the first elections selected "nobles," while current voting patterns brought more egalitarian trends, yet "the influence of the nobles is still strong" (26). One note stated, "The school is the only new institution in the kampong now, and this is the real revolutionary factor. Riekerk is a Socialist and I get the idea that many Dutch in the State of East Indonesia service are left wing. Van Heekeren is also quite liberal. I wonder what the percentage would be" (26).

Kennedy interviewed an "Indo" engineer named Resink, whom he described as "a radical." Kennedy filled several pages of notes with Resink's views, such as his opinion that Indonesian society was divided between "a small upper, rich class" and the "Sjahrir"—a "socialistic" group (221–22). Resink viewed Sukarno as "an opportunist" who would align with whatever interests would maintain his power. Resink described the nature of Indonesian identity politics and the nuances of local shifts in identity from an old ethos aspiring to be "100 percent Dutch" to a new positive longing "to become completely Indonesian" (222). Kennedy reported:

Resink feels that the danger today is that the United States, big business, and the Dutch and others will join with the bourgeois Republic of Indonesia group and sell out the masses. If this happens, the latter will revolt in a few years. They will ask themselves, "Are we better off or not?" And if the answer is not, there will be trouble. He said there are plenty of Communists here and although they are not strong they are ready. They are mainly Chinese trained by Russia. They come via southeast Asia or through Holland. They are largely students. Also, some of the Indonesian students go to Czechoslovakia to study and to get orders there from Moscow. If they are able to ask the people later on if they are any better off, there will be revolution. All is set. Resink's plan is state socialism and development of, for example, bauxite in Riouw, water power in Asahan (for aluminum especially), and textiles in Java. He agreed that if Indonesia goes socialist the United States under big business and propaganda pressure will tag them "communistic." This means America will not help. The thing to do then will be to turn to Russia, and the United States, thus caught, will have to give help even though Indonesia is socialist. This looks like good hard-headed thinking. Certainly the United States won't help a socialist state unless forced to by fear of Russia. Rahim says that the United States is now gypping Indonesia; what happens is that the United States gets rubber (and at a cheaper price than other lands, and insists on this or it won't give exchange), and then forces Indonesia to take a certain percentage of automobiles, instead of machinery, which is really needed. This even applies to busses. The cars are used by the bureaucrats alone, and are hence useless. As for Marshall aid, it has now stopped. This was foolish, he said, and when it is restored it will probably again be channeled via Holland. This is bad because the Dutch have been shamelessly milking Indonesia since the war and will probably continue. Thus, for example, they won't sell yarn, which the folks here could use to weave for themselves and make cheap textiles. Instead they insist that Indonesia buy textiles from them which they can sell at a high price. He is violent on the subject of big business and says that unless the United States realizes that Indonesia needs socialism, they will have Russia and/or revolution there. He also says the United States is being very foolish to spread propaganda (U.S.I.S.) about the virtues of United States capitalism everywhere, and how all people must be like Americans. Such freedom can be afforded only in the United States and the latter must get the idea that poor lands must have a different system. (Can he be a crypto-communist? The line Resink takes could be a Communist one indirectly, and he is clearly trying to get me to tell it. He says the United States believes only Americans, and that is why I am important. On the other hand he may be merely a sincere sociologist.) Anyway it is interesting to see that my point (in the Linton symposium) on former colonies [in R. Linton, editor, *The Science of Man in the World Crisis* to the effect that all poor lands must have state enterprise as there is no private capital and outside capital means outside control], is followed to the letter by this seemingly keen lad. This is very interesting talk, and maybe I'll write something regarding it. (223–24)

Kennedy's ethnographic skills produced rare representations of the political consciousness of villagers in different regions of Indonesia. As an old OSS hand, Kennedy understood the value that such ethnographic details from a region poised to move toward communism provided to American intelligence agencies.

While documents establish Kennedy's work with the OSS, his postwar intelligence work, his political writings on postcolonial Indonesia, the extent to which his ethnographic field notes focused on the emerging political shifts of post-Dutch Indonesia, and the informed speculations of Winks, Cady, and others that he was working with the CIA at the time of his death, we are left without documentation establishing links to the CIA or other intelligence agencies at the time of his murder (see McKinzie 1974: 34; Winks 1987: 50).

Although I found no documents firmly establishing that Kennedy's fieldwork was linked to the CIA at the time of his murder, I identified a CIA operative, funded by the same anthropological research foundation, who was carrying out ethnographic research in Indonesia similar to Kennedy's just months after his murder.

Lloyd Millegan, Replacement Ethnographer?

I first learned of Lloyd S. Millegan's Indonesian research in the 1951 Viking Fund annual report listing him as receiving a predoctoral 1950 fellowship for fieldwork "to aid anthropological studies in Indonesia since independence, and prospects for future studies" (Viking Fund 1951: 157). His project was the only listed grant without a university affiliation, instead listing his affiliation as "Fairfax, Virginia." When I consulted Viking Fund records, I learned that Millegan's CV listed years of CIA employment.

During the war, Millegan worked at OSS for Joseph Ralston Hayden, an adviser to General Douglas MacArthur (see JRH; Gehrke 1976: 204, 216). Millegan worked on several intelligence and insurgency operations, and during the final months of the war he developed recommendations for the U.S. plan "for the cultural reorganization of the Philippines" (JRH, 42–27).[12]

The Viking Fund sponsored Millegan's "Survey of Anthropological Studies in Indonesia since Independence and Prospects for Future Studies," and Millegan expressed interest in undertaking "similar surveys in Burma, Thailand, Malaya and Indonesia'" (LSM, CV 9/6/50). Millegan's Viking Fund grant application listed his employment in the CIA as a research analyst and chief of the Southeast Asia Branch, from 1946 to 1950. The application described his research plan as follows:

> I am scheduled to leave the United States for Indonesia on 30 September to undertake a survey trip for Pacific Books, Inc. to determine the feasibility of establishing a bookstore or chain of bookstores in Indonesia and other Southeast Asian countries. During the two months I expect to be in Indonesia I will be traveling widely and will visit most of the educational and research institutions in the area. The nature of my visit will offer a unique opportunity to undertake the proposed survey. I would contemplate making a detailed report which would be available for publication and as a guide to those interested in anthropological studies in Indonesia. I plan to return to the United States early in December for a short period and contemplate returning to the area to undertake further survey work in Burma, Thailand, Malaya and Indochina. (LSM, 9/6/50 application)

Millegan listed "other personnel involved" as including his consultations with John Embree, Dr. and Mrs. Edward S. C. Handy, and "officials of the Viking Fund."

Millegan requested $3,000 to cover a year of research in Burma, Indochina, Indonesia, Malaya, and Thailand (LSM, 9/6/50 application). Pacific Books, Inc. covered Millegan's travel to Indonesia. Millegan listed John Embree (Yale), Dr. Edward S. C. Handy of Oakland, Virginia, and Mr. David Bernstein as personal references. The same day that Millegan's application was marked as received, Paul Fejos sent an internal Viking Fund memo to Mr. R. C. Hunt recommending that his application for a predoctoral fellowship be approved for $1,500. Millegan had no anthropological training and no academic affiliation, and his project had no identified anthropological content, yet Fejos found "the candidate and aims are worthy of Viking Fund aid" (LSM, PF to RCH 9/8/50). That same day, an award letter and check for $1,500 were sent to Millegan, authorizing Viking Fund grant number 508 (LSM, PF to LM 9/8/50).

One week after Fejos approved Millegan's grant application, the Viking Fund received its first letter of recommendation supporting his application. David Bernstein, of the Federal Security Agency, praised Millegan, noting their work together at the OSS. Bernstein wrote that Millegan would "make a real contribution to anthropological studies. He is intimately familiar with the Indonesian scene and has had many opportunities to establish and strengthen his personal contacts, as well as the possibilities for rapid acquisition of information there" (LSM, DB to PF 9/15/50). Edward Handy's recommendation letter stated that "war service and subsequent work with the Central Intelligence Agency have given [Millegan] a wide acquaintanceship with the whole region of Indonesia and Southeast Asia probably unexcelled by any American at the present time" (LSM, SCH to PF 9/16/50).[13] John Embree wrote that he had known Millegan for "several years" and knew him to be "able and reliable," though he noted, "Mr. Millegan has no formal training in anthropology." Embree believed Millegan would produce a good report on the "current situation in Indonesia" (LSM, JE to PF 11/19/50).

Millegan's résumé, application, and recommendations clearly informed the Viking Fund that it was financing a recent CIA employee. Fejos acted outside of normal Viking Fund protocols by immediately approving a predoctoral fellowship for an individual with no demonstrable plans to enroll in any graduate program and no links to any academic institution.[14] Millegan was not an anthropologist. He had no anthropological training. He had no plans to pursue graduate work in anthropology. It seems likely that Fejos's support for Millegan's application was guided by information not recorded in Millegan's file. While the details of how Millegan came to be funded are unclear, the CIA may have directly encouraged the Viking Fund to support him.

Viking Fund founder Axel Wenner-Gren's postwar problems with the FBI and the State Department (problems involving his reported ties to German war interests) likely made the Viking Fund eager to cooperate with a CIA request, if personnel were discreetly contacted about funding Millegan's "research" in Indonesia.[15] It is also possible that the FBI's extensive investigations of Paul Fejos's wife, Inga Arvad, as a suspected Nazi agent may have led Fejos to assist an apparent CIA operation.[16] There are no records of contacts between Viking Fund personnel and the CIA on this matter.

Exactly what Lloyd Millegan did while in Indonesia is unclear. His son, Kris Millegan, confirmed that his father traveled to Java in 1950. In a telephone interview (KM 9/28/10), Kris Millegan told me that his father's CIA assignment was to establish an American bookstore in Indonesia, which was to function as a CIA front organization where he would run operatives collecting intelligence in the countryside that would monitor shifting political attitudes, especially those relating to the spread of communism (KM 9/28/10).

Millegan's research plan hinged on gleaning information from American and Dutch anthropologists who had conducted fieldwork in Indonesia. In September 1950, before leaving for Indonesia, Millegan met with John Embree and

Harold Conklin at Yale, and with William Thomas at the Viking Fund, each of whom provided him with contact information for Indonesia's top anthropologists ("including, Vand der Hoop, Von Vaal Basil, Hooykas, Cense, Grader and others"). Once he was in Indonesia, Millegan discovered that these anthropologists had left the country (LSM, 6/15/51).

Millegan traveled to Indonesia in October 1950, where he set up his Pacific Book store in Java and began establishing connections with various people (KM 9/28/10). He also worked at an Indonesian museum, where a librarian told him he "would find very little information on current work because of this exodus of the Dutch Anthropologists," but he wrote that he "collected all the material I could and secured some information concerning Indonesians who may be continuing some work in Anthropology." He found that, "in general, it appears that anthropological research is at a low ebb in Indonesia and will continue until some younger Indonesians have been stimulated in developing an interest in this field" (LSM, 6/15/51).

Millegan contracted dysentery, which prevented him from concluding his planned research. When the news of his parents' death in a plane crash reached him in December 1950, he returned to the United States. Millegan went back to Indonesia in early 1951, but in his reports to the Viking Fund he wrote that he did not accomplish the research he had hoped to undertake.[17]

On June 15, 1951, Millegan sent the Viking Fund his brief "Preliminary Report: Survey of Anthropological Studies in Indonesia since Independence and Prospect for Future Studies." This report mirrored established CIA methods for harnessing the field research of others, a process in which the CIA contacted academic experts on the foreign area of interest and these scholars briefed CIA operatives before these operatives traveled abroad (see SII 1983). Millegan used his status as a Viking Fund–sponsored "anthropologist" to gain the confidence of, and access to, Indonesian scholars.

In 1951, the Viking Fund changed its name to the Wenner-Gren Foundation. Once back stateside, Lloyd Millegan and his wife, Eudora, had dinner and other social interactions with William L. Thomas, the Wenner-Gren assistant director of research. Correspondence mentions family dinners and includes indications of a friendly social relationship. Millegan later wrote Thomas on behalf of Frank Sakran, who was working on an upcoming Arab State Exposition, inquiring whether Sakran could receive Wenner-Gren funds for this work (LSM, LM to WT 11/14/52). In other correspondence, Millegan mentioned a "Dr. Eckel," a likely reference to Far East scholar, OSS, and CIA employee Paul Eckel (LSM, LM to WT 9/30/50; see Albright and Kunstel 1990).[18] Thomas wrote

Millegan, asking for information on anthropologist H. R. Van Heekeren's work in Indonesia (LSM, WT to LM 9/4/51). In later correspondence, Millegan inquired about contacts with museum anthropologists and archaeologists working in the Middle East, and Thomas passed along the names of Froelich Rainey, Schuyler Camman, and Carleton Coon (LSM, WT to LM 9/20/52). Millegan's Wenner-Gren file documented several years of correspondence as the foundation struggled to collect Millegan's final report on his Indonesian fieldwork.

Millegan's Wenner-Gren file contains a 1955 pamphlet for a global missionary program launched by Millegan called Missions Unlimited. This pamphlet described his CIA work and other activities under the heading "Central Intelligence Agency, Washington, D.C. 1956–51": "As an Intelligence Analyst, Intelligence Officer and Branch Chief in this agency assisted in the organization and development of a research unit, composed of twelve professionals and three clericals, conducting research on all of the Southeast Asian countries east of India and Pakistan, together with the Philippines, Indonesia, Australia, New Zealand, and all the smaller Pacific Islands. As Chief of this unit participated in the research program for all of Asia" (LSM, 1955 pamphlet). The pamphlet acknowledged Millegan was in the CIA during the period that he traveled to Indonesia with Viking funding. His file also listed his work as president of the Pacific Book and Supply Corporation (New York City and Djakarta, 1951–52) (LSM).

Pacific Book and Supply

It was unusual for the Viking Fund to sponsor a research proposal seeking to establish a bookstore in another country. Pacific Book and Supply was first incorporated in Wilmington, Delaware, in 1946, by Lloyd Millegan (president) and officers of the corporation: Henry H. Douglas (vice president), Guy J. Millegan (secretary and treasurer), and Harry C. Shriever (FBI 100-346660-2, 12/23/46).[19]

In September 1946, the FBI investigated Pacific Book, with suspicions that its interests in publishing books relating to Asia indicated links to international communism.[20] The FBI learned that Pacific Book had accepted five manuscripts for publication and noted links to the East West Association, the China American Council of Commerce and Industry, and the Institute of Pacific Relations (IPR); IPR later became a target of FBI investigations for links between American academics and communism. The FBI reported that "a number of visitors have called at the Pacific Book office, among whom are a number of Chinese military officers and one individual known as Sam Halpern." At that time

Halpern was conducting U.S. military intelligence work, often working with Edward Lansdale in Asia. Halpern would later work on the CIA's Bay of Pigs operations in Cuba. The FBI noted Millegan's and Douglas's connections to Kenneth Langdon of the Department of State (FBI 100-3466601, 9/18/46).[21] In 1951, *Publishers Weekly* listed Lloyd Millegan as the "President of Pacific Book and Supply . . . now living in Djakarta" and identified Cass Canfield, Harold H. Stern, and Edgar Allen Prichard as corporation directors and Alvin Grauer as the corporation manager.[22]

Pacific Book's director, Edgar Allen Prichard, was the mayor of Fairfax, Virginia, a prominent Washington, DC, lawyer, and a veteran of the OSS. Canfield, Grauer, and Franklyn Forkert each established permanent careers in publishing. Cass Canfield's wartime intelligence work included posts at the Office of War Information and the Board of Economic Warfare. Canfield was the president and publisher at Harper and Row, a founder of the journal *Foreign Affairs*, and a member of the Council on Foreign Relations, with long-standing CIA ties. In 1972, Canfield played a role in the CIA's efforts to censor Alfred McCoy's book *The Politics of Heroin*. After McCoy completed the manuscript in 1972 under contract with Harper and Row, he was told by Harper and Row president, Winthrop Knowlton that the CIA sent Cord Meyer Jr. to visit his old friend Canfield, hoping to convince him that McCoy's book represented a national security threat (see McCoy 1991: xvi). In *The Cultural Cold War*, Frances Saunders mentioned a range of passive and active relationships Canfield maintained with the CIA, describing Canfield as having "enjoyed prolific links to the world of intelligence, both as a former psychological warfare officer, and as a close personal friend of Allen Dulles, whose memoirs *The Craft of Intelligence* he published in 1963" (1999: 136). Canfield directed Bantam Books, Grosset and Dunlap, and Harper Brothers, but he also worked with CIA personnel on publishing projects, including facilitating Richard Crossman's CIA-backed book detailing the stories of disillusioned former communists, *Lost Illusion*, and Arthur Koestler et al.'s book *The God That Failed* (Saunders 1999: 64; 136).

Canfield sat on the board of the Farfield Foundation, a CIA funding front directed by CIA agent Frank Platt (Saunders 1999: 136); the Board also included William A. M. Burden, Godfrey S. Rockefeller, Whitelaw Reid, and Charles Fleischmann (see Swanepoel 2007: 143). As a CIA conduit, the Farfield Foundation directed CIA funds to the Council on Cultural Freedom and other organizations the CIA hoped to nurture and influence (see Saunders 1999).

In 1951, Pacific Book produced an eighty-five-page catalog listing and describing about a thousand titles in the company's inventory. The catalog's introduction stressed these books' importance to Indonesia's development. Catalog copy claimed that with the assistance of the U.S. office the company provided books "that will help in the great work of raising Indonesia to her rightful place among the nations of the world" (Indira 1951: iv).

Pacific Book stocked a diverse selection of titles, including collections on the sciences, engineering, technical agricultural, and medicine, as well as current and classic works of literature, history, and political science. This was not just a collection of pro-American books pressing CIA conceptions of anticommunism and democracy; it was a mix of technical books and historical and political analysis, including critical works like Owen Lattimore et al.'s 1950 *Pivot of Asia* and anticolonialism collections, such as volumes of Jawaharlal Nehru's writings. There were also books more obviously aligned with CIA ideology, including John Foster Dulles's *China and America* (1946), Kermit Roosevelt's *Arabs, Oil and History* (1949), T. Cuyler Young's (1951) *Near East Culture and Society*, and Dwight Eisenhower's select speeches. The catalog included a mixture of books on Islamic civilization, ranging from the work of orientalists Harold Lamb, H. A. R. Gibb, Harry St. John Bridger Philby, and Philip Hitti to the writings of Ibn Khaldun. There were books by Will Durant, Aristotle, Bertrand Russell, Pitirim Sorokin, Sigmund Freud, Herbert Spencer, Ashley Montagu, Lewis Mumford, Robert Frost, Walt Whitman, Hortense Powdermaker, John Steinbeck, Gertrude Stein, Cora Du Bois, Kingsley Davis, Anna Louise Strong, Carleton Coon, Mark Twain, and Margaret Mead.

The company's catalog had a predominance of books on engineering and economics, and technological books aligned with the infrastructure needs of new nations, supporting the needs of the coming Rostowian push for modernization. The specific selection of titles stocked by Pacific Book may have been of little importance depending on functional uses of the front. If Pacific Book and Supply primarily served as an outpost for CIA intelligence collection and shipping functions in Indonesia, the book titles stocked may have had little significance.

At Pacific Book in 1951, Millegan became the exclusive Indonesian distributor for Time-Life International publications (*Publishers Weekly* 1951, 160: 2251). *Publishers Weekly* described Millegan's Viking Fund–financed trip to Indonesia as an "exploratory trip to southeast Asia to test the immediate market and perfect his plans for an American company which would purchase books directly in America and sell to its own customers abroad" (*Publishers Weekly* 1952 162: 242). At the time of Millegan's resignation, *Publishers Weekly* announced Franklyn Forkert was "in Indonesia representing the Pacific Book and Supply Corporation and working with Indira, an Indonesian firm, on the sales of American trade and technical books and American education supplies" (*Publishers Weekly* 1952, 162: 242).[23]

Enticements of the Field

While there are several documented instances of anthropologist-spies, few anthropologists have historically used their professional credentials and fieldwork as covers for espionage. Yet, archaeologists and cultural anthropologists have been accused of engaging in spying, and rumors of field-based espionage have long circulated within the field. Rumors of links to the CIA and other intelligence agencies create dangers for those under suspicion and for others working in the field; even scholarly examinations of historical interactions between anthropologists and spies make many in the discipline uneasy. Some anthropologists worry that documenting past disciplinary connections to the CIA could increase suspicion of contemporary anthropologists and archaeologists.

Anthropology articulates with the world it studies through fieldwork. Whether on large, organized archaeological expeditions or small-scale, self-funded research trips undertaken on dilapidated buses or by bush taxi to remote villages, anthropologists during the Cold War frequently traveled to regions of interest to the CIA and Pentagon planners at rates higher than those in most other professions, and the discipline had a mixture of real and imagined interfaces with military and intelligence agencies. Fieldwork scattered hundreds of individual anthropologists in the backwater villages of a world imagined by the Pentagon to soon be the front lines of a global battleground with international communism, and the unobtrusive, often undirected queries of anthropologists seeking knowledge about topics like postmarital residence patterns or language drift brought many legitimate anthropologists and occasionally provided cover for a few anthropologist-spies. Participant observation's approach to cultural understanding gave ethnographers the sort of cultural knowledge that made the discipline attractive to intelligence agencies wanting to understand the hearts and minds of those living in lands of geopolitical interest.[24]

While many anthropologists privately discussed being approached by governmental officials asking for briefings upon their return from fieldwork, and some (like Marvin Harris, discussed earlier in this chapter, and John Allison, discussed in chapter 6) described suspicions that their field notes may have been read or taken by governmental agencies, there has been little scholarly discussion of these possibilities. Some of these activities appear to have continued after the end of the Cold War. In 1995, an American anthropologist writing under the pseudonym "Brooks Duncan" described being approached in the 1990s by FBI, CIA, and State Department personnel requesting information on his research in Russia. When Duncan refused to cooperate, he was harassed by FBI agents; later his research notes disappeared when "the Pan Am bag (supplied to me at the airport by Pan Am for repacking) containing all my scholarly documents, lists of contacts and writings and syllabi materials disappeared en route to my research in Russia and was never found" (Duncan 1995: 9). When he sought help from colleagues, senior professors and civil liberties groups advised him to "do nothing unless I felt like sacrificing my career. They expressed their belief that wherever I applied for a job, someone on the faculty would make things difficult for me" (9).

Even in instances where individuals had witting CIA links that sent them out into the world to gather information or establish networks (cases like John Dimick or the claims of Frank Hibben), they created inverted-duplicitous forms of dual use anthropology. And given the secrecy surrounding CIA operations, we are left with more questions than answers regarding many of these interactions. With the passage of time, scholars will gain access to more archival records and documents under the Freedom of Information Act, which will shed more light on such interactions between anthropologists and intelligence agencies.

Many questions remain about Kennedy, Millegan, and others discussed in this chapter. Though several scholars assert that Kennedy was gathering information for the U.S. government and was linked to the CIA at the time of his death, documentation of this relationship has not been released by the CIA or found in accessible archives. Likewise, there is no documentation establishing that Lloyd Millegan was sent to conduct faux ethnographic research as a direct replacement for the slain Raymond Kennedy. But even with gaps in our knowledge, we can view Kennedy's ethnographic project — like all ethnographic research in Indonesia during this period — as easily fitting into CIA agent Millegan's research plan (as financed by the Viking Fund) of combing existing ethnographic research, looking for information of interest to be synthesized into reports. Such reports have dual audiences and dual uses, and there were likely other reports for other audiences drawing on these same data.

While ethnographic reports from the field were of interest to the CIA and the Pentagon for various reasons, it was the promise of using specific cultural knowledge to inform counterinsurgency operations — as a desired means of controlling other populations through some imagined deep cultural competence — that kept interest in ethnographic research alive in military and intelligence circles.

Unlike efforts to use the eyes and ears of anthropologists to gather reports of developments in distant lands where they conducted fieldwork as a means of gathering specific intelligence, intelligence programs linked to counterinsurgency operations drew more frequently on the funding reports or published academic works of anthropologists writing up the findings of their research long after they had returned home from their fieldwork.

> All social research worthy of the name raises the question of who will use the results, and for what purposes. This is an old question among physical and biological scientists, and it will not [die] down. In the social sciences it carries more explosive implications, as when gangsters make use of studies of an American community to enrich themselves. This has happened more often than some social scientists realize.
>
> DOUGLAS HARING | 1951

TEN COLD WAR ANTHROPOLOGICAL COUNTERINSURGENCY DREAMS

During the Cold War the CIA, Pentagon, and State Department recurrently used anthropological knowledge for psychological warfare and counterinsurgency operations.[1] While ethnographic knowledge had obvious uses, military and intelligence agencies encountered difficulties organizing and retrieving the ethnographic data they sought. One of the more creative efforts to coordinate the retrieval of ethnographic information involved military adaptations of the Human Relations Area Files (HRAF) indexing system as a counterinsurgency tool.

HRAF's bureaucratic approach to cross-cultural research began with the establishment of the "Cross-Cultural Survey" by Yale's Institute of Human Relations (IHR) in 1937. During the Second World War, Lieutenant Commander George Murdock expanded IHR's cross-cultural files to directly meet the needs of the Office of Naval Intelligence for purposes in part linked to counterinsurgency objectives. Murdock helped standardize the production of reports on cultural traits to help military planners better anticipate the cultural variations that U.S. forces would encounter on the Pacific Front (May 1971; Murdock 1961: xii; D. H. Price 2008a: 91–96).

Murdock directed the rapid production of a series of classified Office of the Chief of Naval Operations Civil Affairs Handbooks at IHR on Micronesian cultures. After the war, when IHR became HRAF, it continued governmental contracts to fill "the need by government policy makers for reliable information on strategic areas [that] was fully as great as during World War II" (HRAF 1959: 14, 23; D. H. Price 2008a). These postwar funding opportunities expanded HRAF's coverage. This dual use research strategy met both the strategic needs of the U.S. government and the scientific needs of HRAF's theorists as "much of the work done for the government would also serve the purpose of building basic files on the sample of the world's peoples" (HRAF 1959: 23).

The HRAF indexing system provided an ingenious solution to problems of retrieving a wide variety of textual knowledge in a world without computer search capabilities. By generating a massive universal index of the categories listed in Murdock's *Outline of Cultural Materials* (1961), HRAF facilitated retrieving information on cultural traits in independently produced primary texts. Murdock's system of cross-indexing texts generated by others was the foundation of HRAF research. The data indexed and sorted by HRAF ranged from abstract theoretical analysis of postmarriage residential patterns in matrilineal societies, to the distribution of certain religious beliefs, to (with the expansion of categories by a military-intelligence unit) sorting cultural knowledge to assist counterinsurgency operations.

Dual Use HRAF

During the 1950s, HRAF received significant governmental funding for compiling culture studies of regions of geopolitical Cold War interest.[2] An HRAF report from 1959 noted, "From 1950 to 1955 various government agencies supported work on Southeast Asia, Siberia, Czechoslovakia and Iran. In 1954 the Army offered HRAF one of the largest single government contracts for social science research ever made. Originally for two years and two and three-quarter million dollars, it was extended for an additional two years at a total cost of nearly four million dollars" (HRAF 1959: 24). With this $4 million military contract, HRAF compiled bibliographies, translated foreign texts, and produced a series of "handbooks on more than fifty countries in the Soviet Orbit, the Middle East, and Asia" (24). Between 1958 and 1960, the HRAF Survey of World Cultures Series published volumes on Poland, Jordan, Iraq, Saudi Arabia, Cambodia, China, the USSR, and Laos, nations of Cold War geopolitical importance. Funds for this work were provided by the CIA-linked Rubicon Foundation (Ford 1970: 15; Harwood 1967b).[3]

This dual use role required HRAF to hire personnel who could bridge gaps spanning military-intelligence worlds and the academy. In 1954, retired admiral Edward Lender Woodyard, a decorated naval strategist, was appointed to a new position as HRAF vice president. Donald H. Hunt initially directed a new HRAF office in Washington, DC, but soon Colonel Cary B. Hutchinson was appointed as director in order to "rewrite the [HRAF-subcontracted] monographs into country handbooks," tailoring these texts to meet the needs of military sponsors (HRAF 1959: 24). To oversee these military contracts, HRAF hired Milton D. Graham, whose previous Defense Department work had prepared him to supervise the handbook program, and Graham outsourced handbook sections to more than four hundred scholars at fifteen U.S. universities.[4]

This military sponsorship shifted HRAF's data collection decisions on geographic areas of focus during the 1950s. During the four-year period in which HRAF received $4 million in army funds, it produced "63 unclassified monographs on 50 different countries," along with thirty-four classified country handbooks (of these classified handbooks, twenty-four were "written in Washington and 10 in New Haven"); HRAF produced annotated biographies on forty countries, as well as "20 volumes published by HRAF Press" (HRAF 1959: 24). With the production of almost one hundred military handbooks (and forty annotated bibliographies for military consumption), these military projects dominated, at a ratio of five to one. Some military country handbooks were rewritten, reedited, and republished as part of HRAF's Country Survey Series (HRAF 1959: 26).

In 1958, a governmental committee investigating the national support for behavioral sciences issued a report to Vice President Richard Nixon advocating the formation of an advisory panel to determine which social science projects should receive federal funds.[5] The report recommended federal support to establish an "electronic data storage and retrieval mechanism for the Human Relations Area Files, a compendium of categorized information on several hundred societies of the world" (HRAF 1959: 31; cf. Bauer et al. 1958: 225; Solovey 2013: 95–96).[6] The report supported HRAF playing a direct role in "formulating sound theory" that had potential to influence public policy (Bauer et al. 1958: 222). In the late 1950s, HRAF envisioned itself as serving the geopolitical policy makers, and it considered developing a "six-million-word" encyclopedia on cultures of Asia and organizing "the wealth of material in the files on strategic areas of the Middle East and Southeast Asia" into publications that could offer "guidance" to policy makers (HRAF 1959: 37).

Military-linked personnel were hired at HRAF's Washington office to help secure military funds, and although some military funds went to the production of Pentagon-related or State Department–related resources, these funds also produced purely theoretical anthropological work not directly related to military sponsorship. Military funds allowed HRAF to amass data and code texts, leading to unrelated theoretical work examining social structure and other topics of interest to academics. The dual use nature of this work meant that the military got what it wanted, and funds were also available for unrelated theoretical work of anthropologists' choosing without military interference in the individual projects selected by anthropologists using HRAF materials.

HRAF and the U.S. Army Handbook Program

With a steady flow of military-intelligence funding, HRAF grew rapidly during the 1950s. Between military, intelligence, and State Department funding, HRAF received about $200,000 a year during the early 1950s, and "the Navy, the Army, the Air Force and the Central Intelligence Agency each contributed $50,000 a year to support research on four major areas: Southeast Asia, Europe, Northeast Asia, and the Near and Middle East" (Ford 1970: 13). In 1954, HRAF began producing volumes for the Army Handbook Program, subcontracting each volume to authors using nonclassified materials from academic libraries across the country. After contractors completed their drafts, classified materials were added by army personnel in a process where "the manuscripts prepared at HRAF and at the subcontracted universities were sent to a branch office established at American University, Washington, D.C. where classified information was added to the unclassified material, and the final handbooks were prepared for submission to the Army" (14–15).

The parceling out of Army Handbooks to scholars working with academic library materials was an ideal arrangement for HRAF because it relieved "universities and HRAF from being hampered in any way by security precautions. It also served as a direct link with the Army and was therefore in a position to fashion the final products to Army specifications" (Ford 1970: 15). These funds allowed HRAF to translate a broad collection of foreign language ethnographies and to publish several volumes in the Survey of World Cultures Series (15).

During the 1950s, more than 85 percent of HRAF's funds came from government contracts with the U.S. Army, Air Force, and Navy, while membership dues, gifts, and grants totaled less than 15 percent of HRAF's funds (see table 10.1) (HRAF 1959: 39). A 1959 HRAF report indicated that some of the gifts and grants had ties to the CIA, including grant funds from the Rubicon Foundation (revealed as a CIA front in 1967 [see Harwood 1967c]) and a gift from CIA operative and anthropologist Donald Wilber, whose many years of CIA work included his role as a key architect of the agency's Iran coup in 1953 (Wilber 1954).

TABLE 10.1 Revenue Sources for the Human Relations Area Files, 1949–1959 (Source: HRAF 1959: 39)

MEMBERSHIP DUES
Member Universities..$350,000
GIFTS AND GRANTS
Carnegie Corporation...$162,500
Ford Foundation..$125,000
National Science Foundation..$17,000
Rubicon Foundation...$27,000
Viking Fund (Wenner-Gren)...$5,000
Standard Oil Company..$4,000
National Academy of Sciences..$2,700
Overbrook Foundation..$2,500
Donald Wilber..$1,000
Committee for Promotion of Advanced Slavic Studies.................................$800
GOVERNMENT CONTRACTS
Department of the Army..$4,058,000
Department of the Air Force..$50,000
Department of the Navy...$210,000
Other Departments...$50,000

TOTAL $5,066,000

The writing for the Army Handbooks was outsourced by HRAF to graduate students and professors at Indiana, Chicago, Stanford, Cornell, the University of California, New York University, the University of Washington, American University, Columbia, Johns Hopkins, Yale, and the American Geographical Society. Contributors included Henry Kissinger, Lawrence Krader, Kingsley Davis, Andre Gunder Frank, June Nash, Karl Wittfogel, and Nicholas Poppe (Ford 1970:28–29). Given the formulaic presentation of information in the handbooks, the writers' diverse political perspectives are more of a historical measure of the ubiquitous presence of such projects during this period than a reflection of any particular orientation of the simple narratives of the handbooks.

In 1996, Andre Gunder Frank wrote me that his contribution, as a Chicago graduate student, consisted of nothing more than a few days of library work writing cultural descriptions for HRAF's Slavic Peoples Project, and that he gave little thought to what he was producing mostly because academically it was on the level of a high school textbook (AGF to DHP 7/16/96). He was recruited to the project "by Bert Hoselitz, after he ran out of money to pay me at [the Research Center in Economic Development and Cultural Change], and this came along as a grad student research support possibility. . . . I personally did not know what was going on, except that one day a colonel from the Army Intelligence Service [or the Army Psychological Warfare Division] came to check us out. Chicago subcontracted the 6 projects from Yale which contracted the HRAF directly from the army" (AGF to DHP 7/16/96). Another Chicago graduate student, June Nash, was also recruited by Bert Hoselitz for an HRAF Army Handbook. Nash wrote me that Hoselitz had hired "a staff of mostly Europeans. This included a Czech economist who was supposed to do the piece I did. He sat on it for a year, receiving monthly checks, then one month before publication was due, he decided the data was too biased to use. So I was called in in July and had to produce the report by August, which I did working like a Stakhanovite much to the disgust of the other scholars. It was the only [HRAF] monograph or ms. I did. I didn't get much of an orientation, including issues of classification" (JN to DHP ca. 6/14/95).

Similar forms of contract piecework have employed graduate students in American universities for generations, and given the simple encyclopedia-like entries these graduate students produced, there is no political intrigue in the specifics of what they wrote. The mundane acceptance of anthropologists making cultures legible for the Pentagon and others is one measure of how normal such military-linked relationships were during this period. Anthropologists were comfortable producing these simple narratives to which layers of classified intelligence could later be added. It was a simple exchange in which the anthropologists fed the Pentagon, the Pentagon fed the anthropologists, and the anthropologists went off to do their own work. Yet there remain questions about how such relationships steered the discipline.

Special Operations Research Office, American University

In 1956, a private nonprofit research center producing reports on a variety of topics for the U.S. Army, known as the Special Operations Research Office (SORO), was established at American University. During its eight years of operation, SORO produced "approximately 50 book-length studies of countries in Europe, Asia, the Middle East, Africa and Latin America," as well as studies in "Sub-Saharan Africa and Latin America" (*AAAFN* 1963 4(5): 5).[7] While SORO acknowledged military funding for these ethnographic research projects, most of the anthropologists associated with the office stressed the normal anthropological functions

TABLE 10.2 Anthropologists Working for SORO between 1956 and 1969

NAME	SORO YEARS	SOURCE
George W. Baker	1957–59	(Rohde 2007: 284–93)
William K. Carr	1967–69	(Rohde 2007: 284–93)
Antoinette K. Emrich	1968–69	(Rohde 2007: 284–93)
Edwin E. Erickson	1963	(SORO Box 1, 3/8/63 Roster)
Judith Lynne Hanna	1966–69	(Rohde 2007: 284–93)
George L. Harris	1963	(SORO Box 1, 3/8/63 Roster)
Milton Jacobs	1961–63	(Rohde 2007: 284–93)
Irving Kaplan	1963	(SORO Box 1, 3/8/63 Roster)
Howard Keva Kaufman	1964–66	(Rohde 2007: 284–93)
John D. LeNoir	1965–66	(Rohde 2007: 284–93)
Thomas E. Lux	1963	(SORO Box 1, 3/8/63 Roster)
Bela C. Maday	1963	(SORO Box 1, 3/8/63 Roster)
Felix Moos	1964–65	(Rohde 2007: 284–93)
Hugo Nutini	1964–65	(LOC 1969)
Keith F. Otterbein	1963–64	(Rohde 2007: 284–93)
Peter B. Riddleberger	1963–65	(Rohde 2007: 284–93)
Herbert H. Vreeland, III	1957–67	(Rohde 2007: 284–93)
Irving A. Wallach	1957–58	(Rohde 2007: 284–93)

of analyzing elements of foreign cultures and downplayed SORO's counterinsurgency projects.

Herbert Vreeland recruited anthropologists, writing in the pages of the *AAA Fellows Newsletter* (under his middle name, "Harold") that SORO's "studies are designed to satisfy a military requirement for readily available background information on the society and culture of foreign countries. However, the studies have been in increasing demand by a wide variety of organizations — both governmental and non-governmental for the same purpose" (AAAFN 1963 4[5]: 5–6).[8]

Interdisciplinary teams wrote SORO reports, with anthropologists and other social scientists and area studies and military experts. Originally the reports were classified documents, but by 1963, SORO produced nonclassified documents to be widely distributed and used in a variety of military and nonmilitary agencies (AAAFN 1963 4[5]: 5–6).

While HRAF relied heavily on university-based anthropologists and other social science contractors to write country reports, SORO hired more than a dozen staff anthropologists, whose research tasks were directly linked to SORO's interests in counterinsurgency (see table 10.2). The job announcements in the *AAA Fellows Newsletter* described the job duties in normative research terms and listed salaries that exceeded those of entry-level professorships. But the security dominating the workplace required all SORO employees to undergo background screenings to achieve a "secret" security clearance, which precluded hiring individuals outside of a narrow range of political affiliations (Rohde 2007: 51).

Over a dozen anthropologists were hired by SORO during the early 1960s. Among those holding doctoral degrees were Felix Moos, William Carr, Bela Maday, Howard Kaufman, and Herbert H. Vreeland III, while other staff anthropologists held master's and bachelor's degrees in anthropology. A cadre of sociologists, political scientists, and military personnel at times worked as "anthropologists" on counterinsurgency projects (SORO Box 1, 3/8/63 SORO Roster; Rohde 2013; Lippincott and Dame 1964: i).

In 1963, SORO opened a field office at Fort Bragg, North Carolina, and the following year it established facilities in Seoul, South Korea, and in the Panama Canal Zone, where it conducted "social science research on problems of understanding affecting or supporting foreign people and societies, especially in Latin America, who were involved in or threatened by insurgency and subversion" (Shrader 2008: 200).

A conception of culture emerged from SORO reports expressing what would become recurrent Pentagon misunderstandings about anthropology's ability to contribute elements of cultural engineering to military campaigns. Its Project Prosyms Pakistan tried to construct culturally appropriate counterinsurgency propaganda messages for possible use in Pakistan (Rohde 2013: 42–46). Several SORO projects envisioned using anthropology to control local populations in order to advance American military interests.[9] James R. Price and Paul Jureidini's SORO report "Witchcraft, Sorcery, Magic and Other Psychological Phenomena and Their Implications on Military and Paramilitary Operations in the Congo" (1964) fantasized about weaponizing ethnographic knowledge to manipulate native populations in absurd ways. This report drew on academic anthropological literature, including the work of E. E. Evans-Pritchard, Meyers Forte, Louis Leakey, Jomo Kenyata, John Middleton, George Murdock, C. G. Seligman, and Monica Wilson. Price and Jureidini examined claims that magic was "effective in conditioning dissident elements and their followers to do battle with Government troops. Rebel tribesmen are said to have been persuaded that they can be made magically impervious to Congolese army firepower. Their fear of the government has thus been diminished and, conversely, fear of the rebels has grown within army ranks" (J. R. Price and Jureidini 1964: 1). The report considered whether knowledge of magical beliefs could be used by outsiders to control superstitious natives.

Price and Jureidini claimed that magic-based counterinsurgency campaigns might be potentially so powerful that they could backfire, and that by strengthening and reinforcing local supernatural beliefs, they could accidentally unleash political forces that would be difficult to anticipate or control. They recommended exposing native emic truths of "magical invulnerability" to the etic realities of guns and bullets, writing that "there is every reason to believe that disciplined troops, proficient in marksmanship, and led by competent officers, can handily dispel most notions of magical invulnerability" (Price and Jureidini 1964: 11). These were enticing claims for military and civilian strategists facing historically long odds of success in intractable counterinsurgency campaigns.

Interdisciplinary teams undertook a wide range of SORO projects. Judith Lynne Hanna and her husband, SORO political scientist William Hanna, coauthored *Urban Dynamics in Black Africa: An Interdisciplinary Approach* (1971). Milton Jacobs worked on communications in Thailand (Jacobs, Farzanegan, and Askenasy 1966). William Carr, Howard Kaufman, Robert Suggs, Herbert Vreeland III, and Peter Riddleberger studied Third World insurgent movements (see Molnar et al. 1963; Molnar et al. 1963).[10] From 1964 to 1966, Raoul Naroll, working under a $55,000 SORO "Special Projects" grant, studied "Deterrence in History" (SORO Box 1 Final Report of the Subcommittee on Behavioral Sciences Defense Science Board, 1965 DoD, p. 31; Naroll 1974). In 1965 and 1966, Naroll, working under a $75,000 Department of Navy grant, studied "Intelligence Data Validation" (SORO Box 1 Final Report of the Subcommittee on Behavioral Sciences Defense Science Board, 1965 DoD, 41). Felix Moos studied "Cross-Cultural Relationships between Foreigners and American Military Commanders in Korea" (SORO Box 1 Final Report of the Subcommittee on Behavioral Sciences Defense Science Board, 1965 DoD, 39).[11] The 1964 "Brief Review of Selected Aspects of the San Blas Cuna Indians" calculated the likely impacts of improving health care as a flank of counterinsurgency operations.[12] The primary sources for this report were HRAF and SORO files, and the section on ethnohistory drew on Richard N. Adams's 1957 survey of Panama, Nicaragua, Guatemala, El Salvador, and Honduras (Lippincott and Dame 1964: 1, 3; Adams 1957).

In 1965, anthropologist Milton Jacobs received a $61,000 grant to conduct research at the SORO Panama Field Office (SORO Box 1 Final Report of the Subcommittee on Behavioral Sciences Defense Science Board, 1965 DoD, 40). In 1964, Gerald Hickey received a $92,000 Project Agile grant from the Advanced Research Projects Administration (ARPA) for research on "Motivational Studies" (SORO Box 1 Final Report of the Subcommittee on Behavioral Sciences Defense Science Board, 1965 DoD, 43). Hickey also received ARPA funds ($53,000 in 1964, $26,000 in 1965) for work on a project titled "Advisor-Counterpart Communications" (SORO Box 1 Final Report of the Subcommittee on Behavioral Sciences Defense Science Board, 1965 DoD, 47). Project Agile drew on ARAP funds to pay Charles Osgood $95,000 a year, for three years, to work on his project "Communication, Cooperation and Negotiation in Culturally Heterogeneous Groups" (SORO Box 1 Final Report of the Subcommittee on Behavioral Sciences Defense Science Board, 1965 DoD, 44).

James Price's Counterinsurgency Information and Analysis Center (CINFAC) (and SORO) report titled "Irrigation as a Factor in the Economic Development of Thailand" (1964) described the basic workings of Thai irrigation systems within a "counterinsurgency analysis" framework, focusing on how Thai land tenure systems created stability and weakened insurgents' efforts by vesting farmers in a functioning socioeconomic system (J. R. Price 1964: 6).

In September 1964, the National Academy of Sciences/National Research Council invited ten scholars, including anthropologists Charles Wagley and Leonard Doob, to join an advisory committee that was charged with assisting the Human Factors and Operations Research Division in an unnamed project that was estimated to have a budget of about $600,000 per year (SORO Box 1, NAS memo 9/22/64). Although Project Camelot was never mentioned by name, the letter requesting these scholars' participation described goals that would be at the core of Camelot:

> 1. Identifying and, where possible, measuring indicators of internal war potential, and analyzing the dynamics of their interrelationships.
>
> 2. Determining the effects of various courses of governmental action upon the social processes in the indigenous culture to which the action is directed.
>
> 3. Improving the estimation of internal war potential and devising means of reducing that potential. (SORO Box 1, NAS memo 9/22/64)

In an October 9, 1964, letter addressed to "Fellow SOROns," SORO director Theodore Vallance summarized SORO's activities, including the development of Project Camelot. Among the activities by SOROns was the "loan" of anthropologists Ed Erickson and Bela Maday to Peace Corps training activities held at Brandeis University, assisting in the training of [Peace Corps Volunteers] preparing to be sent to Bolivia (SORO Box 1, Vallance memo 10/9/64).[13]

Project Camelot

In August 1964, U.S. Army leadership called for the formation of a research project to "test in one country the feasibility of designing and developing, for strategic planning and other Army use, an advanced system of early warning of internal conflict or its increased likelihood in foreign nations, together with concepts for early Army reaction systems requirements" (Deitchman 1976: 139). This program was assigned to SORO as Project Camelot (142).

Camelot was conceived as a broad program that would fund social science projects undertaking a variety of tasks, such as predicting outbreaks of violence or episodes of insurgency. Prior to Camelot, SORO consultants conducted reviews of social science literature to develop "800 hypotheses about internal war" (Deitchman 1976: 143). These theories focused on causal variables, including economic inequities, rapid economic growth, elements of "social mobility," reactions to "oppressive governments," toleration of alienation, responses to totalitarianism, and so forth (Deitchman 1976: 143). Some of the social science research at SORO tried to generate social engineering–friendly formulas to predict or prevent political uprisings.

Rex Hooper, a former missionary and a Brooklyn College sociologist with Latin American expertise, was hired by SORO to direct Project Camelot. Camelot was initially an unclassified project, and most of its analysis was to be conducted by independent subcontractor scholars at U.S. and international universities. In October 1964, Vallance and Hooper pitched Camelot to scholars and administrators at SSRC, MIT, Harvard, Columbia, and Princeton and at the Russell Sage and Ford Foundations (SORO Box 1, Vallance memo 10/9/64). Camelot was conceived of as operating on an annual budget of about $1 million for its first three to four years (SORO Box 1, Vallance memo 10/9/64).

The first stage of Project Camelot was to take place during the winter and spring of 1964–65 with U.S.-based "library research on theories of conflict, revolutionary warfare, and processes of change in diverse social systems" covering a broad range of historical and national settings (Deitchman 1976: 145). Among these first planned historical studies identified by SORO were studies of mid-twentieth-century revolutions in Argentina, Cuba, Venezuela, Peru, Colombia, Guatemala, Egypt, Iran, South Korea, and Greece, as well as revolutionary independence movements in Algeria, Turkey, Thailand, Paraguay, Ecuador, Venezuela, Nigeria, Mexico, France, El Salvador, the Dominican Republic, Brazil, Bolivia, and the Congo, and even the Québécois separatist movement, while "Chile was not mentioned as one of the possibilities, although it figured very much in the news later" (145; Solovey 2001: 181).

Chilean-born anthropologist Hugo Nutini was hired by SORO in December 1964, while a professor of anthropology at the University of Pittsburg. Between January and April 1965, Nutini regularly attended "Camelot Monday meetings" in Washington, DC, as a consultant. He was compensated with a payment of seventy-five dollars (plus transportation and a per diem) for each meeting (RB 75, HGN to RB 9/17/66). In April 1965, Nutini traveled to Chile, where he misrepresented his research to Chilean colleagues, telling them it was sponsored by the National Science Foundation. Nutini falsely claimed to colleagues that Robert K. Merton, Kingsley Davis, Seymour Lipset, and other prestigious social scientists were joining the project. After meeting with Nutini, Alvaro Bunster of the University of Chile became suspicious that Nutini was involved in some sort of U.S. spy program.

Nutini asked Hopper for a letter to present to the American embassy in Santiago notifying it of his status, but Hopper refused. Nutini later wrote Ralph Beals that he told Hopper he "would deny any knowledge of Army sponsorship of the project if the situation got sticky. To this they agreed, and nothing was further discussed. I do not remember what I said to [Chilean sociologist Raúl] Urzua on the 29 of April, but I can tell you confidentially that he knew everything about Camelot from the very beginning" (RB 75, HGN to RB 9/17/66).

Norwegian sociologist Johan Galtung was conducting research in Chile when Nutini approached scholars there. In December 1964, SORO had invited Galtung to participate in an August 1965 Camelot conference, but Galtung declined.[14] After Nutini tried recruiting Chilean social scientists with misrepresentations of a program already known to Galtung, Galtung exposed Nutini's activities to the Latin American Faculty of Social Science, which stirred up outrage in the leftist press and with left-wing members of the Chilean Senate. On June 12, 1965, a Chilean Communist newspaper broke the Camelot story with a headline warning, "Yankees Study Invasion of Chile: Project Camelot Financed by U.S. Army" (Deitchman 1976: 157).

The resulting damage and distrust among South American scholars toward their U.S. colleagues were widespread; as Marshall Sahlins observed, "As a tactic of fomenting Latin American unrest and anti–North American sentiment, Camelot would be the envy of any Communist conspiracy. We have heard of the self-fulfilling prophecy; here was the self-fulfilling research proposal" (2000b: 263).

Later, a report by Library of Congress staff for the Congressional Subcommittee on Science, Research and Development indicated that Nutini lied about the sponsorship and scope of Camelot research to Chilean social scientists. This report found Nutini's misrepresentations were premeditated and had taken some preparation, and that he had "erased from the working papers he brought with him all references to DOD sponsorship and represented the project as being funded by the National Science Foundation" (LOC 1969: 132). Nutini later claimed he never said Camelot had NSF funding and that he "was instructed by Camelot officials to say, if asked, that the Project was sponsored by American Government agencies, without giving any details, and that was exactly what I did" (RB 76, Nutini to Beals 9/17/66).[15] The U.S. ambassador to Chile was broadsided by these revelations, and, as Joy Rohde (2013) argues, the fallout and clash between the State Department and the Pentagon exacerbated already tense relations between them, and this had more to do with the termination of Camelot than with any protests launched by academics. As Rohde notes, Camelot collapsed not because of anthropologists' or Chileans' rage but because the Department of State used what might have been a minor scandal to confront the Defense Department in an ongoing struggle over which department should determine foreign policy. Rohde overstates the impact of this, however, claiming that the termination of Camelot "had little to with its intellectual content" (2013: 72), as if the exposed counterinsurgency operation was not at the heart of the trouble it caused the Johnson administration.

Secretary of Defense Robert McNamara terminated Camelot the second week of July 1965, just as Congress prepared to hold hearings on the program (Eder 1965). Theodore Vallance, director of SORO, testified to the House Foreign Affairs Subcommittee that Nutini was the only Camelot social scientist ever sent abroad before the program was terminated (Eder 1965). President Johnson's August 1965 memo to Secretary of State Dean Rusk, responding to the Camelot scandal, said little more than that he did not want the U.S. to be embarrassed again and proclaimed, "No Government sponsorship of foreign area research should be undertaken which in the judgment of the Secretary of State would adversely affect United States foreign relations" (Johnson qtd. in Horowitz 1967: 17). The State Department's Foreign Affairs Research Council subsequently reviewed hundreds of projects to evaluate "the propriety of Government-sponsored social science research in the area of foreign policy" (NAAA 1969 10[1]: 11).

After Harold Pincus published articles critiquing Camelot, George Murdock met with Seymour Deitchman at Murdock's office at the National Academy of

Sciences/National Research Council to discuss the fallout from these revelations for other social science research projects.[16] According to Deitchman, "Out of the discussions with Murdock arose the idea of establishing an NAS/NRC Committee on Social Sciences, to examine DOD's needs and its role, and to see what might be done to improve the situation. The DDR&E [Department of Defense, Research & Engineering] accepted the idea, and in fact felt it would be worthwhile enough that he initiated a request to the NAS to establish the committee" (1976: 203–4).[17]

In 1965, SORO launched Project Colony in Peru and Project Simpatico in Colombia. Both projects repeated elements of Camelot's basic research design, and both used U.S. anthropologists working with local governmental authorities. Project Colony relied on "observation and analysis of Peruvian army efforts to assist the economic development and integration of the Indians in the trans-Andean highlands into the Peruvian economy and society. The results of the study were also intended to assist the U.S. Amy to develop its 'civic action' doctrines for military assistance to the armies of developing nations" (Deitchman 1976: 185). Project Simpatico used social science surveys to measure rural attitudes about the government and rebel groups. There were plans to expand Project Colony into Bolivia, but after Camelot's disastrous publicity, the American ambassador to Bolivia canceled them, even though the Bolivian government remained supportive of the project (186). During the summer of 1965, SORO became involved in protracted legal disagreements with Peruvian workers, and American University settled with five individuals, paying a total of $9,294 for lost wages on a Project Colony contract (SORO, Box 2 contracts/legal; Pincus 1966).

Project Simpatico was codirected by anthropologist Howard Kaufman and used anthropologists and psychologists to design research questionnaires to study political attitudes in rural Colombia. Using structured questionnaires and standardized "thematic apperception tests," Simpatico probed rural Colombian villagers' attitudes concerning current political conditions, the government, rural bandits, the military, and other social forces believed to be contributing to political instability in the country. As elected Colombian officials tried to use Project Simpatico to gather information in an upcoming political election, a scandal developed in Colombia and the United States when news of this project became public, and the program was terminated (see Deitchman 1976: 187; RB 75, Executive Board Minutes 5/20–21/66).

On June 27, 1966, Stephen Boggs, executive secretary of the AAA, testified before the U.S. Senate Hearings for the Subcommittee on Government Research that "an absolutely impassable barrier must be established between the intelligence agencies of the United States Government and the universities, private foundations and international voluntary organizations engaged in research" (Eder 1966b: 5). This public stance by academics wishing to distance themselves from intelligence work further dashed SORO hopes for rehabilitation, and in July 1966 SORO closed down its operations, while some SORO personnel and projects continued at American University at the Center for Research in Social Systems (CRESS).

These revelations about SORO's use of anthropologists and other social scientists brought suspicions on many American researchers working in Latin America and elsewhere. American anthropologists suffered from new forms of guilt by disciplinary association, and some researchers found it difficult to obtain research visas for fieldwork in Latin America and other regions of the underdeveloped world.

The M-VICO *System of Counterinsurgency Taxonomy*

Hoping to efficiently link existing ethnographic literature with the needs of military and intelligence counterinsurgency projects, SORO developed *The M-VICO System of Counterinsurgency Taxonomy*. The M-VICO System adopted HRAF's cross-indexing and classification system to include new categories of counterinsurgency data (J. R. Price et al. ca. 1964–65; Conley 1966). *The M-VICO System* is a 230-page report, 187 pages of which are photocopied reproductions of HRAF documents crudely sandwiched into the main text. Immediately following the title page are eight pages of unaltered photocopies of the fourth edition of Murdock's *Outline of Cultural Materials* (OCM) table of contents (a brief listing of the 88 primary classifications, and hundreds of secondary categories of traits indexed by HRAF), which are followed by a three-page listing of SORO's additional 22 primary trait classifications and a total of 123 secondary cultural traits of interest to military and intelligence personnel engaged in counterinsurgency (see Murdock 1961). The text of M-VICO followed HRAF's indexing methods, with "the Matrix of the outline consists of 80 major divisions or sections, numbered from 10 through 89, and 623 minor divisions or categories, numbered by adding digits from 1 to 9 to the numbers on the sections under which they fall" (J. R. Price et al. ca. 1964–65: intro. 2). The OCM categories end at number 88, and SORO added an eighty-ninth division to HRAF's matrix under the heading "United States Policy Orientation"; this section contained SORO's added "minor divisions or categories" that used HRAF-derived categories to catalog cultural data of interest to SORO's counterinsurgency theorists.

It is unclear what year James R. Price, Barbara Reason Butler, Doris M. Condit, Bert Cooper, Michael Conley, and Richard H. Moore produced *The M-VICO System of Counterinsurgency Taxonomy* for SORO, but a consideration of the years when the authors were at SORO indicates it was produced between 1964 and 1965 (J. R. Price et al. ca. 1964–65).[18] The only two copies of *The M-VICO System* that I located (one in the Pentagon Library, the other in the Georgetown University Library) are undated, but several elements indicate a date in the mid-1960s. We know that SORO was terminated in 1966, the discussion of using *The M-VICO System* at CINFAC, and the known SORO employment dates of authors suggest it was produced sometime during 1964–65.[19]

The M-VICO categories mimicked HRAF's index and could be revised over time as new sources were analyzed (J. R. Price et al. ca. 1964–65: intro. 3–4). The format of M-VICO copied the index format of OCM, with its index divided into the four categories giving it its name, with Matrix sections on "Vulnerabilities," "Insurgency," "Counterinsurgency," and "Outcomes." The focus on these sections was identified as follows:

> Vulnerabilities. This section has been designed to organize information indicating the vulnerabilities of a particular country to subversion of any type. Geographical, demographic, political, economic, military, and psychological conditions are identified in this section, whose categories are preceded by the initial "V," and whose numerical codes are selected from those of the Matrix.
>
> *Insurgency*. The content of this section of a file is indicated by the political or social temperature in a given country. The information categories in this section are organized sequentially to permit either partial or complete activation, category by category, as may be indicated by the progression of events. The categories range from political, economic, or social unrest through organization of underground activities on through progressive degrees of organized violence. All numbered categories in this section are preceded by the initial "I."
>
> Counterinsurgency. This section organizes information about anti-subversive activities ranging from pre-insurgent preventive or reformist political, social, and economic activities on through police, military, and other types of response to organized violence. Information categories in this section are identified by the initial "C."
>
> Outcome. This section covers the settlement of active insurgencies. It organizes information about military, political, economic, and social consequences of a particular insurgency, as well as about the outlook for the future. Categories in this section are preceded by the initial "O." (J. R. Price et al. ca. 1964–65: intro. 4–5)

A 6-page narrative explanation of the M-VICO System of Counterinsurgency Taxonomy detailed how M-VICO adopted and expanded HRAF's methodology; the remaining portions of the report are a verbatim reprinting of 159 pages photocopied from OCM, with OCM text running from page xi of the preface to the end of the index of complete itemized HRAF traits on page 144, ending with trait 888, "Status and Treatment of the Aged." A 65-page section on "M-VICO Information Categories" extends OCM's trait list, starting with the new category, "United States Policy Orientation," and including detailed narrative descriptions following the format used in the preceding 150 pages of OCM text, for a total of 123 cultural traits (see tables 10.3 and 10.4). The report concluded with a photocopied reproduction of the unaltered index to OCM.[20]

The matrix developed in M-VICO mimicked the general structure of Murdock's *Outline of Cultural Materials*, but instead of compiling a database for testing purely theoretical cross-cultural hypothesis, it was designed to organize cultural data to be used by American military or intelligence personnel in suppressing uprisings. The authors of M-VICO appear intoxicated by social engineering dreams. As they promise readers:

> Although sets of files will be compiled about specific countries, the system will also permit the establishment of one entire set of information categories not keyed to any area or country, but which will include non-area-oriented research about functional aspects of insurgency and counterinsurgency.
>
> The M-VICO outline has been structured to permit its users to maintain active information categories to the extent indicated by the degree of insurgency and counterinsurgency in areas under study. Expansion of the degree of subversion or insurgency in a given area can thus be matched by activating the subsequent information categories keyed to the normal progression of insurgent movements. The flexibility of this system can be seen in the organization of its components. (J. R. Price et al. ca. 1964–65: intro. 2)

The M-VICO matrix organized data relating to specific regional counterinsurgency efforts, and it strove to compile a retrievable database for CINFAC social scientists formulating theories of counterinsurgency designed to aid in suppressing insurgent movements arising in cultures around the globe. Identifying core themes of numerous projects at CINFAC and SORO, the introduction expressed hopes that "the accumulation of specialized information about revolutions and their antidotes could eventually result in the beginnings of a possibility for the formulation of a genuinely creative theory of revolutionary behavior" (J. R. Price et al. ca. 1964–65: intro. 6).

TABLE 10.3 Examples of sample cultural trait entries from HRAF's *Outline of Cultural Materials* (563 Ethnic Stratification) and *The M-VICO System of Counterinsurgency Taxonomy* (C-184 Resettlement Programs)

563 ETHNIC STRATIFICATION—alien and immigration subgroups; racial and national minorities; cultural differences between and characteristics of ethnic and minority groups; social and political status of ethnic subgroups; race prejudice and discrimination; assimilation and irredentism; race crossing and amalgamation; racial hybrids and their status; etc. see also:

Racial affinities	144	Ethnocentrism	186
Ethnic composition		Ingroup antagonisms	578
of the population	162	Naturalization	641
Immigration	167	Reservations	657
Acculturation	77	Religious persecutions	798
Degree of subcultural		Race theories	829
differentiation	184	(Murdock 1961: 77)	

C-184 RESETTLEMENT PROGRAMS—gathering of scattered civil population into settlements for greater security from insurgent attack and to bar possible support to the insurgent (e.g. strategic hamlets, protected villages, denial of food, medical, and other essential supplies to insurgent); improvements of living conditions; better use of land resources; screening of settlers; prior planning and specific steps undertaken before actual movement; the settlement of refugees; etc. See also:

Land reform	423	Reform programs	185
State enterprise	474	Organized resettlement	166
State regulation	656	Wartime adjustments.	722
Monopolies	655	Care of refugees	727
Cooperative work groups	476	Living standards	511
Public works	653	Settlement patterns	361
Military participation in resettlement	C-173	(J. R. Price et al. ca. 1964–65: 205)	

What emerged from this patchwork of standard HRAF organization of cultural traits realigned with a militarized focus was a tool not only for the retrieval of cultural information of use to military personnel engaging in counterinsurgency operations, but also one that is even more useful to us in the present: M-VICO survives as a cultural artifact informing us of resilient institutional ways of viewing culture as a counterinsurgency tool. Rather than interpreting

TABLE 10.4 Comparison of the cultural trait format of HRAF's *Outline of Cultural Materials* (Murdock 1961: vii) with M-VICO (J. R. Price et al. ca. 1964–65).

The following are sample index entries from HRAF's *Outline of Cultural Materials*:

59 FAMILY
- 591 Residence
- 592 Household
- 593 Family Relationships
- 594 Nuclear Family
- 595 Polygamy
- 596 Extended Families
- 597 Adoption

60 KINSHIP
- 601 Kinship Terminology
- 602 Kin Relationships
- 603 Grandparents and Grandchildren
- 604 Avuncular and Nepotic Relatives
- 605 Cousins
- 606 Parents-in-Law and Children-in-Law
- 607 Siblings-in-Law
- 608 Artificial Kin Relationships
- 609 Behavior toward Nonrelatives

61 KIN GROUPS
- 611 Rule of Descent
- 612 Kindreds
- 613 Lineages
- 614 Sibs
- 615 Phratries
- 616 Moieties
- 617 Bilinear Kin Groups
- 618 Clans
- 619 Tribe and Nation

The following are sample index entries from M-VICO:

I-10 POLITICAL ASPECTS OF INSURGENCY
- I-101 Political Organizations
- I-102 Political Aims and Techniques
- I-103 Dissident Political Leadership
- I-104 Role of Indigenous Communist Party
- I-105 Organization and Orientation of the Populace

TABLE 10.4 *(continued)*

	I-106	Incidence of Penetration and Infiltration Tactics by Dissident Elements
	I-107	Relationships and Interaction Within and Among Political Insurgent Groups
I-18	OPERATIONS OF COVERT ORGANIZATION	
	I-181	Functions of the Covert Organization
	I-182	Covert Psychological Operations
	I-183	Activities in Controlled Areas and Bases
	I-184	Intelligence and Counterintelligence Operations
	I-185	Antiproperty Operations
	I-186	Antipersonnel Operations
	I-187	Escape and Evasion
C-10	MOBILIZATION OF NATIONAL COUNTERINSURGENCY EFFORTS	
	C-101	Government Response to the Emergency
	C-102	Special Administrative Organization below the National Level
	C-103	Pro-government Political and Social Organizations
	C-104	Organization for National Intelligence/Counterintelligence and Espionage Effort
	C-105	Special Police Organizations
	C-106	Judiciary
	C-107	Paramilitary Organizations
	C-108	Significant Indigenous Personages in the National Mobilization Effort
	C-109	Domestic Information and Propaganda Agencies

The M-VICO System was a misuse of HRAF's OCM, it was a logical extension of HRAF's historical military roots merging with the deep institutional needs for disarticulated cultural knowledge by a military seeking to weaponize culture.

The structure of *The M-VICO System* shows SORO layering its own counterinsurgency data atop existing HRAF information. The project envisioned its "selection and adaptation of completed HRAF files as points of departure for a buildup of counterinsurgency information files [that] will result in great economies of time, effort, and money required for background research in areas and culture if the research must be started from scratch" (J. R. Price et al. ca. 1964–65: intro. 3). M-VICO's adaptations transformed HRAF academic data into a touchstone of American counterinsurgency.

This was going to be a tool used "to respond to customer requests for information and analysis" at SORO's CINFAC (J. R. Price et al. ca. 1964–65: intro. 1), and integrate anthropological notions of social structure by building a collection that would "concentrate upon that which is structural and hence relatively slow to change, and will not include the type of information upon which current intelligence estimates are based" (intro. 1). The introduction to the report stated that M-VICO's taxonomical system came from extensive SORO research into more than fifty case studies of insurgency operations from around the world.

With M-VICO's additions to HRAF trait categories, SORO extended the dual use processes already occurring with HRAF's production of area handbooks. Independent scholars produced basic declassified, publicly available handbooks containing widely available information on cultural, economic, political, geographic, and historical features of individual nation-states as piecework contractors, while others assembled classified versions of these resources used internally by HRAF's military sponsors.

Merging SORO and HRAF data within the M-VICO matrix sought to transform HRAF into a global counterinsurgency matrix; and SORO's plans of adding its own content, presumably a mixture of classified and nonclassified materials, to HRAF sought new levels of ethnographically informed counterinsurgency. (J. R. Price et al. ca. 1964–65: intro. 4). The report's authors stated: "When completed HRAF files are used as the Matrix for a Center file [e.g., the CINFAC file], the inclusion of seeming superfluous material poses no problem. When Center files do not have HRAF material to draw upon, obviously priorities must be established to govern the selection of material to complete the information categories in the Matrix" (intro. 5). As an example of how existing HRAF files and M-VICO files would merge with CINFAC's files, the authors explained how exiting HRAF materials on Cuba would be supplemented with "VICO sections" that would "be separately organized for, say, the Castro revolution against Batista, and the currently smoldering anti-Castro agitation" (intro. 6). This project envisioned a hybrid conjoining of academic and intelligence analysis in ways seeking to convert a broad sample of the ethnographic record into a counterinsurgency weapon to be used by the U.S. military against the populations studied by the unwitting anthropologists who were collecting the linked ethnographic data.

The details of *The M-VICO System*'s demise are unclear, but it appears to have been abandoned soon after its initial formation. The two M-VICO reports that I located (J. R. Price et al. ca. 1964–65; Conley ca. 1966) portray an ambitious project in its early stages that never got off the ground. Yet the importance of M-VICO is not what it accomplished; it is the clarity of its expression of a militarized vision for anthropology that wedded HRAF's approach to the collection and analysis of ethnographic data (an approach that itself was well financed by military-intelligence funds) with an aggressive Cold War counterinsurgency project.

Life after SORO

The Camelot scandal launched SORO's demise, but military efforts to anthropologically inform counterinsurgency continued. Several SORO anthropologists continued counterinsurgency work, some within SORO's institutionally linked American University CRESS and CINFAC groups. Felix Moos approached Project Themis with a research proposal whose "subject was considered too sensitive to risk the possible consequences of the kind of free access and movement that university researchers would demand, and the idea was dropped" (Deitchman 1976: 336). Other anthropologists, such as Howard Kaufman (see Rohde 2007: 256), worked as private contractors, and some anthropologists worked for CINFAC, ARPA, RAND, or other sponsors issuing counterinsurgency-related contracts. In 1966, anthropologist Terry Rambo combined anthropological, psychological, military, and political science approaches to counterinsurgency in his contributions to the *U.S. Army Handbook of Counterinsurgency Guidelines for Area Commanders: An Analysis of Criteria* (Havron, Wittenburg, and Rambo 1966). The handbook's analysis of successful counterinsurgency tactics drew on diverse writings, including those of Raoul Naroll, Mao Tse-tung, Richard Critchfield, Gerald Hickey, Roger Hilsman, Walt Rostow, and Richard N. Adams. In 1967, ARPA provided $3.9 million for behavioral science research "related to military operations in Southeast Asia" (ACGPBS 1968: 64). Stillman Bradfield and William F. Whyte's Peruvian development studies were sponsored by ARPA. When controversy arose over Whyte's Pentagon funding, he allayed concerns by switching his funding source to AID (RB 75, Executive Board Minutes 5/20/66).

Other governmental agencies maintained interest in these anthropologically informed counterinsurgency projects. Documents released in response to my FOIA requests for CIA Camelot records included a memo from May 17, 1967, requesting that Lord, Rosenthal, and Dodson's CRESS report "Communist Theory and Practice in Subversive Insurgencies" be reviewed to determine if it should "be released for open publication" (Lord, Rosenthal, and Dodson 1965; CIA, memo to ASST DCI 5/17/67). This CIA memo stated the paper was based on "overt" sources, and there was no objection to the report's publication.[21]

After SORO closed in July 1966, many of its operations moved to American University's CRESS, which housed the army's CINFAC (Shrader 2008: 200).[22] The Pentagon then relied on CINFAC for the "collecting, storing, retrieving, and analyzing 'information on peoples and cultures of the world as they apply to insurgency setting'" (200). Several CINFAC reports developed synthetic theoretical understandings of counterinsurgency dynamics. As Salemink observed, CINFAC's *Customs and Taboos of Selected Tribes Residing along the Western Border of the Republic of Vietnam* (Fallah 1967) interpreted tribal beliefs in ways that were imagined to help military commanders to "force Montagnards into political and military compliance" (Salemink 2003: 229). *Minority Groups in the Republic of Vietnam* (Schrock et al. 1966), was produced as part of CINFAC's Ethnographic Study Series. It was a synthesis of information from hundreds of academic articles and books, combined to produce a 1,163-page compendium of ethnographic information on tribal and ethnic groups in a format designed to assist military and intelligence personnel interacting with members of these groups in Vietnam. The first eight hundred pages described cultural features of the most prevalent eighteen tribal groups of Vietnam.[23] A detailed index allowed users to locate relevant information on customs, social structure, history, settlement patterns, and other cultural information in the field, as if problems facing military leaders could be solved with an eight-hundred-page cookbook (Schrock et al. 1966: vi).

Using a format similar to that of George Murdock's World War II Office of the Chief of Naval Operations reports, these reports plugged in specific information on tribal groups using a mostly uniform format that allowed field users to quickly access information. Each ethnic or "tribal" group's chapter was divided into the standardized subheadings shown in table 10.5. Oscar Salemink connected the format and material of CINFAC's *Montagnard Tribal Groups in the Republic of South Viet-Nam* directly with Gerald Hickey and John Musgrave's HRAF book *Ethnic Groups of Southeast Asia* (1964), observing that "the notes and bibliographies of the various volumes not only referred to the same sources, but to each other as well, indicating a cross-fertilization of academic and military ethnographies" (2003: 231).

These CINFAC publications's bibliographies blended academic and military literature.[24] Hickey, Thomas, LeBar, et al. were key sources used in most chapters of *Minority Groups in the Republic of Vietnam*, but the work also drew on interviews with missionaries, such as one with the Reverend Charles E. Long, a Mennonite missionary, conducted by members of the U.S. Special Warfare

TABLE 10.5 General Organization Format for *Minority Groups in the Republic of Vietnam** (Source: Schrock et al. 1966)

Section I	Introduction
Section II	Tribal Background
Section III	Individual Characteristics
Section IV	Social Structure
Section V	Customs and Taboos
Section VI	Religion
Section VII	Economic Organization
Section VIII	Political Organization
Section IX	Communications Techniques
Section X	Civic Action Considerations
Section XI	Paramilitary Capabilities
Section XII	Suggestions for Personnel Working with [tribal group]
Footnotes and Bibliography	

*The chapters on the Cao Dai, Binh Xuyen, Hoa Hao, and Indians and Pakistanis do not follow this organizational pattern and instead focus on more recent history, using the following organizational structure:

Section I	Introduction
Section II	Early History and Status during the Indochina War
Section III	Status during the Diem Regime
Section IV	Status since the Diem Regime
Footnotes and Bibliography	

School (Schrock et al. 1966: 718). David Thomas, of the Summer Institute of Linguistics, authored a monograph on "Mon-Khmer Subgroupings in Vietnam," that was cited throughout the book; given the overlapping methods, approaches, and larger goals of contact between missionary and military groups to foreign cultures, the organizational approach used by the SIL had natural applications for American counterinsurgency operatives (see D. Thomas 1962).[25]

Sections 10 through 12 of *Minority Groups in the Republic of Vietnam* used ethnographic knowledge to recommend uses of cultural knowledge for counterinsurgency operations. The listed civic action projects read like an overview of USAID rural Vietnam projects from this period and included programs to improve livestock quality and agricultural yields, programs for rural electrification and rural roads, education programs, and sanitation projects. The book stressed the importance of projects producing results that were "observable, measurable, or tangible" so that U.S. forces could receive credit over their insurgent opponents (Schrock et al. 1966: 40).

A section on paramilitary capabilities described the fighting capacities of different tribal groups, reporting group reputations as trackers and scouts, venturing estimates of a tribe's likelihood of fighting against or capitulating to armed aggressors, and assessing individual tribes' abilities "to absorb military instruction" (Schrock et al. 1966: 4). Reviews of indigenous fighting capacities mixed romantic assessments of local culture with cautionary reminders of the deadly capacities of tribal members.

Chapters provided general recommendations such as that when making "first contact" with tribal groups, military personnel should seek an audience with local leaders and develop relationships of trust and respect. In most chapters, instructions for interactions followed a similar routine in which readers are told to not enter villages where religious ceremonies were taking place, advising them to identify and avoid sacred objects and to not mock villagers' beliefs (see, e.g., Schrock et al. 1966: 204).

But as with other military manuals, the impact of the information was mixed, with some ignoring the information and others adapting behaviors accordingly. With time, the Pentagon moved away from producing outsourced counterinsurgency information at American University's centralized campus and increasingly used contractors who were not linked to universities. The Pentagon also increased efforts to gain knowledge from social science professors with fieldwork expertise in Southeast Asia who were teaching at universities across the United States, a shift in strategy that later generated divisiveness within American anthropology.

Dual Use Knowledge Production in a Land Dreaming of Counterinsurgency Controls

Questions remain concerning HRAF's relationships with the CIA and other intelligence agencies. I failed to locate copies of several Pentagon sponsored HRAF documents that I found referenced. These include the HRAF-published *Army Psychological Warfare Country Plan for Vietnam* (1954), which I have found cited in other works but could not locate in civilian or military libraries, and have not succeeded in acquiring with FOIA requests (SORO 1960:63).[26] When I filed an FOIA request in 1994 for all CIA records on HRAF, the CIA's response stated that while the CIA could neither confirm nor deny "a confidential or covert relationship" between it and HRAF, to the extent that CIA records "might concern such information it is denied pursuant to FOIA exemption (b)(1) and (b)(3)" (CIA to DHP 2/24/94). Over the course of several years, HRAF president Melvin Ember made a series of misleading statements to me and others concerning HRAF's historical relationship with the CIA. In response to my queries concerning HRAF's historical ties to the CIA, Ember first wrote me that he was unaware of any such connections; then, when I informed him of my FOIA inquiries into the historical CIA-HRAF relationship, he wrote me on July 18, 1995, that he had only "inadvertently discovered yesterday that the CIA was an Associate Member of HRAF from 1979 until 1983" (ME to DHP 7/18/95). Ember later misrepresented his written correspondence with me to Richard Shweder. But Shweder confirmed that Ember must have known about these CIA connections because Shweder knew of them from his past term as an HRAF board member (see Shweder 2010: 5; for corrections to Shweder's errors, see: Common Knowledge 2010: 365).[27] As Shweder confirmed, in 1995 Ember had initially misrepresented HRAF's relationship with the CIA to me; Ember told Shweder in 2009 that "the board of course knew about [the CIA being an associate member of HRAF], because all members have to be approved by the board" (Shweder 2010: 5). I received no reply from Ember when I wrote him, asking for a response to Robin Winks's statement that: "HRAF was drawn upon by the CIA at least through 1967, it was widely believed that a full [HRAF] file had been deposited at the agency's new headquarters in Langley, Virginia" (see Winks 1987:45).

This vision of *The M-VICO System* expressed the military's desire for simplistic means of using cultural knowledge for the subjugation of other cultures. The Human Relations Area Files's cataloging of the ethnographic record had historic military roots, and HRAF's penchant for simplifying uniformity and a drive to catalog and standardize the world led the Pentagon to become a significant funder of HRAF during the early Cold War. It is unclear what HRAF did or did not know about SORO's adaptation of the OCM and HRAF methodologies for M-VICO's counterinsurgent ends.[28]

If the creation of HRAF represented, as Tobin argues, "a radical experiment in technological rationality," then SORO's bootlegged expansion of HRAF's methodologies linked this rationality to Pentagon desires for a mechanical theory of counterinsurgency (Tobin 1990: 482). *Outline of Cultural Materials* provided the skeletal structure for this hybrid project, as M-VICO haphazardly mixed HRAF's drive to discover truths devoid of overshadowing political contexts of knowledge production with the military's political mission to subvert indigenous uprisings without regard to anthropologists' usual ethical abhorrence to using ethnography for counterinsurgency. It was all crude and clunky, but it fit in the larger machinery of American Cold War inquiry.

American military culture's reliance on interchangeable parts and its deep reliance on engineering models predisposed military strategists to look to anthropology as a discipline ready-made to supply the military with the needed "culture piece" to be plugged into military operations. These various projects at SORO, CINFAC, and CRESS articulated what would become recurrent military desires of harnessing anthropology—in ways betraying fundamental misunderstandings of culture *and* anthropology—as an imagined tool that could somehow repair things that had been broken by political or military forces, as if cultural knowledge could smooth over the harsh realities of killings, invasions, or occupations. Setting aside the political and ethical issues raised by anthropological contributions to military operations, the impossibility of adapting cultural knowledge for the types of interchangeable armed counterinsurgency operations imagined by SORO and CINFAC should have raised serious questions from the anthropologists affiliated with these projects. Yet the economic contingencies of these relationships precluded the internal development of such internal critiques.

Camelot was a multidimensional failure. It failed to inform the U.S. ambassador to Chile (Ralph Dungan) of its activities. But, most significantly, it failed to seriously consider the ethical and political meanings of using cultural knowledge for counterinsurgency. News of Camelot spread quickly, and given the role this news played in getting members of the AAA to formalize professional ethics, this publicity had a more significant impact on anthropology than Camelot could ever have had on transforming the cultures it sought to study. But news of Camelot also created problems for anthropologists for years to come.

Joy Rohde later blamed academic critics for failing to stop Pentagon social science projects of the sort developed at SORO and CRESS, arguing that by not keeping these militarized projects on campus and not correcting their flawed assumptions and methods, these academic critics helped derivative research grow without the critical supervision it would have received under some imagined watchful professorial eye. Rohde claimed that "instead of taming the military-industrial-academic complex, divestiture fueled the growth of an insular network of think tanks and consulting agencies that would serve the national security state well into the 1980s" (2013: 121). But Rohde's critique identifies a fundamental contradiction that she ignores. While acknowledging that "a researcher's duty was, above all, to fulfill his client agency's needs without being too critical of its policies" (132), she blames academics for removing themselves from such inherently corrupting structures, instead leaving the work to off-campus contractors, who created problems that "only intensified as contract work was removed from academic settings" (133). But the quality of this later off-campus contract work was no better than that of work produced for SORO and CRESS on the campus of American University—regardless of location, both produced the sort of low-quality social engineering work the Pentagon sponsors desired.

Most American anthropologists understood SORO's Project Camelot and other SORO-CRESS campus-based projects as threatening academic freedom on campuses and in the discipline as a whole—threatening their own access to the field and also threatening the people they studied. While later revelations of anthropological contributions to counterinsurgency would divide generations of anthropologists, details about Project Camelot brought the condemnation and concern of the majority of the anthropological community.

> On the advisor question, it seemed impossible
> to hope that thousands of men could be found each year
> who would perform like Lawrence of Arabia.
>
> SEYMOUR DEITCHMAN | ARPA, 1976

ELEVEN THE AAA CONFRONTS MILITARY AND INTELLIGENCE USES OF DISCIPLINARY KNOWLEDGE

America's twentieth-century wars periodically impacted the annual meetings of the American Anthropological Association in ways that mixed disciplinary, ethical, political, and economic concerns. Council meetings, the annual business meeting of the AAA, became the association's central venue for discussing issues pertinent to anthropology's engagement with specific wars, at times functioning as a disciplinary town hall, at other times as an intellectual boxing ring.

After the First World War and during the Second World War, the AAA council meetings hosted discussions on anthropological contributions to warfare (see Stocking 1968; D. H. Price 2000, 2008a). Cold War council meetings at times brought resolutions concerning anthropological interactions with military and intelligence organizations. The Korean War found the AAA advocating for increased funding for language study—while maintaining silence when Gene Weltfish was fired from Columbia while speaking out against the war (D. H. Price 2004b: 109–35). While AAA members served in the Korean War, fulfilling a variety of tasks, the association and the annual council meetings were not used to stage calls for supporting an anthropological wartime mobilization as they did during World War II, nor were these meetings a stage for the sort of protests that would come in the following decades. As the Vietnam War lengthened, the AAA council meetings increasingly became staging grounds for anthropologists' critiques of American militarism.

Two features of the association's bylaws played important roles in the council meetings. First, until the organization's constitution was amended in early 1970, the association had a two-tier division of membership under which only "fellows" had voting rights at the council meetings (NAAA 1970 11[1]: 1; NAAA 1970 11[3]: 1). Although anyone could join the AAA as a member, section 3 of the bylaws defined a "fellow" as someone who had published "significant" anthropological contributions; had a BA, MA, or PhD in anthropology and was "actively engaged in anthropology"; had a doctorate in an "allied field and [was] engaged in anthropology," or was a lifetime member of the AAA (AAAFN 1961 2[1]: 3).[1] Second, section 4 of the bylaws required that "new legislation may be proposed by the Executive Board or by five per cent of the Fellows in good standing, and must be circulated to the Council at least 30 days in advance of the annual meeting if it is to be acted upon at that time" (AAAFN 1961 2[1]: 6).

In 1961, Margaret Mead became the first anthropologist to use the council meeting to push the membership to critically address issues of militarization. Mead offered a resolution, unanimously approved, "calling for anthropological contributions to the search for disarmament and peace" (AAAFN 1961 2[1]: 1–3). Robert Suggs and William Carr complained that Mead distorted notions of war and peace in relation to disarmament, arguing that anthropologists had contributed to the Second World War without the association attempting to limit such work (see AAAFN 1962 3[7]: 3).[2] They maintained that anthropologists should not be held responsible for the uses of their work, arguing that "scientists *are* responsible for what they produce, *in terms of scientific standards*, but once the production is public domain, its use or abuse cannot be controlled nor can the scientist be held responsible for results of such use or abuse" (AAAFN 1963 4[8]: 1).[3]

While this early debate on anthropology, war, and peace indicated disciplinary fissures, borders, and arguments to come, AAA publications of the early 1960s still ran advertisements for counterinsurgency-related positions without member objections. These advertisements were from military-linked contractors like Operations Research Incorporated (AAAFN 1964 5[6]: 8) or the army's Special Warfare School, seeking a psychological operations (PSYOPS) anthropologist (AAAFN 1965 [1]: 8). Until news of Project Camelot broke, such advertisements did not draw organized negative comments from members.

Camelot within the AAA: Ralph Beals's Inquiry and the Road to an AAA Ethics Code

After news of Project Camelot broke in late October 1965, Harold Conklin, Marvin Harris, Dell Hymes, Robert Murphy, and Eric Wolf mailed a statement titled "Government Involvement and the Future of Anthropological Field

Research" to anthropology departments across the United States, Canada, and Mexico. The statement warned that despite President Johnson's assurances that damaging programs like Camelot would not continue, "the general climate of relations between the government and professional anthropological research is such that the possibility of continuing truly independent work is seriously threatened." Anthropologists were experiencing increasing problems conducting fieldwork due to fears of governmental links, and the statement by Conklin and others called for anthropologists to learn more about the impacts of governmental research programs on anthropology (MHP 22; *AAAFN* 1965 6[10]: 1–2). This statement circulated widely, and the political stance staked out by these five anthropologists found support from the majority of AAA members in ways that future debates over the militarization of anthropology for the wars of Southeast Asia would not.

President Alexander Spoehr of the AAA met with the State Department's deputy director of intelligence and research, George Denney, to discuss anthropologists' concerns raised by Camelot. Camelot also dominated the 1965 AAA council meeting, with the Conklin group's handbill framing the council's discussions about using anthropology for counterinsurgency. An adopted resolution charged the Executive Board with gathering information on sponsors and anthropologists relating to "access to foreign areas, governmental clearance, at home and abroad, the people with whom we work, and the sponsoring agencies" (*AAAFN* 1965 6[10]: 1). Records from an executive session of the board at the 1965 AAA meetings included concerns over reports that American anthropologists in Latin America were suspected of being spies, and how "anti-American sentiment in the social sciences in all disciplines was rife everywhere and increasing" (RB 75, 11/17–21/65, 9).[4]

In early 1966, the AAA Executive Board appointed Ralph Beals to "lead the effort to implement the resolution on overseas research and ethics adopted by the Council last November 20th" (*AAAFN* 1966 7[2]: 1). With financial assistance from the Wenner-Gren Foundation, Beals was released from his teaching responsibilities at UCLA during the spring term in order to work on an AAA report exploring political and ethical issues raised by governmental uses of anthropological research (RB 76; *AAAFN* 1966 7[7]: 3).

Beals had served on the AAA's Executive Committee in the 1940s. He had years of experience working with governmental agencies on a range of public policy programs. He had worked for the Institute of Social Anthropology in the 1940s and served as an adviser to the U.S. delegation attending the American Indianist Conference in 1939. Beals's professional background prepared him for his work on the committee; coming from a radical California family, his political background brought a sophisticated critique of power.[5]

Beals chaired the AAA's ad hoc Committee on Research Problems and Ethics, a group that consisted of him and the association's Executive Board (see AAAFN 1966 7[3]: 1). Operating essentially as a one-person committee, Beals used this freedom to quickly compile information and draft a detailed report that would have likely taken a committee of ten people years to negotiate. The resulting report would be commonly known as the Beals Report, but its full title is, "Background Information on Problems of Anthropological Research and Ethics" (AAAFN 1967 8[1]: 9–13).

Beals collected anecdotal accounts of the CIA's infiltration of U.S. foundations and college programs at Michigan State University and elsewhere. He and AAA Executive Secretary Stephen T. Boggs contacted and interviewed two dozen anthropologists, representing various geographic areas, and asked them to serve as resources for their region of expertise, calling them the "volunteer chairmen of world areas" (e.g., Irwin and Burke 1967; RB 75; RB 76) (see table 11.1). Some of these anthropologists declined his invitation, and only a few made significant contributions to the project. They collected information on fieldwork problems they had experienced relating to U.S. government activities (AAAFN 1966 7[3]: 1).

Elizabeth Bacon

After Beals's project was announced by the AAA, several anthropologists wrote him, sharing information on encounters with military and intelligence agencies. John Hitchcock wrote that a fellow anthropologist working in Nepal told him that Nepalese governmental officials suspected anthropologists were engaging in espionage (RB 77, JH to RB 3/25/66). Peter Kunstadter described his involvement with two Department of Defense contracts: "The first was for holding a [1965] conference on the subjects of tribes, minorities, and central governments in Southeast Asia. The second was a [1965] contract for ethnological and ecological field research in Thailand." Kunstadter wrote that he had retained complete academic freedom and had produced no secret reports, and that all his work was publicly available (RB 75, PK to RB 4/5/66).[6]

The most in-depth correspondence relating to Beals's inquiry — a correspondence that stretched beyond the time frame of the Beals Report — was with anthropologist Elizabeth Bacon. Because most of this correspondence occurred while Beals was finishing, or after he had completed, his report for the AAA,

TABLE 11.1 Ralph Beals's List of Anthropologists Invited to Serve as Volunteer Chairmen for World Areas (Source: RB75 and RB76)

ANTHROPOLOGIST	AREA OF EXPERTISE
Richard N. Adams	Central America
Robert M. Adams	Iraq
Ethel M. Albert	South America
Jacques Amyot	Southeast Asia
Conrad M. Arensberg	India
Gerald D. Berreman	Himalayas
James B. Christensen	East and West Africa
Elizabeth Colson	Central Africa
Lambros Comitas	Caribbean
Harold G. Conklin	Philippines
William H. Davenport	Oceania
Henry Dobyns	Peru
Louis B. Dupree	Middle East (Afghanistan)
Lloyd Fallers	East Africa
Morton H. Fried	Taiwan
Clifford Geertz	Indonesia and North Africa
Joel Halpern	Yugoslavia
Robert F. Murphy	Brazil
Laura Nader	Mexico
Leopold J. Pospisil	New Guinea
Ruben E. Reina	Guatemala
Robert J. Smith	Japan
Eric R. Wolf	Austria

Bacon's impact on the report was limited. However, Bacon's descriptions of the methods used by intelligence agencies to contact anthropologists are included in the report and also influenced Beals's book *Politics of Social Research* (1969).

Elizabeth Bacon was a well-respected scholar; educated at the Sorbonne and Smith College in the 1920s and Yale in the 1930s, she earned her PhD at Berkeley in 1951. She was an itinerant academic, teaching at a variety of universities, including UCLA (1948–49), Washington University (1949–54), Cornell (1955–56), and Hofstra (1965–66), and later becoming a professor, then emeritus professor, at Michigan State University.

Bacon began fieldwork in Iran and Kazakhstan in the 1930s, and her war years in the OSS provided her with intelligence contacts, and knowledge about intelligence agencies. Because of her OSS connections and her regular travels in south central Asia, she was contacted by the CIA multiple times, and she was aware of CIA personnel operating in her areas of research. She provided Beals with detailed accounts of how the CIA contacted and used anthropologists working in regions of interest to the agency.

Bacon wrote that Afghanistan, Iran, and Pakistan had long been "spy conscious," adding that ethnographers were "particularly suspect." She described the American academic presence in post–World War II Afghanistan, where a museum archaeological expedition included "an ethnographer and CIA agent." She wrote that the CIA agent "found that he could not operate on his own, and a year later returned to Kabul under an institutional cover. He stayed four years, and returned later for a year on research grants to spell his successor while the latter was on leave" (RB 75, EB to RB 10/10/66).

Bacon wrote that in Afghanistan "an anthropologist went out as a CIA agent in 1959 and has been there off and on ever since. He works for a cover organization, is 'on leave' from a university where he once taught, and is research associate of a very reputable museum" (RB 75, EB to RB 10/10/66).[7] Anthropologists had become so synonymous with spying that when AID began operating in Afghanistan, Bacon recommended not calling the AID social scientists "anthropologists" because they would be assumed to be spies; when she was ignored, "the Afghan officials on the project ruled against employing an anthropologist" (RB 75, EB to RB 10/10/66).

Bacon reported that the CIA monitored anthropological research in Afghanistan and Iran. Anthropologists working independently from the CIA were at times contacted by the agency. When an "anthropologist returns from *Bona fide* field work, done without chores for CIA or any other intelligence agency, he is likely to be approached for an interview. . . . On two occasions, when emerging from the country where I had been working, I reported to American consular officials situations which I felt affected the amity of relations between the United States and the country involved. In both cases, my comments were acted on" (RB 75, EB to RB 10/10/66).

Bacon warned Beals that the CIA would be aware of his AAA report when it was released, noting that the

> CIA regularly sends a recruiter to the annual meetings of the AAA.[8] (The recruiter this year—and perhaps the top man himself—will undoubtedly listen to your report with great interest.) There are individuals on the faculties of certain universities who, I think, do some recruiting among their own students, perhaps guiding

the student's interest toward a research project which would be useful to CIA. More often, however, it is my impression that when word gets about that an anthropologist is considering research in certain areas, someone connected with CIA pounces. If CIA already has someone in the locality, an attempt is made to deflect the prospective field worker to another locality. An individual or committee evaluates the desirability of the project from the CIA point of view; if it approves, assistance of various kinds is offered: helpful leads to officials in the prospective host country; funds to supplement bona fide research grants (in some cases the foundation grant may be only enough to obscure the source of most of the funds); cover affiliation with a reputable academic institution or with some other institution. At one time a CIA operative (not an anthropologist) had for his cover the position of regional officer for the Ford Foundation. The Ford Foundation was presumably unaware of this, although I think CIA had planted a man on the New York staff of the foundation. The Fulbright committee for the Middle East in Washington includes at least two CIA people. (RB 75, EB to RB 11/8/66)

Bacon described four distinct types of anthropologists conducting fieldwork with CIA ties: (1) anthropologists primarily interested in pursuing legitimate field research questions, with legitimate ties to universities and foundations, who agree independently to gather information needed by the CIA (Bacon said these individuals undertook CIA work due to patriotism or a "sense of adventure"); (2) those doing research who are "tempted by the CIA offer of funds"; (3) anthropologists who want to undertake fieldwork in a specific country and use CIA connections to become established in this country; and (4) thrill seekers who "enjoy the excitement and romance of engaging in espionage" (RB 75, EB to RB 11/8/66).

She observed that "many anthropologists" did not know what was "going on around them." She described one incident where a student completing his graduate work was recruited into the CIA by two of his professor's "favorite former students. He did not know that his professor abhorred the idea of using anthropology as a cover for espionage. His professor did not know that the two favorites worked for CIA" (RB 75, EB to RB 11/8/66).

Writing before the investigative journalistic exposés of *Ramparts*, the *New York Times*, and other media revealed CIA infiltration of foundations (see chapters 1 and 7), Bacon presented an accurate account of how such operations worked. She described how private foundations, such as the Ford Foundation, worked hand in hand with the CIA to sponsor area studies research of specific interest to the agency, writing that she knew of a university area program for an area in which CIA was interested, but could find no links between CIA and that program. Recently I brought this up in conversation with someone who has been a part of the university program and who is knowledgeable in the matter of intelligence. He said that two of the top people in the program, who had in the past "been burned" by CIA (whatever that means), had wanted to insert into the terms of a Ford university grant a clause barring any CIA participation, and that the Ford Foundation had refused to accept the clause. This was before the Ford Foreign Area Program man in Pakistan got caught out. The separation of the Foreign Area Program from the Ford Foundation — the personnel moved a few blocks down Madison Avenue to a new office and "Ford Foundation" was dropped from the name — occurred just after the Pakistan debacle. Does this mean that the Ford Foundation is still engaging in fun and games? The move of McGeorge Bundy from the White House to head the Ford Foundation is of some interest. In Washington, Bundy's chief bailiwick was the Security Council, which means that he had very close ties with CIA.

The point I am driving at is that a grant from even such a seemingly solid foundation as Ford could be suspect, although a Ford grant does not necessarily imply CIA commitment. And even if the area program were indirectly financed by CIA through some foundation, this does not mean that all members of the institution staff are knowingly working for CIA. It would be perfectly possible for an anthropologist on the staff of the Department of Anthropology at UCLA teaching courses on the Middle East, to be unaware of what was going on — at least in the beginning. How soon he became aware of the situation would depend on his sophistication in such matters. What he did then would depend on how much opportunity he had had to develop a code of ethics in this matter, and how strong the ethical drive was.

It is probable that a majority of anthropologists and other academics who do field work "for CIA" are doing the kind of research they would do in any event, and some are financed for work they would not otherwise be able to do. Their only contribution to CIA is to report on what they have observed. Some of them, however, undoubtedly do more. (RB 75, EB to RB 12/25/66)

According to Bacon, the CIA's presence in Iran was so ubiquitous that the agency even played a role in parceling out regions of Iran for fieldwork — hoping to achieve a good distribution of data on the countryside; she assumed the Iranians knew about this arrangement and monitored these researchers. She observed that "normally when an anthropologist wants to do field work in a country, he seeks out everyone he can find who has had experience in the area and gets all the information he can about the situation there. If one tries that for Iran, one bumps into CIA at every turn" (RB 75, EB to RB 12/25/66).

Bacon told of a CIA administrator calling on her when she was a professor at Washington University, using the name of a colleague by way of an introduction. He quizzed her about her background, and when Bacon asked why the administrator was so interested, he replied that he hoped she could provide the CIA with information when she returned from her next trip. Bacon wrote: "On my announcement that while I might give relevant information to someone in the State Department I would not trouble CIA, he wished me happy shopping and we parted. Had I realized at the time the growing extent of the CIA tentacles, I might have led him on and learned more. But I think that this is all that CIA expects of the average anthropologist going into the field, although it is always ready to recruit people for special jobs" (RB 75, EB to RB 12/25/66). Bacon explained that while the recent revelations about CIA infiltration of American society had provided valuable information, her "two years in the Research and Analysis Branch of OSS served as a post-graduate course in espionage.... The cultural divergence between those who returned to academia and those who remained in Washington was so gradual that it was a long time before I realized what was happening in CIA. But once I did realize this, I had the background to check details. *American Men of Science* and *Fellow Newsletter* can be very illuminating if you know what you are looking for" (RB 75, EB to RB 12/25/66).

In a letter to Beals, Bacon expressed concerns that UCLA's Near East Studies Center might be operating with a CIA contract (RB 75, EB to RB 12/25/66). Beals followed up this correspondence with queries made to Carl York, of UCLA's Office of Extramural Support, who made a "categorical denial" that UCLA had any classified contracts with the CIA or other intelligence agencies (RB 75, RB to CY 12/29/66; RB 75, CY to RB 1/4/67).

Bacon described being "offered CIA funds for field work" after "a friend in OIR asked me outright if I could use a specified sum from CIA and I said no thank you" (RB 75, EB to RB 1/19/67). She wrote that one of the indirect ways military and intelligence agencies recruited anthropologists into intelligence work was through HRAF contract work:

> You undoubtedly know that the HRAF Handbook Series was financed by Psychological Warfare. The original outline provided by Washington included a couple of chapters that would have caused trouble but I think that all handbook editors omitted these. Everyone employed on the project, including many foreign nationals, knew that they were working on an Army subcontract and many project direc-

tors quite properly informed the Ambassadors of countries whose nationals were being employed. Since the work was open and straightforward, there was not difficulty.... What may be less well known is that at the end of the project, forms were sent out for distribution to American citizens on the staff asking if they would be interested in employment with Psychological Warfare. Thus the program was used as a recruitment device. How successful this was, I have no idea. I do not know of anyone who responded. (RB 75, EB to RB 1/19/67)

In February 1967, Bacon wrote Beals about two anthropologists working in Afghanistan whom she believed were CIA operatives, and she provided a five-page analysis listing six organizations she believed to be CIA fronts funding anthropological research. The organizations identified by Bacon were American Friends of the Middle East, the American University Field Staff (AUFS), the Asia Foundation, the Iran Foundation, the Field Foundation, and Operations and Policy Research, Inc. (RB 75, EB to RB 2/6/67).

Bacon wrote that American Friends of the Middle East "joins with the Asia Foundation in giving financial assistance to a student organization which the head of the CIA network for the area was using within a year of the organization's founding." She described the AUFS as "one of the most obvious covers thought up by CIA," adding that their staff member "in Afghanistan for the last eight years has been an anthropologist, who proclaims himself as such at every step." She wrote that she knew "the Asia Foundation was used as a cover for one CIA agent anthropologist. A senior sociologist, acting as a consultant to the foundation, did field work in a region not his own in West Pakistan during two periods when the Ford Foundation CIA man was busy at graduate school." Bacon described the Iran Foundation as "headed by the head of the CIA network for Iran, Afghanistan, Pakistan. Uses medical work as cover. Set up modern hospital school in Shiraz, Iran and is now active in helping establish a medical school at University of Ahwaz (both areas of CIA interest)." The foundation tracked research by scholars studying Iran and tried "to screen potential field workers according to their abilities and to prevent their getting in each other's way in the field. Because one can do little in Iran without proper accreditation, their control of Persian officials to be approached is important. Presumably anyone who has been vetted by CIA gets full treatment in facilitating research. If CIA wishes to give financial assistance to a field worker, I think this is done through other channels. The chairman of the board of the foundation is on the Fulbright committee in Washington" (RB 75, EB to RB "Cover Organization memo," 2/6/67). Bacon had little information on the Field Foundation, writing that she had only been told by others that it was a CIA cover. She also had no direct evidence that Operations and Policy Research, Inc., had CIA ties, but that organization aroused her suspicions, and she speculated it was conducting psychological warfare operations (RB 75 EB to RB 2/6/67).⁹

Bacon described "new clues" revealing how private foundations with no direct ties to the government funded research projects, at times making inquiries in concert with American intelligence needs. She wrote Beals that she had recently

> received a copy of a report on an important international research program. The list of members of the American committee included the name of an anthropologist who I thought had been "retired" to academia by CIA. Obviously my interpretation of retirement was incorrect. On checking this anthropologist in *American Men of Science*, I found a really impressive record which completely masked his nearly twenty years' service in intelligence—first in MID [Military Intelligence Division], then in CIA. Clearly he had been set up to use his academic position for high level activities. On this committee he could exert influence in favoring projects and individuals sponsored by CIA.
>
> Spotting his name reminded [me] that I had been told recently of the appointment of another CIA alumnus to a committee which awards grants for work in a certain area.
>
> Even more recently I received the annual report of the Social Science Research Council. In reading over the lists of committee members, I noticed that in the committees for strategic areas there was usually one name of interest in this context. In some cases I know that the individual had a CIA background; in one case, I had been told that the individual was high up in CIA; in several cases the individual hailed from a university area program where I know there have been CIA ties. Indeed, as the result of a careful study of some of the key committees, I concluded that the center of gravity for CIA research on one area had shifted from one university to another.
>
> Among grantees, I spotted two people whom I know have CIA ties, and a third who was with British intelligence before he came to the United States. His grant was for research in an area in which CIA is interested.
>
> *This study of committee members gave me a new understanding of how CIA operates in academia. Most members of the committee are undoubtedly clean. Those individuals acting for CIA have solid academic reputations in their field of specialization. Some of them have never been employed by a governmental intelligence organization either in Washington or in the field. One I know of has probably played along with CIA out of ambition. That he has CIA ties I know. Years ago a CIA regional officer*

called on me at his suggestion and he cooled noticeably toward me after I told the CIA *man that I did not want to have anything to do with* CIA. (RB 75, EB to RB 4/10/67, emphasis added)

Bacon recognized that the addition of a single individual working in concert with the CIA to a selection committee could allow the agency to direct funding toward projects likely to collect information of use to the CIA or achieving other agency-desired outcomes.

Evaluating Bacon's Claims

Bacon believed she had identified how the CIA used private foundations to fund research of interest to the agency through processes in which former CIA employees working for foundations or on grant selection committees influenced the selection of anthropological research. She claimed to have found opportunity, motive, and mechanisms for the CIA's intrusion into anthropology. It is difficult to read some of her pronouncements on the depth of CIA intrusion without wondering if she was just being paranoid; yet, several of her theorized connections can be verified. Because of revelations in the press and in congressional hearings in the decades after Bacon made these claims, we can evaluate the veracity of her comment that she had identified six foundations as CIA fronts.

Of the six foundations identified by Bacon in 1966, three were later verified as CIA fronts (American Friends of the Middle East in 1966, the Asia Foundation in 1967, and Operations and Policy Research, Inc., in 1967).[10] The other three foundations claimed by Bacon to have CIA connections (the AUFS, the Iran Foundation, and the Field Foundation) were not later documented to be CIA fronts, though AUFS and the Iran Foundation both had individuals linked to them who had reported CIA connections: Louis Dupree worked with AUFS for more than a decade, and CIA agent Donald Wilber was a member of the Iran Foundation's Board of Directors (Wilber 1986: 150, 186). Some have claimed CIA connections for the Field Foundation (most prominently, Alan Ogden in his 1977 testimony before the U.S. Committee on Foreign Relations), and while this remains a possibility, these claims remain unconfirmed and have established no documented links (see U.S. Senate 1977: 55).[11]

Beals questioned Bacon about her suspicions of the AUFS, in large part because the Crane Foundation (established by Crane Plumbing) had begun funding the organization two decades prior to the creation of the CIA (RB 75, RB to EB 2/20/67).[12] Bacon wrote that when reading Crane Foundation reports, she noticed many names of supposedly "retired" CIA personnel appearing in the reports of committees and grant awardees (RB 75, EB to RB 4/10/67).

Bacon described how she was once invited to contribute to a book on Afghanistan in which "the other American contributors [were] affiliated with CIA. My first reaction was to avoid guilt by association then I decided that I couldn't spend my whole life running away from things, and agreed to write the chapter" (RB 75, EB to RB 12/25/66). She did not identify the book or the contributors, but it was an HRAF-published volume edited by CIA agent Donald Wilber (see chapter 6).[13]

While Bacon's letters to Beals detailed how the CIA established contacts with anthropologists, Beals's report did not name any of the organizations identified by Bacon as having CIA links, nor did he describe how former OSS personnel working in academic settings helped steer funding to individuals and projects of interest to the CIA. Beals's final report contained less direct critiques indicating that unseen, undocumented links between anthropological research likely existed.

The Beals Report and Growing Anthropological Demilitarization

In May 1966, Ralph Beals and former AAA executive secretary Stephen T. Boggs met with Steven Ebbin, chief of staff to Senator Fred R. Harris (D-OK). Beals's notes indicated that Ebbin said, in an off-the-record capacity, that it was his "opinion that little is done with any of the research, domestic or foreign. He cited a new man in education who asked about prior research, and asked to see it. No one could believe that he actually wished to see prior research, but when he insisted, he was taken to a warehouse in southwest Washington where great piles of research reports were stacked on the floor which have never been looked at after their completion" (RB 76, ACNA Notes 5/25/66). Ebbin said that few people in government knew what to do with research.

On June 27, 1966, Boggs and Beals testified before Senate hearings, chaired by Harris, on federal support for social science research and training. Boggs stressed the importance of governmental funding for social science research but supported Harris's position that "any CIA involvement in university research projects abroad damages irreparably the effectiveness of such research and makes us liable to the charge that research is pressured by our government for desired findings" (AAAFN 1966 7[7]: 2). Boggs described how some in the underdeveloped world viewed American social science projects as primarily meeting the needs of the United States rather than the needs of their country. He argued that revelations that Michigan State University was training CIA operatives working in Vietnam, and that MIT conducted CIA-funded research fed fears that other social science research projects had CIA links. He wrote that anthropologists did not want "to become the heir of the colonial administrator's legacy of mistrust. Nothing would more surely doom the opportunity of carrying out any kind of social science research abroad. To avoid this, an absolutely impassable barrier must be established between the intelligence agencies of the U.S. Government and the universities, private foundations, and international voluntary organizations engaged in research" (AAAFN 1966 7[7]: 3).

In July 1966, the AAA's Executive Board adopted Ralph Beals's "Statement on Government Involvement in Research" as the association's interim statement.[14] This report clarified that "except in times of clear and present national emergency, universities should not undertake activities which are unrelated to their normal teaching, research, and public service functions, or which can more appropriately be performed by other types of organizations" (AAAFN 1966 7[8]: 1). It condemned clandestine research and research that did not disclose sponsorship and declared that the "gathering of information and data which can never be made available to the public does not constitute scientific research and should not be so represented" (AAAFN 1966 7[8]: 1–2).

In November 1966, Ralph Beals submitted his "Statement on Problems of Anthropological Research and Ethics" (SPARE) to the AAA Council, where it was amended during a "spirited discussion" and adopted, by a vote of 727 to 59, and later mailed to fellows as a referendum (AAAFN 1967 8[4]: 1; AAA1967).[15] At this council meeting David and Kathleen Aberle ushered in a new era of meetings by introducing an antiwar resolution as a new business item. This was not the sort of generic statement against harmful weapons that Margaret Mead had introduced a few years earlier; the Aberles' resolution opposed U.S. involvement in the Vietnam War and was adopted by a significant majority (AAAFN 1966 7[10]: 2).

The Beals Report focused on three primary areas: "anthropology and government," "sponsorships of anthropological research," and "research in foreign areas." It observed that SORO's and Project Camelot's use of anthropology had pressed AAA members to take action on these issues, but it stressed there were broader issues linking anthropologists to governmental agencies that also needed consideration by the association (AAAFN 1967 8[1]: 3).

The Executive Board worried that links to governmental agencies would limit American anthropologists' safety and their ability to conduct fieldwork in other countries (AAAFN 1967 8[1]: 3). In the Executive Board's discussion of Beals's draft report, Harold Conklin "suggested that the existence, and if possible the names, of foundations which had served as cover for the CIA should be included in the report," but the final document contained no such information (RB 75, Executive Board Minutes 5/20–21/66, 9).

Beals received much feedback from AAA members, with assistance from anthropologists he had written, and extensive interviews on "several university campuses." These interviews did not produce a uniform response. Some anthropologists were outraged by the rise of anthropological contacts with intelligence agencies; others believed the decision to work with military or intelligence agencies should be a matter of personal choice (AAAFN 1967 8[1]: 4).

Beals identified several governmental projects employing anthropologists that did not compromise fundamentals of research ethics or political power relations. His report criticized university-based anthropologists who failed to understand how their work could connect to military and intelligence agencies. While many anthropologists viewed their research as simply being the "pursuit of knowledge solely for its own sake," the report stressed that this work had policy applications, warning that ignoring these issues "plagued basic researchers in such fields as atomic physics" (AAAFN 1967 8[1]: 6). The Beals Report found that private agencies that contracted social science research with governmental agencies, "especially the Department of Defense," had recurrent problems with improper methodologies, excessive costs, government misrepresentation of the competence of personnel, deceiving the public about the purpose of research or the source of funds, and punishing whistle-blowers or dissenters on projects (AAAFN 1967 8[1]: 8).

Beals described growing suspicions that anthropologists were "engaged in non-anthropological activities, or that the information they are collecting will be used for non-scientific and harmful ends" (AAAFN 1967 8[1]: 11).[16] According to Beals, CIA agents had "posed as anthropologists or asserted that they were doing anthropological research, when in fact they were neither qualified as anthropologists nor competent to do basic anthropological studies" (AAAFN 1967 8[1]: 11). In other cases, actual anthropologists were using fieldwork as a cover for espionage, collecting intelligence for the CIA, either as direct CIA employees or by "accepting grants from certain foundations with questionable sources of income, or through employment by certain private research organizations" (AAAFN 1967 8[1]: 11).

Beals's report detailed instances of younger anthropologists who, after failing to secure grants for a particular research project, were "approached by obscure foundations or have been offered supplementary support from such sources, only to discover later that they were expected to provide intelligence information, usually to the Central Intelligence Agency" (AAAFN 1967 8[1]: 11). Other anthropologists reportedly willingly entered into such working relationships, though the report acknowledged that little verification of such interactions was available.

Anthropologists reported being approached by U.S. embassy officials while conducting research abroad, or sometimes by intelligence personnel after returning to the United States, with requests to provide the government with information gathered while conducting fieldwork. Some anthropologists complied with these requests, but others refused to cooperate (AAAFN 1967 8[1]: 11). Some anthropologists who worked for intelligence agencies during World War II later encountered difficulties when applying for research visas, and some universities denied employment to professors with past links to intelligence agencies (AAAFN 1967 8[1]: 12). Suspicions that anthropologists might have CIA connections created conditions where researchers funded by *any* form of governmental funds were sometimes viewed with suspicion.

Project Camelot popularized notions of anthropologist-spies. Beals's report included the account of an anthropologist who, during the course of conducting two years of fieldwork, "was accused variously of being a Castroite, a Chinese communist, a Russian communist, a CIA agent, a FBI agent, a spy for the host nation's taxing agencies, and a Protestant missionary." The punch line was that "only the last caused him serious difficulties, and such an identification given anthropologists generally seems to be the most important field problem in much of South and Central America" (AAAFN 1967 8[1]: 12).

The report did not issue specific recommendations, instead calling for concerted work on these problems. But within the context of the Aberles' resolution adopted at the AAA Council meeting where Beals's report was delivered, growing numbers within the AAA condemned all anthropological contributions to military-intelligence activities in ways that mixed political and ethical critiques of anthropological engagements.

In March 1967, the AAA fellows voted to adopt SPARE, which articulated the values and findings from the Beals Report (AAA 1967). This statement was not a formal ethics code, but it expressed commitment to standards of ethical practice championing the freedom of research, clarifying that anthropologists must disclose "their professional qualifications and associations, their sponsorship and source of funds, and the nature and objectives of the research being undertaken." In response to Project Camelot, the statement proclaimed, "Constraint, deception, and secrecy have no place in science. Actions which compromise the intellectual integrity and autonomy of research scholars and institutions not only weaken those international understandings essential to our discipline, but in so doing they also threaten any contribution anthropology might make to our own society and to the general interests of human welfare" (AAA 1967).

The AAA's condemnation of covert research made SPARE's adoption national news, with the *Washington Post* and other newspapers covering the vote as a significant step in limiting military access to academic knowledge (Reistrup 1967). As an ethics statement, SPARE lacked several features. It was more concerned about the damage that might be done to anthropology's disciplinary reputation than with the well-being of studied populations. The word "harm" appeared nowhere in the statement, and the only use of "damage" appeared in a warning about damages to anthropology's international reputation by false anthropologists (AAA 1967).

In the *Fellow Newsletter*, the AAA leadership sought to alleviate member concerns about anthropologists' links to intelligence agencies with assurances that the new chair of the National Research Council, Division of Behavioral Sciences, was investigating this problem (*AAAFN* 1967 8[2]: 1). But this new chair was George Murdock, whose disqualifications for this task included secretly acting in the past as an FBI informer attacking other anthropologists he believed to be communists. Murdock also had long-standing ties to the HRAF, whose primary sources of funding were the very governmental agencies (including the CIA and Defense Department) that raised these concerns (D. H. Price 2004b: 70–89). While Murdock's role as an FBI informer was unknown at the time, his letters to the *Fellow Newsletter* attacking the Aberles' antiwar resolution and HRAF's receipt of Pentagon funds made no secret of the political positions he would champion in this NRC role (*AAAFN* 1967 8[2]: 7–9).

For the next half year, the *Fellow Newsletter* published letters that argued passionately for and against the Aberles' antiwar resolution. Many opponents argued that it was beyond the proper scope of a professional association to take stances on political issues (*AAAFN* 1967 8[2]: 7–9).[17] David Aberle responded to these arguments, stating, "The question is not whether the Association should be political; it has made itself political. The only question is what kind of political positions it should adopt" (*AAAFN* 1967 8[5]: 7). Lloyd Cabbot Briggs, an OSS veteran, scoffed at the rage over Camelot and concerns over CIA funding (*AAAFN* 8[6]: 8).[18] Betokening Goodwin's law, Sally and Lewis Binford ridiculed claims that the association should not become involved in militarized political decisions, claiming these positions "are unpleasantly reminiscent of the 'good' German scientists during the 1930's who hoped to keep their profession distinct from its political and social matrix" (*AAAFN* 1967 8[6]: 9). Finally, after months of heated debate, a note published by the *Fellow Newsletter* editor announced, in all capitals: "CORRESPONDENCE ON THE ANTI-WAR RESOLUTION IS NOW CLOSED" (*AAAFN* 1967 8[6]: 11).

In July 1967, Thomas L. Hughes, chair of the Foreign Affairs Research Council and the Department of State's director of intelligence and research, assured the AAA Executive Board that the State Department did not want to engage in research that would undermine relationships with foreign countries. Hughes stressed that most of the academic research supported by the department was of a general, basic science type, unrelated to specific political projects (*AAAFN* 1968 9[6]: 9). The federal government's Foreign Area Research Coordination Group issued its "Guidelines for Foreign Area Research" in December 1967, addressing concerns raised by Project Camelot. These guidelines established that the government should not undertake actions that would undermine the integrity of American academics, that academics should acknowledge governmental research support, and that government research should be published. Research should preferably be unclassified, but the report acknowledged that in some cases classified research would be conducted by academics (*AAAFN* 1968 9[5]: 4–7).

In 1967, the AAA amended its bylaws to require resolutions presented at council meetings to "be submitted to the Executive Board at least one week in advance of the annual meeting if they are to be placed on the agenda. A copy of the agenda shall be furnished to all Fellows at the time of registration at the annual meeting or 24 hours before the Council Meeting" (*AAAFN* 1968 9[1]: 1). The year 1967 was a watershed for young AAA activists awakening to the possibilities of organizing the discipline to struggle against American foreign policies and abuses of anthropological knowledge. There were efforts to organize a forum for radical anthropological critiques. Karen Brodkin later recalled that she and a "cohort of grad students from Michigan attend[ed] the 1967 meetings in DC with a plan to create a radical caucus. We had a couple of pretty well-attended evening meetings in hotel conference rooms. There were other efforts in other years and while they didn't leave much of a paper trail, they were places where grad students especially began to form the political networks that underlay the upcoming generation of left anthropology" (2008: 4).

Thai Affair Prequel

Even as the Executive Board finalized the report titled "Background Information on Problems of Anthropological Research and Ethics," ARPA expanded efforts to use ethnographic research for counterinsurgency projects. In one such effort ARPA sought the assistance of University of Washington sociologist Pierre L. van den Berghe for a study of Congo tribal groups.[19] However, van den Berghe immediately wrote the AAA and members of the press expressing concerns that ARPA was trying "to enlist him in intelligence activities for the suppression of Congo tribes in the conflict that was then in its final stages there. Only a firm denial by ARPA that a contract existed or was contemplated allowed the matter to come to rest" (Deitchman 1976: 300). Van den Berghe alerted Ralph Beals of ARPA's efforts to recruit him, and he critically responded to ARPA that he was "morally obligated to publicize" this recruitment effort, adding that he was "deeply distressed at the continued misuse of social science research for purposes which conflict with the generally accepted norms of international relations as expressed in international law and in the United Nations Charter. Beyond the ethical issues involved, the behavior of some of our colleagues is making the pursuit of cross-cultural studies increasingly difficult for most of us. We have a collective responsibility in trying to put an end to this kind of academic colonialism" (RB, PVDB to RB 10/4/66; see D. H. Price 2012c: 6).

Around this time, a group of anthropologists working in Thailand were independently raising their own concerns with the director of a new ARPA program appropriating anthropological knowledge. On Halloween 1966, University of Washington anthropologist Charles F. Keyes wrote to the director of ARPA's Remote Area Conflict Program (RACP) on behalf of himself, Everett Hawkins, Millard Long, Michael Moerman, Gayle Ness, Lauriston Sharp, and Robert Tilman, expressing alarm over RACP's efforts to use anthropological knowledge (RB 75, CFK to ARPA 10/31/66). Keyes warned Seymour Deitchman that some of his "colleagues have even referred to this project as a potential Southeast Asian Camelot." Keyes's group requested a briefing from ARPA before the upcoming AAA annual meeting. Deitchman later wrote that Keyes, Moerman, Herbert Phillips, and Sharp "wanted an explanation, and if they didn't get one, or weren't satisfied with the one they did get, they would go to Congress and the press" (1976: 300).

Ten days later, Keyes expressed concerns to Moerman about RACP's impact on anthropologists' research. Keyes had heard that RACP's Rural Security Systems Study planned to gather information on every village in Nkahon Phanom Province with "the establishment of villager 'reporters' in each village to channel information into a central office in Bangkok, and a general analysis of the 'counter-insurgency' situation in the province." Keyes understood that about fifty social scientists would be hired by contractors at Stanford Research Institute, Abt Associates, and the Atlantic Research Corporation (RB 75, CFK to MM 11/10/66).[20]

Keyes wrote to the six anthropologists he had represented in his letter to ARPA and reported on his recent conversation with Seymour Deitchman, in which Deitchman tried to allay Keyes's concerns without denying the program's counterinsurgency goals. Deitchman's explanations offered only clarifications of minor differences in detail, such as insisting there would be "no system of informants in each village," while not denying the program's broad use of village informants and informers. Some of Keyes's concerns remained, but he felt that rather than withdraw from this flawed project, more good could be accomplished by anthropological engagement and efforts to steer the program in a better direction.[21]

Deitchman wanted to discuss the program with Keyes and his colleagues, and Keyes wrote to the group that he had told Deitchman of his wish to not make public their work until the project "was at least restructured along sounder lines." Keyes was reassured by ARPA's initial reactions to his concerns, and he hoped this would continue "in this vein since *a public airing might produce a backlash effect in the scholarly community*" (RB 75 CFK to EH et al. 11/15/66, emphasis added). Keyes's belief that they could help transform ARPA by working with it quashed his initial desire to blow the whistle on the program. But his prediction that public knowledge of ARPA's program would bring a backlash would later prove to be tragically prophetic.

Deitchman told the Keyes group that the Thai Rural Security Systems Program was in its early stages, and he assured them that this project was in no way linked to Camelot. While administratively it was true that this Thai program had no organizational ties to Camelot, the counterinsurgent goals had strong thematic links. As a Pentagon spokesperson explained to Congress, the Thai counterinsurgency program sought to "gather and collate critical information on the local geography," to create "files on insurgent incidents and operations," to "provide assistance in analyzing the effectiveness of various counterinsurgency programs," and "to plan future CI [counterinsurgency] programs" (Department of Defense, in Deitchman 1976: 301).

Deitchman wrote that these would-be anthropological critics "were reassured" (1976: 302). He pitched the benevolence of ARPA's counterinsurgency program in northern Thailand, stressing the Rostowian progress of the project and claiming that, with one visit with Keyes and the other anthropologist-critics, he had turned them into allies. He wrote:

> Having reached this happy conclusion to a delicate confrontation, I then asked whether, since they were among the recognized American experts on Thai culture and history, they would be willing to help us do a better job by helping in the research. The responses varied. One said that if the work were later to be criticized, he would not want to be associated with it but would rather be free to join the critics (although he later sent us a copy, which was very helpful of his yet-to-be-published Ph.D. thesis on life in Thai village society). Others promised benevolent neutrality. (303)

Keyes believed that by engaging in "dialogue with ARPA," he could "minimize the ill-effects of such projects," though he worried that he might be too naive about the changes he could accomplish (RB 75CFK to EH et al. 11/15/66). This correspondence was darkly prophetic. Four years later, Keyes's concerns about his naïveté regarding effecting change and angry eruptions in the discipline following public knowledge of their contact with ARPA would later bear fruit in the AAA's biggest showdown over the militarization of anthropology.

But even as Moerman, Keyes, and Phillips hoped to steer ARPA's use of anthropological data to help rather than harm people, there was a rising tide within the AAA advocating for complete disengagement from military and intelligence agencies.

AAA Eruptions over AAA Military Advertisements

Even as AAA members increasingly organized opposition to military and intelligence uses of anthropology, the association's official publications carried advertisements for such jobs. A 1967 advertisement for Human Sciences Research, Inc., of McLean, Virginia, sought anthropologists with graduate-level expertise in cultures of Asia and the Middle East (*AAAFN* 1967 8[2]: 12). An advertisement the following year angered a large group of association members to take action.

The back pages of the August 1968 issue of *American Anthropologist* carried a full-page employment advertisement, paid for by the U.S. Navy, with the heading "Research Anthropologist for Vietnam." The ad sought anthropologists to work on a PSYOPS project in Saigon, where they would study "enemy propaganda," "analyze the susceptibilities" and determine "enemy vulnerabilities" of target audiences, and make recommendations. The advertisement specified "qualified professional anthropologists" with "at least three years of progressively responsible experience in anthropological research." The position paid well, with a base advertised salary of "$14,409 plus 25% foreign post differential" and $1,250 to $3,700 a year for dependents.

The next issue of *American Anthropologist* carried a note from the editor, Ward Goodenough, explaining that the AAA had received complaints concerning the navy PYSOP ad in the previous issue. He wrote that despite widespread moral objections to the war in Vietnam held by members of the association, in the absence of any policy banning such ads, AAA publications would continue to publish paid advertisements from the navy and other military branches (Goodenough 1968: vi).

The roots of the formalization of the association's first code of ethics were established in 1968 in a series of meetings of the AAA's ad hoc Committee on Organizations. The committee called for the writing of a formal ethics statement and recommended that a forum on ethics be held at the association's next annual meeting. This push to establish an ethics code influenced elections, as election for seats on the 1968 Executive Board became referendums on the association's stance on the Vietnam War.

David Aberle's campaign statement for an open Executive Board seat declared that the board "seems to regard activities in support of U.S. Government policies as service and activities in opposition to those policies as politics. One of my chief concerns is for the Association to rethink this indefensible position, with a view to deciding its responsibilities to science, the public, the peoples it studies, the problems of our times, and the U.S. Government and other governments with which members of the profession and the Association have relations" (*AAAFN* 1968 9[8]: 3). On the basis of this radical campaign stance, David Aberle was elected to the board.

Attendance at the 1968 AAA meeting was low, most likely because its location in Seattle was distant from many departments (*NAAA* 1969 10[1]: 1). This was the last meeting before the association's voting rules changed so resolutions no longer needed to be submitted a week before the council meeting. But even under the old rules, the council meeting adopted two resolutions that had been submitted in advance (*NAAA* 1969 10[1]: 1).[22] The Wenner-Gren Foundation funded seventy "student delegates" to attend the annual meeting. These delegates attended sessions, held their own meetings, and issued a "combined student statement" to the AAA, called for voting rights within the association and for more attention to professional ethics (*AAAFN* 1969 10[1]: 1).

A loosely organized group of anthropologists calling themselves a "Committee of Concerned Anthropologists" organized a mail campaign to gather signatures and funds for a counteradvertisement to be published in the back pages of *American Anthropologist* (AAAFN 1969 10[3]: 2). A war of words over whether the association should accept military advertisements filled the letters sections of the *Fellow Newsletter* (e.g., AAAFN 1969 10[3]: 3; 1969 10[6]: 2).

The February 1969 issue of *American Anthropologist* contained a paid ad protesting the navy's August 1968 advertisement. To address issues raised by military ads in AAA publications and rising concerns over military and intelligence agencies seeking anthropological knowledge, the AAA Executive Board appointed an ad hoc Committee on Ethics, composed of cochairs David Schneider and David Aberle, Richard N. Adams, Joseph Jorgenson, William Shack, and Eric Wolf. As its first act, the committee issued a policy statement concerning the acceptance of military advertisements for association publications. The statement proclaimed, "The AAA will not accept advertisements or notices for positions involving research or other activities the products of which cannot be made available to the entire scholarly community through accepted academic channels of communication" (AAAFN 1969 10[3]: 1). The Committee on Ethics would review future advertisements that presented possible problems.

During a January 1969 weekend meeting in Chicago, the AAA ad hoc Committee on Ethics rapidly composed a working draft of a code of ethics and sent it to the Executive Board the following week. This draft, which drew heavily on Beals's "Statement on Problems of Anthropological Research and Ethics," incorporated ethical principles identified by the American Psychological Association, the American Sociological Association, and the Society for Applied Anthropology. The ad hoc committee recommended to the board that the membership elect a standing Committee on Ethics immediately (AAAFN 1969 10[4]: 3).

The ad hoc committee's report described the composition of a standing committee in some detail and specified the range of issues it would address. The four general categories were "relations with those studied," "responsibilities to the discipline," "responsibilities to students," and "relations with sponsors" (AAAFN 1969 10[4]: 4–5). Some language in this report remained in the Principles of Professional Responsibility that was adapted by the membership two years later.

The report of the ad hoc Committee on Ethics generated strong opposition from a vocal minority of anthropologists, who argued in the *Fellow Newsletter* that the proposed code attempted to "legislate a socio-ideological system" that was akin to the sort of controlling mechanism used in Nazi Germany, a totalitarian tactic, similar to tactics in Orwell's *Animal Farm*; some derisively referred to the ethics committee as the "Censorship Committee" or the "Ethical Surveillance Committee."[23] This hyperbole reflected some anthropologists' concerns that the association would use the code to police research, but it also prefigured some of the ways that ethics would later be used to bolster political positions. These concerns also expressed many anthropologists' conception of science in an era in which practitioners of that most humanistic of sciences took umbrage at suggestions that anthropologists should be answerable for the impacts of the discipline's search for truth (Wolf 1964:88).

Collisions of Ethics and Politics

The AAA's leadership historically viewed the association as an apolitical professional organization, though what this generally meant was that it helped organize anthropological support for governmental programs (social programs, military programs, etc.), while hesitating to oppose government policies or programs, as if alignment with power was an apolitical stance. After the association coordinated anthropological contributions to the Second World War, it experienced schisms during the 1960s — which widened during the early 1970s — as the annual council meetings became staging grounds for critical political discourse on anthropology and American militarism.

The 1960s opened with Margaret Mead leading a movement within the AAA opposing rising militarism; early in the 1970s, she was backed into a corner, defending anthropological counterinsurgency against a sizable faction of the discipline. While the generation of anthropologists who had served during World War II were less categorically opposed to anthropologists' contributions to counterinsurgency operations in Thailand than their younger colleagues, when news spread of Project Camelot's intentions to use anthropologists for counterinsurgency in South America, anthropologists young and old alike expressed their anger and opposition. Camelot touched a raw nerve in the discipline, as it exposed anthropology as a potentially manipulative instrument for American political gain. But just half a decade later, some anthropologists considered counterinsurgency as a peaceful alternative to, not just a component of, warfare.

Ralph Beals's efforts to describe relationships between military and intelligence agencies and anthropologists identified patterns of ongoing attempts to exploit cultural knowledge in ways that raised significant political and ethical questions. Beals's report prepared the association to oppose secret research and some forms of counterinsurgency, and it laid the groundwork for SPARE and the coming Principles of Professional Responsibility. As his correspondence with Elizabeth Bacon records, Beals collected a good deal of information specifying how the CIA and the Pentagon contacted anthropologists or used anthropological knowledge, but he did not include these details in his final report. This correspondence provides an important view of how CIA efforts to directly and indirectly connect with and use anthropologists worked during the early Cold War. Bacon's account of the ways that CIA personnel contacted and attempted to debrief anthropologists returning from fieldwork fits with the reports of others, and while Bacon rejected offers to provide information to the CIA, other anthropologists during the Cold War held hopes of better informing CIA analysis.

But it was counterinsurgency, rather than spying or the more subtle articulations of academia's soft interfaces with the military-intelligence establishment, that most violently opened the fissures between anthropologists' passionate, if unarticulated, visions of anthropology. While the 1968 advertisements in *American Anthropologist* released volleys of anger opposing the association's alignment with the war in Vietnam, just a few years later, many of those who had opposed these ads would side with the anthropologists assisting counterinsurgency operations in Thailand.

The early exchanges between Seymour Deitchman and Charles Keyes show how supporters of counterinsurgency made humanitarian claims of stability, liberation, and peace, while avoiding the uncomfortable truth that these means of implementing "stability" were warfare by other means. While Keyes showed clear awareness of such critiques in this early correspondence, claims that anthropologists' assistance could lessen harm became a powerful enticement in the military's efforts to recruit anthropologists. Assurances that counterinsurgency was not a weapon of soft power but a tool for assisting those impacted by war were an effective argument for some anthropologists during the Vietnam War. As the next chapter shows, the contingencies supporting anthropological contributions to counterinsurgency helped convince some anthropologists to join these efforts and to overlook the lack of impact their research or recommendations had on the well-being of those they studied.

> "The old formula for successful counterinsurgency used to be
> 10 troops for every guerrilla," one American specialist remarked,
> "now the formula is 10 anthropologists for every guerrilla."
>
> PETER BRAESTRUP | 1967

TWELVE ANTHROPOLOGICALLY INFORMED COUNTERINSURGENCY IN SOUTHEAST ASIA

From the CIA's earliest days in Vietnam, the agency knew the importance of understanding the local culture's mores. Edward Lansdale, Graham Greene's model for CIA agent Alden Pyle in *The Quiet American*, incorporated anthropological knowledge into his CIA counterinsurgency campaigns in the Philippines and Vietnam. In his memoir, *In the Midst of War*, Lansdale described using local superstitions of vampires that roamed the jungles at night as a force multiplier when he trained operatives to kill insurgents and leave their bodies punctured with holes to suggest that vampires had drained their blood (1972: 72–73).

In Vietnam, Lansdale developed counterinsurgency operations that mixed hard power techniques of assassination and organized strategic military assaults with diverse soft power methods such as dispersing economic aid and drawing on existing local Catholic organizations as counterinsurgency tools. The *Pentagon Papers* described Lansdale's work for President Ngo Dinh Diem as relying on the "three withs," consisting of a counterinsurgency approach in which Lansdale and his CIA operatives would "'eat, sleep, and work with the people' — some 1400 to 1800 'cadre' undertook: census and surveys of the physical needs of villages; building schools, maternity hospitals, information halls; repairing and enlarging local roads; digging wells and irrigation canals; teaching personal and public hygiene; distributing medicine; teaching children by day, and anti-illiteracy classes by night; forming village militia; conducting political meetings; and publicizing agrarian reform legislation" (U.S. Department of Defense 1972: 306).

Anthony Poshepny, a CIA agent more commonly known as Tony Poe, who is sometimes credited as an inspiration for elements of Francis Ford Coppola's Colonel Kurtz in *Apocalypse Now*, enacted Lansdale's approach to culturally centered counterinsurgency (Branfman 1975: 56–58; M. Isaacs 1999).[1] Poe's knowledge of Meo culture and his willingness to work within local cultural confines made him an invaluable CIA asset in Laos during America's secret war, though his tendency to follow local customs over CIA rules (e.g., marrying a Laotian "chieftain's daughter" after a village raid, complete with a dowry of one hundred water buffalo and seventy-five goats) repeatedly violated agency procedures, while his efforts to "go native" earned him the respect and support of some locals (M. Isaacs 1999).

Because of the influences of CIA operatives like Poe, Lansdale, and others, the agency and the Pentagon increasingly understood the need for nuanced cultural knowledge when conducting counterinsurgency and military operations in Southeast Asia. This desire for cultural knowledge to be used for conquest and control led to a series of problematic interactions with anthropologists—dual use interactions that often found anthropologists trying to lessen harm to the indigenous groups they lived with and studied, while military and intelligence agencies pursued their own goals.

Several American anthropologists worked in Vietnam, Laos, and Thailand during the 1950s, 1960s, and 1970s. William Smalley, who earned a PhD at Columbia University in the 1950s, mixed anthropological research with missionary work in Laos, Vietnam, and Thailand (Smalley 1994). Forensic anthropologist Robert B. Pickering identified remains of American soldiers at the U.S. Army Central Identification Laboratory in Thailand (BIC 2014d). Terry Rambo studied Vietnamese farming communities with SEADAG and USAID funds (Rambo 1973). But the American anthropologist who most prominently worked in Vietnam before and throughout the war was Gerald Hickey.

Gerald Hickey, the Not-So-Quiet American

In the late 1950s and throughout the 1960s, a rapidly increasing flow of American social scientists from the disciplines of sociology, political science, anthropology, and geography were drawn to the problems of the Vietnam War, and with these scholars came a stream of seemingly endless, futile theoretical approaches to the problems of America's war (Marquis 2000). From 1955 to 1959, Michigan State University had a secret $25 million CIA contract, bringing CIA personnel to campus, where agency personnel and professors trained Vietnamese officials (see Hinckle, Scheer, and Stern 1966). Anthropologist Gerald Hickey began working for the Michigan State University Group (MSUG) while in Vietnam in 1954, and in 1956 he attended MSUG meetings in which CIA personnel were Michigan State advisers to Saigon law enforcement personnel. Hickey later conducted MSUG work in Saigon with anthropologist Frederick Wickert (Hickey 2002: 3, 18–19, 23–24, 57–60), and MSUG designed curriculum for Vietnam's National Institute of Administration to train civil servants, police, and security personnel, programs that included CIA employee Louis Boudrias (Ernst 1998: 64). The MSUG training taught the Vietnamese Bureau of Investigation updated fingerprinting techniques and in 1957 advised the Central Identification Bureau on its new national identity card program (72). John Ernst, historian of MSUG's role in these military and intelligence training programs, wrote that the applications of this training were clear, and "Diem approved of using repressive tactics to purge political rivals and communists from South Vietnam and enlisted Michigan State's aid in doing so" (66).

The initial work by MSUG involved efforts to help refugees fleeing to the South following the 1954 Geneva Accords (Ernst 1998: 29–30). Following Diem's 1956 call for MSUG to research highland peoples, it developed a line of analysis that "compared the situation of the highland peoples to that of the American Indians during the nineteenth century" (30). This comparison was not just an evocative metaphor to generate sympathetic comparisons; it was a reference to be used in developing a political managerial strategy, as Wesley Fishel at MSUG "wrote the United States Bureau of Indian Affairs requesting literature on agency policies. He noted that 'From the Western *and* Vietnamese points of view, the Montagnards are *primitive* in respect to their social and economic way of life and religious beliefs" (31).

Diem cared little about MSUG's recommendations and supported refugee resettlement programs in the highlands with the assistance of MSUG personnel as part of a defensive guerrilla action project. But Michigan State's "role in the refugee resettlement program [was] complex. The MSUG tried to act as a positive force, and most of the Field Administration Division's recommendations were utilized with solid results, but because numerous organizations and factors were involved in the resettlement program, the university's overall impact is difficult to measure" (Ernst 1998: 35). Later, when the university's collusion with the CIA was exposed in 1966, MSU president John A. Hannah claimed the university "did not have a spy operation within its Vietnam Project. It did not have CIA people operating under cover provided by the University, or in secret from the Vietnam government" (82). Hannah's statement stressed this was not a *spy operation* per se; it was a *training operation*. The university had become a CIA-financed training camp where paramilitary operatives learned the harsh tactics they deployed in Vietnam. Michigan State wasn't spying (or an interrogator, a death squad overseer, etc.); it *trained* spies. Even after CIA funds ceased, MSUG continued working on counterinsurgency projects, including "internal security of strategic hamlets, registration and identification of family groups, and controls of the movement of both population and material" (MSUG 1962: 51). The Pike Commission later evaluated these "public safety" training programs run by AID and CIA personnel and concluded that between the early 1950s and 1973, up to five thousand foreign police officers from around the world were trained by the CIA through programs like the one at Michigan State (Pike Report 1977: 228–29).

From the late 1950s throughout the years of America's involvement in the Vietnam War, no other American anthropologist had more fieldwork experience with the cultures of Vietnam than Gerald Hickey. Hickey first conducted fieldwork in Vietnam in 1956 and 1957, at which time he met many of the individuals who would figure prominently in his future research. Hickey was in Vietnam when director Joseph Mankiewicz filmed the original Hollywood production of *The Quiet American* (1958), based on Greene's novel, and he appeared as an extra in a scene shot with Michael Redgrave (Hickey 2002: 48). After earning his doctorate at the University of Chicago in 1959, Hickey became a research associate at Michigan State University, working with MSUG (Elliot 2010: 25). Hickey spent much of the war in Vietnam, working for RAND and other agencies interfacing with U.S. military and intelligence personnel.

Between January and April 1962, Hickey and John Donnell conducted ethnographic research in resettled communities near Saigon, studying "social, economic, and certain political aspects of the strategic hamlet program as seen from the peasants' point of view," for a RAND report on the Strategic Hamlet Program (Donnell and Hickey 1962: iii). This program was a counterinsurgency operation that relocated entire villages in areas where U.S. military personnel could more easily reduce their contacts with the Vietcong. While the stated goal of these new hamlets was to move villagers from the "path" of insurgents, functionally, the new hamlets were locked-down encampments that maintained illusions of open-door free movement (complete with deadly fortified barriers) while isolating and controlling hamlet populations.

The Strategic Hamlet Program targeted village members suspected of being Vietcong supporters and installed village informers who reported to U.S. military and intelligence personnel on subversive activities (Donnell and Hickey

1962: 2–3). As Donnell and Hickey described it, the "program involves the political and social organization of the inhabitants in a way that permits close surveillance of their political activities, of their social participation in such government-controlled mass movements as the Republican Youth, and the contribution to labor projects for community development. Once these programs are established, the system is further designed to serve as a basis for wider programs of rural economic reconstruction, including agricultural credit and extension services" (2–3).

Strategic hamlets created panoptical microcosms that moved villagers from regions of Vietcong movements and redesigned village economic and social dynamics. As inducements for families to leave their traditional village homes, villagers were given small pieces of land to build homes within the perimeter of the strategic hamlet compounds and promised access to farmlands outside the compounds. In some instances farmers were left outside these compounds to collect intelligence (Donnell and Hickey 1962: 6–7).[2]

Hickey did not oppose the Strategic Hamlet Program. He believed that for counterinsurgency to succeed, the military needed to increase the total control of (and reinforcements flowing into) these artificial village environments. Hickey understood that controlling physical space was as important as controlling cultural space, and that "the reorganization of a hamlet's social and administrative organs is regarded by all officials as at least as important as the construction of physical defense facilities" (Donnell and Hickey 1962: 7). Units known as Rural Reconstruction Teams supervised the reorganization of villages and helped install social, agricultural, and economic programs that provided aid but also increased the contingencies of control over and dependency of villagers (see Donnell and Hickey 1962: 7; Millhauser 2008). These Rural Reconstruction Teams also tried "to learn about families with pro–Viet Cong sentiment who should be regrouped near a military post for easier surveillance" (Donnell and Hickey 1962: 7). Under a system of mandatory corvée, farmers built the new hamlet compounds, sometimes being forced to contribute between forty-five and ninety days of labor. This created conflicts with some villagers, as did the loss of valuable farmlands to build the new hamlets among those already living in the settlement region (10–11). Some farmers were forced to "contribute" the entirety of their most marketable crop, bamboo, to the strategic hamlet's fortifications — a demand that at times created years of debt (11).

The scale of the Strategic Hamlet dream was massive. In 1962, the U.S. military planned to install twelve thousand strategic hamlets in a six-month period (Donnell and Hickey 1962: 3). Such increasingly large visions of total control appear as logical and inevitable developments once militaries depend on counterinsurgency for military goals. These contrived "hamlets" installed "council of elders" advisory units composed of wealthy and influential community members whom American planners hoped could be manipulated to steer public opinions and policies (8). Rural Reconstruction Teams began their work by conducting a census, an act that Donnell and Hickey found "often prompts some pro-Communist individuals to flee the hamlet" (7). Hickey envisioned strategic hamlets bringing uniformity and control, and severing connections with preexisting cultural life, supplanting order and control in ways that fit the needs of the U.S. military and kept inhabitants legible to them (see Scott 1998: 37–40).

Donnell and Hickey's report provided U.S. policy makers and military and intelligence agencies with an ethnographic view of why the Strategic Hamlet Program would fail. The report outlined how the debts, disruptions, generated ill will, and economic losses would outweigh any benefits of surveillance and disruption of village aid to the Vietcong. The report made the motives and lives of Vietnamese peasants understandable to agencies seeking to control them. It clarified that these peasants were "more favorably disposed to the side which offers [them] the possibility of a better life," yet the inherent problems in the Strategic Hamlet Program could easily lead these farmers to turn against the program's American designers (Donnell and Hickey 1962: 15).

Donnell and Hickey supported changing portions of the Strategic Hamlet Program to better meet the needs of villagers, while maintaining the U.S. military's control over the hamlets. They recommended manipulating conditions so that farmers living in the strategic hamlets could derive direct benefits from the programs in which they were forced to participate. Donnell and Hickey used concrete examples to illustrate why rational peasants disliked their relocation and the disruption of their normal agricultural activities. They explained that because farmers had short-term views of future payoffs, the immediate reductions in tobacco cash crops were rationally viewed as failures rather than simply as the inconveniences claimed by American Strategic Hamlet proponents. Donnell and Hickey warned that if the cultural views and needs of these people were not accommodated, the villagers' support as allies would be lost. They wrote that "these farmers are the backbone of the village warning and auxiliary guard systems. In our opinion, they will participate in these security activities willingly and effectively only if, in the very near future, they see evidence that the strategic hamlet to which they have made such heavy contributions in time, materials, land, and reduced secondary crop yields is capable of improving their economic, social, and political welfare beyond the narrower aspect of the greater physical security it offers them" (Donnell and Hickey 1962: 16–17). Their report viewed peasants as rational actors whose needs and values should be understood and respected if the Strategic Hamlet Program were to achieve its desired ends of control. They did not recommend the end of the forced relocation of villagers but instead suggested that peasants receive increased compensation for their work and cooperation, as well as more opportunities to participate in actual decision making.[3]

Hickey and Donnell recognized that many of the features of these hamlets alienated the villagers they were designed to protect, but their analysis did not address how long it would take to implement such a program or how difficult and expensive such an effort would be. Their vision of an "improved" hamlet program ignored larger problems of costs and scale. Roger Hilsman, the director of the State Department's Bureau of Intelligence and Research under President Kennedy, later explained that the British counterinsurgency experiences in Malaya taught American policy makers that the Strategic Hamlet Program could work, but it would take a long time. Even decades later, Hilsman insisted, "It would have taken twenty years, but it would have worked. Instead of chasing Communist troops all over the jungles, you would have slowly enlarged the secure areas, like an oil block with strategic hamlets moving out" (National Security Archives 1998). Hilsman's plan would have increasingly locked down Vietnamese peasants in strategic hamlets until well into the early 1980s. Historian Eric Bergerud later observed that Donnell and Hickey understood that unless the Strategic Hamlet Program was overhauled to better fit the cultural and economic needs of the people living within the hamlets, it would fail, and "when Diem was overthrown, the junta in Saigon ended the Strategic Hamlet Program immediately, citing as reasons many of the points raised by Hickey and Donnell" (1991: 52).

Hickey's Other RAND Reports

Though Hickey's 1962 recommendations to RAND on the Strategic Hamlet Program were ignored, he continued producing military-related reports for RAND throughout the decade. In 1964, Hickey published a RAND report describing South Vietnamese highland ethnic groups, drawing on published and unpublished reports and ethnographic writings on the highland tribes. Hickey presented ethnographic information on the Rhadé, Jarai, Mnong, Stieng, Bahnar, and Sedang tribes using a uniform format in which he presented basic cultural information about each group, then described settlement patterns, sociopolitical organization, and religious information. Many of his sources were unpublished and were consulted in France, primarily French ethnographic writings (thirty-eight out of forty-four were written in French, two in Vietnamese) or historical or geographic reports written by scholars who did not anticipate the RAND audience and military uses of this information.

Hickey compared Vietnam's highland and lowland cultural formations, stressing how Indian and Chinese cultural traditions had influenced cultures of the Indochinese lowlands but had had only limited impacts on highland cultures, which "have not become part of any of the great traditions that have touched them; they have not been 'civilized'" (1964: 2). Hickey described highland groups' reliance on swidden agriculture, growing dry rice and other garden crops while also raising livestock.

Hickey identified villages as the basic political unit in highland culture, describing the importance of the village headman and the village council and outlining the basic principles of the "village-centered justice" system and the importance of rituals (1964: 8). He provided an overview of historical traditions of intervillage warfare and traditional institutions of alliance and peacemaking. He noted that, although the French had generally "abolished" highland warfare, it still occurred:

> Institutions such as the aforementioned *toring* of the Bahnar, or clans among the Rhadé and Jarai which create intervillage kinship ties, serve to diminish wars and conflicts between villages. But among all the groups the favored means for avoiding them are the alliances. Through the father-son alliance or the "great *xep*" blood oath, for example, villages can prevent or end wars and other conflicts and can force bonds of co-operation. *By the same token, of course, such alliances can be a means of gaining allies with whom to carry on a war more effectively. And families or clans can ally themselves so as to be able to carry out vendettas.* (9, emphasis added)

Hickey's narrative was designed not as some act of public education but to inform RAND's military-intelligence audience concerned with tasks of domination and control. Hickey situated his presentation on cultural distinctions not only with frames of geography but also with frames of history and domination, writing that "the history of the highlands reveals the persistent role of the area as a buffer zone in the struggles among the Khmer, Cham, Siamese, Lao, Vietnamese, and colonial powers, as well as in the recent war between the French and the Viet Minh, and in the current conflict between the Viet Cong and the government of South Vietnam" (1964: 14). Hickey noted how the Sedang,

Stieng, and Mong tribes successfully resisted French domination and staged revolts, explaining how these groups resisted external control with religious revelations such as the 1935 reincarnation of the Thunder Spirit's son (15). Hickey's historical summary highlighted themes of sorcery, recurrent tales of rumored ghostly spirits undermining colonial efforts, intertribal warfare, revolts, the importance of gifts to highland leaders, and failed efforts of missions to dominate the highlands.

He drew attention to how French efforts, under Léopold Sabatier's administration, to provide services and aid to Darlac Province in the early twentieth century helped subdue resistance in the region, and he summarized French land reform plans for the highlands—and indigenous efforts to resist these plans (Hickey 1964: 25–26). The role of blood oaths in establishing alliances and peace treaties was described in some detail; stressing the importance of proper participation in these acts, he wrote, "To refuse a friendship alliance is an act of bad faith. This was illustrated in the Odend'hal affair, when the French administrator refused to drink the blood-oath mixture prepared by the Sadet of Fire, whose anger at the insult undoubtedly contributed to Odend'hal's subsequent slaying" (40).

Hickey's discussions of the social structure of specific highland groups stressed the particulars of organization, drawing special attention to the roles of elders, headmen, extravillage liaisons, and supravillage power relations. The report's final sections described specific details of different tribal groups. For example, one section of Hickey's summary of Stieng social organization reported that "every village has a headman selected by the household heads. Tribunals for wrongs of varying degrees are organized in the village. Crimes of the first degree, entailing punishments above the value of two buffaloes, are dealt with by a tribunal composed of the village headman and two elderly men versed in traditional customs. When the contesting parties are from different villages, both headmen must sit on the tribunal, and no kinsmen are permitted to attend" (1964: 57). Given the report's military audience and the state of the war, Hickey's discussions of blood oaths, tribunals, and friendship rituals mandating alliances were specifically selected social features that could possibly be leveraged by his readers (see D. H. Price 2011f: 133–38). Hickey made no direct recommendations on how such information might be used, though the Phoenix Program and CORDS would later weaponize such knowledge in armed counterinsurgency campaigns (see Valentine 1990).

As part of a 1965 RAND and ARPA sponsored project assessing military advisors, Hickey interviewed "several hundred" individuals (Hickey 1965: iv). The factors he identified as influencing the effectiveness of American advisers were the ability to recognize cultural differences, spending time in field battle settings, levels of training, linguistic competence in Vietnamese, availability of skilled translators, experience with different forms of military training, and training in the specific conditions that they faced in Vietnam.

Many American advisers misinterpreted Vietnamese behaviors as indicating the Vietnamese were lazy, unreliable, dishonest, dirty, wasteful, and unable to complete complex tasks (Hickey 1965: viii).[4] Hickey tried to counter these impressions by recommending that U.S. military advisers receive specific cultural and language training before being posted to Vietnam, writing that they needed training in "history, economics, government, sociology, ethnic composition, major religious sects, and general customs of the country as well as on the special characteristics of the region to which they are being assigned" (xiii). He also recommended that "language and cultural training centers, similar to those that some missionary societies have found useful, might be set up as a pilot project within South Vietnam. In them, carefully selected personnel would live and study for several months in a community away from Saigon and without contact with other Americans, the instruction to be supplemented by frequent field trips to different regions of Vietnam" (xv).[5] While such suggestions for cultural training continued the sort of work anthropologists had designed and implemented during the Second World War, the political differences between American intervention in Vietnam's civil war and the previous war against fascism and nationalist occupations brought significantly different attitudes regarding the political ends to which anthropology was to serve. These, however, were distinctions not made by Hickey.

RAND *Visions*

At times Hickey's analysis drew on classic sociocultural theory. His RAND report from 1967 contextualized the ethnic and historical complexities of Vietnamese social life with a Durkheimian analysis of the structural pulls at work in Vietnamese society. As he wrote, "Social and political complexity in any given society does not necessarily mean confusion and chaos; given the right circumstances, the interdependence that is intrinsic to such complexity can give rise to a kind of solidarity. It would be similar to Durkheim's organic solidarity which arises out of the interdependence and need to cooperate as the division of labor in society becomes more specialized and diverse. Without this type of solidarity the society would fragment and perhaps collapse" (Hickey 1967a:1).

In September 1967, RAND published *The Highland People of South Vietnam* (1967b), Hickey's most substantial ARPA report on the social and economic development of these people. This was an impressive piece of anthropological work combining data Hickey collected from villages of twenty-one highland ethnic groups (iii). Hickey drew on ethnographic fieldwork he had undertaken throughout the previous decade, as well as field research conducted in the company of Special Forces units (10).

Hickey's writing at times strayed from anthropological analysis to advocating military strategies; for example, in a 1967 report he advocated that the South Vietnamese government end its opposition to the Front Unifie de Lutte des Races Opprimees (FULRO) and support FULRO autonomy. Hickey argued that this alignment would result in

> the immediate acquisition of an estimated 3000 to 5000 armed men skilled in jungle warfare and familiar with the mountain terrain near Cambodia[;] it would greatly help the government's intelligence network at the village level in areas where FULRO has much popular following. Also evidence of FULRO's pro-GVN stand and of the government's willingness to let the Highlanders assume a larger role within the nation would lessen not only the chance of open discontent and protest but also the demand for autonomy and, most important, the Highlanders' susceptibility to the appeal of the Viet Cong, whose presence in the highlands would thus become increasingly untenable. (1967b: vii–viii)

As anthropologist Oscar Salemink notes, Hickey's support for FULRO separated his analysis from "French anthropologists like Dournes and Condominas, as well as critical American scholars, [who] saw FULRO as a movement of tribal mercenaries organized and supported by the CIA" (2003: 247). From the mid-1960s to 1971, Hickey wrote a series of memos advocating that General William Westmoreland and members of the U.S. military command take specific actions (Emerson 1978: 287), including increased highland agricultural assistance and efforts to resolve land tenure disputes with lowlanders as a means of building support for these needed allies.

While Hickey conducted interviews in French or Vietnamese, he also sometimes used translators from the Summer Institute of Linguistics to help with his work (Hickey 1967b: 16–22). Hickey's RAND report titled *U.S. Strategy in South Vietnam: Extrication and Equilibrium* (1969) argued that the United States did not understand the political nature and nuanced history of the war, and outlined American military withdrawal scenarios.

Hickey's final RAND report, from 1971, retreated into a detailed historical analysis of past Vietnamese historical incidents.[6] It generated a narrative (which detailed topics like "recent economic innovation; the French Period to the Present") that was disconnected from the military realities traumatizing the Vietnam of the present (Hickey 1971: 137).[7]

Over the course of a decade, Hickey's work for RAND found him shifting from counterinsurgency support efforts involving the destruction of tribal villages in order to save them, to providing cultural information of strategic value and trying to inform a military-intelligence audience of the cultural intricacies of the world in which they were waging a war they were increasingly losing. Reading Hickey's RAND reports and his memoir, it seems almost as if he did not understand how different his imagined mission (self-conceived of as reducing harm for tribal groups) was from that of the larger military and intelligence institutions that were consuming his reports. Yet this disconnect (and what appears to be an enduring, naive hope of prevailing over deep institutional forces) seems to have propelled him forward and kept him engaged with a military complex that appeared to ignore his recommendations while continuing to sponsor works containing detailed accounts of cultural customs that it likely believed could have militarized uses.

Hickey's Back-Home Retcon

In late 1970, Hickey wrote his dissertation adviser, Fred Eggan, inquiring about the possibility of landing a visiting professorship at the University of Chicago. Eggan expressed excitement at this prospect. But funds were scarce, and when Eggan advised him to try to secure outside funding, Hickey turned to the Ford Foundation and RAND. Eggan warned him that "there is also a strong feeling on the part of some students and a few of the faculty about research for the government and even stronger feeling about classified research" (Hickey 2002: 297). These "strong feelings" were growing concerns within American anthropology over military and intelligence agency uses of anthropological information in Southeast Asia. When Eggan wrote a memo to department chair Bernard Cohn advocating for a yearlong appointment for Hickey, he added that he knew of "no evidence of any violation of ethic standards, as I have practiced them and as I have tried to teach them to graduate students" (298). Eggan wrote Hickey of growing departmental concerns about Hickey's secret RAND or Defense Department research. Hickey replied that his work had been "classified" but not "secret"—missing the larger issue that writing noncirculating reports that military and intelligence agencies could access raised concerns with his colleagues (298). After Chicago's anthropology department voted against offering Hickey a one-year position, the *Wall Street Journal* ran an article characterizing this decision as "McCarthyism of the Left" (301).

Hickey later complained that his advice was largely ignored by RAND and the military, while in the academy he was demonized by his fellow anthropologists. He wrote: "If my accommodation-coalition approach earned me the reputation in some American political [military/policy] circles of being a heretic, my being in Vietnam with the RAND corporation earned me pariah status among my academic colleagues" (Hickey 2002: 296). Yet Hickey's experience of being ignored in Vietnam was not one in which his influence decreased over time; in fact, from his earliest years onward, his experience was that his colleague's "report was suppressed and mine was ignored" (350). Hickey did not give up when his Strategic Hamlet evaluation was ignored, but neither did he seem to question the ethical and political issues raised by such battle fieldwork and contributions to counterinsurgency, nor did he adequately consider that his declared interests in the people of Vietnam were so at odds with the U.S. military's institutional behaviors and values that his contributions stood no chance of accomplishing what he envisioned. But over time, his views seemed to coalesce with the strategic thinking of the military.

There is an otherworldliness in the ethnographic representations in Hickey's later RAND reports. He wrote as if he were living between dimensions in a world where traditional Vietnamese ethnic and linguistic groups maintained an existence outside of the American carpet bombing, napalm, and Agent Orange. Hickey wrote just-so-story vignettes in which hardworking capitalist peasant entrepreneurs rose above their poverty with cash crops like coffee — yet the narrative frame of these peasants' success was not expanded to incorporate capitalism's war raining down on them.

The political and historical context in which Hickey produced his RAND work transformed these reports into works with meanings and uses far beyond the sum of their parts. Meanings hinge on uses, and Hickey took pieces of ethnographic work produced by himself and others and transformed disparate elements into weaponized knowledge — political knowledge that he knew would be used in military contexts to manipulate, as identified in the title of one of his works for RAND, the "major ethnic groups of the South Vietnamese highlands." Despite Hickey's latter-day complaints about military and intelligence agencies' neglect of the "proper" use of his research, his continual participation in this process documents a form of complicity that is difficult to reconcile.

Oscar Salemink's research adds a chilling final chapter to the tragic unintended consequences of Hickey's research. Salemink found that in the years after American military forces left Southeast Asia, Vietnamese scholars used Hickey's ethnographic writings to identify and persecute the Montagnard FULRO village leaders Hickey made identifiable in his book *Fire in the Forest: Ethnohistory of the Vietnamese Central Highlands* (1982). Hickey had published "a list of 'One Hundred Highlander Leaders: Ethnic affiliation, approximate birth date, and religion.' After his books were published and arrived in Vietnam, security officials who were still fighting FULRO started to arrest every person mentioned in the book. Thanks to the courageous intervention of a Vietnamese ethnologist these persons were gradually released" (Salemink 2003: 4). When Salemink later relayed to Hickey these unintended outcomes of his fieldwork and publication, Hickey was "very upset" (4).

Hickey did not understand how different his anthropological purposes were from those of the individuals who consumed his RAND reports. He wanted to protect those he studied while steering the military toward a kinder form of conquest, at the same time arguing that he was serving the needs of those to be conquered. While the contradictions of this approach did not cause Hickey to disengage from his sponsors, this ongoing cross-purpose relationship fundamentally served the military's needs and apparently served as a salve to Hickey's conscience, at least in the short term. Such relationships of cross-purposes and lopsided outcomes favoring sponsors' desires are not unique to military-linked projects and can be found in a variety of ongoing applied anthropology projects throughout the years (see Downing 2002; D. H. Price 1989).

Delmos Jones and the Complicity of All

While Hickey naively sought to reshape American military-intelligence actions in Southeast Asia from within the system, other anthropologists openly resisted such uses of anthropological knowledge for counterinsurgency. Delmos Jones's reaction to U.S. military and intelligence agencies' efforts to use his anthropological field research to assist military actions in Southeast Asia presents a stark contrast to Gerald Hickey's contributions.

In 1965, while a doctoral student in anthropology at Cornell University, Jones was selected for a Ford Foundation Foreign Area Fellowship, which financed his first fieldwork in Thailand. His wife, Linda Jones, and their children accompanied him to Thailand, and his family lived in Chiang Mai while he collected data for his dissertation work examining cultural variation in several Lahu villages in northern Thailand (LJ to DHP 3/3/08; Jones 1967).

The Jones children attended school in Chiang Mai, while their father conducted research in Lahu villages, regularly traveling back and forth between his research sites and his family. Chiang Mai had a small air force installation with significant radar and communications facilities that Jones and others in the community assumed were monitoring Chinese communications. The Joneses and other expatriates assumed some sort of intelligence operation was being run out of Chiang Mai. Delmos Jones's now former wife, Linda Jones, wrote me, almost four decades later, that at the time they "were aware of American activities being conducted out of Chiang Mai. 'Air America' had lots of planes flying in and out of Chiang Mai airport (an otherwise pretty sleepy place). People who ostensibly worked for various American agencies, but who were known to be CIA would board helicopters and go off, sometimes never to return. Their wives could never get any information and were eventually removed from the country" (LJ to DHP 3/3/08).

Efforts were made to maintain a pretense that Chiang Mai was not a covert-ops base, but with the Jones's children attending the area's only English language school and playing with the children of personnel stationed at Chiang Mai, it became apparent from socializing with this community that this base was being used for clandestine operations. These paramilitary activities occurring in the background of his fieldwork troubled Jones, and as these activities later crept into the foreground, the knowledge of military-intelligence interests in his own work became increasingly difficult for Jones to ignore.

After returning from this fieldwork, Jones completed and defended his dissertation at Cornell in 1967 without delving into the political backdrop of his traditional comparative village study. Like so many other anthropologists who were encountering American paramilitary or intelligence activities while conducting fieldwork, he wrote his dissertation without remarking on these events. This has long been the standard practice of the discipline, and to do otherwise would have been unusual and academically inadvisable (see Nader 1997b).

We now know that the CIA was trying to monitor the spread of communist sympathies in the area of northern Thailand where Jones was working. The National Intelligence Estimate report titled "Communist Insurgency in Thailand" (1968) described agricultural programs implemented in the region of Jones's work as vital elements of the region's counterinsurgency campaign. The CIA monitored counterinsurgency operations, giving special attention to the use of

"Mobile Development Units (MDU), teams of specialists working on small-scale projects and attempting to stimulate self-help efforts in selected villages, and the village-level programs of the Community Development Department" and the ARD [Accelerated Rural Development] program they hoped would counter "the economic deficiencies which the Communists attempt to exploit" (CIA 1968a: 8–9).

In 1970 a Fulbright Fellowship allowed Jones to return to Chiang Mai, where he expanded on his earlier village-based research. Once in Chiang Mai, Jones found that American intelligence operations in the region had drastically increased. Linda Jones later wrote me:

> I remember we were quite proud of [the Fulbright Fellowship], but discovered how naive we had been when we discovered that in Chiang Mai we would report to USIS (known to be CIA). Shortly after we settled in Chiang Mai, we went to the Chiang Mai hotel for dinner. While we were eating, an American came over to speak with us. He told Del that he was part of an ARPA program collecting information about the Hill Tribes. Del was uninterested in cooperating. This fellow said it didn't matter. They had computerized and indexed all of his papers and notes anyway. Eye-opening shock number 2! So it went for I think about 5 months when Del had had enough of the situation. He told the head of USIS that we wished to leave Thailand immediately. In return, he was told that our fare home would not be paid. Del threatened to publish what he knew and they backed off. Our fare was paid and we left.
>
> It was out of this ferment that Del began to write and speak about how the work of anthropologists could be used, even if they did not explicitly cooperate with governments. We talked about how it was common for anthropologists to note in their reports the names of village leaders, population counts and geographical locations. These facts could then be used in ways that would not be in the best interests of the tribes. At that time, the tribal villages were suspected of harboring communists. To remove this opportunity, entire villages would just be uprooted and moved against their will. The idea was to get them out of the mountains, but their knowledge of agriculture was geared to that environment, not to that of the valleys. Also, the Thais were very prejudiced against the tribal people. Once they were relocated to the valleys, they were handy targets for mistreatment. (LJ to DHP 3/3/08)

Jones had not looked to become involved in a contentious political issue, but he understood that if he did not withdraw from his planned research project, his work would be used by military or intelligence operatives for purposes that he did not approve, and to which his research participants had not consented.

Jones returned to the United States and began writing about how troubled he was by his experiences in Thailand. His angst was channeled into the short piece "Social Responsibility and the Belief in Basic Research: An Example from Thailand," published the following year in *Current Anthropology*. He identified the dangers facing anthropologists and research participants, not only when anthropologists engaged in military-sponsored research but even when they conducted basic independent research that had potential uses in informing counterinsurgency operations.

Jones described the economic importance of the highland and lowland regions of Vietnam and stressed the military significance of highland villages because they "can be of tremendous strategic importance for storing supplies and establishing camps for guerrilla forces" (1971b: 347). He connected these same dynamics with the situation in Thailand's highlands and lowlands and asked, did "the anthropologists who rushed into the area to do basic descriptive studies consider these political facts? It is safe to say that most of us did not" (347). Jones questioned whether it was a coincidence that funding for research on the cultures of these highland peoples had increased throughout the decade, by ARPA and nonmilitary organizations (348).

He wrote that the Thai Information Center was "controlled and funded" by ARPA, and that it held a collection of more than fifteen thousand documents gathered by the Thai and American governments (Jones 1971b: 348). But Jones's fundamental criticism was not directed at ARPA; he considered all anthropologists culpable, himself included, and argued, "Most of us who have conducted basic research in Thailand have in fact contributed to that end, we might as well have taken ARPA's money. The question of ethics and responsibility may have little to do with the source of funding and much more with the social and political context within which the data are produced" (348).

Jones described specific reports and publications focused on counterinsurgency and the control of highland populations and argued that "the more information there is available, the easier it is to develop new techniques of dealing with the people whom the government is trying to manipulate. The techniques may not be ones the social scientist himself conceives; the results may not be ones he would approve. Nevertheless, those approaches that have been developed and are being developed by the United States and Thai governments to deal with hill peoples have been aided by all of us who have done research on hill culture" (1971b: 348). Because of the political context in which this fieldwork was conducted, Jones saw a clear ethical course of action. He argued that anthropologists should "consider seriously the political implications of research and publication and cease doing both where the situation warrants" (349). Jones insisted that anthropologists needed to embrace their political values and to use their scholarly research to advance political causes they supported. This was not an anticounterinsurgency stance but one insisting that since anthropological work was being used for unintended ends, researchers should clarify their political stance and integrate it into the work they published. He wrote, "Anthropologists who wished to aid the counterinsurgency efforts of the United States in Southeast Asia should do so, and do so with conviction. Such persons can at least be respected. I would class as unethical only those who attempt to hide behind the idea of pure research while their activities aid the preservation of the status quo" (349). Jones's argument bestowed respect on anthropologists like Gerald Hickey, while damning a seeming majority of anthropologists whose silence appeared to support a belief in the neutrality of research.

While Jones's call for anthropologists to acknowledge their research as inevitably embedded within larger political processes that left them without the option of neutrality, his call for anthropologists to acknowledge their political stance helped clarify this situation, but it did not resolve problems of anthropological data being used for ends they did not approve. An anthropologist who clarified his or her anticounterinsurgency stance while continuing to report ethnographic information that could be used for counterinsurgency campaigns still left studied populations vulnerable.

Jones argued that anthropologists should cease chasing funding and publishing opportunities that advanced their careers but could endanger those they studied, arguing that "there is no longer any excuse for any of us to pretend that the results of our research are not being used to help bring about the oppression of groups. This has been the traditional role of the anthropologist, it seems" (1971b: 349).

Anthropologists on the New York Review of Books Warpath

In November 1970, Joseph Jorgensen and Eric Wolf published a lengthy analysis in the *New York Review of Books*, "Anthropology on the Warpath in Thailand," describing military and intelligence efforts to use anthropological knowledge for counterinsurgency operations in Southeast Asia, and offering an important critique of anthropology's historical connections with colonialism, military and intelligence agencies. They described the collection of identifying data on individuals and ethnic groups as a means of tracking and manipulating populations in Thailand, including proposals by the Tribal Data Center, in Chiang Mai,

Thailand to monitor villagers using village data cards. They also championed the recent work of an unnamed anthropologist (Delmos Jones) who resisted efforts to co-opt his fieldwork in Thailand for counterinsurgency programs. Jorgensen and Wolf also wrongly assumed that it was the brouhaha deriving from the Student Mobilization Committee's leaking of documents that led the unnamed Jones to take a stand against what he had seen in Thailand earlier that year (Jorgensen & Wolf 1970; Jones 1971b).

On July 22, 1971, Delmos Jones published a response to Jorgensen and Wolf's essay, clarifying that his decision to speak out against the abuses of anthropological research in Thailand was unrelated to the Student Mobilization Committee's revelations (Jones 1971a). Jones identified himself as the unnamed anthropologist described in their article and explained that he had chosen not to publish his findings because of his concerns that the military would abuse his work. Jones bristled at being cast as the hero of Jorgensen and Wolf's piece, pointing out the article's errors and mischaracterizations both large and small and ending his response by striking back at the authors, writing that "the distortions presented in the Wolf and Jorgensen article are disturbing." According to Jones, "They seized upon the more or less individual examples offered, rather than the general issues which were being discussed. The problem is not restricted to Thailand. The comments which I made about anthropologists were meant to apply to anthropologists in general, not only to those who worked in Thailand. The problem comes even closer to home as we begin to shift our attention to the study of urban areas in the United States" (1971a).

In 1973, after learning that U.S. Special Forces had translated his ethnographic writings and used them in armed campaigns, Georges Condominas acknowledged that anthropologists' writings could be used by military and intelligence agencies in ways anthropologists never intended, but he argued that Jones went too far in suggesting that anthropologists should refrain from publishing altogether. Condominas argued that anthropologists were engaging in what he termed a "double exaggeration": the first exaggeration occurred when they overestimated the military's understanding of how to use anthropological reports against local populations; the second exaggeration was the assumption that even if military or intelligence personnel learned how to exploit anthropological knowledge, it would be difficult to convince anyone within the entrenched military-intelligence bureaucracy to take action using this knowledge (Condominas 1979: 192). Condominas's second point certainly voiced a recurrent experience of many World War II anthropologists (see D. H. Price 2008a: 197).

Condominas believed anthropologists' self-deceptions came from a "lack of modesty" and that the media embraced and spread these ideas. He wrote:

> We all know how difficult it is to convince specialists even with training in the social sciences to admit the practical importance of the cultural frame in a limited program of development. It is difficult to conceive how the military, or their so-called advisors, whose creed is force, would be able to use such data on such a large scale as they fight against counterinsurgency. Even if one of them, as a technically good anthropologist having betrayed his profession, wanted to launch himself into such an operation, he would very soon be blocked by an institution as strictly structured as an army. There are of course some kinds of documents which give information useful for police operations, such as demographic data. But for that job they have no need of anthropologists; a local border police sergeant, such as those in Thailand, is more than enough. (Condominas 1979: 192)

Condominas ridiculed claims that anthropological knowledge could shift counterinsurgency operations as betraying "naïve confidence in science" and revealing a predilection for wasteful military spending (Condominas 1979: 192).

Delmos Jones's admonition that anthropologists "consider seriously the political implications of research and publication and cease doing both" (1971b: 349) to undermine the militarization of anthropological knowledge cut to the heart of Cold War anthropology's dual use problems, but it ignored the political economy that governed the lives of most anthropologists. In academic settings where struggles for tenure and promotion guide many of the contingencies regulating research and publication decisions, such an altruistic call to not publish is doomed (to abuse an evolutionary metaphor) to lead to an evolutionary dead end, as those following this ethical call for silence would inevitably be selected against. Outside the academy, applied anthropologists choosing to not write reports would face even grimmer survival prospects. As Eric Ross observed, "While anthropologists readily profess to be the advocates of the dispossessed, their theoretical tendencies nonetheless have often been in conflict with the needs of the world's poor by failing to clarify the structural sources of injustice or to endorse radical, systemic solutions" (1998a: 497).

On Good Intentions, Naiveté, and Bad Outcomes

While Hickey tried to influence American policy in Vietnam by working within the system to affect incremental change, other anthropologists used less orthodox means to direct attention to the failures of American actions. In August

1965, Marshall Sahlins paid his own way to Saigon and traveled for ten days in South Vietnam, talking with American soldiers and learning about the American presence there (Sahlins 2000a; MS to DHP 8/1/14).[8] Returning home, he published his essay "The Destruction of Conscience in Vietnam" (1966), and his reports of his interactions with some locals and U.S. and South Vietnamese military personnel broke a significant silence, as he wrote: "It is often said of South Vietnam that the day belongs to the government, the night to the 'Vietcong.' Perhaps it is better said of An Phu District that the day belongs to the Neolithic, the night to the Cold War of the mid-twentieth century" (Sahlins 2000a: 229).

Sahlins's contributions were unlike Hickey's efforts to redirect or shore up the failed American military presence by hoping for a less destructive, more effective activities; instead, Sahlins found a corruption of mission so pervasive that regardless of individual intentions, no good outcome could be achieved in a war requiring that the conscience of those fighting "must be destroyed" (2000a: 248). Sahlins understood the intentions of those trying to diminish the impact of the war to be admirable, writing that "the motivation and dedication of American AID people is beyond question and not at issue. Many, I understand, work tirelessly under dangerous conditions to bring a modicum of betterment to the countryside. Likewise the small Special Forces detachment I saw at An Phu was committed to a program of medical and economic aid for the people — the Peace Corps of the War Corps. But these slim measures of good intention have to be put in the balance against the huge, unplanned subsidization of decadence in the cities to determine a final reading on the American presence" (237).

Jones's stance was perhaps even more radical than Sahlins's as his analysis questioned the responsibility of all anthropologists who made their work public. Jones and Hickey offered stark choices to anthropologists with needed expertise during times of war, a choice between either blind optimism that individuals can redirect institutional uses of knowledge or maintain a state of recalcitrant skeptical silence. Hickey believed he could steer the military straight; Jones believed that military and intelligence agencies would rob his and other anthropologists' work for their own ends and that he had no control over these uses. Hickey's memoir chronicled how his reports were used only in selective ways or ignored, yet he did not adequately consider the possibility that structural dynamics governing the military's consumption of anthropological knowledge necessarily led to such outcomes — unless anthropologists front-load their assumptions to meet with military culture, a tendency that often seems to increase over time. Hickey acknowledged that these structural dynamics are rooted in the forms of military and civilian decision making but they also derive from the deeper contingencies bred within forms of warfare in neocolonial states seeking to suppress occupied insurgents.

Hickey was a slow learner. Over the course of a decade he was unable to acknowledge that the larger forces unleashed when he and other anthropologists engaged with military decision makers doomed his ability to control how ethnographic reports would be used. Hickey's cameo in *The Quiet American* leaves us with an ironic moment for viewing his contributions to American military and intelligence policies over the dozen years that followed his film debut, but this afterimage also portrays him as having an early awareness of Graham Greene's critique of the CIA's interventions and intentions in Vietnam. Hickey appears as a tragic figure — but *why* he is tragic changes with different readings. One can read him as a martyr or a willfully ignorant, tragic hero, or as naive, self-serving, or uncaring, but there is no reason for contemporary anthropologists to not learn from his experiences. Some might claim the moral of Hickey's story is that we must work harder to make the military understand what anthropology has to offer, but such an interpretation ignores the importance of institutional culture and the possibility of larger contingencies governing the use of military knowledge. One lesson from Hickey's years trying to protect groups with his failed efforts to redirect American military actions is that in the last instance, motivations can have little impact on outcomes. As Graham Greene's narrator Thomas Fowler said of Alden Pyle, "I never knew a man who had better motives for all the trouble he caused" (1955: 60).

> The days of naïve anthropology are over. It is no longer adequate to collect information about little known and powerless people; one needs to know also the uses to which that knowledge can be put.
>
> JOSEPH JORGENSEN AND ERIC WOLF | 1970

THIRTEEN ANTHROPOLOGISTS FOR RADICAL POLITICAL ACTION AND REVOLUTION WITHIN THE AAA

By the mid-1960s, American anthropologists were at the forefront of growing movements on American campuses to stop the war in Vietnam. In March 1965, Marshall Sahlins led the movement to establish the first teach-in against the war in Vietnam on the campus of the University of Michigan. This was a precipitous cultural moment of anarchic simplicity and power, loosely bringing together scholars with relevant perspectives on the war and American militarism and a large audience hungering for critique. The moment spread like wildfire. "Within weeks of the first teach-in at Michigan," according to Sahlins, "there were over 100 such events in colleges and universities across the country, culminating in mid-May with an all-day National Teach-In in Washington, DC" (2009: 4). Whatever lessons of conformity, silence, and disengagement had been imparted to anthropologist-activists in the 1950s were quickly set aside, as anthropologists became central figures in radical critiques of militarism and the war in Vietnam and played central roles in campus uprisings and national debates (Sanjek 1995; Gough 1968; D. H. Price 2004b: 306–40).

Within the American Anthropological Association, the establishment of the Radical Caucus in 1967 brought the association a firm critical voice, yet until a change was made in the bylaws in 1969, the graduate students who were developing this voice were disenfranchised from voting on association business.[1] The Radical Caucus and, later, Anthropologists for Radical Political Action organized an impressive collection of sessions at AAA meetings in the late 1960s and early 1970s focusing on themes of liberation, anthropological praxis, Marxist theory, and colonial critiques. The AAA's 1969 business meeting demonstrated the power of the Radical Caucus, as members adopted eighteen resolutions, all of which were later ratified in a mail vote (D. H. Price 2008b).

In ratifying the Radical Caucus's 1969 slate of resolutions, the membership supported the following: an investigation of uses made of U.S. arms sent to Latin America (passed by a vote of 1,450 to 573); "developing sanctions against discrimination based on sex" (passed, 1,367 to 633); and Karen Sacks's resolutions that "members shall not engage in secret or classified Research" (passed, 1,077 to 941) and that "field workers shall not divulge information about informants that might endanger their well-being or cultural integrity" (passed, 1,607 to 433) (NAAA 1970 11[6]: 1; NAAA 1970 11[1]: 7). Other resolutions, presented in table 13.1, offered moral support to Alaskan natives in land disputes, took a stand against sex discrimination, and opposed the construction of California's Dos Rios Dam (see NAAA 1970 11[1]: 7; NAAA 1970 11[6]: 1).

While the membership's votes demonstrated that the Radical Caucus's political stances represented a disciplinary norm, these positions were not generally shared by the association's established power base. This schism would come to dominate the dramas to be acted out at the association council meetings in the late 1960s and early 1970s. The AAA leadership's narrative during this period conjured up visions of an undemocratic mob hijacking control of council meetings, while the views of a claimed silent majority of members were not present. But the mail votes of the wider membership in 1969, 1970, 1971, and later demonstrated that when AAA voting members were able to vote on a full docket of radical propositions, they adopted nearly every radical resolution that they had the opportunity to consider.

The Thai Affair

The Student Mobilizer was an "underground" tabloid-size paper published by the national organization, the Student Mobilization Committee to End the War in Vietnam (SMC). The April 2, 1970, cover of the *Mobilizer* proclaimed, "Counterinsurgency Research on Campus EXPOSED," referring to the title of a sixteen-hundred-word exposé based on documents stolen from the UCLA office of anthropologist Michael Moerman. These stolen documents detailed the work of Moerman and three other anthropologists (Herbert Phillips, Steven Piker, and Lauriston Sharp) on ARPA-sponsored counterinsurgency research projects in Thailand, and of the Academic Advisory Committee for Thailand (AACT), USAID, SEADAG, and other organizations. Other *Student Mobilizer*

TABLE 13.1 AAA Resolutions Ratified in 1969 (Source: NAAA 1970 11[6]:1)

1.	Recognition of the legitimacy and importance of research and training in contemporary American Society (1,962 to 1,360).
2.	Recruiting into anthropology members of minority groups (1,847 to 233).
3.	Continuing support of UNESCO (2,030 to 67).
4.	Endorsing the academic freedom and tenure statements of the AAUP and CAUT (1,962 to 123).
5.	Urging just and equitable settlement in the native Alaskan land claims (1,945 to 143).
6.	Demanding investigation of uses made of U.S. arms to Latin America (1,450 to 573).
7.	Urging moral support and professional skills be offered to the Alaskan natives in their land claims (1,971 to 121).
8.	Urging endorsement of the 10-point resolution prepared for the Experimental Session on Women in the Professions (1,231 to 741).
9.	Resolving that the AAA go on record against sex discrimination (1,816 to 260).
10.	Establishing a committee to collect and publish data and to take action on all cases of sex discrimination in anthropology (1,370 to 662).
11.	Publishing data on sex ratios in positions in anthropology in the *Newsletter of the American Anthropological Association* (1,453 to 586).
12.	Developing sanctions against discrimination based on sex (1,367 to 633).
13.	Resolving that AAA members shall not engage in secret or classified research (1,077 to 941).
14.	Resolving that fieldworkers shall not divulge information about informants that might endanger their well-being or cultural integrity (1,607 to 433).
15.	Condemning Jensen's article on racial differences in intelligence (1,795 to 239).
16.	Requesting all anthropologists to use all available media outlets to inform the public on the correct facts of human variability and that reports on such activity be included in a special section in the *Newsletter* (1,803 to 218).
17.	Opposing construction of the Dos Rios dam and its subsequent destruction of human values (1,789 to 171).

articles focused on SEADAG membership, the role of Abt Associates in Project Agile, ending campus-based counterinsurgency research, Michigan State University's past role in Vietnam counterinsurgency research, USAID's role in Thailand, and a geographic listing of Thai experts at American universities (*Mobilizer* 1970).

The stolen documents were quoted at length in the *Mobilizer* and showed how the Defense Department's ARPA used anthropologists and other social scientists to improve the military's understanding of the cultural groups it sought to control in rural Thailand (*Mobilizer* 1970: 3). The *Mobilizer* printed excerpts from a 1967 letter by Herbert Phillips complaining about the poor quality of ARPA social science, which was conducted by "only two professionally trained anthropologists" and a collection of people with bachelor's degrees in subjects such as physics or public administration taking the title of anthropologists, "to provide them with a veneer of legitimacy." Phillips estimated that "there are about eight of these pseudoanthropologists in the entire ARPA project" (*Mobilizer* 1970: 26).

The *Mobilizer's* published documents did not show these anthropologists walking in lockstep with the military. In a letter that Phillips sent to anthropologist William Rittenberg on May 1, 1967, Phillips wrote, "There is little that is particularly secretive, earth-shaking, or CIA'ish about ARPA activities; most of their people are intelligent, but bumbling American bureaucrats trying to obtain basic descriptive materials on aspects of Thai society" (*Mobilizer* 1970: 26). In this 1967 letter Phillips worried about ARPA hiring fake "anthropologists" and about the ineffectiveness of ARPA's governmental bureaucracy, arguing that "there is little that we, as scholars, can do about it, unless we choose to become applied anthropologists or advisors to ARPA — a position that is not without its professional and moral dilemmas, but one that does involve more intellectual and moral responsibility than sitting on the sidelines and simply condemning ARPA for its immorality or ineffectiveness" (*Mobilizer* 1970: 26). These documents showed USAID, ARPA, and AACT buying access to Piker, Moerman, Sharp, and Phillips, as well as economists, political scientists, and geographers, to gain their expertise for Thai counterinsurgency programs operating under euphemisms like "village security" programs. Whether this purchased access meaningfully altered American interactions with Thai populations, or simply addressed the legitimacy concerns raised by Phillips and others that these agencies were only using fake "anthropologists" was open to interpretation; but the revelations of these anthropologists' interactions with these appendages of America's intelligence apparatus shocked the discipline.

The SMC held a press conference in San Francisco and read from a telegram, sent on April 1 by Marshall Sahlins and Eric Wolf, and a statement by Gerald Berreman condemning anthropological contributions to counterinsurgency (EBW, MM to GF 4/24/70). Because Wolf and Berreman were members of the AAA Committee on Ethics, these early condemnations soon became the focus of criticism by the accused anthropologists and their supporters.

On April 3, 1970, in his role as chair of the AAA's Committee on Ethics, Eric Wolf sent letters of inquiry to Michael Moerman, Herbert Phillips, Lauriston Sharp, and Steven Piker informing them that he and Joseph Jorgensen had seen "a number of documents bearing on the involvement of anthropologists in secret research." Wolf informed these individuals that their names appeared on these documents and that the Committee on Ethics was investigating this matter. Wolf wrote that the committee would "deal with cases on as anonymous a basis as possible" and that it was making efforts to "develop an approach to cases without penalizing any individuals." He invited them to make statements "especially in view of the past resolutions of our Association on the subject of clandestine research and restricted, non-public publication of research results" (EBW, EBW to MM 4/3/70).

While the letters sent to these anthropologists were identical, there were some variations in the responses Wolf received. Moerman responded with outrage, others with a tone of personal hurt, having been attacked in the press before receiving Wolf's letter. Each argued that *The Student Mobilizer*'s uses of quotes without context created the false impression that their interactions with ARPA assisted nefarious governmental actions in Southeast Asia. They were angry that others did not interpret their actions as efforts to correct misguided military acts.

The Accused Respond

Moerman wrote Wolf of his unease about how to address him or Sahlins. Moerman knew them as his former professors and friends but now found them "behaving inhumanely . . . and unprofessionally" toward him (EBW, MM to EBW 4/8/70). He insisted he had done nothing against the AAA's Code of Ethics and believed that the telegram to the *Mobilizer* indicated he had been prejudged as guilty. Moerman viewed Sahlins and Wolf's sending the telegram as unprofessional conduct, and he accused Wolf of acting in collusion with the *Mobilizer* (EBW, MM to EBW 4/8/70). Wolf wrote Moerman that on March 30, he and Jorgensen had received copies of the documents later published in the *Mobilizer* and that after reading these, they responded to the ethical implications of this work in a message to the newspaper. Wolf stressed that he had not identified any individuals in his comments to the *Mobilizer*, and that he had no connection to the publication or control over what it published (EBW, EBW to MM 4/14/70).

On April 10, 1970, Charles Keyes circulated a sixteen-hundred word statement to colleagues, explaining both the circumstances under which his name had appeared in *The Student Mobilizer* article and his involvement with SEADAG. He indicated that his research in Thailand was funded by the Ford Foundation's Foreign Area Fellowship program and the NSF, not by the military. Keyes had joined SEADAG to voice concerns about U.S. policies in circles that included policy makers. With time he "grew disillusioned with SEADAG owing to the fact that its structure and leadership have prevented it from being such a forum," and he had not participated in any SEADAG activities for three years (ST 62, 8, 4/10/70). Keyes came to understand that policy makers tended to ignore critiques from scholars not aligned with their preconceptions or with U.S. policies. But Keyes did not completely withdraw from his engagement with USAID policy groups; after disengaging with SEADAG, in early 1968 he joined USAID's Academic Advisory Council for Thailand. Keyes wrote that he had no idea that AACT was involved in counterinsurgency operations until he attended a recent Association for Asian Studies meeting — where he had learned the Regents of the University of California had authorized AACT-USAID counterinsurgency work (ST 62, 8, 4/10/70).

Keyes wrote that he and other AACT members were never asked to contribute to Thai counterinsurgency operations, and that all proceedings of AACT were open to the public and reported in the *Newsletter of the Association of Asian Studies*. He explained that his only interaction with ARPA had occurred in January 1967 when he traveled to Washington, DC,

> to protest the allocation of extremely large sums of money for social science research on counterinsurgency in Thailand. As a result of that meeting, I realized that ARPA was unwilling to reconsider its decision to undertake the work it had projected and thus I wrote to my colleagues warning them that ARPA research was of such a scale that no scholar undertaking field work in Thailand would be able to leave it out of account. *My worst fears have subsequently been realized as it is now apparent that all research by Americans in Thailand has been seriously compromised by the fact that the greatest proportion of research funds spent by Americans in Thailand and the largest number of American researchers involved there have been connected with agencies whose aim it is to further the objectives of counterinsurgency programs*. (ST 62, 8, 4/10/70, emphasis added)

Keyes was concerned about the "size and character of the American presence in Thailand," and he expressed his opposition to counterinsurgency research.

Herbert Phillips wrote angry replies to Wolf (EBW HP to EBW 4/5/70; 4/6/70) and Berreman (EBW HP to GB 4/4/70). After Wolf replied in a lengthy circumspect letter (EBW EBW to HP 4/12/70), Phillips adopted a more measured tone, but he continued to call for Wolf's, Berreman's, and Jorgensen's resignations (EBW HP TO EBW 4/16/70). Phillips complained that he had not seen a copy of the documents taken from Moerman's office until May 19, 1970, and that he had to request these from the committee (EBW, HP to AAA Committee on Ethics 5/19/70). Phillips stressed there was nothing secret about ARPA's relationship with anthropologists working in Thailand, and that "any social scientist who has been in Thailand for a week knows about the role that ARPA — with its annual budget of 5–12 million dollars — plays in subverting the purpose and direction of social science research in that country" (EBW, HP to AAA Committee on Ethics 5/19/70). Phillips told Wolf that he had overstepped his role as chair of the Committee on Ethics and asked him to resign from the committee (EBW, HP to EBW, 4/5/70); he also chided the committee, writing that "if this is the way you treat your informants in the field, God help the anthropological profession" (EBW, HP to AAA Committee on Ethics 5/19/70).

Steven Piker's response to Wolf was calm and nonthreatening (EBW; SP to EBW 4/6/70). Piker replied that he was "happy ... to make known to your committee — and anyone else who might inquire — the specifics of all research and professional work generally in which I have been involved since my association with anthropology began more than ten years ago" (EBW, SP to EBW 4/6/70). To demonstrate his long-standing opposition to American militarism in Southeast Asia, Piker mailed Wolf two academic papers, from 1966 and 1969, voicing his opposition to U.S. military policy in Vietnam and Thailand (EBW, SP to EBW 4/6/70).

On April 8, 1970, Lauriston Sharp sent a memo, titled "Allegations of Professional Impropriety," to the officers of Cornell University and sent carbon copies to a large group of colleagues (ST 62, 8, 4/8/70). Sharp wrote that the "scholarly integrity" of AACT had recently been attacked in *The Student Mobilizer*, making charges that

> AACT conducts, organizes, coordinates, and initiates "counterinsurgency" research on Thailand according to the needs of the Agency for International Development, that its members work "secretly (or semi-secretly) serving as instruments of counterinsurgency programs in Thailand," and that it has "been employed by the United States government as part of a counterinsurgency program directed

against revolution in the Kingdom of Thailand." Charges that AACT in pursuit of its alleged "counterinsurgency" interest improperly intervened in the scholarly meetings of the Association of Asian Studies on April 3, 1970, were rejected by the A.A.S. Program Committee and received and not acted on by the Board of Directors. (ST 62, 8, 4/8/70)

Sharp's enclosed documents described the work undertaken by AACT, as well as copies of *The Student Mobilizer* article and an AACT reply to a *New York Times* story on AACT (see NYT 1970, for original story).

Sharp asked colleagues to examine "selected excerpts from some of the purloined documents as published in *The Student Mobilizer* on April 2, 1970, of which I unfortunately purchased only two copies at the Association for Asian Studies and Committee of Concerned Sian Scholars meeting in San Francisco last week," as well as an AACT press release and other AACT documents (ST 62, 8, 4/9/70). Answering accusations that he and others at AACT had engaged in clandestine activities, Sharp explained that after checking with others attending this meeting, he had confirmed that there were no reports issued (ST 62, 8, 4/9/70). He acknowledged that he was a member of the American Institute for Research, which he described as "a private organization which, I believe, had done classified research in Thailand for ARPA and the Department of Defense, but with which I have never had any communication whatsoever" (ST 62, 8, 4/9/70).

Sharp sent a memo to colleagues across the country. After quoting from passages published in *The Student Mobilizer* claiming that he and AACT engaged in "secret" or "semi-secret" counterinsurgency research, Sharp complained that "nowhere is the term 'counterinsurgency' defined." Sharp conceded that AACT did "advise and consult with staff of the Agency for International Development who are concerned with Thailand," but he clarified that none of this research dealt with "banditry, terrorism, or insurgency" (ST 62, 8, 4/10/70). Sharp claimed that his work with AACT "is totally unlike another kind of relationship in which universities undertook contracts to provide technical assistance directly," specifying that arrangements with AACT were not like "Michigan State University's famous Vietnam Public Administration Institute contract" or Cornell's work in the Philippines. He explained that AACT was a problem-oriented research group drawing on scholars' expertise as part of "U.S. non-military assistance to Thailand" to share information about development for Thailand.

In his memo, Sharp argued this was an innocent study group, completely unconnected with the counterinsurgency campaigns of the wars of Southeast Asia, as if aid programs themselves existed outside of a specific geopolitical framework. He assured colleagues that instead of working on military counterinsurgency operations, "AACT is dealing with problems of agricultural production, land tenure, education, regionalism in North Thailand, population increase, urbanization and the urban-rural gap, investment, and means for supporting more research by Thai in Thailand" (ST 62, 8, 4/10/70). But claims that these development projects in Northern Thailand were removed from the context of counterinsurgency rang false to many anthropologists.

Sharp maintained that none of this research was hidden from the public and that had SMC "been more patient, we would have gladly sent them a full report of this conference published in English and Thai" (ST 62, 8, 4/10/70). He acknowledged that this conference included issues of civil security in isolated villages but claimed that in its "eagerness to depict AACT as sinister," SMC "concludes gratuitously that 'security in this context is really counter insurgency'" (ST 62, 8, 4/10/70).

Because AACT worked with groups with names similar to those recently identified as working with the CIA (e.g., Sharp mentioned AACT's association with the "Asia Society" being confused with the exposed CIA-linked "Asia Foundation"), Sharp argued, it was being accused of "guilt by association."[2] He believed the false claims that AACT did Pentagon research created an "argument as vicious and spurious as any concocted by the late Senator Joseph McCarthy" (ST 62, 8, 4/10/70). Sharp made no effort to distance himself or AACT from USAID's work in Thailand and stated that AACT members "judge its work to be benevolent and on the whole beneficent and wanted by most Thai" (ST 62, 8, 4/10/70). He stressed that AACT had "complete control over their own work," and assured his colleagues that there had "been no improper conduct as defined by my conscience or by the AAA 1967 'Statement on Ethics.'" He explained that he had been "moved to work with AACT" by an interest in seeing if academic knowledge could improve policy, stressing his personal admiration of the Thai people (ST 62, 8, 4/10/70).

Sharp mailed Wolf memos he had sent to colleagues at Cornell in the aftermath of the *Mobilizer* article's revelations. He pointed out several errors in the article (including claims that Sharp had been at a meeting in Bangkok in June and July 1969) and objected to efforts to not differentiate between SEADAG, AACT, and ARPA work and the CIA and other Pentagon programs (EBW, LS to Cornell Anth. 4/9/70). Sharp asked Wolf, Jorgensen, and Berreman to resign from the Committee on Ethics and then to either make specific documented allegations or issue an apology (EBW, LS to EBW 4/17/70).

Questions of Which Party Engaged in Misconduct

Moerman, Phillips, Piker, and Sharp each wrote AAA president George Foster, arguing that if any wrongdoing was to be investigated by the AAA, it should be the behavior of Wolf, Berreman, and Jorgensen, not any accusations against themselves. Sharp wrote President Foster on May 8, 1970, that he would not cooperate with the Committee on Ethics given Wolf's and other committee members' "slanders." He requested that Foster appoint an AAA ad hoc committee to investigate Wolf's, Jorgensen's, and Berreman's unethical behavior (EBW, LS to GF 5/8/70).

Michael Moerman sent President Foster a thirteen-page letter requesting the appointment of an ad hoc committee to investigate the conduct of Wolf, Berreman, Jorgensen, and Sahlins, claiming that "a kangaroo court has been loosed on the profession, and we were only the first to be kicked" (EBW, MM to GF 4/24/70). Moerman explained that once he saw the actual documents,

> it was clear that my files had been stolen — no difficult task since the papers were all personal, and not "secret" in any official sense and since the University cabinet in which they were stored has no lock. That same evening I learned the last name of the man who had first presented my papers to the SMC. His name was the same as that of a married graduate student who had worked for me as a typist under my NSF grant from 12 June to 13 March and who had quit just before I was about to fire her.... Since I had hired and retained this student (whose formal MA committee chairman I had been) only because a colleague had recommended her and because she pled poverty, my suspicions of her (since confirmed) made me feel that I had been used and my trust (I supervised neither her activities nor the honesty of her time-reports) abused. The instantaneous corruption of trust caused by the smear tactics that have been used is also suggested by the suspicions that Phillips and Wilson, long-time friends, had of me. (EBW, MM to GF 4/24/70)

Moerman called for Wolf's, Berreman's, and Jorgensen's resignations, arguing that "since I am accusing about half of the Ethics Committee of unethical behavior, it is clear that the Ethics Committee is not the arena for hearing my charge." He worried that many other documents might have been stolen from his office, some of which could be misinterpreted in a bad light, and that if he made statements about the limits of his work, some forgotten exception could impeach his claims.

Moerman claimed to have evidence that a Committee on Ethics member was part of a conspiracy in which he "knew the kind of case which SMC was assembling, offered to fund it, and is sufficiently a party to these operations to be told where the next files have been stolen from and to be sent copies of them. It is a charming slogan, 'Even paranoids have enemies'" (EBW, MM to GF 4/24/70).[3] Moerman sent a copy of a letter to Foster that he claimed supported this assertion, but soon Moerman dropped this claim from his litany of arguments.[4]

In April 1970, President Foster asked Ralph Beals whether the actions of Keyes, Moerman, Phillips, Piker, and Sharp were improper under the standards Beals identified in the Statement on Problems of Anthropological Research and Ethics (SPARE), which the AAA had adopted in 1967. Beals replied that because this work was not clandestine, he did not identify specific activities as violating SPARE's principles (Wakin 1992: 183). Beals wrote that it was an individual decision whether or not an anthropologist contribute to governmental programs, and he indicated that Wolf, Jorgensen, and Berreman had acted unethically in speaking out as members of the Committee on Ethics and should resign from the committee (183–84).

Public Discourse in the AAA Newsletter and Beyond

In the June 1970 issue of the *AAA Fellow Newsletter*, the Executive Board provided a summary of the purloined documents published in the *Student Mobilizer* and shared concerns raised by two of the (unidentified) professors who feared "their professional reputations have been adversely affected" and who questioned "the propriety of the action of two Ethics Committee members in this matter." The Executive Board reaffirmed the AAA's SPARE document from 1967 and the association's recently adopted resolutions prohibiting "secret or classified research" and research that "might endanger [the] well-being or cultural integrity" of studied populations. The board wrote that Wolf's and Jorgensen's actions "went beyond the mandate of the Executive Board" to the Committee on Ethics, and it admonished the committee to stick to its charge and clarified that personal statements must not be confused with official positions (*AAAFN* 1970 11[6]: 10).

Wolf and Jorgensen responded to the board's criticisms by providing additional information about the documents they received from the *Mobilizer* (NAAA 1970 11[7]: 2). Their response itemized the documents they received, listing minutes of the JASON group, an ARPA counterinsurgency proposal, a 1969 report of a visit to rural Thai villages, a USAID contract, meeting agendas, and minutes. They wrote that because these documents contradicted the AAA's resolution opposing clandestine and secret research, "we feel that they raise the most serious issues for the scientific integrity of our profession." They rejected most of the Executive Board's claims about process and clarified they had not indiscriminately circulated documents (*NAAA* 1970 11[7]: 2). Wolf and Jorgensen stressed that this counterinsurgency research conflicted with the ethical principles identified in Beals's 1967 statement and adopted by the association, and they presented examples of their correspondence.

Frustrated that the Executive Board so narrowly interpreted the Committee on Ethic's charge, Wolf and Jorgensen stressed that while the board was trying to avert conflict, limiting the committee's activities and chastising Wolf and Jorgensen created more conflict. Because of the board's actions, Wolf and Jorgensen closed their letter by resigning from the Committee on Ethics (*NAAA* 1970 11[7]: 19).

The *Newsletter of the AAA* published a letter from David Aberle registering his misgivings over the Executive Board's criticisms of Wolf and Jorgensen. As a board member and the board's liaison with the Committee on Ethics, Aberle had been a part of the board's discussions leading to its criticism of Wolf and Jorgensen while ignoring the problems of anthropologists working for ARPA in Thailand. In frustration, Aberle resigned as the board's liaison with the committee (*NAAA* 1970 11[7]: 19).

The *Newsletter* carried angry letters representing a broad spectrum of members' views, making arguments about ethics, politics, process, fascism, and totalitarianism; one even (mistakenly) claimed that Eric Wolf's book *Peasants* contained a photograph produced by a Soviet propaganda agency (*NAAA* 1970 11[8]: 12). In one letter, Robert Ehrich sounded an alarm that Berreman could win the upcoming AAA presidential election if he split the establishment vote with the three establishment candidates (Albert Spaulding, James Spuhler, and Anthony Wallace) all remaining in the election *(NAAA* 1970 11[7]: 22). The next issue of the *Newsletter* carried an announcement that Spaulding and Spuhler had withdrawn their candidacy (*NAAA* 1970 11[8]: 1). As discussed in the previous chapter, Jorgensen and Wolf raised the public profile of this crisis by publishing "Anthropology on the Warpath in Thailand" in the November 19, 1970, issue of the *New York Review of Books*.

In the November *Newsletter*, David Schneider and David Aberle published (as a "minority report") a lengthy resolution that they had submitted to the Executive Board at its October meeting, but which had failed to garner board support. Their resolution called for the establishment of a fact-finding committee to investigate claims that anthropologists were assisting counterinsurgency campaigns in Thailand, in violation of the AAA's expressed position in the 1967 Beals statement. Some of the accused used the *Newsletter* as a platform for defending themselves. Herbert Phillips attacked the Committee on Ethics in the *Newsletter*, claiming it had "misinformed the membership" and forfeited claims of impartiality (NAAA 1971 12[1]: 2, 7–9). Moerman explained he had been a USAID consultant from 1964 to 1970, out of a conviction that American policy in Thailand was based on ignorance and he wished to improve it (NAAA 1971 12[1]: 9–11). He described his work on USAID's ARD program not as counterinsurgency but as development work, and he explained that his work with JASON (at an unclassified meeting) was an effort to add some understanding of the complex environment in which foreign aid was being directed (NAAA 1971 12[1]: 10).

The 1970 annual report of the Committee on Ethics stated that Wolf had acted properly in calling for more information after he received documents from *The Student Mobilizer*. It found Wolf's statements as a private citizen were appropriate and concluded that "acting as a body, we therefore gave our unanimous support and endorsement to Wolf and Jorgensen at our May 2 meeting, transmitting the first resolution" (NAAA 1970 11[9]: 12). The report's Appendix A was the committee's proposed Principles of Professional Responsibility (PPR).

At the 1970 AAA annual council meeting, the Radical Caucus maintained a forceful presence, passing thirteen resolutions, including ones from Radical Caucus members on gay rights, the status of women, and the treatment of Brazilian Indians.[5] One adopted resolution required the Executive Board to adopt the resolution that Schneider and Aberle initially had failed to pass within the Executive Board (subsequently published in the *Newsletter*) calling for the formation of an ad hoc committee to investigate the Thai affair. In response to this motion adopted at the council meeting, the Executive Board adopted a motion calling for the "establishment of an ad hoc committee of inquiry to deal with the controversy over research and other activities of United States anthropologists in Thailand and their implications for anthropology as a profession and for anthropological research throughout the world" (NAAA 1971 12[1]: 1). The motion clearly stated that the ad hoc committee's charge was to investigate controversies involving U.S. anthropologists working in Thailand; it did not charge the committee with investigating the actions of Wolf, Jorgensen, or the AAA Committee on Ethics — yet the Executive Board would soon take actions to subvert this democratically approved resolution, leading to this result.

Heading toward the Mead Committee

George Foster and most of the Executive Board represented the discipline's older generation, a group that largely opposed the sort of antiwar militancy that Wolf, Sahlins, and many younger anthropologists advocated.[6] Had Foster charged a task force with investigating the propriety of Wolf's, Berreman's, and Jorgensen's actions, there would have been a significant uproar from the AAA's increasingly organized and activist radical members. When Foster first charged the ad hoc committee, its instructions were broad and phrased in such a way that it appeared the committee would primarily investigate the ethical propriety of anthropologists assisting counterinsurgency operations in Southeast Asia. At its February 1971 meeting, the Executive Board decided the inquiry charge endorsed at the 1970 council meeting would have prohibitive costs due to the need to hire attorneys and gather testimony, and the board modified the description of, and charge for, the committee (NAAA 1971 12[3]: 1).

The new charge instructed the committee to use primarily existing documentation, requesting additional written statements as needed from designated parties. The committee was also instructed to "determine what, if any, aspects of these activities violated the principles of that 1967 statement or subsequent resolutions pertaining to ethics and professional conduct passed by the Association" (NAAA 1971 12[3]: 1). The committee was now also charged with investigating the conduct of members of the Committee on Ethics. It was to "prepare a report to the Board for release to members of the Association"; this report was to summarize findings and make recommendations (NAAA 1971 12[3]: 1, 6–7). The committee was to consider whether the approved 1967 ethics statements (SPARE), as well as the pending Code of Professional Conduct (which would become the previously mentioned PPR), had been violated (see Wakin 1992: 202–3). By revising the charge, Foster cleared the way for Mead's committee to attack Berreman, Jorgensen, and Wolf while ignoring the ethical questions raised by anthropologists working on counterinsurgency projects.

The anthropologists appointed to the AAA's Ad Hoc Committee to Evaluate the Controversy Concerning Anthropological Activities in Thailand were Margaret Mead (chair), David L. Olmstead, William H. Davenport, and Ruth S. Freed (executive secretary); the *Newsletter* carried an announcement requesting anyone with pertinent information to send it to Ruth Freed (NAAA 1971 12[4]: 1). The ad hoc committee requested that the *Newsletter* stop publishing letters on the Thai controversy and that all such letters instead be diverted to the committee. The editors of the *Newsletter* cooperated and notified its readers of this decision (NAAA 1971 12[6]: 2).

Mead's committee received a wealth of correspondence and statements from anthropologists working in governmental settings and from opponents to military-linked anthropological work, and its members read a range of published documents and critiques (AAAP 328). The committee submitted its report to the Executive Board in September 1971, requesting that the board not release it to the AAA membership until after the annual meeting in November. When board member David Aberle objected to this request, he was told by the AAA executive director that should he or anyone else leak their copy of the report, they would be detected because "there were distinct mistakes on each copy to allow for the tracing of leaks" (Wakin 1992: 204). Aberle continued to pressure the board to officially release the document to AAA members, and it was only mailed to the membership in the weeks before the annual November meeting (Wakin 1992: 204).

The ad hoc committee's report had two sections; the first covered "anthropological activities in Thailand," and the second offered "guidelines on future policy."[7] The report acknowledged that all members of the ad hoc committee found the Indochina war to be "unconstitutional, unwise, and unnecessary," but the committee did not find the activities of the accused anthropologist consultants to be unethical under either the AAA's SPARE or the proposed PPR. The report described a range of "optimistic" consultancy relationships of anthropologists working with organizations such as USAID, SEADAG, and AACT but found these to not be secret or clandestine relationships. The committee stressed that none of the stolen documents printed in the *Mobilizer* were classified as secret. As acknowledged in the report:

> It is very likely that secret and clandestine intelligence work among Thai people has been conducted at the instigation of special U.S. military and government intelligence units. The ad hoc committee has no information about such covert work, nor could it be expected to have. The committee has been informed about some American anthropologists who have been approached with proposals that they engage in such intelligence activity and who report that the proposals were refused. We mention this only in order clearly to distinguish such clandestine intelligence from the applied anthropology or mission-oriented research and consultation that American anthropologists, as well as anthropologists from other countries, have openly pursued. (qtd. in Wakin 1992: 288)

The committee explicitly rejected the premise that anthropological contributions to war zone counterinsurgency operations are "sinister" (288). The report described American academia's historical problems with McCarthyism, anti-intellectualism, and other factors that limited the availability of nondirective governmental research funds. There instead developed problem-related research funds from governmental agencies focusing on contemporary issues such as "communications" or "mental health" that provided funds for the problems of an era.

The report argued that community development and counterinsurgency were simply the contemporary issues providing funding opportunities for anthropologists. It noted that while anthropological contributions to community development or rural public health projects were counterinsurgent insofar as they reduced the likelihood of revolutionary uprisings "such activity is well within the traditional canons of acceptable behavior for the applied anthropologist, and is counterinsurgent only for present funding purposes; a decade ago it might have been 'mental health'" (qtd. in Wakin 1992: 289). The report also argued that soft power anthropological contributions to military operations were all part of applied anthropologists' historical legacy and therefore were not to be judged as ethical violations regardless of their contributions to military actions. This historical argument was used to normalize counterinsurgency work, and instead of questioning the ethical nature of this past work, the present was excused without critical examination.

The report stressed that all anthropologists need to be aware of the dangers that their work could be reused by others for military action, citing the Tribal Research Centre at Chieng Mai as a possible example of how centralized files could be used for targeted military strikes (qtd. in Wakin 1992: 290).

The committee reserved its criticism for the unnamed members of the Committee on Ethics (Berreman, Jorgensen, and Wolf) who had publicly criticized the anthropologists identified in *The Student Mobilizer* and other documents. The report found their "unauthorized identification of themselves as members of [the ethics] committee in connection with their public denunciations," their use of stolen documents, and accusations without due process to be "reprehensible" (qtd. in Wakin 1992: 291). The report's conclusions exonerated the anthropologists contributing to counterinsurgency projects of any wrongdoing but found members of the Committee on Ethics to have "acted hastily, unfairly, and unwisely in making public statements" (293).

The Mead Committee understood that the report would generate controversy among the AAA membership, and when its efforts to suppress the public distribution of the report failed, the stage was set for a public showdown. Since the 1968 meeting, there had been a broad coalition of radical members who organized before and during the annual meetings and, despite earlier association rules limiting the political participation of younger members, to use organization skills and their numbers to make their voices heard.

The 1971 AAA Council Meeting

Eric Wolf contacted anthropologist Richard Lee in the months leading up to the 1971 AAA annual meeting. Wolf was upset that the Mead Committee's report found more fault with Wolf and Jorgensen than it did with the anthropologists who contributed to counterinsurgency projects, and he asked Lee to "organize colleagues to lead a floor fight at the business meeting raising objections to the Mead Report's equal apportioning of blame" (Lee 2008: 1). Lee joined forces with anthropologist Steve Barnett and others to organize opposition to Mead's report at the meeting.[8]

At the November 19, 1971, AAA council meeting at the New York Hilton Hotel, Wolf and Jorgensen passed out a lengthy rebuttal statement to attendees.[9] Their statement disagreed with the Mead Report's characterization of their work and findings, and they objected to the report's claim that the operations of anthropologists in Thailand were "well within traditional canons of acceptable behavior for the applied anthropologist." They rejected the claim that "counterinsurgency" was merely a trendy buzzword for funding, and that it had no more necessary links to military or intelligence research than did "mental health" or "communication" research in earlier decades.[10] They were "appalled by the degree to which the committee tries to disguise human and cultural realities through the use of an Orwellian language which turns phenomena into their very opposites. We are as much dismayed by the callousness of the report as by its factual and theoretical faults" (NAAA 1972 13[1]: 3).

The day before the council meeting, the Executive Board officially accepted (without approving or rejecting) the committee's report. When the discussion of the report came forward at the council meeting, Mead asked that the report not be voted on, but only that it be received; she was greeted by hisses from many of the seven hundred in attendance.

From the floor, Berreman and Wolf read potions of their rebuttal, and Wolf stirred up outrage in the audience by reading sections from a 1965 report titled "Low-Altitude Visual Search for Individual Human Targets: Further Field Testing in Southeast Asia" that he told the crowd had been written by a member of the AAA. Wolf explained to the assembly that this report sought optimal ways of identifying and killing human targets in Southeast Asian rice fields. While Wolf did not identify the author by name, it was later determined, by Herbert Phillips, that Wolf had confused the nonanthropologist author Donald Blakeslee with an AAA member archaeologist of the same name. While Wolf's reading of this report angered his listeners, it remains unclear what effect this mistake had in galvanizing the crowd in opposition to the Mead report; some claimed it was a decisive factor, others that it was but one small piece of a larger picture. As Eric Wakin observed two decades later, "The importance attributed to the name confusion seems to correlate with one's position on the Thailand Controversy" (1992: 211).[11]

A motion from the floor divided the report into three sections, for discussion and approval, and over the course of the long evening, the sections were successively rejected by floor votes (the first section, by a vote of 308 to 74; the second, 243 to 57; the third, 214 to 14), with attendance dwindling as the meeting continued past midnight. More than three decades later, Richard Lee recounted the evening's drama:

> Mead entered the hall, a striking matriarchal figure, with her shepherd's crook and flowing robes, and was seated at the front with her committee members in tow. When the agenda inched its way and the Mead Report was tabled for consideration by the membership, I rose and summoning my limited eloquence, pointed out the gross injustice of equating anthropological actions which contributed to the killing of real people with actions of Wolf and Jorgensen that brought the wrong-doing to light; employing the idiom of the day, I commended the whistleblowers for bearing witness to evil, and for speaking truth to power. I moved that Part One of the Mead Report be struck down, and Steve Barnett quickly and with far more eloquence, seconded the motion. A furious floor fight followed with Mead's backers vigorously defending her position and lauding the report's even-handedness. Defenders of Wolf and Jorgensen spoke with equal passion. (2008: 2–3; cf. Lee 1972)

The rejection of the Mead Committee report exposed generational fissures within the association and indicated a shift in the AAA establishment's ability to maintain top-down policy making for the association. Stephen Isaacs's story on the clash for the *New York Times* characterized Margaret Mead as being "furious" and insisting that the report was never intended to be voted on by the association; he wrote that Mead "indicated that she had been tricked by the board." Isaacs observed that "what became clear in the meeting was that the association's younger members see the 69-year-old Dr. Mead as a kind of anthropological Uncle Tom. And it became obvious very quickly, the younger members had the votes" (1971: A10).

Mead joined the majority in voting to reject the report for which she had been the primary author (*NAAA* 1972 13[2]: 1). Some weeks after the 1971 meeting, Ester Goldfrank wrote Mead:

> I have been wanting to tell you since the meetings ended that your Ad Hoc Report said just what needed to be said. I sensed things would go the way they did when

I learned in the afternoon that [Gerald] Berreman had been elected to a three year term on the Board. The Radical Caucus in the evening, you will remember, had an attendance of about 700 and the applause for the speakers [who authored the report] was certainly not exuberant. I had enough by 8:30 and left. I wasn't surprised to learn that the meeting ended at 1:20 A.M. The vote was 248 to 14 against your report. So almost 500 persons who had been at the earlier meeting that evening had melted away. There is a good old Communist tactic — you wear down your opponents with endless and not too relevant discussion and amendments, and when you are sure you can win, you call for a vote.

In the afternoon Pete Murdock said if he were ten years younger he would start a new scientific association. Perhaps what we ought to try first is to organize a Scholarly Caucus so that our membership could be kept informed regarding what is really at issue. . . . I wanted to resign when I learned what had happened on the Night of Infamy in November, but my younger friends have been urging me not to — to see if something can't be done to overcome the politicization of our Association — a process that has gone far already. (EG, EG to MM 1/3/72)

Goldfrank described articles in a recent edition of *Liberation* magazine detailing the growth of radical Marxist anthropology and tracing the crypto-Marxian elements of Leslie White's and others' anthropology (see Moore 1971). She signed off, writing, "If you are interested in a concerted move to offset the damage being done by what I think is a small but well-integrated minority I would be glad to hear from you. Yours for a better — but not a politicized — anthropology" (EG, EG to MM 1/3/72). Goldfrank's claim to want an anthropology without politics was ironic given her own role and that of her husband, Karl Wittfogel, as FBI informers who secretly attacked anthropologists and colleagues whose politics they disliked by reporting their suspicions that they might be Communists (D. H. Price 2004b, 2008c).

Mead replied to Goldfrank that she was "glad to have the references you sent. After all there has been boring from within before, as you and I well know." This may have been a reference to the 1948 AAA meeting in Toronto, which led George Murdock to become an FBI informer after he incorrectly imagined that a group of fellows speaking out for the academic freedom of a colleague (Richard Morgan), suffering a McCarthyistic attack, were part of a Communist plot to take over the association (EG, MM to EG 1/25/72; see D. H. Price 2004b: 70–89).

Mead's views were shared by many of the older generation of American anthropologists whose views on making disciplinary contributions to warfare had been shaped by their contributions to the Second World War. Mead's papers contain a series of letters she received following the 1971 AAA meeting supporting the position taken in her committee's report. Among those writing with support were L. Pospisil, M. Estelleie Smith, Murray Wax, Raoul Naroll, and Douglas Oliver (MM E12). Max Gluckman wrote that he was "inclined to resign from the AAA, to persuade other Foreign Fellows to do so," and he asked Mead if she believed this would be the correct stance to take (MM E12, MG to MM 12/21/71). Mead replied that no one should resign from the AAA because it was "in a sense a disavowal of democracy to get out instead of stay in and fight" (MM E12, MM to MG 1/23/72). L. Cabot Briggs wrote Mead that he and Robert Ehrich were thinking of leaving the AAA to break off and form their own professional association (MM E12, LCB to MM 11/21/71).

A few days after the council meeting, Joseph Jorgensen sent a curt note to "Mead's Ad Hoc Committee" that read, "I want to thank you for your unwitting efforts to smite imperialist anthropology. I suspect the clincher was the subtle counter insurgency–mental health analogy, but the overall high comic presentation may well have turned the trick. Whatever the case may be, thanks for your excessive help." In a postscript he asked, "Mead, did you really say all of those nasty and condemning things about Eric and me between the time that our NYR article was published and you accepted the post as chairwoman of your unbiased committee?" (MM E12, JJ to MM 11/24/71). Mead replied that she did not know what nasty and condemning things he was referring to, adding that if Jorgensen was still at the council meeting when the voting occurred, he would know that "the motion in favor of continuing vigilance on the part of the American Anthropological Association was seconded by me" (MM E12, MM to JJ 12/30/71).

The schisms of the 1971 meeting remained powerful within the AAA and affected association business for years to come, although in ways that were not always visible. After the meeting, Mead oversaw the destruction of the seven thousand pages of materials that had been collected for the report, thereby limiting the understanding and analysis of future generations of anthropologists (Davenport 1985: 68).

Anthropologists for Radical Political Action: Reorganizing the Radical Caucus

Years later, Richard Lee recalled a festive mood and late-night parties throughout the hotel following the rejection of the Mead Committee's report and noted, "From the critical writing that has grown up around it, the rejection of the

Mead Report was a pivotal moment in American Anthropology" (2008: 3). This sense of coming change led a group of radical anthropologists to organize an ongoing anthropological resistance to the war in Vietnam, following organizational models developed by the Union of Radical Political Economy (URPE) (3). During the months after the rejection of the Mead Report, there were efforts to maintain the momentum by developing a network of anthropologists working for radical activist change. Lee's datebook records that on January 27, 1972, he was "standing at a bus stop somewhere on the Upper West Side of Manhattan with Marvin Harris and Eleanor Leacock discussing the new organization. It was Harris who said let's call it Anthropologists for Radical Political Action, ARPA, an ironic dig at the Pentagon's Advanced Research Projects Administration, an agency which funded academic research on a wide range of the sciences including way at the bottom of the list, Anthropology. It was a branch of ARPA [Advanced Research Projects Administration] that had funded the original research on Thailand that had launched Wolf and Jorgensen's careers as whistleblowers" (3). Anthropologists for Radical Political Action drew on the strategies and base of the AAA's Radical Caucus, using decentralized local collectives to work on issues throughout the year.[12]

In April 1972, Stanley Diamond hosted an Anthropologists for Radical Political Action meeting at the New School for Social Research at which attendees pooled resources, generated names of hundreds of progressive anthropologists across the country, and organized a mailing campaign that resulted in "over four hundred responses" and the creation of Anthropologists for Radical Political Action "collectives" in several cities (Lee 2008: 4). In the *ARPA Newsletter*, which was established in the fall of 1972, Lee outlined the four basic anarchistic principles of the organization as decentralization, nonsectarianism, combining theory and practice, and facilitating communication (Lee 1972).

In 1972, Lee left New York for a position at the University of Toronto, where he organized a Canadian Anthropologists for Radical Political Action chapter. James Faris returned to the United States from fieldwork in the Sudan, where, he later wrote, he "consequently became a rabid anti-imperialist" (2008: 3). When Anthropologists for Radical Political Action made its first appearance at the 1972 AAA council meeting, it pushed through nine motions — successes that led the AAA leadership to limit members' ability to set association policy from the council meeting floor. But that year, the AAA's old guard was battling a significant demographic shift. In 1972, "the majority of anthropologists at the meeting were young—fully half (1520) of the 3106 registrants were students; only 649 were Fellows and 475 Voting Members—yet in most sessions, even in the

Council Meeting, members were largely in accord" (*NAAA* 1973 14[1]: 14). When the AAA's elected leaders realized that opening up the voting membership beyond the exclusive fellow category had weakened the older generation's grip on power, they began enforcing rules governing the council meetings that the Executive Board had violated for years.

At the 1972 council meeting, the present members passed "nine motions brought before them there, but defeated the one resolution which was submitted a week prior to the meeting as required by the constitution of the Association" (*NAAA* 1973 14[1]: 1). The AAA leadership wrote in the *Newsletter*, "This year, council members followed the constitutional requirement and all legislation proposed at the sessions was in the form of motions—advisory to, but not binding upon, the Executive Board and not needing mail referendum to the Council at large. Texts of the motions with their authors and co-signers, all passed by voice vote, are given below. They were released to the press and distributed to appropriate organizations by the Executive Office as many of the motions specifically requested and the Board then moved should be done" (*NAAA* 1973 14[1]: 1). Still stinging from the Radical Caucus's role in leading the rejection of the AAA's ad hoc committee's Thailand Report, AAA staff and the Executive Board maneuvered to strictly interpret the association's bylaws so that the ongoing practice of allowing motions passed at the council meeting to be passed along to the membership for a mail vote would no longer occur (see *NAAA* 1973 14[1]: 1). In 1969, the Executive Board had violated these same rules it now sought to enforce (*NAAA* 1970 11[1]: 7).[13] Now that the violation of these rules was being effectively used to weaken the power of the Executive Board, the board enforced the rules to suit its own purposes.[14]

The Executive Board Limits Floor Democracy

After the Radical Caucus demonstrated its control over the agenda at council meetings, and Anthropologists for Radical Political Action's successes at the 1972 meeting, in October 1973 the AAA's Executive Board, under AAA president Joseph Casagrande, took direct action to limit the impact of the group at upcoming council meetings. The October 1973 *Newsletter* carried a statement, "at the request of" AAA executive director, Edward J. Lehman, by Daniel Whitney, chairman of the AAA Resolutions and Motions Committee, and Robert Benjamin, AAA parliamentarian. The statement specified the procedures that would be followed at that year's annual meeting (*NAAA* 1973 14[8]: 1, 8).

Whitney and Benjamin notified AAA members that Section 4 of the association's bylaws stated that "new legislation or resolutions proposed by members of the Council" must be submitted to the Executive Board "at least one week in advance of the annual meeting if they are to be placed on the agenda." This was indeed the language of the bylaws, but the Radical Caucus had successfully argued, with a two-thirds majority at the meeting, that under the bylaws members could add resolutions and other items to the agenda, and these should be sent to the general membership in a mail ballot as had been done in previous years. Whitney and Benjamin noted that the bylaws also allowed for the passage of a "referendum" under the following conditions: "A referendum vote may be held by mail ballot at any time upon the initiation of the Executive Board or a signed petition of fifty (50) of the Council members in good standing" (*NAAA* 1973 14[8]: 1, 8; D. H. Price 2008b).[15]

The AAA leadership's monopoly on interpreting rules restricted the radical group's ability to set association policy from the floor of business meetings. The inability of members to send motions from the meeting floor to all members for a mail vote diminished the AAA business meetings' central importance and initiated a trend of diminishing attendance. At the 1973 meeting, activist members of the association again submitted one resolution (on conditions in Chile), and fifteen motions were passed from the floor, including resolutions on civil liberties under the Chilean military junta and ones on issues of gender equality.

The years following 1973 marked a decline in efforts by activists to pass resolutions at council meetings. The two resolutions raised in 1974, which passed easily, were the least political of any passed at AAA meetings in years: one was a friendly blanket resolution encouraging "research across national borders"; the other supported "archaeological excavations for educational purposes." The absence of political motions was conspicuous, but not surprising, given that the decision to hold the meeting in Mexico City meant that Anthropologists for Radical Political Action's base could not afford the expense of traveling to these distant locations; it was as if the AAA business meeting had been relocated within the walls of a gated community.

By 1975, the central political purpose for mobilizing radical anthropologists, the war in Vietnam, was no longer the pressing issue it had once been: the public had turned on the war, and the American retreat from Vietnam was under way. In 1975, the *Newsletter* observed that council meeting attendance "was light, with observers almost as numerous as Council members." Even as the AAA leadership achieved its goal of alienating radicals attending the meeting,

Rayna Reiter (later Rayna Rapp) pushed back with a resolution directing the Executive Board "to inform the membership through the newsletter of action taken and not taken on all resolutions and motions passed at the Council meeting and/or by mail ballot" (NAAA 1976 17[1]: 1, 9). The resolution was itself a commentary on the Executive Board's disdain for bottom-up democracy in the association; the AAA leadership had succeeded in killing members' interest in attending the business meeting (D. H. Price 2008b).

Because Anthropologists for Radical Political Action was a decentralized movement, the exact date of its dissolution is unclear. Jim Faris wrote that ARPA's end "coincided with the end of the Vietnam War as well, and ARPA finally went the way of many radical organizations of the time — into quiet abandon. By the later 1970s, it was gone, short-lived as it was, our weak and largely under-organized struggles within the AAA essentially defeated. Working for USAID, DOD, the World Bank and others was no longer even remotely considered the unethical or morally wrong thing to do. Money flowed uphill in the opposite direction to what most of us would consider a principled way to practice our craft" (2008: 7–8). As America retreated in defeat from Vietnam, the group's moment passed, though anthropologists' opposition to war, and more specifically their opposition to applying anthropology as an instrument of warfare of oppression, left deep impacts on the AAA. Yet like most institutional reforms, many of the changes initiated in opposition to the war would be short-lived.

Not with a Bang, but a Whimper

The deep divisions among AAA members that were exposed at the 1971 council meeting were not easily repaired in the years that followed. Reactions to the political and ethical issues involved in deploying anthropology in the service of counterinsurgency largely, though not entirely, split the association along generational lines and were embedded in the contemporary struggles of America's imperial wars in Southeast Asia, yet these issues were much deeper. The Mead Report's claim that anthropologists' contributions to soft power campaigns to quell uprisings or maintain power relations were in fact common features of applied anthropology projects revealed a profound truth, yet this observation could just as easily have been used to condemn many other applications of anthropology as to excuse, as the Mead Committee did, the counterinsurgency activities of these anthropologists.

Whatever gains had been made in rejecting the Mead Committee's report were short-lived and established little counter-inertia against the push of larger political economic forces steering the future course of the association. In 2008, James Faris reflected, "We currently have something of a statement, but no sanctions prohibiting members from doing the work of DOD and other sinister agencies. Margaret Mead, indeed, won. She kept the AAA safe for the America we know today and the AAA safe from us" (2008: 4–5).

In response to the insurgent movements of the Radical Caucus and Anthropologists for Radical Political Action, the AAA leadership used its power to subvert the democratic will of the majority of association members. The Executive Board worked hard to wrestle power from the Radical Caucus and other bottom-up manifestations of the membership's power — and the Radical Caucus and Anthropologists for Radical Political Action proved they could use association rules to seize power at the annual business meeting. One measure of the success of these grassroots groups in exerting their political will on the larger association is seen in the leadership's legalistic response of reinterpreting extant rules to limit their power at the AAA's annual meetings.[16]

These historical events had mixed outcomes. On the one hand, during the late 1960s and early 1970s, the radical anthropologists effectively pushed the AAA to adopt official public policies opposing the militarization of the discipline and the Vietnam War, and supporting positions of gender, racial, and economic equality. On the other hand, the AAA's power structure effectively disarmed this rebellion by selectively using association rules.

It is somewhat ironic that an essentially anarchistic group was in part subdued by institutional rules, but this was only a small part of what occurred. In truth, Anthropologists for Radical Political Action was more than a mechanism for controlling the AAA business meeting. Most members cared little about the legitimacy of getting their floor measures adopted by the AAA's rank and file in a mail ballot; most important, by the time the AAA power structure coordinated its defensive efforts and enforced rules to minimize their use of the business meeting to set association-wide policy, the American withdrawal from Vietnam was already under way. Any statement Anthropologists for Radical Political Action wanted to make, it could still make from the council meeting floor as a motion, and in the short term it mattered little if these motions were voted on by the entire membership. But there were long-term consequences of adopting this approach.

Perhaps the most enduring outcome of this history was the steady decline in AAA members' participation in the annual council meetings. The AAA membership's lack of interest in the annual business meetings was not an accidental occurrence; it was initiated as an intentional design feature of the sort Laura Nader (1997a) refers to as "controlling processes," enacted to thwart a flare-up of troublesome democracy through processes of institutionalized disenfranchisement.

The radical critique of the militarization of anthropology and the adoption of disciplinary ethical standards born of this critique remain important disciplinary connections to this period. But many of the fundamental issues raised during this period remain unresolved. Anthropology could not save itself, much less the world it studied. While the moral outrage of the period was connected to the privileges of wealth that produced it, it cannot be reduced to this. These concerns of social justice and abuses of power reflected growing domestic awareness of the abuses of the peoples subjected to American military power, an awareness at least in part funded by programs hoping for more hegemonic analysis.

> "But," says Arthur, "I wouldn't be proud of your clothes
> For you've only the lend of them, as I suppose
> But you dare not change them one night, for you know
> If you do, you'll be flogged in the morning
> And although that we are single and free
> We take great delight in our own company
> We have no desire strange places to see
> Although that your offers are charming
> And we have no desire to take your advance
> All hazards and dangers we barter on chance
> For you would have no scruples for to send us to France
> Where we would get shot without warning."
> "ARTHUR MCBRIDE AND THE SERGEANT" |
> early nineteenth-century traditional Irish folk song

FOURTEEN UNTANGLING OPEN SECRETS, HIDDEN HISTORIES, OUTRAGE DENIED, AND RECURRENT DUAL USE THEMES

The shift in America's military mission from the Second World War's fight against fascism and totalitarianism to Cold War policies supporting neocolonialism, militarism, and an expanding American empire helped transform American anthropologists' attitudes to align with collaborations with military and intelligence agencies. Many of these changes were under way soon after the Second World War, but such shifts in mission were apparent to few Americans, as there was no public awareness of the secret policy developments driving American Cold War strategies. The public had little understanding of the National Security Act of 1947 and no knowledge of NSC-68's plan for global containment of communism or Kennan's "Policy Planning Study 23," much less of the CIA's covert and illegal activities: assassinations, foreign coups, interrogation experiments, kidnappings, and subversion of foreign democratic movements threatening American corporate interests. In 1968, Kathleen Gough wrote that while "in the Fifties, it looked to some of us as though much of the non-Western world might gain genuine political and economic independence from the West by peaceful means, this is no longer the case" (1968: 17). In the short span of just over two decades, American anthropologists' high hopes for global changes favoring the peoples they so frequently studied shifted from postwar optimistic alignment with U.S. government programs to growing support for revolutionary movements opposing American hegemony. While many debates over the militarization of anthropology focused on professional ethics, this political shift was the taproot of this movement.

By the time Dell Hymes published *Reinventing Anthropology* in 1972, growing numbers of American anthropologists challenged the discipline's relationships to power, though not all anthropologists shared these critiques. As the generational confrontation over the Mead Committee's report on the Thai Affair demonstrated, deep schisms had developed. In his review of *Reinventing Anthropology* for the *New York Review of Books*, Sir Edmund Leach appeared offended that these crass Americans would bring political concerns to the fore of their anthropology in ways that he believed oversimplified complex systems of oppression. Leach wrote:

> The trouble with all the essays in Hymes's collection is their denial of historical reality. The authors have been shocked by the fact that, in south-east Asia and South America, professional anthropologists have functioned as intelligence agents on behalf of the CIA and the American armed forces, from which they have inferred that a politically neutral anthropology is an impossibility. They take it for granted that the "others" whom anthropologists study are, by definition, in a state of political subjugation. Since they hold that attempts at objectivity in social studies are positivist illusions, it follows that the anthropologist must always be "involved" in his research situation. He then has a simple moral choice: he can side either with the oppressors or with the oppressed. From this it is readily deduced that it is always morally deplorable to serve any established authority and always morally virtuous to side with liberation movements. That sympathies may be divided or solutions elusive does not seem to occur to these writers. All the anthropologist's actions must be immediately relevant to the manifest problems of those whom he observes. (1974: 35)

Leach's dismissive slaps at a movement challenging the discipline's historical complacency and its default siding with (to use Leach's terms) the oppressed over oppressors revealed a generational dividing line marking many anthropologists' responses to these issues, with many older anthropologists' experiences during the Second World War tempering their responses to these new critiques.

You Like It, It Likes You: Did the CIA and the Pentagon Get What They Paid For?

The ways that Cold War CIA- and Pentagon-aligned funding impacted anthropology were nonmonolithic and inconsistent, and at various times they produced desired, undesired, direct, distant, or no meaningful outcomes of direct use to governmental regimes of power. There were ample funds aligned with strategic interests coming from private foundations and governmental agencies for anthropological work ranging from classroom language study to fieldwork research projects. These funds financed a theoretically and geographically broad range of research activities, with the work of conservatives, conformists, liberals, progressives, Marxists, Maoists, and other radicals (during the late 1960s and the 1970s) financed by public and private sources. But even with the rise of critical anthropological analysis in the late 1960s and early 1970s, anthropology still produced enough knowledge of use to the national security state for it to comfortably justify these expenditures, and the independence of peer reviewed scholarship had a value that could not be produced within governmental structures (see Eickelman 1986:39).

Government and foundation funding programs spread their resources broadly. While much of the research funded in the postwar 1940s and throughout the 1950s aligned well with the needs and ideologies of the American Cold War state, in the 1960s and 1970s radical voices used these funds to generate their own critiques. The links between Cold War funds and outcomes were often not just nonlinear; at times they were oppositional, as scholars like Andre Gunder Frank and June Nash financed their graduate work, leading to powerful radical critiques, with funds from military-linked projects. While such unintended consequences had real significance in the development of American anthropology, these outcomes do not argue against payoffs for the national security state's gambit — which still produced knowledge of use to national priorities and helped train generations of younger scholars, including some who would work within these governmental systems.[1] Regardless of the analytical or political orientation of a particular work, anthropological writings informed a larger intellectual zeitgeist and supported the training of a broad universe of area specialists outside the discipline.

Cold War agendas shaped anthropological research projects — sometimes in direct ways (e.g., anthropologists funded at SORO, CRESS, the Research in

Contemporary Cultures project, the Russian Research Center, the Human Ecology Fund), and other times in secondary ways (working in critical geographic areas, even if conducting radical analysis), but there were still either large or small political dimensions of this work. The Cold War's progression at times influenced funding opportunities and analytical approaches.

In the postwar 1940s and throughout the 1950s, there was little room for critical work challenging American domestic or international policies. Threats of McCarthyism's punishments clarified the narrow range of allowable critiques, and at times "the wandering dialogue of science with the unknown [was] straightjacketed for petty military projects" (Goodman 1967:18). In the 1960s, a greater breadth of critical analysis was allowed, even while some (at SORO, HRAF, CRESS, etc.) did work that was directly aligned with meeting military-intelligence needs. Often, both researchers and the national security state got something they wanted — though frequently this was something as nonnefarious as generating general knowledge about geographic regions of general potential national security interest, and field research opportunities for the anthropologist. Anthropology's knowledge of "strategic cultures" and other topics enticed military interests, while funding opportunities provided enticements that directed some anthropological inquiries. But recognizing that multiple parties gained is not to claim that all these anthropologists would have pursued the same projects had different funding opportunities or different political pressures existed.

In the end, the CIA, the Pentagon, and a host of civilian programs mostly got what they paid for — though I suspect many contemporary scholars misjudge what it was that the military-industrial complex understood it was buying. The desired outcomes were clearly stated in the numerous postwar reports envisioning coming funding streams of public and private funds (see Pool 1963; Steward 1950; Wagley 1948). These reports called for the establishment of ongoing funding to train scholars and finance research projects around the globe that would have general and potential applications to strategic American policy issues — programs to establish a body of knowledgeable experts in regions of geopolitical interest. These postwar plans for area studies and increased governmental and foundational support for international research acknowledged that much of what was funded would be general scholarship contributing to the formation of the American academic brain trust. The directive nature of foundation funding helped shape the scope of research, but it only inconsistently succeeded in winning the hearts and minds of funded anthropologists. Functionally, this was only a minor inconvenience. Anthropologists produced enough useful knowledge to justify these relationships; loyalties were of minor importance. These interactions transformed anthropology in ways large and small. And while much remains unknown about all of the ways that the CIA and the Pentagon used these contacts, we know enough to map some of the ways these agencies *and* anthropologists each, though dual use processes, used these interactions.

As dual use partners, anthropology and the national security state both gained from Cold War relationships. Military and intelligence agencies, other civilian branches of government, and aligned private foundations gained a steady supply of well-trained specialists with linguistic, cultural, and political expertise covering the globe. Scholars were sometimes free to pursue a broad range of ideas, yet regardless of whether these scholars' work aligned with military or diplomatic policies, it engaged with and informed academic environments feeding these operations. Sometimes scholars knowingly served as consultants to the CIA or the Department of State, or in ongoing consultancies like the Princeton Consultants. Some anthropologists used open sources to write copy for army handbooks, to which classified materials were later added. Sometimes, the CIA or the Department of Defense asked professors at top universities to have graduate students unwittingly pursue questions of interest to the government, later secretly sharing these findings with governmental agencies. Harvard's Weberians and Parsonians embraced "value-free science" while hitching their wagons to an impressive array of value-laden Cold War–linked projects.

Anthropologists supported by the CIA through funding fronts contributed as unwitting subcontractors to larger projects — projects that included research informing the work of those producing the CIA's interrogation manual, and numerous projects establishing contacts in developing nations; in other instances, fronts financed esoteric anthropological research to provide needed illusions of legitimacy. The academic projects financed by CIA funding fronts generated publications and reports that were generally indistinguishable from non-CIA-funded projects.

Anthropologists' fieldwork in underdeveloped nations produced reports on peoples courted by the Soviets and the Americans as potential clients or players in the Cold War's proxy wars; it generally mattered little what analytical perspective was used in their writings. The CIA's "Family Jewels" report showed that USAID field projects provided "a major source of information" to the agency. Some anthropologists worked on economic assistance projects distributing soft power gifts and loans, achieving counterinsurgent ends while cultivating clients, debt, and dependence.

Agencies like RAND, CRESS, and SORO drew on anthropologists' ethnographic reports to synthesize counterinsurgency plans for operations in South

America and Southeast Asia. At times, military and intelligence organizations simply stole anthropologists' work for their own purposes—purposes frequently linked to counterinsurgency programs. This included instances like the U.S. Special Forces' unauthorized translation and pirating of George Condominas's book, or the ARPA program uncovered by Delmos Jones reading unpublished reports from northern Thailand to model counterinsurgency plans: anthropological knowledge fed a range of counterinsurgency operations. The Human Relations Area Files's academic research provided military and intelligence agencies with a dual use retrieval system to locate cultural information of value to counterinsurgency operations, hoping to transform ethnographic literature into knowledge that could control others.

Elisabeth Bacon's correspondence with Ralph Beals described the steps used by the CIA to contact anthropologists returning from the field, hoping to debrief them on what they saw and learned. Bacon's knowledge of scholars with OSS backgrounds bridging transitions to the CIA, and appearing on grant selection committees and boards, shows how the agency influenced the selection of anthropologists' field research. The CIA's fake anthropologists, like Lloyd Millegan, at times gained access to developing nations or used claims of anthropological research to gather information from actual anthropologists working in these countries. Sometimes embassy personnel pumped anthropologists for insights on what they knew from the remote villages where they lived.

During the Cold War, the AAA occasionally provided valuable information to the CIA. At times, the agency sent personnel, unannounced, to AAA meetings. The CIA secretly helped design the collection of information for the AAA's first comprehensive cross-indexed membership roster; CIA computers compiled, collated, and stored all the private data the AAA had collected on its members for the roster. Using the Asia Foundation as a front, the CIA collected information on the AAA's Asian anthropologists. The CIA also used the Asia Foundation to provide generous travel funds for Asian anthropologists traveling to conferences, settings where foundation staff seeking further information had opportunities to approach them. Even while most American anthropologists during the early Cold War had little direct contact with military or intelligence agencies, these Cold War dynamics indirectly impacted their work.

Military and intelligence agencies were not the only ones that benefited; anthropologists also profited from these interactions. Area study centers, private foundations, and governmental grants funded anthropologists' research in developing nations. In some instances, these field research opportunities, as in the case of Louise Sweet, had hidden links to military or intelligence agencies;

usually, however, no such duplicity occurred, as other more general gains in the development of a pool of regional experts were achieved.

Anthropologists benefited from new centrally funded, multischolar or interdisciplinary collaborative research projects like the Modjokuto Project, CIMA, or the Research in Contemporary Cultures project. These projects held theoretical significance to participating scholars that was unrelated to governmental interests. The CIA's secret funding of academic books provided new publishing opportunities for anthropologists and other scholars. Millions of dollars in contract funds allowed HRAF to translate and code ethnographic works; dual use processes provided the army with the basic unclassified texts it needed for its handbook series, while HRAF used the resulting funds to buy materials it used in its basic theoretical research completely unrelated to these military and intelligence projects.

When the CIA secretly placed personnel in key positions within foundations, or maintained contacts with foundations funding projects focusing on underdeveloped nations, anthropologists were among the scholars who benefited from such arrangements. The paper trail is necessarily incomplete, but examples showing CIA-linked personnel at the Asia Foundation suggesting who should, and who should not, present at an academic conference on Southeast Asia, or seeding funds within the AAA to gain access to young Asian scholars demonstrates the CIA shifting discourse and gaining access in ways that we can assume occurred elsewhere with other organizations. Likewise, SEADAG funded anthropological research by scholars employing a broad range of political and theoretical frameworks. Even anthropologists who were unwittingly supported by CIA funding fronts like the Asia Foundation or the Human Ecology Fund at times worked on projects of their own design, undertaking research of interest to them without noticeable constraints from their funders.

The Cold War made previously unimaginable levels of funding available for diverse research topics — topics ranging from studying culture at a distance, to village studies in remote contested regions, to Russian economic studies, to physical anthropological studies of somatological typologies. There were funds to attend high-status junkets in New York, Washington, DC, Moscow, Salzburg, Hawaii, and elsewhere. Asian anthropologists received virtually free AAA memberships and at times were given money to attend academic conferences, and the AAA received a small fortune in free computer time from the CIA when completing work on its first comprehensive membership roster.

Some anthropologists found steady work outside of universities at places like RAND, CRESS, SORO, USAID, the CIA, and the Department of Defense.

Archaeologists, anthropologists, and other scholars working in the developing world with CIA links, like Donald Wilber, John Dimick, or James R. Hooker, mixed their travels with agency work. Frank Bessac gained valuable experiences as a CIA agent, exploring remote regions of Central Asia that he would otherwise have not visited, experiences that established the foundations of his later academic research.

Perhaps anthropology's greatest gains from these dual use relationships came from the wealth of governmental and private funds available for language training and basic research in regions of the world deemed geopolitically significant. Anthropology graduate students had scholarships, fellowships, grants, and tuition waivers subsidized by federal and private programs supporting the production of expertise on geographic regions of strategic interest. Likewise, a range of programs with few direct ties to national security programs funded field research around the globe, with no commitments for scholars to contribute directly to governmental programs, yet the establishment of these programs during the postwar period was explicitly rationalized to support national security.

Cold War anthropologists' research followed shifts in funds favoring specific geographic regions or languages. It has never been particularly difficult for research funders to redirect scholars' interests and inclinations. Shifting the availability of specific language funds, at times favoring programs directing an influx of work in Latin America, Africa, Russia, or China, produced visible results that changed with Cold War geopolitical developments.

Yet, beyond the anthropologists, foundations, and military and intelligence agencies that gained from this work were the people who were studied and impacted by these relationships. To the extent that American foreign policies, military actions, and covert activities damaged the autonomy and interests of anthropologists' subjects, anthropologists' contributions to the knowledge systems supporting such outcomes undermined primary anthropological commitments to research participants.

Situating Interpretations

In many cases scholars were relatively free to pursue questions of interest to them with a mix of government and private foundation funds assuring the maintenance of a brain trust generating regional expertise, or knowledge on topics of interest to governmental agencies or policy makers. These funds helped stock universities with regional expertise. Anthropologists often studied theoretical questions of their choosing, yet in instances where hidden or open governmental funds supported specific forms of research, we must question whether these choices were always as free as is often assumed. This leaves us with contested interpretations of relationships between anthropologists, sponsors, military and intelligence agencies, and their research outcomes.

While my interpretation of military and intelligence agencies' impacts on the development of American anthropology and other disciplines aligns with the work of other scholars (see Diamond 1992; González 2010; Ross 1998a, 2011; Wakin 1992; and Jorgensen and Wolf 1970), still others find little impact of these interactions on anthropology and other branches of academia. During the two decades since the publication of Sigmund Diamond's breakthrough book *Compromised Campus* (1992), scholars have added more peer-reviewed research establishing how links between the CIA, the military, and social scientists functioned during the Cold War. After Diamond and other critical scholars began documenting and critiquing these Cold War intrusions into academia, a first wave of academic critics responded with skepticism, but as more documented examples were published (e.g., Bundy 1977), there has been a perceptible shift from disbelief, to critics adopting a dismissive commitment to downplaying the significance of such relationships. Countering conservative positions shifting from skepticism to dismissive revisionist acceptance can be a bit like loading a truck full of mercury with a pitchfork (Brautigan 1976). Today, a new group of scholars acknowledge many of these links but discount their significance, arguing that CIA or Pentagon ties did not meaningfully alter the nature of academic research. These scholars find few significant connections between Cold War dynamics and the produced work.

Intellectual historians now analyze Harvard's Russian Research Center, acknowledging CIA funding without meaningfully probing its influence (Engerman 2009); or argue that the CIA's covert funding of political and academic movements supported rather than altered intellectual and political trajectories (Wilford 2008, 2013); or interpret Ruth Benedict, Margaret Mead, and Geoffrey Gorer's postwar culture and personality work as if they might have freely chosen this exact research path without the enticement of previously unimaginable levels of military funding (Mandler 2013); or find minimal impacts of institutional framing in government-funded war zone ethnographic research (Oppenheim 2008). Some who lived through this period insist that they "did not tailor . . . theories to suit Walt Rostow or to serve the interests of the CIA, nor did we busy and bury ourselves in irrelevant projects in order to avoid controversy" (H. Lewis 2005: 108; cf. Rauch 1955). Some argue that the many examples of Cold War era anthropological work that cannot be tied to military or intelligence agendas mitigate the significance of established connections. But such arguments are reminiscent of the claim by piano virtuoso Glenn Gould (a notoriously bad driver) that "it's true I've driven through a number of red lights on occasion, but on the other hand I've stopped at a lot of green ones but never gotten credit for it" (Hafner 2008: 203). As Laura Nader argues in her essay "The Phantom Factor: Impact of the Cold War on Anthropology" (1997), most of the anthropologists who came of age during the early Cold War gave little thought to these processes shaping them and their work. That some who developed and prospered in this world later refused to acknowledge its impact is not surprising; if cultural insiders had sufficient insight to analyze the culture in which they live, there would be no need for anthropology itself.

From outside the Pentagon and the CIA, it remained difficult to access the fruits of many CIA- and Pentagon-funded projects. But a 1963 CIA memo from Asia Foundation president Russell Smith reporting on his first year as foundation president indicates that some CIA-funded programs that from a distance appeared disconnected from CIA matters often had agency uses that were not apparent to outsiders. As the CIA reported, "Mr. Smith acknowledged that a small percentage of the [Asia] Foundation's programs were for the sake of 'window-dressing,' public relations, or entrée into fields of interest. In discussing such projects, however, Mr. Smith remarked that since becoming President he has learned that some projects which, at first appearance seem to be frivolous, may have concealed edges [of] potential" (FOIA CIA-1705143 1/28/63, DTPILLAR 3, 24 p. 2).

Rewarding individuals whose work aligned with or informed larger projects of the American national security state helped some scholars "freely" choose topics or theoretical approaches of interest in ways that maintained certain illusions of academic free will. Most academics spend their lives agreeably working within the confines of their disciplines, departments, and universities, content enough with the parameters delimiting the boundaries of mainstream scholarship. For those who seldom question the directions of funded research, there is little to see that does not appear as freely chosen areas of study. To some degree, all people create illusions of agency and choice while reinforcing cultural norms. To argue that the dominant cultural milieu and political-economic forces did not shape anthropologists' work would place the discipline of anthropology outside of the sort of usual influences of culture that anthropologists normally take for granted when studying other cultures. From the postwar rush to follow the funding of area studies onward, the Cold War brought recurrent episodes of anthropologists shifting their work to align with the era's funding opportunities, and instances of governmental agencies acquiring and consulting the work these anthropologists produced; yet Ralph Beals's account of Senator Fred Harris's chief of staff describing warehouses in Washington with "great piles" of unread research reports (see chapter 11) offers some relief in the consolation of government incompetency.

There are high stakes for the discipline itself concerning how to interpret the writings of generations of anthropologists who traveled to the field and theorized using funds mixing academic pleasures with the business of empire. If, for example, we find that the writings of prominent Harvard scholars such as Clyde Kluckhohn and Talcott Parsons were in some way elevated because of their alignment with a power elite (explicitly rejected by Parsons) that included the CIA and the FBI, while others (Gene Weltfish, Richard Morgan, Richard Armstrong, Jack Harris, etc.) who opposed such regimes of power were driven to the edges of the discipline by the FBI, then we are left to confront new questions about this work.

I would not argue that the work of Kluckhohn, Wilber, Mead, Benedict, or others whose research aligned with the interests of CIA or the Pentagon was necessarily of an inferior quality, or that it should not be taken seriously simply *because* of these relationships, only that it should be read and interpreted with these relationships firmly in mind. Anthropologists study contexts, and these relationships are important elements of the context in which this work was produced and consumed. Clifford Geertz's *Agricultural Involution* should not be dismissed as nothing more than a piece of CENIS-influenced propaganda; it is something more than that, yet the context in which it was produced is part of the text that must be brought to the surface if we are to understand it. Burying the political context of this and other work obscures important elements of its meanings. While the political context of Jack Stauder's essay "The 'Relevance' of Anthropology under Imperialism" (1972), Kathleen Gough's "Anthropology and Imperialism" (1968), Marshall Sahlins's "The Destruction of Conscience in Vietnam" (2000a), or Marvin Harris's *Portugal's African Wards* (1958) might seem obvious to most readers, these texts are no more or less political than *Agricultural Involution*; it is their clarity of political position — as well as their opposition to elite power structures — that creates illusions that they are somehow more political than those texts with more hidden political orientations.

Anthropology needs to concretely consider how regimes of power influence disciplinary developments in ways large and small. Such considerations necessitate formulating the sort of metanarratives of power that declined with the rise of some popular postmodern strains. Anthropologists who adapted Lyotard's "incredulity towards metanarratives" had no means of systemically interpreting recurrent intrusions of military and intelligence agencies on the discipline, leaving anthropology vulnerable to recurrent episodes of exploitation (Lyotard 1984: xxiv). As William Roseberry observed, "'Grand narratives'... are never sufficient, but they remain necessary" (1996: 22). While many anthropologists are stepping back from the extremes of postmodern reflexivity, a clear focus on anthropology's relationship to the military economies in which it is embedded remains elusive, and the footprint of this inward turn remains deep. Even with recent calls for renewed attention to ontological developments, the discipline's postmodern avoidance of grand narratives of power fosters notions that the Cold War political economy did not meaningfully alter the production of knowledge.

Social theory (or anti-theory stances) can selectively blind anthropologists, even as it fuels interpretation and understanding. During the Reagan years, anthropologists became increasingly entranced with postmodern inward-focused narratives and particularist versions of disciplinary history that, while ritualistically poking at colonialism, power, and othering, led us away from confronting ongoing disciplinary links to American militarism and other pressing political issues. Many postmodern and interpretivist narratives focus indulgently on the meanings and subjective engagements of ethnographers, even, as Geertz's experiences show us, to the extent of missing massive bloody genocidal campaigns.[2]

With time, the programmatic rejection of metanarratives ironically become an unacknowledged metanarrative undermining explanatory paths of inquiry not taken in ways that made it difficult to identify and confront recurrent power relations. David Graeber recently critiqued this reflective turn as "vulgar Foucauldianism, which simultaneously developed the subjective experience of professional-managerial work arrangements as the basis for a universal principle of human sociality, and denied the central importance of either capitalism, or the threat of direct physical violence, at exactly the moment the threat of direct physical violence was becoming central to the operation of capitalism" (2014: 84).

Anthropologists' research choices are routinely shaped by regimes of punishment and reward. During the 1950s, McCarthyism effectively corralled anthropological inquiry, limiting research that challenged tenets of American Cold War dogma; anthropologists learned to disengage from analysis focusing on stratification, open Marxist-derived analysis, applying anthropological research on racial equality to activist campaigns, and postwar anticolonial campaigns (D. H. Price 2003b, 2004b). As the Cold War progressed beyond the scare tactics of the McCarthy era, funding seeds were cast broadly, with little effort to limit critical analysis.

It would be instructive to study the variety of research projects that were *not* funded during the 1950s, or at least not funded more than once, but beyond tallying numbers of unfunded proposals, foundations do not usually retain the records of rejected grant applications. Foundations named after dead tycoons paid anthropologists to study peasants, princes, and displaced peoples around the globe, with few funds forthcoming to study the public and private lives of Western elites. Governmental funding bodies expressed clear concerns about supposed left-wing biases and certain political uses of social research. At the National Science Foundation, specific policies were adopted, according to the NSF's Harry Alpert, to "eschew identification with social reform movements and welfare activities, and especially, the unfortunate phonetic relationship to socialism" (qtd. in Solovey and Pooley 2011:250). Such policies meant governmental funding programs supported social science research seeking only specific types of social change, while dooming others.

Some progressive social research was unfundable during this period because of negative associations with "activism," yet social research providing yeoman's service to the national security state rarely suffered such setbacks. There were more funding opportunities for scholars to support the debt-laden regimes of modernization than to question them. Cold War biases against materialist theoretical perspectives during the 1950s caused several analysts to cloak their theoretical writings in obscure references and cumbersome logic. Leslie White hid his Marxist roots, while Julian Steward encrypted the notions of base and superstructure to such an extent that his model of human ecology at times contradicted itself (see Peace 2004). It took Karl Wittfogel, a committed anticommunist and FBI informer, to openly reintroduce anthropology to Marx's Asiatic mode of production during the darkest days of McCarthyism (D. H. Price 2008c).

Anthropological Ambivalences

An evaluation of anthropologists' efforts to effect positive change within governmental and nongovernmental agencies linked to American wars in Southeast Asia would have difficulties finding positive measurable outcomes in which anthropologists had the desired impacts on the agencies with which they engaged. Anthropologists hoping to correct or reshape what they viewed as misguided policies had little success. These general failures had thematic connections with many anthropologists' contributions to the Second World War and today's contemporary militarized engagements. The prospects for anthropologists working within military or intelligence agencies to change policies do not appear promising, though I suppose renewed interest and funding opportunities may present new ways for enthusiastic anthropologists to reconceive such measures.

Charles Keyes's early correspondence with ARPA in 1966 expressed concerns that anthropologists' contributions to ARPA's project could lead to an Asian Camelot-like scandal. He threatened to expose the program in the press, but Seymour Deitchman convinced Keyes that he could help reshape the Rural Security Systems Study. With similar motivations, Gerald Hickey began working for RAND, in hopes of helping the U.S. military do less harm in Vietnam. Keyes, Hickey, Moerman, Piker, Sharp, and others expressed similar motivations for their work on these projects, and I found no records or correspondence contradicting this. Yet, their work with these military or advisory groups showed little impact on these groups, their participation brought a desired layer of legitimacy to these programs, and they had no control over the uses of their contributions. Effecting internal change on a bureaucratic organization as robust as the Pentagon is daunting even under the most favorable conditions, and when advocated changes cut against the grain of the core beliefs and behaviors of the Pentagon and the larger military-industrial economy, it is unlikely that any meaningful change will occur. Continuing to work under such conditions raises questions about the naïveté or cynicism of scholars who remain in such well-paid positions while effecting no significant change.

American anthropologists' experiences with military and intelligence agencies trying to harness anthropological knowledge have spawned several efforts to limit these incursions by strengthening professional ethics codes. From the Society for Applied Anthropology's post–World War II code, to the AAA's Vietnam era efforts to establish ethics codes, war forced the discipline to grapple with these issues of identity and meaning (see D. H. Price 2011f: 11–31). Warfare recurrently tempts anthropologists to betray assumed and assured trusts with those with whom they have lived and studied; but warfare does not create unique opportunities to betray trusts so much as it reveals raw components of existing relationships and weaknesses that exist in most anthropologists' research interactions.

Professional ethics codes establish social norms, mark disciplinary borders, and affirm shared values and agreed-upon best practices. Clarifying professional ethics codes becomes an important project for professional associations during or after times of war, yet in times of war these codes have also been used to avoid *political* discussions. Constructing ethics codes declaring the importance of voluntary informed consent, mandating disclosure, and prohibiting reports that studied populations cannot access can help delineate appropriate activities for anthropologists conducting research in any research context, yet such prescriptive guidelines ignore the core political questions raised by anthropologists within the Radical Caucus, the Committee of Concerned Anthropologists, Anthropologists for Radical Political Action, and other waves of critical anthropology that developed during the late 1960s and early 1970s. Unless professional associations like the AAA can address these core political issues (which they are loath to do, precisely because they are *political* issues),[3] associations like the AAA will continue to sidestep core issues of what anthropology is, what it *should* be used for, and what is it good for, by addressing only ethical research issues.

While attention to research ethics remain vital for all anthropologists, the AAA's compartmentalization of concerns with disciplinary militarization as primarily an ethical problem fails to address the political issues raised by practicing anthropology in an American political economy and within an international policy of escalating militarization. The AAA and other professional organizations need to address the political problems necessarily embedded in practicing anthropology in settings dominated by a growing military-industrial complex, neocolonial militarization, and expanding fears of terrorism. There is no single answer to these political questions. But until anthropologists confront and hash out these political issues directly, the discipline seems doomed to recurrently suddenly discover militarized misappropriations of what it self-conceives of as its heart and soul, with repeated crises and misguided efforts to solve political problems using ethics, not politics.

As the generation of 1960s and 1970s activists retires and dies off, universities increasingly find themselves without a generation of professors who know firsthand the history of CIA and Pentagon intrusions on our campuses and in our disciplines. With the loss of this institutional memory, the remaining generations of scholars need to study this history to understand why these relationships endanger prospects of free inquiry. Those who bother learning this history will struggle against an incoming tide, as three decades of neoliberal programs' impacts on student loan debt, campus austerity programs, and new enticements of military funding converge to transform American universities into even greater extensions of military and intelligence programs, as increasingly the remaining tenured faculty respond with silence.

Today's anthropology students face increasing student debt, with new funding opportunities carrying direct or indirect links to military and intelligence projects. Programs like the National Security Education Program, the Pat Roberts Intelligence Scholars Program, and the Intelligence Community Scholars Program now fund undergraduate and graduate students (in some instances, secretly) while requiring recipients to work in national security sectors at some future date (D. H. Price 2011f: 33–90). Some older funding programs without mandated future payback stipulations, like the former National Defense Foreign Language Fellowships, now renamed the Foreign Language and Area Studies (FLAS) fellowships, continue to fund students studying "strategic languages" that are assumed to have importance in military, intelligence, and policy circles. While these programs exist as part of the broader national security apparatus, the lack of restrictions on participants' work raises more passive than active forms of dual use issues and does not tie students to future work for governmental agencies.

Biologists' and other researchers' awareness of dual use issues at times forces them to consider potential unintended dual use outcomes for their research as part of their research design process. Anthropologists can follow these examples and develop protocols for considering how our work can be weaponized by others at later dates. There is too much history of such interactions to ignore these possibilities. Anthropology needs to develop historical and contemporary critiques of how its research interfaces with the political economy in which it is embedded. American anthropologists cannot proceed as if disciplinary links with military and intelligence agencies are not part of the social milieu in which we work; there can be no ignorance that such agencies (and industry) have made unintended uses of our work. But what this awareness means and how we use this knowledge to proceed is unclear beyond maintaining a heightened awareness to consider how such agencies may selectively harvest the analysis we produce. In some instances it may mean that anthropologists withhold material from publication if we have reason to believe work can be used against studied populations. In other instances it may mean that the discipline's professional associations identify, confront, and try to alter the ways that knowledge informs military and intelligence agencies.

It is not that anthropology can or should disengage from political issues. As anthropologists' journalistic and academic writings clarify, the discipline has a lot to offer international policy discussions (see González 2004; Besteman and Gusterson 2005). And while anthropologists have contributed to policy developments, historically, military operations have looked to anthropology for assistance with the cultural problems that arise with conquest, occupation, and counterinsurgency. While current militarization trends render unlikely any significant anthropological contributions to national policy decisions in the United States in the near future, anthropology and American policy would be strengthened by renewed efforts to establish the forms of independent social science research funding advocated by Senator Fred Harris in the 1960s. Such an independent funding source could focus on problems of domestic and global poverty, stratification, health care, police brutality, education reform, participatory democracy, peace studies that are something other than war studies by another name, racism, sustainable agriculture, and many other social issues. Yet under a political economy so devoted to warfare, such independence often remains a distant yet worthy goal.

The contradictions of working within a political economic system operating in a state of perpetual warfare create difficulties for those who do not want to produce work that may inadvertently feed back into this system. The dominance of the militarized backdrop creates conditions in which even humanitarian efforts to assist war victims increasingly become tools of counterinsurgency or control (see Feldman 2007; D. H. Price 2014a).

The solutions to these problems are not simple, but acknowledging their existence is a vital step. Anthropology needs metanarratives of power relations that expose recurrent episodes of the weaponization of the field. Part of this metanarrative includes explicit understanding that funds for language and area specialization study have historically been granted with expectations that gained expertise and knowledge will later be available for national militarized projects, often directed against the people anthropologists study, and those they are generally ethically committed to not harm. Anthropologists must come to grips with the limits of individual agency, acknowledging the unlikelihood that individuals working within agencies devoted to warfare and conquest can meaningfully alter the core functions of these organizations.

At a minimum, anthropology must develop dual use research protocols, identifying harm that may come from work should others use research findings, and disengage from research or publications that present significant prospects of such harmful outcomes. As the AAA's current code of ethics argues: "Anthropologists should not only avoid causing direct and immediate harm but also should weigh carefully the potential consequences and inadvertent impacts of their work. When it conflicts with other responsibilities, this primary obligation can supersede the goal of seeking new knowledge and can lead to decisions to not undertake or to discontinue a project" (PPR 2012). I see these processes as broad and far-reaching, and do not remove my own work, including this book, from such considerations.[4] While such measures are imperfect and incomplete, they are necessary as a minimal step connecting our work with the world we study, inhabit, share, and inevitably alter.

Revisiting the Gift

During the Cold War, foundations and governmental agencies were able to "decide which problem areas merited their support and reward those scholars whose research fits the approved categories. The impetus for new directions that formerly came from collegial discussions now came from directives issued by the agencies" (Denich 1980: 173). It is surprising that a discipline that embraced Marcel Mauss's (1925) notion that gifts necessarily entail obligations paid so little attention to the obligations accompanying the precious gifts it received and became increasingly reliant upon. Instead, these gifts were widely sought and welcomed on university campuses with little concern about these matters. As Sigmund Diamond observed, during the early Cold War years, the U.S. government became an "invited guest in campuses and quadrangles, and there is precious little evidence that the universities objected to, or even thought much about, the price that was being exacted for the benefits they sought. In a sense, a great potlatch was being celebrated: the government brought gifts, highly visible ones; the universities also brought gifts, research results in permissible areas" (1992: 275). Participants in the kula ring, potlatches, or other gift exchange systems generally reject nontraditional explanations for failing to recognize the meanings of these transactions to participants, and anthropological explanations focusing on the counterflow of goods, other economic functions, or created social relations generate greater interest among outsiders than among members of these cultures. Such analysis tends to strike participants as crass, claiming participants are following cultural illusions and reducing complex personal motivations to unidimensional mercenary transactions removing individual autonomy.

Anthropology has its own gifts to offer the world. Even with fundamental epistemological disagreements in the discipline, we produce unique knowledge and ways of understanding our species, the human condition, the nature of culture, and humanity's place in the universe. Anthropologists' contributions to studies of language, culture, primatology, human prehistory, gender, hominid evolution, stratification, political economy, power relations, warfare, peace, culture contact, kinship, social movements, the cultural construction of race, culture change, biocultural interactions, and a long list of other topics have been significant and remarkably different from those of any other discipline. Cold

War anthropologists made tremendously important contributions to these and other areas of inquiry, yet many still lost sight of how, while the discipline accomplished its half of the dual use bargain, some disciplinary gaze was selectively diverted.

In 1972, Radical Caucus leader Jack Stauder described some of the direct links between social science funding and the work produced, observing that anthropologists' belief in political "semi-autonomy" from the government funding their research was "an illusion."[5] Stauder predicted that "to the degree they are dependent on government money, anthropologists will be increasingly pressed into service to do work more relevant to short-term imperialist interests. The pressures are likely to be subtle, mainly taking the form of selective funding and the greater availability of money for 'relevant' research. The appeal of 'relevance' capitalizes on the ambiguity of the term to enlist students and faculty who, often from different interests, also want 'relevance'" (1972: 78). While not specifying a time scale, Stauder accurately described the coming shift in funding opportunities that would develop in the next four decades, with a decline in traditional graduate funding opportunities, reduced state and federal tuition subsidies, and the expansion of new "payback" programs (such as the National Security Education Program) linking graduate funds to future national security work (see D. H. Price 2011f).

In 1973, Gerald Berreman summarized the AAA's Vietnam War era ethics conflicts, detailing efforts to prohibit anthropologists from conducting secret research. Because the struggle within the association had been largely waged along generational lines, he predicted that the generational "reverberations will be felt for many years for the demand that anthropological research be relevant and socially responsible is increasing. The age structure of the Association and the mortality of its members virtually assure that these demands will win out in the end" (Berreman 1973: 8). Berreman's optimism was understandable, but history finds that he misjudged the power of economic forces to shape the attitudes not of some distant unborn generation but of his own generation and the academic generation to follow. A decade and a half later, the AAA revised its ethics code, once again opening the doors for anthropologists to do covert research and to produce secret proprietary reports that studied populations could not access (D. H. Price 2011f: 11–31). The motivations for these changes had everything to do with market forces leading anthropologists to increasingly conduct proprietary corporate research, and little to do with seeking employment with the Pentagon or the CIA. But once they were propped open, these doors would be used soon enough by anthropologists seeking validation for their work in military and intelligence agencies. Berreman failed to realize just how powerful the economic forces of America's military-industrial complex would be in shaping the attitudes of anthropologists needing to eat and pay off student loans in an era of limited employment possibilities.

While the economic contingencies governing university departments favor the careers of successful grant writers, there remains an elusive rare freedom for those who find ways to pursue unfunded, or alternatively funded, research programs. Anthropologists need to consider the high price of surrendering intellectual independence for the projects of others with agendas both known and unknown. The luxuries of remaining independent and free to keep our own company have immeasurable value.

Anthropologists can learn from this history. We can develop standards to maintain some independence from militarized agendas and remain aware of how our work can be abused. I don't know if we can learn that attempting to mitigate harm by joining and trying to change military and intelligence organizations has little chance of even limited success (see Hastings 2015; Price 2011f: 155–72). Some steps toward the demilitarization of the discipline may be easy to identify; others are fraught with complexities. It is not that lines of participation or disengagement can always be clearly drawn — if anything, this history shows the difficulties in understanding when knowledge production has links to militarized projects. Yet, if anthropologists do not try to disambiguate these lines, there is no hope of not contributing to the militarization of the discipline with these endemic dual use relationships.

Resistance is not futile. There is much in the history of anthropologists' efforts to confront the militarization of the discipline that can inform campaigns to limit such encroachments. One important lesson is that organized resistance matters. This resistance can occur both within and outside of professional organizations like the AAA. The successes in the 1960s and 1970s of Anthropologists for Radical Political Action, the AAA's Radical Caucus, the Committee of Concerned Anthropologists, and groups like the Union of Concerned Scientists were models for the formation of the Network of Concerned Anthropologists, in 2007, as an organizational tool for pressuring the AAA to limit military and intelligence incursions into the discipline (see NCA 2009). While far from a panacea, the formation of the NCA as a loose collective pressed the AAA to address concerns of militarization, and as an identifiable organization, it gave the AAA's bureaucratic structure a body to approach when addressing relevant association policy changes.

In 2009, pressure from AAA members concerned about increased uses of anthropological knowledge by military and intelligence agencies led the association to reinstate bans on secret research, which itself led to an overhaul of the AAA's ethics code (DeSantis 2012; Jaschik 2009; D. H. Price 2011f: 11–31). Along with the renewed prohibition against producing reports that studied populations cannot access, the AAA's new code (the Principles of Professional Responsibility) contains new language that stresses the importance of considering unintended uses of research, and a new focus on the ethical problems of compartmentalized research, stating: "Compartmented research by design will not allow the anthropologist to know the full scope or purpose of a project; it is therefore ethically problematic, since by definition the anthropologist cannot communicate transparently with participants, nor ensure fully informed consent. Anthropologists have an ethical obligation to consider the potential impact of both their research and the communication or dissemination of the results of their research. Anthropologists must consider this issue prior to beginning research as well as throughout the research process" (PPR 2012). Although it remains difficult for researchers to definitively know how others may use their work, this insistence that anthropologists avoid research projects that compartmentalize and repurpose their field research is a meaningful step toward addressing some of the historical abuses of anthropological research by military and intelligence agencies. While institutional efforts to address dangers of militarization are important, many of the most important efforts to resist come from individuals.

In 2013, Marshall Sahlins resigned from the National Academy of Sciences over objections that the NAS was using its anthropologist members to seek applicants for research projects to be funded by the Army Research Institute. In his resignation letter, Sahlins described his growing awareness of the ways that the NAS contributed to the legitimization of militarized social science, which had led him to a point where he did not "wish to be a party to the aid, comfort, and support the NAS is giving to social science research on improving the combat performance of the US military, given the toll that military has taken on the blood, treasure, and happiness of American people, and the suffering it has imposed on other peoples in the unnecessary wars of this century" (D. H. Price 2013a). With the post-2001 shifts to normalize militarized uses of anthropology, such principled resignations are rare occurrences, yet this is the sort of stance anthropologists need to take to mark the appropriate uses of the discipline.

The outrage and hope expressed in writings by members of the Radical Caucus and Anthropologists for Radical Political Action mark the moral conscience of a generation resisting militarized political uses of disciplinary knowledge. These reactions were rooted in social movements outside the discipline, but these were specific anthropological expressions of critical resistance that offer hope to other generations of anthropologists facing new abuses of our work. Most of these discipline-specific elements grew from bonds of responsibility linking anthropologists to the individuals and communities that share their lives with them.

While the challenges facing current and future generations of anthropologists differ from those faced by past generations, there remain important connections concerning questions of what is to be done with the fruits of anthropologists' labors — questions whose answers must acknowledge, as Cora Du Bois expressed after the Second World War, that "there is no end to the intricate chain of responsibility and guilt that the pursuit of even the most arcane social research involves" (1960: iv–v).

NOTES

Preface

1. For more information on my use of FOIA in this Duke University Press series, see Price 2004b: 355–61.

2. For information on the Cambridge Working Group, see http://www.cambridgeworkinggroup.org/; information on Scientists for Science is available at http://www.scientistsforscience.org/. Accessed 8/15/14.

3. I am grateful to Roberto González for suggesting the theme of dual personality features after reading an early draft of this preface.

ONE Political Economy and Intelligence

1. President Truman used the fifty-six-page, top secret "Park Report" to discredit, and disband, the OSS as an amateurish outfit, infiltrated by communists.

2. IRIS later became the Bureau of Intelligence Research.

3. The span of time between the dissolution of the OSS (October 1, 1945) and the establishment of the CIA (July 26, 1947) was 664 days.

4. While the CIA viewed the rising anticolonialist movement as a potential threat, anthropologists like John Embree, Raymond Kennedy, and Jack Harris championed these transformations as hopeful developments. Ironically, the CIA had tried to recruit Jack Harris, though he declined its offer in part because the OSS had broken promises to individuals who had helped him out of "difficult situations" during the war (Melvern 1995: 55).

5. The 1954 Doolittle Commission was appointed by President Eisenhower to evaluate the range of secret work undertaken by the CIA.

6. Peter Richardson reports that the CIA undertook retaliatory action against *Ramparts*, including increased surveillance on the magazine's staff and a range of "dirty tricks to hurt their circulation," and other acts that included considerations of blackmail against vulnerable staff (Richardson 2009: 79–80).

7. These *New York Times* articles included De Onis 1967; Emerson 1967; Farnsworth 1967; Flint 1967; Fox, 1967; Herbers 1967; Kenworthy 1967a, 1967b; Lelyveld 1968; NYT 1967a, 1967b, 1967c; Reed 1967; Sheehan 1967a, 1967b, 1967c, 1967d; and Turner 1967.

8. In 1974, John Marks published a methodologically improved effort to identify CIA agents in his essay "How to Spot a Spook," which focused particularly on identifying embassy "political officers" (Marks 1974).

9. John Ehrlichman and H. R. Halderman met with Helms on June 23, 1972, to request that the CIA disrupt the FBI's Watergate investigation (Powers 1976: 54).

10. The committee was chaired by Rockefeller and consisted of John T. Connor, C. Douglas Dillon, Erwin N. Griswold, Lane Kirkland, Lyman L. Lemnitzer, Ronald Reagan, and Edgar F. Shanon Jr.; attorney David W. Belin served as executive director.

11. After publishing *Inside the Company*, Agee faced ongoing CIA surveillance and harassment while living abroad (Agee 1987). The State Department revoked Agee's passport in 1979, but he continued to travel on Grenadian, Nicaraguan, and German passports, returning to the United States in the early 1990s.

12. This passage is not suggesting that "the big three" (Ford, Rockefeller, and Carnegie) did not also collaborate with the CIA; this is simply not under consideration here.

13. A CIA memo from a few years earlier expressed agency concerns that Ford Foundation applicants were asked to affirm that they were not linked to American intelligence agencies (FOIA CIA-RDP80B01676R004000140025–8, 5/2/53).

14. In 1998, CIA historian Gerald Haines published an analysis drawing on internal CIA documents and other sources on the Pike and Church committees' investigations. Haines contrasted Pike's independence with Church's cooperative work with CIA staff, observing that the Pike Committee "and its staff never developed a cooperative working relationship with the Agency or the Ford administration" (Haines 1998: 81). This animosity and contempt for the CIA's lawless behavior created difficulties in obtaining documents, which impacted their analysis.

TWO *World War II's Long Shadow*

1. The AAA recorded that in 1948, seventy-nine U.S. colleges and universities offered anthropology courses (*NBAAA* 1948 2[1]: 22).

2. The book was never completed.

3. Leighton described the riots at the 1948 Bogotá Inter-American Conference and noted that the CIA had warned the State Department that such protests were likely, adding that "no use was made of his findings" (Leighton 1949: 128).

4. On October 10, 1951, the Marshall Plan was replaced by the $7.5 billion Mutual Security Act.

5. Emilo Morán observed the Marshall Plan had "little use for anthropologists" (1996: 27).

6. The CIA's archives contain records of an OSS interview, a month after the Nazis' surrender, in which Claude Lévi-Strauss told the OSS agent that with the war over in France, "it might have been better to kill 50,000 collaborationists immediately" than to face these quislings in the years to come or let the French judicial system deal with them (Mehlman 2000: 181).

7. The "new Ruth Benedicts" showed few positive measurable results, designing and joining programs like Human Terrain Systems (see González 2010; NCA 2009).

8. This work stands in contrast to the national character studies conducted by Gorer, Mead, and others, which essentialized culture and personality in ways that did not allow such rapid shifts and adaptations due to deep cultural trends.

9. From 1949 to 1951, John W. Bennett was the chief of the Public Opinion and Sociological Research Division of the Civil Information and Education Section at GHQ, working under the supreme commander for the Allied powers in Japan. In 1951, Bennett was funded by the ONR for Japanese field studies (Bennett 1951).

10. Tami Tsuchiyama was the first Japanese American woman to earn a PhD in anthropology at the University of California, Berkeley. During the war she conducted covert research among Japanese Americans interned at the Poston, Arizona, camp, assisting sociologist Dorothy Thomas's Bureau of Sociological Research and the Japanese American Evacuation and Resettlement Study (D. H. Price 2008a: 143–70).

11. For more on these processes, see Steven Millhauser's short story "The Next Thing" (2008).

12. One 1951 advertisement for a job at Maxwell Air Force Base notified applicants that "security clearance is necessary" (*NBAAA* 1951 5[4]: 4).

THREE *Rebooting Professional Anthropology*

1. The Temporary Organizing Committee consisted of Homer Barnett (chair), Julian Steward, John Provinse, Clyde Kluckhohn, and Frank Roberts (Frantz 1974: 9).

2. In 1993, I learned of David Stout's reported history of American anthropology during the Second World War; my correspondence with members of the anthropology department at SUNY and with Stout's widow failed to locate this manuscript.

3. This study was authored by a group dominated by Princeton scholars: Ansley J. Coale (Office of Population Research, Princeton University); W. Phillips Davison (Council on Foreign Relations); Harry Eckstein (Center of International Studies, Princeton University); Klaus Knorr (Center of International Studies, Princeton University); Vincent V. McRae (Office of Special Assistant for Science and Technology, Washington, DC); Lucian W. Pye (CENIS, MIT); Thomas C. Schelling (Center for International Affairs, Cambridge, MA); Wilbur Schramm (Institute for Communications Research, Stanford University).

4. Huizer and Mannheim observed that "each foundation is controlled by a single family, such as Ford, Duke, Rockefeller, Carnegie, Kellogg, etc. To prevent the loss of family-controlled businesses through inheritance taxes, large blocks of stock are entrusted under the name of the foundations. The family members then place themselves, or their representatives, as trustees of the foundation. In this way foundations exist on the outer fringe of the capitalist system and experiment constantly with new 'nonviolent' ways by which the social organization of the society can better serve the economic needs of the ruling class" (1979: 481).

5. Steward's concerns about the politicization of the discipline betray a narrow conceptualization of political action. At the 1949 AAA annual meeting, a resolution was passed by the membership supporting Point IV, even while the AAA was taking extremely weak protective actions for Richard Morgan and Morris Swadesh, appointing FBI informer George P. Murdock to the association's committee protecting members' academic freedom (Price 2004b: 71–80).

6. See http://www.foia.cia.gov/sites/default/files/document_conversions/5829/CIA-RDP 80R01731R003400050047-3.pdf. During the postwar period, there were other efforts to compile rosters of anthropologists. In 1947, the Viking Fund and the AAA provided grants to the NRC's Committee on International Cooperation in Anthropology for the production of an international anthropological roster (AA 1948, 50[1]: 176).

7. In 1947, the NRC compiled a list of "anthropologists outside of the United States" (NBAAA 1[3]: 25).

8. Prior to approaching the Executive Board with this proposal, Johnson had privately told David Stout of the CIA's involvement with this project. In February 1951, Johnson briefed Stout about the roster. Johnson wrote: "Shortly I shall prepare a memorandum for the Executive Board which will explain a proposal made by the [handwritten: "Central"] Intelligence Agency. In essence they propose to do all the work connected with compiling a roster except for the mailing. Also the roster will be officially a project of the Association. Please do not jump to conclusions about this nor broadcast the idea until I can get the memorandum distributed" (AAA 36, FJ to DS, 2/19/51; more correspondence in D. H. Price 2003a).

9. This appears to refer to the following individuals: [Marshall T.] Newman, [William N.] Fenton, [Henry B.] Collins, [George] Foster, [Regina] Flannery, [F. H. H.] Roberts, and [Matthew] Stirling. The reference to "Jim Andrews" likely refers to archaeologist James Madison Andrews IV, then working at the CIA (see chapter 6).

10. My FOIA requests for CIA and FBI records pertaining to the AAA produced limited results, and statements that records relating to the association had been destroyed.

11. It is possible that the "Francis Kelly" referenced here and earlier is the Francis J. Kelley identified by Ray et al. (1979: 518) as working for the CIA in Liberia and Cyprus during the 1960s and 1970s.

12. In 1945, Johnson had instructed Steward, "It might be a good idea to add [provisions within the restructuring of the AAA] permitting balloting on questions by mail in the event that an annual meeting cannot be held. You will remember I did this with the SAA when we raised our dues. It was illegal as hell but practical and necessary so nobody kicked — but they could have done so and upset the whole thing" (AAAP 131, 10/5/45).

13. My FOIA requests for CIA records on the AAA were denied, "to the extent that [my] request seeks records that would reveal a covert connection between CIA and the [AAA's 1952 roster project]." The CIA claimed these records should remain undisclosed despite Executive Order 12958 (CIA to DHP 8/14/98).

14. Kenneth Holland worked for Nelson Rockefeller at the Committee on International Activities Abroad during the war and later became president of the Institute of International Education (IIE). At IIE he compiled lists of scholars working on international research for the Central Index of Education Exchanges. Holland oversaw the compilation of a list of more than two hundred thousand students participating in international education program (see BAAA 1955 3[1]: 13). Gerald Colby and Charlotte Dennett described Holland's IIE years during the 1960s as functioning as a "CIA conduit that administered the Fulbright Scholarship and student exchanges from its offices at U.N. Plaza. Holland had served on the [Organization of American States] Task Force

on Education and was considered well informed on student affairs during the tumultuous 1960s" (1995: 832). A *CounterSpy* article linked Holland to the American Institute for Free Labor Development (AIFLD), a CIA asset (*CounterSpy* 1975 2[2]: 42). In 1952, Holland joined the Board of the Foundation of Youth Student Affairs, where he "not only provided cover for the CIA but also annually screened applicants for [the National Student Association's] International Student Relations Seminar, a summer program that recruited (secretly) and trained future NSA international-staff" (Paget 2006: 77). Under FOIA, the CIA released documents establishing correspondence and meetings between DCI Dulles and Holland during the early 1960s (CIA-RDP80B01676R003500110024-8).

15. http://www.foia.cia.gov/sites/default/files/document_conversions/1705143/SYMPHONY%20%20VOL.%201_0011.pdf. Another CIA-released document described Maday being sent to Vienna in early 1946 to reorganize the Hungarian Red Cross office, noting that "he seems to be honest, but dumb and apparently is being used by the others, who staff the section." http://www.foia.cia.gov/sites/default/files/document_conversions/1705143/SYMPHONY%20%20%20VOL.%202_0009.pdf (CIA FOIA doc. 1705143, 4/27/46, Julius Schulz to Nikolaus Korda).

FOUR *After the Shooting War*

1. For Rockefeller, see Stocking 1985.

2. Among exceptions to this trend were several Bureau of Indian Affairs projects and Carnegie's Yucatan Community Studies' Maya Program (Redfield 1948).

3. The conference was held in New York on November 28-30, 1947, and had 106 participants (75 university faculty, 17 from federal government, 5 from foundations, and 9 from scholarly institutions) of which 24 were anthropologists, from nineteen universities and about two dozen academic departments (Wagley 1948: 3). Columbia, Yale, and Harvard sent the most individuals (14, 12, and 11 respectively); the State Department sent 9 individuals (Wagley 1948: 53–57).

4. Among those attending the conference were A. E. Hindmarsh (U.S. Naval Intelligence School); Elbert G. Matthews (Division of South Asian Affairs, Department of State); John A. Morrison (National War College); Howard Piquet (Select Committee on Foreign Aid, U.S. House of Representatives); Henry Lee Smith Jr. (Foreign Service Institute); Llewellyn E. Thompson Jr. (Division of Eastern European Affairs, Department of State); Rudolph A. Winnacker (National War College) and Bryce Wood (Rockefeller Foundation) (Wagley 1948: 53–57).

5. http://www.foia.cia.gov/sites/default/files/document_conversions/5829/CIA-RDP80 R01731R003100040052-1.pdf (accessed 5/18/13).

6. http://www.foia.cia.gov/sites/default/files/document_conversions/5829/CIA-RDP80 R01731R003500150016-5.pdf (accessed 5/18/13).

7. Friedrich's considerable linguistics skills and his father's prominence at Harvard contributed to his selection for this work. His father, Harvard political theorist Carl Friedrich, studied totalitarianism and coauthored the classic *Totalitarian Dictatorship and Autocracy* (1956) with Zbigniew Brzezinski.

8. http://www2.gwu.edu/~nsarchiv/NSAEBB/NSAEBB78/propaganda%20034.pdf, accessed 5/23/13.

9. Sweet later taught anthropology for many years at the University of Manitoba.

10. There is conflicting information surrounding who created the Modjokuto Project. Geertz remembered it originating with Oliver (see Handler 1991: 604–5), while Oliver remembered Kluckhohn's and Millikan's involvement in the project's conception (Oliver interview 7/10/95; Geertz phone interview 7/19/95). In 1952 the *News Bulletin of the* AAA announced, "Rufus Hendon will replace Douglas Oliver as director of a Gadjah Mada U. (Djokdjakarta)–Harvard University Project" (*NBAAA* 1952 6[4]: 8).

11. The Modjokuto Project fieldworkers were Alice Dewey, Donald Fagg, Clifford Geertz, Hildred Geertz, Rufus Hendon, Robert Jay, and Edward Ryan.

12. For more on CENIS and the political context of "the three I's," see Blackmer 2002: 67–69.

13. Gilman observed that "Geertz nowhere made his political position explicit" (2002: 15). But Geertz's silences, his opposition to applying academic knowledge to political movements opposing the Vietnam War, and his Council of Foreign Relations membership shed some light on his political engagements and orientation (see Rosen 2005).

14. Paul Rabinow described the Committee for the Comparative Study of New Nations as "one of numerous Third Way attempts that marked the twentieth century" (2006: 6), but this missed how analyses by Geertz, Fallers, and other project participants restated Rostow's modernization theory in ways that expanded dependencies and had nothing to do with progressive visions of "Third Ways."

15. The Council on Intercultural Relations, later known as the Institute for Intercultural Studies, was created during the Second World War as a clearinghouse for anthropologically informed work on national character research of enemy cultures "at a distance" (Mandler 2013: 68–70; Métraux 1980: 362).

16. Mead and Bateson described the roots of their interdisciplinary approach as influenced by pre- and postwar Macy Conferences, which pioneered studies of cybernetics and other innovative work (Brand 1976).

17. The political bias of this culture and personality work was critiqued by Soviet and Chinese anthropologists for its oversimplifications, and in China, it was said to "hide racist assumptions about the superiority and inferiority of different peoples. Mead's championing of the American model seemed to declare American culture a cut above others and worthy of imitation" (Guldin 1994: 121–22).

18. Wolff wrote Mead in 1940 concerning his research on "psychobiological aspects of peptic ulcer" (MM C6, HW to MM 9/3/40). Mead later suggested to Edwin Embree that Wolff join Gregory Bateson, Lyman Bryson, Mead, and Embree on a project (MM M1, MM to EE 3/5/43). Mead asked Wolff to help Mark Zborowski get NIMH funding in 1951 (MM M17, MM to HW 3/21/51).

19. Instead of celebrating or protecting Steinbeck's free speech rights, the FBI undertook extensive surveillance and harassment for his critiques of American capitalism (H. N. Smith 1949: 35–36; FBI HQ-9-4583, HQ 100–106224).

20. Kluckhohn and Parsons helped bring Nicholas Poppe, a Russian scholar of Mongolian ethnography, to the United States. At the war's end, Poppe was held by the Soviets as a Nazi collaborator. Poppe later claimed he had only translated for the Nazis "in the interest of the local people" (Poppe quoted in Oppenheimer 1997:77), but others found he assisted "the Nazis at the Wannssee Institute and his research helped round up Jews and Gypsies for the death squads," and that he was "a kind of 'Nazi sociologist'" (Porter 1996: 606, 608; see also O'Connell 1990; Oppenheimer 1997). Documents released under the CIA Sources Methods Exemption 382B Nazi War Crimes Disclosure Act confirm CIA knowledge of Poppe's Nazi connections even as the CIA worked to bring him to the United States without detection (FOIA CIA, vol. 1_0001, outline of Poppe movements 5/17/49–4/2/50). Parsons, Taylor, and Kluckhohn helped Poppe establish a teaching position at the University of Washington (GET 1/34: GET to Clyde Kluckhohn 7/18/49; GET 1/34: CK to GET 7/27/49, http://www.foia.cia.gov/sites/default/files/document_conversions/1705143/POPPE%2C%20NIKOLAI%20%20VOL.%201_0056.pdf). A 1949 CIA cable stated, "Taylor has made a firm offer which Poppe . . . has accepted, anything that we might do would be after the fact of the contract" (FOIA CIA "Secret CK NR 194 to: Seattle from Washington/ from [Lyman B.] Kirkpatrick," 7/21/49). Another CIA cable documents that Taylor was not told of the CIA's contact with Poppe (FOIA CIA, 7/21/49, L. B. Kirkpatrick to Acting Chief, Seattle Office; Poppe vol. 1_0057).

21. Rauch wrote, "The [Viking] Fund's founder, Axel L. Wenner-Gren, is a Swedish-international industrialist and financier who in May–July, 1939, figured in international politics. He was the non-publicized contact man in the Goering-Chamberlin efforts towards an English-German rapprochement based upon a common enmity towards the Soviet Union. *Documents on British Foreign Policy, 1919–1939*, 3rd series, VI (London, 1953), 736–42. More recently, Wenner-Gren has been spending $10 million on a Bahama Island playground for international aristocracy. *Time*, March 22, 1954, 39–40. Mr. Wenner-Gren also has purchased major holdings in the Ruhr steel producing firm manufacturing 25% of West Germany's annual output and, after his meeting with Alfred Krupp, speculation has been rife that Wenner-Gren will gain control of Krupp's important Constantine coal mine. *New York Herald-Tribune*, October 1, and 23, 1954" (Rauch 1955: 416).

FIVE *Anthropologists and State*

1. Results of my 1999 Defense Information Systems Agency FOIA request for defense projects indexed as involving "anthropology" located 237 projects, 18 percent of which were archaeological projects (DTIC-RSM, FOIA 99–125, 4/19/99); other identified projects included CIMA and SORO projects and a range of ethnographic studies, including ONR-sponsored Tlingit research—exemplifying dual use research unarticulated from direct militarized ends, furthering culture and personality models (de Laguna 1952: 1).

2. Fischer's arguments were identical to those made by contemporary anthropologists' explanations of their reasons for engaging with Pentagon and intelligence agencies:

arguments that they are not "tools" (cf. Fischer 1951: 133), claimed abilities to mitigate "the amount of natural disturbance" (133), to "serve as a channel of communication from the people to the administrator" (133).

3. Because John Embree died as he was developing this critique, questions remain about where his critique would have gone next. When he died, Embree was undergoing an extensive FBI background check as part of his clearance relating to a governmental employment opportunity. Given his radical critique, had Embree lived, he might have been the target of McCarthyist attacks, with the same sort of career problems as those faced by anthropologist critics such as Richard Morgan, Gene Weltfish, Jack Harris, and Morris Swadesh.

4. In August 1953, remaining IIAA projects were transferred to the TCA and the FOA.

5. Stephen Reed, Lucien Hanks, John Useem, David Mandelbaum, Lauriston Sharp, and Fred Eggan were associate editors for the manual project (*AA* 1951 [3]: 449; *AA* 1952(2)287).

6. In 1949, Willey consulted with Wendell Bennett, Julian Stewart, John H. Rowe, Harry Tschopik, Frederick Johnson, Cora Du Bois, and Edward Kinnard about Point IV plans.

7. Rostow later wrote that this memorandum was essentially "a rough first draft" of what would become their 1957 book, *A Proposal: Key to an Effective Foreign Policy* (see Rostow 1972: 89).

8. http://www.foia.cia.gov/sites/default/files/document_conversions/5829/CIA-RDP80 B01676R000100100032-7.pdf.

9. Anthropologists listed in the 1969 SEADAG directory are William L. Bradley (Rockefeller), Edward M. Bruner (Illinois), Clark Cunningham (Illinois), Fred Eggan (Chicago), Clifford Geertz (Chicago), Peter R. Goethals (University of North Carolina), Joel M. Halpern (UMass), Gerald Hickey, Jasper Ingersoll (Catholic University), Robert R. Jay (Brown), Charles Fenton Keyes (Washington), A. Thomas Kirsch (Princeton), Melvin Mednick (Temple), Michael Moerman (UCLA), Manning Nash (Chicago), Herbert P. Phillips (Berkeley), Lauriston Sharp (Cornell), Wilhelm G. Solheim II, Robert B. Textor (Stanford), and Aram A. Yengoyan (Michigan).

10. In 1968, SEADAG hosted its Asian-American Research Conference in Honolulu in late January (SEADAG 1969: x).

11. Marchetti and Marks (1974: 76) described the CIA convincing unwitting National Student Association officers to sign what they believed to be normal nondisclosure agreements, before revealing that the association had secret links to the CIA.

SIX *Cold War Anthropologists at the CIA*

1. See also *NBAAA* 1948 2[1]: 22. Andrews had worked with Hooton analyzing somatotype photographs of members of the U.S. military (*NBAAA* 1[3]: 49).

2. Dubberstein committed suicide in 1983 while facing charges claiming in 1977 he had passed along sensitive intelligence about regional military capacities to Muammar Gadaffi (Ayres 1983).

3. Lepowsky (2000: 162–63) suggested that Gower began working for the CIA in part because of widespread gender discrimination on American university campuses.

4. Worman became an international art expert, serving as president of the American Historical Print Collectors Society, and specialized in and collected the work of British orientalist travel illustrator William H. Bartlett. The Smithsonian's Archives of American Art holds the Eugene C. Worman Research Material on William H. Bartlett, 1835–1995, in the Archives of American Art (see ECW).

5. William Johnson identified Worman as the author of the CIA's internal "five volume unpublished transcript" history, deposited at the CIA archives in 1971: *History of the Office of Current Intelligence* (see Johnson 1976: 27n18).

6. The CIA refused to release records on James Madison Andrews IV under FOIA, replying that "to the extent [my] request might concern records containing information that would divulge the identity of an unacknowledged employee, it is denied" (CIA to DHP 6/3/98).

7. The memo described Andrews as "(Edward) WYLLYS ANDREWS IV, #2769, a former OSS/CIA employee who has lived in Mexico for many years and has continued to have social contacts with representatives of this Agency in Mexico as well as with Agency employees from Headquarters who visit him from time to time. ANDREWS, like CAIN, was born in Chicago of parents who also were born in the general area of Chicago" (CIA 104-10419-10321).

8. Bessac's claim of joining the CIA, prior to its creation in September 1947, presents its own problems. As Laird argues, while the CIG was the official governmental intelligence institution in July 1947 when these events occurred, "CIG's name was changed to the CIA informally as early as May 1, 1947, though it would not be formalized until September" (2002: 23).

9. Bessac later told people in Tibet he was not an official U.S. representative but was instead "a lost Fulbright scholar," thereby using his Fulbright status as a cover for his CIA-linked work (Laird 2002: 220).

10. Bessac claimed that soon after he resigned from the CIA, he "continued his language studies and applied for a Fulbright scholarship." The legal prohibitions against CIA agents using Fulbright fellowships as a cover for intelligence work present the most parsimonious explanation for Bessac's inconsistencies (Laird 2002: 98).

11. Bessac knew that "recipients of Fulbright grants were explicitly warned not to use their research as cover for intelligence work for the CIA" (Bessac and Bessac 2006: 79).

12. Laird rejects the possibility that Bessac resigned, citing information from Mongol and American sources. A former CIA agent told Laird that "Bessac would not have been allowed to quit after being sent back to China as a contract undercover agent" (Laird 2002: 57).

13. In the late 1970s, the AUFS's institutional members were the University of Alabama, the Asia Society, the Aspen Institute for Humanistic Studies, Brown University, the Institute for the Study of World Politics, the University of Kansas, Michigan State University, the University of Pittsburgh, Rampo College of New Jersey, and the University of Wisconsin (JLA, Box 10, LD to JLA 11/23/78).

14. See chapter 11 for a discussion of Elizabeth Bacon's suspicions of the AUFS as a CIA front.

15. Fischel was a key player in MSUG's CIA work in Vietnam (Ernst 1998). At Michigan State, Hanifi initially studied police administration, later taking up anthropology. When I asked Hanifi about the CIA's presence in international policing studies during this period, he replied: "I doubt that the choice of my studying police administration involved the CIA. As I remember this decision was grabbed out of the air by the Afghan minister of finance (Abd al-Malik Abdulrahimzai) on the spot. He and my father were friends and of the same Paxtun tribe. I guess they both thought (or hoped) I could become rich like all other customs high officials in the country!" (MJH to DHP 11/5/05). Hanifi recalled "large numbers of Vietnamese who were brought to MSU for police training" (MJH to DHP 11/5/05).

16. John Allison's fieldwork in Afghanistan in the 1960s led to his recruitment for Human Terrain Systems in 2009 (see D. H. Price 2011f: 155–72).

17. John Allison later reflected: "I think it was Jack (John) Shroder at University of Nebraska, Omaha, who told me this story that typifies the swash-buckling clown version of Dupree's image: There was a major dinner for Europeans and [Americans] with Afghan political leaders and privileged members of the ruling class, maybe even the King was there. Dupree was one of the main [American] guests. At the time dinner began, Louis and Nancy had not arrived. Then, when dinner was over, and the drinking was beginning, there is a knock at the door. When the door is open, Louis leaves a well-dressed Nancy standing at the door and comes running in and does a series of forward hand flips across the marble floor, and ends up standing in front of the Afghan and Euro-American dignitaries, smiling. He is more or less well dressed, but, he has on a red dress shirt and has pulled the shirt front through the zipper of his pants suit and zipped it up so the red shirt is sticking straight out through the zipper, resembling, for all to see, a dick" (2012).

18. However, a 1980 congressional investigation of the Soviet invasion of Afghanistan mentions a Soviet who "falsely" identified Dupree as a CIA operative (U.S. Congress 1980: 121).

19. Examples of such dubious assertions include his claims to have originated the idea of moving the monuments at Abu Simbel displaced by the Aswan Dam, and engaging in wife sharing in the Egyptian village of Gurna (Wilber 1986: 15, 17).

20. Other American anthropologists working in Iran during this period include Elizabeth Bacon, Henry Field (summer 1950) (*NBAAA* 1950 4[3]: 4), and Carleton Coon (summer 1949) (*NBAAA* 1949 3[3]: 5).

21. Roosevelt claimed he designed the CIA's coup plan, though Wilber's (1986: 187–95) CIA account, released in the *New York Times*' FOIA request, shows Wilber's central role.

22. In his book *Countercoup*, Roosevelt described Wilber's involvement in the planning of the coup, though it did not identify him by name. Roosevelt wrote, "Another Persian expert—an exceptionally thin man with a razor-sharp mind and less guilt-ridden than our other professional friend—participated in a key role during preparation of much of the plan. He enjoyed it thoroughly and in return gave much enjoyment to his co-workers. Soon after I had first met him, he unnecessarily informed me that he had a

'lithp.' He was not, in appearance, anyone's idea of a secret operator, being very tall and *very* shy, with a diffident air and a modest almost, self-deprecating grin. His sense of humor was deceptively casual, and even after one knew him well, it was difficult to be sure whether he was serious or teasing in his proposals" (1979: 128). Wilber later confirmed that this passage referred to him (Wilber 1986: 188).

SEVEN *How Funding Fronts Shaped Research*

1. In 1961, Frederick Praeger offered to publish a book by Allen Dulles, but Dulles declined (FOIA CIA-RDP80B01676R003500210012-0, 8/19/61).

2. Fodor's distributors denied CIA connections, but Hunt claimed that Eugene Fodor was "a former agent for the C.I.A. in Austria" (Hersh 1974a: 4). Fodor admitted he "had cooperated with the Central Intelligence Agency" but denied Hunt's accusation he was a CIA agent in Austria, while refusing to comment on Hunt's claim that he used his status as a travel writer as cover for CIA operations (Van Gelder 1975).

3. Hunter's intelligence links stretched back to the war, when his OSS service overlapped with that of Gregory Bateson, Julia Child, and Cora Du Bois at the OSS installation in Kandy, Ceylon (Hunter 1959: 12, 14).

4. The CFA's board included presidents of the University of California, Stanford, and Standard Oil and the novelist James A. Michener (Defty 2004: 207; Cummings 2010: 48–49).

5. This quote by John F. Sullivan comes from a cover letter, dated March 25, 1953, found in the interlibrary loan copy I read (in 2010) of *Land Reform: Communist China, Nationalist China, Taiwan, India, Pakistan*.

6. Ekvall, born to American missionaries, spent decades in China and undertook graduate studies in anthropology at the University of Chicago.

7. This was the Conference of the Western Regional American Assembly on the United States and the Far East (RB 1,6).

8. The foundation personnel and the assigned geographic regions listed in the directory were President Robert Blum, Robert B. Hall (Japan), Laurence G. Thompson (Korea), Earl Swisher (Taiwan), James T. Ivy (Hong Kong), L. Albert Wilson (Philippines), Edgar N. Pike (Viet Nam), Leonard C. Overton (Cambodia), Noel F. Busch (Thailand), Patrick Judge (Malaya), Raymond V. Johnson (Indonesia), John H. Tallman (Burma), William T. Fleming (Ceylon), Richard J. Miller (Pakistan), and Harold L. Amoss Jr. (Afghanistan) (Morehouse 1957: 52–53).

9. Sources in Morehouse 1957: Association of Asian Studies (56); Boy Scouts of America (64); East Asia Teacher Training (70); Burmese scholars (56); Japanese scholars (71); book buying (83); citizen education (86–87); business education (143); summer study (239); radio commentaries (289); economic analysis (395).

10. I first reported this CIA-AAA relationship at the 2011 AAA annual meeting (D. H. Price 2011a).

11. The AAA's Asia Foundation grant committee was composed of David Mandelbaum, Richard K. Beardsley, Cora Du Bois, and Edward Norbeck.

12. This count of 413 individuals includes some who participated for multiple years. The gaps in the AAA's records suggest that the total number of recipients was likely higher than the recorded 413 (AAAP 73).

13. One AAA document from 1958 records that Kwang-Chih Chang was awarded $205.90 to travel from Cambridge to Memphis and back to observe a Peabody Museum excavation that was under way (AAAP 49, Du Bois to Godfrey 4/17/58). In 1959, the following Asian anthropologists were provided hundreds of dollars in Asia Foundation grants to enable them to attend the AAA annual meeting in Mexico City: R. P. Srivastava, Yih-yuan Li, K. N. Sharma, Hiroko Sue, and Alfredo Villanueva (AAAP 73, BM to DM 10/19/59). Another Asian anthropologist at a New England university received ninety-eight dollars to attend the AAA annual meeting in Chicago in 1958 (AAAP 49, M. Nag to W. Godfrey 1/27/58); in 1959, five Asian anthropologists were provided hundreds of dollars to attend that year's AAA annual meeting in Mexico City (AAAP 73, BM to DM 10/19/59).

14. For Robert Spencer, see BIC 2014c; for Agehananda Bharati, see Bharati 1970: 263; for Wilton Dillon, see *AAAFN* 1966 7[7]: 8. While several conspiracy-minded writers have attempted to connect President Obama's mother to the CIA through Asia Foundation funding or other means, I know of no evidence supporting such a connection. Stanley Ann Dunham received Asia Foundation funds in 1972 for Indonesian research more than five years *after* the CIA stopped funding the Asia Foundation (for misleading claims of Obama-Dunham CIA links, see Madsen 2012).

15. Asia Foundation board members identified by the *New York Times* were President Haydn Williams (former U.S. assistant secretary of defense); Robert B. Anderson (former secretary of the Treasury); Barry Bingham (publisher); Ellsworth Bunker (U.S. ambassador to South Vietnam); Arthur H. Dean (State Department); Mortimer Fleishhacker Jr. (San Francisco businessman); Caryl O. Haskins (president, Carnegie Institute of Washington); Charles J. Hitch (vice president, University of California); Paul Hoffman (former president, Ford Foundation), Grayson L. Kirk (president, Columbia University); Turner H. McBain (San Francisco lawyer); Walter H. Mallory (former executive director; Council on Foreign Relations); Robbins Milbank (New York advertising professional); Mrs. Maurice T. Moore (chair, Institute of International Education); Lucian W. Pye (professor of political science, MIT); Edwin O. Reischauer (former U.S. ambassador to Japan); Russell G. Smith (vice president, Bank of America); J. E. Wallace Sterling (president, Stanford University); Adlai Stevenson (U.S. representative to the UN); and J. D. Zellerbach (U.S. ambassador to Italy) (Turner 1967: 17).

16. The 303 Committee — named after National Security Action Memorandum No. 303 establishing its existence on June 2, 1964 — was the oversight body reviewing CIA covert actions. The 303 Committee reported to the president; it was first chaired by McGeorge Bundy and was succeeded by the 40 Committee.

17. See http://www.state.gov/r/pa/ho/frus/johnsonlb/x/9062.htm 8/5/66 (accessed 8/23/12).

18. Marchetti and Marks (1974: 200–201) report the foundation secretly received a large severance package.

19. Attending the April 17–18 meeting in New York City were Irving Rouse (president), Cora Du Bois (president-elect), Harold Conklin, David French, Conrad Arensberg, Helen Codere, Dell Hymes, David Schneider, Charles Frantz (executive secretary), Ward Goodenough, and Edward Lehman (business manager).

EIGHT *Unwitting CIA Collaborators*

1. Without direct evidence, McCoy speculates that Stanley Milgram's research was covertly funded by the CIA under such programs; Milgram's biographer rejects this possibility (cf. McCoy 2006: 49; Blass 2006).

2. Expenses for the Society for the Investigation of Human Ecology's expenses included a high-rent townhouse ($1,200 a month) and $180,000 a year in salaries and other operating expenses; the organization spent $5 million of CIA funds during its last three years (G. Thomas 1989: 153–54).

3. In 1935, Wolff experimentally induced and measured controlled headaches in research subjects at Cornell (Science News 1935).

4. DCI Dulles wrote Wolff a personal reply after receiving a copy of the interrogation article "Every Man Has His Breaking Point" (1960) (FOIA CIA-RDP80B01676R003700110110, 3/28/60).

5. Some Human Ecology Fund records survive in Wolff's professional papers at Cornell Medical School. Draft materials for the 1957 report, cut from the final report, include a list of six proposed studies considered for funding : (1) studying "comparable groups of frequently ill and essentially healthy people drawn from a homogeneous working population"; (2) social mobility among business executives; (3) studying the population of New York's National Diabetes Association camp; (4) ecological factors contributing to coronary occlusions; (5) lab research on functions of the central nervous system; (6) publish data from previous Human Ecology studies (HW 6, 15).

6. Organizations that financially supported Human Ecology included Baird Foundation, Broad-High Foundation, Derwent Foundation, Foresight Foundation, Littauer Foundation, Michigan Fund, Phoenix Foundation, Social Research Foundation, Sonnabend Foundation, and Southern and Western Foundation (HEF 1963: 10). Organizations that received Human Ecology funds included the Academy of Science for East Africa (SFIHER 1963); the African Research Foundation (SFIHER 1963); Dunlap and Associates, Inc. (Suggs 1962; Yarnold and Suggs 1961); the Foundation for Instrumentation Education and Research (Slater 1961); and Panoramic Research Inc. (SFIHER 1963).

7. Rhodes participated in a series of unethical drug experiments, including efforts to dose unsuspecting people with an aerosol of LSD supplied by an MK-Ultra research program (Marks 1979: 156–57, 99).

8. Mead maintained a friendship with Wolff for several decades; they had known each other since at least the mid-1940s (MM M3, HW to MM 5/24/45). A story in the November 1951 issue of the *News Bulletin of the AAA* stated that Mead was the "representative of anthropology" at the NIMH-sponsored Work Conference in Mental Health Research, where she worked alongside Wolff (NBAAA 1951 5[4]: 4–5). In 1951, Mead corresponded

with Wolff regarding Mark Zborowski's anthropological studies of pain (MM M17, MM to HW 4/21/51). In 1958, she alerted Wolff to Daniel Gadjusek's research into Kuru among the Fore of New Guinea (MM C41, MM to HW 7/21/58). Wolff, who was on the board of IFIS, received funds from the Research in Contemporary Cultures project for "a medically oriented project, studies in Human Ecology–China" that he directed (R. Métraux 1980: 362).

9. See also *AAAFN* 1966 7[2]: 8; erratum *AAAFN* 1967 8[4]: 8.

10. In the "Ticker Tape USA" section of *JET* magazine (10/26/61, 23), under a headline reading, "Africa Needs U.S. Negro Teachers, Says Scholar," a notice mentioned Kennedy's Human Ecology–funded project.

11. Stephenson received a grant from the SIHE in 1956–57 (BIC 2014a).

12. These catatonics are reminiscent of the precogs that had appeared in Philip K. Dick's short story "The Minority Report" (Dick [1956] 1987).

13. Stover wrote elsewhere about science fiction's potential for illuminating anthropological findings (Stover 1968, 1973).

14. Human Ecology–funded grants appearing to fit this model include Janet Hartle's $948.75 grant to reexamine Central Mongol skulls (HEF 1963: 19); Robert C. Suggs's $700 grant to compare Marquesan behavior with that found on various Polynesian islands (HEF 1963: 18); ethnomusicologist William Kay Archer's study of "the ecology of music" (Archer 1962, 1964); a study on psychological impacts of circumcision on Turkish boys — though it is possible that this and other studies provided information on cultural elements of separation, trauma, and reintegration that are core elements of the interrogation literature (Marks 1979: 158). Human Ecology's interest in funding research by Dr. Beatrice Berle (wife of Human Ecology board member Adolf Berle) on family illnesses in Harlem remains unclear (HEF 1963: 41). It may be that the fund provided a board member's spouse with a nepotistic kickback unrelated to MK-Ultra's interests.

15. Charles Osgood later stated he did not know he was receiving CIA funds for his Human Ecology–sponsored cross-cultural communications research. These communications projects aligned with larger MK-Ultra projects studying effective propaganda techniques, with specific emphasis on cultural barriers to effective cross-cultural communication (see Tanaka, Oyama, and Osgood 1963).

16. The Human Ecology Fund provided funds to B. F. Skinner to write an autobiographical essay for his Festschrift (Skinner 1970: 1n1). Human Ecology funds also supported Skinner's work for the Symposium on the Application of Operant Conditioning at the 1964 annual meeting of the American Psychological Association (see Skinner 1966: 13).

17. The emphasis occurs in the original document and likely signified that these terms were cross-indexed in the CIA files.

18. From 1959 to 1964, Samuel B. Lyerly (former editor of *Psychometrika*) was the research director of the Human Ecology Fund, a position that likely required knowledge of the CIA's involvement in the fund (POQ 1964).

19. Prior to receiving this grant, Carr produced papers such as "China's Young Communist League, Functions and Structures" (see Franke 1959: 549). In March 1964, Carr

joined Human Ecology's staff (*AAAFN* 1964 5[5]: 6; see also Carr and Tullock 1965). Years later, Human Ecology grant recipient Leon Stover (1974) wrote on Chinese cultural ecology, but this work appears unconnected to these projects.

20. Hall previously taught cultural sensitivity at the Department of State and the Strategic Intelligence School (Coffield 1959).

21. In *The Silent Language,* Hall discussed the role played by cultural expectations in the interrogation of Japanese prisoners during World War Two (E. T. Hall 1959: 77).

22. In 1959, the CIA's journal, *Studies in Intelligence,* reviewed Hall's book *The Silence Language,* stressing that "the understanding of foreign cultures is critical to intelligence operations and to intelligence analysis; and such a considerable contribution to new thinking as *The Silent Language* makes can but stimulate more progress toward this understanding" (Coffield 1959).

23. Air Force contract No. AF 18(600)1797.

24. Marvin Opler arranged Anderson's Human Ecology support (Anderson 1965: 181n1).

25. Sociologist Jay Schulman was part of Human Ecology's program studying Hungarian refugees (see U.S. Senate 1977: 60). There may be a publication by Schulman describing his work with Human Ecology that I am unaware of, or Scott may have been thinking of Stephenson's account (1978) or the article by Greenfield (1977) that quotes Schulman.

26. Another Human Ecology research project undertaken by Howard organized data he collected in fieldwork studying Rotuman sexuality (Howard and Howard 1964: 282). Almost two decades later, Howard coauthored a paper (with no connection to Human Ecology) examining symbolic and functional features of torture traditionally practiced by the Huron on prisoners of war and other cultural groups (Bilmes and Howard 1980).

27. Howard and Scott's 1965 article acknowledged the help of Leonard Cottrell Jr., who had chaired the Defense Department's advisory group on psychological warfare and sat on similar boards at the air force and army (Simpson 1994: 61).

28. DCI Stansfield Turner mistakenly testified that the Privacy Act prevented the identification of all scholars working on MK-Ultra projects at Human Ecology (U.S. Senate 1977: 13). At least one witting researcher, Harold Wolff, was dead and thus had no Privacy Act protections.

29. Among Wolff's surviving papers is correspondence with a Bureau of Narcotics officer, George H. White, on the topic of political prisoner abuse (e.g., HW 6; GHW to HGW 12/27/56). White was later exposed during the Church Committee hearings, and Kennedy's Subcommittee on Health and Scientific Research Senate hearings for his role in doping unsuspecting members of the public with LSD and other powerful drugs, and operating a safe house at 225 Chestnut Street in San Francisco.

NINE Cold War Fieldwork

1. Howell observed that "an indicator of the degree of trust and good will of the local population is probably found in the frequency with which investigators are accused of

spying, a charge that is difficult to defend against when one is there in search of information, and the uses to which it will be put cannot easily be explained to the locals" (1990: 97).

2. The CIA sometimes monitored foreign anthropologists in their own countries. A 1954 CIA report on the Sociedad de Amigos de Guatemala identified Mexican anthropologist Dr. Alfonso Caso as supporting Jacobo Árbenz, noting Caso's presence at the 1949 Mexico City and 1952 Montevideo Continental Peace Congresses (CIA 1953). "Sociedad de Amigos de Guatemala," DOC_0000914527, 12/21/53.

3. http://www.foia.cia.gov/sites/default/files/document_conversions/5829/CIA-RDP80 R01731R000500020001–8.pdf (accessed 4/20/13).

4. http://www.foia.cia.gov/sites/default/files/document_conversions/5829/CIA-RDP80 R01731R000500020005–4.pdf (accessed 4/20/13).

5. See CIA, MORI DocID: 242535, Roland Dulin to R. C. Read 1/4/46; CIA MORI DocID: 242537, RD to RCR 1/9/46.

6. Kennedy's classroom attacks on religion, as a "matter of ghosts, spirits and emotions," in his "Introduction to Anthropology" course so offended his undergraduate student William F. Buckley that Buckley wrote *Man and God at Yale*, in part as a reaction to Kennedy (Buckley 1951: 14).

7. During the 1950s, Kattenburg regularly briefed the Intelligence Advisory Committee (CIA 2/5/55 CIA-RDP85S00362R000200060028–3; http://www.foia.cia.gov/sites/default /files/document_conversions/5829/CIA-RDP85S00362R000200060028–3.pdf).

8. Kattenburg speculated that Darul Islam might have been involved in the murders or that Kennedy and Doyle may have been "victims of local thugs intent on capturing the several thousand U.S. dollars that many in West Java knew Kennedy had with him" (Gardner 1997: 68n50).

9. http://www.trumanlibrary.org/oralhist/cadyjf.htm.

10. In a 2012 conversation, Harold Conklin told me he had not known Kennedy, but as a graduate student at Yale with a working knowledge of Indonesian, he was asked to edit Kennedy's notes; see also Conklin 1998: xxiv.

11. For example, one entry in his field notes read: "The KNIL [Koninklijk Nederlandsch Indisch Leger] is about 40,000 strong, highly trained, consisting mainly of Ambonese, Minahasans and Indos" (1953b: 222).

12. Between the war and his work for the CIA, Millegan briefly worked for the Department of State (see *Far Eastern Quarterly* 1948, 7[4]: 411; Millegan 1942; J. W. Hall 1952: 294).

13. Handy founded Genethnics Inc., a corporation collecting data on heredity, personality, and environmental data on individuals with hopes of developing explanatory theories.

14. Nine years later, Millegan's master's thesis (1959) examined Indonesian heterogeneity and the political context of Indonesian Protestantism, exploring Indonesian Protestants' alignment with the Indonesian state's opposition to communism.

15. Axel Wenner-Gren's FBI file began in 1940 with a report monitoring the travels of his yacht, *The Southern Cross*, and his reported contacts with Nazis. One letter from J. Edgar Hoover to Assistant Secretary of State Adolf Berle expressed concern over Wenner-Gren's "contacts with Field Marshal Herman Goering of Germany" (FBI 65-885783,

9/10/40). George Dixon's story in the *Washington Times Herald* (3/22/49) on Wenner-Gren's successful campaign to get his name removed from the State Department's blacklist, described Wenner-Gren as a "one time crony of Herman Goering" and as having pulled "every wire at his command to have the barrier lifted" (FBI 65-8857-A). Dixon credited former New York state senator John A. Hastings with helping remove Wenner-Gren from the blacklist.

FBI reports summarized Wenner-Gren's financial dealings with the Nazis during the war as linked to his financial control of the Bofors Armament Works (previously held by Krupp). One FBI report quoted a "confidential source" who reported "hearing Goering say in 1933 that Wenner-Gren was one of the most powerful instruments which the Nazis would be able to use in their economic operations with important people in England, France, and the United States" (FBI 100-769-33538, 1/16/61). The report stated: "Goering allegedly claimed that Wenner-Gren mentioned important connections in the United States and England, claimed he was personally acquainted with the President of the United States and indicated he might negotiate a peace settlement. Goering allegedly stated that Wenner-Gren's peace plan was regarded by Hitler as a very confused project and was rejected. Goering further was reported to have stated that he personally believed Wenner-Gren was an opportunist, who, when in Berlin, was very flattering concerning the National Socialist system and its successes, but undoubtedly was just as critical of National Socialism when he was talking with persons not sympathetic to Nazism" (FBI 100-769-33538, 1/16/1961; FBI 65-8857-862).

We are left with more questions than answers concerning Axel Wenner-Gren's alleged links to the Nazis; but regardless of the veracity of these allegations, his foundation would likely have complied with government requests made during these postwar years. Like other postwar foundations, some Viking Fund projects in this period had links to governmental concerns (see Ross 1999), including projects such as the $10,000 provided in 1947 to the National Research Council and the "Pacific Science Board for anthropological work in Micronesia" linked to CIMA and ONR funding (Viking Fund 1951:15).

16. Inga Arvad's extensive FBI file (exceeding one thousand pages) documents FBI investigations of her wartime sexual relationship with John F. Kennedy and her meetings with Adolf Hitler, Joseph Goebbels, and other high-ranking Nazis (FBI 65-39058).

17. Fejos wrote Millegan in 1954, requesting a final report for his 1950–51 (no. 508) fellowship. Millegan responded that his parents had died in a plane crash in December 1950; that his "preliminary work" in Indonesia was carried out between September and October 1950; and that illness, the death of his parents (December 1950), and housing problems prevented him "from completing the survey and publishing the results" (LSM, LM to PF 1/19/55). Fejos requested more information on Millegan's accomplishments and an accounting of funds for the Board of Directors (LSM, PF to LM 1/27/55). Millegan again sent a copy of his June 15, 1951, preliminary report, which Fejos accepted as a final report (LSM, PF to LM 2/12/55).

18. "Dr. Eckel" was apparently Paul Edward Eckel, who may have had contact with Millegan while both conducted OSS Asian intelligence work during the war. Eckel worked at the U.S. Foreign Broadcast Intelligence Service and was with the CIA for years.

He was reportedly the CIA agent who assisted in South Africa's arrest of Nelson Mandela in August 1962 (see Albright and Kunstel 1990).

19. An otherwise unknown individual identified as George Nievel was listed as providing start-up funds (FBI 100-346660-1, 8/26/46).

20. Pacific Book's incorporation date of 1946 predates the establishment of the CIA, though this was a period in which Lloyd Millegan's son Chris reports his father was associated with one of the military intelligence branch units bridging the transition between OSS and CIA (KM 9/28/10).

21. This appears to be Kenneth Landgon, whose wife, Margaret Langdon, wrote *The King and I*, in part based on their years in Thailand in the diplomatic corps.

22. See *Publishers Weekly* 1951, 160: 1904, 2252; *Publishers Weekly* 1951, 160: 768. The business address is identified in *Publishers Weekly* as Pacific Book and Supply Corporation, 667 Madison Avenue, New York, NY; see also BDNA 1956: 109.

23. *Publishers Weekly* identified Franklyn R. Forkert as Pacific Book and Supply's late-1950s "sales manager and treasurer in New York City" (see *Publishers Weekly* 1965, 188: 84). A 1957 *Publishers Weekly* article from 1957 announced Pacific Book's Joseph Culbertson was operating a "portable model American Book Shop" with five thousand books in Indonesia (*Publishers Weekly* 1957, 172: 16). Joseph L. Culbertson's involvement is listed in the 1987 membership directory of the Association of Former Intelligence Officers (AFIO 1987).

24. Anthropologists gathered other forms of Cold War–linked data from remote corners of the world. For example, some of Napoleon Chagnon's fieldwork among the remote Yanomami of Brazilian-Venezuelan rain forests was funded by the Atomic Energy Commission as he assisted James Neel's efforts to retrieve blood samples from the Indians to measure levels of trace fallout radiation from distant nuclear weapons tests (see Ferguson 1995).

TEN Cold War Counterinsurgency Dreams

1. One 1951 CIA memorandum on "intelligence support for psychological operations" stressed the importance of anthropological research for such operations. The memo described anthropologists providing information on topics such as "level of education, standard of living, political views or cultural ties of various groups such as French labor, Uzbek tribesmen, etc." (FOIA CIA-RDP80R01731R003500180010-8, 6/14/51).

2. HRAF was founded in 1948 as a "cooperative interuniversity organization" originally consisting of ten universities and the Office of Naval Research (Roe 2007: 53).

3. See Barnett 1958; Harris 1958a, 1958b; Lipsky 1959; Steinberg 1959; Changdu 1960; Fitzsimmons 1960; LeBar and Suddard 1960.

4. Graham was the former executive secretary of the Department of Defense's Committee on Psychological and Unconventional Warfare. At the Brookings Institute, Graham studied how military and intelligence organizations could better access academic research (see Graham 1954; HRAF 1959: 24).

5. Committee members included Robert K. Merton, Clyde Kluckhohn, Max Millikan, and Samuel A. Stouffer.

6. HRAF's use of this quote in its annual report stopped short of stating that years of HRAF data collection and classification had "been supported by grants from the military departments" (Bauer et al. 1958: 225).

7. The production of these reports later shifted from HRAF to SORO's Foreign Area Studies Division (FASD).

8. Vreeland was a student of Owen Lattimore and a scholar of Mongolian society. Despite his marriage to a White Russian and pro-military associations, he was suspected by the FBI of being a Communist after Lattimore's 1952 perjury indictment (FBI 128–5130).

9. After HRAF's subcontractors completed the initial text for the Army Handbooks, SORO oversaw revisions and expansions of the handbooks for military consumption (SORO Box 1, SORO memo, Standing Operating Procedures for the Production of Foreign Area Handbooks under Contract DA-49-083-OSA-2427, 10/16/63).

10. Riddleberger later became a spokesperson at the World Bank.

11. In 1965, while on leave from the University of Kansas, Moos received a $61,000 Unconventional Warfare and Counterinsurgency Research SORO grant to study "SORO Elements of Human Factors and Operations" (associated with the "Research Office—Korea") (SORO Box 1 Final Report Subcommittee on Behavioral Sciences Defense Science Board, 1965 DoD, 40; see also *AAAFN* 1965 2 [1]: 7).

12. The report acknowledged assistance from SORO "staff anthropologists," Herbert H. Vreeland III, and Howard K. Kauffman and Dr. Ritchie P. Lowry (trained in sociology) (Lippincott and Dame 1964: i).

13. See the discussion of Maday in chapter 3.

14. Horowitz wrote that Galtung rejected the premise that the military could be involved in reducing conflict and "was deeply concerned about the possibility of European scholars being frozen out of Latin American studies by an inundation of sociologists from the United States. Furthermore, he expressed fears that the scale of Camelot honoraria would completely destroy the social science labor market in Latin America" (1965: 5).

15. Nutini told Ralph Beals that he "absolutely never said that Camelot would be financed by NSF" (RB 75, HGN to RB 9/17/66).

16. Murdock was then the head of the NAS/NRC Social Science Division.

17. The NRC's Advisory Committee on Government Programs in the Behavioral Sciences (ACGPBS) included psychologists, sociologists, geographers, economists, and political scientists, as well as anthropologists: Allen Holmberg, George Foster, Alexander Spoehr, and Donald R. Young (chair) (see Deitchman 1976: 206). The committee argued that, while military and intelligence agencies sought specific forms of behavioral science knowledge, "the primary responsibility for government support for behavioral science research and training conducted in foreign countries by universities in the United States [should] be placed in agencies and programs committed to basic research and research training, particularly the National Science Foundation, the National Institutes of Health, and the proposed Center for Educational Cooperation under the International

Education Act" (ACGPBS 1968: 9). The committee recommended increased general NSF funding for social sciences.

18. Rohde (2007: 284–93) indicates the credited M-VICO authors were at SORO during the following periods: James Price (1962–69), Barbara R. Butler (1962–65), Doris Condit (1956–70), Bert Cooper (1961–69), Michael Conley (1964–69), and Richard H. Moore (1964–68). From this information we can fix the date of M-VICO as between 1964 (when Conley and Moore began working for SORO) and 1965 (when Butler left SORO). None of the M-VICO authors were anthropologists, and the authors came from the following disciplines: Price, Butler and Cooper: international relations; Condit and Conley: history; Moore: military science (SORO 2 roster; Rohde 2007).

19. The introduction to M-VICO refers to CINFAC in the future tense, writing that it "will be conceived and organized along pragmatic lines" (J. R. Price et al. ca. 1964–65: intro. 1).

20. It is unclear whether HRAF was aware that SORO had adopted and republished its copyright-protected OCM as a governmental document.

21. A CIA memo, "Unauthorized Release of OCR Intelligence Publication Index (IPI) to Department of Army Contractor" (1967), indicated that from 1962 to 1965, CRESS had access to the DIA's classified *Intelligence Publication Index* (CIA documents, sent 6/25/09).

22. Rohde identified CRESS's director, psychologist Preston Abbot, as continuing this director role at the American Institute for Research (AIR) (2007: 250). Abbot had been director of Research Programs at the Human Ecology Fund; in 1975 he left AIR, founding Abbot Associates, which produced intelligence policy reports on the Middle East (Rohde 2007: 256; AAAFN 1966 7 [2]: 8).

23. The eighteen identified "tribal groups" were the Bahnar, Bru, Cua, Halang, Hre, Hroi, Jarai, Jeh, Katu, Koho, Ma, M'nong, Muong, Raglai, Rengao, Rhade, Sedang, Stieng; the seven chapters on "other minority groups" discussed the Binh Xuye, Cao Dai, Cham, Chinese, Hoa Hao, Khmer, and Indians and Pakistanis (Schrock et al. 1966).

24. Among the social scientists whose work was cited were Gerald Hickey (Schrock et al. 1966: 52), Frank LeBar, Gerald Hickey, and John K. Musgrave (88), David Thomas (52), Georges Coedés (87), Georges Condominas (523), George Devereux (647), Frederic Wickert (649), John D. Donoghue (717), and Paul K. Benedict (1119).

25. Suspicions and accusations of links between the SIL and the CIA are widespread among anthropologists. Most claimed links are circumstantial. I made extensive CIA FOIA requests for SIL records (resulting in the release of cables relating to reports of kidnapped missionaries and other news accounts) and have read the published literature critiquing SIL and made several archival inquiries. Although Colby and Dennett and Stoll establish a series of clear symbiotic relationships between the SIL and American economic, military, and intelligence ventures, there remains a lack of firm documentation establishing direct, directive connections between the CIA and the SIL (see Colby and Dennett 1995; Stoll 1982).

26. References to this 1954 CINFAC and HRAF document can be found in Schrock et al. 1966: 920, 929.

27. Ember misrepresented his knowledge and that of others at HRAF about HRAF's CIA connections by claiming that the board had not been told (while Shweder confirmed that as a HRAF board member he was aware of HRAF's CIA links). Ember wrote to me that "the CIA was an Associate Member of the HRAF consortium between 1979 and 1983, and I don't think that the Board of Directors was told about it" (ME to DHP 7/18/95).

28. There are enough instances of the military republishing and translating the published writings of unaware anthropologists that it is possible they did not consult HRAF about this adaptation of their rubrics — though SORO's relationship with HRAF at American University reduces this likelihood (see Condominas 1973).

ELEVEN *Uses of Disciplinary Knowledge*

1. The provision granting fellow status to some anthropologists holding bachelor's degrees did not mean that most graduate students could vote; it meant that working anthropologists (frequently archaeologists), "actively engaged in anthropology," might be granted voting rights.

2. Suggs and Carr received Human Ecology Fund grants, and in 1964 Carr joined the Human Ecology Fund's staff (*AAAFN* 1964 5[5]: 6).

3. See also *AAAFN* 1962 3[7]: 4–6; *AAAFN* 1962 4[5]: 2.

4. After the 1965 AAA annual meeting, Peter Kunstadter protested to the Executive Board what he misunderstood to be an official resolution by the AAA Council disapproving of anthropologists' "negotiations with the Department of Defense to carry out research" (RB 75, EB Minutes 5/20–21/66). After Kunstadter received more information on the board's position, he withdrew his complaint.

5. Beals came from a family with radical political roots. During his childhood, his mother had run for state office and was a Socialist; Beals fled to Mexico with his brother Carleton during the First World War, as Carleton sought to avoid the draft (AB to DHP 1/16/05).

6. Because of his government contract work, Kunstadter was viewed by some anthropologists with suspicion during the 1970 Thai controversy (see Wakin 1992: 181).

7. Without hesitation, the three anthropologists working in Afghanistan I asked to speculate on the identity of this individual named Louis Dupree as the anthropologist referenced here, though Dupree began his Afghanistan work in 1949, not 1959.

8. My FOIA requests for CIA records on the AAA led to the limited release of documents but included the (undated) CIA's "Report on the Annual Meeting of the American Anthropological Association," in which it was reported to the CIA that "prominent at the meeting in the lower-level organizational roles were individuals from ▮▮▮▮ and the Committee of Returned Volunteers (CRV), a group of largely Peace Corps returnees active in the protest movement. A CRV member said ▮▮▮▮ that they had sponsored a trip of an individual to Thailand" (CIA FOIA F94-1900).

9. The Institute for Cross-Cultural Research was a division of Operations and Policy Research Inc., Washington, DC (*AAAFN* 1969 10[2]: 7–8).

10. For the following sources on these foundations as CIA fronts: for American Friends of the Middle East, see Eveland 1980: 125; Wilford 2008: 126; 2013. For the Asia Foundation, see Turner 1967; for Operations and Policy Research, Inc., see Sheehan 1967b.

11. Testifying in 1977 before the U.S. Senate's Committee on Foreign Relations, holding confirmation hearings for Andrew Young's appointment as UN ambassador, Alan Ogden (U.S. Labor Party) expounded on several far-fetched conspiracy theories pertaining to Young's background, including claims of Field Foundation CIA links and Trilateral Commission plots (U.S. Senate 1977: 50–55).

12. This concern was addressed by later press and congressional investigations establishing that long-standing foundations channeled the CIA's funds to front foundations.

13. The other contributors to this volume (there were two editions, from 1956 and 1962) were Charles A. Ferguson, Dr. Peter G. Franck, and Dr. Pieter K. Roest. Ferguson was a linguist with strong governmental and military connections. He established an Arabic language training program for U.S. foreign service officers in Beirut in 1947, and in 1953–55, the Foreign Service Institute Field School of Arabic Language and Area Studies Department of State from 1953–1955 (Rouchdy 1992: 209). Peter G. Franck was a diplomatic adviser to Afghanistan in 1948–60. Pieter K. Roest served in postwar occupation of Japan, where he was a lieutenant colonel. He had a PhD in anthropology and sociology from the University of Chicago and had done postdoctoral international relations work at USC (Koikari 2008: 55–56).

14. The AAA's statement was printed in the *Washington Post* on July 8, 1966.

15. The *New York Times* and international news coverage of Beals's findings renewed international concerns about anthropologist-spies. News of the CIA sold newspapers, and the *New York Times* did a story on Beals warning that "secrecy and pressures by United States intelligence agencies were eroding the effectiveness and prestige of American scholarly research abroad" (Raymont 1966: 1).

16. See the letter from Mario C. Vásquez and Julio Romani Torres, president and secretary, respectively, of the Asociación Peruana de Antropólogos, voicing concerns about anthropologists and counterinsurgency research (*AAAFN* 1967 8[1]: 14).

17. For example, see letters by Robert W. Ehrich, John P. Gillin, George P. Murdock, Alexander Spoehr, and Arthur Neihoff (*AAAFN* 1967 8[2]: 7–9) or by Raoul Naroll (*AAAFN* 8[4]: 10).

18. See also letters by Richard Frucht (*AAAFN* 1967 8[6]: 8), Stephen P. Dunn (*AAAFN* 1967 8[6]: 9), Raoul Naroll (*AAAFN* 1967 8[4]: 10), and Kathleen Gough Aberle (*AAAFN* 1967 8[6]: 11).

19. Van den Berghe was contacted because he was raised in the Congo and because of his academic expertise.

20. Abt Associates was a contractor, based in Cambridge, Massachusetts, that developed computer models for counterinsurgency operations (see Herman 1998: 118; Klare 1972: 104–5).

21. Deitchman wrote of Kunstadter's concerns that the Defense Department had so "saturated the area with social scientists studying the local people for 'applied' reasons, [Kunstadter] would not be able to continue his research on the culture in the existing

state. Our interpretation was that, in effect, he was concerned that we would be spoiling his museum" (1976: 302). Deitchman's Spenserian logic insisted that modernization was coming to northern Thailand, "and that if the DOD were supporting research on how the changes affected people and on how to ease the inevitable burdens of their cultural evolution, this was an objective which they would not condemn" (303).

22. Under the 1968 rules, resolutions to be voted on at the AAA council meeting had to be mailed out to all AAA voting members before the meeting was held.

23. The sources of these characterizations are as follows: "legislate a socio-ideological system" (Anthony Leeds, AAAFN 1969 10[6]: 3); Nazi comparisons (Laura Thompson, AAAFN 1969 10[7]: 4); totalitarian tactic (Esther Goldfrank, AAAFN 1969 10[7]: 4); *Animal Farm* (Otto von Mering, AAAFN 1969 10[7]: 5); "Censorship Committee" (Joe Pierce, AAAFN 1969 10[8]: 2); "Ethical Surveillance Committee" (Igor Kopytoff, AAAFN 1969 10[10]: 8).

TWELVE *Counterinsurgency in Southeast Asia*

1. Francis Ford Coppola indicated his contemporary source for Kurtz was not Poe but Green Beret commander Colonel Robert Rheault (Branfman 1975: 56–58; M. Isaacs 1999).

2. Rostow viewed strategic hamlets as a laboratory for proving his theories of modernization, and while Rostow never acknowledged the failures of the program, in the years after its failure, as an advisor to President Johnson, he advocated Operation Rolling Thunder, the Vietnam War's showcase of armed hard power (Milne 2008: 200–203).

3. If we compare these recommendations with those made by World War II anthropologists at the War Relocation Authority camps, we find groups advising that better management and control could be achieved by adding more elements of normalcy to the daily lives of these constrained populations (D. H. Price 2008a: 142–70).

4. Anthropologist Lieutenant Colonel Donald Marshall, PhD, had joined the military after a failed tenure effort at Harvard (see Elliott 2010: 328; Salemink 2003: 241). Marshall supported Hickey's efforts.

5. Hickey worked with Dr. Richard Pitman and David Thomas, of Wycliffe Bible Translators. Hickey drew on these relationships when he later needed translators to produce RAND counterinsurgency reports (Hickey 2002: 68).

6. This report acknowledged his reliance on the Institute for Defense Analysis, ARPA, USAID, and the CORDS program and made development recommendations for highlander economic programs.

7. Hickey's final work in Vietnam was for the "Herbicide Study Group," in which he documented the horrors Agent Orange brought to highland villages. This report was highly critical of U.S. military action and was submitted to the U.S. Senate in February 1974 (Hickey 2002: 341–46).

8. Sahlins's trip to Vietnam "was self-financed, but it was suggested by a meeting of those involved in the Vietnam Teach-In in Washington, the National Teach-In in May" (MS to DHP 8/1/14).

THIRTEEN *Anthropologists for Radical Political Action*

1. This bylaw change allowed graduate students and individuals with PhDs from aligned fields to vote and extended fellow status to non-PhD-holding anthropologists. (This amendment passed by a vote of 546 to 119 [73 percent to 27 percent] [NAAA 1970 11(3): 1].) All AAA members became voting members in early 1970; this ended a two-tier membership system in which elder anthropologists' voices determined AAA policies and opened the door for more activism within the association.

2. While the Asia Society's funding was not connected to the CIA (not to be confused with the Asia Foundation), as a pet project of John D. Rockefeller III, the Asia Society was aligned with the same sort of counterinsurgency "state-building" strategic philosophy that pervaded the CIA-funded Asia Foundation (Colby and Dennett 1995: 572).

3. The copy of the letter I consulted was located in Wolf's papers, so Wolf eventually learned of these accusations.

4. I have not found a copy of this letter in the archives I consulted.

5. These thirteen resolutions were sent to the membership for ratification. Four other floor motions were adopted but not sent to the membership in mail ballots (NAAA 1971 12[1]: 2).

6. After reading tens of thousands of pages of FBI reports on hundreds of anthropologists, I find the FBI's 1969 report entertaining the possibility that an antiradical like George Foster might be a Communist to be illustrative of the routine comedic levels of paranoid blindness that prevailed in Hoover's FBI (FBI SF 105-24157 C 1/7/69).

7. The report recommended how the AAA could better respond to contemporary and future problems. Recommendations included changes to the proposed ethics code, stressing that bans on secrecy did not address issues of nonsecret data being used to harm studied populations, and proposing that applied anthropologists follow a separate ethics code from the AAA's (Wakin 1992: 293-98).

8. The Radical Caucus organized multiple sessions on Marxist anthropology at the 1971 AAA meeting. One session, organized by Peter Newcomer and James Faris, featured Marvin Harris as a discussant and included papers by Brian Turner, Harold Hickerson, Brian Hill, Karen Sacks, James Faris, and Peter Newcomer; the second session featured discussants Harry Magdoff (*Monthly Review*) and Stanley Diamond, with papers from Jack Stauder, Judy Torres, Kathleen Gough, Eric Larson, Bernard Maguband and John O'Brien, and David Epstein (MM E11).

9. The statement distributed by Wolf and Jorgensen at the 1971 AAA council meeting was later published in the *Newsletter of the AAA* (NAAA 1972 13[1]: 3).

10. Given Mead's role on the advisory board of the CIA's MK-Ultra-funded *Research in Mental Health Newsletter* (Marks 1979: 159), there is some irony that she would use this "mental health" research as her example of harmless trendy research (see also NBAAA Nov. 1951: 4-5).

11. In December 1971, Herbert Phillips wrote Donald Blakeslee, at the University of Wisconsin–Milwaukee Department of Anthropology, asking about the ARPA report Eric Wolf claimed Blakeslee had written titled "Low-Altitude Visual Search for Indi-

vidual Human Targets." Blakeslee replied that he was a graduate student working in North American archaeology, with no connection to Thailand or ARPA (MM E12, HP to DB 12/15/71; MM E12, DB to HP 1/27/72). Wolf had confused him with another Donald Blakeslee who was not an anthropologist.

Phillips wrote James Gibbs and the AAA Executive Board, informing them that Wolf had misidentified Blakeslee. Phillips wrote Gibbs about two other AAA members with ARPA connections, Lee Huff and Bob Kickert, adding that Kickert "resigned from ARPA a few months before the Cambodian invasion because he refused to complete and submit his ethnography of the Akha to ARPA — a resignation that they initially refused to accept, but eventually did. He has since been unemployed living in Vienna. It is possible that he may eventually try to publish his Akha materials and other data from Thailand" (MM E12, HP to JG 12/29/71).

12. To avoid confusion between the two groups known as ARPA, in this book I refer to the Advanced Research Projects Administration as ARPA and spell out Anthropologists for Radical Political Action, though both were known simply as ARPA.

13. This previous violation had occurred when a floor motion opposing the construction of the Dos Rios Dam in California passed and the board then sent this resolution to the full AAA membership in a mail ballot.

14. See Marvin Harris's article "Why a Perfect Knowledge of All the Rules One Must Know to Act Like a Native Cannot Lead to the Knowledge of How Natives Act" (1974), which argues that all organizations operate under conflicting sets of rules, and that rather than focusing primarily on rules as if they governed human behavior, anthropologists should also study *behaviors* and differential power relations if they want to understand why some rules are selected for enforcement over others.

15. Whitney and Benjamin admitted that while it was "not explicit in the By-Laws" the association had apparently come to an informal understanding that there were assumed differences between what a "motion" or "resolution" was (NAAA 1973 14[8]: 1, 8). The AAA leadership's distinction between "motions" and "resolutions" was not found in *Robert's Rules of Order*, the guiding rules of AAA council meetings. Had Anthropologists for Radical Political Action members used *Robert's Rules* to fight the establishment's assertion of authority, they might well have prevailed (or at least muddied the waters to a satisfying degree), but as radicals committed to using any means necessary, their use of prim rules of order as a line of defense was far less attractive than continuing to organize and carry out a floor takeover of the council meetings, even if the results of this political theater were less officially binding. The parliamentary procedural ruling did not diminish their ability to control the business meetings — it only diminished their ability to set official association policy.

16. Under the 1971 AAA By-Laws (Annual Meeting, Section One), "new legislation or resolutions proposed by members of the Council" had to submit these to the Executive Board "at least one week in advance of the annual meeting if they are to be placed on the agenda" (NAAA 1973 14[8]: 1). Members could still add agenda items from the floor (following the procedure in *Robert's Rules of Order*). Thus, in the early 1970s, AAA members could add motions from the floor of the AAA's annual business meeting.

FOURTEEN *Untangling Open Secrets*

1. One example of these distant influences is found in future DCI William Colby's interest in anthropology courses while he was a freshman at Princeton, which his biographer speculated influenced his approach to "pacification" in Vietnam in later years (Prados 2003: 24–25).

2. Other theoretical schools had similar blind spots. Orin Starn (1991) observed that ecological and structural Andean anthropologists working in Peru were so focused on exploring and refining the details of their paradigmatic analysis that they equally (catastrophically) failed to anticipate the coming of the Sendero Luminoso's revolutionary upheaval in that country.

3. Because the AAA leadership traditionally has conceived of the association as primarily not involved in political matters, it has refrained from taking official stances opposing anthropologists' involvement in military and intelligence operations. The inconsistency of the AAA's claims of remaining removed from political statements can be seen in its adoption of policies and position papers for a number of political issues (e.g., race, gay marriage, refugees) and its having officially mobilized in *support* of specific military operations (such as World War II).

4. I have disengaged from analysis and critiques that I am concerned might have other, unintended uses for military and intelligence readers, yet I also understand my work may inform military and intelligence training in unforeseen ways (see D. H. Price 2007c: 21–22).

5. After Stauder was suspended from his professorship in Harvard's Department of Social Relations in 1969 over political fallout stemming from his "Radical Perspectives in Social Change" course, anthropologists from across the country rallied to support him (see Goldhaber 1969a, 1969b). For more on Stauder's post-1960s political journey, see Stauder 1995.

REFERENCES

Archival and Manuscript Sources

AAAP Papers of the American Anthropological Association. National Anthropological Archives, Smithsonian Institution.
EBW Eric B. Wolf Papers. Michigan Historical Collections, Bentley Historical Library, University of Michigan.
ECW Eugene C. Worman Research Material on William H. Bartlett. Smithsonian Institution, Archives of American Art.
EG Esther Goldfrank Papers. National Anthropological Archives, Smithsonian Institution.
GET George Edward Taylor Papers. University of Washington Library Manuscripts, Special Collections, University Archives.
GWU-NSA George Washington University, National Security Archives.
HPSSS Harvard Project on the Soviet Social System digital collection: Interviews and Manuals, 1950–1953. Harvard University, Russian Research Center. H. C. Fung Library. http://oasis.lib.harvard.edu/oasis/deliver/~fun00001.
HW Harold G. Wolff Papers. Cornell Medical School.
HWA Harold Weisberg Archive. Beneficial-Hodson Library, Hood College. Frederick, Maryland.
ISA Papers of the Institute of Social Anthropology. National Anthropological Archives, Smithsonian Institution.
JLA John Lawrence Angel Papers. National Anthropological Archives, Smithsonian Institution.
JRH Joseph Ralston Hayden Papers, 1854–1975. Bentley Historical Library, University of Michigan.
KM Telephone Interview with Kris Millegan, son of Lloyd and Eudora Millegan. September 28, 2010.
LSM Lloyd S. Millegan File held by Viking Fund on Millegan's 1950 predoctoral fellowship application. Funded September 8, 1950. Wenner-Gren Foundation, New York.
MHP Papers of Marvin Harris. National Anthropological Archives, Smithsonian Institution.
MJ Melville Jacobs Papers. University of Washington Library Manuscripts, Special Collections, Seattle, Washington.
MM Margaret Mead Papers. Manuscript Division, Library of Congress.
NARA National Archives, and Records Administration.
RB Ralph Beals Papers. National Anthropological Archives, Smithsonian Institution.
RBP Robert Blum Papers. MS 87. Yale University Library Manuscripts and Archives.

RK Raymond Kennedy Papers. Yale University Library Manuscripts and Archives.
SORO Special Operations Research Office Archival Records. American University.
ST Sol Tax Papers. University of Chicago, Special Collections.

Citation Abbreviations Used in Text

AA *American Anthropologist*
AAAFN *American Anthropological Association Fellow Newsletter* (January 1960–June 1968)
AN *Anthropology Newsletter* (September 1974–May 1999)
BAAA *Bulletin of the American Anthropological Association* (April 1953–December 1959)
NAAA *Newsletter of the American Anthropological Association* (June 1968–June 1974)
NBAAA *News Bulletin of the American Anthropological Association* (April 1947–January 1953)

Books, Journal Articles, and Reports

AAA. 1947. "Statement on Human Rights." *American Anthropologist* 49 (4): 539–43.
———. 1967. "Statement on Problems of Anthropological Research and Ethics." http://www.aaanet.org/stmts/ethstmnt.htm.
ACGPBS (Advisory Committee on Government Programs in the Behavioral Sciences, National Research Council). 1968. *Behavioral Sciences and the Federal Government*. National Academy of Sciences, Publication 1680. Washington, DC: National Academy of Sciences.
Adams, Richard N. 1957. *Cultural Surveys of Panama, Nicaragua, Guatemala, El Salvador, Honduras*. Scientific Publications No. 33. Washington, DC: Pan American Sanitary Bureau.
AFIO (Association of Foreign Intelligence Officers). 1987. *AFIO Membership Directory*. McLean, VA: AFIO.
African-American Institute. 1956–1959. "African Special Report." Vol. 1–4. Washington, DC: The Institute.
Agee, Philip. 1975. *Inside the Company: CIA Diary*. New York: Bantam.
———. 1987. *On the Run*. London: Bloomsbury.
Albright, Joseph, and Marcia Kunstel. 1990. "Ex-Official: CIA Helped Jail Mandela." *Chicago Tribune*, June 10, accessed July 3, 2012, http://articles.chicagotribune.com/1990-06-10/news/9002170271_1_anti-apartheid-activities-gerard-ludi-cia-spokesman-mark-mansfield.
Allison, John. 2012. "The Goat Caught in Bushkazi: Personal Effects of One's Role in the Great Game." *Zero Anthropology*, July 31, accessed August 13, 2012, http://zeroanthropology.net/2012/07/31/the-goat-caught-in-bushkazi-personal-effects-of-ones-role-in-the-great-game/.
Alterman, Jon B. 2002. *Egypt and American Foreign Assistance, 1952–1956*. New York: Palgrave Macmillan.

AMWS. 2005. *American Men and Women of Science*. 23rd ed. New Providence, NJ: Bowker.

Anderson, Barbara Gallatin. 1965. "Bereavement as a Subject of Cross-Cultural Inquiry." *Anthropological Quarterly* 38 (4): 181–200.

Archer, William Kay. 1962 "Reflections on Buying Records in Tashkent." *American Record Guide* 28 (6): 436, 496–502.

———. 1964. "On the Ecology of Music." *Ethnomusicology* 8 (1): 28–33.

Ayrout, Henry Habib. 1963. *The Egyptian Peasant*. Boston: Beacon Press.

Asad, Talal, ed. 1973. *Anthropology and the Colonial Encounter*. London: Ithaca Press.

Ash, Timothy Garton. 1998. *The File*. New York: Vintage.

Ayres, B. Drummond. 1983. "Indicted Expert on Mideast Is Found Dead in Virginia." *New York Times*, April 30, accessed August 3, 2015. http://www.nytimes.com/1983/04/30/us/indicted-expert-on-mideast-is-found-dead-in-virginia.html.

Baker, Paul T. 1958. "Anthropology and the Army." In *Anthropology in the Armed Services*, ed. Louis Dupree, 22–32. University Park: Pennsylvania State University Press.

Barnett, Clifford. 1958. "Poland, its People, its Society, its Culture." *Survey of World Cultures*, No. 1. New Haven, CT: HRAF Press.

Battistini, Lawrence. 1956. *The Postwar Student Struggle in Japan*. New York: Gotham Foundation.

Bauer, R. A. 1962. *Some Views on Soviet Psychology*. Washington, DC: American Psychological Association.

Bauer, Raymond A., George P. Berry, Paul H. Buck, Ralph W. Gerard, H. Bentley Glass, C. Leslie Glenn, Clyde K. Kluckhohn, Donald G. Marquis, Robert K. Merton, James G. Miller, Max F. Millikan, Frank Stanton, Samuel A. Stoffer, Ralph W. Tyler, John C. Whitehorn. 1958. "National Support for Behavioral Sciences." *Behavioral Sciences* 3 (3): 217–27.

BDNA (Book Dealers in North America). 1956. *Book Dealers in North America, 1956–57*. Sheppard Press.

Beals, Ralph. 1966. "Committee on Research Problems and Ethics." SFAA Report. April 7. Ralph Beals Papers, Box 76.

———. 1967. "Cross-Cultural Research and Government Policy." *Bulletin of the Atomic Scientist*, October 1967, 18–24.

———. 1969. *Politics of Social Research*. Chicago: Aldine.

Bell, Terrence. 1989. "The Politics of Social Science in Post-war America." In Larry May, ed., *Recasting America*, ed. Larry May, 76–92. Chicago: University of Chicago Press.

Belshaw, Cyril. 1957. *The Great Village*. London: Routledge.

Benedict, Ruth. 1946. *The Chrysanthemum and the Sword*. Boston: Houghton Mifflin.

———. 1956. "The Growth of Culture." In *Man, Culture, and Society*, ed. Harry L. Shapiro, 182–95. New York: Oxford University Press.

Bennett, John W. 1951. "Community Research in the Japan Occupation." *Clearinghouse Bulletin of Research in Human Organization* 1 (3): 1–5.

———. 1958. "Economic Aspects of a Boss-Henchman System in the Japanese Forestry Industry." *Economic Development and Cultural Change* 7 (1): 13–30.

Bennett, John W., and Iwao Ishino. 1955. "Futomi." *Rural Sociology* 20 (1): 41–50.

Benson, Miles. 1976. "Pike Says Dr. K. Doesn't Believe in Democracy." *San Francisco Chronicle*, February 29, A12.

Bergerud, Eric. 1991. *The Dynamics of Defeat*. Boulder, CO: Westview Press.

Berlin, Louis, Thomas Guthrie, Arthur Weider and Hellen Goodell, et al. 1955. "Studies in Human Cerebral Function: The Effects of Mescaline and Lysergic Acid on Cerebral Processes Pertinent to Creative Activity." *Journal of Nervous and Mental Disease* 122 (5): 487–91.

Berreman, Gerald D. 1973. "The Social Responsibility of the Anthropologist." In *To See Ourselves*, ed. Thomas Weaver, 8–10. Glenview, IL: Scott, Foresman.

———. 1981. *The Politics of Truth*. New Delhi: South Asian Publishers.

Bessac, Frank B., as told to James Burke. 1950. "These Tibetans Killed an American and Get the Lash for It." *Life*, November 13, 130–41.

Bessac, Frank Bagneell, and Susanne Leppmann Bessac. 2006. *Death on the Chang Tang*. Missoula: University of Montana.

Besteman, Catherine, and Hugh Gusterson, eds. 2005. *Why America's Top Pundits Are Wrong*. Berkeley: University of California Press.

Bharati, Swami Agehananda. 1970. *The Ochre Robe*. New York: Doubleday Anchor.

BIC (Biography in Context). 2014a. "Richard M(anning) Stephenson." *Contemporary Authors Online*. Detroit: Gale, 2002. *Biography in Context*. Web, accessed May 5, 2014.

———. 2014b. "Richard W. Howell." *Contemporary Authors Online*. Detroit: Gale, 2001. Accessed May 5, 2014.

———. 2014c. "Robert Francis Spencer." *Contemporary Authors Online*. Detroit: Gale, 2003. Accessed May 5, 2014.

———. 2014d. "Robert B. Pickering." *Contemporary Authors Online*. Detroit: Gale, 2006. Accessed May 5, 2014.

———. 2014e. "Robert Brainerd Ekvall." *Contemporary Authors Online*. Detroit: Gale, 2003. Accessed May 5, 2014.

———. 2014f. "Thomas A. Sebeok." *Contemporary Authors Online*. Detroit: Gale, 2002. *Biography in Context*. Accessed May 5, 2014.

Biderman, Albert D. 1956. *Communist Techniques of Coercive Interrogation*. AFPTRC Development Report TN-56-132. Lackland Air Force Base, U.S. Government. TX.

———. 1960. "Social-Psychological Needs and 'Involuntary' Behavior as Illustrated by Compliance in Interrogation." *Sociometry* 23 (2): 120–47.

———. 1963. *March to Calumny: The Story of American POW's in the Korean War*. New York: Macmillan.

Biderman, Albert D., and Herbert Zimmer, eds. 1961. *The Manipulation of Human Behavior*. New York: Wiley.

Bilmes, Jacob, and Alan Howard. 1980. "Pain as Cultural Drama." *Anthropology and Humanism* 5 (2–3): 10–13.

Blackmer, Donald M. 2002. *The MIT Center for International Studies*. Cambridge, MA: MIT Press.

Blanchard, Frank, and Mark Scheinbaum. 1977a. "Latin American Center Attempts to Shake CIA Stigma." *Independent Florida Alligator*, March 10, 14–15.

———. 1977b. "Lemarchand Rebuff CIA." *Independent Florida Alligator*, March 3, 101, 10–11.

Blass, Thomas. 2006. "Milgram and the CIA — NOT!" Accessed February 8, 2007. http://www.stanleymilgram.com/rebuttal.php.

Blau, J. N. 2004. "Harold G. Wolff: The Man and His Migraine." *Cephalalgia* 24 (3): 215–22.

Bloch, Maurice. 1985. *Marxism and Anthropology*. Oxford: Oxford University Press.

Blum, William. 1995. *Killing Hope*. Monroe, ME: Common Courage Press.

Bonosky, Phillip. 2001. *Afghanistan — Washington's Secret War*. New York: International Publishers.

Braden, Thomas W. 1967. "I'm Glad the CIA Is 'Immoral.'" *Saturday Evening Post*, May 20, 10–14.

Braestrup, Peter. 1967. "Researchers and Thai Rebels Fight: U.S. Defense Unit Develops Antiguerilla Devices." *New York Times*, March 20, 7.

Brand, Stewart. 1976. "For God's Sake, Margaret: Conversation with Gregory Bateson and Margaret Mead." *CoEvolution Quarterly* 10:32–44.

Branfman, Fred. 1975. "The President's Secret Army: A Case Study — the CIA in Laos, 1962–1972." In *The CIA File*, ed. Robert L. Borosage and John Marks, 46–78. New York: Grossman.

Brautigan, Richard. 1976. *Loading Mercury with a Pitchfork*. New York: Simon and Schuster.

Brodkin, Karen. 2008. "Radical Anthropology Back in the Day: ARPA and Anti-imperialist Anthropology in the 60s and 70s." Paper presented at the annual meeting of the American Anthropological Association, San Francisco, November 20.

Brookings Institution. 1962. *Development of the Emerging Countries*. Washington, DC: Brookings Institution.

Brooks, Oakley. 2008. "One Reporter's Odyssey Tracking His Uncle's Legacy in Laos." *Christian Science Monitor*, April 22, accessed August 13, 2015. http://www.csmonitor.com/World/Asia-South-Central/2008/0422/p20s01-wosc.html.

Browman, David L., and Stephen Williams. 2013. *Anthropology at Harvard: A Biographical History, 1790–1940*. Cambridge, MA: Peabody Museum Press.

Brugioni, Dino A. 2010. *Eyes in the Sky*. Annapolis, MD: Naval Institute Press.

Buchwald, Art. 1967. "Pull Up the Covers: There Are All Sorts of Excuses for the CIA Priming the NSA." *Washington Post*, A17, February 19.

Buckley, William F., Jr. 1951. *God and Man at Yale*. Chicago: Regnery.

———. 2007. "Howard Hunt, R.I.P." *National Review*, January 26. http://nrd.nationalreview.com/article/?q=MDYzM2MyMDIwMjRiNWZlY2RlZjc3ZDY4YjAxMjBiM2Q=.

Bundy, McGeorge. 1977. "Letter to Editor." *New York Review of Books*, July 14, 39.

Burks, Ardath. 2011. *The Government of Japan*. New York: Routledge.

Caffrey, Margaret M. 1989. *Ruth Benedict*. Austin: University of Texas Press.

Carr, William K., and Gordon Tullock. 1965. "Fifteen Years of Communist China." *China Quarterly* 23:174–76.

Cavanagh, John. 1980. "Dulles Papers Reveal CIA Consulting Network." *Forerunner*, April 19, accessed August 7, 2010. http://www.cia-on-campus.org/princeton.edu/consult.html.

CFA (Committee for Free Asia). 1953. *Land Reform: Communist China, Nationalist China, Taiwan, India, Pakistan*. San Francisco: Committee for Free Asia.

Changdu, Hu. 1960. *China: Its People, Its Society, Its Culture*. Survey of World Culture Series, No. 6. New Haven, CT: HRAF Press.

Chapple, Eliot D. 1953. "The Liquidation of Point Four." *Human Organization* 12 (3): 2–3.

Chriswell, Joan. 1958. "Anthropology and the Navy." In *Anthropology in the Armed Services*, ed. Louis Dupree, 15–21. University Park: Pennsylvania State University Press.

CIA. 1948. "The Break-up of the Colonial Empires and Its Implications for US Security." [Confidential] CIA Report. September 3, accessed May 14, 2011, http://www.foia.cia.gov/sites/default/files/document_conversions/89801/DOC_0000258342.pdf.

———. 1953. "Sociedad de Amigos de Guatemala," FOIA DOC_0000914527, 12/21/53, http://www.foia.cia.gov/sites/default/files/document_conversions/89801/DOC_0000914527.pdf.

———. 1954. "RQM/OIS Support of PBSUCCESS." CIA Report, released in 2003.

———. 1959a. "Advisory Committees memo." March 9. (Classified Secret) FOIA CIA-RDP80B01676R004300020010-4.

———. 1959b. "Central Intelligence Agency, Office of National Estimates, Staff Memo No. 53-59: 'Meeting of the Consultants at Princeton, 19 and 20 November [1959].'" FOIA CIA DOC 0001088874 (classified Secret).

———. 1959c. "Memorandum: Strengthening United States Government Activities among Free World Youth." FOIA CIA-RDP80B01676R002900220001-8.

———. 1961. "Soviet Policy toward the Underdeveloped Countries." Current Intelligence Staff Study. (Reference Title: CAESAR XIII-61) OCI No. 1803/61 April 28 (Classified Secret).

———. 1963a. "Agency Newsletter." [Classified Secret] 11/6/63. FOIA CIA-RDP80B01676R001400110004-3.

———. 1963b. *Kubark Counterintelligence Interrogation*, July 1963.

———. 1963c. [Program for CIA's] "Midcareer Course, October 7–November 15, 1963." CIA-FOIA RDP80B01676R001400110004-3.

———. 1963d. MKULTRA Document Labeled: "REPORT OF INSPECTION OF MKULTRA/TSD." 1–185209, cy 2 See D, July 26, 1963.

———. 1966a. "Communist Cultural and Propaganda Activities in the Less Developed Countries." CIA Intelligence Report, classified Secret. January, CIA/RR EE 66-1.

———. 1966b. "The Asia Foundation: Proposed Improvements in Funding Procedures." Memorandum from the Central Intelligence Agency to the 303 Committee. Foreign Relations of the United States, 1964–1968. Volume X, National Security

Policy, Document 132. 6/22/66, accessed June 14, 2014, https://history.state.gov
/historicaldocuments/frus1964-68v10/d132.
———. 1968a. "Communist Insurgency in Thailand." National Intelligence Estimate
No. 52-68.
———. 1968b. "Student Reaction to CIA Recruitment Activities on Campus." CIA report
classified Confidential. FOIA CIA DOC_0001468660.
———. 1973. "The Family Jewels." May 16. CIA MORI DocID: 14518.
———. 1983. Human Resource Exploitation Training Manual. [Declassified 1997].
National Security Archive, George Washington University. http://www.gwu.edu
/~nsarchiv/NSAEBB/NSAEBB122/index.htm#hre.
CIAA (Committee on Information Activities Abroad). 1960. "Conclusions and Recommendations of the President's Committee on Information Activities Abroad." CIA.
December. CIA-RDP86B00269R001400210001-2.
CLAANRC (Committee on Latin American Anthropology of the National Research
Council). 1949. "Research Needs in the Field of Modern Latin American Culture."
American Anthropologist 51 (1): 149–54.
Coe, Michael D. 2006. *Final Report: An Archaeologist Excavates His Past*. New York:
Thames and Hudson.
Coffield, D. N. 1959. "Book Review, Edward T. Hall's *The Silent Language*." *Studies in
Intelligence*, [page and volume numbers redacted by CIA].
Colby, Gerard, with Charlotte Dennett. 1995. *Thy Will Be Done*. New York:
HarperCollins.
Common Knowledge. 2010. "Corrections." *Common Knowledge* 16 (2): 365.
Condominas, Georges. 1973. "Ethics and Comfort: An Ethnographer's View of His
Profession." In *AAA Annual Report 1972*, 1–17. Washington, DC: American Anthropological Association.
———. 1977. *We Have Eaten the Forest*. New York: Hill and Wang.
———. 1979. "Notes on the Present-Day State of Anthropology in the Third World." In
The Politics of Anthropology, ed. Gerrit Huizer and Bruce Mannheim, 187–99. The
Hague: Mouton.
Conklin, Harold. 1998. "Language, Culture and Environment: My Early Years." *Annual
Review of Anthropology* 27: xiii–xxx.
Conley, Michael C. ca. 1966. *An Alphabetical Index to the VICO Counterinsurgency
Taxonomy*. Washington, DC: SORO.
Cook, Ralph E. 1983. "The CIA and Academe." *Studies in Intelligence*, Winter, 33–42.
Copeland, Miles. 1989. *The Game Player*. London: Aurum Press.
Corn, David. 1994. *Blond Ghost*. New York: Simon and Schuster.
Corson, William R. 1968. *The Betrayal*. New York: Norton.
———. 1977. *The Armies of Ignorance*. New York: Dial Press.
Cotter, George. 1981. "Spies, String and Missionaries." *Christian Century* 98 (1): 321–24.
CQ (*Congressional Quarterly*). 1967. "Foundations, Private Organizations Linked to
CIA." CQ *Special Report on CIA Disclosures*, February 24, 1–2.

Crewdson, John, with Joseph B. Treaster. 1977. "Worldwide Propaganda Network Built by the CIA." *New York Times*, December 26, A1, A37.

Cumings, Bruce 1999. *Parallax Visions: Making Sense of American-East Asian Relations*. Durham, NC: Duke University Press.

Cummings, Richard H. 2010. *Radio Free Europe's "Crusade for Freedom."* Jefferson, NC: McFarland.

Darling, Arthur Burr. 1990. *The Central Intelligence Agency: An Instrument of Government, to 1950*. University Park: Pennsylvania State University Press.

Davenport, William. 1985. "The Thailand Controversy in Retrospect." In *Social Contexts of American Anthropology, 1840–1984*, ed. June Helm, 65–72. Washington, DC: American Ethnological Society.

DeFleur, Melvin. 1964. "Occupations Roles as Portrayed on Television." *Public Opinion Quarterly* 28 (1): 57–74.

DeFleur, Melvin, and Frank Westie. 1963. "Attitude as a Scientific Concept." *Social Forces* 42 (1): 17–31.

Defty, Andrew. 2004. *Britain, America, and Anticommunist Propaganda, 1945–53*. New York: Routledge.

Deitchman, Seymour J. 1976. *The Best-Laid Plans: A Tale of Social Research and Bureaucracy*. Cambridge, MA: MIT Press.

de Laguna, Frederica. 1952. "Some Dynamic Forces in Tlingit Society." *Southwestern Journal of Anthropology* 8 (1): 1–12.

DeLillo, Don. 1982. *The Names*. New York: Knopf.

———. 1997. *Underworld*. New York: Scribner's.

Denich, Bette. 1980. "Bureaucratic Scholarship." In *Hierarchy and Society*, ed. Gerald M. Britan and Ronald Cohen, 165–75. Philadelphia: Institute for the Study of Human Issues.

De Onis, Juan. 1967. "Ramparts Says CIA Received Student Report." *New York Times*, February 16, 26.

DeSantis, Nick. 2012. "Anthropology Group Approves Overhaul of Its Ethics Code." *Chronicle of Higher Education*, November 6.

De Vries, Tity. 2012. "The 1967 Center Intelligence Agency Scandal: Catalyst in a Transforming Relationship between State and People." *Journal of American History* 98: 1075–92.

Diamond, Sigmund. 1988. "Informed Consent and Survey Research." In *Surveying Social Life*, ed. Hubert J. O'Gorman, 72–99. Middletown, CT: Wesleyan University Press.

———. 1992. *Compromised Campus: The Collaboration of Universities with the Intelligence Community, 1945–1955*. New York: Oxford University Press.

———. 1993. "Compromising American Studies Programs and Survey Research." *International Journal of Politics, Culture and Society* 6 (3): 409–15.

Diamond, Stanley. 1974. *In Search of the Primitive: A Critique of Civilization*. New Brunswick, NJ: Transaction Books.

Dick, Philip K. (1956) 1987. "The Minority Report." In *The Minority Report and Other Classic Stories by Philip K. Dick*, 71–102. New York: Kensington.
Dimick, John. 1968. *Episodes in Archaeology*. Barre, MA: Barre.
Divale, William Tulio, with James Joseph. 1970. *I Lived Inside the Campus Revolution*. New York: Cowles.
Djilas, Milovan. 1957. *The New Class*. Praeger.
Donnell, John, and Gerald Hickey. 1962. "The Vietnamese 'Strategic Hamlets.'" RAND Research Memorandum, RM-3208-ARPA.
Doolittle, James H., William B. Franke, Morris Hadley, and William Pawley, with S. Paul Johnston. 1954. "Report on the Covert Activities of the Central Intelligence Agency." Classified, Top Secret. http://www.foia.cia.gov/helms/pdf/doolittle_report.pdf.
Dower, John W. 1999. *Embracing Defeat: Japan in the Wake of World War II*. New York: Norton.
Downing, Theodore. 2002. "Creating Poverty." *Forced Migration Review* 12:13–14.
Du Bois, Cora. 1960. *The People of Alor*. Cambridge, MA: Harvard University Press.
Dujmovic, Nicholas. 2008. "Amnesia to Anamnesis: Commemoration of the Dead at CIA." *Studies in Intelligence* 52 (3): 3–16.
Duncan, Brooks [pseudonym]. 1995. "Anthropological Perils: Dilemmas in the Cold War's Wake." *Political and Legal Anthropological Review* 18 (2): 7–15.
Dupree, A. Hunter. 1957. *Science in the Federal Government*. Cambridge, MA: Harvard University Press.
Dupree, Louis, ed. 1958. *Anthropology in the Armed Services*. University Park: Pennsylvania State University Press.
———. 1976. "Anthropology in Afghanistan." *Field Staff Reports, Asia*. Vol. 22, no. 5. LD-5-'76.
———. 1980a. *Red Flag over the Hindu Kush, Part V: Repressions, or Security through Terror Purges*. AUFs Reports. 28, LD-4-'80.
———. 1980b. *Red Flag over the Hindu Kush, Part VI: Repressions, or Security through Terror*. AUFs Reports. 29, LD-5-'80.
Ecklund, George. 1965. "Guns or Butter Problems of the Cold War." *Studies in Intelligence* 9 (Fall): 1–11. [Classified: SECRET]
Edelman, Marc. 2009. "Synergies and Tensions between Rural Social Movements and Professional Researchers." *Journal of Peasant Studies* 36 (1): 245–65.
Eder, Richard. 1965. "Pentagon Drops Insurgency Study." *New York Times*, July 9, 8.
———. 1966a. "National Foundation on Social Science Proposed in Senate Bill." *New York Times*, October 10, 25.
———. 1966b. "Peril Called Inherent in Scholars' Work for C.I.A." *New York Times*, June 28, 5.
Ege, Konrad. 1980. "CIA Intervention in Afghanistan." *CounterSpy*, Spring, 22–38.
Eickelman, Dale F. 1986. "Anthropology and International Relations." In *Anthropology and Public Policy*, ed. Walter Goldschmidt, 33–44. Special Publication of the AAA, No. 21. Washington, DC: American Anthropological Association.

Eisenhower, Dwight. 1961. "Farewell Radio and Television Address to the American People." January 17. http://www.eisenhower.archives.gov/all_about_ike/speeches/farewell_address.pdf.

Elliott, Duong Van Mai. 2010. *RAND in Southeast Asia; A History of the Vietnam War Era*. Santa Monica: RAND.

Ellis, Robert A., and W. Clayton Lane. 1967. "Social Mobility and Social Isolation." *American Sociological Review* 32 (2): 237–53.

Embree, John F. 1949. "Some Problems of an American Cultural Officer in Asia." *American Anthropologist* 51 (1): 155–58.

———. 1950. "A Note on Ethnocentrism in Anthropology." *American Anthropologist* 52 (3): 430–32.

Emerson, Gloria. 1967. "Cultural Group Once Aided by C.I.A. Picks Ford Fund Aide to Be Its Director." *New York Times*, October 2, 17.

———. 1978. *Winners and Losers: Battles, Retreats, Gains, Losses and Ruins from the Vietnam War*. New York: Harcourt Brace Jovanovich.

Engerman, David C. 2009. *Know Your Enemy*. New York: Oxford University Press.

EOA (Encyclopedia of Associations). 1961. *Encyclopedia of Associations: National Organizations of the United States*. Detroit, MI: Gale.

Epstein, Jason. 1967. "The CIA and the Intellectuals." *New York Review of Books*, April 20, 16–21.

Ernst, John. 1998. *Forging a Fateful Alliance: Michigan State University and the Vietnam War*. East Lansing: Michigan State University Press.

ETS (Educational Testing Service). 1955. *Annual Report to the Board of Trustees*. Lawrence, NJ: Educational Testing Service.

Eveland, Wilbur. 1980. *Ropes of Sand*. New York: Norton.

Eysenck, H. J., R. A. Willett, and Patrick Slater. 1962. "Drive, Direction of Rotation, and Massing of Practice as Determinants of the After-Effects from the Rotating Spiral." *American Journal of Psychology* 75 (1): 127–33.

Falgout, Suzanne. 1995. "Americans in Paradise: Anthropologists, Custom, and Democracy in Postwar Micronesia." *Ethnology* 34 (2): 99–112.

Fallah, Skaidrite Maliks. 1967. *Customs and Taboos of Selected Tribes Residing along the Western Border of the Republic of Vietnam*. Washington, DC: CRESS.

Faris, James. 2008. "ARPA and the AAA: One History and Commentary." Paper presented at the annual meeting of the AAA, American Anthropological Association, San Francisco, November 20.

Farnsworth, Clyde H. 1967. "2 Donors Named by Student Group; Units Linked to C.I.A. Listed by Conference Abroad." *New York Times*, February 18, 14.

Feldman, Ilana. 2007. "The Quaker Way: Ethical Labor and Humanitarian Relief." *American Ethnologist* 34 (4): 689–705.

Fenton, William N. 1947. *Area Studies in American Universities*. Washington, DC: American Council on Education.

Ferguson, Brian. 1995. *Yanomami Warfare*. Santa Fe, NM: SAR Press.

Fischer, John L. 1951. "Applied Anthropology and Administration." *American Anthropologist* 53 (1): 133–34.

———. 1979. "Government Anthropologists in the Trust Territories of Micronesia." In *The Uses of Anthropology*, ed. Walter Goldschmidt, 238–252. Washington, DC: American Anthropological Association.

Fitzsimmons, Thomas. 1960. *USSR: Its People, its Society, its Culture*. Survey of World Culture Series, No. 7. New Haven: HRAF Press.

Flint, Jerry M. 1967. "Reuther Concedes Union on One Occasion Took $50,000 from Agency." *New York Times*, May 8, 1, 37.

Ford, Clellan S. 1970. "Human Relations Area Files, 1949–1969: A Twenty Year Report." *Behavior Science Notes*, 5: 1–33.

Fox, Sylvan. 1967. "Stephen Spender Quits Encounter." *New York Times*, May 8, 1.

Frank, Andre Gunder. 1997. "The Cold War and Me." *Bulletin of Concerned Asian Scholars* Vol. 29 (3): 79–82.

Franke, Herbert. 1959. "News of the Profession." *Journal of Asian Studies* 18 (4): 535–49.

Frantz, Charles. 1974. "Structuring and Restructuring of the American Anthropological Association." Paper presented at the annual meeting of the American Anthropological Association, November 22.

Friedrich, Carl J. and Zbigniew K. Brzezinski. 1956. *Totalitarian Dictatorship and Autocracy*. Cambridge, MA: Harvard University Press.

Fuller, Steve. 2000. *Thomas Kuhn*. Chicago: University of Chicago Press.

Gaillard, Gérald. 2004. *The Routledge Dictionary of Anthropologists*. New York: Routledge.

Gardner, Paul F. 1997. *Shared Hopes, Separate Fears: Fifty Years of U.S.-Indonesian Relations*. Boulder, CO: Westview Press.

Geertz, Clifford. 1963a. *Agricultural Involution*. Berkeley: University of California Press.

———. 1963b. *Peddlers and Princes*. Chicago: University of Chicago Press.

———. 1995. *After the Fact*. Cambridge, MA: Harvard University Press.

———. 2010. *Life among the Anthros and Other Essays*. Princeton, NJ: Princeton University Press.

Gehrke, Velma Odeal Sexton. 1976. *Story of a Sexton Family*. Portland, OR.

Gendlin, Eugene T., and Jerome I. Berlin. 1961. "Galvanic Skin Response Correlates of Different Modes of Experiencing." *Journal of Clinical Psychology* 17–18:73–77.

Gerhardt, Uta. 1996. "Scholarship, Not Scandal." *Sociological Forum* 11 (4): 623–30.

Gilbert, William H. 1951. "Report: Anthropological Society of Washington." *American Anthropologist* 53 (2): 308–10.

Gilman, Nils. 2002. "Involution and Modernization: The Case of Clifford Geertz." In *Economic Development*, ed. Jeffrey H. Cohen and Norbert Dannhaeuser, 3–22. Walnut Creek, CA: AltaMira.

———. 2003. *Mandarins of the Future*. Baltimore: Johns Hopkins University Press.

Ginzberg, Carlo. 1992. *The Cheese and the Worms*. Chicago: University of Chicago Press.

Glander, Timothy. 2000. *Origins of Mass Communications Research during the American Cold War*. Mahwah, NJ: Erlbaum.

Glass, Andrew J. 1967. "Foundations Fail to File Reports." *Washington Post*, February 21, accessed February 3, 2010, http://jfk.hood.edu/Collection/Weisberg%20Subject%20 Index%20Files/C%20Disk/CIA%20Foundations/Item%20220.pdf.

Gleason, Herbert P. 1949. "Student Council Sponsored Salzburg Seminar Explains American Civilization to Europeans." *Harvard Crimson*, September 26.

Goldhaber, Samuel Z. 1969a. "Profile Jack Stauder." *Harvard Crimson*, November 15.

———. 1969b. "Stauder Gets Soc Rel OK for 1970–71." *Harvard Crimson*, December 5.

Golinger, Eva. 2006. *The Chávez Code*. Northampton, MA: Olive Branch Press.

González, Roberto, ed. 2004. *Anthropology in the Public Sphere*. Austin: University of Texas Press.

———. 2010. *Militarizing Culture*. Walnut Creek, CA: Left Coast Books.

Goodenough, Ward. 1968. "Editorial Note." *American Anthropologist* 70 (5): vi.

Goodman, Paul. 1967. "A Causerie at the Military-Industrial." *New York Review of Books*, November 23, 14–19.

Gordon, Nathan J., and William L. Fleisher. 2006. *Effective Interviewing and Interrogation Techniques*. 2nd ed. Amsterdam: Elsevier.

Gough, Kathleen. 1968. "Anthropology and Imperialism." *Monthly Review*, April, 12–27.

Graeber, David. 2014. "Anthropology and the Rise of the Professional-Managerial Class." HAU: *Journal of Ethnographic Theory* 4 (3): 73–88.

Graham, Milton D. 1954. "Federal Utilization of Social Science Research." Washington, DC: Brookings Institution.

Graves, Theodore D. 2004. *Behavioral Anthropology*. Walnut Creek, CA: Altamira.

Gray, Geoffrey. 2005. "Australian Anthropologists and World War II." *Anthropology Today* 21 (3): 18–21.

Green, Fitzhugh. 1988. *American Propaganda Abroad*. New York: Hippocrene Books.

Greene, Graham. 1955. *The Quiet American*. New York: Viking.

Greenfield, Patricia. 1977. "CIA's Behavior Caper." *APA Monitor*, December, 1, 10–11.

Greenfieldboyce, Nell. 2014. "Biologists Choose Sides in Safety Debate over Lab-Made Pathogens." Morning Edition, National Public Radio. August 13.

Greenwald, Glen. 2014. *No Place to Hide*. New York: Metropolitan Books.

Greider, William. 1969. "Unions Turn to AID after CIA Pullout." *Washington Post*, April 21, A1.

Guldin, Gregory Eliyu. 1994. *The Saga of Anthropology in China: From Malinowski to Moscow to Mao*. Armonk, NY: M. E. Sharpe.

Hafner, Katie. 2008. *Romance on Three Legs*. New York: Bloomsbury.

Hailey, Foster. 1964. "Kaplan Fund, Cited as C.I.A. 'Conduit,' Lists Unexplained $395,000 Grant." *New York Times*, September 3, 10.

Haines, Gerald K. 1998. "The Pike Committee Investigations and the CIA: Looking for a Rogue Elephant." *Studies in Intelligence*, Winter 81–92.

Hall, Edward T. 1959. *The Silent Language*. Greenwich, CT: Fawcett.

———. 1966. *The Hidden Dimension*. Garden City, NY: Doubleday.

Hall, John Whitney. 1952. "News of the Profession." *Far Eastern Quarterly* 11 (2): 287–94.

Halpern, Joel. 1960. "The Lao Elite: A Study of Tradition and Innovation." RAND Report, RM-2636-RC.
Handler, Richard. 1991. "An Interview with Clifford Geertz." *Current Anthropology* 32 (5): 602–13.
Hanna, William John, and Judith Lynne Hanna. 1971. *Urban Dynamics in Black Africa: An Interdisciplinary Approach*. Chicago: Aldine Atherton.
Hardy, Timothy S. 1976. "Intelligence Reform in the Mid-1970s." *Studies in Intelligence* 20 (2): 1–15.
Haring, Douglas. 1951. "Re: Ethnocentric Anthropologists." *American Anthropologist* 53 (1): 135–37.
Haronian, Frank, and A. Arthur Sugerman. 1965. "A Comparison of Sheldon's and Parnell's Methods for Quantifying Morphological Differences." *American Journal of Physical Anthropology* 23:135–42.
Harris, Marvin. 1958. *Portugal's African Wards*. New York: American Committee on Africa.
———. 1968. *The Rise of Anthropological Theory*. New York: Crowell.
———. 1974. "Why a Perfect Knowledge of All the Rules One Must Know to Act Like a Native Cannot Lead to the Knowledge of How Natives Act." *Journal of Anthropological Research* 30 (4): 242–51.
———. 1998. *Theories of Culture in Postmodern Times*. Walnut Creek, CA: AltaMira.
Harwood, Richard. 1967a. "CIA Probe to Take in New Areas." *Washington Post*, February 19. A4.
———. 1967b. "CIA Reported Ending Aid to Some Groups." *Washington Post*, February 22. A3.
———. 1967c. "8 More Groups Linked to CIA's Fund Activities." *Washington Post*, February 21, A6.
———. 1967d. "O What a Tangled Web the CIA Wove." *Washington Post*, February 26, E1.
———. 1967e. "Public Service Union Abroad Aided by CIA." *Washington Post*, February 23, A1.
Havron, M. D., J. A. Wittenburg, and A. T. Rambo. 1966. *U.S. Army Handbook of Counterinsurgency Guidelines for Area Commanders*. Prepared under subcontract by Human Sciences Research, January 1966 (Unclassified). AD 478–301. SORO.
Hays, D. G. 1962. *Simulations: An Introduction for Anthropologists*. November. RAND Publications P-2668.
HEF (Human Ecology Fund). 1963. *Report*. Forest Hills, NY: Society for the Investigation of Human Ecology.
Henderson, John P. 1989. *Studies in the African Diaspora*. Dover, MA: Majority Press.
Henry, Jules. 1951. "National Character and War." *American Anthropologist* 53 (1): 134–35.
Herbers, John. 1967. "President Bars Agency Influence over Education." *New York Times*, February 16, 1, 26.
Herman, Ellen. 1998. "Project Camelot and the Career of Cold War Psychology." In *Universities and Empire*, ed. Christopher Simpson, 97–133. New York: New Press.

Hersh, Seymour. 1974a. "Hunt Tells of Early Work for a CIA Domestic Unit." *New York Times*, December 31, 1, 4.

———. 1974b. "Huge CIA Operation Reported in U.S. Against Antiwar Forces, Other Dissidents in Nixon Years." *New York Times*, Dec. 22, 1974. 1; 26.

Hickey, Gerald C. 1964. *The Major Ethnic Groups of the South Vietnamese Highlands*. RAND Corporation, ARPA Memorandum RM-4041-ARPA. April.

Hickey, Gerald C., with W. P. Davison. 1965. *The American Military Advisor and His Foreign Counterpart: The Case of Vietnam*. RAND Memorandum, RM-4482-ARPA. March.

———. 1967a. *Accommodation in South Vietnam: The Key to Sociopolitical Solidarity*. RAND report. P-3703.

———. 1967b. *The Highland People of South Vietnam: Social and Economic Development*. Prepared for the Advanced Research Projects Agency, APRA Order No. 189–1. RAND RM-5381/1-ARPA. September.

———. 1969. *U.S. Strategy in South Vietnam: Extrication and Equilibrium*. RAND No. D-19736-ARPA. Project No. 9793. December 15.

———. 1971. *Some Recommendations Affecting the Prospective Role of Vietnamese Highlands in Economic Development*. RAND. September.

———. 1982. *Fire in the Forest: Ethnohistory of the Vietnamese Central Highlands*. New Haven, CT: Yale University Press.

———. 2002. *Window on a War*. Lubbock, TX: Texas Tech University Press.

Hinckle, Warren, Robert Scheer, and Sol Stern. 1966. "The University on the Make." *Ramparts*, April, 11–22.

Hinkle, Lawrence. 1961. "The Physiological State of the Interrogation Subject as It Affects Brain Function." In *The Manipulation of Human Behavior*, ed. A. D. Biderman and H. Zimmer, 19–50. New York: Wiley.

———. 1965. "Division of Human Ecology, Cornell Medical Center." *BioScience* 15 (8): 532.

Hinkle, L. E., Jr., J. W. Gittinger, L. Goldberger, A. Ostfeld, R. Métraux, P. Richter, and H. G. Wolff. 1957. "Studies in Human Ecology: Factors Governing the Adaptation of Chinese Unable to Return to China." In *Experimental Psychopathology*, ed. Paul H. Hoch and Joseph Zubin, 170–86. New York: Grune and Stratton.

Hinkle, L. E., Jr., and Harold G. Wolff. 1956. "Communist Interrogation and Indoctrination of 'Enemies of the State.'" *American Medical Association Archives of Neurology and Psychiatry* 76:115.

———. 1957. "The Nature of Man's Adaptation to His Total Environment and the Relation of This to Illness." *American Medical Association Archives of Internal Medicine* 99:442–60.

Hoffman, David H. 2015. *Independent Review Relating to APA Ethics Guidelines, National Security Interrogations, and Torture*. Report to the Special Committee of the Board of Directors of the American Psychological Association. Chicago: Sidley Austin LLP.

Hogan, Michael J. 1987. *The Marshall Plan*. Cambridge: Cambridge University Press.

Hogbin, Ian. 1951. *Transformation Scene: The Changing Culture of a New Guinea Village*. London: Routledge and Paul.

Hooker, James R. 1963. "The Anthropologists' Frontier: The Last Phase of African Exploitation." *Journal of Modern African Studies* 1 (4): 455–59.

Horowitz, Irving Louis. 1965. "The Life and Death of Project Camelot." *Transaction* 3 (1): 3–7, 44–47.

———. 1967. "Introduction: The Rise and Fall of Project Camelot." In *The Rise and Fall of Project Camelot*, ed. I. L. Horowitz, 3–44. Cambridge, MA: MIT Press.

Howard, Alan, and Irwin Howard. 1964. "Pre-Marital Sex and Social Control among the Rotumans." *American Anthropologist* 66 (2): 266–83.

Howard, Alan, and Robert A. Scott. 1965. "A Proposed Framework for the Analysis of Stress in the Human Organism." *Behavioral Science* 10:141–60.

———. 1965–66. "Cultural Values and Attitudes toward Death." *Journal of Existentialism* 6:161–74.

Howell, Nancy. 1990. *Surviving Fieldwork*. Washington, DC: American Anthropological Association.

HRAF. 1959. *1949–1959, Human Relations Area Files, Inc. Report*. New Haven: HRAF.

Huizer, G., and B. Mannheim, eds. 1979. "Appendix: Foundations on the Move." In *The Politics of Anthropology*, ed. G. Huizer and B. Mannheim, 481–94. The Hague: Mouton.

Hunter, Edward S. 1959. *The Past Present: A Year in Afghanistan*. London: Hodder and Stoughton.

Hymes, Dell, ed. 1972. *Reinventing Anthropology*. New York: Pantheon.

Indira. 1951. *Indira Selects*. Pacific Book and Supply catalog, October 22. Library of Congress, Washington, DC.

Ingersoll, Jasper C. 1968. Human Dimensions of Mekong River Basin Development: A Case Study of the Nam Pong Project, Northeast Thailand, 1967–1968. AID Report.

Irwin, Don, and Vincent J. Burke. 1967. "21 Foundations, Union Got Money from CIA." *Los Angeles Times*, February 26, B3.

Isaacs, Matt. 1999. "Agent Provocative." *SF Weekly*, November 17, accessed August 13, 2015, http://www.sfweekly.com/sanfrancisco/agent-provocative/Content?oid=2137417.

Isaacs, Stephen. 1971. "Anthropologists Battle over Role in Thailand." *New York Times*, November 25, A1, A10.

ISB (Intelligence Science Board). 2006. *Educing Information*. Washington, DC: NDIC.

Ishino, Iwao. 1956. "Motivational Factors in a Japanese Labor Supply Organization." *Human Organization* 15:12–17.

Jackson, David P. 2004. "The Life and Works and Writings of Robert Brainerd Ekvall (1898–1983)." In *Three Mountains and Seven Rivers*, ed. Shoun Hino and Toshihiro Wada, 609–35. Delhi: Motilal Banarsidass.

Jacobs, Milton, Farhad Farzanegan, and Alexander Askenasy. 1966. "A Study of Key Communicators in Thailand." *Social Forces* 45:192–99.

Jagchid, Sechin. 1999. *The Last Mongol Prince*. Studies on East Asia, Vol. 21. Bellingham: Western Washington University Press.

Jaschik, Scott. 2009. "Anthropologists Toughen Ethics Code." *Inside Higher Ed*, February 19, accessed December 23, 2014. https://www.insidehighered.com/news/2009/02/19/anthro.

Jeffreys-Jones, Rhodi. 1985. "The Socio-educational Composition of the CIA Elite." *Journal of American Studies* 19 (December): 421–24.

———. 1989. *The CIA and American Democracy*. New Haven, CT: Yale University Press.

Johnson, William R. 1976. "Clandestinity and Current Intelligence." *Studies in Intelligence* 20 (3): 15–69.

Jones, Delmos. 1967. "Cultural Variation among Six Lahu Villages, Northern Thailand." Doctoral PhD diss., Cornell University.

———. 1970. "Towards a Native Anthropology." *Human Organization* 29:251–59.

———. 1971a. "Reply to Jorgensen and Wolf." *New York Review of Books*, July 22, accessed June 2, 2014. http://www.nybooks.com/articles/archives/1971/jul/22/anthropology-on-the-warpath-an-exchange/.

———. 1971b. "Social Responsibility and the Belief in Basic Research." *Current Anthropology* 12 (3): 347–50.

Jorgensen, Joseph G., and Eric R. Wolf. 1970. "Anthropology on the Warpath in Thailand." *New York Review of Books*, November 19, 26–35.

Kahin, George McT. 1997. "The Making of Southeast Asian Studies." *Bulletin of Concerned Asian Scholars* 29 (1): 38–42.

Kaiser, David. 2002. "Cold War Requisitions, Scientific Manpower, and the Production of American Physicists after World War II." *Historical Studies in the Physical and Biological Sciences* 33:131–59.

Kalb, John. 2001. *Adventures in the Bone Trade*. New York: Copernicus Books.

Kay, M. 1969. *The Computer System to Aid the Linguistic Field Worker*. May. RAND P-4095.

Keating, Joshua. 2014. "Rich Countries Got More Generous Last Year." *Slate* April 9, accessed August 13, 2015, http://www.slate.com/blogs/the_world_/2014/04/09/new_oecd_figures_the_surprising_country_that_gives_the_most_foreign_aid.html.

Keesing, Felix. 1947. "American Island Territories in the Pacific." In *America's Future in the Pacific*, ed. John Carter, et al., 59–81. New Brunswick, NJ: Rutgers University Press.

Kelber, Harry. 2004. "AFL-CIO's Dark Past." *Labor Educator*, November 22. http://www.laboreducator.org/darkpast3.htm.

Kelman, Herbert C. 1965. *International Behavior: A Social-Psychological Analysis*. New York: Holt, Rinehart and Winston.

Kennan, George F. (1948) 1983. "Review of Current Trends [in] U.S. Foreign Policy." Policy Planning Study 23. In *The State Department Policy Planning Staff Papers 1947–1949*, 2:103–34. New York: Garland.

Kennedy, Raymond. 1944. "Applied Anthropology in the Dutch East Indies." *Transactions, New York Academy of Sciences*, 2nd ser., 6:157–62.

———. 1945a. "The Colonial Crisis and the Future." In *The Science of Man in the World Crisis*, ed. Ralph Linton, 306–46. New York: Columbia University Press.

———. 1945b. "Indonesian Politics and Parties." *Far Eastern Survey* 14:129–32.

———. 1953a. *Field Notes on Indonesia: Flores, 1949–50*. Behaviour Science Monographs. New Haven, CT: HRAF.

———. 1953b. *Field Notes on Indonesia: South Celebes, 1949–50*. Behavior Science Monographs. New Haven, CT: HRAF.

———. 1953c. *Field Notes on Indonesia: West Borneo, 1949–50*. Behaviour Science Monographs. New Haven, CT: HRAF.

Kennedy, Raymond, and Paul M. Kattenburg. 1948. Indonesia in Crisis. *Foreign Policy Report* 22 (15): 174–87.

Kenworthy, E. W. 1967a. "Hobby Foundation of Houston Affirms CIA Tie." *New York Times*, February 21, 32.

———. 1967b. "Witney Trust Got Aid from a Conduit of C.I.A." *New York Times*, February 25, 1.

Kimble, Gregory A. 1979. "Harold Schlosberg." In *International Encyclopedia of the Social Sciences, Biographical Supplement*, no. 18, 704–7. New York: Macmillan.

Kipling, Rudyard. 1922. *Kim*. Garden City, NY: Doubleday.

Kirsch, Stuart. 2006. *Reverse Anthropology*. Palo Alto, CA: Stanford University Press.

Kiste, Robert C., and Mac Marshall. 2000. "American Anthropology in Micronesia, 1941–1997." *Pacific Science* 54 (3): 265–74.

Klare, Michael T. 1972. *War without End: American Planning for the Next Vietnam War*. New York: Vintage.

Kleinman, Steven M. 2006. "KUBARK Counterintelligence Interrogation Review: Observations of an Interrogator." In *Educing Information*, 95–140. Washington, DC: NDIC. http://www.fas.org/irp/dni/educing.pdf.

Knight, G. R. 1982. "Introduction: 'Involution' and the Spread of Capitalism in Rural Java." In *Capitalism and Commodity Production in Java*, ed. H. Alavi, P. L. Burns, G. R. Knight, P. B. Mayer, and Doug McEacher, 119–59. London: Croom Helm.

Koikari, Mire. 2008. *Pedagogy of Democracy*. Philadelphia: Temple University Press.

Kurzman, Dan. 1963. *Subversion of the Innocents*. New York: Random House.

La Barre, Weston. 1945. "Some Observations on Character Structure in the Orient—the Japanese." *Psychiatry* 8:319–42.

———. 1946a. "Some Observations on Character Structure in the Orient: II. The Chinese, Part One." *Psychiatry* 9:215–37.

———. 1946b. "Some Observations on Character Structure in the Orient. Part II: The Chinese, Part Two." *Psychiatry* 9:378–80.

Laird, Thomas. 2002. *Into Tibet: The CIA's First Atomic Spy and His Secret Expedition to Lhasa*. New York: Grove Press.

Lancaster, Roger N. 1992. *Life Is Hard*. Berkley: University of California Press.

Lansdale, Edward. 1972. *In the Midst of Wars*. New York: Harper and Row.

Larsen, Otto. 1992. *Milestones and Millstones: Social Science at the National Science Foundation, 1945–1991*. New Brunswick, NJ: Transaction.

Lawrence, Ken. 1979. "Academics: An Overview." In *Dirty Work 2*, ed. Ellen Ray, William Schapp, Karl Van Meter, and Louis Wolf, 80–93. Secaucus, NJ: Lyle Stuart.

Leach, Edmund. 1974. "Anthropology Upside Down." *New York Review of Books*, April 4, 33–35.

LeBar, Frank M., Adrienne Suddard, and HRAF. 1960. *Laos: Its People, Its Society, Its Culture.* Survey of World Culture Series, No. 8. New Haven, CT: HRAF Press.

Lee, Richard B. 1972. "Notes on the Prehistory of ARPA." *ARPA Newsletter*, no. 1. (November): 1–3.

———. 1979. *The !Kung San.* Cambridge: Cambridge University Press.

———. 2008. "The Anti-imperialist Tradition in North American Anthropology: Vietnam, the Left Academy, and the Founding of ARPA." Paper presented at the annual meeting of the American Anthropological Association, San Francisco, November 20.

Leighton, Alexander. 1945. *The Governing of Men.* Princeton, NJ: Princeton University Press.

———. 1949. *Human Relations in a Changing World: Observations on the Use of the Social Science.* New York: Dutton.

Lelyveld, Joseph. 1968. "Asia Foundation Banned by India." *New York Times*, February 16, 9.

Lepowsky, Maria. 2000. "Charlotte Gower and the Subterranean History of Anthropology." In *Excluded Ancestors, Inventible Traditions*, ed. R. Handler, 12–170. HOA vol. 9. Madison: University of Wisconsin Press.

Lewis, Herbert. 2005. "Anthropology, the Cold War, and Intellectual History." In *Histories of Anthropology Annual*, ed. Regna Darnell and Frederic W. Gleach, 99–113. Lincoln: University of Nebraska Press.

Lewis, Michael. 2002. "Scientists or Spies? Ecology in a Climate of Cold War Suspicion." *Economic and Political Weekly*, June 15–21, 2322–32.

Life. 1950. "In Pursuit of News." *Life*, May 8, 42.

Lippincott, Aubrey E., and Hartley F. Dame. 1964. "A Brief Review of Selected Aspects of the San Blas Cuna Indians." Washington, DC: SORO.

Lienhardt, Godfrey, Dennis Duerden, John Nagenda, and Lewis Nkosi. 1966. "The Oral Tradition." *New African*, July, 124–25.

Lipsky, George A. 1959. *Saudi Arabia: Its People, Its Society, Its Culture.* Survey of World Culture Series, No. 4. New Haven, CT: HRAF Press.

Liss, Arlene. 1953. "Seminar Studies Major Near Eastern Problems." *Michigan Daily* November 21, 10.

LOC (Library of Congress). 1969. "Technical Information for Congress: Report to the Subcommittee on Science, Research and Development of the Committee on Science and Astronautics." U.S. House of Representatives. Ninety-First Cong., 1st sess. Prepared by the Science Policy Research Division Legislative Reference Service Library of Congress. April 29.

Lord, John M., Carl F. Rosenthal, and James M. Dodson. 1965. *Communist Theory and Practice in Subversive Insurgencies.* Washington, DC: SORO.

Lu, David John. 1996. *Japan: A Documentary History.* Vol. 1. Armonk, NY: M. E. Sharp.

Lyerly, Samuel B., and Preston S. Abbott. 1966. *Handbook of Psychiatric Rating Scales (1950–1964).* Public Health Service Publication No. 1495. Washington, DC: U.S. Government Printing Office.

Lyotard, Jean-François. 1984. *The Postmodern Condition*. Translated by Brian Massumi. Minneapolis: University of Minnesota Press.

Macgregor, Gordon. 1955. "Anthropology in Government." In *Yearbook of Anthropology*, ed. W. L. Thomas, 421–435. Chicago: University of Chicago Press.

MacGregor, Morris J., Jr. 1985. *Integration of the Armed Forces, 1940–1965*. Washington, DC: Center of Military History, U.S. Army.

Mader, Julius. 1968. *Who's Who in the CIA*. Berlin: W 66, Mauerstrasse 69.

Madsen, Wayne. 2012. *The Manufacturing of a President: The CIA's Insertion of Barak H. Obama, Jr. into the White House*. N.p.

Mandler, Peter. 2013. *Return from the Natives: How Margaret Mead Won the Second World War and Lost the Cold War*. New Haven, CT: Yale University Press.

Mannheim, Karl. 1936. *Ideology and Utopia*. New York: Harcourt, Brace.

Marchetti, Victor, and John D. Marks. 1974. *The CIA and the Cult of Intelligence*. London: Coronet Books.

Marks, John. 1974. "How To Spot a Spook." *Washington Monthly*, November, 5–11.

———. 1979. *The Search for the "Manchurian Candidate."* New York: Times Books.

Marquis, Jefferson P. 2000. "The Other Warriors: American Social Science and Nation Building in Vietnam." *Diplomatic History* 24:79–105.

Mars, Gerald. 2003. "The CIA and the KGB: Paranoia Is a Two-Way Mirror." *Anthropology Today* 19 (4): 22–23.

Marshack, Alexander. 1952. "The Unreported War in Indonesia." *American Mercury* 74 (February): 37–47.

Marshall, Donald S. 1957. *Songs of the Sea Kings*. Salem, MA: Peabody Museum.

———. 1961. *Ra'ivavae: An Expedition to the Most Fascinating and Mysterious Island in Polynesia*. New York: Doubleday.

———, ed., 1966. *Program for the Pacification and Long Term Development of South Vietnam*. 2 vols. Washington, DC: U.S. Army.

Martin, William G. and Michael O. West. 1999. "The Ascent, Triumph, and Disintegration of the Africanist Enterprise, USA." In *Out of One, Many Africas*, eds., W. G. Martin and M. O. West, 85–122. Urbana: University of Illinois Press.

Marx, Karl. (1894) 1993. *Capital, Volume III*. New York: Penguin Classics.

Mason, Leonard. 1953. "Anthropology in American Micronesia." *Clearinghouse Bulletin of Research in Human Organization* 2 (3): 1–5.

May, Mark A. 1971. "A Retrospective View of the Institute of Human Relations at Yale." *Behavioral Science Notes* 6:141–72.

McCoy, Alfred. 1991. *The Politics of Heroin*. Brooklyn, NY: Lawrence Hill Books.

———. 2006. *A Question of Torture*. New York: Henry Holt.

McGehee, Ralph W. 1983. *Deadly Deceits: My 25 Years in the C.I.A.* New York: Sheridan Square Publications.

McGranahan, Carole. 2010. *Arrested Histories: Tibet, the CIA, and Memories of a Forgotten War*. Durham, NC: Duke University Press.

McKinzie, Richard D. 1974. "Oral History Interview with John F. Cady." Truman Library. http://www.trumanlibrary.org/oralhist/cadyjf.htm.

Mead, Margaret. 1947. "The Salzburg Seminar in American Civilization." Report by Margaret Mead to the Harvard Student Council, accessed July 2, 2011. http://www.salzburgglobal.org/reports/1947_MeadArticle.pdf 5/23/10.

———. 1951. *Soviet Attitudes toward Authority*. January. Unclassified RAND Publications R-199.

———. 1959. *An Anthropologist at Work: Writings of Ruth Benedict*. Boston: Houghton Mifflin.

———. 1962. "The Underdeveloped and the Overdeveloped." *Foreign Affairs* 41 (1): 78–89.

———. 1979. "Anthropological Contributions to National Policies during and Immediately after World War II." In *The Uses of Anthropology*, ed. Walter Goldschmidt, 145–57. Washington, DC: AAA.

Medsger, Betty. 2014. *The Burglary*. New York: Knopf.

Mehlman, Jeffrey. 2000. *French Intellectuals in Wartime Manhattan, 1940–1944*. Baltimore: Johns Hopkins University Press.

Melvern, Linda. 1995. *The Ultimate Crime: Who Betrayed the UN and Why*. London: Allyn and Busby.

Mendenhall, Joseph. 1969. "U.S. Governance, USAID and U.S. CORDS Objectives and Organization in Vietnam." USAID Report. Washington, DC. July 22.

Métraux, Alfred. 1951. "United Nations Economic and Security Council, Statement by Experts on Problems of Race." *American Anthropologists* 53 (1): 142–45.

Métraux, Rhoda. 1980. "The Study of Culture at a Distance: A Prototype." *American Anthropologist* 82 (2): 362–73.

Meyer, Alfred G. 2000. *The Ritchie Boys*. Accessed March 18, 2011, http://www.ritchieboys.com/DL/fish205.pdf.

Michael, Donald N. 1960. "The Beginning of the Space Age and American Public Opinion." *Public Opinion Quarterly* 24 (4): 573–82.

Millegan, Lloyd S. 1942. "Census of the Philippines: 1939." *Far Eastern Quarterly* 2 (1): 77–79.

———. 1959. "The Protestant Church in Indonesia." Master's thesis, American University.

Miller, Seumas, and Michael J. Selgelid. 2008. *Ethical and Philosophical Consideration of the Dual-Use Dilemma in the Biological Sciences*. New York: Springer.

Millhauser, Steven. 2008. "The Next Thing." *Harpers*, May 2008, 71–78.

Millikan, Max F., and Donald L. M. Blackmer, eds. 1961. *The Emerging Nations*. Boston: Little, Brown.

Millikan, Max M., and Walt W. Rostow. 1957. *A Proposal: Key to an Effective Foreign Policy*. New York: Harper and Brothers.

Mills, Ami Chen. 1991. *CIA Off Campus*. 2nd ed. Boston: South End Press.

Mills, C. Wright. 1959. *The Sociological Imagination*. New York: Oxford University Press.

Milne, David. 2008. *American Rasputin; Walt Rostow and the Vietnam War*. New York: Hill and Wang.

Mintz, Sidney. 1985. *Sweetness and Power*. New York: Viking Books.

Mitchell, Philip H. 1958. "The Future of Anthropology in the Department of Defense." In *Anthropology in the Armed Services*, ed. Louis Dupree, 45–51. University Park: Pennsylvania State University Press.

Mitchell, Timothy. 2002. *Rule of Experts: Egypt, Techno-Politics, Modernity*. Berkeley: University of California Press.

Molnar, Andrew R., William A. Lybrand, Lorna Hahn, James L. Kirkman and Peter B. Riddleberger. 1963. *Undergrounds in Insurgent, Revolutionary, and Resistance Warfare*. Washington, DC: SORO.

Montague, Ludwell Lee. 1992. *General Walter Bedell Smith as Director of Central Intelligence, October 1950–February 1953*. University Park: Pennsylvania State University Press.

Moore, John. 1971. "Perspective for a Partisan Anthropology." *Liberation*, November, 34–43.

Morán, Emilo. 1996. *Transforming Societies, Transforming Anthropology*. Ann Arbor: University of Michigan Press.

Morehouse, Ward, ed. 1957. *American Institutions and Organizations Interested in Asia: A Reference Directory*. New York: Taplinger.

MSUG (Michigan State University Group). 1962. *Final Report Covering Activities of the Michigan State University Vietnam Advisory Group, May 20, 1955–June 30, 1962*. Saigon: MSUG.

Mullen, Jay. 1979. "I Was Idi Amin's Basketball Czar." Pts. 1 and 2. *Oregon Magazine*, May, 54–65; June, 66–77.

Murdock, George Peter. 1956. "How Culture *Changes*." In *Man, Culture, and Society*, ed. Harry L. Shapiro, 247–60. New York: Oxford University Press.

———. 1961. *Outline of Cultural Materials*. 4th rev. ed. New Haven, CT: HRAF.

Murphy, Robert F. 1976. "Introduction: A Quarter Century of American Anthropology." In *Selected Papers from the American Anthropologist*, ed. R. Murphy, 1–22. Washington, DC: American Anthropological Association.

Nader, Laura. 1972. "Up the Anthropologist—Perspectives Gained from Studying Up." In *Reinventing Anthropology*, ed. Dell Hymes, 284–311. New York: Pantheon.

———. 1997a. "Controlling Processes: Tracking the Dynamic Components of Power." *Current Anthropology* 38 (5): 711–37.

———. 1997b. "The Phantom Factor: Impact of the Cold War on Anthropology." In *The Cold War and the University*, 107–46. New York: New Press.

Naroll, Raoul. 1974. *Military Deterrence in History*. Albany: SUNY Press.

Narvaez, Alfonso A. 1989. "Louis Dupree, 63, Anthropologist and Expert on Afghanistan, Dies." *New York Times*, March 23, accessed June 12, 2009, http://www.nytimes.com/1989/03/23/obituaries/louis-dupree-63-anthropologist-and-expert-on-afghanistan-dies.html.

Nash, June. 1979a. "Ethnology in a Revolutionary Setting." In *The Politics of Anthropology*, ed. Gerrit Huizer and Bruce Mannheim, 353–70. The Hague: Mouton.

———. 1979b. *We Eat the Mines and the Mines Eat Us*. New York: Columbia University Press.

———. 2007. *Practicing Ethnography in a Globalizing World*. Lanham, MD: AltaMira.

National Review. 1957. "Did CIA Take the Senate?" *National Review*, February 2, 103.

National Security Archives. 1998. Interview with Roger Hilsman. December 6, accessed April 15, 2009. http://www.gwu.edu/~nsarchiv/coldwar/interviews/episode-11/hilsman1.html.

NCA (Network of Concerned Anthropologists). 2009. *Counter Counterinsurgency Manual*. Chicago: Prickly Paradigm Press.

Nelkin, Dorothy. 1972. *The University and Military Research*. Ithaca, NY: Cornell University Press.

Nesbitt, Paul H. 1958. "Anthropology and the Air Force." In *Anthropology in the Armed Services*, ed. Louis Dupree, 4–14. University Park: Pennsylvania State University Press.

Newberry, Larry. 1971. "Soldiers and the Land to the Tiller Program in Military Region 4 of Vietnam." Control Data Corporation. AID-730-3449.

Newbold, Stokes [pseudonym, Richard N. Adams]. 1957. "Receptivity to Communist Fomented Agitation in Rural Guatemala." *Economic Development and Cultural Change* 5:338–61.

New Scientist. 1982. "Cold War, Commerce and the Lucy Trail." *New Scientist*, December 2, 552.

Newsweek. 1967. "The Administration: House of Glass." *Newsweek*, March 6, 28–30.

Norman, Bob. 2005. "Finding Gary." *New Times*, August 11, accessed August 3, 2015, http://www.browardpalmbeach.com/news/finding-gary-part-2-6314519.

Nugent, David. 2002. "Introduction." In *Locating Capitalism in Time and Space*, ed. David Nugent, 1–59. Stanford, CA: Stanford University Press.

———. 2010. "Knowledge and Empire." *Identities* 17: 2–44.

Nye, Joseph S. 2005. *Soft Power: The Means to Success in World Politics*. New York: Public Affairs.

NYT (*New York Times*). 1950. "Guggenheim Fund Lists 158 Awards." *New York Times*, April 17.

———. 1964. "Misusing CIA Money." *New York Times*, September 4.

———. 1967a. "Arab Magazine Shuts Down, Citing Reports of CIA Aid." *New York Times*, May 22.

———. 1967b. "Harvard Programs Received CIA Help." *New York Times*, April 16.

———. 1967c. "Praeger Published '15 or 16' Books at CIA Request." *New York Times*, February 24.

———. 1970. "War Protestors Score Thai Link." *New York Times*, April 5.

———. 2000. "Overthrow of Premier Mossadeq of Iran: November 1952–August 1953." *New York Times*, April 16. [Declassified Secret CIA document], accessed March 2, 2011. http://www.nytimes.com/library/world/mideast/iran-cia-intro.pdf.

OCNO (Office of the Chief of Naval Operations). 1948. *Handbook on the Trust Territory of the Pacific Islands*. Washington, DC: Navy Department.

O'Connell, Charles Thomas. 1990. "Social Structure and Science: Soviet Studies at Harvard." PhD diss., UCLA.

Oliver, Douglas, ed. 1951. *Planning Micronesia's Future*. Cambridge, MA: Harvard University Press.

Opler, Marvin K. 1965. "Report on the First International Congress of Social Psychiatry in London, England, August 17–22, 1964." *Current Anthropology* 6 (3): 294.

Oppenheim, Robert. 2008. "On Locations of Korean War and Cold War Anthropology." *Histories of Anthropology Annual* 4 (1): 220–58.

Oppenheimer, Martin. 1997. "Social Scientists and War Criminals." *New Politics*, n.s. 6 (3): 77–87.

Osgood, Cornelius. 1951. *The Koreans and Their Culture*. New York: Ronald Press.

Paget, Karen M. 2006. "From Cooperation to Covert Action: The United States Government and Students, 1940–52." In *The U.S. Government, Citizen Groups and the Cold War*, ed. Helen Laville and Hugh Wilford, 66–82. New York: Routledge.

Parsons, Talcott. 1973. "Clyde Kluckhohn and the Integration of Social Science." In *Culture and Life*, ed. Walter W. Taylor, John L Fischer and Evon Z. Vogt, 30–57. Carbondale: Southern Illinois University Press.

Patterson, Thomas. 2003. *Social History of Anthropology in the United States*. Oxford: Berg.

Patterson, Thomas C., and Antonio Lauria-Perricelli. 1999. "Julian Steward and the Construction of Area-Studies Research in the United States." In *Julian Steward and the Great Basin*, R. O. Clemmer, L. D. Myers, and M. E. Rudden, 219–40. Salt Lake City: University of Utah Press.

Pauker, Guy J. 1967. "Political Consequences of Rural Development Programs in Indonesia." SEADAG Paper No. 26. December 9.

Paulson, Joy Larsen. 2010. *Family Law Reform in Postwar Japan*. Xlibris.

Peace, William. 2004. *Leslie A. White: Evolution and Revolution in Anthropology*. Lincoln: University of Nebraska Press.

Pearce, R. Michael. 1965. *Evolution of a Vietnamese Village: Part One. The Present, after Eight Months of Pacification*. RAND RM 4552–1.

Pearson, Drew. 1967. "Patman Balked in Probe of CIA Funds." *Washington Post*, March 1, E17.

Perkins, John. 2004. *Confessions of an Economic Hitman*. New York: Plume.

Peterson, Mark Allen. 2005. *Communication*. New York: Berghahn Books.

Phillips, H. P., and David A. Wilson. 1964. *Certain Effects of Culture and Social Organization on Internal Security in Thailand*. RAND RM-3786-ARPA.

Pike Report. 1977. CIA: *The Pike Report*. London: Spokesman Books.

Pincus, Walter. 1966. "Operation Simpatico: Pentagon in New Latin Row." *Washington Star*, January 31.

Pool, Ithiel de Sola. 1967. "The Necessity for Social Scientists Doing Research for Governments." In *The Rise and Fall of Project Camelot*, ed. I. L. Horowitz, 267–80. Cambridge: MIT Press.

Pool, Ithiel de Sola and others. 1963. *Social Science Research and National Security.* Under Office of Naval Research Contract 1354(08) Task No. NR 170-379. Washington, DC: Smithsonian Institution.

Poppe, Nicholas. 1983. *Reminiscences.* Edited by Henry G. Schwarz, Bellingham: Western Washington University.

POQ (*Public Opinion Quarterly*). 1964. "News and Notes." *Public Opinion Quarterly* 28 (1): 169-77.

Porter, Jack Nusan. 1996. "Talcott Parsons and National Socialism: The Case of the 'Ten Mysterious Missing Letters.'" *Sociological Forum* 11 (4): 603-11.

Powers, Thomas. 1976. "The Rise and Fall of Richard Helms." *Rolling Stone*, December 16, 46-55.

Poyer, Lin. 2004. "Dimensions of Hunger in Wartime: Chuuk Lagoon, 1943-1945." *Food and Foodways* 12:137-174.

PPR. 2012. Principles of Professional Responsibility, American Anthropological Association. Accessed December 23, 2014, http://ethics.aaanet.org/category/statement/.

Prados, John. 1986. *Presidents' Secret Wars.* New York: Morrow.

———. 2003. *Lost Crusader: The Secret Wars of CIA Director William Colby.* Oxford: Oxford University Press.

Preston, Douglas. 1995. "The Mystery of Sandia Cave." *New Yorker*, June 12, 66-83.

Price, David. 1989. *Before the Bulldozers.* Washington, DC: Seven Locks Press.

Price, David H. 1998. "Cold War Anthropology: Collaborators and Victims of the National Security State." *Identities* 4 (3-4): 389-430.

———. 2000. "Anthropologists as Spies." *Nation*, November 20, 24-27.

———. 2002. "Interlopers and Invited Guests." *Anthropology Today* 18 (6): 16-21.

———. 2003a. "Anthropology *Sub Rosa*: The AAA, the CIA and the Ethical Problems Inherent in Secret Research." In *Ethics and the Profession of Anthropology*, ed. Carolyn Fluehr-Lobban, 29-49. Walnut Creek, CA: AltaMira.

———. 2003b. "Subtle Means and Enticing Carrots: The Impact of Funding on American Cold War Anthropology." *Critique of Anthropology* 23 (4): 373-401.

———. 2004a. "Academia under Attack: Sketches for a New Blacklist." In *Anthropologists in the Public Sphere*, ed. Roberto González, 243-26. Austin: University of Texas Press.

———. 2004b. *Threatening Anthropology: The FBI's Surveillance and Repression of Activist Anthropologists.* Durham, NC: Duke University Press.

———. 2005. "El FBI y las ciencias sociales." *Historia Antropología y Fuentes Orales* 34 (3): 29-46.

———. 2007a. "André Gunder Frank, the FBI, and the Bureaucratic Exile of a Critical Mind." *CounterPunch* 14 (12): 1-4.

———. 2007b. "Buying a Piece of Anthropology, Part One: Human Ecology and Unwitting Anthropological Research for the CIA." *Anthropology Today* 23 (3): 8-13.

———. 2007c. "Buying a Piece of Anthropology, Part Two: The CIA and Our Tortured Past." *Anthropology Today* 23 (5): 17-22.

———. 2008a. *Anthropological Intelligence: The Deployment and Neglect of American Anthropology in the Second World War.* Durham, NC: Duke University Press.

———. 2008b. "Limiting Democracy and Reining-In ARPA at the Annual Business Meeting." Paper presented at the annual meeting of the American Anthropological Association, San Francisco, November 20.

———. 2008c. "Materialism's Free Pass: Karl Wittfogel, McCarthyism and the 'Bureaucratization of Guilt.'" In *Anthropology at the Dawn of the Cold War*, ed. Dustin Wax, 37–61. London: Pluto.

———. 2010a. "Counterinsurgency." In *The Routledge Encyclopedia of Social and Cultural Anthropology, 2nd ed.* Allan Bernard and Jonathan Spencer, 162–164. London: Routledge.

———. 2010b. "Governing Fear in the Iron Cage of Rationalism: Terry Gilliam's Brazil through the 9/11 Looking Glass." In *Reframing 9/11: Film, Popular Culture and the "War on Terror,"* ed. Jeff Birkenstein, Anna Froula, and Karen Randell, 167–82. New York: Continuum.

———. 2011a. "The CIA, the Asia Foundation, and the AAA: How the AAA Linked Asian Anthropologists to a CIA Funding Front." Paper presented at the session "Anthropologies of the Covert" at the annual meeting of the American Anthropological Association, Montreal, Canada, November 19.

———. 2011b. "Counterinsurgency, Vietnam, Thailand, and the Political Uses of Militarized Anthropology." In *Dangerous Liaisons*, ed. Laura McNamara and Robert Rubinstein, 51–76. Santa Fe, NM: School for Advanced Research Press.

———. 2011c. "How the CIA and Pentagon Harnessed Anthropological Research during the Second World War and Cold War with Little Critical Notice." *Journal of Anthropological Research* 67 (3): 333–56.

———. 2011d. "Mark Zborowski in a World of Pain." Pts. 1 and 2. *CounterPunch* 18 (12): 1, 5–8; 18 (13): 1, 4–7.

———. 2011e. "Uninvited Guests: A Short History of the CIA on Campus." In *The CIA on Campus*, ed. Philip Zwerling, 33–60. Jefferson, NC: McFarland.

———. 2011f. *Weaponizing Anthropology: Social Science in Service of the Militarized State*. Petrolia, CA: CounterPunch Books.

———. 2012a. "Connecting Wartime Anthropology's Trajectories with the Birth of Area Studies." Paper presented at Columbia University's Heyman Center conference "OSS, Intelligence, and Knowledge of the World," April 13. New York.

———. 2012b. "Counterinsurgency and the M-VICO System." *Anthropology Today* 28 (1): 16–20.

———. 2012c. "Resistance's Half-Life." *CounterPunch* 19 (11): 1, 5–7.

———. 2013a. "The Destruction of Conscience in the National Academy of Sciences." *CounterPunch*, February 26, accessed April 19, 2014, http://www.counterpunch.org/2013/02/26/the-destruction-of-conscience-in-national-academy-of-sciences/.

———. 2013b. "Raymond Kennedy: Unanswered and Ignored Questions of Early Cold War Ethnography." Council on Southeast Asia Studies Seminar Series, MacMillan Center, Yale University, February 13.

———. 2013c. "A Social History of Wiretaps." *CounterPunch* 20 (6): 10–14.

———. 2014a. "Counterinsurgency by Other Names: Complicating Humanitarian Applied Anthropology in Current, Former, and Future War Zones." *Human Organization* 75 (2): 95–105.

———. 2014b. "On Using Ethics to Avoid Politics." Engaged Scholarship Workshop: "Embedded! Archaeologists and Anthropologists in Modern Landscapes of Conflict." Engaged Scholarship Workshop, Middle East Studies, Brown University, May 1.

Price, James R. 1964. "Irrigation as a Factor in the Economic Development of Thailand." SORO/CINFAC 1–64, Washington, DC: SORO.

Price, James R., and Paul Jureidini. 1964. "Witchcraft, Sorcery, Magic and Other Psychological Phenomena and Their Implications on Military and Paramilitary Operations in the Congo." SORO/CINFAC 6–64. August 8. Washington, DC: SORO.

Price, James R., Barbara Reason Butler, Doris M. Condit, Bert Cooper, and Michael Conley, under the Supervision of Richard H. Moore. Ca. 1964–65 *The M-VICO System of Counterinsurgency Taxonomy*. Washington, DC: SORO, American University.

Price, William A. 1967. "CIA Funds Had a Role in Downfall of Jagan." *Guardian*, March 4.

Prince, Raymond H. 1962a. "Frequency of Depression in African Natives." *Review and Newsletter: Transcultural Research in Mental Health Problems* 13:42–50.

———. 1962b. "Functional Symptoms Associated with the Study of Nigerian Students." *West Africa Medical Journal* 11:198–206.

———. 1964. *Ifa: Yoruba Divination and Sacrifice*. Ibadan, Nigeria: Ibadan University Press.

———. 1995. "The Central Intelligence Agency and the Origins of Transcultural Psychiatry at McGill University." *Annals of the Royal College of Physicians and Surgeons of Canada* 28:407–13.

Pyle, Christopher. 2002. "Domestic Spying — Again?" *Hartford Courant*, November 32. http://www.mtholyoke.edu/offices/comm/oped/spying2.shtml.

Quirk, John Patrick, David Atlee Phillips, Ray Cline, and Walter Pforzheimer. 1986. *The Central Intelligence Agency: A Photographic History*. Guilford, CT: Foreign Intelligence Press.

Rabinow, Paul. 2006. "Steps toward an Anthropological Laboratory." Laboratory for the Anthropology of the Contemporary, draft discussion paper. February 2. http://www.ram-wan.net/restrepo/teorias-antrop-contem/Rabinow_Laboratory.pdf.

Rambo, A. Terry. 1973. *A Comparison of Peasant Social Systems of Northern and Southern Viet-Nam: A Study of Ecological Adaptation, Social Succession and Cultural Evolution*. Monograph Series III. Center for Vietnamese Studies Southern Illinois University at Carbondale.

Rambo, A. Terry, and Neil L. Jamieson III. 1973. *Cultural Change in Rural Vietnam: A Study on the Effects of Long-Term Communist Control on the Social Structure, Attitudes, and Values of the Peasants of the Mekong Delta*. SEADAG Report, 73–74.

Ramparts Magazine Editors. 1967. "How the CIA Turns Foreign Students into Traitors." *Ramparts*, April, 23–24.

Ramsey, Diane. 1965. "Information and Control Processes in Living Systems." *Science*, July 23, 459.

RAND. 1948. *Conference of Social Scientists: September 14 to 19, 1947—New York*. Project RAND (USAF Project MX-791), RAND Publication R-106. Santa Monica, CA: RAND Corporation.

Ransom, David. 1975. "Ford Country: Building an Elite for Indonesia." In *The Trojan Horse: A Radical Look at Foreign Aid*, ed. Steve Weissman and members of Pacific Studies Center and the North American Congress on Latin America, 93–116. San Francisco: Ramparts Press.

Raper, Arthur F., Tami Tsuchiyama, Herbert Passin, and David L. Sills. 1950. *The Japanese Village in Transition*. GHQ Report No. 136. Tokyo: GHQ.

Rappaport, Roy. 1984. *Pigs for the Ancestors*. New Haven, CT: Yale University Press.

Rauch, Jerome S. 1955. "Area Institute Programs and African Studies." *Journal of Negro Education* 24 (4): 409–25.

Ray, Ellen, William Schaap, Karl van Meter, and Louis Wolf, eds. 1979. *Dirty Work 2: The CIA in Africa*. Secaucus, NJ: Lyle Stuart.

Raybeck, Douglas. 1996. *Mad Dogs, Englishmen, and the Errant Anthropologist: Fieldwork in Malaysia*. Long Grove, IL: Waveland.

Raymont, Henry. 1966. "Spy Agencies Held Danger to Research." *New York Times*, November 18, 1–2.

Read, Kenneth. 1947. "Effects of the Pacific War in the Markham Valley." *Oceania* 18 (2): 95–116.

Redfield, Robert. 1948. *Folk Culture of the Yucatan*. Chicago: University of Chicago Press.

Reed, Roy. 1967. "President Orders C.I.A. to Halt Aid to Private Groups." *New York Times*, March 30, 1.

Reistrup, J. V. 1967. "Anthropologists Vote 12 to 1 to Oppose Joining in Secret Intelligence Work." *Washington Post*, April 21.

Reuter, M. 1978. "*New York Times* Investigated CIA Ties to Book Industry." *Publishers Weekly*, January 16, 213:18.

Rév, Istán. 2002. "The Suggestion." *Representations* 80:62–98.

Reyna, Stephen P. 1998. "Right and Might: Of Approximate Truths and Moral Judgment." *Identities* 4 (3–4): 431–66.

Richardson, Peter. 2009. *A Bomb in Every Issue*. New York: New Press.

Rockefeller, Nelson (Chair). 1975. *Report to the President by the Commission on CIA Activities within the United States*. Washington, DC: Government Printing Office.

Rockefeller Foundation. 1952. *The Rockefeller Foundation Annual Report*. New York: Rockefeller Foundation.

Roe, Sandra K. 2007. "A Brief History of an Ethnographic Database: The Collection of Ethnography." *Behavioral and Social Sciences Librarian* 25 (2): 47–77.

Roelofs, Joan. 2003. *Foundations and Public Policy: The Mask of Pluralism*. Albany: SUNY Press.

Rohde, Joy Elizabeth. 2007. "The Social Scientists' War: Expertise in a Cold War Nation." PhD diss., University of Pennsylvania.

———. 2009. "Gray Matters: Social Scientists, Military Patronage, and Democracy in the Cold War." *Journal of American History* 96:99–122.

Roosevelt, Kermit. 1979. *Countercoup: The Struggle for the Control of Iran*. New York: McGraw-Hill.

———. 2013. *Armed with Expertise: The Militarization of American Social Research during the Cold War*. Ithaca, NY: Cornell University Press.

Roseberry, William. 1988. "Political Economy." *Annual Review of Anthropology* 17:61–185.

———. 1996. "The Unbearable Lightness of Anthropology." *Radical History Review* 65:5–25.

Rosen, Lawrence. 2005. "Passing Judgment: Interpretation, Morality, and Cultural Assessment in the Work of Clifford Geertz." In *Clifford Geertz by His Colleagues*, ed. Clifford Geertz, Richard A. Shweder, and Byron Good, 10–19. Chicago: University of Chicago Press.

Rosenbaum, Ron. 1995. "The Great Ivy League Nude Posture Photo Scandal." *New York Times Magazine*, January 15, 26–31.

Ross, Eric B. 1998a. "Cold Warriors without Weapons." *Identities* 98 (3–4): 475–506.

———. 1998b. *The Malthus Factor: Poverty, Politics and Population in Capitalist Development*. London: Zed.

———. 1999. "Axel Wenner-Gren and the Nazi Connection: An Ethical Dilemma for Anthropology." Paper presented at the annual meeting of the American Anthropological Association, Chicago, November 18.

———. 2011. "Reflections on Vicos." In *Vicos and Beyond*, eds. Tom Greaves, Ralph Bolton, and Florencia Zapata, 129–61. Walnut Creek, CA: AltaMira.

Ross, Thomas B. 1976. "Surreptitious Entry: The CIA's Operations in the United States" in *The CIA File*, ed. Borosage, Robert L. & John Marks, 93–108. New York: Grossman.

Rostow, Walt W. 1960. *Stages of Economic Development: A Non-Communist Manifesto*. Cambridge: Cambridge University Press.

———. 1972. *The Diffusion of Power*. New York: Macmillan.

Rouchdy, Aleya. 1992. *The Arabic Language in America*. Detroit, MI: Wayne State University Press.

Russell, Roger V. 1971. "Soldiers and the Land to the Tiller Program in Military Region 1 of Vietnam." Control Data Corporation. Sponsored by ADLR, USAID, Vietnam under Contract No. AID-730-3449.

Ryback, Timothy W. 2009. "The Salzburg Seminar — A Community of Fellows." Salzburg Global Seminar website, accessed May 24, 2010. http://www.salzburgglobal.org/2009/history.cfm.

Sade, D. S. 1997. "Earle W. Count, 1899–1996." *Anthropology News* 38 (3): 25.

Sahlins, Marshall. 2000a. "The Destruction of Conscience in Vietnam" (1966). In *Culture in Practice: Selected Essays*, 229–60. New York: Zone Books.

———. 2000b. "The Established Order: Do Not Fold, Spindle, or Mutilate" (1967). In *Culture in Practice: Selected Essays*, 261–68. New York: Zone Books.

———. 2000c. "What is Anthropological Enlightenment? Some Lessons of the Twentieth Century" (1999). In *Culture in Practice: Selected Essays*, 501–26. New York: Zone Books.

———. 2009. "The Teach-Ins: Anti-war Protest in the Old Stoned Age." *Anthropology Today* 25 (1): 3–5.
Salemink, Oscar. 1991. "Mois and Maquis: The Invention and Appropriation of Vietnam's Montagnards from Sabatier to the CIA." In *Colonial Situations*, ed. In G. W. Stocking, 243–84. Madison: University of Wisconsin Press.
———. 2003. *The Ethnography of Vietnam's Central Highlands*. Honolulu: University of Hawai'i Press.
Sanjek, Roger. 1995. "Politics, Theory, and the Nature of Cultural Things." In *Science, Materialism, and the Study of Culture*, ed. Marty Murphy and Maxine Margolis, 39–61. Gainesville: University Press of Florida.
Saunders, Frances Stoner. 1999. *The Cultural Cold War*. New York: New Press.
Saxton, Wolfgang. 1994. "Richard Starr, 94, Middle East Expert and Archaeologist." *New York Times*, March 17. Accessed September 11, 2011. http://www.nytimes.com/1994/03/17/obituaries/richard-starr-94-middle-east-expert-and-archeologist.html.
Schafft, Gretchen. 2004. *From Racism to Genocide*. Urbana: University of Illinois Press.
Schein, Edgar. 1961. *Coercive Persuasion: A Socio-Psychological Analysis of the "Brainwashing" of American Civilian Prisoners by the Chinese Communists*. New York: Norton.
Scheper-Hughes, Nancy. 1995. "The Primacy of the Ethical: Propositions for a Militant Anthropology." *Current Anthropology* 36 (3): 409–40.
Schlesinger, James R. 1963. "Strategic Leverage from Aid and Trade." In *National Security: Political, Military, and Economic Strategies in the Decade Ahead*, ed. D. M. Abshire and R. V. Allen, 602–701. New York: Praeger.
Schlesinger, Stephen C., and Stephen Kinzer. 1983. *Bitter Fruit*. Cambridge, MA: Harvard University Press.
Schmidt, Petra. 2005. "Law of Succession." In *History of Law in Japan since 1868*, ed. Wilhelm Röhl, 305–29. Leiden: Brill.
Schneider, David M., and Richard Handler. 1995. *Schneider on Schneider*. Durham, NC: Duke University Press.
Schnell, Jane. 1961. "Snapshots at Random." *Studies in Intelligence* 5:17–23.
Schorr, Daniel. 1976. "The Report on the CIA That President Ford Doesn't Want You to Read." *Village Voice*, February 16, 69–92.
———. 1977. *Clearing the Air*. Boston: Houghton Mifflin.
Schrock, Joann L., William Stockton Jr., Elaine M. Murphy, and Marilou Fromme. 1966. *Minority Groups in the Republic of Vietnam*. Ethnographic Study Series, Department of the Army Pamphlet No. 550–105. CINFAC AD 649 980.
Science. 1935. "Science News: Experimental Headaches." *Science* 82 (2119, suppl.): 8.
Scott, James C. 1975. "Exploitations in Rural Class Relations: A Victim's Perspective." SEADAG Report, 75–1.
———. 1985. *Weapons of the Weak*. New Haven, CT: Yale University Press.
———. 1998. *Seeing Like a State*. New Haven, CT: Yale University Press.
SEADAG. 1969. *SEADAG Directory, 1968–1969*. New York: Asia Society.

Seymour, Susan. 2015. *Cora Du Bois: Anthropologist, Diplomat, Agent*. Lincoln: University of Nebraska Press.
Shackley, Ted, and Richard A. Finney. 2005. *Spymaster: My Life in the CIA*. Dulles, VA: Potomac Books.
Shane, Scott. 2007. "Soviet-Style 'Torture' Becomes 'Interrogation.'" *New York Times*, June 3. 4, S3.
Sheehan, Neil. 1967a. "Aid by CIA Put in the Millions." *New York Times*, February 19, 1.
———. 1967b. "5 New Groups Tied to CIA Conduits." *New York Times*, February 17, 1.
———. 1967c. "Harvard Dean's Fund Aided." *New York Times*, February 19, 1.
———. 1967d. "A Student Group Concedes It Took Funds from CIA." *New York Times*, February 14, 1, 7.
Sheets, Payson. 2001. "The CIA." *Anthropology News* 42 (1): 3.
Shiloh, Ailon. 1959. *Peoples and Cultures of the Middle East*. New York: Random House.
Shrader, Charles R. 2008. *History of Operations Research in the United States*. Vol. 2, *1961–1973*. Washington, DC: Government Printing Office.
Shweder, Richard. 2010. "Intellectuals and 'Humanity as a Whole.'" *Common Knowledge* 16 (1): 1–6.
SIHE (Society for the Investigation of Human Ecology). 1957. *1957 Annual Report: Society for the Investigation of Human Ecology, Incorporated*. Forest Hills, NY: Society for the Investigation of Human Ecology.
———. 1958. *The Hungarian Revolution of October 1956, Second Seminar*. June 6. New York: Society for the Investigation of Human Ecology.
———. 1960. *Brainwashing, a Guide to the Literature: A Report*. Forest Hills, NY: Society for the Investigation of Human Ecology.
———. n.d. *Report*. Forest Hills, NY: Society for the Investigation of Human Ecology.
Simpson, Christopher. 1994. *Science of Coercion*. New York: Oxford University Press.
Siskiyou. 2011. "Retired SOU Professor Was a Former CIA Operative." *Siskiyou*, October 26, 1.
Sjoberg, Gideon. 1967. "Project Camelot: Selected Reactions and Personal Reflections." In *Ethics, Politics and Social Research*, ed. Gideon Sjoberg, 141–61. Cambridge, MA: Schenkman.
Skinner, B. F. 1966. "What Is the Experimental Analysis of Behavior?" *Journal of the Experimental Analysis of Behavior* 9 (3): 13–18.
———. 1970. "B. F. Skinner: An Autobiography." In *Festschrift for B.F. Skinner*, ed. P. B. Dews, 1–21. New York: Irvington.Smalley, William A. 1994. *Linguistic Diversity and National Unity*. Chicago: University of Chicago Press.
Smith, Gaddis. 1999. "Yale and the Vietnam War." University Seminar on the History of Columbia University. October 19, accessed May 3, 2008, http://beatl.barnard.columbia.edu/cuhistory/yale.htm.
Smith, Henry Nash. 1949. "The Salzburg Seminar." *American Quarterly* 1:30–37.
Smith, Marian. 1946. "Notes from Bengal." *American Anthropologist* 48 (40): 574–92.
Soley, Lawrence C. 1989. *Radio Warfare: OSS and CIA Subversive Propaganda*. New York: Praeger.

Solovey, Mark. 2001. "Project Camelot and the 1960s Epistemological Revolution." *Social Studies of Science* 21 (2): 171–206.

———. 2012. "Senator Fred Harris's National Social Science Foundation Proposal." *Isis* 103 (1): 54–82.

———. 2013. *Shaky Foundations: The Politics-Patronage-Social Science Nexus in Cold War America*. New Brunswick, NJ: Rutgers University Press.

Solovey, Mark and Jefferson D. Pooley. 2011. "The Price of Success: Sociologist Harry Alpert, the NSF's First Social Science Policy Architect." *Annals of Science* 68(2):229–60.

SORO. 1965. "The Cham." SORO/CINFAC R-0118-65. Washington DC: SORO.

Spoehr, Alexander. 1951. "Anthropology and the Trust Territory." *Clearinghouse Bulletin of Research in Human Organization* 1(2): 1–3.

Staley, Eugene. 1961. *The Future of Underdeveloped Countries*. New York: Praeger.

Starn, Orin. 1991. "Missing the Revolution: Anthropologists and the War in Peru." *Cultural Anthropology* 6 (1): 63–91.

Stauder, Jack. 1972. "The 'Relevance' of Anthropology under Imperialism." *Critical Anthropology* 2:65–87.

———. 1995. "Changing Course: Teaching Both Sides of Environmental Issues." *Liberal Education* 81 (3): 36–41.

Steinberg, David J. 1959. *Cambodia, Its People, Its Society, Its Culture*. Survey of World Cultures, No. 5. New Haven, CT: HRAF Press.

Stephenson, Richard M. 1978. "The CIA and the Professor: A Personal Account." *American Sociologist* 13:128–33.

Stern, Sol. 1967. "A Short Account of International Student Politics and the Cold War with Particular Reference to the NSA, CIA, etc." *Ramparts*, March, 29–38.

Steury, Donald P., ed. 1994. *Sherman Kent and the Board of National Estimates*. Washington, DC: History Staff, Center for the Study of Intelligence, Central Intelligence Agency.

Steward, Julian. 1948. "Comments on the Statement on Human Rights." *American Anthropologist* 50 (2): 351–52.

———. 1950. *Area Research: Theory and Practice*. New York: Social Science Research Council.

Stille, Alexander. 2003. "Experts Can Help Rebuild a Country." *New York Times*, July 19, A15, A17.

Stirling, Matthew W. 1973. "E. Wyllys Andrews IV, 1916–1971." *American Anthropologist* 75 (1): 295–98.

Stocking, George W., Jr. 1968. "The Scientific Reaction against Cultural Anthropology, 1917–1920." In *Race, Culture, and Evolution*, ed. George Stocking, 270–307. Chicago: University of Chicago Press.

———. 1985. "Philanthropoids and Vanishing Cultures." In *Objects and Others*, ed. G. W. Stocking, 112–45. History of Anthropology Series, Vol. 3. Madison: University of Wisconsin Press.

———. 2004. "A. I. Hallowell's Boasian Evolutionism. "*Significant Others*, ed. R. Hander, 196–260. HOA Vol. 10. Madison: University of Wisconsin Press.

Stockwell, John. 1991. *The Praetorian Guard*. Boston: South End Press.

Stoll, David. 1982. *Fishers of Men or Founders of Empire? The Wycliffe Bible Translators in Latin America*. London: Zed.

Stork, Joe. 1980. "U.S. Involvement in Afghanistan." MERIP *Reports* 89 (July–August): 25–26.

Stover, Leon E. 1968. "Afterword." In *Apeman, Spaceman: Anthropological Science Fiction*, ed. Leon Stover and Harry Harrison, 311–51. New York: Doubleday.

———. 1972. "What We Have Here Is Too Much Communication." In *Above the Human Landscape*, ed. Willis Everett McNelly, 193–204. Pacific Palisades, CA: Goodyear.

———. 1973. "Anthropology and Science Fiction." *Current Anthropology* 14 (4): 471–74.

———. 1974. *The Cultural Ecology of Chinese Civilization*. New York: Pica Press.

Student Mobilizer, The. 1970. "Counterinsurgency Research on Campus EXPOSED," *The Student Mobilizer* 3(4):1–31. April 2, 1970.

Sugerman, A. A. Arthur, and Frank Haronian. 1964. "Body Type and Sophistication of Body Concept." *Journal of Personality* 32 (3): 380–94.

Suggs, Robert. 1962. *Survival Handbook*. New York: Macmillan.

Swanepoel, Petrus Cornelius. 2007. *Really Inside Boss: A Tale of South Africa's Late Intelligence Service (and Something about the CIA)*. Pretoria: P. C. Swanepoel.

Sweet, Louise. 1960. *Tell Toqaan: A Syrian Village*. Anthropological Papers, Museum of Anthropology, No. 14. Ann Arbor: University of Michigan.

Taft, Ronald. 1966. *From Stranger to Citizen*. Perth: University of Western Australia Press.

Takeyama, Michio, and Richard H. Minear. 2007. *The Scars of War*. Lanham, MD: Rowman and Littlefield.

Tambiah, Stanley. 2002. *Edmund Leach: An Anthropological Life*. Cambridge: Cambridge University Press.

Tanaka, Yasumasa, Tadasu Oyama, and C. E. Osgood. 1963. "A Cross-Cultural and Cross-Concept Study of the Generality of Semantic Space." *Journal of Verbal Learning and Verbal Behavior* 2: 392–405.

Taylor, Jay. 2000. *The Generalissimo's Son*. Cambridge, MA: Harvard University Press.

Tenenbaum, Joseph. 1948. *In Search of a Lost People*. New York: Beechhurst Press.

Thomas, David. 1962. "Mon-Khmer Subgroupings in Vietnam." Grand Forks, ND: University of North Dakota, Summer Institute of Linguistics.

Thomas, Gordon. 1989. *Journey into Madness*. New York: Bantam.

Time. 1967a. "Pandora's Cashbox." *Time*, March 3, 23–24.

———. 1967b. "The Silent Service." *Time*, February 24, 13–17.

Tobin, Joseph. 1990. "The HRAF as Radical Text?" *Cultural Anthropology* 5 (4): 473–87.

Tolley, Hoard B., Jr. 1994. *The International Commission of Jurists*. Philadelphia: University of Pennsylvania Press.

Trento, Joseph J. 2001. *The Secret History of the CIA*. New York: Carroll and Graf.

Troy, Thomas F. 1981. *Donovan and the CIA*. Frederick, MD: University Publications of America.

Truman, Harry. 1949. "Truman's Inaugural Address, January 20, 1949." Truman Library website, accessed March 22, 2011, http://www.trumanlibrary.org/whistlestop/50yr_archive/inagura120jan1949.htm.

Turner, Stansfield. 1985. *Secrecy and Democracy*. Boston: Houghton Mifflin.

Turner, Wallace. 1967. "Asia Foundation Got CIA Funds." *New York Times*, March 22, 17.

UNESCO. 1969. *Four Statements on the Race Question*. Paris: Oberthur-Rennes.

University of Michigan. 2000. "The University of Michigan, an Encyclopedic Survey." Edited by Wilfred B. Shaw. University of Michigan, http://name.umdl.umich.edu/AAS3302.0006.001.

U.S. Congress. 1964. "Tax-Exempt Foundations." Hearings before Subcommittee No. 1 on Foundations. Select Committee on Small Business House of Representatives. 66th Cong., 2nd sess. Washington, DC: U.S. Government Printing Office.

———. 1980. "United States–Western European Relations in 1980." Hearings before the Subcommittee on Europe and the Middle East of the Committee on Foreign Affairs, House of Representatives, 96th Cong., 2nd sess. Washington, DC: U.S. Government Printing Office.

U.S. Department of Defense. 1972. *The Pentagon Papers*. Boston: Beacon Press.

U.S. House. 1952. "Tax Exempt Foundations." Hearings before the Select Committee to Investigate Tax-Exempt Foundations and Comparable Organization, on House Resolution 561, 82nd Cong., 2nd sess., November–December, 344–46.

U.S. Senate. 1976. *Final Report of the U.S. Senate Select Committee to Study Governmental Operations with Respect to Intelligence Activities, Book One [Church Committee]*. Senate Report, 94th Cong. 2nd sess. No. 94-755. Washington, DC: Government Printing Office.

———. 1977. "Project MKULTRA, the CIA's Program of Research in Behavioral Modification." Joint Hearings before the Select Committee on Intelligence and the Subcommittee on Health and Scientific Research of the Committee on Human Resources United States Senate. 95th Cong., 1st sess. August 3. Washington, DC: Government Printing Office.

———. 1989. "A Tribute to the Late Dr. Louis Dupree." S4649. Congressional Record, 101st Cong. (1989–90). Washington, DC: Government Printing Office.

Valentine, Douglas. 1990. *The Phoenix Program*. New York: Avon Books.

Van Gelder, Lawrence. 1975. "Fodor Denies Being Agent but Says He Helped C.I.A." *New York Times*, January 9, 21.

Verdery, Katherine. 1996. *What Was Socialism, and What Comes Next?* Princeton, NJ: Princeton University Press.

Viking Fund. 1951. *The First Ten Years: 1941–1951*. New York: Viking Fund.

Wachman, Marvin. 2005. *The Education of a University President*. Philadelphia: Temple University Press.

Wagley, Charles. 1948. *Area Research and Training*. Pamphlet. New York: Social Science Research Council.

Wakin, Eric. 1992. *Anthropology Goes to War: Professional Ethics and Counterinsurgency in Thailand*. Monograph No. 7. Madison: University of Wisconsin Center for Asian Studies.

Wallace, Henry. 1948. "The Wallace Plan vs the (Hoover) (Dulles) Marshall Plan." Testimony by Henry A. Wallace before the House Committee on Foreign Affairs, Tuesday, February 24. New York: National Wallace for President Campaign. [Reprint.]

Warner, Michael. 1995. "Origins of the Congress for Cultural Freedom, 1949–50." *Studies in Intelligence* 38 (5): 89–98.

Washington Post. 1966. "CIA Front?" *Washington Post*, January 12 [date unclear, difficult to read], accessed August 14, 2015, http://jfk.hood.edu/Collection/Weisberg%20Subject%20Index%20Files/C%20Disk/CIA%20General/Item%20109.pdf.

Weinstein, Harvey. 1990. *Father, Son, and CIA*. Halifax, NS: Goodread Biographies.

Weissman, Steve. 1974. "Foreign Aid: Who Needs It?" In *The Trojan Horse: A Radical Look at Foreign Aid*, ed. Steve Weissman, 15–34. San Francisco: Ramparts Press.

Weissman, Steve, and John Shoch. 1972. "CIAsia Foundation." *Pacific Research and World Empire Telegram*, September–October, 3–4.

Western Australian (Perth). 1950. "American Murdered by Indonesian Gang." *Western Australian*, April 29, 1.

Westie, Frank R. 1965. "The American Dilemma: An Empirical Test." *American Sociological Review* 30 (4): 527–38.

Wilber, Donald 1954. "Overthrow of Premier Mossadeq of Iran, Nov. 1952–August 1953." CIA Clandestine Service History. Accessed March 2, 2011, http://www.nytimes.com/library/world/mideast/iran-cia-intro.pdf.

———. 1986. *Adventures in the Middle East*. Princeton: The Darwin Press.

———. 2014. *Iran, Past and Present*. 9th ed. Princeton: Princeton University Press.

Wilford, Hugh. 2008. *The Mighty Wurlitzer: How the CIA Played America*. Cambridge, MA: Harvard University Press.

———. 2013. *America's Great Game: The CIA's Secret Arabists and the Shaping of the Modern Middle East*. New York: Basic Books.

Winks, Robin. 1987. *Cloak and Gown: Scholars in the Secret War, 1939–1961*. New York: Morrow.

Wittfogel, Karl. 1950. "Russia and Asia: Problems of Contemporary Area Studies and International Relations." *World Politics* 2:445–62.

Wolf, Eric R. 1964. *Anthropology*. Englewood Cliffs, NJ: Prentice Hall.

Wolff, Harold G. 1960. "Every Man Has His Breaking Point." *Military Medicine* 125:85–104.

Worman, Eugene C. 1946. "The Problem of a Neolithic Culture in India." PhD diss., Harvard University.

Wright, Peter. 1988. *Spy Catcher*. New York: Penguin.

Yarnold, Kenneth W., and Robert C. Suggs. 1961. "Thinking Ahead: Business Can Save 70,000,000 Lives." *The Harvard Business Review* Nov.-Dec. 1961, 6–25.

Zborowski, Mark. 1952. "Cultural Components in Responses to Pain." *Journal of Social Issues* 8(4): 16–30.

———. 1969. *People in Pain*. San Francisco: Jossey-Bass.

Zipperstein, Steven J. 2010. "Underground Man: The Curious Case of Mark Zborowski and the Writing of a Modern Jewish Classic." *Jewish Review of Books*, Summer, 38–42.

INDEX

Aaron E. Norman Fund, 169
Abbot, Preston, 202, 206, 390n22
Aberle: David, 75, 289, 291–92, 297–98, 334–35, 337; Kathleen Gough 289, 291–92, 392n18. *See also* Gough, Kathleen
Abt Associates, 295, 325, 392n20
Academic Advisory Council for Thailand (AACT), xxiii, 324, 326, 328–31
Academy of Science for East Africa, 200
Accelerated Rural Development (ARD), 316–17, 335
Accusations of being spies, 221–22
Acheson, Dean, 33
Adams, Richard N., 230–32, 269, 298. *See also* Newbold, Stokes
Adams, Robert M., 280
Advanced Research Projects Administration (ARPA), xxiii, 257, 269, 293–96, 309, 311, 316–18, 324–31, 333–34, 343, 346, 354, 362, 393n6, 394n11, 395n12
Afghanistan, 138, 152–57, 159, 175, 183, 280, 281, 285, 288, 380n16–18
AFL-CIO, 124, 133, 170
African-American Institute, 167, 170, 172, 174
African Research Foundation, 170, 200, 383n6
Agee, Philip, 3, 20, 132, 372n11
Air America, 132, 315
Albert, Ethel M., 280
Algeria, 7, 258
Allison, John, 153–55, 157, 245, 380n16, 380n17
American Anthropological Association (AAA) xxi–xxiii, 41–42, 54–60, 62–75, 79–80, 89, 116–18, 146, 147, 164, 170, 176–93, 202, 205, 254–55, 261–62, 274, 276–300, 323–48, 354–55, 362–63, 365, 367–69, 372n1, 373n12, 373n5, 374n6, 374n8–13, 381n10–11, 392n12–13, 383n8, 391n4, 391n8, 392n14, 393n22, 394n1, 394n7–11, 395n13–16, 396n3; AAA Committee on Non-Nazi Anthropologists, 63–65; Annual AAA Meetings, xxvi, 56–57, 63–65, 189–90, 276–78, 281, 289–91, 293–94, 297–99, 323–28, 334–48, 354, 373n5, 374n12, 381n10, 382n13, 391n4, 393n22, 394n8–9, 395n15–16; Anthropologists for Radical Political Action, 135, 323, 342–47, 363, 368–69, 395n12, 395n15; Asia Foundation CIA funding, xxii, 176–93; Beals Report—Committee on Research Problems and Ethics (Beals Report), 277–93, 298–300, 333–34, 354, 359, 389n15, 391n5, 392n15; CIA and AAA xxvi 10, 41, 53, 54–60, 62–75, 79–80, 146, 147, 164, 170, 381n10; CIA role in AAA roster xxvi, 67–75, 179; CIA front funds and AAA, 170, 179–81; Committee on Ethics, 89, 279, 291, 297–99, 326–27, 329, 331–36, 338, 350, 362–63, 365, 367, 369, 394n7; Committee on Anthropology and Point IV, 116–18; Declaration of Human Rights 65–67; Military Advertisements, 296–300, 373n12; Postwar reorganization 54–60, 62–67, 79–80; Principles of Professional Responsibility (PPR), 335–37, 365, 369; Project Camelot, xiii, xxii, 59, 60, 257, 258–62, 269, 274–75, 277–79, 291–92, 293, 295, 299, 362, 389n14, 389n15; Radical Caucus, AAA, 293, 323–25, 341–45, 347, 363, 367, 369,

American Anthropological Association (AAA) (*continued*) 394n8; Resolutions, 63, 65, 71, 276–78, 289, 291–93, 297, 324–25, 327, 333–36, 344–46, 373n5, 391n4, 393n22, 394n5, 395n13, 395n13, 395n15–16; Selective Political Advocacy of AAA, 62–67, 79–80; 396n3; Statement on Problems of Anthropological research and Ethics (SPARE), 289, 291–92, 300, 331, 333, 336–37, 339; Thai Affair, 293–96, 314–21, 324–44, 391n6, 394n11

American Anthropologist, xxvi, 31, 73, 112, 179–91, 296–300; Asia Foundation, 179–91; military advertisements in, 296–300

American Committee for Émigrés in the Professions, 170

American Council for the International Commission of Jurists, 166, 170

American Council of Learned Societies (ACLS), 62, 72–73, 106, 138

American Federation of State, County and Municipal Employees, 170

American Friends of the Middle East, 167, 170, 285, 287, 392n10

American Fund for Free Jurists, 170

American Geographical Society, 252

American Institute for Free Labor Development, 124, 375n14

American Institute for Research (AIR), 330, 390n22

American Museum of Natural History, 47, 227

American Museum of Natural History in Afghanistan, 152

American Newspaper Guild, 170

American Society of African Culture, 170, 174

American University, 79, 251–75, 391n28

American Universities Field Staff (AUFS), 152, 155, 146, 285, 287, 379n13, 380n14; CINFAC, xxii, 257, 263–64, 267–70, 274,

390n19, 390n26; CRESS, 262, 269–70, 274–75, 351–53, 355, 390n21–22; Special Operations Research Office (SORO), xxii, 79, 253–70, 272–75, 289, 351–53, 355, 377n1, 389n6, 389n9, 389n11–12, 390n18, 390n18, 390n10, 391n28

Anderson: Barbara Gallatin, 211, 385n24; Robert, 229, 382n15

Andrew Hamilton Fund, 15, 133–34, 168, 172–73

Andrews: Edward Wyllys, 144, 148, 379n7; James Madison IV, 34, 69, 71, 147–48, 374n9, 379n6

Angleton, James Jesus, 131–32, 177

Anthropological theory, xxii, xvi, xvii, xix, xxi–xxii, 27, 42, 51, 59, 80–81, 84, 90, 91, 94, 97, 99, 111, 118–21, 128, 130, 135, 211, 216, 218, 224, 249–25 1, 258, 264, 270, 273, 310, 315, 355–61, 376n14, 393n2, 396n2; Comtian social physics, 56; Counterinsurgency Theory, xviii, 39–44, 59, 119, 121–28, 133, 246, 248–75, 295, 299–300, 305–7, 339; Culture and personality, 35, 60, 100–102, 357, 372n8, 376n17, 377n1; Cultural evolutionary theory, 49–50, 119, 129–30, 145, 393n21; Ecological anthropology, 46, 49, 129–30, 279, 396n2; Functionalism, 43, 46, 51, 230, 264, 384n19, 385n26; Game theory, 59, 99; Kinship, 43, 49, 51, 266, 308, 366; Marxist theory, xix, 27, 122, 224, 323–24, 341, 351, 360, 361, 394n8; Materialism, xix, 119, 361; Military desires for mechanical models of culture, 40, 41, 45, 119, 255, 258, 264, 275; Modernization Theory, 7, 62, 94, 97, 118–22, 128–29, 135–36, 145, 230, 244, 361, 376n14, 393n21, 393n2; Parsonian influences, 42, 86–87, 94, 97–98, 108, 119, 128, 353, 369, 377n20; Postmodernism, xii, 359–60; Rituals 42–43, 205, 236, 308, 309; Social structure, 49, 97, 129–30, 204, 236, 251, 268, 270, 271,

309; Structuralism, 396n2; Structural functionalism 46; Symbolic Anthropology, 27, 94–98, 385n26
Anthropologists for Radical Political Action, 135, 323, 342–47, 363, 368–69, 395n12, 395n15
Anticolonialism, 5–6, 107, 110–13, 232–34, 236–37, 244, 360, 371n4
Anticommunism, 125, 161, 173, 184, 292, 341, 361
Appalachian Fund, 168
Applied anthropology, xvi, 34, 41, 48, 51, 53, 72, 75–79, 107–14, 135–36, 152, 298, 314, 320, 326, 337–39, 346, 362, 394n7
Apter, David, 119
Archaeological Institute of America, 73
Archaeology, xviii, xix, xxii, 49, 54, 72, 73, 77, 81, 87, 89, 109, 144, 145, 147, 148, 152, 153, 157–58, 160, 162, 163–64, 225, 228–29, 242, 245, 281, 339, 345, 356, 374n9, 377n1, 391n1, 395n11
Area studies, xix, xxii, 13, 59–62, 81–82, 84–98, 105–8, 111, 123 138–39, 143, 254, 282–84, 352, 354, 358, 364, 389n7, 392n13; Harvard's Russian Research Center, 84–87; MIT's CENIS xix, 59, 89–98, 118–21; Rauch's critique of, 106–8; University of Michigan's Near East Study Center, 87–89
Arensberg, Conrad, 100, 117, 280, 383n19
Armour, Norman, 11
Armstrong: Hamilton Fish, 11; Richard, 359
Arvad, Inga, 240, 387n16
Asad, Talal, xii, xix
Ash, Timothy Garton, 13
Asia Foundation, xxii, 67, 166, 168, 169, 173–74, 176–93, 231, 285, 287, 331, 354–55, 358, 381n11, 382n,13, 382n14, 382n15, 392n10, 394n2; and the AAA, 179–81; Radio Free Asia, 176, ; Committee For Free Asia, 176
Asia Society, 127–28, 331, 379n13; 394n2
Asian Development Bank, 123

Association of Asian Studies, 179, 328, 330, 381n9
Association of Hungarian Students in North America, 170
Atlantic Research Corporation, 295
Atwater Research Program in North Africa, 170
Australia, 32–33, 58, 65, 103, 147, 203, 223, 233, 242
Austria, 41, 156, 174, 280, 381n2
Ayrout, Henry Habib, 163

Bacon, Elizabeth, xix, 137–39, 181, 279–88, 300, 354, 380n14, 380n20
Baird Foundation, 169, 383n6
Baker, George W., 254
Baker, Paul T., 76–77
Bannigan, John, 182
Barrett, Edward W., 87–88
Bateson, Gregory, xvi, 63–65, 82, 100, 376n16, 376n18, 381n3
Beacon Fund, 15, 168
Beaglehole, Ernest, 66–67
Beals, Ralph, xxii, 82, 83, 137–39, 181, 186, 225, 259–60, 277–81, 284–91, 294, 298–300, 333–34, 354, 359, 389n15, 391n5, 392n15
Beardsley, Richard K. 381n11
Belo, Jane, 100
Bemis, Samuel 11
Benedict, Ruth, 39, 55, 76, 82, 83, 99–101, 145, 357, 359, 372n7
Benjamin, Robert, 344–45, 395n15
Benjamin Rosenthal Foundation, 169
Bennett: John 42–43, 46, 75–76, 109, 373n9; Wendell C., 75, 83, 116, 378n6
Berle: Adolf, 384n14, 386n15; Beatrice, 202, 384n14
Berlin, Louis, 198
Berliner Verein, 167, 170
Bernstein, David, 239–40
Berreman, Gerald, xii, 280, 326, 329, 331–34, 336, 338–39, 341, 367, 368

Bessac, Frank, 148–52, 356, 379n8–12
Bessaignet, Pierre, 38
Bharati, Agehananda, 178, 181, 382n14
Biderman, Albert D, 207–9, 213
Billington, James, 11
Billy Graham Spanish-American Crusade, 171
Binford, Lewis and Sally, 292–93
Bissell, Richard, 11, 133
Black, Cyril, 10–11, 119
Blackmer, Donald, 90–93, 145, 376n12
Blakeslee, Donald, 339, 394n11
Blum, Robert, 67, 176–80, 185–86, 381n8
Boas, Franz, 67, 101
Boggs, Stephen T. 180, 187, 261–62, 279, 288–89
Bolivia, xiv, 223–24, 257, 258, 261
Books for Asian Students Program, 183
Borden Trust, 15, 168
Boston University 123
Bothmer, Bernard V., 73
Boudrias, Louis, 303
Bowie, Robert, 11
Bowles, Gordon, 116
Boy Scouts, 179, 381n9
Bradfield, Stillman, 269
Brainwashing, 29, 175, 195, 198, 206, 209
Brand, Stewart, xvi
Brazil, 79, 124, 258, 280, 335, 388n24
Brew, John, 68
Briggs, Lloyd Cabbot, 292, 342
Broad High Fund, 168, 383n6
Brodkin, Karen, 293. *See also* Sacks, Karen
Brookings Institution, 102, 145, 388n4
Brown and Pappas Foundation, 166
Brown University, 199, 379n13
Brunder, Jerome, 91
Buchwald, Art, 16
Buck, Paul, 84, 90
Buckley, William F. 92–93, 173, 386n6
Bundy, McGeorge, 61, 81, 166, 283, 357, 382n16

Bunster, Alvaro, 259
Bunzel, Ruth 100
Burden, William A.M., 243
Burma, 7, 31, 51, 58, 64, 78, 177, 200, 239, 381n8
Bush, Vannevar, 11, 55
Butler, Barbara Reason, 263, 290n18

Cady, John F. 234, 238
Cambodia, 177, 180–81, 249, 311, 381n8, 396n11
Cambridge Working Group, xv, 371n2
Camelot, see Project Camelot
Cameron, George C., 87–88
Camman, Schuyler, 147, 242
Campbell, Richard, 103–4
Canadian Union of Students, 170
Canfield, Cass, 243, 388n22
Carnegie Endowment for International Peace, 179, 224
Carnegie Corporation, 11, 21, 60–62, 166, 252, 372n12, 373n4; and CIA, 166
Carter, James E., 27
Carr, William K., 202, 203, 207, 254, 255–57, 384n19, 391n2
Castro, Fidel, 19, 20, 268, 291
Catherwood Foundation, 169
Center for Christian Democratic Action, 170
Center for International Studies (CENIS, MIT), xix, 59, 62, 89–98, 106, 118–21, 359, 373n3, 376n12
Center for Research in Social Systems (CRESS), 262, 269–70, 274–75, 351–53, 355, 390n21–22
Central Intelligence Agency (CIA), xiii–xiv, ixx–xxiii, xv–xvii, 3–30, 59–62, 67–75, 78–79, 82, 84–86, 89–96, 98, 101–6, 108, 118–26, 130–220, 222–34, 238–46, 248, 249, 251, 269, 272–73, 279–92, 300–304, 311, 315–16, 322, 326, 331, 349–59, 363, 367, 371n1–9, 372n10–14, 372n3, 372n6, 374n8–14, 375n15, 377n20,

436 | INDEX

378n11, 378n1-2, 379n3-13, 380n14-22, 381n1-11, 382n12-18, 383n1-8, 384n9-19, 385n22-29, 386n2, 386n12, 387n18, 388n20, 388n1, 390n21-22, 390n25, 391n27, 391n8, 392n10-12, 392n15, 394n2, 394n10; AAA and Asia Foundation, 179-94; AAA roster, xxvi, 67-75, 179; Anthropologists' CIA careers, 143-64; Anthropology and CIA Training, 145-46; Asia Foundation, xxii, 67, 166, 168, 169, 173-74, 176-93, 231, 285, 287, 331, 354-55, 358, 381n11, 382n,13, 382n14, 382n15, 392n10, 394n2; and the AAA, 179-81; Assassination programs, 19-20; Frank Bessac, 148-52, 356, 379n8-12; Brainwashing Research, 29, 175, 195, 198, 206, 209; *Break-up of the Colonial Empires* 5-9; CIA Campus Recruitment, 9-13, 226-27, 284-85; CENIS, xix, 59, 62, 89-98, 106, 118-21, 359, 373n3, 376n12; CIA Publishing, 172-74; Elizabeth Bacon on CIA, 137-39, 279-88; Family Jewels, 19-20, 130-34; Fieldwork and CIA, xvii, 89, 148, 152-53, 157-60, 162-163, 225-29, 238-47, 282-87, 315-16; Ford Foundation and CIA, 22, 61-62, 89, 93, 106, 118, 166, 192, 282-83, 285, 372n13, 382n15; The Forty Committee, 5, 25-26; Funding fronts, 15-19, 102, 106, 132-33, 138, 165-94, 195-220, 240, 242-45, 251, 285-88, 290-91, 353-55, 380n14, 381n1-11, 382n12-18, 383n19, 383n1-8, 384n9-19, 385n20-29, 392n10, 392n12; Harvard's Russian Research Center, 84-87, 88, 357; Human Ecology Fund, xxii, xxvi, 102, 168, 195-220, 352, 355, 383n2, 383n5-6, 384n8, 384n10, 384n14-16, 384n18-19, 385n24-29, 391n2; Journalistic Revelations About, 14-20, 25, 167, 181-82, 191, 282, 371n6; *Kubark Counterintelligence Interrogation* manual 195-197, 199, 206-19, 213, 215-19; HRAF 251, 272-73, 391n27; Lloyd S. Millegan, 238-45; 246, 354, 386n12, 386n14, 386n17, 386n18, 388n20; MK-Ultra, 27, 29, 102, 195-220, 383n7, 384n14-15, 385n28, 394n10; Office of National Estimates, 10, 82; Operation Ajax, 159; Operation Artichoke, 197; Operation Bluebird, 197; Operation CHAOS 19-20; Princeton Consultants, 10-11; Technical Services Division, 195-96, 205; University Associates Program, 9; USAID and CIA, 20, 26, 122-23, 126, 131-34, 304

Ceylon, 31, 34, 180, 381n3, 381n8
Challinor, David, 225
Chapple, Elliot D., 57, 118
Charles Price-Whitten Trust, 168
Chen, William, 100
Chesapeake Fund, 168
Chile, 20, 125, 259-61, 274, 345; Project Camelot, xiii, xxii, 59, 60, 257, 258-62, 269, 274-75, 277-79, 291-92, 293, 295, 299, 362
China, 23-24, 31, 34, 51, 56, 60, 78, 82, 100, 107, 110, 121-22, 148-51, 161-62, 176, 178, 180, 183, 184, 199, 206-7, 225, 229, 242, 244, 249, 256, 356, 376n17, 379n12, 381n5-6, 383n8, 384n19
China American Council of Commerce and Industry, 242
Christensen, James B., 280
Chriswell, Joan, 76
Church Committee, 20-29, 60, 134, 167, 185, 193, 226, 372n14, 385n29
Church, Frank, 21
City College of New York, 17
Civil Operations and Revolutionary Development Support (CORDS), 125-26, 133, 309, 393n6
Cleaveland H. Dodge Foundation, 169
Cline, Ray and Marjory, 144-45
Clothier, William, 225
Coe, Michael D. 160-62

COINTELPRO, 18, 21
Colby, William, 19–20, 25, 396n1
Collins, Henry B., 69, 374n9
Colonialism, 5–9, 33, 37, 48, 51, 56, 60, 94, 97, 107, 110–11, 119–20, 221, 225, 232–33, 289, 294, 308–9, 318, 324, 360
Colombia, 258, 261
Colson, Elizabeth, 280
Columbia, University, 9, 11, 18, 47, 48, 62, 80, 83, 84, 100–102, 106, 211, 252, 258, 276, 302, 382n15
Comitas, Lambros, 280
Commentary Magazine, 170
Committee for Self-Determination, 170
Committee for the Comparative Study of New Nations, 97, 376n14
Committee for Promotion of Advanced Slavic Studies, 252
Committee of Concerned Anthropologists, 298, 363, 368
Committee of Correspondence, 167, 170
Communism, 5–9, 14–17, 23, 33, 78–79, 82, 86, 88, 91–93, 96, 99, 110, 118–23, 128–29, 151, 173, 207–9, 231, 235–37, 238, 240, 242–45, 269, 291–92, 303, 306–7, 315–16, 341, 349, 371n1, 381n5, 384n19, 386n14, 389n8, 394n6
Conant, James B., 103
Condit, Doris M., 263, 390n18
Condominas, Georges, 311, 319–20, 354, 390n24
The Congo, 20, 255, 258, 294, 392n19
Congress for Cultural Freedom, 16, 61, 170, 172
Congress of Anthropological and Ethnological Sciences, 188
Conklin, Harold, 235, 241, 277, 278, 280, 290, 383n19, 386n10
Conley, Michael, 262–63, 390n18
Connick, Louis, 180, 185
Conspiracy theories, xiv, 29, 392n11
Coon, Carleton, 63–65, 83, 242, 244, 380n21

Cooper, Bert, 263, 390n18
Cooper, John, 55
Coordinated Investigation of Micronesia (CIMA), xviii–xix, 35, 38, 46–51, 76, 355, 377n1, 387n15
Copeland, Miles, 158–59
Coppola, Francis Ford, 28, 302
Cornell University, 83, 96, 100, 177, 197, 199, 206, 211, 213, 222, 252, 280, 314, 315, 329–331, 378n9, 383n3, 383n5
Corson, William, 10, 133, 177
Cotter, George, 109, 134–35
Council for Intercultural Relations, 101, 376n15
Count, Earle, 63–65
Counterinsurgency, xviii, xxii–xxiii, 20, 22, 36, 39, 44, 59, 78, 80, 89, 93, 114, 116, 119–30, 132–33, 135, 221, 246–47, 248–75, 277–78, 294–95, 299–300, 301–22, 324–31, 333–39, 346, 353–54, 364–65, 389n11, 392n16, 392n20, 393n5, 393n6, 394n2; Academic Advisory Council for Thailand (AACT), xxiii, 324, 326, 328–31; Accelerated Rural Development (ARD), 317, 335; CINFAC xxii, 257, 263–64, 267–70, 274, 390n19, 390n26; CORDS, 125–26, 133; Delmos Jones Critique of, 314–18; M-VICO System, 262–69, 273, 390n18–19; Project Camelot, xiii, xxii, 59, 60, 257, 258–62, 269, 274–75, 277–79, 291–92, 293, 295, 299, 362, 389n14, 389n15; RAND, 307–14; SORO, xxii, 79, 253–70, 272–75, 289, 351353, 355, 377n1, 389n6, 389n9, 389n11–12, 390n18, 390n18, 390n10, 391n28; Strategic Hamlet Program, 126, 265, 304–7, 313, 393n2; The Thai Affair, 324–44; USAID 122–27
Counterinsurgency Information and Analysis Center (CINFAC), xxii, 257, 263–64, 267–70, 274, 390n19, 390n26
Crane Foundation, 152, 287–88

Critchfield: James, 162–63; Richard, 162–63, 269
Crossman, Richard, 243
Cuba, 20, 144, 224, 243, 258, 268
Cumings, Bruce, 52, 62, 105–6
Cybernetics, xvi, 376n16
Cyprus, 25, 158, 374n11

Dalai Lama, 151, 176
Danielsson, Bengt, 49
Davenport, William H., 280, 336, 342
Davis, Kingsley, 85, 244, 252, 259
Davison, F. Trubee, 227
Debevoise, Eli Whitney, 166
Debt, 27, 120, 121, 123, 126, 135–36, 187, 189, 190, 236, 305, 306, 353, 361, 363
Deitchman, Seymour, 260–61, 276, 294–96, 300, 362, 392n21,
DeLillo, Don, 194
Denny, George, 278
Dept. of Social Relations, Harvard, 80–97, 396n5
Desai, M. J. 170,
Devereux, George, 390n24
Dialogue, 170
Diamond, Sigmund, 8, 85–86, 106, 357, 366
Diamond, Stanley, 224, 225, 343, 394n8
Dick, Philip K., 384n12
Diem, Ngo Dinh, 20, 271, 301, 303, 307
Dillon, Wilton S., 181, 382n14
Dimick, John M., 228–29, 246, 256, 356
Divale, William T., 18
Dobyns, Henry, 280
Dominican Republic, The, 20, 258
Donnell, John, 304–7
Doob, Leonard, 257
Doolittle Commission, 9–10, 371n5
Doughty, Paul, 226–27
Douglas, Henry H., 242–43
Dower, John W., 39–42
Doyle, Robert, 233–35, 386n8
Drucker, Phillip, 51

Dual use, xiii–xx, xxiii, xxvi, 27, 36, 46 81, 84, 89, 95–96, 98, 106–7, 108, 122–29, 159, 198, 206, 220, 225, 246, 249, 251, 268, 272, 302, 320, 353–56, 364–65, 367–68, 377n1
Dubberstein, Waldo, 144, 378n2
Du Bois, Cora, 31–32, 82, 83, 110, 189–90, 244, 370, 478n6, 381n3, 381n11, 383n18
Duke Foundation, 373n4
Duke University, 11
Dulles, Allen, 7, 22, 61–62, 106, 110, 120–21, 137–38, 147, 166, 177, 187, 197–98, 227, 243, 375n14, 381n1, 383n4
Dulles, John Foster, 138, 165, 244
Duncan, Brooks, 246
Dupree, Louis, 75–77, 152–57, 280, 287, 380n17, 380n18, 391n7

East West Association, 242
Ebbin, Steven, 288
Eckel, Paul, 241, 387n18
Edsel Fund, 15, 168
Ehrich, Robert, 334, 342, 392n17
Eisenhower, Dwight, 13–14, 244
Eggan, Fred, 83, 312, 378n5, 378n9
Egypt, 7, 25, 33, 58, 157–58, 163, 228–29, 258, 380n19
Ekvall, Robert B., 78, 176, 381n6
Elliot, William, 104
El Salvador, 225, 256, 258
Ember, Melvin, 273, 391n27
Embree, John, xix, 110–14, 116–17, 239–41, 371n4, 378n3
Emrich, Antoinette, 147, 254
Epstein, Jason, 174, 192, 194
Erickson, Edwin E., 254, 247
Ethics, xx, xxii–xxiii, 64, 67, 89, 99, 111, 113, 143, 150, 155, 220, 232, 273–74, 276–79, 283, 289–94, 297–99, 312–13, 317–18, 320, 326–27, 329, 331–38, 346, 348, 350, 362–63, 365, 367, 369, 383n7, 393n23, 394n7; AAA failure to differentiate between ethics and politics,

Ethics (*continued*)
63–65, 362–66, 396n3; SPARE: Principles of Professional Responsibility (PPR), 299, 335–37, 365, 369; 299, 89, 298–99, 326–27, 329, 331–36, 338
Ethnogeographic Board, 63, 67, 70, 81, 83, 107
Evans-Pritchard, E.E., 255
Eveland, Wilbur, 228, 392n10

Fahs, Burton, 11
Fallers, Lloyd, 280, 376n14
Family Jewels, 19–21, 25, 130–32, 185, 353
Farfield Foundation, 16, 169, 243
Faris, James, 343, 346–47, 394n8
Federal Bureau of Investigation (FBI), xiii, xix–xxi, 18–21, 28–29, 58, 65, 73–74, 78–79, 84–86, 99–100, 110, 123, 224, 229, 240, 242–43, 246, 291, 292, 341, 359, 361, 371n9, 373n5, 374n10, 376n19, 378n3, 386n15, 387n16, 388n19, 389n8, 94n6; Absurd paranoia of, 110, 394n6; Media, PA break-in 18–19, 72–73; Surveillance of AAA members, 72–73; Harvard's Russian Research Center, 84–87
Fejos, Paul, 239–40, 387n17
Fenton, William, 69, 81, 374n9
Ferguson, Charles, 110, 392n13
Field Foundation, 285–86, 287, 392n11
Field, Henry, 380n20
Figueiredo, Antonio, 174
Fischel, Wesley, 153, 380n15
Fischer, John, 112–13, 377n2
Flanagan, Patricia, 188–89
Flannery, Regina, 69, 374n9
Fleischmann, Charles, 243
Florence Foundation, 169
Fodor Travel Guide, 173, 381n2
Ford Foundation, xix, 21, 22, 60–62, 63, 75, 80, 89, 91, 93–98, 106, 118, 138, 166, 192, 224, 252, 258, 282–83, 285, 312, 314, 328, 372n12, 372n13, 372n14, 373n4, 382n15; and CIA, 22, 61–62, 89, 93, 106, 118, 166, 192, 282–83, 285, 372n13, 382n15
Foreign Affairs, 11, 145, 243
Foreign Morale Analysis Division, 36–37
Foreign Policy Research Institute, 170
Forkert, Franklyn 243–44, 388n23
Forman, Lawrence t., 187–88, 193
Forte, Meyers, 255
Forty Committee, The, 5, 25–26, 27, 382n16
Foster, George, 41, 69, 80, 92, 116–17, 147, 179, 332–33, 335336, 374n9, 389n17, 394n6,
Foundations, xii, xix, 15–16, 21–22, 59–63, 82, 105–6, 134, 165–67, 181–83, 186, 192, 258, 262, 279, 282, 286–91, 351, 353–56, 361, 366, 373n4, 375n3, 387n15, 392n10, 392n12. *See also* Funding fronts
Foundation for Youth and Social Affairs, 166, 168
France, 7, 38, 56, 100, 156, 158, 176, 258, 308, 372n6, 387n15
Frank, Andre Gunder, 252, 351
Franklin Press, 173–74
Frantz, Charles, 67–68, 186–90, 373n 1, 383n19
Freed, Ruth, 336
Freedom of Information Act (FOIA), xiii, 72–73, 78, 104, 145, 148, 159, 192, 195, 197, 223, 229, 233, 269, 272, 273, 371n1, 374n10, 374n13, 377n1, 379n6, 390n25, 391n8
Frente Department de Composinos de Puno, 170
Fried, Morton, 129, 280
Friedrich, Paul, 86–87, 375n7
Friends of India Committee 170
Frucht, Richard, 392
Fulbright, William, 23, 57
Fulbright Fellowships, 57, 58, 77, 80, 82, 122, 149–52, 282, 285, 316, 374n14, 379n9–11; CIA connections, 151–52, 282, 379n9–11
Fund for International Social and Economic Education, 166, 167, 170

Funding fronts, 15–19, 102, 106, 132–33, 138, 165–94, 195–220, 240, 242–45, 251, 285–88, 290–91, 353–55, 380n14, 381n1–11, 382n12–18, 383n19, 383n1–8, 384n9–19, 385n20–29, 392n10, 392n12
Furniss, Edgar, 33

Gajdusek, Daniel, 102, 383n8
Galtung, Johan, 259, 389n14
Geertz, Clifford, xix, 94–98, 128–29, 234, 280, 359, 360, 376n10, 376n11, 376n13, 376n14, 378n9
Germany, 13, 41, 56, 63–65, 85, 86, 156, 158, 174, 176, 230, 240, 292, 372n11, 377n21, 386n15
Geschickter Fund for Medical Research, 169
Ghana, 158, 203
GI Bill of Rights, 27, 34, 80
Gibson, McGuire, 89
Gilligan, Thomas J. Jr., 171
Gillin, John, 60, 68, 83, 392n17
Gittinger, John, 202, 209, 214, 219
Gladwin, Thomas, 46, 47, 50
Goering, Herman[n], 377n21, 386n15
Gökçe, Cansever, 200
Goldfrank, Ester, 340–41, 393n23
Golinger, Eva, 123
González, Roberto, 48, 364, 371n3
Goodell, Helen, 198
Goodenough, Ward, 46, 47, 48, 49, 297, 383n19
Gorer, Geoffrey, 82, 100, 357, 372n8
Gotham Foundation, 15, 168, 169
Gottlieb, Sidney, 196, 199
Gough, Kathleen, xii, 350, 359, 394n8. See also Kathleen Aberle
Gower, Charlotte, 144, 379n3
Graeber, David, 360
Graham, Milton D., 250, 388n4
Granary Fund, 133–34, 169
Grauer, Alvin, 243
Graves, Theodore, 226

Gray, Gordon, 11
Great Brittan, 7, 56, 65, 145, 156, 158, 387n15
Greece, 58, 158, 228, 258
Green Revolution, 61, 135
Grew, Joseph, 11
Grinnell College, 17
Guatemala, 91–92, 225, 228, 230–32, 258, 280; CIA coup, 91–92, 230–32
Guggenheim Foundation, 34, 77, 144
Guthrie, Thomas, 198

Hall, Edward T., 109, 208–9, 385n20, 385n21, 385n22
Hallock, Richard, 144
Hallowell, A. I., 57, 82, 83
Halpern: Joel, 280, 378n9; Sam, 242–43
Handy, Edward S.C., 239–40, 386n13
Hanifi, M. Jamil, 153, 157, 380n15
Hanna: Judith Lynne, 254, 256; William, 256
Hannah, John A., 303–4
Haring, Douglas, 41, 82, 83, 113, 248
Haronian, Frank, 202, 210
Harris: Fred, 59–60, 288, 365; Jack, 108, 359, 371n4, 378n3; Marvin, xii, xx, 129, 174, 224, 245, 277–78, 343, 359, 394n8, 395n14
Harrisson, Tom, 102, 227
Hart, C.W.M., 75–76
Hartle, Janet A., 200, 384n14
Harvard Law School Fund, 171
Harvard University, 9, 11, 17, 34, 47, 48, 49, 77, 80, 83–87, 88, 90, 94, 97, 103–4, 108, 109, 144, 145, 146, 148, 152, 160–62, 166, 171, 177, 184, 225, 258, 353, 357, 359, 375n3, 375n7, 376n10, 393n4, 396n5; Dept. of Social Relations, 80, 97, 396n5; FBI 84–87; International Summer School and CIA, 104; Refugee Interview Project, 85–86; Russian Research Center 84–87, 88, 357; Salzburg Seminars 102–4, 355
Haskins, Caryl 11, 382n15

Hawkins, Everett, 294,
Hayden, Joseph Ralson, 238
Heights Fund, 168
Heller, Clemens, 103–4
Helms, Richard, 17, 19, 183, 196–97, 371n9
Henry: Barklie, 11; Jules, 113
Hersh, Seymour, 19, 29, 173, 381n2
Herskovits, Melville, 63–65, 83
Hertzberg, H.T.E., 75
Hibben, Frank, 229, 246
Hickey, Gerald, 256–57, 269, 270, 302–14, 318, 320–22, 362, 378n9, 390n24, 393n4, 393n5, 393n7
Hilsman, Roger, 123, 269, 307
Hinkle, Lawrence, 198, 206–8, 212–13, 219
Hiroshima, 35–36, 63
Hitchcock, John, 279
Hobby, William P., 166–67
Hobby Foundation, 166–67, 169
Hoblitzelle Foundation, 169, 172
Hoebel, E.A., 58, 68
Hoffman, Paul, 182, 186
Hofstra University, 280
Holland, Kenneth, 75, 374n14
Hong Kong, 58, 176, 177, 381n8
Hooker, James, R., 173, 226
Hooper, Rex, 258–59
Hooton, E. A. 34, 144, 378n1
Hoover: Calvin, 10–11; J. Edgar, 386n15, 394n6
Howard, Alan, 201, 211–18, 220, 385n26–27
Howell: Nancy, 221, 385n1; Wesley, 78
Howells, W.W., 69–72, 75
Hsu, Francis L.K., 100
Hughes: Charles and Jane, 205; Stuart, 86; Thomas L., 293
Hughes-Ryan Act, 15
Human Ecology Fund, xxii, xxvi, 102, 168, 195–220, 352, 355, 383n2, 383n5–6, 384n8, 384n10, 384n14–16, 384n18–19, 385n24–29, 391n2. *See also* Society for the Investigation of Human Ecology

Human Relations Area File (HRAF), xxii, 59, 76, 235, 248–54, 256, 262–70, 272–73, 284–85, 288, 292, 352, 355, 388n2, 389n6, 389n7, 389n9, 390n20, 391n27, 391n28; Army Handbooks, 250–53; M-VICO System, 262–69, 390n19; Washington, D.C. HRAF Office, 250–51
Human Sciences Research, Inc., 296
Humphrey: Gordon J. 157; Hubert, 167
Hungary, 78–79, 170, 375n15; Refugees, 199, 200, 207, 385n25
Hunt: Donald H., 250; E. Howard, 24–25, 93, 173, 318n2
Hunter, Edward S., 175–76, 381n3
Hymes, Dell, 277, 350, 383n19

Independence Foundation, 16, 168
Independent Research Service, 171
India, xvii, 7, 24, 35, 34, 60, 66, 82, 83, 93, 95, 114, 146, 158, 159, 163, 174, 176, 179–80, 188, 191, 225, 242, 280, 308, 381n5; Closing Asia Foundation Office 188, 191
Indiana University, 153–55, 252
Indochina, see Vietnam
Indonesia, xix, 7–8, 31–32, 33, 57, 60, 80, 94–98, 128, 177–78, 180, 232–46, 280, 381n8, 382n14, 386n10, 386n14, 387n17, 388n23
Ingersoll, Jasper, 130, 378n9
Institut d'Historie Sociale, 171
Institute for Intercultural Studies, 100–102, 203, 376n15, 384n8
Institute for International Peace, 179
Institute of East Asiatic Studies, 179
Institute of Human Relations, 51, 76, 248
Institute of Inter-American Affairs, 114–16
Institute of International Education, 75, 167, 171, 374n14, 382n15
Institute of International Labor Research, 171
Institute of Pacific Relations, 242,

Institute of Public Administration, 171
Institute of Social Anthropology, 80, 83, 117, 278
Inter-American Police Academy (USAID), 123
Interdisciplinary research, 43–46, 80–82, 88–90, 94, 101, 105, 195, 202, 254, 256, 355, 376n16; Macy Conferences 376n16; OSS roots, 105–6; RAND Conference 99–100
Internal Revenue Service, 15, 165–66
International Commission of Jurists, 166, 171
International Committee of Women, 16
International Confederation of Free Trade Unions, 171, 176
International Cooperation Administration, 114–15, 175–76
International Cooperative Development Fund, 171
International Development Foundation, 168, 171
International Federation of Petroleum and Chemical Workers, 171
International Food and Drink Workers Federation, 171
International Marketing Inst., 168, 171
International Monetary Fund, 135
International Student Conference, 171
International Union of Socialist Youth, 171
Interrogation, 195–220
Iran, 58, 87–88, 118, 145, 157–60, 170, 249, 251, 258, 280, 281, 283–85, 287, 380n20; Donald Wilber and CIA Coup, 157–60
Iran-American Relations Society, 158
Iran Foundation, 158, 285, 287
Iraq, 39, 87, 88–89, 146, 228, 249, 280
Italy, 7, 58, 95, 158, 228, 382n15

J. Frederick Brown Foundation, 16, 169
Jackson, William H., 11
Jacobs, Melville, 102
Jacobs, Milton, 254, 256

James Carlisle Trust, 168
James O'Donnell Foundation, 168, 169
Jamieson, Neil, 130
Jandy, Edward T. 109
Japan, 6, 7, 39–44, 50, 51, 55, 60, 76, 78, 110–11, 169, 172, 178, 179–80, 188, 201, 204–5, 232, 280n9, 381n8, 382n15, 392n13; postwar occupation 39–46, 56, 98–99
Japan Society, 179
JASON Group, 333, 335
John Hay Whitney Trust, 172
Johns Hopkins University, 123, 252
Johnson: Frederick, 54–57, 62–63, 68–75, 116, 374n8, 374n8, 374n12, 378n6; Lyndon B., 17–18, 25, 166–67, 260, 278, 393n2
Jones, Delmos, 314–19, 320–21, 354
Jones, Linda, 314–16
Jones O'Donnell Foundation, 168–69
Jones, Shepard, 87
Jorgensen, Joseph, xiii, 298, 318–19, 327, 329, 331, 332–36, 338–40, 342–43, 357, 394n9
Josiah Macy, Jr. Foundation, 169, 376n16
Jureidini, Paul, 255–56

Kalb, Jon, 222–23
Kahin, George McT., 177–78, 234,
Kaplan, Irving, 254
Kaplan Fund, 15, 16, 169
Kardiner, Lawrence, 82
Kattenburg, Paul, 233–34, 386n7–8
Katzenbach, Nicholas, 17, 184
Kaufman, Howard Keva, 254, 255, 256, 269
Kazakhstan, 149–50, 280
Keeney, Barnaby C., 199
Keesing, Felix, 49, 83
Kennan, George, 3–4, 9, 11, 37, 349
Kennard, Edward, 110, 219, 385n29
Kennedy: John F., 148, 166, 167, 307; Raymond, 83, 232–38, 246, 371n4, 386n6, 386n8, 386n10; Robert, 167

INDEX | 443

Kentfield Fund, 15, 168
Kenya, 171, 174, 221
Kenya Federation of Labor, 171
Kenyata, Jomo, 255
Keyes, Charles F., 294–96, 300, 328, 333, 362, 378n9
Khrushchev, Nikita, 121, 175
Kidder, Alfred, 160, 228
Kiefer, Tom, 181
Killian, James, 90
Kirk, Grayson, 182, 382n15
Kirsch, Stuart, 223
Kissinger, Henry, 104, 177, 252
Kluckhohn, Clyde, xix, 55, 82, 83, 84–86, 88, 90–91, 94–95, 100, 104, 108, 109, 160, 359, 373n1, 376n10, 377n20, 389n5; CIA recruiter and contact, 160, 359
Kluckhohn, Florence, 130
Knickerbocker Foundation, 168
Knorr, Klaus, 10–11, 373n3
Knowlton, Winthrop, 243
Koestler, Arthur, 243
Korean War, 33, 109, 160–61 199, 209, 276
Kossuth Foundation, 171
Krader, Lawrence, 252
Kubark Counterintelligence Interrogation manual, 195–97, 199, 206–19, 213, 215–19
Kuhn, Thomas, xiv
Kunstadter, Peter, 279, 391n4, 391n6, 392n21

La Barre Weston, 34–35
Labor Unions and CIA, 133–34
Lancaster, Roger, 223–24
Langdon, Kenneth, 243, 388n21
Land reform, 41, 44, 125, 176, 230, 265, 309
Langer: Paul, 61, 106; William, 11
Lansdale, Edward, 243, 301–2
Laos, 132, 177, 185, 249, 302
Lapham, Roger, 186
Lasswell, Harold, 91, 99
Lattimore, Owen, 110, 244, 389n8

Lazarsfeld, Paul, 62, 91
Leach, Edmund, 130, 350–51
Leacock, Eleanor, 343
Leakey, Louis, 221, 255
LeBar, Frank, 47, 270, 388n3, 390n24
Lebanon, 109, 158, 221
Lee, Richard, xiv, 339–40, 342–43
Lehman, Edward, 190–91, 344, 383n19
Leighton: Alexander, 35–37, 84, 372n3; Dorothea, 205
Lemarchand, Rene 226
LeNoir, John D., 254
Lerner, Daniel, 119
Lessa, William, 46, 47
Levi-Strass, Claude, 66–67, 372n6
Lewis: Kepler, 110; Oscar, 224
Li an-Che, 83
Library of Congress, 35, 161, 260
Liberia, 203, 374n11
Libya, 7, 141
Lienhardt, Godfrey, 172
Lincoln, George A., 11
Linder, Harold F. 11
Linguists, xvii, 27, 50, 67, 69, 72, 78, 98, 106, 110, 144, 153, 157, 271, 310–11, 313, 353, 375n7, 392n13
Linton, Ralph, 82, 83, 237–38
Lipset, Seymour, 259
Lockard, Derwood and Barbara, 145
Long: Charles E., 270; Millard, 294
Loomis, Henry, 22–23
Lovestone, Jay, 16
LSD, 197–98, 383n7, 385n29
Lucius N. Littouer Foundation, 169
Lux, Thomas E., 254
Lumumba, Patrice, 19–20

MacArthur, Douglas, 39, 238
Macisco, John, 200
Mackiernan, Douglas, 149–51
Maday, Bela, 78–79, 254, 255, 257, 375n15, 389n13
Mader, Julius, 18

Malaysia, 31, 58, 79, 222, 239, 307,
Malinowski, Bronislaw, xix
Malta, 58
Madagascar, 7, 107
Mandelbaum, David, 83, 110, 188, 378n5, 381n11
Mandler, Peter, 116,
Manning, Robert, 166
Mao, Tse-tung, 149, 161, 269
Marchetti, Victor, 132, 133, 183–84, 378n11. 382n18,
Marks, John, 132–33, 183, 195, 198, 219, 371n8, 378n11, 382n18
Marshack, Alexander, 234
Marshall: Donald Stanley, 77–78, 393n4; George, 37
Marshall Foundation, 169
Marshall Plan, 37–38, 40, 53, 114, 372n4–5
Marxism, xix, 27, 122, 160, 224, 323, 351, 360, 394n8
Massachusetts Institute of Technology, xix, 59, 62, 89–98, 106, 118–21, 258, 289, 359, 373n3, 376n12
Materialism, xix, 361
Matthiessen, Peter, 173
McBaine, Turner, 186, 382n15
McCarthyism, xix–xxi, xxv, 53, 86, 101, 102, 108, 110, 113, 331, 337, 341, 352, 360–61, 378n3
McClellan, John, 58
McCloy, John 61, 166
McCone, John, 104
McCoy, Alfred, 195–97, 243, 383n1
McGehee, Ralph, 26
McGregor Fund, 169
McNamara, Robert, 162, 260
McQuown, Norman, 80
M. D. Anderson Foundation, 169,
Mead, Margaret, 55, 76, 82, 100–103, 145–46, 203, 244, 277, 289, 299, 335–36, 338–43, 346–47, 350, 357, 359, 372n8, 376n16, 376n17, 376n18, 383n8, 394n10; Mead Committee, 335–42

Mendenhall, Joseph, 125–27
Merton, Robert K., 259, 389n5
Métraux: Alfred, 63–65, 67; Rhoda, 101–2, 206–7
Mexico, 20, 93, 148, 224, 258, 278, 280, 345, 379n7, 382n13, 386n2, 391n5
Meyer: Alfred, 85; Cord, Jr., 243
Michael, Donald N., 102
Michigan Fund, 15, 168, 383n6
Michigan State University, 153, 173, 279, 280, 289, 302–4, 325, 330, 379. 330, 379n13, 38n15
Michigan State University Group (MSUG), 303–4, 380n15
Michener, James, 381n4
Micronesia, xviii–xix, 33, 35, 38, 46–51, 76, 111–12, 248, 355, 377n1, 387n15
Middle East Research Associates, 159
Middleton, John, 255
Millegan: Eudora, 241; Guy, 242; Kris, 240; Lloyd S., 238–45; 246, 354, 386n12, 386n14, 386n17, 386n18, 388n20
Millikan, Max, 7, 11, 23, 58, 90–98, 119–20, 145, 376n10, 389n5
Mills, C. Wright, 86–87, 108
Minority Groups in the Republic of Vietnam, 270–71
Mintz, Sidney, xii
Missionaries, 78, 111–12, 113, 134–35, 146, 158, 176, 242, 258, 270–71, 291, 302, 310, 381n6, 390n25, 393n5
Mitchell: Philip H., 77; Timothy, 162–63
Mitrione, Dan, 131
MK-Ultra, 27, 29, 102, 195–220, 383n7, 384n14–15, 385n28, 394n10
Modernization Theory, 7, 62, 94, 97, 118–22, 128–29, 135–36, 145, 230, 244, 361, 376n14, 393n21, 393n2
Modjokuto Project, xix, 80, 94–98, 106, 355, 376n9–13
Moerman, Michael, 294, 296, 324, 326–27, 329, 332–33, 335, 362, 378n9
Mongolia, 149–51, 229, 377n20, 389, n.8

Monroe Fund, 168
Montagnards, 270, 303, 314
Montagu, Ashley, 66–67, 244
Moore: John, 97, 341; Richard H., 263, 290n18
Moos, Felix, 254–56, 269, 389n11
Morgan, Richard, 108, 341, 359, 373n5, 378n3
Morocco, 7, 33
Mosely, Philip, 11, 62, 106
Mossadegh, Mohammad, 159–60
Mount Pleasant Fund, 169
Mullen, Jay, 226
Munich Institute, 168
Murdock, George P. 47, 49, 51, 57, 83, 107, 111, 145, 146, 248–49, 255, 260–62, 264, 270, 292, 341, 373n5, 389n16, 392n17
Murphy, Robert, 277–78, 280
Musgrave, John, 270, 390n24
Mutual Security Agency, 109, 113–18, 122
M-VICO System, 262–69, 273, 390n18–19

Nader, Laura, xi, 280, 315, 348, 358
Nagasaki, 63
Naroll, Raoul, 256, 269, 342, 392n17, 292n18
Nash: June, xii, xiv, 221, 223, 224, 230–32, 252, 253, 351; Manning, 230–32; 378n9; Philleo, 109
Nasser, Gamal Abdel, 228–29
National Academy of Sciences, 252, 257, 261, 369, 389n16
National Association of Foreign Student Advisors, 179
National Council of Churches, 171
National Education Association, 171
National Institute of Health, 80, 102
National Foundation on Social Science, 59–60
National Science Foundation, 57–60, 67, 79–80, 80, 222–23, 252, 259, 260–61, 328, 332, 361, 389n15, 389n17

National Research Council, 35, 41, 46, 49, 55–57, 60, 67, 83, 117, 146, 257, 261, 292, 374n6–7, 387n15, 389n16–17
National Review 92–93
National Security Act of 1947, 4–5, 349
National Security Agency, 13, 16, 23, 30, 78, 191, 375n14
National Student Association, 15–16, 25, 132, 167, 171, 181–82, 375n14, 378n11
National Geographic Society, 144
Nationalist movements, 6–9, 50, 150, 161
Nazis, 32, 51, 63–65, 79, 104, 107, 240, 298, 372n6, 377n20, 386n15, 387n16
Neocolonialism, 5–9, 122–35, 143, 232–33
Nepal, 121–22, 163, 177, 279
Nesbitt, Paul, 76
Ness, Gayle, 294
Netherlands, The, 58, 176, 200, 234
New Guinea, 32–33, 102, 223, 280, 384n8
New School for Social Research, 343
New York University, 252
New Zealand 77, 242
Newbold, Stokes [pseud. for Richard N. Adams], 231–32
Newman, Marshall, 69, 75, 374n9
Nieman Foundation for Journalism, 179, 184
Nigeria, 7, 58, 203, 205, 258
Nixon, Richard M., 19, 250
Norbeck, Edward, 381n11
North Korea, 147, 161, 184, 199, 209, 199, 209, 276, 381n8
Northcraft Educational Fund, 168
Norway, 58, 156
Nuclear Weapons, xvi–xv, 25, 35–36, 40, 59, 63, 99, 149–50, 200, 220, 229, 388n24
Nugent, David, 61, 105
Nuristani, Mohammad Alam, 153–56
Nutini, Hugo, 259–60, 389n15

Office of the Coordinator of Information, 67 137, 157

Office of National Estimates (CIA), 10, 82
Office of Naval Intelligence, 34, 83, 144, 146, 248
Office of Public Safety, 123, 131
Office of Strategic Services (OSS), xvii, 4–5, 9, 31–32, 34–35, 43, 63, 64, 67, 78, 81, 101, 105, 110, 137–38, 145, 148–49, 157–58, 176, 190, 229, 232–34, 238, 239, 241, 243, 281, 284, 288, 292, 354, 371n1, 371n3–4, 372n6, 379n7, 381n3, 387n18, 388n20
Office of War Information (OWI), 43, 101, 107, 137, 143, 243
Oliver, Douglas, 48, 50, 94–95, 160, 342, 376n10
Olmstead, David L., 336
Operation Ajax, 159
Operations and Policy Research Inc., 171, 285–86, 287, 391n9, 292n10
Opler: Marvin, 203, 386n24; Morris, 68
Orne, Martin, 202, 207, 208
Osgood: Charles E., 202, 205, 257, 384n15; Cornelius, 33, 147
Otterbein, Keith F., 254
Outline of Cultural Materials, 249, 262–67, 273, 390n20
Overbook Foundation, 252

Pacific Book and Supply, 239, 241, 242–45, 388n20, 388n22, 388n23
Pacific Science Board, 41, 46, 49, 387n15
Pahlavi, Mohammad Reza, 159
Pakistan, 118, 156, 158, 175, 176, 180, 242, 255, 251, 281, 283, 285, 381n8, 390n23
Pan-American Foundation, 171
Pappas Charitable Trust, 166, 169
Parson, Talcott, 42, 86–87, 94, 98, 103–4, 108, 119, 128, 359, 377n20
Passin, Herbert, 43
Patman, Wright, 15–16
Patterson, Thomas, xii, 80
Pauker, Guy, 96, 97, 128–29

Pax Romana, North American Secretariat, 171
Peace Corps, 257, 391n8
P.E.N., 171
Perkins, John, 120
Peru, 225, 258, 261, 280, 396n2
Philby, Harry St. John Bridger, 244
Philippines, The, 33, 48, 51, 57, 114, 152, 176, 177, 180, 238, 242, 280, 301, 330, 381n8
Phillips, Herbert, 294, 296, 324, 326–27, 329, 332, 332–33, 335, 339, 378n9, 394n11
Phoenix Program, 133, 309
Physical anthropology, xvii, 72, 76–77, 210, 355
Pickering, Robert B., 302
Pike Committee, 25–29, 60, 134, 185, 193, 304, 372n14
Pike, Otis, 25–26, 60
Piker, Steven, 324, 326–27, 329, 332–33, 362
Platt, Frank, 243
Plimpton: Francis T.P., 166; George, 173
Poe, Tony, 132, 302, 393n1
Point IV, 88, 113–18, 373n5, 378n6
Pool, Ithiel de Sola, 59, 62, 91, 93, 143
Poppe, Nicholas, 104, 252, 377n20
Pospisil, Leopold J., 280, 242
Postcolonial issues, 5–9, 32–34, 94–97, 235, 238
Postmodernism, 359–60
Praeger, Frederick D., 173–74, 381n1
Praeger Press, 24, 171, 173–74
Price, Don K., 22
Price, James R., 255–57, 262–69, 390n18, 390n18
Price Fund, 15, 16, 168
Prichard, Edgar Allen, 243
Prince, Raymond H., 196, 201, 203, 205–7
Princeton Consultants, 10–11, 28
Princeton Research Council, 172
Princeton University, 10–11, 107, 159, 166, 258, 373n3, 396n1
Principles of Professional Responsibility (PPR), 335–37, 365, 369

Project Agile, 256–57, 325
Project Camelot, xiii, xxii, 59, 60, 257, 258–62, 269, 274–75, 277–79, 291–92, 293, 295, 299, 362, 389n14, 389n15
Project Colony, 261
Project Simpatico, 261
Project Themis, 269
Project Troy, 90–91
Propaganda, 3, 7, 17, 22, 24, 26, 64, 87–88, 90, 92, 104, 121, 159, 173–74, 176, 183, 221, 232–33, 237, 255, 267, 296, 334, 359, 384n15
Provinse, John, 373n1
Public Services International, 171
Pye, Lucian, 11, 93, 119, 373n3, 382n15
Pyle, Christopher, 18

Rabb Foundation, 16, 169
Race, 60, 65–67, 86, 366, 396n3
Radical Caucus, AAA, 293, 323–25, 341–45, 347, 363, 367, 369, 394n8
Radio Free Asia, 176
Radio Free Europe, 167, 171, 176
Rainey, Froelich, 68, 242
Rambo, Terry, 129–30, 269, 302
Ramparts, 15–17, 25, 167, 181–82, 191, 282, 371n6
RAND Corporation, xxii, 98–102, 269, 304, 307–14, 353, 355, 362, 393n5
Raper, Arthur, 41–42, 43–45
Rappaport, Roy, xiv, 129
Rauch, Jerome, xix, 47, 53, 106–8, 377n21
Raybeck, Douglas, 222
Refugees, 78–79, 85–86, 126, 163, 197, 199, 200, 206–7, 223, 225, 265, 303, 396n3; Chinese Refugees, 206–7; Harvard Refugee Interview Project, 85–86; Hungarian Refugees, 199, 200, 207, 385n25; Project Symphony 78–79; Soviet Refugees 85–86; Tibetan Refugees, 163, 225; Vietnamese Refugees, 303
Reid, Whitelaw, 243
Reina, Ruben E., 280

Research in Contemporary Cultures, 100–102, 352, 355, 384n8
Retail Clerks International Association, 133–34, 171
Riddleberger, Peter B., 254, 256, 389n10
Ripley, S. Dillon, xvii
Robert E. Witherspoon Fdn., 172
Roberts, F.H.H., 69–70, 373n1, 374n9
Rockefeller: Godfrey S., 243; Nelson, 20, 116, 372, 374n14
Rockefeller Commission, 20
Rockefeller Foundation, 11, 21, 60–62, 80, 103, 118, 127–30, 166, 372n12, 373n4, 375n1; and CIA, 118, 166
Rodd, William, 207
Rogers, Karl, 205
Rohde, Joy, 260, 274–75
Rohdes, David, 199
Roosevelt: Franklin D., 4; Kermit, 158–59, 229, 244, 380n21–22
Roseberry, William xii, 360
Ross, Eric, xii, 136, 320
Rostow, Walt, 7, 58, 90, 92–93, 96–98, 118–22, 128, 135, 145, 183, 244, 269, 295, 357, 376n14, 378n7, 393n2
Rouse, Irving, 189–90, 193, 383n19,
Rowan, Carl, 16–17
Rubicon Foundation, 166, 169, 249, 252
Rusk, Dean, 61, 260,
Russell Sage Foundation, 212, 258

Sacks, Karen, 324, 394n8. *See also* Brodkin, Karen
Sahlins, Marshall, 119, 259, 320–21, 323, 326–27, 332, 336, 359, 369, 393n8
Sakran, Frank, 241
Salemink, Oscar, 270, 311, 314, 393n4
Salzburg Seminars, 102–4
San Blas Cuna Indians, 78, 256
San Jacinto Fund, 16, 158
San Jose State, 17
San Miguel Fund, 168

Sarason, Seymour, 50
Sarawak, 227
Savage, Charles, 205
Schafft, Gretchen, 65
Scheper-Huges, Nancy, 98
Schlesinger, James R. 19, 131–32
Schneider, David, 47, 49, 51, 298, 334–35, 383n19
Schorger, William, 89
Schorr, Daniel, 19–20, 26–27
Scott, Robert, 201, 211–18, 220, 385n26–27
Schroeder, Bruce, 221
Schulman, Jay, 211, 385n25
Schwantes, Robert, 180
SEADAG. *See* Southeast Asia Development Advisory Group
Sebeok, Thomas, 78
Secrecy and anthropology, 10, 67–75, 84–87, 88–89, 95–97, 104, 133, 137–39, 150, 158–59, 163, 165–94, 195–220, 226, 246, 291–92, 299–300, 302–3, 324–33, 337, 353–55, 364, 367, 369, 381n22, 392n15, 394n7
Seligman, C.G., 255
Service Educational Foundation, 171
Service, Elman, 129
Shack, William, 298
Shackley, Ted, 132
Sharp, Lauriston, 83, 294, 324, 326–27, 329–33, 362, 378n5, 378n9
Sheets, Payson, 225
Sheldon, William Herbert, 210
Sherif, Muzafer, 198, 202
Shills, Edward, 91, 98, 119
Shriever, Harry C., 242
Silberman, Leo, 224
Sills, David, 43
Skinner, B.F., 205, 384n16
Smalley, William, 302
Smith College, 280
Smith: Henry, 110; M. Estelleie, 342; Marian W., 83; Robert J., 280; Russell, 231, 358, 382n15; Walter Bedell, 147–48

Smithsonian Institution, xvii, 63, 78, 81, 117, 225, 379n4
Snowden, Edward, 13
Social Science Research Council, 35, 62, 63, 75–77, 80, 82, 106, 258, 286; CIA and, 62, 106, 286
Society for Applied Anthropology, 53, 75–79, 79–80, 152, 298, 362
Society for the Investigation of Human Ecology, 102, 195–220. *See also* Human Ecology Fund
Southeast Asia Development Advisory Group (SEADAG), 127–30, 302, 324–25, 328, 331, 337, 355, 378n9, 378n10
Soviet Union, 6–10, 14, 20, 25, 27, 35, 58, 78, 82, 84–87, 90–91, 98, 100–103, 120–23, 144, 149–50, 156–59, 161, 173, 175–76, 198, 199, 203, 206–7, 230, 249, 334, 353, 376n17, 377n20–21, 380n18; VENONA intercepts 144, 159, 173–76, 199, 230
Sontag, Raymond, 11
Southeast Asia Development Advisory Group (SEADAG), 127–30, 302, 324, 325, 328, 331, 337, 355, 378n9, 378n10
South Korea, 33, 109, 147, 160–61, 177, 179, 180, 199, 255–56, 258, 276, 381n8, 389n11
Spain 147, 228
Spaulding, Albert, 334
Special Operations Research Office (SORO), xxii, 79, 253–70, 272–75, 289, 351–53, 355, 377n1, 389n6, 389n9, 389n11–12, 390n18, 390n18, 390n10, 391n28
Spencer, Robert F., 181, 382n14
Spicer, Edward H., 68
Spiro, Rosemary, 47, 100
Spoehr, Alexander, 47, 48, 50–51, 75, 278, 389n17, 392n17
Sprague Report, 13–14
Spuhler, James, 334
Sputnik, 58, 102
Staley, Eugene, 145
Stallings, William Sidney, 144
Standard Oil, 252, 381n4

INDEX | *449*

Standing, Alexander, 11
Stanford Research Institute, 172, 179, 295
Stanford University, 83, 252, 373n3, 381n4
Starr, Richard Francis, 144
Stassi, 13, 18
Statement on Problems of Anthropological research and Ethics (SPARE), 289, 291–92, 300, 331, 333, 336–37, 339
Stauder, Jack, 195, 359, 367, 394n8, 396n5, 396n5
Stephenson, Richard, 203, 207, 384n11, 395n25
Stern, Bernhard: 108; Harold H., 243; Sol, 15–17, 167, 168–69
Stevenson, Adlai, 182, 186
Steward, Julian, xix, 54–59, 66–67, 81–82, 83, 108, 129, 361, 373n1, 373n5, 374n12, 378n6
Stirling, Matthew, 69, 374n9
Stockwell, John, 10, 12, 222
Stone, Shepard, 61
Stouffer, Samuel A., 389, n.5
Stout, David B., 75, 146, 373n2, 374n8
Stover, Leon, 201, 204–5, 384n13, 385n19
Strategic Hamlet Program, 126, 265, 304–7, 313, 393n2
Strayer, Joseph, 11
Strong, William Duncan, 57, 70, 83
Student Mobilization Committee, 319, 324, 327, 328
Student Mobilizer, 324, 327–30, 333, 335, 338
Students for a Democratic Society, 18
Sugerman, A. Arthur, 210
Suggs, Robert, 200, 256, 277, 384n14, 391n2
Summer Institute of Linguistics (SIL), 270, 270, 271, 311, 390n24–25, 393n5
Swadesh, Morris, 373n5, 378n3
Swanepoel, P. C., 172, 243
Sweden, 156, 174, 377n21
Sweet, Louise, 89, 354, 367n9
Synod of Bishops of the Russian Church Outside Russia, 172
Syracuse University, 41, 83

Taiwan, 176, 280, 381n8
Tax, Sol, 60, 179
Taylor, George, 84, 377n20
Teach-In, 323, 393n8
Technical Cooperation Administration, 113–18, 122, 378n4
Tenenbaum, Joseph, 32
Thai Affair, 293–96, 314–21, 324–44, 391n6, 394n11
Thailand, xxii–xxiii, 78, 98, 130, 177, 180, 239, 256–58, 279, 293–96, 299–300, 302, 314–20, 324, 325–31, 334–40, 343–44, 354, 381n8, 388n21, 391n8, 393n21, 395n11
Thomas, David, 270, 271, 390n24, 393n5
Thomas, Howard C. Jr., 166
Thomas, William L., 241–42
Thompson, Robert, 123
303 Committee, The, 182–83, 185, 382n16
Tibet, 150–51, 163, 176, 225, 379n9
Tilman, Robert, 294
Titiev, Mischa, 83
Title VI, xviii, 82
Torture, 20, 28, 30, 131, 156, 195–97, 209, 216, 385n26; *Kubark* Manual, 195–97, 199, 206–19, 213, 215–19
Tozzer, Alfred, 160
Tower Fund, 16, 168
Trager, George, 110
Transcription Center, 172
Trujillo, Rafael, 19, 20
Truman, Harry, 4, 9, 37, 109, 116, 371n1
Tsuchiyama, Tami, 43, 373n10
Tulane University, 148
Tunisia, 7
Turkey, 145, 158, 228, 258
Turner, Stansfield, xi, 219, 385n28

United Fruit, 228, 230
United Nations, 7, 65, 66–67, 110, 116, 149, 156, 161, 166, 294, 325
UNESCO, 66–67
United Auto Workers, 172
United States Youth Council, 172

University Associates Program, 9
University of California, Berkeley, 11, 151, 224, 280, 373n10
University of California, Los Angeles, 83, 139, 181, 226, 252, 278, 280, 283, 284, 324, 328; UCLA Middle East Center, 139, 283, 284
University of Chicago, 47, 78, 97, 144, 157, 224, 252, 304, 312–13, 381n6, 392n13; Committee for the Comparative Study of New Nations 97, 376n14
University of Colorado, 226
University of Florida, 226–27
University of Michigan, 47, 86, 87–89, 100, 179, 323; Near East Study Center, 87–89; Teach-in, 323
University of New Mexico, 65
University of Pennsylvania, 47, 48, 83, 228
University of Southern California, 47, 48, 172
University of Toronto, 343
University of Washington, 78, 252, 294, 377n20
University of Wisconsin, 47–48, 151, 379n13, 394n11
Urzuna, Raúl, 259
Useem, John, 48, 378n5
US Agency for International Development (USAID), xxiii, 23–24, 26, 109, 114–16, 121–36, 156, 185, 271, 281, 302, 324–26, 328, 331, 333, 335, 337, 346, 353, 355, 393n6; USAID and Counterinsurgency, 122–27; CIA Family Jewels and USAID, 130–34; USAID Police Training Programs 26, 122–23, 130–31, 380n15; USAID Pacification Program 133–34; CIA/USAID Office of Public Safety, 20, 26, 122–23, 126, 131, 133, 304, 389n9, 390n21
US Air Force, 23–24, 75–77, 84–86, 199, 209, 251, 252, 315, 373n12, 385n23, 385n27
US Air Force Intelligence, 23–24, 84

US Army, xvii, xviii, xxii, 11, 18, 23, 35, 37, 41, 61, 76–79, 82, 103, 109, 133, 137, 152, 161, 208, 249–75, 277, 284, 302, 320, 353, 355, 369, 385n27; Army Handbook Program, 251–52; Army Intelligence 61, 103; CINFAC, xxii, 257, 263–64, 267–70, 274, 390n19, 390n26; SORO, xxii, 79, 253–70, 272–75, 289, 351–53, 355, 377n1, 389n6, 389n9, 389n11–12, 390n18, 390n18, 390n10, 391n28
US Army Intelligence, 61, 103, 137, 143, 253, US Dept. of Defense, xiii, 26, 29, 75–79, 93, 137–38, 202, 250, 260, 261, 279, 290, 292, 295, 301, 312, 325, 330, 353, 346–47, 355, 382n15, 385n27, 391n4, 392n21, 393n21
US Dept. of Interior, 50, 51, 76, 81
US Dept. of State, 9, 37–38, 61, 63, 65, 76, 78–79, 83–87, 90, 94, 103, 104, 108–38, 144, 149, 156, 190, 191, 195, 208, 230–34, 240, 246, 248, 250–51, 260, 278, 284, 293, 307, 372n3, 372n11, 372n3, 375n3, 382n15, 387n15. *See also* US Agency for International Development, US Information Agency
US Information Agency (USIA), 173–74, 208
US Strategic Bombing Survey, 35–36, 63

Vallance, Theodore, 257–60
van den Berghe, Pierre, 294, 392n19
Vann, John Paul, 133
Vayda, Andrew, 129
Vekeman, Roger, 125
Venezuela, 124, 258, 388
Vernon Fund, 168
Vicos Project, 136
Victoria Strauss Fund, 169
Vietnam, xxiii, 8, 17, 18, 20, 25, 57, 78, 97–98, 123–25, 129, 132–33 177, 184, 185, 239, 337, 270–72, 276, 289, 296–300, 301–4, 307–14, 317, 320–25, 329–30, 343, 345–47, 359, 362, 367, 376n13, 380n15,

Vietnam (*continued*)
  382n15, 393n2, 393n7–8, 396n1; Sahlins' walkabout, 320–21, 393n8
Viking Fund, 80, 233, 238–42, 244, 246, 252, 374n6, 377n21, 387n15. *See also* Wenner-Gren Foundation
Voegelin, Carl F., 57, 75
Vreeland, Herbert H. III, 254–56, 389n8, 389n12

Wagley, Charles, 60, 81–82, 83, 257
Wakin, Eric, 340
Wallace, Anthony, 334
Wallace, Henry, 37–38, 53
Wallach, Irving A., 254
War Relocation Authority, 118, 393n3
Warbasse, Anne, 200
Warden Trust, 168
Wares, Evelyn, 190
Washburn, S., 57
Washington University, 280, 284
Watt, Norman F., 111, 200
Wax, Murray, 342
Weider, Arthur, 198
Weissman, Steve, 122–23, 176
Weltfish, Gene, 108, 276, 359, 378n3
Wenner-Gren, Axel, 107, 240, 377n21, 386n15
Wenner-Gren Foundation, 41, 49, 80, 107, 240–42, 252, 278, 297. *See also* Viking Fund
Wertime, Theodore Allen, 78
West, Robert, 82
Westerling, Raymond Pierre Paul, 234–35
White, George H., 385n29,
White, Leslie, 57, 129, 341, 361
Whitney, Daniel 344–45, 395n15
Whyte, William F., 269
Wickert, Frederick, 303, 390n24
Widerkehr, Doris, 223
Wilber, Donald, 157–62, 251, 252, 287–88, 356, 359, 380n19, 380n21, 380n22

Wilford-Telford Fund, 168
Willey, Gordon, 82, 116–17, 180, 378n6
Williams, Haydn, 382
Wilson, Edwin P., 144
Wilson, Monica, 255
Wilson, Sam, 132–33
Winks, Robin, 105, 148, 234, 238, 273
Wisner, Frank, 133
Wittfogel, Karl, xix, 107, 252, 341, 361
Wolf, Eric, xii, xiii, 100, 129, 277–78, 280, 298, 318–19, 326–27, 328–29, 331–36, 338–40, 342, 343, 357, 394n3, 394n9, 394n11
Wolfenstein, Martha, 102
Wolff, Harold, 100–102, 197–99, 203, 206, 211–14, 219, 376n18, 383n3, 383n4, 383n5, 383n8, 384n8, 385n28, 385n29
Woodyard, Edward Lender, 250–51
World Assembly of Youth, 172, 176
World Bank, 123, 135, 346, 389n10
World Confederation of Organizations of the Teaching Profession, 172
World Federation of Trade Unions, 8
World War II, xvii, xxi, 3–4, 7, 9, 30–37, 54–55, 67, 75–80, 81–83, 102, 106–7, 137–38, 143, 145, 148, 152, 176, 225, 232–33, 270, 284, 299, 319, 342, 349, 352, 362, 370, 392n6–8, 373n10, 373n2, 376n15, 385n21, 393n2, 396n3
Worman, Eugene Jr., 144, 146–47, 164, 379n4–5
Wynnewood Fund, 168

Yale University, 9, 11, 111, 160–62, 177, 233, 241, 248, 252, 280, 375n3, 386n6, 386n10
York, Carl, 284
Young, T. Cuyler, Sr., 11, 83, 244

Zborowski, Mark, 102, 208, 376n18, 384n8
Zemurray, Sam, 228
Zimmer, Herbert, 200, 207, 213

www.ingramcontent.com/pod-product-compliance
Lightning Source LLC
Chambersburg PA
CBHW070817250426
43672CB00031B/2753